UNRELIABLE SOURCES

UNRELIABLE SOURCES

A Guide to Detecting Bias in News Media

Martin A. Lee

and

Norman Solomon

A Lyle Stuart Book

Published by Carol Publishing Group

To our parents

Copyright © 1990 by Martin A. Lee and Norman Soloman

A Lyle Stuart Book
Published by Carol Publishing Group

Editorial Offices
600 Madison Avenue
New York, NY 10022

Sales & Distribution Offices
120 Enterprise Avenue
Secaucus, NJ 07094

In Canada: Musson Book Company
A division of General Publishing Co. Limited
Don Mills, Ontario

Manufactured in the United States of America
10 9 8 7 6 5 4 3 2 1

Library of Congress Cataloging in Publication Data

Lee, Martin A.
        Unreliable sources : a guide to detecting bias in
news media / by Martin A. Lee and Norman Solomon.
            p.   cm.
        "A Lyle Stuart book."
        Includes bibliographical references (p.   ) and index.
        ISBN 0-8184-0521-X (cloth) : $19.95
            1. Journalism--United States--Objectivity. 2. Mass
media--United States--Objectivity. I. Solomon, Norman.
II. Title.
PN4888.025L44   1990
302.23'0973--dc20   90-2229
                                                            CIP

Contents

The most sacred cow of the press is the press itself.

—George Seldes

Foreword

For five years on television, I played newsman Lou Grant, a crusty city editor for the mythical *Los Angeles Tribune*. He was a tough journalist, Lou—from the old school. For him, the only job was informing the public through the *Trib*'s stories, even if those stories—the truth—offended the rich and powerful.

Are there any real-life Lou Grants out there? Sure there are, and they bring their ethics to work with them every day: "To pursue the truth without fear or favor... To publish everything that's fit to print... To fight for the public's 'right to know' even if it offends the powers that be." I know journalists who unerringly follow that credo.

But I'm worried. I fear the Lou Grants of this world are a dying breed, a species failing to adapt to a rapidly changing environment. I don't want the Lou Grants to become the dinosaurs of American journalism.

As with any "endangered species," independent journalists find their environment becoming inhospitable. The atmosphere of greed and corporate mergers is choking out these journalists as "media managers" take over—managers more concerned with making a buck than reporting the news.

While the mythical *Tribune* was locally owned by the independently wealthy "Mrs. Pynchon," you don't find that very often today—by now, she would have been bought up by some distant conglomerate. And chances are, that conglomerate would have financial interests in nuclear reactors or Wall Street firms or factories producing guided missiles. Farfetched? You have only to look at some of the owners of our television networks, newspaper chains, and radio stations. What's most disturbing, these takeovers have taken place without any serious debate in the media about what impact they would have on journalism—and, more important, on the public's right to know.

Not long ago, such takeovers would've been impossible. In 1966, for example, when the ITT conglomerate set its sights on the ABC network, the deal was broken up after public debate raised concerns that such a merger would "compromise ABC's news coverage." In many ways, news standards were different then. That same year the president of CBS News resigned in disgust when network bigwigs chose to air an "I Love Lucy" rerun instead of an important Senate hearing on the Vietnam War. Guys like that executive are becoming extinct, as well: Today, programmers often put entertainment and ratings far ahead of news, and news executives take such priorities in stride. So, while things are changing in the world of journalism, I wouldn't say they're "evolving"—it looks to me like things are getting worse.

What can we do? As citizens, it's our duty to demand that the press present the news fairly, completely and accurately. Each of us, regardless of our individual political points-of-view, has an interest in seeing to it that the news media give us a faithful picture of the world around us.

Unreliable Sources reveals how and why the U.S. news media are distorting current events—whether down the street or around the world. As media corporations grow in size and shrink in number, they are becoming more powerful and less accountable to the public. Exposing the vested interests behind this trend, the authors have provided a vital handbook for seeing through media bias. People will find themselves equipped with a set of tools for reading between the lines of news reports by newspapers, magazines, radio and television.

Unreliable Sources gives a rundown of some of the most important news stories you didn't hear about over the past decade. I think you'll be surprised at some of the things the authors have turned up. These are stories that were effectively censored, made unavailable to the average citizen. You might be outraged that you didn't hear about them earlier. And you might be interested in the many suggestions this book offers regarding what active citizens can do to promote fairness and pluralism in the media.

Years ago you were considered an informed citizen if you kept up with the news by reading two or three diverse publications. Today, when the media are as big a part of the story as the story itself, you're not truly informed unless you're up on the media as well. This book is an excellent place to start.

Edward Asner

Introduction

Imagine turning on the television to watch the evening news on a major network. You're familiar with the anchor and many of the correspondents, but there is something different about this particular broadcast. Instead of the usual lineup of corporate sponsors, tonight's news is brought to you by the United Mine Workers, the Machinists Union, the American Federation of Teachers, and Teamsters for a Democratic Union. You switch to another network news program and there are commercials for Greenpeace, the Natural Resources Defense Council and the Sierra Club.

If we saw only commercials from labor organizations or environmental groups on television it would doubtless strike us as odd, out of kilter. Yet we rarely give it a second thought when we see one commercial after another from corporate sponsors. They are so prevalent and so routine that we hardly pause to dwell on their implications. A whole generation of Americans has come of age in a TV environment so conditioned by corporate sponsors that it's hard to envision any other state of affairs.

Popular legends assure us that the American press is committed, above all, to seeking and speaking the truth—no matter who might be offended. This is a familiar pose for a profession that prides itself on being feisty, independent and unbiased. The story goes that the news media, though flawed, are free to function as fairly neutral guardians of the public trust. Such myths gain acceptance through the press itself.

Amidst all the high-sounding goals, we're apt to forget that mass media are corporate enterprises. Since most media are funded largely by advertising or corporate sponsorship, their ability to make money depends on delivering an audience for advertisers, who pay the owners of TV and radio outlets, newspapers, and magazines more than $70 billion every year in the United States. Repetition has a cumulative impact; that's why some TV commercials are aired on national networks many hundreds or thousands of times. To the hard-nosed media biz, people exist most of all as potential customers. In that role, our most desirable qualities are gullibility and compliance with media advice.

Such widespread huckstering is ominous enough. But most publishers and broadcasters are no longer just under the influence of big-money interests.

Increasingly, media companies are *themselves* big-money interests—part of global corporations with millions or billions of dollars invested in a variety of industries. These are the main institutions linking us to the wider world beyond our firsthand knowledge.

The same corporations that report the news are often deeply involved in shaping current events before they become news. But our mass media don't readily acknowledge this. NBC, for example, is owned by General Electric, a leading military contractor that reaps huge profits from producing nuclear bombs and conducting Star Wars research; yet NBC News never discloses these financial interests when reporting on Star Wars and nuclear weapons issues. Local utility companies are often represented on the boards of big-city newspapers; yet this isn't mentioned in their coverage of utility rate hikes and related subjects.

Journalists are said to be constantly on the lookout for "man bites dog" stories. But we would have to search long and hard through the country's most prestigious newspapers to find a story by a reporter biting the hand that signs the paychecks. While some news dailies employ insightful TV critics, no major paper in the United States pays a staff writer to be a vigorous *newspaper* critic. By the same token, TV networks rarely showcase any strong self-criticism. Retractions of errors and corrections of the record are almost never seen in television news.

Under the circumstances, it would be naive and foolhardy to accept at face value what news media say. We have written this book to encourage people to become their own press critics. The first section examines prevalent journalistic practices that distort the news. The second section analyzes two key institutional factors that limit the scope and content of American media: concentrated corporate ownership and the role our government plays in dominating the news agenda. In the third and fourth sections, we dissect news coverage of a wide range of domestic and international issues. And the postscript discusses ways to invigorate the First Amendment and instill some much-needed *glasnost* in the U.S. press. Above all, our hope is to provide a guide that will help people to scrutinize the media with a sharp and skeptical eye.

Martin A. Lee and Norman Solomon
January 15, 1990

PART I

The Story Behind the Story

1

Mixed Messages

The news, and the journalists who provide it to us, can't be understood outside the context of the media industry as a whole. If we're off to see the wizard of media oz, we will find no single set of controls, no almighty men behind the curtain. Conglomerates—bringing us the news, weather and sports, along with all kinds of marketed entertainment—do not operate at the behest of lone individuals. The most famous TV anchors or network executives wield "power" only to the extent that their performances seem to help efforts to increase the company's profit margin—that's the bottom line.

In pursuit of higher ratings that bring higher earnings, TV programmers have honed mesmerizing techniques—described by one critic as "constant violence, gratuitous sex and deliberate manipulation of split-second change of images and sounds to make an emotional and sensory impact that leaves no time for reflection." More than ever, what's on the screen is in constant motion, with a style of eventfulness and a lack of substance—designed to minimize the risk that viewers will think long enough to tune out.

Television flows as freely and cheaply as tap water, and in many households it's turned on much more often. Nationwide, in a 24-hour period, an American home has a TV on for an average of nearly seven hours. Individual viewing averages 31 hours each week. By age 16 the typical American has already witnessed some 200,000 televised acts of violence—as well as 300,000 commercials. A majority of adults say they get most of their news from television.

TV affects the thinking and behavior of more people in our society than any other information technology. Yet for all the hype about television as the ultimate communications medium, the picture turns grim if we consider what it has actually been best at communicating. A survey in mid-1989 found that only 29 percent of adult Americans were able to name even one member of the Supreme Court, and a mere nine percent could identify the Chief Justice. But 54 percent of the same group could name the TV star of *The People's Court*, Judge Joseph Wapner.

Are American viewers just getting what they want? "That is the biggest fallacy in our business," says TV journalist Linda Ellerbee. "That's the argument that people on our side use to put dreck on the air... The American public didn't ask for trash television. They'll watch it the same way we go out and watch a fire. It's not all they want." But it's most of what we get, even with social conditions crying out for creative and diligent media.

"Television has created a vacuousness in American public life," *Los*

Angeles Times reporter Stanley Meisler lamented in 1989. After five years in Paris, he was dismayed by a Washington scene of fast-paced slogans: "While I thought I was arranging lengthy interviews with officials, they assumed that I was setting up quick phone calls to catch pithy quotes. Television had instilled the idea that reporters needed no more than 15-second bites."

"I have felt anguish," Meisler wrote, "about the irrefutable evidence of deterioration in America: Surveys rank U.S. schoolchildren at the bottom in math when tested against South Koreans, Canadians, Spaniards, Britons and Irish." Studies show that 17 western industrialized countries have a better infant-mortality rate than the United States. "Such reports make me feel I have returned to an America that feels good about tinsel and helpless before the scourges that matter."

When nightly TV news shows portray serious issues, the dramatic footage and narrations are apt to be authoritative—yet simplistic. And poignant events too easily become national palliatives. Recall, for example, how the news covered the rescue of Jessica McClure, an 18-month-old girl who was stuck in an abandoned well in Midland, Texas, for a few days in 1987. Her dire situation was, of course, a human-interest story that merited attention. But as Howard Rosenberg noted in the *Los Angeles Times*, "TV made it *the* story, made the plight of a single child bigger than the plights of the multitudes whose stories were not being covered. There were untold millions of dying or suffering children in October, 1987, children whose stories were going untold, for whatever reasons. But the Jessica story was accessible. It was less complex. It had a discernible beginning and end. And it offered the opportunity for self-promotion, for stations to use this tragedy to ingratiate themselves to viewers. It was not enough for them to rely on the networks or CNN. They felt the need to send in their own personnel, in order to establish themselves as extensions of the rescue effort."

Plenty of drama is available in the lives of those "untold millions of dying or suffering children." Abandoned wells do not rank high on the list of dangers to our country's babies; malnutrition, homelessness and untreated disease do. (Government statistics place one-fifth of all American children below the official poverty line.) Even when focusing on victims, TV producers prefer to avoid taking on those who benefit from inequity.

A SMOKING GUN

The media business operates with a pair of avowed purposes—to provide a public service and to make money. As a result, mixed messages are typical.

America's three major newsweeklies, for instance, have published occasional articles critical of the tobacco habit. Yet most of their back covers in 1989 were advertisements for cigarettes. Despite the reassuring myth that ads don't affect news content, neither *Time* nor *Newsweek* nor *U.S. News &*

World Report have gone on any crusades against cigarette smoking. The massive ad budgets of R.J. Reynolds, Philip Morris and other tobacco sellers provide a clue as to why a cigarette industry with an annual death toll of 390,000 Americans doesn't get more bad press.

Mixed messages: front and back covers of *Newsweek*, February 5, 1990

The threat of retaliation is more than conjecture. In 1980, tobacco companies pulled their ads from *Mother Jones* after that magazine ran a series of articles about cigarettes as a major cause of cancer and heart disease. Eight years later, butt-pushers pointedly disciplined the largest ad-agency group in the world when one of its subsidiaries strayed from the nicotine-stained road by having the temerity to produce a TV commercial that dramatized passenger applause for the advent of Northwest Airline's strict no-smoking rule. RJR Nabisco, makers of packaged goods ranging from Shredded Wheat to Winstons and Camels, cancelled its account with a Saatchi & Saatchi ad agency. Executives at Saatchi were not about to make the same mistake twice; when their company bought an ad agency putting together antismoking messages for the Minnesota Department of Health, Saatchi nixed that million-dollar arrangement rather than jeopardize its $35 million fee for advertising Kool cigarettes.

In 1989, U.S. Surgeon General C. Everett Koop angrily alleged that many magazines and newspapers thick with cigarette ads remain unwilling to publish articles on smoking dangers—a charge that received scant media mention, and no appreciable follow-up. Koop was right on target.

Consider *TV Guide*—a weekly magazine picked up by 42 million American adults plus 5.6 million teenagers—with a total circulation of more than 890 million copies per year. Each one of those copies contains cigarette ads. Federal law has banned cigarette commercials from the airwaves since 1971, but viewers consulting *TV Guide*—now the property of Fox Television Network owner Rupert Murdoch—keep getting plenty of color pitches for cigs. While receiving more than $30 million each year from tobacco advertisements, *TV Guide* does not publish any articles critical of the television networks' gentle treatment of the cigarette industry. Purchasing ads in *TV Guide* to the tune of about $590,000 a week, tobacco companies also buy the magazine's silence.

"I think it would be naive to expect publications that take a lot of revenue from the tobacco industry to go after them vigorously," *TV Guide*'s assistant managing editor Andrew Mills said in an interview for this book. Mills acknowledged that television has ducked the cigarette story—"It doesn't seem to me that TV has done much with it"—but his magazine wouldn't touch the subject with a ten-foot antenna. "I don't recall that this has ever come up at *TV Guide*," he told us. "My personal opinion is that it wouldn't look good for *TV Guide* to go after the networks when *TV Guide* runs cigarette ads in every issue." Such criticism would be "not becoming"—and would risk loss of revenue from cigarette advertisers. Periodicals with cigarette ads "are all in the same situation." When we thanked Mills for his candor, he replied: "Facts are facts, right?"

Some publications go further to protect cigarette advertisers. The September 1989 *Playboy* featured an attorney's essay denouncing proposals to restrict cigarette ads. The article advocated the right of cigarette companies to advertise without further legal restraints—and specifically defended a Camels ad campaign aimed at teens. Filling the first two pages of that month's *Playboy* was a full-color spread for Camels. The back cover was an advertisement for Merit Ultra Lights, headlined "Tasty little number." All told, the issue contained twelve full pages of cigarette ads, along with a tear-out postcard for three free packs of Marlboro Menthol. In 1989, *Playboy* received about $900,000 a month from cigarette advertisements—a quarter of all its ad revenue.

Playboy is hardly the only mass-circulation magazine going out of its way to be more sensitive to the well-being of tobacco hawkers than human lung tissue. On the rare occasions that either *Time*, *Newsweek* or *U.S. News & World Report* schedules a negative article about smoking, spokespersons for those magazines reluctantly admitted to us, the policy is to give the cigarette companies advance notice—and the option of moving, or removing, their ads in that issue, lest readers associate them with the unsavory publicity. Other unpleasant articles—precipitated by plane crashes, reports on auto safety hazards, studies of alcoholism and the like—trigger the same early warning system, giving advertisers such as airlines, car manufacturers and liquor marketers the chance to pull or rearrange ads that week.

This "courtesy" reflects broader incentives to publish articles that will attract rather than repel advertisers. The news magazines routinely notify advertisers about upcoming special reports or theme editions that might be a draw. Clearly, editors must satisfy ad executives. Speaking for *Newsweek*, Gary Gerard likened journalism and advertising to "separation of church and state"—but the barriers are porous.

Ties between articles and advertiser patronage become more direct in projects called "special sections" or "advertising supplements." In those cases, Gerard informed us, "the advertising sales people at *Newsweek* commission the content of those special sections"—a practice that, he conceded, "has occasionally raised concerns." In theory the articles on these pages are distinct, set in a different typeface on specially marked pages, but readers might easily make the mistaken assumption that they're looking at journalism. Actually they're reading articles that exist only because of specific sponsorship. *Time* magazine's publicity manager, Brian Brown, spelled out the fundamentals: "We're not going to run a special section that doesn't have advertising. In the past they've killed sections when they haven't gotten the advertising."

After a third of a century in journalism, former *Washington Post* editor Ben Bagdikian has concluded what the prevalent media myths deny—that mass advertising "deeply influences the subjects dealt with in the nonadvertising sections of newspapers and broadcast programs."

SEX SELLS

A wholesome image has always been central to the facade of *USA Today*, which accumulated more than six million daily readers during the 1980s. Yet zeal to capture readers and marketing dollars has entailed reliance on mixing messages. Vehement instructions about front-page photos came from the top boss, Allen Neuharth, who got the attention of editors one day by repeatedly slamming a newspaper rack in a conference room. "When you run a picture of a nice clean-cut all-American girl like this," he lectured, "*get her tits above the fold.*"

Neuharth's edict, of course, was meant only for *USA Today* editors' ears. But planned titillation to boost mainstream publications is commonplace—paralleling the misuse of women's bodies as sales props in printed ads. Meanwhile, on TV, the sexual pandering in many programs is an echo of commercials' more blatant and sometimes subliminal methods that would have kept Sigmund Freud glued to a slow-motion VCR.

The exploitation of sexuality, to create allure for products that have nothing in particular to do with sexual fulfillment, seems to involve no moral dilemmas for corporate journalism. Ethics take a back seat—or, more accurately, trail behind the back bumper—of the stretch-limos that lead the way for media magnates. The success of ad campaigns is gauged financially, by advertising companies and the news media dependent on them.

In the spring of 1989, St. Pauli Girl beer mounted a $5 million advertising blitz. Print ads with several pictures of long-necked beer bottles ran under the headline: "When you meet the *Right* Girl, how should you treat her?" Captions provided the answers: "Open the door for her. Tip your cap to her. Admire her body. Appreciate her good taste. Propose a toast to her. Introduce her to your friends."

The *New York Times'* advertising column—a daily feature in the business section—takes for granted the appropriateness of brandishing sexual imagery as a marketplace tool. Ethical considerations go unmentioned. So, in 17 paragraphs about the St. Pauli Girl promo drive, the *Times* discussed the new ad campaign only in terms of potential for boosting sales with its "suggestive humor"; the ads were "using coy word plays about how a young man should treat the 'right Girl' when he brings her home." The advertising firm handling the account, the *Times* reported, "nicknamed the target market the Charmed Winner. The target's psychological profile: confident, stable, full of fun, not married but with female friends."

"Suggestive" advertising in search of "target markets" may on the surface seem savvy and lusty—and its detractors perhaps unduly prudish. But in reality the methodical use of sexual metaphors—so central to American advertising for cars, cigarettes, alcohol, packaged foods, soda pop, toothpaste, chewing gum and any number of other products—is a high-intensity assault, feverishly seeking to wring maximum monetary gain out of the populace's sexual desires. Yearnings for personal connection are grist for the advertiser's next few mill. Under this perennial media barrage, it may slip Americans' unconscious minds that eroticism has no special relevance to buying a new automobile or a particular brand of soft drink, other than the linkage supplied by an ad-mad culture toying with deep human emotions.

The continuous stream of advertising, news and entertainment imparts paradoxical concepts: Problems are individual, and so are solutions—yet you should strive to live (and buy) as others do. The mixed message, while self-contradictory, is powerful: To be truly yourself, imitate others. Repetition has rendered even absurd rhetoric quite familiar, and unlikely to raise eyebrows, as when commercials entreat viewers to break through and express their real individuality by buying the new car that millions of other people will also be driving.

Mass media's forte—explicit among advertising execs—is the capability to induce large numbers of disparate people to want the same things. Other effects on audiences are incidental to the economic mission: Selling advertisers direct access to receptive readers, listeners and viewers.

ELLERBEE'S CONFESSION

A maverick TV journalist is rare enough that when one cracks a national network, the result can be a media novelty item. Linda Ellerbee gained a reputation as a witty no-nonsense critic of tele-vacuities. But, taking measure of such winsome determination not to be a commodity, the big-time TV business sees opportunities for marketing another commodity. Like a torturer in a late-night B-movie, sooner or later media conglomerates convey a chilling message to a recalcitrant professional: *Ve have vays to make you talk.* The scripted outcome is that quasi-renegades wind up trading on their outsider reps to develop leverage as insiders. Only weeks after appearing on the cover of *Mother Jones* magazine as a go-your-own-way pathbreaker, Ellerbee was on national television commercials selling Maxwell House coffee.

"Had another journalist mugged for Maxwell, it would have raised enough eyebrows," *Village Voice* columnist Leslie Savan wrote, "but Ellerbee is supposed to be some kind of keeper of journalistic cynicism, most biting about the hypocrisies of the TV news industry itself. Which is why Maxwell House wanted her in the first place—and paid her half a million dollars for two days' work."

Savan put her finger on the symbolism: "Although the public ranks reporters right next to politicians on the sleaze spectrum, news types are still associated with 'facts,' especially in pop-up appearances like ads. Anacin had an actor play a reporter—standing in front of a printing press no less—to announce 'the news about aspirin.' Shearson Lehman paid a real reporter, Richard Valeriani, to pretend to interview a Shearson-paid spokesman, Henry Kissinger, about the economy. But General Foods' coffee-achieving company has outdone those previous press plugs by hiring someone who could be sold as someone who could not be bought."

Linda Ellerbee's testimonial did much more than demonstrate that celebrity sincerity is available for the right price. That concept has long been established in the ad world—paralleling the vital advertising precept that a person can never have "enough" money or possessions. Commercials say so explicitly, as do the myriad TV shows glorifying the rich and famous. Celebs-for-hire on commercials convey the message by example too, so that spectacles like James Garner peddling many a Mazda, or Bill Cosby cashing in as he smiles for everything from pudding to stockbrokers, are endorsements of specific products as well as of insatiable zeal for ever more wealth. The subtext was unmistakable, for instance, in gas commercials starring Bob

Hope—already one of this country's richest men—seemingly determined to prime his fiscal pump with Texaco's largess until (and perhaps, with residuals, even past) his dying day.

But Ellerbee's work as a pitchwoman also spoke high volumes about mass media's capacity to housebreak rebellious souls, who might aspire to get some semblance of substance onto the networks. More telling than her cameo role for Maxwell House was her rationale for it: "I did it for the money—I make no bones about it." Having founded a new company for producing quality documentaries, she explained, the need for an influx of cash was crucial. "I had three choices—get an investor, which would mean giving up control; accept an offer to do a daily syndicated talkshow; or do this commercial." So she did the commercial to avoid having commercial pressures compromise the integrity of her work.

Such is the whiplash of TV's corporate power. It is necessary to destroy integrity in order to save it. Low achievers can only hope to go on sale for low prices; successes command more impressive price-tags. The role models, on the surface encouraging, commonly turn out to be dispiriting. Reinforced is the idea that all people have their price; some come higher than others.

Like Ellerbee doing her good-to-the-last-drop spot, TV newscasters are well paid. The process is more circuitous than with a commercial, but the requirement of pleasing a CEO and board of directors is no less stringent—and obedience no less lucrative. Salaries of TV journalists have spiraled since the early 1970s, when the top yearly wages were in the $100,000-$150,000 range. By the time Roger Mudd left NBC News in the mid-1980s, his annual salary had reached $1.2 million. He complained that "network television news has become an increasingly difficult place to be for those of us who came to it in the 1950s. Money is everything nowadays."

What appears on TV screens often looms so large that the people who live next door may seem less "real" to us than Dan Rather, or the Golden Girls, or even a pleasant woman who's endorsing a pain reliever for the hundredth time. Journalism's widest reach is via television, providing vivid images of "reality." In retrospect, Walter Cronkite's famed closing line was an ominous trademark for a TV news industry with the power and arrogance to squeeze slanted versions of events through the Tube and then underscore its pretensions with the matter-of-fact declaration: "And that's the way it is."

A LEXICON OF MEDIA BUZZWORDS

What we hear over and over again shapes our language and guides our thoughts. As with ad jingles, the drumbeat of repeated news lingo stays with us and takes on a life of its own. In the long run, what's repeated endlessly becomes social "reality." For every exceptional media item (notable as an *exception*), hundreds of stories solemnly present recycled clichés as truisms. Too often, American journalism is not "reporting the news" so much as reinforcing timeworn attitudes.

To consume the news dished out every day is to partake of a steady offering of buzzwords and catch-phrases that range from the vaguely factual to the questionable to the ridiculous. For example:

- *Acting presidential*
  A grandly nebulous description by TV news correspondents, giving a favorable review to some bit of presidential acting.

- *Bailout*
  Huge amounts of taxpayers' money going to wealthy financiers with souring investments in industries like auto production or Savings and Loans.

- *Believed to be, Considered to be*
  Using the passive voice, the journalist can generalize at will, as though anyone knowledgeable shares the same belief.

- *Big government*
  A pejorative for regulatory agencies limiting corporate activities, or for social service programs aiding poor and middle-class people—but not for the government's enormous military expenditures.

- *Brought to you by*
  A roundabout way of plugging commercial sponsors.

- *Caller claimed responsibility*
  Mysterious phone tip to a news organization, usually impossible to verify. Who really made the call? The CIA? The KGB? An autonomous lunatic? We'll never know.

- *Clean up*
  A scenario for setting right oil spills, nuclear pollution, chemical releases and the like. The phrase sounds comforting—it implies a magical vacuum cleaner at work—except that most ecological disasters can't be undone.

- *Dangerous drugs*
  Illegal substances, as distinct from other damaging consumables—alcohol, cigarettes and overprescribed pharmaceuticals—also widely used.

- *Defense spending*
  Military spending.

- *Deterrent*
  Nuclear weapons pointed at the Soviet Union. (Nuclear weapons pointed at the United States never get the U.S. media's "deterrent" tag.)

- *Efficiency*
  Frequently shorthand for corporate management's preferences, maybe involving layoffs, firings, wage cuts and/or union-busting.

- *Experts*
  A common noun handy for promoting a favored point of view.

- *Extremists, Fanatics, Fringe groups*
  Political individuals or groupings that meet with U.S. government and media disapproval.

- *Instability*
  Code for situations overseas where the U.S. State Department is unhappy with current events.

- *Intelligence community*
  A way of making cloak-and-dagger specialists at the CIA and other spy agencies sound like friendly neighbors.

- *Military leader*
  A foreign military dictator whom the White House doesn't mind a whole lot.

- *Military strongman*
  A foreign military dictator out of favor with the White House. (In 1989, Military Strongman seemed to be the first names of Panamanian General Manuel Noriega. A few years earlier, when he was on the CIA's payroll, he was "military leader.")

- *Moderate*
  In domestic politics, this favorable adjective is conferred for not rocking the status-quo boat. As a moniker for foreign regimes, "moderate" denotes little inclination to disrupt U.S. government plans. Thus, Saudi Arabia's monarchy is "moderate"—which would surprise the hundreds of torture victims inside Saudi prisons.

- *Modernization* (of nuclear weapons)
  The United States and NATO proceed to "modernize" nuclear arsenals with new missiles. But American media never apply the benign-sounding term to newly devised Soviet nuclear arms.

- *National security*
  Confined to subjects like weapons, soldiers and espionage, the connotations bypass vital aspects of true national security—such as environmental protection, public health, social cohesion and a strong economy.

- *Observers*
  The observers taken most seriously by news media.

- *Radical*
  Although students protesting in, say, China are "pro-democracy," in South Korea pro-democracy students in the streets are "radical" demon-

strators—with the reasons behind their anti-U.S. protests rarely explained.

- *Reform*
In journalese, "reform" can mean just about anything. "Tax reform" during the 1980s was a euphemism for legislation that gave the wealthy major tax cuts.

- *Senior administration officials, Sources close to the investigation*
The people putting out the line are only willing to do so anonymously—refusing to publicly answer for whether they've leaked truth or lies.

- *Special interests*
This phrase used to be applied to wheeler-dealers relying on big bucks instead of grassroots supporters to sway the democratic process. But in recent years, mass media have turned the "special interests" label upside down and plastered it elsewhere—on large numbers of people with less money and less power—groups of black and Hispanic Americans, labor union members, feminist women, seniors, lesbian and gay rights backers, and other organized constituencies.

- *Stability*
A codeword for situations overseas where the U.S. State Department wouldn't mind if conditions stayed the same.

- *Terrorism*
A label very selectively applied, in keeping with U.S. government definitions. So—in the mediaspeak lexicon—bombings, assassinations and kidnapings are "terrorism" if done by Arabs, but not if done by Israelis.

- *U.S. analysts, Western diplomats*, etc.
These phrases are broad and pliable enough to serve as springboards for the opinions of American officials and their allies, while obscuring the sources and motives behind the words.

The power to label is key to manipulation.

THE McPAPERING OF AMERICA

Many journalists are less than enthralled with their product. In 1989, the American Society of Newspaper Editors conducted a survey of over 1,000 newspaper reporters, copy editors, photographers and executives, randomly chosen from among the country's 1,600 dailies. Three out of five gave their paper a rating of "adequate but not outstanding." Only one-third rated their product "very high."

One might think that these conclusions would be worrisome to top editors.

But apparently not. The head of the newspaper editors society "said that so self-critical an attitude is healthy and reflects the idealism of journalists," Associated Press reported. Such verbal pats-on-the-head express a somewhat patronizing attitude toward working journalists, whose "idealism" is tolerated as long as it does not interfere with the designs of corporate management. After all, media moguls are far more concerned about the balance sheet than the candid assessments of journalism's work force.

Daily routines often leave idealism more wistful than realized. One limitation is the fact that the "news hole"—the space for articles and pictures—is not determined in the news department. As any editor knows, news is wrapped around advertising: the more ads the more room for articles; the less advertising the fewer pages. That's why, judging from a daily paper, the world appears more eventful between Thanksgiving and Christmas, with a sharp drop-off in print-worthy news when January begins.

The spectacle of a lame newshorse following a profit-laden cart is nothing new. Yet pressure has tightened for reporters to make coverage shorter and breezier, with newspapers across the country battling for circulation in the throes of the McPapering of America. Ever since its auspicious start as a nationwide five-days-a-week paper in 1982, *USA Today* has avoided messy complexities. There's nothing wrong with bright color graphics—except that they often accompany the proliferation of skimpy articles, brief and not necessarily to the point, while in-depth original reporting diminishes. (The ultimate McPaper might contain only photos, drawings, charts and headlines, with no articles at all.) Stuffed with celebrity gossip and other bite-sized light items, the innards of many newspapers largely resemble fluffy bon-bons. Although not hesitant to denigrate—while simultaneously hyping—"trash TV" and superficial "infotainment," daily newspapers have devoted little critical ink to their own metamorphosis.

Even at the presumed antithesis of a McPaper—the *New York Times*—the message from above has been unmistakable, as in a 1988 memo from managing editor Arthur Gelb: "Non-readers who fit our reader profile—people we'd like to attract—invariably say The Times puts them off because they don't have 'enough time' to read it. One clear message is that front-page stories should be shorter. We ought to try for an average of 900 words, with an occasional 600- or 700-word change of pace." These trends are likely to make America's "journal of record" more disappointing than ever.

Within such constraints, journalists in every community of the United States labor with intelligence and vigor each day. Many are conscientious, skillful, and idealistic. From newsrooms to cutting rooms, from editorial suites to overseas bureaus, individual employees may have any number of personal and professional motivations. But they are harnessed to giant combines, working in a media industry that has about as much to do with independent journalism as Safeway has to do with family farming.

2

Consider the Sources

"The news" usually comes to us as a finished product—smooth and tidy, neatly fitting within printed pages, a TV program or a radio slot. We're likely to assume that well-reasoned logic determines what we will see and hear. And it's true that a lot of professional criteria are at work in selecting what to report as news. Every journalist, facing blank paper or an empty computer screen, constantly makes choices about what to put in and what to leave out. We might wonder why the results tend to be so homogenized.

After all is said and done, the world according to American mass media is carefully screened for our eyes and ears. Spanning the globe with far-flung news gatherers, our country's most pervasive media nevertheless manage to be remarkably insular. Clichés, timeworn or instant, spin like wildfire through the crackly timber of the nation's press. As *Los Angeles Times* journalist David Shaw admitted, "A reporter sitting in his office or in a hotel room can watch Cable News Network and, simultaneously, call up on his computer screen several wire service reports of an event, even as he sits writing his own version. The tendency to conformity can be all but irresistible." Shaw added: "There are far fewer *enfants terribles* than *enfants timids* in the contemporary press corps," working in an environment that has become "both more corporate and more conformist."

Aspiring journalists get started by imitating established journalists, and most of the careers that follow consist largely of echoing others in the profession. The criteria that determined yesterday's coverage are being used to put together today's news, in a self-referencing—and self-perpetuating—process. A newsroom ritual is to spread out a set of clippings from "the morgue"—a collection of past articles on the subject. These days the files may be computerized, but the meaning is the same: Journalists draw heavily on previous stories by reporters who, in turn, probably relied on still earlier stories...

All too often, the media circle is unbroken. Facts pass into circulation swiftly—but so do inaccuracies, distortions, skewed frames of reference, and outright lies. Once published or broadcast, they are much more likely to be repeated than corrected.

Erroneous data may be the least of our worries. Many reporters keep their facts straight with admirable regularity. But piled-up facts do not ensure insight; a key omission can make an entire story misleading. A phone book, or a list of yesterday's stock market closings, or a newspaper's front page might contain lots of factual information—but perhaps no significant truth.

Lacking direct contact with the events and people prominent on the evening news or in the daily papers, we depend on media to enable us to "experience" them. But the supervisors with authority to decide what goes over the Associated Press national wires tonight, or into *Time* magazine next week, are ordinarily far-removed from the scene of events. Firsthand observations by reporters may have little to do with the final copy. In New York suites, editors are slashing and rewriting stories filed from Moscow or Addis Ababa or Managua or Bonn. Reporters in the field are apt to take into account the proclivities of higher-ups back home.

In theory, objective journalism—unaffected by favoritism or prejudice—informs the public about relevant facts, so that citizens can make up their own minds about current issues. Yet value judgments infuse everything in the news media. Ben Bagdikian lays out some of the subjective choices that go into a daily newspaper: "Which of the infinite number of events in the environment will be assigned for coverage and which ignored? Which of the infinite observations confronting the reporter will be noted? Which of the facts noted will be included in the story? Which of the reported events will become the first paragraph? Which story will be prominently displayed on page 1 and which buried inside or discarded? None of these is a truly objective decision." Mass media not only report the news—they also literally *make* the news. Familiar types of coverage can come across as "objective" precisely because they're so ubiquitous, blending in with the customary media landscape.

Like any other human being, a reporter has personal biases, whether or not they affect media products. Many news-media professionals claim to perform impartially. Connie Chung went a step further when she spoke with an interviewer in June 1989, while upheaval raged in Beijing. "Because she feels so strongly about what's going on in China, Chung said she feels the desire to 'take sides' for the first time in her journalistic career. She said it would create a serious 'inner struggle' for her to cover the story objectively." Imagine covering thousands of news stories without ever having felt a desire to "take sides." Either such self-portrayals of internal neutrality are disingenuous, or requisite career pretenses have been creating genuine moral ciphers within the media industry.

"BLOOD BROTHERS TO THE ESTABLISHMENT"

On a typical weekday evening, more than 29 million households tune in for a half-hour news show on one of three national TV networks. Most people tend to believe what comes across the luminous screen.

Occasional spicy clashes can disguise the conventional flavor of news reporting on television. ABC's Sam Donaldson has jousted with presidents, while adhering to limits that make the networks active participants in presidential media strategies. "I preach a good line, but I practice what most people in my profession practice," Donaldson told a Southern California newspaper. "Once in a while, I like to think that I get a little bit further down the road, but so do other reporters. As a rule, we are, if not handmaidens of the establishment, at least blood brothers to the establishment... We end up the day usually having some version of what the White House...has suggested as a story."

When reporters aren't listening to government officials they're usually consulting a few anointed authorities on political issues. In 1989, CBS anchor Dan Rather admitted that—like so many other journalists—he kept going back to "a shockingly small...circle of experts [who]...get called upon time after time after time." The selection process is hardly innocent of bias. *Los Angeles Times* staff writer David Shaw, a specialist in examining media practices, has found that "reporters often call a source because they want a quotation to illustrate a particular point, and they are sure to get exactly what they want if they call a source whose attitudes they already know."

High-level journalists and high-placed sources need each other. Whatever the tensions, cooperation is routine. "The elites who make most of the national news," scholar Robert Entman observes in a 1989 book, "are the ones who control policy outcomes in Washington... News reports can advance or undermine the policy proposals they want enacted or privileges they want maintained. The information they provide is tainted."

But ever-present. "Very few newspaper stories are the result of reporters digging in files; poring over documents; or interviewing experts, dissenters, or ordinary people," Walter Karp wrote in an incisive *Harper's Magazine* article in mid-1989. "The overwhelming majority of stories are based on official sources—on information provided by members of Congress, presidential aides, and politicians... The first fact of American journalism is its overwhelming dependence on sources, mostly official, usually powerful." Various studies bear out this assertion. For example, a sampling of 2,850 articles in the *New York Times* and the *Washington Post* found 78 percent to be primarily based on the words of public officials. The same sources dominate TV news.

When millions of listeners tune in National Public Radio (NPR), what they're likely to get is a lengthier replica of the same old skewed picture. Without a doubt the noncommercial radio network's feature narratives can be sensitive and discerning. However, when covering highly-politicized matters of foreign policy, NPR reporters at the State Department, Pentagon, Congress and White House are prone to do little but raptly transmit the utterances of politicians and their appointees. The tilt is against non-officials, and against officials not on the president's team. When media critics in Minneapolis studied the *All Things Considered* program for a five-week period in late 1988, they found that "administration sources outnumbered responses to administration sources by nearly two-to-one."

Beat sweeteners

Journalists on a beat are loath to alienate powerful sources, who might retaliate by freezing them out. Summing up the hazards of "aggressive challenges to the official version of things," Tom Wicker of the *New York Times* listed "lost access, complaints to editors and publishers, social penalties, leaks to competitors, a variety of responses no one wants." In order to get responses they want, reporters often cater to public officials. "Especially useful sources...are rewarded with occasional 'beat sweeteners,'" wrote Jonathan Alter in *Newsweek*. Puff pieces about powerful figures "are written partly out of hope for *future* morsels from an important source."

Contrary to all the hype, journalists who gain renown for breaking torrid stories about the federal government may be among those most enmeshed in a mutually-reinforcing web connecting them with power brokers on the inside. "It is a bitter irony of source journalism," Karp remarked ruefully, "that the most esteemed journalists are precisely the most servile. For it is by making themselves useful to the powerful that they gain access to the 'best' sources."

With officials dispensing each leak as "a gift," Karp wrote, "'Exclusives' are less a sign of enterprise than of passive service to the powerful." The norm is for journalists' tales to be wagged by sources inside the entrails of the mighty. "So pervasive is the passivity of the press that when a reporter actually looks for news on his or her own it is given a special name, 'investigative journalism,' to distinguish it from routine, passive 'source journalism.' It is investigative journalism that wins the professional honors, that makes what little history the American press ever makes, and that provides the misleading exception that proves the rule: the American press, unbidden by powerful sources, seldom investigates anything."

In this context, usually a media breakthrough on the national political scene is officially authorized. Washington's ongoing turf wars, personal rivalries and political agendas generate profuse motives for leaks that are damaging to some while bolstering others behind the scenes. This has been going on for a very long time. A classic example: FBI chief J. Edgar Hoover went into a tizzy when he got wind of a plan by a rival U.S. intelligence agency, the Office of Strategic Services (the CIA's wartime predecessor), to continue as a peacetime outfit. In the summer of 1945 Hoover planted a story in the *Chicago Tribune* about OSS plans for an "American gestapo." The ensuing public uproar forced President Truman to disband the OSS. Peeved that other U.S. spies were trodding on what had been exclusively his turf, the FBI director scored a decisive coup with a single well-placed news leak.

The "damage control" trade

Negative news may have more to do with covering up than revealing the truth. Such is the deceptive logic of "damage control." U.S. officials will sometimes disclose information that is truly scandalous—yet ultimately serves as a lightning rod that distracts attention from more damaging revelations. For instance, in 1983 the U.S. news media widely reported on findings of a Justice Department investigation that American intelligence agencies had protected Klaus Barbie, a notorious Nazi war criminal, and helped engineer his escape to South America after World War II. But the Barbie affair was depicted as an isolated case. What the Justice Department didn't say—and what the media ignored—was that Barbie was one of hundreds of Nazi spies on the CIA's payroll during the Cold War.

In effect, a source offers journalists what amounts to a deal: *I'll keep furnishing some dirt if you stay away from publicizing other dirt.* In their trades, officials get news coverage they want and reporters get fresh stories that seem dramatic. "Government sources and journalists," Professor Entman points out, "join in an intimacy that renders any notion of a genuinely 'free' press inaccurate."

At times a journalist's usage of anonymous sources serves the public interest, reassuring informants deep in the bureaucracy that they can reveal information without losing their jobs. Otherwise, as reporter David Johnston observed in the *Columbia Journalism Review*, "News organizations that use only on-the-record quotes run the risk of providing only the official version of events." But when mass media disseminate the trial balloons and calculated leaks of sources insisting that their identities remain secret, usually those sources aren't whistleblowing—they're policy makers blowing their own political horns. And officialdom's hot air winds up on the front pages of America's most influential newspapers, presented as the most profound news going.

PAPERS OF RECORD

More than any other publications, the *Washington Post* and the *New York Times* exert tremendous impact on American political life. Every day these newspapers contain more comprehensive coverage than any other U.S. media. While enjoying reputations for hard-hitting journalism, both papers are integral to the prevailing political power structure. They publish exclusive news stories and eminent punditry that greatly influence the direction and tone of other media. And their printed words carry heavy weight within the government's "national security" leviathan.

James McCartney, a Washington correspondent for Knight-Ridder Newspapers, is blunt: "The *New York Times* and the *Washington Post* play the unnamed sources game relentlessly—the *Post* uses more goddamned unnamed sources than just about anybody—but they don't get much out of it. Far too often they use unnamed sources to let the administration spread its bullshit."

The *Post* and *Times* have enormous clout not only because of overriding influence in the Northeast power corridor, but also because their high-prestige articles appear in hundreds of dailies across the United States and in many other countries. What's more, the two newspapers set much of the news agenda for the TV networks. For good measure, the ostensibly alternative National Public Radio habitually puts a *Post* or *Times* reporter on the air to analyze fast-breaking events from an overseas capital.

"People around the country may not be aware that they're 'reading' the *Washington Post* or *New York Times* every time they turn on the TV news or listen to NPR," says Jeff Cohen, founder of the media watch group FAIR. "Those newspapers are sanctifying what is an issue, what isn't an issue, and who the experts are who should address each issue."

The Washington Post eases off

Washington Post executive editor Ben Bradlee—a dozen years after being immortalized by Jason Robards as a courageous journalist in the movie *All the President's Men*—exhibited suspender-busting pride in the *Post*'s news operation. But Bradlee conceded that more recent approaches had been less inspiring: "You know, initially after Watergate, the public was saying about the press, 'Okay, guys, now that's enough, that's enough.' The criticism was that we were going on too much, and trying to make a Watergate out of everything. And I think we were sensitive to that criticism much more than we should have been, and that we did ease off."

Post reporter Scott Armstrong—who co-authored with Bob Woodward *The Brethren*, a book about the Supreme Court—eventually quit the paper. "I was never unaware at the *Washington Post* that my principal job was to increase the return on investment for the Graham-Meyer family," Armstrong recalled in an interview with FAIR's newsletter *Extra!*. "This was reflected in the way the *Post* was organized, the way it treated its employees. Anything that might be mistaken for investigative journalism was allowed if it boosted sales. But there was never any question in my mind that if protecting the First Amendment became more expensive than the return on investment, the First Amendment would be the loser."

At first glance, the *Washington Post* seems rigorous in pursuit of the truth. But America's premier symbol of investigative journalism frequently—and intentionally—leaves many stones unturned. Armstrong explained, "I should make clear that the *Post* is one of the better organizations; they did bring five Freedom of Information lawsuits on my behalf, for example. But there were 200 other instances when the *Post* was illegally denied access to information and did not challenge the government. That's the way it is at most newspapers. They aren't prepared to go after stories that require a major investment of time. They're oriented toward short-term daily journalism, which—if you read between the lines—means increasing the profit margin."

In 1971 the *Post* began issuing public stock, and during the decade profits jumped for stakeholders, foremost among them publisher Katharine Graham and her son Donald Graham. Determined to reduce costs, *Post* management became more combative against its own work force, and a pivotal 1975 strike by printing-press operators ended with their union crushed. The triumph of hardball tactics gave *Post* executives firm control of dealings with employees. The paper became a protracted financial success story, while hewing to a more conservative course in its newsroom and editorial suites.

The *Post*'s "ombudsman" has embodied this momentum. Created in 1970, the job first went to the *Post*'s national editor at the time, Richard Harwood. Far from being a freewheeling critic of the *Post*, Harwood was so cozy with its top echelon that when the Washington Post Company purchased the *Trenton Times* in the mid-1970s, management put him in charge of running it. At the close of the 1980s, Harwood was doing another stint as the *Post*'s ombudsman—by then a role of farcical dimensions. In contrast with the dictionary definition of "one who investigates complaints, as from consumers, and helps to achieve settlements," the ombudsman was functioning as a faithful spear-carrier for *Post* chieftains.

In a July 1989 *Post* column, amid seething labor-management tensions, Ombudsman Harwood wrote caustically about the Newspaper Guild representing 1,400 people on the company payroll. Harwood—who'd formally represented *Post* management during seven years of negotiations with the Guild—denounced the union. A week later the ombudsman column on the *Post*'s editorial page was again promoting the company line: "A certain kind of virtue, by accident or by design, is overtaking us. The prosperity of our great media empires has made them more or less invulnerable to economic subversion or bullying tactics by big government, big labor or big business." Harwood added that "you can be reasonably certain these days that the news brought into your homes is not propaganda that has been bought and paid for by a lobbyist, politician or advertiser."

Its public rationales aside, the *Washington Post*, says Ralph Nader, has become "a corporate conglomerate...with a bottom-line mentality."

UNFIT TO PRINT

The mightiest of daily papers can find journalistic independence intolerable when mega-bucks are at stake, as demonstrated by the saga of the *New York Times* and Sidney Schanberg.

On August 20, 1985, page 18 of the newspaper carried a cryptic announcement: "After four years of writing his twice-weekly 'New York' column on the Op-Ed page of The New York Times, Sydney Schanberg has been asked to accept another assignment, which is now under discussion."

The *Times* was obfuscating a delicate matter, with phraseology well illustrating how the newspaper that claims to publish All the News That's Fit to Print can fog up the simplest realities when it prefers to avoid undue clarity. Of course the wording wasn't a lie—Schanberg had in fact "been asked to accept another assignment"—but that was as close as the *Times* was willing to get to stating the more significant truth: The *New York Times* cancelled Schanberg's column about New York City.

Schanberg had plenty of credentials after 15 years of working for the *Times*. In New York he'd been a city desk reporter, then covered the state capital. He'd filed in-depth dispatches from many Asian nations. His reporting from Cambodia won him the Pulitzer Prize, and his book about that country formed the basis for the movie *The Killing Fields*. Back in Manhattan, Schanberg worked for three years as the *Times* metropolitan editor. In the early 1980s, he began writing the first local column to appear on the *Times* op-ed page. Without warning, one day in August 1985, Schanberg received word that the column was finished.

What was the problem? Journalist Pete Hamill later described the evolving focus of Schanberg's op-ed pieces: "the homeless, the injured, the casualties of the indifference and greed of big builders, bankers, and other pillars of the Establishment..." His twice-a-week column had been spotlighting the financial beneficiaries of various social ills—"taking on some of the people and institutions for whom the *Times* itself was edited. Schanberg was following one of the most fundamental journalistic intentions: to comfort the afflicted and afflict the comfortable. But Schanberg's column made some people in the *Times* hierarchy as uncomfortable as his chosen targets... The powerful people afflicted by Schanberg squealed loudly."

After the *Times* terminated his column, Schanberg resigned from the paper. (He since became a columnist for *Newsday*.) Notwithstanding all the lofty rhetoric about the integrity of its mission as a great newspaper, the *New York Times* had muzzled an articulate journalist who refused to heel. As Schanberg said in an interview with a small community newspaper, "The closer you may step on toes, the closer the toes get to the headquarters of the journalistic organization, the more loudly are the protests registered and the more loudly are they heard."

Replying to hundreds of readers' irate letters about the axing of Schanberg's column, *Times* vice-chairman Sydney Gruson summarized the whole sequence of events this way: "We have come to conclude after four years that a better column might be produced by another writer."

THE WIRES

A few wire services provide the vast majority of newspapers with windows on the world beyond the local horizon. For glimpses past their circulation areas, most daily papers depend on the major wires. While readers of the

New York Times or the *Washington Post* see comparatively little reportage from Associated Press or United Press International, readers in small towns may see little else in terms of national and foreign news. And for radio and TV stations, where "rip 'n' read" is something of a job description for newscasters, a clacking AP or UPI teletype is the essential fount of information.

America's most conservative major wire service, Associated Press, is also the most far-reaching—with its articles and photos running in more than 1,400 daily papers, about 85 percent of all the dailies in the country. AP machines also chatter inside about 6,000 of the nation's TV and radio stations. In 112 foreign countries, AP wires are hooked into 8,500 news outlets. AP's global audience: a billion people a day.

Technically a "nonprofit news cooperative," AP is owned by the media companies using and contributing to its coverage. With an annual budget of $275 million, and a total of more than 300 bureaus at home and abroad, Associated Press "is often on the scene first, covering for virtually everyone until other media outlets can get their people there," a *Los Angeles Times* analysis concluded in 1988.

But AP rarely digs deeply into stories. The *Los Angeles Times*, which teams up with the *Washington Post* to operate a news service marketed as a supplement to Associated Press, reported that "clichés and superficiality often abound" in AP copy. "Reporters who like to write investigative stories or other stories that challenge the Establishment generally complain the most about AP; many walk away from AP unhappy, convinced that AP is reluctant to break ground on certain kinds of controversial stories for fear of being criticized by editors of member newspapers—who are, simultaneously AP's employers and its paying customers."

While repeating official words by the millions, AP is hesitant to venture along any untrodden path. Owen Ullmann, a reporter who went on to cover the White House for Knight-Ridder, has been frank about his prior experience at Associated Press. "Ullmann says that when he worked in the AP's Washington bureau from 1977 to 1983, he detected a subtle discouragement, by management, of reporting that might seem overly critical of those in power, especially the President," the *Columbia Journalism Review* informed its readership. "By yielding such stories to others, he says, the AP avoided complaints from editors and publishers who might think the agency was going out of its way to attack the President."

Associated Press holds back

If the choice had been left to AP, Americans would not have learned about some very important stories that eventually emerged via other news media. When Secretary of Defense Caspar Weinberger urged AP not to report what it had discovered about a U.S. military satellite being launched in December 1984, AP bosses obeyed. So did NBC News. (The *Washington Post*, which

later broke that story, is itself more than willing to give in to "national security" arguments for suppressing news. For almost half a year, at U.S. government request, the *Post* sat on a story about Ronald Pelton's alleged spy
activities for the Soviet Union—and then expurgated much of the story
before publishing it in May 1986. The *Post* also agreed to remove 150 words
from an article about Pelton's trial before printing it.)

Moments before a radio speech in August 1984, President Reagan joshed
about attacking the USSR—"My fellow Americans, I'm pleased to tell you
today that I've signed legislation that will outlaw Russia forever. We begin
bombing in five minutes." An AP reporter handed in an article on the
episode, only to see the scoop killed by top AP editors. The information
reached the light of day only after he gave it to another news organization.

Two AP reporters based in Washington, Robert Parry and Brian Barger,
were among the first to delve into Oliver North's behind-the-scenes funnel-
ing of illegal aid to the Nicaraguan contras. They were the first mainstream
U.S. reporters to expose that the contra arms supply network was also
trafficking in cocaine. But the AP hierarchy impeded some of their stories
and blue-penciled out a lot of the substance of others. Much of the interference came from AP's Washington bureau chief, Charles J. Lewis, who was
frequently meeting with North at the same time he was passing judgment
on—and interfering with—the Parry-Barger investigative pieces about
North's operation. Associated Press bigwigs blocked one of those pieces for
over a month in spring 1986, and only budged it onto the AP wire after the
Miami Herald broke a similar exposé by pathbreaking journalist Alfonso
Chardy. In the summer of 1986, Parry and Barger quit AP in disgust.

In November—the same month that ended in an uproar as Attorney
General Edwin Meese publicly admitted that profits from selling weapons to
Iran had been going to the contras—AP's executive editor Walter Mears
issued remarkable written orders to high-ranking editors. "We will do no
investigative reporting about the inside details of efforts to gain freedom for
American hostages still held in Lebanon," Mears directed. His memo
asserted: "Reporting about secret channels of communication...can only hurt
the people who have been kidnaped."

The four million words moving on AP wires every day are wholesale
products of a news agency that asks few probing questions and provides
plenty of standard answers. Sometimes AP's warmed-over official fare is too
rancid for newspaper editors to stomach—as when, on the fifth anniversary
of the U.S. invasion of Grenada, the *Boston Globe* found an AP news dispatch to be so propagandistic and celebratory that the paper assigned a staff
writer to clarify whether the U.S. military action in 1983 had actually turned
the Caribbean Island into Heaven on Earth. In the article the *Globe* printed,
half of the dozen paragraphs were its own, surrounded by brackets; the headline summarized AP's gloss—"Grenada celebrates anniversary of U.S. inva-

sion"—while the subhead encapsulated the *Globe*'s findings: "Countrymen say nation is in trouble." But for the overwhelming majority of newspapers which publish AP articles intact and unbalanced by divergent sources, Associated Press is the Wonder Bread of reporting.

United Press International

United Press International used to give AP a run for its money. But, beset by financial woes, UPI has slipped steadily, retaining only a few hundred client newspapers in the United States. Reputed to be more speedy than accurate—its spring 1986 news flash about 2,000 immediate deaths from the Chernobyl nuclear power disaster in the USSR turned out to be totally bogus—UPI nonetheless has occasionally churned out some aggressive and high-quality journalism. But other wire services have been proving successful as competitors. The *New York Times* put a sizable dent in United Press International's income by dropping a million-dollars-a-year contract with UPI in 1986; it was a shrewd business move for the *Times*—proprietor of its own news service, which could only benefit from UPI's demise.

Teetering amid rumors of imminent collapse during the last half of the '80s, UPI survived a series of ownership changes, staff cutbacks and brisk turnover of key editors. Late in the decade, the news service showed incipient signs of solvency. But there were ominous signs as well.

In 1988, UPI became a possession of Earl W. Brian, founder of cable TV's Financial News Network, a man linked to questionable business dealings with then-Attorney-General Meese. That same year, UPI made a deal with the United States Information Agency to distribute USIA stories, thus joining forces with an overt propaganda arm of the government. In mid-1989, UPI management moved to quash criticism from within; reporter Gregory Gordon lost his job because he co-authored a book about UPI and then refused to submit the manuscript to higher-ups for approval prior to the book's scheduled publication in early 1990. Gordon, a 17-year employee, contended that UPI was trying to engage in censorship out of fear "the manuscript has some unflattering things to say."

NIGHTLINE: A CASE STUDY

The ABC TV News program *Nightline* is widely thought of as the cutting-edge of media inquiry. "In a half hour each week-night, the show identifies what's in the wind, bottles it and helps set the tone and intensity of the ensuing public debate," *Newsweek* declared, deeming *Nightline* "a conduit for ideas from around the world." Yet, after proclaiming that "where the program's heart lies" is "in serious, searing journalism," the magazine noted a disparity between the image and function of *Nightline* host Ted Koppel: "The anchor who makes viewers feel that he is challenging the powers that be on their behalf is in fact the quintessential establishment journalist." The magazine meant no offense.

Koppel has ruminated about similarities between watching *Wheel of Fortune* and *Nightline*. "As in the case of Vanna White...many of *Nightline*'s viewers project onto me those opinions that they would like me to hold, and then find me compatible..." he remarked to a graduation audience at Duke University in 1987. "We have been hired, Vanna and I, to project neutrality. On television, ambiguity is a virtue."

But after a contributing editor of *Columbia Journalism Review* watched 30 consecutive *Nightlines*, he concluded that the pattern was disappointing. "On many nights I found the program flat and predictable," Michael Massing recounted. "Important points of view were excluded; the range of opinion was kept very narrow. *Nightline* may serve as a national town meeting, but not everyone is invited. In fact, judging from the programs I viewed, it would seem that *Nightline*'s neutrality is more apparent than real."

Off-camera, Ted Koppel proudly counts among his best friends a man he believes to be possessed of nonpareil genius—Henry Kissinger—a frequent *Nightline* guest. "Henry Kissinger is, plain and simply, the best secretary of state we have had in 20, maybe 30 years—certainly one of the two or three great secretaries of state of our century," Koppel said in an interview, adding: "I'm proud to be a friend of Henry Kissinger. He is an extraordinary man. This country has lost a lot by not having him in a position of influence and authority." In summer 1989, during an upsurge of publicity about American hostages in Lebanon, Koppel's ultra-deference led him to turn the moderating role of the *Nightline* program over to Kissinger so that the revered diplomat could direct the panel discussion himself.

The adoration is mutual. In 1975, Kissinger offered Koppel the post of State Department spokesman; Ted declined. A dozen years later, Kissinger commented that given the opportunity, he'd still offer Koppel a major State Department position: "It would be a substantive one—say, assistant secretary for Europe." But Koppel's close friend Marvin Kalb objected that "Ted could do better than that, and I would be surprised if he would not want to. He is a man of great talent and considerable ambition." In 1988, *Nightline*'s host acknowledged that he had some qualifications to be secretary of state. "Part of the job," Koppel said, "is to sell American foreign policy, not only to Congress but to the American public. I know I could do that." As an ABC newsman, Koppel certainly has amassed plenty of that kind of experience.

The FAIR study of Nightline

In 1989 the media watch group FAIR—Fairness & Accuracy In Reporting—issued the results of a painstaking tabulation of 40 months of *Nightline* shows—a total of 865 programs with 2,498 guests. FAIR chose to study *Nightline* because of its acclaim as one of the best TV news programs.*

"The narrow range of guests," the FAIR report concluded, "makes *Nightline* a fundamentally conservative political program." The leading guests, with 14 appearances each, were Henry Kissinger and another former secretary of state, Alexander Haig. Next came State Department official Elliott Abrams and the Moral Majority's Jerry Falwell (12 appearances each). Out of the 19 American guests who could be termed *Nightline* "regulars" (more than five appearances), all were men, all but two were white, and 13 of the 19 were conservatives. "*Nightline*'s coverage of domestic and foreign affairs results in significant distortions," said the study, compiled for FAIR by Boston College sociologists William Hoynes and David Croteau.

Over 10 million Americans watch *Nightline* on a given weekday night; the offerings they see are out-of-balance to an extreme. Most of *Nightline*'s participants are movers and shakers from powerful institutions, interpreting the world for viewers. "Essentially absent from the guest list are representatives of civic and community organizations, popular social movements, minority communities, and so on," the report found. "*Nightline*'s guest list is heavily weighted in favor of government spokespeople, assorted 'experts,' and journalists."

Out of all the U.S. guests, a full 80 percent were professionals, government officials or corporate representatives. Only five percent spoke on behalf of "public interest" constituencies (peace, environmental, consumer organizations, etc.); less than two percent were leaders of labor or racial/ethnic groups. "Working, middle class and poor people and their representatives are provided virtually no opportunity to speak out. *Nightline* thereby reinforces the notion that non-elites must play by the rules set by the upper classes which have the power to define reality for society as a whole."

The report documented that 89 percent of U.S. guests on *Nightline* were men; 92 percent were white. When the show dealt with economic issues, corporate representatives outnumbered labor spokespeople seven-to-one. On shows about media and politics, which had potential for some critical candor, *Nightline* was true to form—the commentators were 95.5 percent white, 97.5 percent American, and 90 percent male. "On the whole," the study summed up, "*Nightline* serves as an electronic soapbox from which white, male, elite representatives of the status quo can present their case. Minorities, women, and those with challenging views are generally excluded."

"With respect to foreign policy," the FAIR report noted, "the 'solutions' Koppel seeks are essentially outcomes that the U.S. government finds desirable. When Koppel puts on the hat of a diplomat and assumes the role more of a statesperson than a journalist, it becomes evident that the worldview

---

*The authors of this book were on the FAIR staff during the late 1980s.

From FAIR's *Nightline* study

informing *Nightline*'s international coverage is little different from that of the U.S. government."

As ABC News anchor Peter Jennings has said, "Television seems to give people an instant set of credentials. Just appearing on the box, whether you're a guest or being quoted, has its own set of electronic credentials, and sometimes they don't match reality." But they *do* end up fabricating *political* reality. And in the media game of defining whose opinions matter, *Nightline* is a champion.

"WHEEL OF GUESTS"

Reactions to FAIR's study of *Nightline* were quite illuminating. Many TV columnists publicized the report in daily newspapers, praising the significance of its data. But from *Nightline*'s decision-makers came some fascinating defenses:

• "*Nightline* is a news program, not the op-ed page," executive producer Richard Kaplan said. And Koppel told the *Los Angeles Times* that the FAIR study was "missing the larger point. Ours is a news program. It is not meant to be a forum to give all divergent views in the United States equal access. When we are covering the news, we try to go to the people involved in the news."

FAIR's director, Jeff Cohen, responded that "FAIR would be thrilled if *Nightline* acted as a news program, not simply as a forum for those in power and their pundits. Good journalism requires calling on wide-ranging sources of information, not the same narrow base day after day."

• "When you have a conservative government elected by the people of this country, as a news broadcast that's what we have to deal with," said producer Kaplan. Koppel pursued the same point. "What they have reflected is that over the 40 months, we've been dealing with a rather conservative Reagan Administration."

Unwittingly, *Nightline*'s top strata was enunciating its subservience to those wielding government power. As Cohen replied, "This explanation could have been uttered by a Soviet TV news programmer—pre-*glasnost*. American television news, however, is not supposed to be strictly a forum for representatives of the state. FAIR does not criticize *Nightline* for inviting policy makers to appear on the show, but for its exclusion of forceful American critics of the policy. Critics, and critical sources, are part of a news story."

• "If we had a liberal administration in office, you would suddenly see an enormous disparity in the other direction," Koppel claimed.

"That would be equally lamentable," Cohen shot back. "The administration in power should not set TV's news agenda."

• Koppel insisted that "if you want to critique U.S. foreign policy, you don't bring on the opponents of U.S. foreign policy and let them speak their minds. What you do is bring on the architects of U.S. foreign policy and hold them to account, which is what we try to do on this broadcast."

But as anyone who has caught a single episode of Koppel's holding Henry Kissinger "to account" can attest, he is not inclined to be tough on admired guests. "As skilled an interviewer as he is, Koppel's questions rarely challenge the fundamentals of American policy," Cohen pointed out. "He seems particularly soft when interviewing Kissinger and other favored members of the foreign-policy establishment. Even as a devil's advocate, Koppel almost never expressed such positions as the bilateral nuclear freeze or opposition to contra aid (both favored by 70 percent of the public)." Cohen remarked that "Koppel's interviewing skill is not the issue. There are dozens of articulate representatives for peace and public interest groups who would welcome the opportunity to handle Koppel's 'tough questions.' The American public has a right to hear their answers."

Philadelphia columnist Chuck Stone, a longtime outspoken civil rights advocate, wrote that FAIR's report was "a great public service." Yet, he said, "most disheartening of all is Koppel's lame response to the analysis. It's hard to believe that this unarguably superb journalist was reduced to such an embarrassingly inept defense." Calling *Nightline* "the voice of the white American male establishment," Stone added that "I began to lose interest in *Nightline* four years ago when it became painfully apparent every show was a disguised reprise."

The Rolodex Syndrome

Clarence Page, a columnist for the *Chicago Tribune*, calls it "the Rolodex Syndrome. For all the competition among the nation's news shows, there is precious little competition for new faces or viewpoints to illuminate old problems. In a pinch—and up against tight deadlines—editors and news directors are most comfortable with familiar names and faces... As a result, the same spokespersons pop into public view again and again, where they often are spotted by other editors and producers who expand the circle of fame even more."

Howard Rosenberg has dubbed the phenomenon "Wheel of Guests"—"Spin the wheel and Henry Kissinger lands on ABC. Spin it again and he lands on CBS. No wonder that network newscasts and morning shows tend to look and sound alike especially when a major story is breaking." As if by rote, "the media—particularly TV—break out the same portable experts. It's musical-guests time."

When the Iran-contra story became officially scandalous in late November 1986, Rosenberg wrote that the networks' response was to "dust off the roster of talking heavyweights. You know the names: Former Secretaries of State Kissinger and Alexander M. Haig Jr., former national security advisers Zbigniew Brzezinski and Richard V. Allen, former CIA director Stansfield Turner and so on and so on. The buttons were there for the pushing. It was Haig/Brzezinski on Tuesday's *MacNeil/Lehrer NewsHour* and Haig/Kissinger on Tuesday's *Nightline* and Haig alone on NBC's *Today* and Kissinger alone on the *CBS Morning News* and Brzezinski alone on ABC's *Good Morning America* and Turner and Allen on NBC's *Today* and Allen alone on CNN's *Crossfire*."

Overall, Rosenberg contended in his *Los Angeles Times* column, "Those mustered by networks to comment on breaking stories are basically the gray-suited, gray-talking crowd. That's because networks are mainstreamers. Hence, sameness." And, in times of media crisis or no, "From *Meet the Press* to Meet the Morning Shows, the message is Meet the Mainstream. If anything, moreover, TV's definition of mainstream might well be rightstream." Former assistant secretary of state Charles William Maynes, a frequent television guest expert, acknowledged that TV networks defer to the outlooks of those in power. "Articulate dissidents of the left don't get on at all," Maynes said.

Roger Wilkins, a former editor at the *Washington Post* who has been one of the few black commentators to reappear on network television, attests that in TV discussions "the left is just left-out. I've never seen Noam Chomsky on television. I don't even think I know what Chomsky looks-like, though I know from his writing he's an extremely articulate critic of U.S. foreign policy." And Chomsky—a linguistics professor at the Massachusetts Institute of Technology and a prolific author—is also a gifted speaker, although Americans have had little chance to find that out via their TV sets. Except for a notable pair of 1988 interviews with Bill Moyers on PBS, throughout the 1980s television bookers continued to virtually bar Chomsky from the national airwaves. Yet when Chomsky travels abroad, foreign journalists constantly seek him out and solicit his opinions on current events.

Exclusions are based on race and gender as well as ideology. "I think the TV people all assume that standard-brand white people can talk in sound bites," Wilkins commented. "When you get to non-standard Americans, like blacks or Hispanics or women who aren't Jeane Kirkpatrick, there isn't that assumption."

In a rut, news programming stays more or less the same. *Nightline* is symptomatic of what ails TV coverage in general, as news and public affairs shows feature a narrow spectrum of viewpoints, again and again. When choosing portions of interviews or participants for round-table discussions, the networks see to it that real diversity is rare.

3

Media Con Games: How to See Through Them

A ll of us at one time or another have read a newspaper story or seen a news broadcast that we know misses the real story. Perhaps we have been present at an event, only to find the next day's news account far removed from our firsthand experience. The more one understands about the world, the more often one sees how our news media deliberately or inadvertently fudge the facts and distort key issues.

Reading between the lines and seeing through media con games isn't a natural talent, it's an acquired skill. Obviously if a person has expertise in a particular area, he or she will be better equipped to ascertain the strengths and weaknesses of news coverage of that subject. However, most of us aren't experts in the nuances of international diplomacy, military strategy, corporate mergers and leveraged buyouts, or a hundred other topics that media report on regularly. "Of course, it is possible for any citizen with time to spare, and a canny eye, to work out what is actually going on," said novelist Gore Vidal, "but for many there is no time, and the network news is the only news even though it may not be news at all but only a series of flashing fictions intended, like the avowed commercials, to keep docile huddled masses, keep avid for products addled consumers."

One can learn to be a more critical consumer of the news. Toward this end, it helps to survey a wide range of news media, especially publications that question conventional wisdom. The irascible media critic I.F. Stone used to read everything he could get his hands on. He pointed out the mainstream media's contradictions and omissions in his journal, *I.F. Stone's Weekly*, which tweaked the nose of the American establishment during the 1950s and '60s.

Stone's method is easy to apply to today's media. One doesn't have to be an expert on macroeconomics, for example, to figure out that something is amiss when a *New York Times* headline reads, "April Job Growth Eased Decisively, Stirring Concern," and a *USA Today* headline two days later says, "Jobless Rate Increase Seen As Good News." Or compare New York *Newsday*'s headline of April 13, 1989—"City School Dropout Rate Is Up"—to the *New York Times* on the same day: "Dropout Rate Unchanged, Despite More Spending."

A weather forecaster would have a hard time reconciling these headlines about relations between Nancy Reagan and Raisa Gorbachev: "Frost in the White House for 2 First Ladies" (*New York Times*, December 10, 1987) and

"A warming trend seen between Nancy, Raisa" (*Boston Globe*, December 10, 1987). Readers of the *New York Times* and the *Washington Post* on September 30, 1988, must have been puzzled by the different versions of how peace talks were progressing in Southern Africa. "Accord on Cuban Pullout From Angola Reported," the *Times* headline proclaimed, whereas the *Post* played it this way: "Talks on Cuban Pullout Adjourn Without Accord."

Mixed messages sometimes appear in the same newspaper. On April 30, 1989, the *St. Louis Post-Dispatch* headlined on two different pages: "Jesse Jackson Hints At Running for D.C. Mayor" and "Jackson Has No Plans For Mayor Race." Conflicting assertions ran on the same page of the *New York Times* (June 15, 1989); the headline stated, "Uganda After Its Years of Terror: A New Stability," but the subhead disclosed, "300 Rebels Reported Killed In Clash With Uganda Army."

Every so often a media outlet will commit a blatant error that raises fundamental questions about journalistic procedure. Anyone who heard the tragic news that the airplane carrying United Nations Secretary-General Dag Hammarskjold crashed en route to Northern Rhodesia on September 17, 1961, must have been surprised to read an AP dispatch that ran the next day in the *New York Times*. Headlined "Tshombe Confers With U.N.'s Chief On Katanga Truce," the article reported that "Hammarskjold and President Moise Tshombe of Katanga Province met for more than an hour... Separate planes brought Mr. Tshombe and Mr. Hammarskjold to Ndola, 130 miles southeast of the Katanga capital of Elisabethville... Mr. Hammarskjold's chartered DC-4 from Leopoldville landed about four hours after Mr. Tshombe arrived."

But Hammarskjold's plane never arrived from Leopoldville. The meeting between the U.N. Secretary-General and Tshombe—described in detail by AP—never happened. Someone at AP faked the entire story, and it got out on the wires before Hammarskjold's death was announced.

For those who read more than one daily paper, it can be instructive to compare how the same wire service report is presented in different papers. For example:

• An AP dispatch appearing in the *San Juan Star*, Puerto Rico's English-language paper, on August 20, 1989, led as follows: "Police used whips and dogs to disperse hundreds of blacks, including Archbishop Desmond Tutu, during mass protests Saturday at two whites-only beaches." The *New York Times*, meanwhile, ran a watered-down version of the same AP dispatch: "South African police dispersed hundreds of blacks during protests today at two whites-only beaches." Whoever edited the AP copy for the *Times* took a bite out of the article, omitting any reference to police dogs.

• Also on August 20th, the *Times* and the *San Juan Star* both ran AP stories on anticommunist mujahadeen rebels bombing Kabul, the capital of

Afghanistan. The *Times'* matter-of-fact account was only one-paragraph long: "Fourteen rockets slammed into Kabul today, and hospital officials said at least 18 people were wounded. Kabul has been hit almost daily by rocket attacks since late June, and Islamic guerrillas have claimed responsibility for some of the attacks." The same sentences appeared in the *San Juan Star* which featured 16 additional paragraphs of AP copy, including pertinent gory details neglected by the *Times*, such as: "Rebels say they aim for military targets, but unofficial estimates say 98 percent of the rockets have hit non-military targets including schools, homes, crowded bus stops and bazaars. One rocket Saturday went through the roof of the home of a family in Karte Parwann... Young boys and girls wailed and the brother of [an] injured woman said the United States was responsible for the deaths of innocent Afghans... U.S. officials have promised new arms shipments to the mujahadeen but have not disclosed the types of weapons."

• In September 1988 the *New York Times* Sunday magazine ran an article by two Native American writers, Louise Erdrich and Michael Dorris, about government land grabs and white economic control squeezing Indian people at the White Earth reservation in Minnesota. The article—a rather mild portrait of the wrongs still being visited on Native Americans—quoted Indians and whites in an effort to present both sides of the White Earth land conflict. Distributed by the *New York Times* wire service, it was picked up and reprinted by Minnesota's biggest newspaper, the *Minneapolis Star Tribune*—but only after the paper removed almost everything that gave the Indians' side of the story. Furious, Erdrich and Dorris declared in a letter-to-the-editor: "The point of our article was that historically Indian people in Minnesota were treated as if they were invisible, and had no voice. You have done it again. The *Star Tribune* has intentionally or unintentionally misrepresented the spirit...perspective...and facts we endeavored to present."

• It's also interesting to observe when important wire stories are picked up by certain newspapers and ignored by others. On July 22, 1989, the *San Juan Star* ran a lengthy AP dispatch with the headline, "North Contra-support network linked to drugs in Costa Rica." According to this report, a Costa Rican congressional commission found that the Nicaraguan contra support network created by Lt. Col. Oliver North had been involved in cocaine trafficking in Costa Rica. A short item in the *Washington Post* the next day noted that Costa Rica officially barred North, Richard Secord and former U.S. national security adviser John Poindexter from entering its territory because of their role in fostering the contra drug connection. None of this information was reported by the *New York Times* or the major TV networks, even though they all subscribe to AP.

What follows is a run-down of various types of media con games that active and skeptical news consumers should be constantly on the alert for.

HEADLINE HANKY-PANKY

A good way to begin detecting and decoding biased news coverage is to take a close look at how accurately headlines encapsulate the stories that follow. The headline is the most important aspect of a news story, serving as an index for the reader who is "shopping" the paper. Most people, when reading a newspaper or magazine, scan the headlines but only actually read a few articles that perk their interest. Our "take" on the news is, therefore, largely formed by fleeting glances at headlines and subheads that may or may not accurately reflect the accompanying stories.

Reporters don't write the headlines for their own stories; editors do. This, in part, may explain why headlines sometimes contradict news stories. Headlines not only can mislead people who merely skim a page, they also give a particular slant to a story and establish a mind-set or predisposition that influences how we read the text. Keep an eye out for deceptive headlines and titles that don't jibe with the ensuing articles. A few examples:

• During the June 1988 U.S.-Soviet summit in Moscow, the U.S. media bent over backwards to portray President Ronald Reagan in a flattering light. "Reagan Impresses Soviet Elite" read the subtitle of a prominent front-page story in the *New York Times* even though the piece indicated that the President had fallen asleep while meeting with Soviet officials. In another *Times* article on the summit, British Prime Minister Margaret Thatcher was quoted saying of Reagan, "Poor dear, there's nothing between his ears." The headline: "Thatcher Salute to the Reagan Years."

• An article by Julia Preston in the *Washington Post* described a predawn contra attack on a Nicaraguan farming cooperative, where a rebel bullet hit a six-year-old girl who was left "lying in a ditch screaming for help." The headline of the article: "Combat Performance of Contras Said to Improve."

• The *Miami Herald* reprinted a story about Philippine mail-order brides that appeared originally in the *Orange County Register.* The *Herald*'s headline was "U.S. men wed more Filipinos," followed by the subhead, "Mail-order marriages said to be successful." Reading further one learned that many of these marriages are not so successful after all: "Some husbands are wife-beaters and others force their wives into prostitution." (The rosy headline did not reflect the fact that mail-order marriages are a form of trafficking in women, akin in many ways to slavery. Filipino women are bought and sold, yet this commercial activity is sanctioned by the U.S. and Philippine governments.)

• A more subtle kind of distortion occurs when headlines exaggerate stories, transforming dubious allegations into facts. This happened frequently in the U.S. during the anticommunist witch-hunts of the 1950s. Senator Joseph

McCarthy made wild charges about communist infiltration of the U.S. State Department, and newspaper headlines treated his allegations as if they had already been proven: "Reds in High Places Face Senate Quiz" (*Oakland Tribune*), "Probers to Check State Department Reds" (*Stockton Record*), and "McCarthy Insists Truman Oust Reds" (*New York Times*).

Headlines that exaggerate the truth or treat official assertions as hard facts continue to proliferate in today's newspapers.

EDITORIALS VERSUS NEWS STORIES

Another category of media bias involves editorials that contradict news stories appearing in the same newspaper. By editorials, we mean unsigned commentary on the left side of the editorial page—as opposed to op-eds and opinion pieces that run with bylines usually on the right side of the editorial spread.

On the whole, editors tend to be somewhat more conservative than beat reporters. This is especially true at a newspaper like the *Wall Street Journal*, where the editors and reporters often seem to inhabit different planets.

Sometimes editorials conflict with news stories appearing the same day in the same paper. On other occasions, information reported in the news pages will be conveniently ignored in an editorial published days, weeks or even months later.

• A *Washington Post* editorial critical of the Nicaraguan government referred to "38 Nicaraguans who were arrested in a peaceful protest at Nandaime last July 10." Checking the *Post*'s news coverage during that period, we find that the protest was anything but "peaceful." The incident was described in a *Post* news article headlined "Protest Rally Turns Violent in Nicaragua" which stated that anti-government demonstrators, emboldened by the presence of U.S. Embassy officials, "threw rocks, sticks and bottles" at the police.

• A May 1988 *New York Times* editorial, titled "The Superpowers vs. South Africa," correctly blamed South Africa for destabilizing neighboring states in the region. But the title and gist of the editorial misleadingly implied that both superpowers, the U.S. and Soviet Union, were geopolitical adversaries of South Africa. As the *Times* previously reported in its news pages, the U.S. has for years facilitated South Africa's destabilization schemes by sharing intelligence with the apartheid regime and supplying military aid to South African-backed UNITA guerrillas waging war against Angola.

LOADED LANGUAGE

This category of media distortion is broad and far-ranging. It could include a peculiar—or politically dubious—use of a word or phrase that might stand reality on its head. Or it might entail the selective application of phrases that, when compared in different contexts, display a pattern of bias. Such patterns are rampant, yet not always easily discernible unless one scrutinizes the media closely. For example, in its coverage of anti-government demonstrations in then-Communist-ruled East Germany, the *San Francisco Examiner* described protesters throwing rocks at police as engaged in "civil disobedience." When is the last time the *Examiner* or other mainstream media used the phrase "civil disobedience" to describe Palestinian youths in the Occupied Territories throwing rocks at Israeli soldiers?

"In trying to describe a foreign political landscape, language is everything," former *New York Times* correspondent Jo Thomas wrote in the *Columbia Journalism Review*. Thomas, who covered Great Britain for the *Times*, was critical of her colleagues for adopting loaded terminology when reporting on Northern Ireland. In particular, Thomas noted the predilection on the part of American journalists to use the word "Ulster" as a synonym for "Northern Ireland." "Ulster is used interchangeably with Northern Ireland," said Thomas, "*only* by the British and by the Protestant unionists who want to maintain their union with the Crown at any cost." Catholics and Irish nationalists, however, consider the term an insult and reject its usage. "To call the place 'Ulster' is to choose sides," Thomas concluded. Yet that's exactly what the *New York Times* did in an August 1989 article headlined, "After 20 Years, Ulster's Hopes Fade"—to mention only one of countless examples.

• Another example: Serge Schmemann's front page article in the *New York Times* was headlined, "Moscow Cautions NATO on Replacing Missiles in Europe; Weighs Violating Treaty." The article asserted that the Soviet Union was "prepared to *violate* the American-Soviet treaty banning medium- and short-range nuclear missiles from Europe" if NATO upgraded its own missiles. Two days later, A.M. Rosenthal beat the same drum in his *Times* opinion column: "Gorbachev's Foreign Minister warned that Moscow was ready to *violate* a U.S.-Soviet treaty…"

Compare this language to a *Times* news story by Michael R. Gordon: "The Bush Administration has not said whether it accepts the strict reading of the ABM treaty…or whether it endorses a much more permissive reading of the agreement developed by the Reagan Administration." In Timespeak, the Soviets *violate* arms treaties; the U.S. government merely reinterprets them—permissively.

Permissive readings were in vogue in the U.S. media a few years ago when President Reagan pushed the Star Wars program. Accepting Reagan's "broad" interpretation of the Anti-Ballistic Missile (ABM) Treaty, *Nightline* host Ted Koppel derided as a "clever move" a Soviet journalist's insistence that the 1972 treaty prohibits Star Wars deployment. Apparently Koppel was unfamiliar with Article 5 of the ABM Treaty, which states in no uncertain terms that each party must not "develop, test or deploy ABM systems or components which are sea-based, air-based, *space-based* or mobile land-based [emphasis added]."

• When it comes to nuclear issues, it appears we need a doctor in the press room. A few years ago, the *Washington Post* editorial page reported a link between anti-nuclear sentiment and physical affliction. When New Zealand opted for "nuclear-free" status in 1984—banning nuclear weapons from its shores—the *Post* said that New Zealand had contracted a "nuclear allergy."

The *Post* editors broke new medical ground when they diagnosed a "similar nuclear allergy" in Australia, as if allergies were somehow contagious. This was related symptomatically to another *Post* diagnosis: "New Zealand, it appears, has a touch of Hollanditis." Holland had made the *Post*'s sick list the year before when it considered banning U.S. missiles.

The *Post*'s contaminated language seems to have infected the *New York Times*, as well. A *Times* editorial described the South Pacific as a region "where nuclear allergy is widespread." And a *Times* news story by Clyde Haberman, showing similar symptoms, was headlined: "Sardinia Catches the Nuclear Jitters." But the roots of this illness apparently go back to Japan, a country which has long been "haunted by a 'nuclear allergy' growing out of the atomic devastation it suffered in the last days of World War II," according to the *San Francisco Chronicle*.

That efforts to rid a country or region of nuclear weapons might be a sign of mental or social health is obscured by such slanted language.

• Another instance of loaded language appeared in a *New York Times* editorial, headlined "Hiding Behind Hormones in Milk." The editorial lambasted the National Farmers Union for opposing a genetically-engineered growth hormone that makes cows produce 15 percent more milk than untreated cows. The Farmers Union was trying to ignite public concern about the adverse health impact of "unnatural milk," but according to the *New York Times*, all they really cared about was keeping inefficient dairy farmers in business.

"There are too many dairy farmers," said the *Times*, admitting that "huge productivity gains from bovine growth hormone could have a harsh social impact." As many as 15,000 dairy farms "might be forced out of business." The editorial concluded by rejecting the prospect of "hoist[ing] a permanent umbrella over a privileged few." That's how the *Times* referred to the 15,000 dairy farmers who may lose their livelihood because of a DNA-rigged growth hormone: "a privileged few." To our knowledge, the *Times* has never described America's wealthy agribusiness elite as "a privileged few."

• The *Washington Post* argued in favor of giving "humanitarian aid" to the Nicaraguan contras. However, according to the Geneva Conventions and

Protocols and the International Red Cross, the right to "humanitarian aid" is not available to members of a military force. It must be distributed by humanitarian groups, not an interested party such as the U.S. government. Such aid must be applied impartially to all civilians who need it, not just those on one side. These criteria automatically disqualified the contras. But one wouldn't know this from the *Washington Post* and other U.S. news media, which ignored international legal standards as they endorsed more aid to the contras.

POLITICALLY-CHARGED LABELS

This is actually a subset of the previous category of loaded language. By politically-charged labels we mean designations that are used gratuitously or improperly, resulting in distortion, deception or the reinforcement of time-worn prejudices. More often than not, misleading labels are explicitly political in nature. Some examples:

• A *Miami Herald* article about abortion rights activist Bill Baird was headlined: "Pro-abortion crusader won't quit." The label "pro-abortion" reflects a biased political vocabulary since no one crusades for abortion as such, but rather, the legal right to choose abortion. Similarly, the *International Herald Tribune* referred to a "huge pro-abortion rally in Washington" in April 1989. The *Herald Tribune* could have called it a "Keep abortion legal rally." A WNBC-TV correspondent in New York spoke of "pro- and anti-abortion activists," when he could have said "pro- and anti-choice activists."

• How a political group is labeled by the press often says more about the journalist doing the labeling than the group itself. *New York Times* correspondent Serge Schmemann, reporting on the results of municipal elections in Berlin, stated: "Both the extreme left and the extreme right gained... The left-wing Alternative List, as the West Berlin chapter of the Greens is called, gained about two percentage points, getting 11.7 percent of the vote... But most surprising was the eight percent of the popular vote garnered by the Republican Citizens Party, a far right group" that campaigned on a racist anti-immigrant platform.

Calling the anti-nuclear, ecology-oriented Greens an "extreme" political party says a lot about bias at the *Times*. Schmemann never explains in what way the Greens are "extreme"—a term laden with negative connotations. By lumping the nonviolent Greens together with a neo-Nazi party, he implies a moral equivalence between the so-called extremes. Such smear tactics are particularly reprehensible in view of the fact that the Greens have long been at the forefront of anti-racist, anti-Nazi movements in Germany and elsewhere in Western Europe.

• Even worse than words like "extreme" or "radical" in U.S. political discourse is the label "communist." A *New York Times* news story by Jonathan Fuerbringer referred matter-of-factly to "the communist regime of Nicaragua." The characterization was biased and inaccurate, as FAIR noted in a letter to the *Times*: "What communist regime allows approximately half of the economy to remain in the private sector as in Nicaragua—a higher percentage than in Mexico or Brazil?" After complaints from readers, the *Times* ran a terse correction: "While Nicaragua is Marxist, it does not operate on the Soviet model of communism."

In contrast to "Marxist" Nicaragua, the *Times* and other U.S. media routinely referred to neighboring states as "the democratic countries in Central America." During Mikhail Gorbachev's visit to Cuba in 1989, CNN correspondent Tom Mintier wondered whether Gorbachev would prevail upon Fidel Castro to stop subverting "the budding democracy in El Salvador," a nation where government-sponsored death squads make a mockery of the rule of law.

Times writers habitually refer to "the Marxist Government of Angola," as if this were the official title of that country's governing body. But Angolan officials do not call themselves "the Marxist Government of Angola." To them, Angola is simply Angola. The *Times* and other U.S. mass media, however, never referred to General Augusto Pinochet's regime as "the Fascist Government of Chile" or to the apartheid regime as "the Racist Government of South Africa."

An AP story appearing in the *Times* stated that the Korean peninsula was divided "into Communist North Korea and pro-Western South Korea." Such a dichotomy implies that communism is an anti-Western ideology, when actually it is rooted in Western thought and associated with Western intellectuals Karl Marx and Friederich Engels.

Appellations such as "Marxist," "Communist" and "extreme left" conjure up negative images in the minds of many Americans. Exactly what the media mean when they use these labels is not clarified. In a three-part series in February 1989, the *New York Times* belatedly acknowledged what had been widely understood elsewhere for many years: "Communism" no longer describes a "single set of beliefs" or any "universally accepted ideological canon."

As Jim Lobe stated in a letter to the *Times*: "If 'Communists' cannot agree on the definition of 'Communism,' then what is the use of words such as 'anti-Communist'?... Without more explanation, how are we to interpret these adjectives? How are we to understand the use of the word 'anti-Communism' when applied to Jonas Savimbi's followers in Angola? Or 'Marxist-led' when applied to Salvadoran insurgents or the Sandinista Government of Nicaragua? Do these terms tell us much of anything?"

Lobe's comments haven't sunk in with the editors at the *Times*. The words "anticommunist" and "Marxist" still frequently appear in the paper of record. Although the vocabulary is fuzzy, imprecise and open to multiple interpretations, such politically-charged labels continue to mislead and confuse U.S. citizens.

In addition to "democratic," "Marxist" and "anticommunist," another selectively-used label is "terrorist"—a subject to which we'll return later in the book. And there's also the catch-phrase "Soviet-made weapons," which doesn't mean a lot these days, in light of the underground arms market where all sorts of military hardware is available to anyone with sufficient funds. "Soviet-made" is a pejorative when describing Nicaragua's military arsenal, but it rarely appears when referring to contras who carry Soviet AK-47 machine guns.

THE "WE WE" PHENOMENON

It's embarrassing to watch a TV reporter making "we we" on national television. It's embarrassing because the "we we" phenomenon belies a cherished myth of U.S. journalists, who in the past have been quick to criticize their Soviet counterparts for speaking on behalf of the State. Of course, American journalists speak for themselves, not for the U.S. government—or so goes the myth. Keep your ears tuned for when U.S. radio and TV reporters slip into another guise and begin speaking for their government.

• During the U.S. invasion of Panama in December 1989, CNN's Mary Laughlin abandoned all semblance of neutrality and objectivity when she asked George Carver, a former CIA officer, "Noriega has stayed one step ahead of us. Do you think *we'll* ever be able to find him [emphasis added]?"

• *NBC Nightly News* anchor Tom Brokaw started to "we we" when he asked the network's Pentagon correspondent about the on-launch explosion of the Atlas-Centaur rocket: "And what about the loss of the military communications satellite? *We're* kind of short-handed up there already, aren't *we* [emphasis added]?"

• ABC correspondent Sam Donaldson made "we we" about the White House position on the Soviet Union's nuclear test moratorium in the mid-1980s. Said Donaldson: "*We* have not completed our tests to modernize our weapons, and if *we* were to stop testing now, *we* would be at a distinct disadvantage [emphasis added]."

Is that Sam or Uncle Sam speaking? Sometimes it's hard to tell the difference.

UNATTRIBUTED ASSERTIONS

Unattributed assertions often paint with a broad brush and are of questionable validity. For example, *CBS Evening News* anchor Dan Rather, introducing a story about a Palestine Liberation Organization conference in Algiers, said: "Bert Quint reports that the show was orchestrated by Moscow." How did Quint manage to figure out Moscow's role in this affair? Obviously no one stood up and began waving a conductor's wand. Quint's claim that Moscow "orchestrated" the PLO conference was not attributed to any source. When questioned by FAIR, a CBS producer conceded that the word "orchestrated" may have been ill-chosen.

SUSPICIOUS SOURCES

Occasionally reporters need to speak with sources "off the record" or on a "not-for-attribution" basis. This makes it possible for people to provide news without risking their job, safety or reputation. Sources need to know they can trust a journalist before sharing confidentialities. This is especially true for whistleblowers in government or corporate spheres.

Unfortunately, journalists often grant anonymity to people who should be publicly accountable. Instead of a bond of trust, the relationship becomes an indentured contract, as reporters look to government and corporate elites for their daily dose of news.

By "suspicious sources," we mean instances when reporters cite unidentified sources, like "top U.S. officials say..." or "according to Western diplomats..." This happens so often that it's difficult to know who's really talking, and why. What's the hidden agenda?

One should be alert to journalists' use of unnamed official sources. If the unnamed source is a whistleblower speaking accurately and truthfully about his or her boss or agency, the information can be considered a "leak," and in all likelihood the reporter will be serving the public interest. If, on the other hand, the unnamed source is the voice of a government agency and there's no legitimate reason for the source to be unnamed, the information can be considered a "plant," and in all likelihood the reporter will be serving the interest of the agency, not the public.

There is ample reason for suspicion whenever unnamed intelligence sources are invoked: "CIA officials warned..." or "U.S. intelligence experts believe..." When unnamed intelligence sources are cited, lies and disinformation often follow. For example:

• Relying on unnamed U.S. intelligence sources, most major media reported in November 1984 that Soviet MIG fighter jets were being unloaded in Nicaragua. The story turned out to be a big hoax.

• James LeMoyne of the *New York Times* quoted unnamed "American officials" who claimed that the Medallin cocaine cartel "has close ties...to some Sandinista officials in Nicaragua." How does our friendly American official know this? And why didn't he want to be publicly associated with his remarks? Perhaps it had something to do with the fact that the U.S. Drug Enforcement Administration publicly debunked allegations of a Sandinista drug connection, as reported by *Times* correspondent Joel Brinkley.

Another dubious practice by reporters involves imbalanced sources. Reporters don't usually interject their own opinions in stories; this would be a blatant violation of journalistic codes, which stipulate that reporters must remain "objective." Instead, bias is transmitted by the way sources are chosen. An article about an important foreign policy or domestic issue might quote only official U.S. sources—named and unnamed. The spectrum of opinion is narrowly framed by the kinds of "experts" who are featured in print and broadcast news reports—and by those who are left out.

• Suspicious sources were utilized by *New York Times* correspondent Paul Lewis in an article headlined "U.N. Human Rights Group Faces a Key Test." Lewis began with the following: "An American-led campaign to make the U.N. Human Rights Commission a less political and more effective watchdog against oppressive governments is facing its most critical test in years, diplomats say." Lewis cited only unnamed "Western diplomats" and "experts" in his 15-paragraph piece, except for a single comment attributed to U.S. delegate Vernon Walters.

Opposing views were snubbed by Lewis, who dutifully repeated the assertion that the U.S. was simply trying "to get the [U.N.] commission working in a less political manner." In view of strenuous U.S. efforts to initiate U.N. investigations of its enemies while blocking probes of allied countries, independent human rights experts objected to Lewis' gullible portrayal of the U.S. as a neutral watchdog. Lewis ignored "the substantial role the U.S. has played in politicizing U.N. human rights work," wrote Human Rights Watch deputy director Ken Roth in a letter to the *Times*. "It is misleading to portray the U.S. as the champion of impartiality when its own participation in the commission has been so politically charged."

• Reports about nuclear weapons and disarmament often quote U.S. and Soviet officials, without including comments from representatives of peace and anti-nuclear groups. When non-government sources are included they tend to be conservative rather than progressive critics. These patterns are rampant throughout the mainstream news media in the U.S. On several *MacNeil/Lehrer* discussions of nuclear weapons issues in the late 1980s, for example, the most dovish "expert" interviewed was Senator Sam Nunn, a Pentagon booster.

• Here's how Ted Koppel introduced an ABC *Nightline* program on superpower relations in January 1985: "Tonight, live from Geneva, the two Richards, Perle and Burt—Perle, the Pentagon hardliner, Burt, the State Department moderate. They will tell us how and why the U.S. and the

Soviets have agreed to resume arms talks. And another view of the arms control talks and the latest White House staff realignment from a man who knows the ins and outs of both, former White House Chief of Staff and former Secretary of State Alexander Haig." (Richard Burt, a hardline Cruise missile advocate, is to Koppel a moderate.) As FAIR's *Nightline* study noted, "This kind of 'debate' leaves virtually intact every Reagan administration assumption about foreign policy. Any notion of a left progressive or even liberal critique is missing."

When *Nightline* and other U.S. media occasionally present dissenting views on foreign policy, it is usually the leaders—the elites—of foreign countries who are invited to render their opinions, not representatives from popular U.S. movements. These opposing views are foreign by definition, and often anti-American by implication. When U.S. officials square off with their Soviet or Iranian or Nicaraguan counterparts, it may seem like we're getting a balanced discussion of the issues at stake. But the choice of official experts frames the debate in a biased manner. A U.S. audience is likely to be more receptive to the views of American officials who are pitted in debates against leaders of "enemy" states. Missing are the voices of citizen action groups in the U.S. that oppose various aspects of American foreign policy.

BURYING THE LEAD

Even when journalists include a range of sources in their reports, bias is sometimes conveyed by the placement of important sources or information. A lengthy TV news report with a particular slant might go on for a few minutes, only to be contradicted by a significant statement that is buried as an afterthought or a throwaway line at the tail end of the story. A newspaper might run a long story with an addendum or brief passage buried at the bottom that flies smack in the face of everything previously reported.

• In November 1987, *New York Times* reporter Lindsey Gruson puffed the popularity of the Nicaraguan contras in a 50-paragraph article that featured a front page above-the-fold photo of a contra soldier holding an adoring child. Buried near the end of the piece was a passing reference to a just-released Americas Watch report stating that "the contras systematically engage in violent abuses…so prevalent that these may be said to be their principal means of waging war." Then why weren't contra abuses, which included the murder of hundreds of innocent children, a bigger focus of Gruson's article?

• A year and a half prior to the U.S. invasion of Panama, truth was relegated to a footnote when *CBS Evening News* devoted several minutes to what steps the U.S. government should take to deal with Panamanian General Manuel Noriega, who ruled for years with CIA support until he no longer served the needs of U.S. foreign policy. CBS discussed a range of tactics from economic sanctions to a military invasion of Panama. Mentioned in passing at the end of the segment was a brief postscript, which could have been the main story: Twenty-two Latin American and Caribbean countries—from Chile to Cuba—had adopted a resolution calling for an end to U.S. economic sanctions and other coercive measures against Panama.

STENOGRAPHY OR JOURNALISM?

It happens all the time: A government official says something, reporters take down every word, and whatever is said—whether truth or lie—ends up as a sound bite on the evening news or a quote in hundreds of newspapers and magazines. A lot of journalists apparently feel that government officials are there to dish out the facts, and reporters merely have to come and get them.

Of course, journalists have an obligation to accurately report what high-level officials say. But a good reporter should also indicate when an official says something of questionable veracity or when an official out-and-out lies. Unfortunately, qualifying comments that note when official statements cannot be corroborated by independent sources are rarely included by journalists when they quote the high and mighty.

Journalists often act more like stenographers than reporters, duly transcribing lies, half-truths, disinformation and propaganda without attempting to put remarks in perspective or pointing out when something is amiss. Journalists continue to do this even when U.S. officials have been publicly discredited. A classic example:

• In December 1989, CNN and other prominent American news media reported that several months earlier two high-ranking representatives from the Bush administration—National Security Adviser Brent Scowcroft and Deputy Secretary of State Lawrence Eagleburger—had secretly visited Beijing and met with China's hardline leaders. The July 1989 meeting occurred only a few weeks after the Chinese government massacred hundreds of pro-democracy demonstrators in Tiananmen Square. It was embarrassing for Secretary of State Jim Baker to admit that he "misled" the public about Bush's covert China diplomacy. But this hardly tarnished his reputation among the Washington press corps.

A few days after news of the China visit was disclosed, the U.S. invaded Panama; true to form, reporters eagerly conveyed Baker's explanation for the military assault—to promote democracy in Panama. Such noble rhetoric didn't square with U.S. support for the Chinese tyrants who crushed the democracy movement in their country. But instead of asking Baker why they should believe him about Panama when he had lied about China, journalists merely repeated what the Secretary of State said.

THE KISSINGER-HAIG DISEASE

Symptoms of the Kissinger-Haig disease—unlike nuclear allergies—are easily discernible on TV news and public affairs programs. It's a disease that stems from U.S. journalists' unhealthy reliance on official sources and experts, to the exclusion of critical, nongovernmental dissenting views. Advanced stages of this illness afflict the Sunday snooze shows: ABC's *This Week With David Brinkley*, NBC's *Meet the Press*, and *Face the Nation* on CBS.

ABC *Nightline* host Ted Koppel has a bad case of the Kissinger-Haig disease; the two former Secretaries of State were the most frequent guests on *Nightline* during the 40-month period surveyed by FAIR. But the Kissinger-Haig syndrome need not involve these particular gents; it could involve other media-certified experts who are regularly called upon to comment on events. "Whenever anything significant happens, the networks round up the usual suspects," remarked *Newsday* media critic D.D. Guttenplan. "Newspaper reporters often operate the same way."

Oftentimes, former U.S. officials go into business as private consultants after leaving the government. Kissinger, for example, served as a paid consultant in dealings with China's rulers before and after the June 1989 Tiananmen Square massacre. His firm, Kissinger & Associates, represents multinational corporations that profit from a friendly investment climate in China. Kissinger also heads China Ventures, a company engaged in joint ventures with China's state bank. But none of these connections were mentioned when Kissinger, posing as an independent foreign policy expert, apologized for Chinese government atrocities and urged the Bush administration not to impose economic sanctions against that country.

Washington Post columnist Richard Cohen sounded an urgent appeal: "Will someone please ask Henry Kissinger the 'C' question?"—the "C" signifying conflict-of-interest. Most TV viewers who heard Kissinger pontificate on China had no inkling of his business ties to the same government which murdered hundreds of student protesters. These business ties help to explain why Kissinger publicly came to the defense of the Chinese regime. A network news program like *Nightline* commits a great act of cowardice and deception by allowing hired guns like Kissinger to pass themselves off as independent pundits.

PHOTOGRAPHIC SLEIGHT-OF-HAND

We all know the saying, "Every picture tells a story." But pictures don't always tell stories accurately. Pictures and/or their captions sometimes lie.

Manipulative photo journalism can assume various guises. Photographs might have erroneous captions, or two photos might be juxtaposed in such a way as to create a misleading impression. The selection of photos is significant, for a picture sends a cue about how to view an article before we actually read it.

• In his book *Who Killed CBS?*, Peter Boyer tells how network executive Van Gordon Sauter let correspondent Lesley Stahl file critical reports on the Reagan administration, while CBS producers illustrated her words with pictures that contradicted the message. A story focusing on the adverse impact of Reaganomics on the elderly, for example, would be accompanied by a picture of President Reagan opening a new nursing home.

Much to her surprise, Stahl at one point got a phone call from a Reagan aide who thanked her for a story that she thought was critical of the President. Indeed, her words were critical, but the accompanying pictures chosen by CBS News producers (not by Stahl) were viewed favorably by the Reagan team.

• This photo head ran in the *New York Times*: "Pinochet to Seek Third Term." The ensuing caption read, "President Augusto Pinochet of Chile, nominated to run in the Oct. 5 single-candidate election, in Santiago on Monday." (See next page.)

What's wrong with this picture? For starters, General Pinochet wasn't running for a third term in office. He'd never been elected to any office, having taken power in a bloody U.S.-backed coup. He was, however, holding a plebiscite designed to perpetuate his dictatorship for another eight years. Nor was he "nominated" in any sense that most Americans understand the term. He was hand-picked behind closed doors by a clique of military officers.

• CNN *Headline News* aired a story about the use of donations received by the Palestine Aid Society, which supplied food, medical aid and other humanitarian assistance to Palestinians in the Occupied Territories. Comments by members of the Palestine Aid Society were followed by an interview with an unidentified man (his voice was altered and his face hidden in shadows) who alleged without giving any evidence that the Society's money purchased weapons for the Palestinians. As the voice spoke, CNN film footage showed bloodied Israelis being carried to ambulances. The visuals seemed to substantiate the mystery man's claim that Palestinians equipped with weapons were responsible for lethal violence in the West Bank and Gaza Strip. In fact, the film footage actually showed scenes from a West Bank village where a 15-year-old Jewish girl had been killed by an Israeli settler months earlier. CNN later acknowledged the mistake.

When it's words against pictures, the pictures carry the day. Watch for news stories with conflicting words and images.

Agence France-Presse

Pinochet to Seek a Third Term

President Augusto Pinochet of Chile, nominated
yesterday to run in the Oct. 5 single-candidate
election, in Santiago on Monday. Page A3.

From the *New York Times*, August 31, 1988

SPECIAL EFFECTS

The use of background music can manipulate people by orienting them in a certain way during a news report. National Public Radio's *All Things Considered* once did a segment on the different kinds of music that set the tone for its news coverage. There were bouncy tunes for funny stories and cerebral sounds for serious reports. A gloomy melody served as mood music for "sad stories" about life in Soviet-dominated Eastern Europe—but not in reports about poverty-stricken Third World countries allied geopolitically with the U.S.

PASSIVE PHRASES AND GLOSS-OVER EUPHEMISMS

This linguistic technique can impart a subtle bias to news coverage. While the press sometimes has a penchant for hype and sensationalism, reporters and editors frequently choose words that end up neutralizing events that are controversial. Euphemistic phraseology can convey a skewed impression about current events by blurring realities.

Passive phrases and gloss-over euphemisms were invoked by some U.S. reporters in writing about the 1973 military coup in Chile. It was often said that Chilean President Salvador Allende "died" in the presidential palace, when he was murdered by the armed forces. According to the *New York Times*, Allende's policies caused "chaos" which "brought in the military." This obscures the fact that the U.S. government and corporations like ITT were instrumental in fomenting chaos and backing the coup. The notion that "chaos" prompted the Chilean military to move in and restore order implicitly downplays and neutralizes the brutality of the coup, in which tens of thousands of people were killed, tortured and "disappeared."

Michael Parenti cites other examples of this kind of manipulative language in his book *Inventing Reality: The Politics of the Mass Media*.

• Heinous acts of repression by the military government in U.S.-allied Turkey—including the torture, murder and incarceration of trade unionists and other serious human rights abuses—were characterized in the *Washington Post* merely as "controversial measures." Turkey's military despot pursued a "down-to-earth approach" as he sought to deal with "the rough and tumble of everyday politics," according to the *Post*.

• Referring to political violence in El Salvador, the *Christian Science Monitor* stated euphemistically, "Death and destruction still loom high in the saddle in El Salvador," without indicating who—in this case, the U.S.-backed Salvadoran government—was responsible for tens of thousands of political killings in that country.

The use of passive phrases and gloss-over euphemisms results in what Parenti described as the "scanting of content." "By slighting content and dwelling on surface details, the media are able to neutralize the truth while giving an appearance of having thoroughly treated the subject."

CONTRA COMMON SENSE

Whereas the previous technique of media manipulation is rather subtle, this category involves obvious and gross misstatements of fact that defy common sense.

• For example, the lead sentence of a *New York Times* article by Matthew Wald in the aftermath of the Exxon oil spill in Alaska stated: "What man has done and has tried fecklessly to undo here for almost a month, nature is doing instead." The article was based on Exxon assertions that two-thirds of the millions of gallons of oil spilled by the tanker *Valdez* "is gone, most by natural action." Where did all the oil go? Did it magically disappear through the hole in the atmosphere's ozone layer? Why give any credence whatsoever to an absurd Exxon PR ploy?

• The *Miami Herald* reprinted an article by *New York Times* science writer Jane Brody headlined, "'Chemophobia' may be as bad as chemicals." Reports of health hazards in common foods due to pesticides and environmental chemicals are causing "chemophobia," according to Brody. "But this mounting 'chemophobia' is, in turn, raising fears among many scientists... [who] say few people appreciate the benefits of chemicals or the potential negative consequences of rapidly spreading chemophobia."

Brody continues with a whopper: "According to the best available scientific estimates [which she never cited in her article], 99.9 percent of carcinogens in the diet come from natural sources [which she never identified]. Synthetic chemicals account for only 0.01 percent of the carcinogens Americans consume." Another insult to common sense. What was Brody trying to say? That food laced with pesticides and other chemical poisons is healthier than organically-grown produce? When we called to ask Brody to supply evidence to back up her statements, we were told she doesn't respond to inquiries from readers.

ADS THAT DON'T ADD UP

It's not uncommon to come across advertisements and commercials that cynically contradict news stories in the same publication or on the same TV program. This was certainly the case when ABC *Nightline* did a program commemorating Martin Luther King's birthday which was sponsored by De Beers, the notorious South African diamond monopoly.

• Sometimes commercials clash with entertainment television, such as when ABC broadcast *Roots*, the chronicle of a black family's history—from Africa through slavery to emancipation. As *Variety* commented: "It was a bit disconcerting to cut from the anguished screams of a mother whose oldest son had been enslaved to a blurb for Ben-Gay, for use 'when pain is at its worst.'"

• A *Wall Street Journal* news story disclosed: "General Motors unveiled aggressively big price increases on 1988-model cars, apparently in a bid to bolster revenue and earnings." On the same day, the *Journal* carried an ad which boasted: "Now, GM's Most Popular Cars, Equipped the Way You Want, Cost Less in 1988."

• Other ads that don't add up are those that project a public image which grossly contradicts the company's actual practices. A September 1987 "Good Health" supplement of the *New York Times* Sunday magazine was replete with ads from pharmaceutical companies extolling remedies for hay fever, laxatives or simply their benevolent corporate philosophy. The *Times* supplement did not allude to the fact that many of its advertisers had knowingly sold dangerous or ineffective products in the U.S. and the Third World. Example: Upjohn, whose ad featured four cute kids and the slogan "A second century of caring," dumps hazardous chemicals in various Third World countries. Upjohn's product Panalba was withdrawn from the U.S. market after twelve people died from the antibiotic; nevertheless, Upjohn continues to sell Panalba in 33 countries under the brand name Albamycin-T.

• *National Geographic* featured a holographic cover story about whether humanity can "save this fragile Earth." On the back cover, also holographic, was an ad with the golden arches of McDonald's. That McDonald's should advertise in a magazine with any kind of environmental message is ironic given that the fast food chain uses annually more than 70 million pounds of liquid polystyrene, a petroleum product in styrofoam cups and containers. Polystyrene, according to the Citizens Clearinghouse for Hazardous Waste, is not biodegradable and can't be burned without releasing poisonous gases. If buried, chemicals will leach into soil, water, and eventually the food chain. It appears that McDonald's doesn't feel planet Earth also deserves a break today.

• In May 1988 General Electric sponsored a TV movie, *To Heal A Nation*, about Vietnam veterans. The show aired on NBC, the network owned by GE, which grossed over $12 billion from military contracts during the Vietnam War.

• There was also the ad campaign, seen on TV and in major weekly magazines, which featured a Vietnam vet amputee named Bill Denby, who plays basketball on artificial legs supplied by DuPont. The Denby ads are particu-

larly insidious given DuPont's highly profitable role as a military contractor during the Vietnam War. Between 1964 and 1972, DuPont and its affiliates earned several billion dollars in Pentagon contracts, producing such items as napalm, anti-personnel bombs and heavy equipment for the U.S. war effort.

THE NUMBERS RACKET

The numbers racket is a category of media bias that includes rigged statistics, inflated or deflated estimates of attendance at political demonstrations, contradictory tallies and numerical tricks. For instance:

• Each month, the federal Bureau of Labor Statistics (BLS) releases national unemployment figures. These statistics, dutifully reported by mass media, hide the true extent of unemployment in the United States. Not counted are people without jobs who haven't looked for work for over a month because the prospects are discouraging, as well as those who are forced to retire early. Moreover, the BLS inflates the number of employed by counting those who work only one hour a week as fully-employed people.

The BLS actually compiles two sets of statistics. The bureau's "U-7" rate, which factors in "discouraged" employment seekers and early retirees, is a

For Bill Demby, the difference means getting another shot.

When Bill Demby was in Vietnam, he used to dream of coming home and playing a little basketball with the guys.

A dream that all but died when he lost both his legs to a Viet Cong rocket.

But then, a group of researchers discovered that a remarkable Du Pont plastic could help make artificial limbs that were more resilient, more flexible, more like life itself.

Thanks to these efforts, Bill Demby is back. And some say, he hasn't lost a step.

At Du Pont, we make the things that make a difference.

Better things for better living. **DU PONT**

much more accurate reflection of unemployment percentages in the U.S. Thus in 1986, when the media reported the average national unemployment rate was 6.2 percent, 14.3 percent of the labor force actually experienced unemployment. The U-7 rate is available to journalists, who typically ignore the higher figures. "In the end," wrote former *New York Times* labor correspondent William Serrin in *The Nation*, "the press almost always takes the easy way out and uses the conventional numbers, a tendency historically encouraged by the government because it puts the best face on unemployment."

• The headline of an un-bylined *New York Times* story on December 31, 1989 read: "15,000 Jews and Palestinians Join Jerusalem Peace Rally." The figure cited in the headline was based on estimates provided by Israeli police. In fact, the number of demonstrators was significantly higher, as the unidentified *Times* correspondent noted in the fifth paragraph of the article: "The Peace Now movement, which organized the rally, put the number at closer to 35,000. With crowds 10 to 12 deep along much of the route, the Peace Now figure did not seem inflated." Then why was the deflated number featured in the headline?

• During the mid-1980s, journalists frequently repeated State Department claims that Nicaragua hosted some 2,500 to 3,500 Cuban military personnel and 6,000 Cuban civilians. The *New York Times* upped the figure to 3,500 to 5,000 Cubans in combat support roles in Nicaragua. But when a Cuban general, Rafael del Pino Diaz, defected to the U.S. in the summer of 1987, he indicated that only 300 to 400 Cuban military personnel were posted in Nicaragua (the amount claimed all along by Cuba and Nicaragua). Although del Pino Diaz was trumpeted as the most important military defector in Cuban history and was highly regarded by U.S. intelligence, his assessment of the level of Cuban support for Nicaragua was ignored by *Times* correspondent Bernard Trainor who continued to write about "thousands of Cuban military advisers in Nicaragua."

POLLS MADE TO ORDER

Polling data is often deceptive. Results can be skewed in one direction or another depending on what questions are asked and what procedures are used to gather the data. This may explain why polls on the same subject may yield markedly different results.

Herbert I. Schiller, author of *The Mind Managers*, noted: "Opinion-polling as practiced in the United States...presents itself as a means of registering opinions and expressing choices but, in reality...it is a *choice-restricting* mechanism. Because ordinary polls reduce, and sometimes eliminate entirely, the...true spectrum of possible options, the possibilities and preferences they express are better viewed as 'guided' choices."

As Schiller explained, "Those who dominate governmental decision-making and private economic activity are the main supports of the pollsters. The vital needs of these groups determine, intentionally or not, the parameters within which polls are formulated."

• Pollsters often slant questions to increase the likelihood of getting a particular response that will please whoever commissioned the poll. At one point, the Television Information Office hired the Roper polling agency to survey opinion about commercials during children's shows. Note how Roper posed the question: "How do you feel—that there should be *no* commercials on any children's programs or that it is all right to have them if they don't take unfair advantage of children?" The final clause—"if they don't take unfair advantage"—predetermined the results that were announced in a press release by the National Association of Broadcasters and reported widely in the mass media: "Roper Finds Three Out of Four Americans Approve Principle of Commercial Sponsorship for Children's Television Programs."

• The page-one lead story in the *New York Times* on April 4, 1989, was headlined, "Majority in Israel Oppose PLO Talks Now, A Poll Shows." The first sentence referred to "an overwhelming majority of Israeli Jews" as opposed to peace negotiations with the PLO. Yet a day earlier, the *Miami Herald* reported the results of a poll that indicated "two thirds of Israelis favor talks with the PLO if it recognizes the Jewish state's right to a secure border and ceases terrorist acts." A slight change in the phrasing of the question can result in a dramatic change in results.

• Interdisciplinaria en Desarrollo, a Costa Rican-based affiliate of the Gallup polling organization, was commissioned in 1985 by the U.S. Information Agency (the U.S. government's official propaganda arm) to poll Costa Rican attitudes toward neighboring Nicaragua. The poll found that most Costa Ricans viewed Nicaragua as a threat. But National Public Radio subsequently disclosed that this conclusion was reached after eliminating all respondents with less than seven years of education and anyone else who, in the judgment of the pollsters, was "not knowledgeable about the subject being investigated." In other words, it is likely that only the wealthier and more conservative segment of the population was counted.

The results of this poll were widely cited by officials of the Reagan administration, which had commissioned the survey in order to gather more ammunition for its propaganda war against Nicaragua. U.S. journalists also reported the results of this poll, even though Gallup's U.S. headquarters in Princeton, New Jersey, disassociated itself from the Costa Rican firm and refused to vouch for the latter's polling methods. This same Gallup affiliate has done polling throughout Central America that tends to produce results sought by the U.S. Embassy.

OBIT OMIT

Obituaries about the wealthy and the powerful (and who else are most obituaries about?) often whitewash key biographical facts. Examples:

• When longtime CIA operative Irving Brown died, the *New York Times* and the *Washington Post* tried to sidestep his career as a spy, suggesting that allegations of a CIA link were communist-inspired misinformation. Said the *Times*: "Mr. Brown was at times denounced by right-wing Americans as a communist sympathizer, while the communists branded him an agent of the

Central Intelligence Agency." Well, Brown couldn't have been both, so he must have been neither—that was the implicit message. But it wasn't just "communists" who spoke of Brown's CIA association. A range of sources, including former CIA agent and CNN *Crossfire* host Tom Braden, ex-CIA operative Philip Agee and labor organizer Walter Reuther, has confirmed Brown's pivotal role in CIA labor operations in Western Europe after World War II.

• When former Black Panther Party leader Huey Newton was gunned down in Oakland, stories and obituaries about Newton omitted important facts about his political history. According to the *Miami Herald*, "The Panthers eventually died out because of infighting, arrests, deaths, imprisonments and differing philosophies" among leaders of the group. The article made no reference to the FBI's COINTELPRO program which secretly targeted the Black Panther Party for destruction. Nor did the *Herald* mention the assassination of key party leaders, including Fred Hampton, who was murdered in bed by Chicago police.

• When actress Lucille Ball died, *The Nation* magazine pointed out what mainstream obituaries refused to acknowledge. Lucy was registered to vote as a member of the Communist Party in 1936. This earned her a visit before the House Committee on Un-American Activities in its Red-hunting heyday in the 1950s. During her testimony, Ball steadfastly refused to name any friends or colleagues who had also been party members. The failure of obits to point this out is "consistent with the failure to report on the blacklist in the first place," *The Nation* editorialized.

Conclusion

"Despite the wonders of communications technology, the news often seems little more than folklore, a steady stream of nursery tales for adults," says British journalist Ed Harriman. Why is this so?

Some prefer to blame the media's inadequacies on lousy reporters. But criticism should also be directed at the institutional framework in which journalists try to do their job. The most serious and pervasive distortions in the U.S. media are not only the result of deadlines, inadequate space, poor judgment, a lack of skill, or the idiosyncratic nature of professional news people. Such factors cannot explain the larger patterns of bias that persist. As upcoming chapters discuss, these patterns have a lot to do with the corporations that own and control the media, as well as our government's role in shaping and manipulating the news.

PART II

The Media Elite

4

The Media Cartel:
Corporate Control of the News

Do the business priorities of their corporate bosses affect the way journalists cover the news? Consider network news coverage of the 1988 Winter Olympics in Calgary, Canada. All three network news divisions had to decide how much attention the Olympics warranted. NBC devoted a total of 33 minutes of national news coverage to the games, while CBS News provided 17 minutes of coverage. Compare these figures to ABC, which found the Winter Olympics worthy of 47 minutes on its nightly newscasts. Is it merely coincidental that ABC also televised the Winter Olympics and a heavy news focus helped build ratings and profits? Are we to believe that such concerns had no bearing on the "independent news judgment" of ABC producers?

ABC News found the 1988 Summer Olympic Games in Seoul, South Korea, less newsworthy than the winter games. That's because ABC didn't televise the Summer Olympics—NBC did. As it turned out, NBC News considered the summer games and their Korean hosts far more newsworthy than the other networks. NBC's inflated news coverage was geared toward attracting a larger audience—which translated into greater earnings for the network. So much for the hallowed precept that news choices are based solely on the intrinsic importance of a story and are immune to financial considerations.

The truth of the matter is that financial interests play a major role in determining what we see—and don't see—on television. Most of the top network sponsors are powerful multinational corporations. These global mammoths dominate our broadcast and print media far more extensively than most people realize. They exert tremendous leverage over the media industry because they are its principal source of revenue: TV and radio get nearly 100 percent of their income from advertisers, newspapers 75 percent, and magazines about 50 percent.

Corporate sponsors clutter the airways and presses with lies, half-truths, conflicting signals, disconnected factoids, and self-serving come-ons all geared toward reaping mega-bucks from consumers. Between 60 and 70 percent of newspaper space is reserved for ads, while 22 percent of TV time is filled with commercials.

It's obviously a very profitable venture for all concerned; otherwise sponsors wouldn't be willing to sink a quarter of a million dollars into producing a single TV commercial—and that's not counting network airtime, costing an average of $134,000 for a 30-second prime-time spot on a major network. (Half-minute commercials during the 1990 Super Bowl sold for $700,000.) Total spending on TV ads reached nearly $25 billion in 1988.

Although network executives are quick to deny it, commercials are often louder than other on-air programming. Most people have probably noticed this at one time or another. In response to numerous complaints about the volume of TV commercials, the Federal Communications Commission (FCC) looked into the matter but claimed the results were inconclusive—"the causes of apparent loudness remained a mystery." As for the suggestion that the FCC "should simply require that commercials not be loud," the consensus within the Reagan administration was that "imposing regulations in this area would be at odds with the Commission's current deregulatory philosophy." The amplified volume of commercials is yet another indication of how giant corporations intrude on our lives as they dominate mass media.

ADVERTISER MUSCLE

Dependent on corporate sponsors for financial sustenance, TV networks and print media are under tremendous pressure to shape their product in a way that best accommodates the needs of their advertisers. "I would say they are always taken into account," Herman Keld of CBS acknowledged. An obvious example of sponsor intrusion in regular network programming occurs when corporate logos and brand name products appear as props in game shows, sporting events and other entertainment media. For the most part, however, advertisers wield influence by restricting and watering down show biz content, rather than by adding to it. One way they do this is by yanking—or threatening to yank—financial support from certain programs.

In 1989, for example, a television special produced by the National Audubon Society was aired without commercials on a cable channel owned by Turner Broadcasting System after eight advertisers pulled out because of pressure from the logging industry. The special, *Ancient Forests: Rage Over Trees*, was deemed too radical by U.S. logging companies. Meanwhile, Domino's Pizza cancelled its advertising on NBC's *Saturday Night Live* because of the show's alleged anti-Christian message.

These days, no commercial TV executive in his or her right mind would produce a program without considering whether it will fly with sponsors. Prospective shows are often discussed with major advertisers, who review script treatments and suggest changes when necessary. Adjustments are sometimes made to please sponsors. This riles a lot of TV writers, who complain of frequent run-ins with network censors in the "program standards" department, which monitors sex, violence and obscene language, as well as the social and political content of dramatic programs. A poll of the Writers Guild of America disclosed that 86 percent of queried members said they knew from personal experience that entertainment programs are raked over by censors.

It may come as a surprise to many Americans that censorship is so prevalent on network television. But corporate sponsors figure they are entitled to call the shots since they foot the bill—an assumption shared by network executives, who quickly learn to internalize the desires of their well-endowed patrons. For starters, they are likely to frown upon programming that puts a damper on the "buying mood" that advertisers require. Network censors admit that loss of advertising revenue is one of their main concerns. These are the principal guidelines, explicitly spelled out by big-league sponsors, that TV censors follow:

• **Make sure nothing in a script undermines the sales pitch for the advertised product.** For example, a gas company sponsoring a TV version of *Judgment at Nuremberg* demanded that producers delete references to "gas chambers" from accounts of Nazi concentration camps. Pharmaceutical firms won't tolerate scenes in which someone commits suicide by overdosing on pills. On a lighter note, a writer was forced to delete the line "She eats too much"—a concept anathema to the breakfast food manufacturer that sponsored the show. This kind of script tampering is endemic in television entertainment.

• **Portray Big Business in a flattering light.** Sponsors are adamant about this. Procter & Gamble, which spends over a billion dollars a year on advertising, once decreed in a memo on broadcast policy: "There will be no material that will give offense, either directly or indirectly to any commercial organization of any sort." Ditto for Prudential Insurance: "A positive image of business and finance is important to sustain on the air." If a businessman is cast as the bad guy, it must be clear that he is an exception, and the script must also include benevolent business folk so as not to leave the wrong impression. Corporate sponsors are unlikely to underwrite programs that engage in serious criticism of environmental pollution, occupational hazards or other problems attributable to corporate malfeasance.

Marshall Herskovitz, co-executive producer of ABC's *thirtysomething*, had to knuckle under when censors insisted that a character embroiled in a political discussion not say the government cut safety regulations "so that car companies can make more money." Entertainment programs aren't a forum for political debate, Herskovitz was told, and besides it would upset advertisers. "One of the most dangerous, subversive, destructive forces in our country today is advertising," said Herskovitz—not just its hold over commercial TV, but the ads themselves. "I would rather have the messed-up and occasionally confused motivations of television producers than I would to have

the very simple motivations of corporate sponsors making decisions of what
we should see on television."

• **Cater to the upper crust.** Sponsors don't want just any audience; they
want affluent viewers with buying power. To impress potential sponsors,
ABC once prepared a booklet with a section called, "Some people are more
valuable than others." If the elderly and low-income counted for more in the
advertising department, their particular concerns would figure more prominently in the tone and content of TV programming. But the fixations of mass
media are far more demographic than democratic.

• **Steer clear of overly serious or complex subjects and bleach out controversy whenever possible.** DuPont, a major advertiser, told the FCC that
commercials are more effective on "lighter, happier" programs. Comedy,
adventure and escapism are standard fare, as advertisers push mass media
toward socially insignificant content that offends as few viewers as possible.
"You can't take up real problems seriously," complained Charles Knopf, a
TV scriptwriter and former president of the Writers Guild. Acutely sensitive
to sponsor proclivities, many writers and producers automatically avoid controversial topics. When a dicey story is proposed, it is usually killed before it
gets written. Scripts that survive the editing process often bear little resem-
blance to the original concept.

The 1988 season-opening episode of the dramatic series *MacGyver* was
censored by ABC in response to complaints by the National Rifle
Association (NRA). The episode in question included flashbacks of a shooting accident that took the life of MacGyver's boyhood friend. The show was
to have closed with an alert providing statistics as to how many children are
killed each day in handgun accidents. But this was vetoed by ABC's program
practices division, prompting producer Steve Downing to ask, "How much
influence does the NRA have in censoring this show?"

In recent years, network dramas that took too liberal a stand on abortion
rights and the death penalty have also been watered down and neutralized,
much to the chagrin of the writers. Said a network executive: "We will not
allow our programs to be used for advocacy of any kind." Except if it's the
day-to-day advocacy of consumerism and sexism that dominates network
television.

"Things have opened up as far as four-letter words are concerned, but as far
as political content goes, I don't see anything changing," said Tommy
Smothers. Two decades after CBS kicked the Smothers Brothers off the air for
expressing unauthorized opinions about the Vietnam War, the duo was back on
that network—but without illusions. In 1989, Smothers remembered that "four
or five years ago, Lou Grant [Edward Asner] was put off the air because of his
opinions on Nicaragua. I'm sure not going to start getting on their case now
about getting out of Central America. I'll be out of work for another 20 years."

TV programming is often criticized for being bland and superficial, but network executives claim this is what the public wants. Actually, it is what sponsors want. The challenge for TV producers is to keep viewers glued to the Tube while serving up endless varieties of pap. This is accomplished by seasoning prime-time with a mixture of sex and violence. There has to be enough titillation to lure an audience, but not too much, lest the networks provoke a backlash.

Sponsors perk up when right-wing religious crusaders complain loudly about what they see as distasteful or immoral telecasts. Such rumblings have prompted ad agencies to circulate "hit lists" of shows deemed unacceptable to their major clients. "Advertisers have a perfect right to decide where their money is being spent," an advertising executive told the *Wall Street Journal*. The prevailing sentiment within the media industry was summed up by an ad exec quoted in *USA Today*: "I don't believe advertisers have a moral obligation to put their products on the line for the benefit of free speech."

Corporate coercion

From the domineering vantage point of corporate sponsors, broadcast media are first and foremost "advertising vehicles." As an NBC News employee told FAIR, "We learn in this trade when there's a TWA crash, for example, TWA ads will be pulled off the air that day."

Newspapers and magazines are in a similar bind; their economic fortunes are tied more to their advertising base than their subscription base. Magazine editors admit they must adapt to the regimen prescribed by advertisers. "We had to deliver a more high-quality [read: wealthier] reader," said a manager at *Rolling Stone*. "The only way to deliver a different kind of reader is to change editorial."

The *New York Times* has also been dancing to a marketing beat, as Doug Henwood, editor of *Left Business Observer*, noted:

> The title of the *Times* 1987 Annual Report is "The Marketing of Excellence." In his introduction, *Times* executive editor Max Frankel boasted that "The News Department of The New York Times does not wince at the thought of 'marketing'...their many products."
>
> True to the title's promise, the report is a homage to the fruitful marriage of advertising and editorial content. Frankel celebrates the new single-theme pages ("Keeping Fit," "Eating Well," "Consumer's World") and a new focus on "lifestyle patterns." The editorial environment of such pages is, of course, extremely attractive to specialized advertisers.

A *Business Week* appeal for blue chip corporate backers minced no words in a large ad in the *New York Times*: "We reach more executives earning more than $100,000 than any other magazine. More power to you." In the

Times a few days earlier was the paid boast that *"Newsweek* has a higher percentage of readers who are professionals/managers than any other
newsweekly." Simultaneously, a similar ad in the *Los Angeles Times* touted
Newsweek as "the smartest way to talk to college graduates" since the magazine "has a higher percentage of college graduates than any other
newsweekly." Advertisers are after people with money to spend, and editors
are under pressure to deliver—and deliver to—those people.

The immense power of advertisers bends the content as well as the form of
print media. The *New York Times* news department, which prides itself on
independent journalism, has submitted to pressure from advertisers. The
automobile industry is a major advertiser in the *Times*, and consequently
Times coverage of auto safety and pollution has been skewed. According to a
Times staffer, the paper of record ran stories "more or less put together by the
advertisers," as the industry lobbied for looser safety standards in the 1970s.
Times publisher and CEO Arthur Sulzberger admitted that he leaned on his
editors to present the auto industry's position because it "would affect advertising."

Many journalists feel they have been reduced to writing "on the back of
advertisements," as one press representative put it. This is certainly the case
at upscale magazines like *Vanity Fair*, which boosted its bank account by
running a succession of puff pieces about its advertisers, including New York
tycoon Donald Trump. One feature spread accounted for 37 full-page ads in
early 1989 at up to $25,000 a pop.

Drawn by Art Young, December 1912

The Freedom of the Press

"Many trade publications and local papers have long offered favorable editorial coverage to story subjects who agree to purchase ads," wrote Jonathan Alter in *Newsweek*. "On TV, implicit deals for kid-glove treatment are an almost everyday practice."

PREFAB NEWS

It has long been a sacred edict among media professionals that news and advertising ("church and state") are supposed to be kept separate. Most newspaper publishers maintain that their ad directors don't shape the stories and columns produced by their writers and editors. They say it would be unethical for moneyed interests to influence news choices, which ought to rest on unbiased objective criteria.

But this golden rule of journalism is broken all the time. "The wall of separation between American news and the business interests is being systematically dismantled at institutional levels of journalism," asserts Ben Bagdikian, former dean of the School of Journalism at the University of California in Berkeley. "The practice of selecting news in order to make advertising more effective is becoming so common that it has achieved the status of scientific precision and publishing wisdom."

The blurring of distinctions between news and advertising raises troubling questions that aren't being asked by the major media. Isn't it misleading and ethically dubious for famous TV journalists to participate in commercials? Yet there was no outcry when ABC's Sam Donaldson lent his voice and prestige for a slick new form of TV advertising known as the "video news release."

"Television segments that look like news spots but subtly tout products are flooding into newsrooms for airing as part of regular news programming," wrote Pacific News Service (PNS) correspondent Susan Davis in mid-1989. Produced by corporate PR firms, these videos feature expert commentary, dramatic visuals and the voices of top TV anchors, punctuated by a glimpse of the company's product or name. On one video news release, Sam Donaldson was heard introducing a segment on airport security systems that featured a new chemical sensing device for detecting plastic explosives. This well-produced piece was actually an ad for the American Chemical Society.

Every week, hundreds of local TV stations, beset by budget and staff cutbacks, air these free, ready-made news releases, which look increasingly realistic. Even veteran media observers often fail to distinguish between video PR spots and station-produced news. "It's just appalling," University of California sociologist Todd Gitlin told PNS. "Most local news is simply a matter of reporters going to obvious sources and accepting what's spoonfed. But this is one more step on the slippery slope to accepting someone else's prefab news blip."

PR deluge

Newspapers are also inundated by corporate PR. A study by Scott M. Culip, ex-dean of the School of Journalism and Mass Communications at the University of Georgia, found that 40 percent of the news content in a typical U.S. newspaper originated with public relations press releases, story memos, or suggestions. PR copy from real estate agents, developers and industrial firms typically masquerades as authentic news stories. It's not unusual for articles about fashion, for example, to be lifted straight from press releases by designers and fashion shows. Food editors rely heavily on food company blurbs for recipes and stories. Sections on home improvement, travel and entertainment are likewise filled with PR-related fluff. "The growing trend among newspapers to turn over sections of the 'news' to the advertising department usually produces copy that is not marked 'advertising' but is full of promotional material under the guise of news," explained Bagdikian.

The business pages are especially fertile turf for corporate PR operations. "Quite a lot of our business stories originate from press releases," acknowledged Seymour Topping, formerly managing editor of the *New York Times*. "It's impossible for us to cover all of these organizations ourselves."

Charles Staebler, former assistant managing editor of the *Wall Street Journal*, estimated that up to 50 percent of the *Journal*'s stories are generated by press releases. But he quickly added, "In every case we try to go beyond the press release." Apparently the *Journal* hasn't tried hard enough. The *Columbia Journalism Review*, which scrutinized a typical issue of America's leading business paper, found that more than half the *Journal*'s news stories "were based solely on press releases." Oftentimes the releases were reprinted "almost verbatim or in paraphrase," with little additional reporting, and many articles carried the slug, "By a *Wall Street Journal* Staff Reporter."

Corporate PR maestros have at their disposal a formidable array of instruments to promote a company's interests and influence public opinion. PR Newswire, a wire service specializing in business press releases, transmits 150 stories daily to some 600 newsrooms around the country, including the *Wall Street Journal, New York Times, Newsweek, Washington Post, USA Today*, the three major TV networks and other big media outlets. Now partners with CapCities/ABC, PR Newswire is also picked up by AP, UPI, Reuters, and Knight-Ridder Financial News.

In addition to product promotion, corporate PR plays an important role in damage control and crisis management. When scientists disclosed in the mid-1970s that fluorocarbons from aerosol spray products destroy the ozone layer, the aerosol industry launched a PR campaign that emphasized "knowledge gaps" instead of gaps in the Earth's atmospheric shield. Industry press releases formed the basis for articles in numerous newspapers and magazines that questioned the ozone depletion "theory," enabling aerosol spray manufacturers to buy additional time before their product was banned. In this case, industry profits were deemed more important than the prevention of skin cancer.

Faced with rising public concern over dioxin contamination, Dow Chemical's PR team sought to obscure the hazards of this deadly carcinogen by churning out a barrage of misleading data. Dow's attempt to muddle an otherwise clear-cut issue was reflected in a July 1983 *Newsweek* article, titled "Dioxin: How Great a Threat?" "No wonder people are confused about dioxin," said *Newsweek*. "Skeptics downplay its danger, calling it the latest inductee in the environmentalists' 'chemical of the month club.'" And *Fortune*, as usual, came to the defense of big business: "Where lies the truth in the wide gulf between Dow Chemical Co.'s view of itself as a model environmental citizen and the lurid accusations in the press that it is a reckless polluter of its own nest, Midland, Michigan? Closer to Dow's side of the shore..." Dow, which had long known of dioxin's dangers, eventually agreed to an out-of-court settlement of a suit brought by Vietnam veterans who were exposed to dioxin in Agent Orange during the war.

Another example of crisis PR involved Union Carbide's effort to downplay responsibility for the gas leak at its plant in Bhopal, India, that killed over 2,500 people and injured over 250,000 in December 1984. Not content with contaminating the city of Bhopal, Union Carbide poisoned the media environment as well. CBS *60 Minutes* aired a segment echoing Union Carbide's position, which shifted the blame for neglecting the injured from the company to the government of India. Reporter Ed Bradley said Union Carbide "prides itself on its safety record," but he didn't mention the company's history of toxic leaks, accidents and other safety violations, including serious infractions at its plant in Institute, West Virginia, which prompted the Reagan administration to levy a $1.4 million fine.

Another Union Carbide propaganda ploy was the theory that blamed the Bhopal accident not on the company's well-documented negligence, but on sabotage by an unidentified "disgruntled worker." This dubious alibi garnered headlines in the *New York Times* ("Union Carbide Says Upset Worker Set Off the Bhopal Plant"), *Newsday* ("Bhopal Blamed on Sabotage") and other major dailies, even though the company offered no evidence to back up its claim.

Image polishing

Events such as the Bhopal gas leak, Exxon's Alaska oil spill or radiation exposure at DuPont's Savannah River nuclear weapons plant in South Carolina underscore the need for corporate image-polishing. Toward this end, business firms have resorted to purchasing "ad-itorials" in major dailies and news magazines. Pioneered by Mobil Oil's PR wiz Herbert Schmertz, these "advocacy advertisements" are designed not to sell products, but to promote the politics and benevolent image of multinational corporations—and to attack anything that sullies this image.

Mobil spends $5 million annually on such ads (written off as a business expense) to tell us, for example, why it is in America's best interest to sell missiles to Saudi Arabia. Mobil didn't share a significant detail: it makes millions each year from business dealings in that country. Until recently one of the biggest investors in South Africa, Mobil used advocacy ads to voice its opposition to divestment from the apartheid state, despite the pleas of black leaders like Bishop Desmond Tutu that divestment is a key tool against South African oppression.

Portrayed as a phenomenon of media openness, advocacy ads actually reflect just the opposite. Yes, you can buy the bottom right quarter of the *New York Times* op-ed page, but only if you are able to pay $13,000 a shot. Full-page ads are also available to express various points of view in newspapers, to the tune of thousands of dollars even in a mid-sized city. The redoubtable Schmertz calls advocacy ads a return to "the ancient and honorable art of pamphleteering"—a description that *USA Today* liked very much, using it as the caption for a graphic with an article about the increased income newspapers were receiving from such ads.

There's only one catch to this so-called democratic pamphleteering: advocacy ads are possible only for institutions with budgets big enough to shell out millions every year purely for propaganda purposes. Tom Paine had other things in mind.

TIME WARNER TANGO

"It looks like the Rolling Stones are coming here next week," remarked a security guard as he eyed a mob of would-be spectators waiting outside a packed Delaware courthouse. They were there to witness in person the Delaware Supreme Court's historic decision on the fate of Time Inc., target of one of the year's fiercest takeover battles. But only those with special passes were permitted inside on July 24, 1989; the rest had to settle for watching the courtroom drama unfold on Cable News Network. It was the first time ever in Delaware corporate law that TV cameras were allowed in a courtroom.

Even in an era of deregulated merger mania, this corporate tryst was remarkable for the attention it generated. It began in March 1989, when Time and Warner, two communications giants, announced a major stock swap as part of a friendly deal which would have effectively combined the companies, forming the largest—and arguably the most influential—media conglomerate in the world. The business profile of Time Inc., America's biggest magazine ad revenue earner and publisher (*Time, Life, Fortune, People, Sports Illustrated,* etc.), meshed particularly well with Warner, the number-one record and TV production company in the United States. With combined assets somewhere between \$25 and \$30 billion, they also controlled a major chunk of the cable, motion picture and book markets, including Home Box Office (the nation's largest pay TV channel), Lorimar Studios and the Book-of-the-Month Club.

Such an amalgam of lucrative components gave Time Warner distinct advantages for promoting their products in a multiplicity of media. A magazine article with the company copyright, for example, could be expanded into a Time Warner book. It could serve as the basis for a film made at an in-house studio, which would then be distributed through a movie theater chain owned by the same company. The movie doubtless will be reviewed in widely-read magazines also published by Time Warner, and the soundtrack would be issued on a company record label. To catch a re-run, turn to one of Time Warner's cable channels. "More and more, we will be dealing with closed loops," predicts Ben Bagdikian, as a handful of mega-conglomerates squeeze out others in the field.

The prospect of Time Warner commanding such a dominant position in the news and entertainment universe made executives at Paramount, another media titan, hyperactive with envy. It soon became a three-ring circus, as Paramount leaped into the fray, waving top dollar for Time Inc. stock, which shot up 45 points in a single day. Time was suddenly "in play," as market euphoria carried clusters of media stock skyward, followed by a period of wild fluctuation as rumors swept through Wall Street that other corporate heavyweights, including General Electric, might join the battle for Time.

The well-planned Time Warner merger quickly degenerated into a full-fledged corporate scramble, involving investment bankers, blue chip law firms, PR strategists and a fleet of private detectives hired to dig up dirt on the other parties. Time execs rejected Paramount's hostile takeover bid and announced their intention to buy Warner outright. Paramount countered by upping its offer. There was even talk of a reverse takeover—the so-called Pac Man defense—in which Time would turn around and swallow up Paramount. Sensing opportunity amidst all the turmoil, Australian media magnate Rupert Murdoch hovered in the wings, ready to grab any loose assets shed during the scuffle. At stake were commercial empires so vast it staggered the imagination.

While Wall Street movers and shakers were having a field day, those who punched the clock day-in and day-out at Time Inc. grew increasingly nervous. Someone would have to pay for the huge debt amassed by the company, as it sought to stave off Paramount's maneuvers. Given that well-heeled executives and publishers aren't in the habit of volunteering cuts in their seven-figure salaries, it seemed likely that Time's rank-and-file would bear the brunt of the inevitable belt-tightening, layoffs and restructuring that a debt-laden company must undertake.

When the dust finally settled, the Delaware Supreme Court upheld Time's proposed $14 billion buyout of Warner, leaving Paramount to search elsewhere for media industry prey. Most of the press covered the entire ordeal simply as a business story without dwelling on the social and political consequences of such a merger. The main criticisms were voiced by big media execs concerned about facing an even bigger bully on the block. A *New York Times* article, headlined "Time Deal Worrying Competitors," featured comments to that effect by Robert Wright, president of NBC, owned by little ol' GE. Journalists covering the Time Warner merger rarely featured statements by public interest critics warning that mass media concentration in fewer and fewer corporate hands poses a serious threat to pluralism, democratic discourse and the First Amendment.

Media monopoly

The Time Warner tango was only the latest episode in an accelerating march toward media monopolization that is transforming news and entertainment. In 1982, according to Ben Bagdikian, 50 corporations controlled most of the media business. As of January 1990 that number was 23, and shrink-ing fast. Time Warner co-chairman J. Richard Munro predicted that within a few years a half dozen vertically-integrated media mammoths will dominate the industry not just in the U.S. but globally, and he vowed his company would be one of them.

Cross-owner and cross-border patterns are woven through intricate webs of high-finance, as media companies indulge in an incestuous romp spurred by lax regulatory policies. The trend is unmistakable: key players in one venue are buying up other kinds of media properties at home and abroad. Today about a dozen corporations control most of America's daily newspa-per circulation; only three firms account for a majority of magazine earnings; and six publishing houses have a lock on most of the book business. The motion picture scene is dominated by four film studios. A half dozen corpo-rations control 90 percent of domestic record sales. Even computer database services are controlled by a few large companies.

The major TV networks, which continue to capture the lion's share of viewers and revenue, have also succumbed to the forces of merger and con-solidation. In the mid-1980s, as a result of eased ownership rules drafted by Reagan's FCC, the Big Three came under new management even less inter-ested in creative broadcasting than in harnessing the bottom line. ABC fell to CapCities, a wealthy but unimpressive news chain. Shortly thereafter General Electric, a leading military contractor and union-buster, gobbled up NBC.

Laurence Tisch, a hard-nosed hotel and tobacco tycoon, grabbed the reins at CBS after it barely survived a couple of hostile takeover attempts. Following the path blazed by CapCities and GE, Tisch ordered deep staff and budget cutbacks. Ratings sank along with morale, particularly in the news division, once considered to be the cream of the network crop, which began closing overseas bureaus to save money. It didn't help much when Tisch announced that he had struck a deal with K-Mart to promote CBS.

Aided by fiber optics, satellites and other advanced technologies, today's media masters are able to publish and broadcast news across the world at faster speeds and lower costs than ever before. But this has not improved news coverage or other TV fare. "Put the blame where you will, or spread it around generously, but the truth is that the networks are getting worse," said *San Francisco Chronicle* television critic John Carman. "None of these newly restructured entities have shown any genius for programming, a line of endeavor that, after all, is still more art than science."

In the race to maximize profits, the media industry is little different than other business ventures. Newspapers are especially lucrative—which is why they frequently become takeover targets. There are about 1,600 daily papers in the U.S., but local monopolies with a captive audience and no competition exist in 98 percent of U.S. cities. The Gannett Corporation, America's largest chain, has a particular fetish for one-newspaper cities and towns. In addition to *USA Today* (with an estimated readership of 6.3 million), Gannett owned 121 newspapers around the nation, including 86 dailies, in 1989. Other Gannett spoils include ten TV and 16 radio stations, a news service, the Louis Harris & Associates polling agency and, for good measure, the country's second-largest billboard company.

"Wall Street didn't give a damn if we put together a good paper in Niagara Falls. They just wanted to know if our profits would be in the 15-20 percent range," confessed Gannett rudeboy Al Neuharth. By hiking subscription rates and running more advertisements, a cost-conscious manager could expand annual earnings to 40 percent—a temptation many newspaper owners find irresistible. But higher profits don't necessarily add up to a better publication. Numerous surveys indicate that the quality of a newspaper usually deteriorates when it is bought by a major chain. Charles K. McClatchy, former editor and chairman of the board of the Sacramento-based McClatchy Newspapers, decried the wave of mergers and acquisitions making media conglomerates more powerful and less responsive to people's needs. "The public and the government increasingly seem ready to accept what used to be unacceptable," said McClatchy.

The lack of concern among the public is in large part attributable to the silence of mass media, which rarely probe the dangers of concentrated ownership as it pertains to their own industry. The insidious impact of merger mania is not readily apparent to the casual consumer who sees newsstands stocked with lots of publications and bookstores filled with different titles. Equally misleading is the fact that broadcast and cable channels continue to proliferate, and thousands of radio stations operate throughout the country.

"Free TV" versus cable

On the surface it seems that a tremendous variety of media are available to us. Yet appearances are deceptive, for only a handful of multinational corporations control what most Americans see, hear and read. These highly centralized information outlets are remarkably uniform in what they offer. TV news has become so standardized that rival networks often report on the same stories in identical sequence. "CBS, NBC, ABC—they're all the same," Sam Donaldson quipped on the David Letterman Show.

With few exceptions, cable TV serves up imitative programming hardly different from the major networks. Most cable systems are owned by companies that already control other media. The parent firms of ABC and NBC, for example, have big investments in cable. As a result, the turf-war tensions between broadcast network "free TV" and cable network "pay TV" are of little consequence.

"Through your free-TV window, you've been witness to triumph and tragedy, to love, laughter, learning and life," Walter Cronkite told more than 50 million Americans one night in July 1989, in a National Association of

...rs spot aired simultaneously on more than a thousand TV stations. ...wers to "join us in the coming months as we celebrate and ...V." But regular network programming is hardly "free." It's ...by sponsors who factor ad budgets into the cost of their ...ency representative told *Broadcasting* magazine in ...pot, "What we ultimately care about are advertis- ... *Broadcasting*'s words, "whether the availabilities ar... ...able is not a major issue."

Predic... ...edia

Reinfor... by mass advertising, newspaper content has also become increasingly homogeneous—the end result of "assembly-line journalism." The "news" sections of most papers are filled with a similar mix of wire service copy and prefab corporate puffery, while a narrow array of columnists parade their opinions on the editorial pages. It's not uncommon for dailies in smaller cities and towns to run canned editorials provided by syndicated word factories. Even astrologers and homespun advisers are mass marketed through the press.

And then there are the three main newsweeklies: *Time* (4.6 million circulation), *Newsweek* (3.2 million) and *U.S. News & World Report* (2.3 million). Bruce Porter, associate professor at the Columbia School of Journalism, doesn't see much innovative journalism happening at the weeklies: "News magazines once gave readers the feeling that you could get some information in them that you weren't going to get elsewhere, not from a straight story by the Associated Press or a straight newspaper story, or from TV. But if you read what the papers provide today, what can you find in the newsmagazines that is any different?" Porter's sentiments are shared by many independent media critics.

"We Americans like to think of ourselves as rootin' tootin' individualists," the irrepressible journalist I.F. Stone observed, yet we "read the same news-agency reports in the same kind of newspapers, take in the same ideas from the same big national magazines, and listen solemnly to the same platitudes from the two big—and very much the same—political parties." Stone wrote those words in 1952, for the independent New York *Daily Compass*, which folded before the year was out, leaving eight local dailies in New York City. Today only four local news dailies circulate in the Big Apple, the most of any U.S. city. Washington has only two competing papers, the *Post* and the *Washington Times*, whose corporate parent is controlled by Rev. Sun Myung Moon's Unification Church. Compare this to other capitals: Rome has 18 dailies, Tokyo 17, London and Paris 14.

Blunt talk about the foreign press

Ironically, one of the rare instances in which the *New York Times* addressed the social and political implications of media mergers was in an article on media concentration in Italy. Appearing on the front page of the business section, Clyde Haberman's piece noted that all of Italy's important newspapers had been "snatched up by a handful of industrial titans with interests that extend far beyond the gathering of news." Haberman mentioned a resolution issued by journalists and other print media workers, which asserted that "the concentration of publications under the control of industrial and financial groups constitutes a total setback for the system of democratic guarantees in our country."

Fiat automobile magnate Giovanni Agnelli now owns *Corriere della Sera*, once his country's premier newspaper. Its editor insists—like most U.S. editors—that he "never had any interference from the owner on the running of the paper, not once." But many Italian reporters maintain that Agnelli's views are certainly taken into account. "There's no need for interference," a *Corriere della Sera* reporter stated, "because there's total self-censorship."

Italian journalists told Haberman that financial concentration "produces bland journalism, especially on economic and political issues close to their owners' hearts or pocketbooks." The *New York Times* could have quoted U.S. journalists airing the same complaint about American mass media. But the stultifying influence of media mergers in this country is not a hot topic in the paper of record—or in any major U.S. media, for that matter.

"Concentrated power over public information is inherently anti-democratic," said Ben Bagdikian. "If a nation has narrowly controlled information, it will soon have narrowly controlled politics... In a world of multiple problems, where diversity of ideas is essential for decent solutions, controlled information inhibited by uniform self-interest is the first and fatal enemy."

In a key decision on mass media (Associated Press v. United States in 1945), the Supreme Court ruled that the First Amendment "rests on the assumption that the widest possible dissemination of information from diverse and antagonistic sources is essential to the welfare of the public." But cannibalistic mergers, financial monopolies and the rearrangement of media structures have dramatically limited the spectrum of viewpoints to which U.S. citizens have ready access. Functioning as a "Private Ministry of Information," a small group of media corporations wields enormous power in our society. They tell the rest of us how to live, what to fear, what to be proud of, how to be successful, what to think about. "More than media managers," writes Donna Woolfolk Cross, "they are mind managers... Never before in human history have so few imposed so much of their thinking on so many."

Of course, there are alternative sources of information. Some small-circulation local and national periodicals, along with listener-supported noncommercial radio stations, provide vital options for the public. Yet with minuscule funding, they're doing battle against media Goliaths who play a pivotal role in setting the national agenda. Not surprisingly mass media owners promote policies that enhance their own power. "What the public learns is heavily weighted by what serves the economic and political interests of the corporations that own the media," Bagdikian concludes. "Since media owners are now so large and deeply involved in the highest levels of the economy, the news and other public information become heavily weighted in favor of all corporate values."

Free speech for sale

Through well-coordinated lobbying efforts, media corporations have succeeded in obtaining tax-breaks and exemptions from anti-trust laws. The FCC's deregulatory campaign during the Reagan administration culminated in the scuttling of the "Fairness Doctrine," which stipulated that broadcasters should air opposing views on controversial issues. Media moguls claimed this rule (rarely enforced since its inception in 1959) constituted undue government meddling and had a chilling effect on free speech. This was essentially the same objection raised by the tobacco industry when cigarette commercials were banned from the airwaves. Indeed, whenever television is criticized—even the blatant commercialization of children's TV—broadcasters cry foul and plead that their First Amendment right of free expression is threatened.

But just how deeply are media corporations committed to free speech? The record of Time Inc. and Warner Communications prior to their merger is not encouraging. In 1974, Time's Fortune Book Club was set to distribute Gerard Zilg's well-reviewed book, *DuPont: Behind the Nylon Curtain.* But the club broke its contract and dropped the project after DuPont threatened to withdraw its ads from Time publications. A year earlier, a Warner subsidiary had published *Counter-Revolutionary Violence,* a hard-hitting critique of U.S. foreign policy by professors Noam Chomsky and Edward S. Herman. But all 10,000 copies were destroyed when a conservative executive at Warner learned of the book's contents.

The classic axiom provided by A. J. Liebling—"freedom of the press is guaranteed only to those who own one"—neatly explains how media monopolies can gut the spirit of the First Amendment while it technically remains law of the land.

MILITARY-INDUSTRIAL-MEDIA COMPLEX: THE CASE OF GENERAL ELECTRIC AND NBC

In January 1961, shortly before he handed over the formal reins of power, President Dwight Eisenhower issued a blunt warning to the American people about the "immense military establishment" whose "total influence—economic, political, even spiritual—is felt in every city, every state house, every office of the federal government." The departing chief added: "We must guard against the acquisition of unwarranted influence...by the military-industrial complex. The potential for disastrous rise of misplaced power exists and will persist."

General Electric, a financial and industrial behemoth with annual sales topping $50 billion, has long been a key player in the military-industrial complex. Ranked second among U.S. military contractors, GE makes the detonators for every nuclear bomb in America's arsenal. There are few modern weapons systems that GE has not been instrumental in developing. In addition to nuclear and conventional arms, GE manufactures refrigerators, electric motors, medical equipment, plastics, light bulbs and communications satellites. It also owns the Wall Street firm Kidder-Peabody. When it acquired RCA, the parent company of NBC, for $6.28 billion in 1986—at that point the largest non-oil corporate merger in U.S. history—GE added a formidable media component to its worldwide business empire.

The saga of GE—marked by fraud, scandals, labor strife and contempt for the natural environment—illustrates the dangers of misplaced power that Eisenhower spoke about, but which the U.S. media rarely probe at length. Here are a few examples: In 1932, GE initiated a policy of planned obsolescence and cut the life of light bulbs in order to boost sales during the Depression. During World War II, GE was convicted of illegally collaborating with Germany's Krupp company, a linchpin of the Nazi war machine. And in 1961, GE was convicted of price-fixing, bid-rigging and antitrust violations, for which it had to pay a large fine in addition to a $57 million settlement with the U.S. government and other customers. Three GE officials served brief jail terms. But GE's attorney Clark Clifford (chair of the CIA's Foreign Intelligence Advisory Board and a future Defense Secretary) convinced the IRS that the damages GE had to pay for its criminal activities could be written off as a tax-deductible business expense!

With the IRS doling out favors to big business, the pattern of corruption continued. In 1981, GE was found guilty of bribing a Puerto Rican official to obtain a $92 million contract to build a power plant on the island. GE paid no income tax that year, even though its pre-tax earnings were a nifty $2.66 billion; what's more, GE somehow qualified for a $90 million rebate from the IRS. (Is that what they mean by "free enterprise"?) In 1985, GE became the first weapons contractor to be found guilty of defrauding the U.S. government by overcharging on military contracts.

Ronald Reagan: GE front-man

GE's well-documented record of deceit should have been grounds for the Justice Department to disqualify the company from acquiring NBC. But GE had friends in high places and the deal went through without a hitch. The fact that Ronald Reagan had previously spent eight years on GE's payroll as the company's chief PR spokesman undoubtedly helped matters. Publicist

Edward Langley, who has written on Reagan's GE years, described GE as "a company so obsessed with conservatism that it was not unlike the John Birch Society."

Reagan signed on with GE in 1954, when his acting career was floundering. He hosted and occasionally starred in the long-running *General Electric Theater* series that aired on CBS. Soon Reagan began touring the country at GE's behest, making speeches against communism, labor unions, social security, public housing and, of course, corporate taxes. These GE-sponsored lectures laid the groundwork for Reagan's political career, and the rest, as they say, is history.

A number of Reagan cabinet officials had close relations with GE. William French Smith, Reagan's personal attorney, joined GE's board of directors shortly after leaving the administration. It was during Smith's tenure as U.S. Attorney General in the mid-1980s that the Justice Department modified antitrust regulations, thereby enabling GE to buy NBC.

It wasn't always so easy to pull off this kind of merger. ITT's attempt to acquire ABC in 1966-67 provoked a public outcry; the plan was nixed after the Justice Department found that ITT control "could compromise the independence of ABC's news coverage of political events in countries where ITT has interests." The same logic could have been applied to GE, which operates in 50 foreign countries, but its purchase of NBC in 1986 was hardly debated in Washington or the U.S. media.

NBC is one of GE's most profitable assets, largely due to austerity measures such as reducing the news division staff from 1,400 to 1,000. This was par for the course at a GE-owned company. In less than a decade since John Welsh became GE's CEO in 1981, over a hundred thousand employees were laid off—25 percent of GE's total work force. These cutbacks occurred at a time when the company was earning record profits. Welsh has been nicknamed "Neutron Jack" because, like the neutron bomb, he makes people disappear but leaves the buildings standing.

The nuts and bolts of censorship

How has ownership by GE influenced what we see—or don't see—on NBC News programs? NBC has repeatedly insisted that its relationship to GE does not affect its news coverage. But certain incidents suggest otherwise.

For example, a reference to the General Electric Company was surgically removed from a report on substandard products before it aired on NBC's *Today* show on November 30, 1989. The report focused on a federal investigation of inferior bolts used by GE and other firms in building airplanes, bridges, nuclear missile silos and equipment for the NASA space program. It said that 60 percent of the 200 billion bolts used annually in the U.S. may be faulty. The censored portion of the *Today* show included this passage: "Recently, General Electric engineers discovered they had a big problem.

One out of three bolts from one of their major suppliers was bad. Even more alarming, GE accepted the bad bolts without any certification of compliance for eight years."

Peter Karl, the journalist who produced the segment, called NBC's decision to eliminate references to GE "insidious." He cited the "chilling effect" on a network that is "overprotective of a corporate owner."

In March 1987, NBC News broadcast a special documentary, "Nuclear Power: In France It Works," which could have passed for an hour-long nuclear power commercial. In an upbeat introduction, NBC anchor Tom Brokaw neglected to state that his corporate patron is America's second-largest nuclear energy vendor, with 39 nuclear power reactors in the U.S., and the third-leading nuclear weapons producer—facts which gave rise to the moniker "Nuclear Broadcasting Company" among disgruntled NBC staff.

Herein lay a fundamental conflict of interest, which Brokaw didn't own up to. Citizens' fear of nuclear technology could cut into GE's profits—and these fears were a key target of this so-called "News Special." An NBC crew toured France as if on a pilgrimage to the atomic land of Oz, off to see the wizardry of safe nuclear power plants. "Looking at a foreign country where nuclear power is a fact of life may restore some reason to the discussion at home," said correspondent Steve Delaney. "In most countries, especially the U.S., emotions drive the nuclear debate and that makes rational dialogue very difficult."

Having sung the praises of the French nuclear industry, NBC News bluffed when discussing what to do with radioactive waste, some of which remains lethal for dozens of centuries or longer: "The French will probably succeed in their disposal plan for the same reasons the rest of their nuclear program works... The French have more faith than we do in the government's competence to manage the nuclear program, and the French government has less tolerance for endless dissent."

Unfortunately, faith and lack of tolerance for dissent will not solve critical nuclear problems, even in France. One month after NBC aired its pro-nuclear broadcast, there were accidents at two Franch nuclear power installations, injuring seven workers. The *Christian Science Monitor* wrote of a "potentially explosive debate" in France, with polls showing a third of the French public opposing nuclear power. While the accidents were widely discussed in the French media and some U.S. newspapers, NBC TV did not report the story.

A telling sidelight to this incident occurred the following year when NBC's pro-nuke documentary won first prize for science journalism in a competition sponsored by the Westinghouse Foundation, an affiliate of Westinghouse Electric Company. Like GE, Westinghouse is a military-industrial powerhouse with large investments in nuclear power and weapons, as well as in broadcast media. Westinghouse owns Group W Cable and is the second largest radio station operator in the United States.

THE FRENCH LESSON

Can the French teach us
a thing or two about atomic
power? America's nuclear
industry is stumbling, but
France's generates three-
quarters of that nation's
electricity. And French
townspeople welcome each
new reactor with open arms.

Where did France go right?
Tonight's NBC News Special
comes up with intriguing
answers.

10 PM:
NUCLEAR POWER—
IN FRANCE IT WORKS

NBC NEWS 4

Westinghouse gave NBC its journalism trophy not long after GE was publicly implicated in yet another major scandal. A member of the Nuclear Regulatory Commission (NRC) resigned, charging that GE had "struck a deal" with the NRC to keep secret the contents of a 1975 GE internal report critical of its faulty nuclear reactor design. The report—which documented problems such as earthquake hazards and radiation dangers for plant workers—prompted suits by three Midwest utility companies which claimed that GE knowingly installed unsafe systems. Ironically, Jim Lawless, the *Cleveland Plain Dealer* reporter who first exposed the GE nuclear cover-up, was yanked from the utilities beat after the parent company of Cleveland's powerful electric utility complained to the *Plain Dealer*'s management about alleged "bias" in coverage by Lawless.

In 1986, New York State officials banned recreational and commercial bass fishing after GE had polluted the Hudson River with 400,000 pounds of carcinogenic PCBs. Moreover, according to EPA's 1989 Superfund list, GE was responsible for 47 toxic waste sites around the country—the most of any firm cited.

Not surprisingly, NBC News staffers haven't shown much zeal for investigating environmental abuse by the company that pays their salaries. Nor have they done much digging into Kidder-Peabody, GE's brokerage subsidiary, which has been implicated in insider trading scandals on Wall Street. And the worldwide consumer boycott of GE products launched by INFACT, a group opposed to nuclear profiteering, hasn't been a hot topic on NBC News either. INFACT's TV commercials, urging consumers not to buy GE products, were banned by NBC and other television broadcasters.

Conflicts of interest

GE and other military contractors made out like bandits during the Reagan administration, which presided over the largest peacetime military build-up in U.S. history. And bandits is exactly what they are, as the Pentagon procurement scandal, involving dozens of military contractors, amply demonstrates. GE was pegged with a 321-count indictment in November 1988 for trying to defraud the Department of Defense.

Despite such shenanigans, GE continued to receive hefty Defense Department contracts. Star Wars research was a veritable cash cow for GE and other high-tech weapons manufacturers. An article in the *New York Times* business section pointed out that the Stars Wars program (and, by implication, GE contracts) could be scuttled if a major arms control agreement were reached or if a Democrat got elected to the White House. Star Wars subsequently became an issue during the 1988 presidential campaign; Bush was for it and Dukakis was against it. Thus NBC's owner had a material interest in the outcome of the election. NBC President Robert Wright donated money to the Bush campaign, as did GE chief "Neutron Jack"

Welsh. NBC News employees didn't have to be told that a Dukakis victory—or tough, critical reporting on Star Wars—could cost GE millions of dollars.

Given GE's far-flung, diversified interests, there aren't many subjects that NBC News could cover that would not have a direct or indirect bearing on its corporate parent. Conflicts of interest are unavoidable as long as GE owns NBC. "As a newswriter I'm constantly aware who my boss is," a disaffected NBC News staffer told the media watch group FAIR shortly before he was laid off by the network.

Of course, NBC News doesn't completely ignore embarrassing stories about its owner. That would be too blatant, particularly when other news outlets refer in passing to GE corruption. When GE was indicted for its role in the 1988 Pentagon procurement scandal, *NBC Nightly News* gave a straightforward report—that lasted about ten seconds. There was little follow-up on this scandal by any of the major networks. The corporate zeitgeist doesn't encourage a sustained, in-depth investigation of such matters.

It would be an overstatement to say that the topic of GE's ownership is banned entirely from NBC broadcasts. Occasionally, David Letterman will make a few joking references to GE on his late-night show. In that ha-ha context, a bit of lampooning about corporate daddy is permissible. At first glance a concession to openness and self-criticism, such quips may be just the reverse—a kind of inoculation, making light of potential conflicts of interests and ethical quagmires. Like the Fool in a Shakespeare play, Letterman is allowed to utter some jestful references to what's really going on beneath the pretenses. But as for serious examination by NBC News, forget it...

Nor are the other major networks in much of a position to cast the first stone. CapCities/ABC and CBS are interlinked with other huge conglomerates that are part of the military-industrial complex. The boards of directors of the Big Three are composed of executives, lawyers, financiers and former government officials who represent the biggest banks and corporations in the U.S., including military and nuclear contractors, oil companies, agribusiness, insurance and utility firms.

So too with leading newspapers and other major media. The *New York Times*, for example, is not only the newspaper of record for the Fortune 500; it is also a member in good standing of that elite club. There are numerous interlocks between the board of directors of the *New York Times* and the nuclear industry, which partially explains why it has been a fanatical supporter of nuclear weapons and atomic power plants.

Among the 14-member *New York Times* corporate board is George B. Munroe, retired chair and CEO of Phelps Dodge, a notorious anti-union company involved in uranium mining. Munroe and another *Times* board member, George Shinn, are also directors of Manufacturers Hanover, a bank that lent money to bail out LILCO, a New York utility, as plans for the

Shoreham nuclear power plant fell to widespread citizen opposition. (The *Times* steadfastly backed the Shoreham project in dozens of strident editorials, without letting its readers know of these corporate links.) In addition, *Times* board member William R. Cross is vice chairman of the credit policy committee of Morgan bank, another LILCO creditor. And Marian S. Heiskell, sister of *Times* publisher and CEO Arthur Ochs Sulzberger, sits on the board of Con Edison, another nuclear utility.

Time Warner, the world's biggest media corporation, has so many interlocks with Fortune 500 companies that its board reads like a Who's Who of U.S. business and finance. Directors include representatives from military contractors such as General Dynamics, IBM and AT&T, as well as movers and shakers from Mobil Oil, Atlantic Richfield, Xerox and a number of major international banks. But Time Warner and other mass media won't discuss conflicts of interest inherent in interlocking directorates and how these may affect the selection and presentation of news stories. That subject is strictly taboo.

Three cheers for the war economy

Blueblood media and their corporate cousins have a vast stake in decisions made by the U.S. government. Through elite policy-shaping groups like the Council on Foreign Relations and the Business Roundtable, they steer the ship of state in what they deem to be a financially advantageous direction. (GE, CapCities, CBS, the *New York Times* and the *Washington Post* all have board members who sit on the Council on Foreign Relations.) They have much to gain from a favorable investment climate in Third World countries and bloated military budgets at home.

This was made explicit by former GE President Charles Wilson, a longtime advocate of a permanent war economy, who worked with the Pentagon's Office of Defense Mobilization during the 1950s. In a speech before the American Newspaper Publishers Association, he urged the media to rally behind the government's Cold War crusade. "The free world is in mortal danger. If the people were not convinced of that, it would be impossible for Congress to vote vast sums now being spent to avert that danger," said Wilson. "With the support of public opinion, as marshalled by the press, we are off to a good start... It is our job—yours and mine—to keep our people convinced that the only way to keep disaster away from our shores is to build America's might."

Nowadays, General Electric doesn't need to marshall the press to persuade the masses; it owns the press—or at least a sizable chunk of it. Moreover GE's board of directors interlocks with various media, including the Washington Post Company, Harper & Row (book publishers), and the Gannett Foundation. GE also owns a cable channel (CNBC) and sponsors news programs on other networks, such as ABC's *This Week With David*

Brinkley, CNN's *Crossfire*, and the *McLaughlin Group* on PBS. As a communications manager at GE explained, "We insist on a program environment that reinforces our corporate messages."

In what has become standard operating procedure for mega-corporations, GE spends millions of dollars each year sprucing up its image. But behind the catchy PR slogan, "We bring good things to life," lurks a legacy of faulty nuclear reactors, toxic waste dumps, bribery, cheating and cover-up. The chasm between this reality and GE's heroic self-image underscores an essential point: advertising is institutionalized lying, and such lies are tolerated, even encouraged, because they serve the needs of the corporate establishment. Network news is brought to us by sponsors that lie routinely, matter-of-factly, as it were. Under such circumstances, how truthful can we expect the news to be?

The think tank scam

In an effort to get the corporate message across and maximize sympathetic public opinion, GE and like-minded business firms fill the coffers of influential conservative think tanks. Representatives from these well-heeled organizations are quoted regularly in the press and they often pose as unbiased "experts" on television news and public affairs shows. In this capacity they directly serve the interests of the corporations which hold their purse strings.

The American Enterprise Institute (AEI) runs a highly effective PR operation. AEI resident scholars, such as would-be Supreme Court justice Robert Bork and former U.N. ambassador Jeane Kirkpatrick, generate a steady flow of opinion columns on political, social and economic issues that are syndicated in hundreds of news dailies; other AEI associates serve as paid consultants for the three main TV networks. AEI "quotemaster" Norman J. Ornstein claimed to have logged 1,294 calls from 183 news organizations in 1988.

AEI receives financial support from various news media, including the *New York Times*, the Philip L. Graham Fund (*Washington Post*) and Times-Mirror (parent company of the *Los Angeles Times*). Among AEI's favorite whipping boys is Jesse Jackson, whose populist, anti-corporate presidential campaigning undoubtedly annoyed the high-brow business executives from Mobil Oil, Proctor & Gamble, Chase Manhattan, Citibank, Rockwell International and GE who sit on AEI's board of trustees.

GE also supports the Center for Strategic and International Studies (CSIS), an AEI spinoff based in Washington. CSIS functions as a way station for U.S. intelligence operatives as they shuttle back and forth through the revolving door that links the public (or at least as public as spooks can be) and private sectors. Representatives from CSIS and the Rand Corporation, another CIA-linked think tank, frequently appear on TV to comment on terrorism and other "national security" issues. Directors of GE and CBS sit on the Rand Corporation board. During one six-week period, CSIS fellows tallied 650 media "contacts"—TV appearances, opinion columns and quotations in news stories.

The Heritage Foundation, which functioned virtually as a shadow government during much of the Reagan administration, is another media favorite, according to a survey of news sources conducted by the University of Windsor. Burton Yale Pines, formerly a *Time* magazine associate editor and AEI "resident journalist," went on to become vice president of Heritage. GE director Henry H. Henley Jr. is a Heritage board member. Funders include Henley's company—Cluett, Peabody—along with Joseph Coors, the Reader's Digest Foundation (which also finances AEI), Mobil Oil and other major corporations. According to *The Nation* magazine, Heritage also received money on the sly from South Korean intelligence to support its Asian Studies Center.

It's another closed loop: Analysts from think tanks funded by GE and the Fortune 500 elite appear as "independent experts" on TV networks owned and sponsored by the same corporations. When the networks want someone to ratify corporate news and opinion, they turn to a stable of approved think tank specialists. Not surprisingly these well-paid sluggers go to bat for big business and the national security state, confirming biases already deeply-ingrained in U.S. media. Thus we see a lot of "hot spot" coverage on TV that gives the impression that the world is not a safe place for Americans; this unsettling picture is invariably confirmed by the same coterie of pundits who exude a false aura of objectivity as they define security in terms of brute military force rather than a healthy environment, workplace safety and a strong, equitable economy. The prevalence of conservative think-tank mavens on TV and in the press is yet another symptom of corporate domination of the mass media.

PBS: PRO-BUSINESS SERVICE?

Public television, as originally conceived by its proponents, was supposed to make room on the airwaves for risky, innovative programming—the kind that might not inspire big league commercial sponsors to open up their wallets. This was public TV's initial mandate.

In its promotional literature, the Public Broadcasting Service (PBS) offers unabashed self-praise: "PBS, alone among the world's public television organizations, is entirely independent of political and governmental control or interference." But is this true? Is PBS really as "independent" as it claims?

PBS was founded in 1967 when President Lyndon Johnson embraced a plan for a public broadcasting system put forward by the Carnegie Commission on Educational Television. The plan called for government support of public TV and radio, and recommended the formation of a

Corporation for Public Broadcasting (CPB) to oversee the disbursement of federal funds. But there was a catch: Johnson created—and Congress approved—the year-to-year funding that put PBS on a very short leash and compromised its independence from the outset.

A veritable news junkie, Johnson often watched three network news broadcasts simultaneously, and he badgered reporters when he didn't like their coverage of the Vietnam War. He appointed Frank J. Pace Jr., formerly Secretary of the Army and chief executive of General Dynamics (one of the biggest U.S. military contractors), as CPB's first chairman. Upon accepting the post, Pace announced that he had already commissioned research on using public television for riot control.

Angered that public television occasionally aired programs critical of the Vietnam War, President Nixon slashed CPB funding while unleashing one of his media thugs, Patrick Buchanan (then Special Assistant to the President), to lobby publicly and behind the scenes in an effort to run reporters like Bill Moyers and Elizabeth Drew off the noncommercial airwaves. In 1972, public television pulled the plug at the last minute on a show written by comedian Woody Allen because it lampooned a Henry Kissinger-like character and other members of the Nixon administration. Commenting on PBS censorship, Moyers warned that public broadcasters might convince themselves "not that it's dangerous to take risks, but that it's wise to avoid them."

The Petroleum Broadcasting Service

It was during Nixon's tenure as commander-in-chief that big business emerged as a visible force in public television. Burdened by serious image problems because of windfall profits reaped from the "energy crisis" in the early 1970s, oil companies like Mobil began pumping funds into cultural and public affairs programming on PBS. Business support for public TV increased sixfold between 1973 and 1980. With oil companies "underwriting" in full or in part 72 percent of prime-time PBS shows in a typical week in 1981, the initials PBS seemed to stand more appropriately for Petroleum Broadcasting Service. Although PBS commands only four percent of the viewing audience, the network flaunts its upscale demographics, which appeal to corporate donors who gave a record $70 million for PBS programs in 1989. Twenty big firms forked up more than a million dollars each.

The sad truth is that PBS and National Public Radio (NPR) are "made possible" to a large degree by the same corporate sponsors that bring us commercial programming. With corporate contributions for NPR rising from $2.7 million in 1983 to $10.6 million in 1988, its news programming began to imitate commercial formulas. A mainstay of public radio's weekly listenership of 11 million, NPR is a favorite of advertisers—oops! we mean "underwriters"—because of its disproportionately affluent audience. An NPR news employee, who asked not to be identified, explained that "as we've gotten a larger audience, we've tended to be more mainstream. We used to be a lot more alternative and talk to different people."

While many NPR reporters have concentrated more on quality journalism than ratings, higher-ups were long accustomed to fixating on Nielsen or Arbitron figures. In 1989, for instance, both the executive producer of NPR's *Morning Edition* and the vice president for news at NPR were former top producers at CBS News. Anne Garrels, a hawkish correspondent for ABC and then NBC News, became NPR's chief diplomatic correspondent. And the door was swinging both ways. ABC News hired NPR congressional reporter Cokie Roberts, one of several NPR journalists who went to the major networks. (In a unique arrangement, Roberts was able to keep reporting for NPR and ABC at the same time.) Whether on public radio or commercial TV, Roberts' analysis and reporting were unlikely to disturb the status quo.

PBS documentaries

According to former CBS News president Fred Friendly, "corporations exercise a kind of positive veto" by financing and promoting programs of their choice. Political influences are also a factor, despite claims to the contrary by PBS and NPR officials. During the Reagan era, the Corporation for Public Broadcasting board, which allocates PBS funding, was reduced in size and packed with conservative ideologues, who were particularly stingy when it came to supporting independent projects. As a result, independent film and video had an increasingly difficult time getting on PBS. Corporate-financed programming was not similarly encumbered.

PBS programs with corporate backing have gotten special preference. Documentaries on health and medicine, for example, are usually funded by pharmaceutical firms such as Eli Lilly, Squibb and Bristol-Myers. (Not surprisingly, these programs emphasize high-tech medical remedies rather than alternative health approaches.) This is not considered a conflict of interest by the CPB board. But when unions provided money for shows on labor themes, the CPB board frequently objected, citing ethical conflicts. In the mid-1980s, labor unions offered to put up seed money for a multimillion-dollar film series, *Made in USA*, about working people's history—not about labor unions per se—to be made by an independent filmmaker who would be responsible for the show's content. PBS said such funding would be grounds for not carrying the series because of a conflict of interest. Meanwhile, the Bechtel Corporation got a wink and a nod from CPB when it donated money to Milton Friedman's PBS series, *Free to Choose*, a conservative primer in free market economics.

"What's appalling is that public television has never carved out a distinctive role as an information medium and public forum," Pat Aufderheide wrote in *The Progressive* magazine. "Caught in funding contradictions, it is now stuck with an ad-hoc mandate to round up the most viewer-subscribers possible to tempt the underwriters of programming. CPB fulfills that mandate with programs that function more like mental interior decoration than compensation for what's missing from advertising-driven television."

The *de facto* mission of public TV, said Aufderheide, is "to avoid the controversial...to entertain without stooping to vulgarity, and to inform without confronting the assumptions that keep us from knowing the obvious." Public television "is not designed to raise public debate, to ask questions about why our world looks and moves the way it does," Aufderheide concluded. "Of course it doesn't. What corporate underwriter would pay for that?"

This became abundantly clear to WNET, New York's big public TV station, when one of its corporate benefactors—Gulf + Western (now called Paramount)—abruptly withdrew funding in 1985. Gulf + Western executives were peeved at WNET's support for the documentary *Hungry for Profit*, which strongly criticized multinational corporations for their role in exacerbating food and hunger problems in the Third World. WNET officials acknowledged that before the documentary aired, they "did all they could to get the program sanitized." The London *Economist* put the incident in perspective: "Most people believe that WNET will not make the same mistake again." In other words, WNET would work even harder to sanitize programs in an effort to win corporate backing.

Haunted by the specter of short-tempered corporate funders and vocal conservative lobbies, public TV officials have refused to broadcast programs such as *Sun City*, a documentary about the making of a music video by Artists United Against Apartheid. PBS claimed it was biased—against apartheid! Mobil Oil, GE and other PBS-underwriters with heavy investments in South Africa at the time were likely pleased by the decision.

MacNeil/Lehrer doesn't rock the boat

While PBS sometimes presents challenging documentaries, its most glaring weakness is in news programs and public affairs talkshows. This is where the impact of corporate sponsorship is most evident. The *MacNeil/Lehrer NewsHour* is funded by AT&T, a military contractor; it has become a virtual clone of commercial news shows—albeit a half-hour longer. A Conservative Political Action Conference poll ranked *MacNeil/Lehrer* as the "most balanced network news show," which speaks volumes about *MacNeil/Lehrer*'s biases. Like *Washington Week in Review*, another PBS program, its narrow guest-list insures against novel or unconventional insights. TV, said co-host Robert MacNeil, "does not enjoy rocking the boat, politically or commercially."

MacNeil/Lehrer's one-hour news hole allows for more lengthy discussions of the day's events than the three major networks, but the *NewsHour*'s spectrum of experts is often even more narrow than the other networks. Preoccupied with politicians traversing Pennsylvania Avenue, *MacNeil/Lehrer*

MacNeil/Lehrer dwarfed by AT&T: New York City billboard, 1990

features "both sides" of issues that, like diamonds, actually have many sides; ensuing "debates" run the gamut of political opinion from A to C.

MacNeil/Lehrer has presented countless panels in which right-wing Democrats represent the furthest left position: Pro-contra Senator David Boren from Oklahoma has been the "dove" in discussions of the Iran-contra scandal or the CIA, while hawkish Senator Sam Nunn of Georgia has been the "dove" on panels about the nuclear arms race. The only suspense in such "debates" is who will emerge as the true conservative: the Republican or *MacNeil/Lehrer*'s Democratic "oppositionist." According to *NewsHour* staffers, co-anchor Jim Lehrer dislikes interviewing genuine oppositionists from peace and public interest organizations. He refers to such people as "moaners" and "whiners."

Right-wing tilt at PBS

As for political talk shows on PBS—it's a virtual sweep for right-wingers. William Buckley, editor of the conservative *National Review* magazine, has long hosted the weekly PBS program *Firing Line*. And John McLaughlin, one of Buckley's ex-colleagues at *National Review*, hosts two weekly shows, the *McLaughlin Group* and *One on One*.

Described by Jody Powell, President Carter's press secretary, as "an ideological foodfight," the *McLaughlin Group* is carried on two-thirds of PBS stations. It reserves three chairs for outspoken right-wing pundits and none for progressives, the kind of numbers that resonate favorably with GE, the sole underwriter of the program. GE has also tapped McLaughlin, formerly a special assistant to President Nixon, to host a prime-time public affairs show every day on its CNBC cable channel. *American Interests*, a weekly PBS show offering a conservative look at foreign policy, was spawned by the American Enterprise Institute, whose "experts" appear frequently on PBS.

Shortly before the 1988 elections, PBS aired a pair of one-hour specials on the two major political parties. The Democratic special was hosted by Ben Wattenberg, an AEI fellow and right-wing Democrat who had supported much of the Reagan agenda. The view from the Republican side was represented by ex-Reagan-aide David Gergen, also once an AEI fellow. This is what passes for a spectrum of opinion on public broadcasting.

Business viewpoints are certainly well-represented on PBS. In addition to the *Nightly Business Report* (underwritten by Shearson Lehman Hutton, the stock brokerage firm), PBS regularly airs *Wall $treet Week*, hosted by anti-labor commentator Louis Rukeyser, and *Adam Smith's Money World*, both of which have corporate backing.

In a presentation to a PBS review committee, FAIR director Jeff Cohen criticized the conservative, big business tilt of PBS public affairs panel shows. He pointed out the glaring imbalance in the PBS talkshow lineup. "Why is there no regular PBS show hosted by a progressive or a partisan of the left?" asked Cohen. "Would it not serve the public good to provide a public affairs show that reflected the concerns of those constituencies that sometimes conflict with big business—namely, the consumer, environmental and labor movements?" Cohen added: "PBS public affairs shows are populated almost exclusively by white males. Shouldn't minorities and women be better represented as hosts and panelists?"

PBS officials acknowledged a political imbalance. "There happens to be an oversupply of entertaining, glib, right-wing commentators," said Barry Chase, head of news and public affairs programming for PBS. But this glib remark dodged the real issue. A bombastic conservative like John McLaughlin is a fixture on PBS not because he fulfills a quota for responsible news analysis, but because GE puts up the money for his show. Indeed, corporate backing is the main reason for McLaughlin's metamorphosis from a fringe right-wing columnist in the late 1970s to one of the most prominent faces on public affairs TV.

After PBS subscribers and public interest activists complained about the lack of diversity in the network's news and talkshow lineup, some PBS stations began to air the *Kwitny Report*. This hard-hitting weekly show was hosted by Jonathan Kwitny, formerly an ace investigative reporter with the

GE's news sponsorship reaches beyond its ownership of NBC

Wall Street Journal. Kwitny soon ran into political resistance from higher-ups at WNYC, the New York PBS station which launched the show. "There are occasions when the accepted wisdom handed down by the government and corporations is wrong," he told the *Los Angeles Times* shortly after WNYC cancelled his program, claiming a lack of funds.

According to Kwitny, one of the station managers was hostile because he linked Jonas Savimbi, leader of the U.S.-backed UNITA rebels in Angola, to terrorism—a charge supported by human rights and church groups. "He's just one more bloodstained autocrat on the U.S. taxpayers' payroll," said Kwitny. Station management was also upset by an episode that charged the Reagan administration with undermining grand jury and congressional probes of drug smuggling by the U.S.-supported contras fighting the

Nicaraguan government. As of late 1989, Kwitny was seeking financial support and another flagship station with the hope that PBS executives would
live up to their promise to distribute his show nationally.

Business on the attack

One of the most absurd moments in the history of public television
occurred in April 1987, when PBS aired a documentary called "Hollywood's
Favorite Heavy: Businessmen on Prime Time TV." Funded and promoted by
Mobil Oil, the program portrayed businessmen as the oppressed minority of
prime-time entertainment TV. For "evidence" it drew heavily upon a survey
by the Washington-based Media Institute, a pseudo-scientific monitoring
operation funded by big business and conservative foundations.

An example of an anti-business smear cited in the PBS documentary was a
Dallas episode involving J.R. Ewing's scheme to overthrow a foreign government.

> Lieutenant to J.R.: I will try to deliver a new government for you, Mr.
> Ewing. It could get messy.

> J.R.: I don't want to know the details.

Why this should qualify as a smear is unclear given the well-documented
involvement of U.S. corporations in foreign military coups: for example, the
United Fruit Company in Guatemala in 1954, or ITT in Chile in 1973.

The Media Institute, which has received grants from the U.S. Information
Agency (the official propaganda vehicle of the U.S. government), also surveyed the U.S. press and determined that it was biased against nuclear
power. When reporting the results of this survey, journalists typically
neglected to mention that among the Media Institute's principal benefactors
are big oil companies, which by the early 1970s controlled 45 percent of
American uranium reserves.

The media's alleged left-wing bias is another recurring topic that corporate-financed monitoring groups (such as the misnamed Accuracy in Media)
continually hammer away at. Mobil Oil has led the attack against the press
for its supposed anti-business slant. It began harping on this theme in advocacy ads during the early 1970s. Said Herb Schmertz, Mobil's PR wun-
derkind, "We don't think we should leave all the informing of the public up
to the media, because they don't do an adequate job."

Mobil Oil is irked even when superficial items about corporate malfeasance
appear in the press. For the most part, however, critical coverage of big business tends to be piecemeal, focusing on isolated cases rather than the larger
picture. Corporate wrongdoing, when reported at all, is presented as an aberration, not a systemic problem. As Ben Bagdikian observed in his book *The*

Media Monopoly, "There have been ugliness and injustice in corporate wielding of power—bloody repressions of workers who tried to organize unions, corruption of government, theft of public franchises. But through it all, most of the mass media depicted corporate life as benevolent and patriotic."

Most captains of industry privately agree with Bagdikian's assessment of how business is portrayed by the press. A survey by Ruder and Finn, a major PR firm, disclosed that two-thirds of leading industrial execs in the U.S. believed the media treatment of their companies was good to excellent, while only six percent felt it was poor. These are their sincere beliefs, admitted in private. In public, however, Mobil and other Fortune 500 companies continue to bash the media in an effort to intimidate journalists.

"No sacred cow has been so protected and has left more generous residues in the news than the American corporate system," Bagdikian remarked. How ironic that the harshest attacks on the news media should come from U.S. corporations, which "are not only hostile to independent journalists," said Bagdikian. "They are also their employers."

CENSORED, SPIKED & SNUBBED:
WHAT THE NEWS MEDIA LEAVE OUT

The most powerful media institutions in the U.S. have encouraged us to believe that an unfettered Fourth Estate pursues stories without fear or favor. But the much-ballyhooed "Free Press" belongs to corporations operating as rigid hierarchies, with no pretense of being internally democratic. As with any profit-making enterprise, the media industry's chain of command runs from top down, with beat reporters on the bottom of the pecking order.

At the apex of the media pyramid are the owners who wield authority by assuming top executive posts or by hiring and firing those who hold these positions. Their power to replace management if it does not perform as they wish gives them control over policy and editorial direction. Ultimately, it is the media owners and managers who determine which ideas and which version of the facts shall reach the public. They have virtually unlimited power to suggest or veto stories. "In the final analysis," writes Professor Michael Parenti, "the news is not what reporters report but what editors and owners decide to print."

Former FCC commissioner Nicholas Johnson commented on the implications of hierarchical media structures: "The First Amendment rights belong to the owners, and the owners can exercise those rights by hiring people who will hire journalists who don't rock the boat, who don't attack advertisers, who don't challenge the establishment. That's a form of censorship."

Far from being neutral institutions, U.S. media corporations have their own political agendas. With few exceptions, the chief executive officers of major media are conservatives (usually Republicans) who aren't squeamish about using their publishing and broadcasting clout to further their own interests. As Bagdikian noted, major news chains such as Scripps-Howard (seventh largest in U.S. circulation) and Cox Enterprises (ninth) have ordered their papers to adopt a uniform editorial position on key issues, including which candidates to endorse for national office.

Corporate owners, as well as advertisers, are not likely to underwrite a worldview fundamentally at odds with their own. Otis Chandler, publisher of the *Los Angeles Times*, admitted as much: "I'm the chief executive. I set policy and I'm not going to surround myself with people who disagree with me... I surround myself with people who generally see the way I do."

Not surprisingly, Chandler's employees have avoided mentioning certain facts that might embarrass Times-Mirror Inc., the parent company of the *Los Angeles Times*, which also owns cable systems, book publishing houses, printing plants, other newspapers, urban real estate and agricultural land. For many years the *Los Angeles Times* has been a staunch advocate of state and federal subsidies for rural water projects, including a multibillion-dollar, tax-paid canal system, that would directly benefit Times-Mirror land holdings. This profitable connection to Times-Mirror was reported in other California newspapers, but not in the *Los Angeles Times*, the most powerful media outlet in the state.

Flirting with fascists

Media owners have ways of making their presence felt among working journalists. Time-Life publishing magnate Henry Luce, well-known for his conservative politics, used to flood his editors with story ideas. Prior to World War II, media critic George Seldes took Luce to task for devoting "an entire issue of *Fortune* to glorifying Mussolini and Fascism, and...permit[ting] an outright pro-fascist, Laird Goldsborough, to slant and pervert the news every week" in *Time*. Seldes also exposed a secret $400,000-a-year deal between Hitler and press baron William Randolph Hearst, which resulted in pro-Nazi articles in all Hearst papers. As late as December 1940, Hearst was ordering his editors not to include "unnecessarily offensive" cartoons of Hitler and Mussolini in his papers.

Described as the founder of yellow journalism and a debaucher of public taste, Hearst is perhaps the most notorious of the 20th century press barons. Instead of telling the news, Hearst headlines were intent on selling the news. He routinely invented sensational stories, faked interviews, ran phony pictures and distorted real events. Having begun his career as a reform-minded socialist, Hearst ended up a right-wing megalomaniac whose papers carried on the most sustained campaign of jingoism in U.S. history. Hearst propaganda masquerading as journalism played a major role in starting the Spanish-American War in 1898. His media empire also was instrumental in backing Senator Joe McCarthy when he launched his anti-Red crusade in 1950.

Hearst wasn't the only media mogul who supported the anticommunist witch-hunts during the Cold War. A majority of U.S. newspapers, including the Scripps-Howard and Gannett chains, applauded McCarthy's baseless diatribes about alleged communists in the U.S. government. But McCarthy's rise to prominence cannot be attributed solely to the proclivities of press barons like Hearst. The Wisconsin Red-baiter was adept at exploiting a perennial weakness of U.S. reporters who allowed themselves to function as stenographers for those in power. Trapped by their own "objective" techniques, most journalists covered the McCarthy story straight, reporting his hysterical charges without commenting on their accuracy. "There was very little opportunity in those days to break out of the role of being a recording device for Joe," said John L. Steele, formerly a correspondent with the United Press wire service. Indeed, this was how much of the press corps felt and acted at the time.

While a few courageous editors consistently denounced McCarthy, it wasn't until he began attacking President Eisenhower that the press turned against him. In a case of better late than never, CBS aired Edward R. Murrow's TV documentary on McCarthy in 1954, and then it was all downhill for Joe. By this time, thousands of patriotic Americans had been hounded out of their jobs, and groups advocating for civil rights and social justice were tarred as "subversive." Nevertheless, certain media owners felt that McCarthy had served a useful purpose by alerting the American public to the Red Menace. "His methods have been bad," said Joseph Pulitzer, publisher of the *St. Louis Post-Dispatch*, but "have not the results on the whole been good?"

Annenberg's thugs

Another press magnate who favored the McCarthy witch-hunts was Walter Annenberg, publisher of the *Philadelphia Inquirer* and, later, *TV Guide*. Young Walter had inherited a formidable media empire from his father, Moe, who began his newspaper career as circulation manager of the Hearst daily in Chicago during the bloody news wars of the early 1900s. With a gang of street toughs on his payroll, Moe made sure Hearst's product got maximum distribution. Trucks delivering competing papers were wrecked and 30 newsboys were murdered, but Annenberg's hoodlums escaped arrest.

Resorting to similar goon squad tactics while working for Hearst's *New York Daily Mirror*, Moe solicited the services of fledgling gangsters, including Meyer Lansky and Lucky Luciano. "I used to think of the *Mirror* as my kind of paper," Luciano fondly reminisced. "I always thought of Annenberg as my kind of guy." With the Mob's muscle at his disposal, Annenberg started to acquire his own newspapers, eventually amassing what *Fortune* magazine called the largest annual income in the U.S. When Annenberg went to jail for tax evasion in the 1930s, his son, Walter, took over the family business.

Described by Philadelphia attorney Harry Sawyer as "the greatest institutional force for evil" in the city of brotherly love, Walter Annenberg did not hesitate to throw his weight around the editorial room. He maintained a blacklist of people and organizations he didn't like (including Ralph Nader and the American Civil Liberties Union) and ordered that their names never be mentioned in *Philadelphia Inquirer* news stories. Annenberg also reportedly gave Frank Rizzo, Philadelphia's brash right-wing mayor in the late 1960s and 1970s, veto power over certain stories. And he used his paper to attack a gubernatorial candidate who opposed plans that would have boosted the profits of the Pennsylvania Railroad, but Annenberg did not inform his readers that he was the railroad's biggest stockholder.

Murdoch meddles

The Annenberg publishing dynasty came to an end in 1988 when Australian media mogul Rupert Murdoch purchased *TV Guide*. With far-flung media operations spanning three continents, Murdoch's News Corporation ranks fifth among the world's largest media conglomerates. As such, it is part of an emerging international media cartel that includes companies even bigger than Murdoch's—Time Warner, the German-based Bertelsmann empire, CapCities/ABC, and Canada's Thomson newspaper chain—along with publishing firms controlled by British tycoon Robert Maxwell and French arms merchant Jean-Luc Lagardere. If predictions by U.S. media executives are correct, these few gigantic corporations will dominate the global communications market as we enter the 21st century.

When asked why he kept buying up more media organs, Murdoch explained: "It's the challenge of the game. It gives me a great thrill." It was doubtless quite a thrill for Murdoch to have used his British newspapers to help install Margaret Thatcher as Prime Minister and keep her in power. News stories and editorials in Murdoch's drug-and-crime-crazed *New York Post* were unabashedly slanted to please the likes of Mayor Ed Koch and President Ronald Reagan during the 1980s.

Murdoch's most ambitious project to date is the launching of a fourth TV network in the U.S., Fox Broadcasting. In June 1988, Fox heavily censored "The Nelson Mandela 70th Birthday Tribute," a rock concert held at London's Wembley stadium to promote human rights and freedom in South Africa. Unbeknownst to the performing artists, most of their political comments were not heard by millions of people watching the show on U.S. television. Fox TV had surgically removed "the most passionate and especially the most political moments of the day," according to the *Boston Globe*.

Among the anti-apartheid statements deleted by Murdoch's network were Dire Straits' dedication of the song "Brothers in Arms" to the imprisoned Mandela and Peter Gabriel's remark that "South Africa is the only country in the world which has racism enshrined in its constitution." South African singer Miriam Makeba was totally omitted. Little Steven (Van Zandt) and other musicians who performed at Wembley were angry when they learned what happened. "This was the ultimate Orwellian sort of event," said Little Steven. "We did one show and America saw a different show."

Fox refused to identify who was responsible for censoring the concert, but the version that it broadcast probably pleased Murdoch. An outspoken conservative, Murdoch doesn't try to hide his penchant for editorial meddling. "To what extent do you influence the editorial posture of your newspapers?" queried a reporter with *Cosmopolitan* magazine. "Considerably," he responded. "The buck stops on my desk. My editors have input, but I make final decisions."

Such candor is rare among media owners who seek to exert maximum control over the news product with a minimum of direct interference. Unlike the audacious press barons of old, today's news execs prefer the velvet muzzle to the iron fist. They meet on a regular basis with editors hand-picked to fulfill the role of loyal gatekeepers. Editors decide what to feature on the front page, which articles to assign and not to assign, whether to cut, rewrite or kill a story.

Ownership influence on the news

Former managing editor of the *New York Times* Turner Catledge noted in his memoirs how he frequently conveyed publisher Arthur H. Sulzberger's comments to his staff as if they came from himself in order to avoid the impression that the top boss "was constantly looking over their shoulders. In truth, however, he was."

Despite assurances to the contrary, media owners continue to promote self-serving content into the news and banish subjects they dislike. As Bagdikian, formerly national editor at the *Washington Post*, has written, "When an editor makes a news decision based on corporate commands, or knowledge of ownership wishes, the editor seldom states the real reason." This would "violate the prevailing dogma of American journalism that serious news is the result of whatever is true and significant, let the chips fall where they may."

The extent of ownership influence on the news was indicated by a 1980 survey by the American Society of Newspaper Editors. Thirty-three percent of all editors employed by newspaper chains admitted that they would not feel free to publish news stories that were damaging to their parent firm. Years have passed since this survey was taken, and the parent firms are now bigger and more powerful than ever before. TV producers have expressed similar misgivings about news broadcasts that might conflict with the economic or political interests of their parent company.

Covering up for the Gipper

In the course of selecting what to air on the evening news, many stories get "spiked"—an old newspaper term that refers to rejected stories that were literally jammed onto the editor's filing spike. During the months prior to the 1984 presidential election, ABC *World News Tonight* spiked three exposés that could have proved damaging to the Republican campaign. As Mark Dowie later disclosed in *Mother Jones* magazine, producers and reporters at ABC's special investigative unit had documented serious health and safety violations at nursing homes owned by U.S. Information Agency director Charles Wick, an intimate friend of Ronald Reagan; an FBI cover-up of Labor Secretary Raymond Donovan's association with organized crime figures; and an attempt by Senator Paul Laxalt, a close Reagan ally, to persuade the Justice Department to stop an undercover probe of his campaign contributors.

Although considerable resources had been devoted to developing these stories, higher-ups at ABC got cold feet. "It was political pressure...classic spiking," said senior producer Marion Goldin, who worked on the Wick investigation. Someone at ABC didn't want to embarrass the Reagan administration.

At the time the stories were killed, according to *Mother Jones*, ABC executives were preparing to lobby the Republican-controlled FCC to change the so-called 7-7-7 rule, which stipulated that a corporation or network could own no more than seven television stations, seven AM and seven FM radio stations. With big sums of money at stake, ABC executives sought an amended ruling which would expand the allowable number of holdings to 12 in each broadcasting category. The FCC did replace the "7-7-7 rule" with a "12-12-12 rule" in early 1985, thereby greatly enhancing ABC's financial status and making it much more attractive to CapCities, which subsequently acquired the network in a friendly buyout.

There is a clause in the ABC News policy manual which states the following: "Those of us who work in the news share a paramount responsibility to maintain our reputation for fairness, accuracy and impartiality... We must never be obligated to any interest other than the public's interest in the full, fair and accurate reporting of the news." This high-sounding principle was abused by ABC bigwigs who were more concerned about maximizing profits than providing full and unbiased news coverage.

Censorship on political grounds affects a wide range of media—even cartoons, which often convey the most insightful commentary on social and political issues published in many daily newspapers. *Cathy*, a popular comic strip, was temporarily dropped from the *Los Angeles Times* when it expressed anti-Republican views shortly before the November 1988 elections. *Doonesbury* has encountered similar problems. Editorial cartoonist Bill Schorr was sacked by the *Los Angeles Herald-Examiner* after several of his sharpest barbs at the Reagan administration had been censored.

Some stories are spiked by TV news executives because they reflect poorly on the network or its corporate cousins. Meredith Vieira, formerly

CBS Midwest Bureau Chief and later a correspondent for the weekly TV news magazine *West 57th*, recounted how a story on sexual harassment in the workplace was rejected by a local CBS affiliate: "We were going to do it on CBS Records because we had received so many calls from employees there… We really had a good story." But it never came to pass. Instead they "ended up doing it on a cosmetics firm, and it destroyed them," Vieira explained. "Networks are notorious for this. Pointing the finger at someone else… But never can you point the finger at CBS or NBC or ABC."

There have also been instances in which journalists omit sensitive information out of deference to other media. For example, the *New York Times* magazine ran a laudatory cover story on the Newhouse family (which owns *Vanity Fair*, *Vogue*, *GQ* and other publications) without mentioning that Donald and Si Newhouse were awaiting a court decision on charges that they failed to pay over a billion dollars in back taxes.

Self-censorship

Although it is not often publicly discussed, the pervasive nature of news censorship is evident to many media professionals. "I daresay anyone who has been in the business for more than a few months can cite plenty of examples of editorial compromises due to pressure, real or imagined, from publishers, owners and advertisers," said Chris Welles, a former journalist who teaches at the Columbia School of Journalism.

But the brazen intrusion of media owners into the editorial process is not the main impediment to good journalism. A more insidious and widespread form of censorship occurs when reporters give up trying to write about subjects they know will not be acceptable. Alert to the preferences of their higher-ups, journalists learn they must adjust to the constraints of the corporate workplace. For some, this entails a rude awakening and profound career choices; others conform unconsciously, believing in earnest that they are free to express themselves with little managerial control. In either case, as Ralph Nader has stated, "Self-censorship is alive and well in the American media."

Ex-FCC-chief Nicholas Johnson summed up the problem of self-censorship this way: "The story is told of a reporter who first comes up with an investigative story idea, writes it up and submits it to the editor and is told the story is not going to run. He wonders why, but the next time he is cautious enough to check with the editor first. He is told by the editor that it would be better not to write that story. The third time he thinks of an investigative story idea but doesn't bother the editor with it because he knows it's silly. The fourth time he doesn't even think of the idea anymore."

While sometimes thought of as fierce newshounds and watchdogs always on the lookout for a scoop, mass media often act like tired lapdogs. Self-serving myths about the Free Press conjure up images of a journalistic Superman, ready to do battle for truth, justice and the American way. But the reality is much closer to Clark Kent, the mild-mannered reporter who duti-fully does what the boss wants.

Concerned about the mainstream media's propensity for self-censorship, Professor Carl Jensen at Sonoma State University in California initiated "Project Censored," a tally of each year's top ten under-reported stories. Chosen by a prestigious panel of judges, many of these stories were pub-lished in small-circulation newspapers and magazines but got scant coverage in the corporate-owned press. As Jensen explained, "Censorship is the sup-pression of information by any means. It doesn't have to be direct, official government censorship. It could mean overlooking a story, or under-covering a story, or rejecting a story because it would alienate a sponsor."

Suppressed stories cited by Project Censored in recent years include drug trafficking by the CIA-directed Nicaraguan contras, biological warfare research in university laboratories, the dangers of food irradiation, and the abuse of children incarcerated in U.S. prisons. Ironically, most Americans haven't heard of Project Censored, for it, too, is an under-reported story.

The story about NASA's preparations for Project Galileo, the plutonium-laden space shuttle, made Jensen's Top Ten list three years in a row. Hundreds of thousands of people could die from exposure to lethal pluto-nium if an accident occurred. Yet a year before the scheduled launch in October 1989, former NBC News president Reuven Frank flatly denied the existence of Project Galileo. "You know this kind of paranoia masquerading as journalism really doesn't interest me," Frank told journalist Dennis Bernstein. "I don't believe it exists. If there was a plan to do that it would be reported." Frank should have checked with NBC's parent company, GE, which took in over $130 million building generators for Project Galileo.

Editorial flak

A news producer who worked at CBS and NBC for nine years discussed how concentrated corporate ownership encourages self-censorship: "People are even more careful now, because this whole notion of freedom of the press becomes a contradiction when the people who own the media are the same people who need to be reported on. There are political limits I perceive, and you have to work within those limits, because ultimately it's unacceptable to stray beyond them."

Aggressive, independent journalists invariably run into hassles with their superiors. Consider the case of *New York Times* correspondent Raymond Bonner, who risked his life on many occasions while reporting from war-torn El Salvador. Bonner dared to visit the dumping grounds near the Salvadoran capital where government-sponsored death squads left their mutilated victims in the early 1980s—at a time when the Reagan administration was proclaiming that country a "fledgling democracy." As a result, Bonner was yanked from Central America, and he resigned from the *Times* shortly thereafter. The incident sent a chilling message to other journalists at the *Times* who told Bonner as he departed, "I don't want the same thing to happen to me. I'm going to be careful."

The shabby treatment of Bonner and *Washington Post* correspondent Alma Guillermoprieto, who was also pulled from El Salvador after she reported on massacres by U.S.-backed forces, served as a vivid reminder that journalists who stray off the beaten path too often will be demoted or fired. In this sense the newspapers of record are no different than other U.S. media, as William Kovach found out when he left the *Times* in 1987 to become editor-in-chief of the *Atlanta Journal-Constitution*—one of the most powerful and prestigious papers in the South.

Before he took the job, Kovach was told he would have free rein to do whatever he thought was necessary to make the *Journal-Constitution* the best newspaper in the United States. Soon his paper was publishing hard-hitting stories about racial problems in Atlanta, illegal political solicitations by the Georgia Power nuclear utility, discriminatory practices by the city's banking industry, and other flaws in the establishment. As a *Journal-Constitution* reporter told *In These Times*, "Under Kovach, there was a feeling that there were no more topics that were off limits, no more stories that we knew better than to write."

Kovach didn't last long as editor. Under constant pressure from Cox Enterprises (the chain that owns the *Journal-Constitution*) to reshape the paper into a trivialized *USA Today*-type format, Kovach quit in disgust in November 1988. Atlanta's corporate leaders were thrilled to see him go, as noted by reporters who covered Kovach's resignation.

Immediately after Kovach's departure, newsroom staffers had a stormy meeting with management. Investigative journalist Bill Dedman angrily confronted publisher Jay Smith. "What confidence do we have," Dedman asked, "that we won't step back into what we all know was the case before [Kovach], which was not so much where stories get spiked, but people know which stories not to write?"

The situation described by Dedman is par for the course at major U.S. media. Concentrated ownership and economic bonding with advertisers exert an indisputable influence over the kind of information that "freely" circulates in our society. The main problem with today's news media is not the proliferation of explicit falsehoods (though plenty of that goes on); it has more to do with what gets left out of the news when the field of possibilities is circumscribed by vested interests. "Few viewers know what may be missing from the picture window, for their idea of the world is increasingly formed by that window," said TV historian Erik Barnouw.

As FAIR's *Nightline* study showed, a key ingredient lacking in mass media are voices of the public interest community—namely peace, environmental, labor, consumer and civil rights groups, whose perspectives often clash with big business. These groups don't have sufficient funds to purchase their own TV station or daily newspaper. Consequently, whole classes of people are effectively prevented from using the mass media to convey their views to a wide audience. That's why we don't see many people on prime-time television who forcefully challenge corporate America.

News media are not monolithic entities. They occasionally report things that cast big business and other powerful interests in an unfavorable light. But corporate control of the media limits the spectrum of news coverage and, by implication, the range of options available to the U.S. public. This has weakened our ability to respond imaginatively, and appropriately, to the daunting problems our country faces. "It is ownership of the mass media by the wealthy," said Robert Cirano, "rather than a conspiracy of any kind, that explains why the important decisions usually favor viewpoints that support things as they are, rather than viewpoints that support fundamental changes in society."

5

Fourth Estate or Fourth Branch of Government?

B ritish press lord Robert Maxwell got the urge to throw a party while passing through Washington in May 1989. So he hired a top PR firm to round up some VIPs. Three days later, Washington's movers and shakers gathered on Maxwell's 190-foot luxury yacht for some drinking and socializing. CIA director William Webster was there, along with former Defense Secretary Frank Carlucci and ex-Attorney General Edwin Meese. Other luminaries on board included National Security Adviser Brent Scowcroft, White House chief of staff John Sununu and Supreme Court Justice Sandra Day O'Connor.

It was, by Washington standards, an "A-list" party, meaning it attracted Capitol Hill power-brokers—both Dems and Republicans—as well as cabinet members and publishing bigwigs who mixed business with pleasure while sipping champagne and nibbling caviar against a twilit skyline on the Potomac. "It was difficult to tell just who was eyeballing who," remarked one reporter who covered the affair. That a star-studded cast would turn up on such short notice for a stint on Maxwell's yacht underscored the amount of respect that mass media owners command among political heavyweights.

Maxwell himself was a guest at another power-broker bash later that summer hosted by Malcolm Forbes, publisher of *Forbes* magazine. The occasion was Forbes' 70th birthday. Dubbed "the party of the century," nearly 1,000 notables flew to Tangier for a weekend extravaganza that featured Moroccan cavalry units firing rifles in the air as they galloped full speed across the lawns of Forbes' plush seaside estate. "I'm here because so many of my friends are here," said former Secretary of State Henry Kissinger. Others in attendance included former President Jimmy Carter and various U.S. officeholders; corporate honchos such as Donald Trump; big-name journalists like Walter Cronkite, Barbara Walters and A.M. Rosenthal; and a clatch of media moguls: Al Neuharth of Gannett, Katharine Graham of the *Washington Post*, Mort Zuckerman of *U.S. News & World Report*, Jann Wenner of *Rolling Stone*, and the ever-fashionable Rupert Murdoch.

A media controversy erupted as word circulated that Forbes might write off the party's $2 million tab as a tax-deductible business expense. Because of the media industry's overwhelming dependence on advertisers, it made perfect sense to Forbes that his birthday fling should qualify for a heavy subsidy by U.S. taxpayers. Hundreds of his corporate colleagues who partook of the festivities were both sources of advertising income and possible subjects for articles. But the publicity snafu prompted Forbes to reconsider, and he grudgingly announced at a post-birthday press conference that he would foot the bill himself.

Lost amidst all the hubbub over tax loopholes for the rich and famous were other serious issues ignored by most journalists, who tend to report on such gatherings mainly as social events—gossip columns dressed up as news. While Forbes' fete was all the rage, mass media eschewed any probing analysis of what it means when media stars and big politicos chum it up at various hooplas. Does the press function as an independent Fourth Estate or as a fourth branch of government? Are media adversaries of the State or its accomplice?

TV's top journalists are part of the wealthy and influential elite, often socializing with people they're supposed to be scrutinizing. At an awards banquet for the Radio & Television Correspondents Association during Reagan's second term, Kathleen Sullivan (at the time with ABC) was photographed on the arm of then-Defense Secretary Caspar Weinberger, while CBS *Face the Nation* host Lesley Stahl greeted the Republican Party's national chairman Frank Fahrenkopf with a kiss. Vice President Bush serenaded the crowd with a speech and journalists got prizes ostensibly for good reporting.

David Broder of the *Washington Post*, often described as the dean of American political reporting, has won many awards in his day. Upon accepting a prize for lifetime service to journalism at Washington's National Press Club in 1988, Broder stated: "I can't for the life of me fathom why any journalists would want to become insiders, when it's so much fun being outsiders—irreverent, inquisitive, incorrigibly independent outsiders, thumbing our nose at authority and going our own way." Applauding Broder's remarks was an audience of insiders, including James Baker, soon-to-be Secretary of State, who got a flattering profile in Broder's column.

This kind of sycophantic behavior made investigative reporter I.F. Stone's blood boil. Izzy, as his friends called him, was a real outsider. He had one cardinal rule: don't pal around with the folks you write about, don't fraternize with people in power. That's what he always told young people who wanted to be reporters. But his was a voice in a journalistic wilderness. When he died in 1989, Stone was lauded by many high-profile journalists who never listened to his advice.

THE MIGHTY PR ARSENAL

When we turn on the TV, we don't expect to see a government spokesperson reading officially-sanctioned news reports. Most U.S. citizens who hear about a state-controlled press think of something that exists in faraway places, not in their own country. Some of our political leaders, however, have a less sanguine view of American journalism. "Reporters are puppets," said Lyndon Johnson. "They simply respond to the pull of the most powerful strings."

While claiming to be independent, U.S. journalists rely heavily on official sources who don't necessarily deserve the credence they are given. "For all its bluster and professed skepticism, the press is far too willing to take the government at its word," said *Newsday* editor Anthony Marro. Consequently, mass media are often little more than vehicles through which those in power pontificate to the American public. *New York Times* columnist Tom Wicker has described the dependence on official sources as "the gravest professional and intellectual weakness of American journalism." Bill Moyers, who has worked in the White House as well as in print and broadcast media, emphasized a similar point: "Most of the news on television is, unfortunately, whatever the government says is news."

The sheer quantity of information churned out by the U.S. government is a major factor in its ability to set the news agenda. The White House and Pentagon each host two daily press briefings; the State Department holds one. The White House produces 15 to 20 press releases a day. (The Air Force alone issued over 600,000 news releases in 1980—the last year such statistics were made public.) These are supplemented by interviews, off-the-record background briefings, leaks, tips, staged events, photo opportunities, speeches by top officials, and the well-timed release of reports, "white papers" and other documents.

As many as 13,000 PR people work for the federal government, at a cost of more than $2.5 billion a year in taxpayers' money. Every member of Congress has a PR staff. So does an alphabet soup of government agencies: FDA, EPA, DEA, NASA, etc. Dispatched throughout the hallowed halls of officialdom are Washington reporters "whose primary exercise," as Alan Abelson of *Barron's* put it, "is collecting handouts from those informational soup kitchens."

White House occupants have long been adept at dishing out the news. But no president pursued a more sophisticated and vigorous media strategy than Ronald Reagan. Every morning, Reagan's White House staff would meet to decide what news to promote that day and how they wanted the press to cover it. Within minutes after the decision, all senior administration officials and thousands of PR personnel throughout the government would learn via computer link-up what the "line of the day" was. Then the White House News Service kicked into gear, electronically transmitting press releases, official statements and texts of speeches to hundreds of newsrooms around the country.

Reagan's PR team created special events to fit into 30-second or minute-long sound bites on the evening news. "We'd be crazy if we didn't think in those terms," said Reagan aide Michael Deaver. As a follow-up, Deaver and other White House PR-spinners called the networks before the nightly news telecast to check on what was slated to run. If they didn't like what they saw, they called the networks again to complain about specific stories and reporters.

Pentagon public relations

During the Reagan era, Pentagon PR operations grew to include a $100 million annual budget and 3,000-plus staff, which bombarded the American public and much of the world with endless rounds of official information. With their skimpy budgets, non-profit peace and disarmament groups that frequently criticize U.S. military policy were hardly a match for the Pentagon's PR armory. Moreover, big media typically side with big government, giving Department of Defense (DOD) officials veto power over which guests appear with them on TV and radio public affairs shows. DOD spokespeople, for example, refused to participate in National Public Radio discussions of military issues if experts from the Center for Defense Information, a peace organization run by retired admirals and generals, were on the program.

But the Pentagon usually doesn't have to bully the media. Journalists have a long history of cooperating with U.S. military officials. During World War II, the American press functioned as a virtual PR arm of the government. "Public relations, of which war correspondents were considered a part, became another cog in the massive military machine the Americans constructed to defeat Hitler," wrote Phillip Knightley in his book on wartime press coverage. "The supreme commander, General Eisenhower, spelled it out very clearly. 'Public opinion wins wars,' he told a meeting of American newspaper editors. 'I have always considered as quasi-staff officers, correspondents accredited to my headquarters.'"

Hostilities didn't cease when the U.S. bombed Hiroshima and Nagasaki; instead the conflict segued into the Cold War, with the Soviets replacing the Nazis as America's principal enemy. Reporters promoted the needs and strategies of the U.S. government as it engaged in a protracted struggle against a communist foe depicted as ruthless and implacable. An era of permanent nuclear emergency fostered what William Dorman has described as "a journalism of deference to the national security state." "Not surprisingly, the mainstream news media...have performed during the Cold War as they always have during hot ones," Dorman wrote in the *Bulletin of the Atomic Scientists.* "The media have moved further and further away from the watchdog role democratic theory assumed they would play in affairs of state where national defense and foreign policy are concerned."

With few exceptions, reporters have faithfully repeated the Pentagon's exaggerations about Soviet military might and spending. The much-discussed "missile gap" of the early 1960s turned out to be a hoax, as the *New*

York Times finally acknowledged a quarter of a century after the so-called fact. "The charge was untrue," the *Times* editorialized about allegations that the U.S. lagged far behind the Soviet arsenal. "At the time of the missile crisis, the United States had 2,000 long-range missiles, the Soviet Union less than 100." This is but one example of lies disseminated by national security "experts" that received wide circulation—and acceptance by the American public—thanks to a compliant news media. Later came "the ABM gap," "the hard-target-kill gap," "the spending gap" and "the laser gap." As a result, U.S. taxpayers were hoodwinked into squandering their money on bloated military budgets.

Vietnam: a patriotic spin

True to form, big-league reporters coddled official sources throughout the Vietnam War. Producers at NBC and ABC had an explicit policy of deleting graphic footage of the conflict from evening news broadcasts. CBS played by similar rules, thereby helping to "shield the audience from the true horror of the war," according to Fred Friendly. "I must confess that in my two years as CBS News president," said Friendly, "I tempered my news judgment and tailored my conscience more than once."

In times of crisis—defined by the White House and accepted by dominant media—anointed correspondents figuratively salute the Flag raised over American soldiers ordered to their battle stations. Some journalists have dispensed with any pretense of objectivity, leaping headlong into the fray. Arnaud de Borchgrave described his combat role while covering the Vietnam War for *Newsweek*: "Carroll pulls the pin from a grenade and hurls it over my head, throws three more before going back to his radio. I toss another one for good measure..." De Borchgrave, who now edits the *Washington Times*, received a war hero's welcome upon returning to *Newsweek* headquarters in New York.

U.S. media often gave Vietnam War coverage a "patriotic" spin. Typical was NBC's *Huntley-Brinkley Report*, which described "the American forces in Indochina as 'builders' rather than 'destroyers'"—a "central truth" that "needs underscoring." Much of the press was intent on underscoring this "truth"—which explains why reporter Seymour Hersh had to send his account of the My Lai massacre to the Dispatch News Service, a little known media outlet, after wasting more than a year trying to get the major media to cover the story. Hersh subsequently won a well-deserved Pulitzer Prize for the My Lai revelations.

Journalists kept chomping at the government bit, even when it should have been apparent that something was seriously amiss about the official version of the Gulf of Tonkin incident in 1964, which served as a pretext for dramatically escalating the war in Vietnam. Early calls for U.S. withdrawal from Vietnam by Senator Ernest Gruening, one of the two dissenting votes against the Tonkin Gulf Resolution, went unreported in the *New York Times* and the *Washington Post*.

When the *Times* published Harrison Salisbury's 1966 year-end eyewitness accounts of civilian devastation from the U.S. bombing of Hanoi, the *Washington Post* railed at this momentary breach of state journalism. On the Pentagon beat, *Post* reporter George C. Wilson informed readers that Salisbury's statistics on casualties were "identical to those in a communist propaganda leaflet." *Post* reporter Chalmers Roberts described Salisbury as an accessory of North Vietnam and its leader Ho Chi Minh—"Ho's chosen instrument." The *Post* also condemned Salisbury editorially, as an unwitting tool of the North Vietnamese. In spite of the vitriol, within weeks independent verification forced the U.S. government to admit the truth of Salisbury's articles.

Washington Post Company president Katharine Graham counted among her best friends some of the key architects of the Vietnam War, including Defense Secretary Robert McNamara (who later joined the board of directors of the Washington Post Company). President Lyndon Johnson appreciated all the gung-ho editorials about the war that *Post* editor Russell Wiggins was writing. As an apt reward, a presidential appointment made Wiggins the U.S. ambassador to the United Nations the last few months of 1968—"a plum from Johnson to a loyalist," recounts author Howard Bray.

In early 1968, the *Boston Globe* surveyed 39 major American newspapers with a combined circulation of 22 million. Not a single one had called for U.S. withdrawal from Vietnam—this at a time when millions of Americans were demanding an immediate pull-out. The *Washington Post* and the *New York Times* held firm until a big chunk of the corporate establishment had grown disenchanted with the war. Only then did the papers of record assume a more critical editorial stance toward the war. In June 1971, the *Times* and the *Post* crossed the Nixon White House by publishing the Pentagon Papers, which showed that the U.S. government had deceived the public about Tonkin Gulf events and consistently lied about American involvement in Vietnam. The three commercial networks, fearing recrimination by the Nixon administration, had turned down a chance to break the story first.

For a number of years, CBS News anchor Walter Cronkite had been a staunch supporter of the war, routinely reciting statements made by the President and other top U.S. officials without any suggestion that the information ought to be balanced by independent sources. However, as the war dragged on and the deceptions became too obvious to ignore, Cronkite and other journalists began to adopt a more skeptical attitude. A dramatic break came during the Tet Offensive of 1968, when Cronkite began to challenge official assurances of an impending U.S. victory. But the American media never became an advocate of the grassroots antiwar movement, which viewed the war not only as unwinnable, but morally repugnant.

While Cronkite may have cast doubt on proclamations about light at the end of Vietnam's tunnel, neither he nor any other big-name journalists had the gumption to call the U.S. military assault on Vietnam what it really was—an invasion. This central truth was skirted in media debates between hawks and doves, as described by MIT professor Noam Chomsky: "The people called hawks said, 'If we keep at it we win.' The people called doves said, 'Even if we keep at it we probably can't win, and besides, it would probably be too costly for us, and besides maybe we're killing too many people.'" Despite their tactical differences, the mass media's hawks and doves never questioned America's right to carry out aggression against Vietnam. "In fact," said Chomsky, "they didn't even admit that aggression was taking place. They called the war the 'defense' of Vietnam, using 'defense' for 'aggression' in the standard Orwellian manner."

Right to the bitter end, major U.S. media supported additional military aid for the tottering regime in Saigon. Even as the last American forces made a hasty retreat in 1975, the U.S. press was still serving as a credulous conduit for CIA news plants. "The whole idea of a bloodbath was conjured out of thin air. We had no intelligence to indicate that the South Vietnamese were facing a bloodbath," said CIA operative Frank Snepp. But reporters played it the way the government wanted—and rarely said a word about other matters when the American government demanded silence.

Knowing but not reporting: Koppel does Laos

No U.S. government agency exercises a formal right of censorship over the American media. Yet many stories are withheld or slanted because journalists choose not to contradict the official version of events—even when they know it is false.

That was the case when Ted Koppel, then ABC's Southeast Asian bureau chief, paid several visits to Pakse in Southern Laos between 1969 and 1971. Strategically located on the Mekong River at the edge of a plateau, Pakse was a key site where CIA and U.S. military personnel were training, assisting, and directing the Royal Lao Air Force for continuous bombing runs along the diffuse Ho Chi Minh Trail. Koppel was aware that the CIA and members of the U.S. armed forces were in the thick of activities at the Pakse air base—but he never reported the U.S. government's involvement.

Instead, on the ABC television network Koppel simply repeated the official cover story about the Americans at Pakse. "These guys were all in civilian clothes," Koppel told us in a January 1990 interview. "None of them admitted to being in the military, or with the CIA for that matter. They all claimed to be civilian contract employees." Koppel acknowledged that at the time he knew the facts were otherwise: "I may have known that, but I wasn't in a position to prove it."

The United States, in cooperation with a Laotian regime receiving 100 percent of its military budget from the U.S. government, subjected Laos to the most intensive bombing in world history. The bloodshed in that country widened in February 1971 with the "incursion" of 20,000 South Vietnamese and 9,000 U.S. troops accompanied by heavy American air support. Weeks later Ted Koppel returned to Pakse—to do a "profile" on a young Royal Lao Air Force pilot. The ABC newsman rode in the back seat of a T-28 fighter plane as the pilot went on a bombing raid. But in his news report Koppel still made no mention of the CIA and U.S. military involvement, even though it was central to the bombardment that he witnessed.

The U.S. government role in that region was not difficult to discern. A book by Peter Dale Scott, written the same year as Koppel's ride in the T-28, referred matter-of-factly to "the CIA operations headquarters at Pakse." But Koppel is unapologetic about his failure to inform the American people that the bombing runs based in Pakse were anything other than Laotian operations, helped by hired American civilians.

Not everyone who was there looks back contentedly on the deception. Walter J. Smith, a U.S. Air Force noncommissioned officer at Pakse, remembers the day in early 1971 when Koppel showed up with a cameraman at the Royal Laotian Officers' Club, the favored watering hole for a large contingent of U.S. and Laotian military men at the base. Smith told us in an interview that Koppel had made clear he would do nothing to dislodge the official fig-leaf. "In effect, he was saying, 'I'm not going to tell the truth no matter what happens,'" recalls Smith, now an instructor in American studies at the University of California at Santa Cruz. "It seemed that everyone knew what was going on in Laos, except for the American public. And Americans didn't know about it because the media were willingly keeping it secret."

Koppel and other mainstream journalists apparently see no contradiction between their professed independence and their willingness to suppress troublesome stories at the behest of U.S. authorities. While the American people are frequently told of the media's courage to disclose, they rarely hear about the way news is censored out of existence. As Walter Karp observed, "The obligation of a free press to 'act as a check on the power of government' is checked itself by the power of government."

Barbara Walters, shuttle diplomat

Sometimes the line between government and news agencies becomes so blurred that reporters forget which side they're on. Not long after the Iran-contra scandal broke, ABC News star Barbara Walters secretly provided the White House with documents from Manucher Ghorbanifar, an Iranian arms merchant, about the diversion of weapons sales profits to the Nicaraguan insurgents. Claiming that Walters' conduct was "a rather unusual thing," ABC News executive Richard Wald said that the network had not been informed of her decision to pass messages from Ghorbanifar to President Reagan.

Walters' intimate relationship with the White House could have been summed up by the character in a Marx Brothers movie who implored, "Come closer, come closer." To which Groucho responded, "If I get any closer, I'll be behind you."

REVOLVING DOOR: BIG GOVERNMENT, BIG MEDIA

The *New York Times* headline was just what the Nicaraguan contras needed: "Nicaraguan Rebels Say They Won Biggest Victory Over Sandinistas." Datelined Washington, the story by Bernard Trainor was based on a phone conversation with a contra source in Honduras, who claimed the contras had captured the Nicaraguan garrison at San Jose de Bocay "in their biggest victory in the six-year war." Without citing a source, Trainor asserted that "the population of the region is generally sympathetic to the contra movement."

Two days later, the story crumbled. Journalists arrived at the scene and reported that while the contras hardly damaged any military targets, they did kill three children and a pregnant woman, wounded 18 civilians after spraying houses with machine gun fire, and then burned dozens of homes. Apparently these civilians were not "sympathetic to the contra movement."

Where did Trainor go wrong? As usual, Trainor relied only on sources allied with the U.S. military. That's in keeping with his background. He became the *New York Times* military correspondent in 1986 after a 40-year career in the Marine Corps. This was announced in a brief item, "Ex-General to Join The Times."

One of the main reasons why the *Times* hired Trainor was because he had good access to Pentagon insiders. The cooperation of official sources within the Pentagon is considered a major plus if you are a mainstream journalist covering U.S. military affairs. This factor was sufficiently impressive to *Times* management, which ignored possible conflicts of interest inherent in Trainor's situation. Did it ever occur to the *Times* higher-ups that Trainor, a lifelong military man, might be partial to the U.S. military establishment? By the same token, why not hire someone from Greenpeace to report on environmental issues? Or a labor organizer to report on the American workplace?

Foggy Bottom journalism

Trainor is hardly the only journalist at the *New York Times* to travel through the revolving door that links media and government. Jack Rosenthal, editor of the *Times* editorial page since 1986 (and deputy editor for ten years prior to that), had been a high-ranking official in Lyndon Johnson's State Department. Leslie Gelb, another State Department veteran, edits the *Times* op-ed page. Gelb's former boss, ex-Secretary of State Cyrus Vance, currently sits on the board of directors of the Times Company.

It appears that matriculating from the State Department greatly enhances the prospects for getting a job with the *Times* editorial staff. Gelb took a break from the *Times* national security beat to serve in the Carter State Department as director of the Bureau of Politico-Military Affairs. In 1978, he helped set in motion a covert CIA program designed to get the European press to write approvingly about the neutron bomb. Government service was nothing new for Gelb, who had previously worked as a press officer for the Department of Defense.

The same revolving door that brought Gelb back to the *Times* sent his replacement, national security correspondent Richard Burt, into government service as a nuclear strategist for the Reagan administration. In 1989, Burt became President Bush's chief arms negotiator in Geneva. Conservative Burt and moderate Gelb, like two wings of a Stealth bomber, symbolize the complementary roles of their employers. Squabbling over how fast to proceed with the arms race, the wisdom of seeking to enforce a thermonuclear *Pax Americana* was not at issue.

The *Times* ran a piece by Gelb in 1985 which discussed how the U.S. had unilaterally devised wartime contingency plans to deploy nuclear depth charges in Canada and three other countries. This information had already been published in newspapers abroad, and a State Department official helped Gelb prepare the version that appeared in the *Times*. As Gelb later explained, "The *Times* editors and I were concerned about genuine national security as well as news. Therefore, we agreed at the outset to limit the story to those four countries where the contingency plans had already been publicly disclosed." Gelb said he had more sensitive information which he didn't include in the story.

The State Department also employs journalists from other major media. NBC News correspondent Bernard Kalb was a State Department spokesperson during the Reagan administration. He resigned in a huff during the summer of 1986 when an unauthorized leak disclosed that Reagan's National Security Council had manipulated the U.S. press by planting false information about Libyan leader Moammar Qadaffi's alleged belligerent intentions. Another PR man for Reagan's State Department was John Hughes, who subsequently took a job as an editorial columnist for the *Christian Science Monitor*. It's hard to tell the difference between Hughes' diatribes on Central America and State Department positions.

State propagandists

U.S. citizens don't often think of their government as promoting propaganda, but that's the acknowledged function of the Voice of America (VOA) and the United States Information Agency (USIA), both of which are subsumed within the State Department bureaucracy. The notion of serving openly as a State propagandist did not deter *NBC Nightly News* reporter John Chancellor from becoming VOA director during the Johnson administration.

Nor did it deter Sid Davis, VOA program director under Reagan and Bush, who had been the White House correspondent and Washington bureau chief for NBC News. Edward R. Murrow of CBS News and columnist Carl Rowan took turns as USIA director when John F. Kennedy was President.

American Presidents have often chosen as their press secretaries people who later assumed prominent positions within the mass media. Pierre Salinger, currently chief foreign correspondent of ABC *World News Tonight*, was JFK's press secretary. Bill Moyers served in this capacity for Lyndon Johnson and later became a commentator and reporter for CBS and PBS. Ron Nessen, Gerald Ford's press secretary, is now vice president for news at the Mutual Broadcasting System.

Ironically, President Richard Nixon, an outspoken foe of the so-called liberal media, employed a number of people in his administration who ended up making it big in journalism. William Safire, Nixon's special assistant and speechwriter, became a *New York Times* columnist. CNN *Crossfire* and *Capital Gang* host Pat Buchanan shuttled back and forth through the revolving door, starting at the *St. Louis Globe-Democrat* before joining Nixon's team as a Special Assistant to the President. Buchanan, a widely syndicated columnist, also served as communications director for the Reagan White House.

Another news celeb with enduring fondness for Richard Nixon is Diane Sawyer. Prior to emerging as a network news star, Sawyer's professional experience consisted of a couple of years as a local TV weather forecaster in Louisville and eight years as his assistant. "She had not only been a Nixon aide but a Nixon loyalist of the highest order," Peter Boyer wrote in *Who Killed CBS?* "When Nixon finally resigned in disgrace, she was one of the faithful on the plane that took Nixon on his long journey to exile at San Clemente."

In 1978, Sawyer began working for CBS News. A decade later, a lucrative contract lured her to ABC as co-host of *Primetime Live* with Sam Donaldson. Said sardonic Sam: "I'm not going to sit up nights thinking of something nasty to say about Richard Nixon and see how she can handle it."

Journalists have also filled important posts in the Reagan and Bush administrations. David Gergen, Reagan's communications director, became editor of *U.S. News & World Report* in 1983; that year Gergen's deputy, Joanna Bistany, left the White House to become a top executive at ABC News. Reaganite Richard Perle, formerly Assistant Secretary of Defense, is a contributing editor and columnist for *U.S. News*. And prancing through the revolving door in the other direction was Peggy Noonan, who cut her teeth scripting CBS radio commentary for Dan Rather before writing speeches for Reagan and Bush.

George Will in outer space

During the 1980 presidential campaign, commentator George Will coached candidate Reagan in preparation for his debate with Jimmy

Carter—and then praised Reagan's performance while covering the debate for ABC News without mentioning his association with the Reagan campaign team. When this fact came to light during the short-lived "Debategate" scandal in 1983, Will was subjected to a round of polite scolding by other journalists. But the incident didn't hurt his career; on the contrary, it enhanced his reputation among media mavens. "What brought him to outer space was exactly the thing many thought would bring him down: coaching Reagan," said Jeff Greenfield of ABC *Nightline*. "To the skill and style he'd always had it added the insider magic."

While quick to proclaim their independence, many reporters find it easy to empathize with Washington's concerns and are quite comfortable working for the U.S. government. Cronyism and careerism help keep the revolving door spinning, but more important is the fact that both journalists and elected officials tend to view the world in ways that conform to the national security establishment. Within this dominant framework, personal opinions about policy specifics are less important than common biases about what constitutes legitimate "national interests." Whether conservative, moderate or liberal, mainstream journalists function within a media system dominated by government and corporate elites. Constrained by rigid institutional structures and narrow cultural assumptions, most reporters are not predisposed toward bucking the status quo.

Personnel shifts between the press and the government are not part of a planned conspiracy to slant the news. Nor should the brisk traffic through the revolving door be interpreted as proof that beat reporters get explicit marching orders directly from U.S. officials. This is usually not necessary when they share similar assumptions about America's role in the world.

High-level interlocks

One could cite many other examples of journalists who have hitched a ride with Uncle Sam for a while. But the revolving door that matters most spins in much loftier circles, connecting big government with big media executives and upper-level management. Robert McNamara, Defense Secretary under Kennedy and Johnson, recently retired from the board of directors of the Washington Post Company, and ex-Attorney General Nicholas Katzenbach currently sits on the Post board. Former cabinet-rank officials also populate the boards of other major print media, including the *New York Times*, *Los Angeles Times* and the Reader's Digest Association. (Published in 16 editions for a worldwide readership of 100 million, *Reader's Digest* is the most widely-circulated U.S.-based periodical.) These high-placed executive interlocks are far more influential than job-hopping journalists who flit back and forth between politicos and the press with hardly a blink.

The corporate boards of the three major television networks are studded with government power-brokers. Harold Brown, Carter's Defense

Secretary, is a director of CBS, along with former Secretary of State Henry Kissinger. General David Jones, Chairman of the Joint Chiefs of Staff during the Reagan years, is on the board of GE/NBC; so is former Attorney General William French Smith. And prior to becoming CIA Director in 1981, William Casey held sway as chief counsel and an original board member of CapCities, which gobbled up ABC early in Reagan's second term.

Casey, who had been Securities and Exchange Commissioner under Nixon, continued to own $7.5 million in CapCities/ABC stock until his death in 1987. A gung-ho advocate of covert operations and a mover-and-shaker in corporate politics, Casey was part of a network of spooks who had frequently used American companies—including mass media—for espionage purposes. Disgruntled CIA officers disclosed that the Agency had fudged intelligence data to bolster U.S. foreign policy initiatives when William Casey was director—something rarely mentioned on ABC or the other corporate networks, which also worked closely with the CIA.

For many years, CBS supplied cover for CIA agents posted overseas, as well as out-takes of news footage and access to its extensive photo library. General Electric, owner of NBC, was contracted by the CIA to provide estimates of Soviet military strength—a dubious arrangement given that GE reaps huge profits from the arms race and therefore has a vested interest in perpetuating it by inflating the data. As we shall see, the links between the CIA and the three main TV networks are just the tip of a very spooky iceberg.

THE CIA-MEDIA IMBROGLIO

When CIA director William Webster reads his morning paper over toast and coffee, he may be ingesting "news" that was cooked up by his own spy agency. So might millions of other Americans.

Manipulating the media for propaganda purposes has long been a major aspect of clandestine operations conducted by the CIA, which often doesn't have to use subterfuge to get news organizations to do its bidding. Since the CIA was formed in 1947, publishers and executive management have eagerly volunteered their services for the benefit of the Agency.

"There is ample evidence that America's leading publishers allowed themselves and their news organizations to become handmaidens to the intelligence services," wrote investigative journalist Carl Bernstein in *Rolling Stone*. "American publishers, like so many other corporate and institutional leaders at the time, were willing to commit the resources of their companies to the struggle against 'global communism.' Accordingly, the traditional line separating the American press corps and government was often indistinguishable."

As far as America's spymasters were concerned, a natural affinity existed between the cloak-and-dagger trade and the news business, since both professions emphasize information gathering. Debriefing journalists has always been one of the CIA's most effective ways of getting intelligence. Time-Life publisher Henry Luce, a close friend of CIA director Allen Dulles, was debriefed by the CIA after traveling overseas, and he privately encouraged his correspondents to cooperate with the Agency. Malcolm Muir, editor of *Newsweek* during much of the Cold War, was also regularly debriefed after visits abroad.

At times reporters, photographers and camera crews will visit obscure locales that are off-limits to most people. A well-placed journalist can act as the Agency's eyes and ears, obtaining hard-to-come-by data. "One journalist is worth 20 agents," a high-level CIA officer told Bernstein. Former CIA deputy director Ray S. Cline, now a mainstay at the Center for Strategic and International Studies in Washington, called the American news media the "only unfettered espionage agencies in this country."

In addition to swapping information, reporters have killed or altered stories and disseminated propaganda at the request of the Agency. The CIA, in turn, has given friendly journalists career-enhancing scoops and leaks. When a correspondent for the San Diego-based Copley chain learned that CIA-backed anti-Castro Cubans were training for the ill-fated Bay of Pigs invasion, he not only held the story but published misleading information fed to him by the Agency that dismissed rumors of an impending attack. As a gesture of gratitude, the CIA gave Charles Keely a big scoop about Soviet missile bases in Cuba. Keely subsequently won an award for breaking the Cuban missile story.

Foreign news bureaus provided excellent cover for full-time spies posing as reporters. For a while, the CIA ran a formal training program to teach agents how to act like (or be) reporters. Not everyone needed tutoring; Richard Helms, CIA director in the mid-1960s and early 1970s, had previously worked as a UPI correspondent. And the revolving door turned both ways, as CIA agents like William F. Buckley burrowed into media niches after their stint with U.S. intelligence formally ended.

Bernstein estimated in 1977 that at least 400 journalists had lived double lives, maintaining covert relationships with the CIA that went beyond the normal give-and-take between reporters and their sources. Media professionals occasionally were paid for their CIA-related services. Some even signed secrecy agreements while they performed non-journalistic tasks for the Agency, such as keeping an eye out for potential recruits and passing messages or money to CIA contacts. Trusted reporters were dispatched on special undercover assignments, almost always with the consent of their editors. As former CIA director William Colby stated, "Let's not pick on some poor reporters. Let's go to the managements. They were witting."

Old boy networks

The CIA cultivated high-level contacts within the most prestigious media in the U.S., including the three TV networks and the newspapers of record. More than 20 other American news organizations occasionally shared a bed with the CIA, including AP, UPI, Scripps-Howard, the Hearst papers, *Reader's Digest, Wall Street Journal, Christian Science Monitor* and the Mutual Broadcasting System.

Relationships between CIA officials and media execs were often social, dating back many years. For instance, *Washington Post* owners Philip and Katharine Graham were best friends with Frank Wisner, a pivotal figure in the Agency's worldwide propaganda apparatus. Wisner ran CIA covert operations from the early days of the Cold War until shortly before he committed suicide in 1961.

The CIA's global propaganda operation was headed initially by Tom Braden. After leaving the Agency, Braden worked as a syndicated columnist and co-host of CNN *Crossfire* (representing "the left"). Braden once wrote a piece in the *Saturday Evening Post* called "Why I'm Glad the CIA is Immoral." One of Braden's CIA protégés, Philip L. Geyelin, eventually became editor of the *Washington Post* editorial page. At times critical of the Reagan administration for squandering its credibility because it lied so much about Central America, Geyelin nonetheless affirmed the virtue of official deception: "We will get nowhere without first stipulating that, while circumstances alter almost any case you can think of, the President has an inherent right—perhaps an obligation in particular situations—to deceive."

Oftentimes the lie is in the omission—and the *Post* has been a willing participant in keeping the lid on touchy disclosures. "There have been instances," admitted publisher Katharine Graham, "in which secrets have been leaked to us which we thought were so dangerous that we went to them [U.S. officials] and told them that they had been leaked to us and did not print them."

The CIA's most important print media asset has been the *New York Times*, which provided press credentials and cover for more than a dozen CIA operatives during the Cold War. Arthur Hays Sulzberger, publisher from 1935 to 1961, was a close friend of CIA director Allen Dulles. After Dulles' successor John A. McCone stepped down as CIA chief in the mid-1960s, the *Times* continued to submit articles to McCone for vetting and approval. McCone removed certain elements of stories before they went to press. Such groveling by the *Times* suggests that instead of "All the News That's Fit to Print," perhaps its motto should be "Print to Fit."

A particularly egregious case of CIA tampering involved *Times* foreign affairs columnist C.L. Sulzberger, the boss's nephew. Several CIA sources told Bernstein that Sulzberger was given a CIA briefing paper on Soviet intelligence, which ran almost verbatim under the columnist's byline in the *Times* in September 1967.

Domestic fallout

The CIA's propaganda apparatus includes a far-flung network of foreign media outlets. The *New York Times*, which ran a three-part series on the CIA and the media in 1977 (partly in response to the embarrassing revelations by Carl Bernstein in *Rolling Stone*), disclosed that at various times the Agency has "owned or subsidized" more than 50 newspapers, news services, radio stations, periodicals, book publishers and other communication entities, most of which were overseas. "We had at least one newspaper in every foreign capital at any given time," a CIA official told the *Times*. Those not owned or substantially underwritten by U.S intelligence were infiltrated by paid agents or other staff who pushed stories at the behest of the CIA and sometimes blocked articles viewed as detrimental to the Agency.

A favored method of disseminating "black" or unattributed propaganda was through overseas English-language newspapers operating as CIA proprietaries. CIA personnel knew that some of the bogus stories they planted in the foreign press would inevitably get picked up by U.S. media and relayed as hard news back home. American spymasters acknowledged there was no way to avoid the problem of "blowback" or "domestic fallout," in which news tainted with "disinformation," as it is known in espionage parlance, reaches an unwitting American audience.

Once-classified CIA documents suggest that the American public was a prime target of CIA propaganda. A memo dated July 13, 1951, described the CIA's fledgling mind control operations as "broad and comprehensive, involving both domestic and overseas activities." Another CIA document from the same period indicates that high-level CIA officers met on a regular basis to exchange ideas on "the broader aspects of psychology as it pertains to the control of groups or masses rather than the mind of an individual." Specifically, the conversation focused on "determining means for combatting communism and 'selling' democracy."

Americans have grown accustomed to dire warnings about Soviet disinformation plots directed against the United States. But there has been far less media scrutiny of anticommunist propaganda promoted by the CIA. Over the years, the Agency has fabricated stories about Soviet nuclear bomb tests that never happened and forged portions of speeches by Soviet leaders for publication in friendly media assets. At one point, the CIA faked the diary of an alleged Soviet defector; published as a book by Doubleday, *The Penkovsky Papers* portrayed the USSR in the worst possible light.

CIA mind control

CIA director Dulles counselled a Princeton University audience on "how sinister the battle for men's minds had become in Soviet hands." Soviet spies, Dulles warned in April 1953, had developed "brain perversion techniques...so subtle and so abhorrent to our way of life that we have recoiled from facing up to them." Ironically, three days later Dulles authorized Operation MK-ULTRA, the CIA's main drug testing and behavior modification project, involving hallucinogenic chemicals, hypnosis, sensory deprivation, electronic brain stimulation, lobotomy, etc.—the same abhorrent methods he accused the Soviets of employing. But secret CIA memoranda explicitly stated that there was "no indication of Red use of chemicals" during this period. "Apparently their major emphasis is on the development of specially-trained teams without the use of narcotics, hypnosis, or special mechanical devices," concluded a CIA document dated January 14, 1953.

Fully cognizant of these intelligence reports, high-level CIA officials fed false information to Henry Cabot Lodge, then U.S ambassador to the United Nations, who proceeded to denounce the communists for brainwashing American POWs captured during the Korean War. A once-classified document, dated May 11, 1953, described how Lodge had shown "great interest in the potentiality of Chinese and Soviet use of 'brainwashing' as a propaganda weapon." Lodge was particularly enthusiastic about the term "brainwashing," the document explained, because he wanted "to use a very dramatic word which would indicate horror and would condemn (by its sound) Soviet practices of attacking people's minds."

The word "brainwashing" was coined by Edward Hunter, a CIA-employed journalist who authored many emotionally-charged books and articles on the subject. Hunter joined the Agency at its inception after serving as a propaganda specialist with the Office of Strategic Services (OSS), the CIA's World War II predecessor. When he launched his crusade to bring "the facts about brainwashing...to the people," Hunter was working for U.S. intelligence. Popularizing the concept of brainwashing was part of his job as a CIA operative, despite U.S. Army studies which "failed to reveal even one conclusively documented case of the actual 'brainwashing' on an American prisoner of war in Korea." Indeed, it appears that the communist brainwashing scare was a propaganda ploy, a kind of "brainwashing" or mind control in its own right designed to dupe the American people.

As part of its extensive, multimillion-dollar behavior modification program, the CIA experimented with subliminal methods of control in American movie theaters. CIA scientists understood that television and motion picture media are especially conducive to subliminal manipulation, which bypasses rational defense mechanisms through split-second imagery. A once-secret document dated November 21, 1955, noted how "psychologically the general lowering of consciousness during the picture facilitates the phenomenon of identification and suggestion as in hypnosis." According to another CIA report, subliminal techniques have "achieved some success in commercial advertising, as 'Eat Popcorn' or 'Drink Cola' projected on a screen in certain movie theaters for 1/3000 of a second at five second intervals." In a scheme reminiscent of a recent John

Carpenter film, *They Live!*, the CIA document recommended testing whether subliminal projection "can be utilized in such a way as to feature a visual suggestion such as 'Obey [deleted]' or 'Obey [deleted]' with similar success."

The Agency proceeded to test its subliminal hypothesis in a number of movie theaters in the U.S. On one occasion, the CIA admonished an audience in Alexandria, Virginia, to "buy popcorn," prompting many viewers to line up at the drinking fountain because the suggestion made them thirsty. Upon learning of this incident, then-Vice President Nixon quipped that such a technique might be "politically useful," but not if movie-goers were given a subliminal command to "vote for X" only to search for a name on the ballot which began with the letters "For." Quite a sense of humor, that Tricky Dick.

Nazi assets

On the international front, the CIA operated Radio Liberty and Radio Free Europe (aimed at the Soviet Union and Eastern Europe) throughout the Cold War. With several former Nazis and fascists on staff, these were among the largest and most expensive psychological warfare operations ever undertaken by the U.S. government. They generated an onslaught of virulent anti-Red propaganda, at times lifting fraudulent material straight from Hitler's security services in an effort to rouse the Central and East European masses against the Soviets. One Nazi-inspired propaganda piece—"Document on Terror"—did the near-impossible, accusing Stalin of crimes he hadn't actually committed.

Back in the United States, the CIA set in motion the Crusade for Freedom, a multimillion-dollar PR project which served as a domestic counterpart to the Agency's global propaganda effort. As such, it constituted a violation of the National Security Act of 1947, which explicitly prohibited the CIA from engaging in domestic propaganda activity. Designed to mobilize public opinion in support of the government's Cold War policies, this exercise in mind control depended on the cooperation of big media personalities in the United States. It was rather convenient that people like Henry Luce of Time-Life, C.D. Jackson of *Fortune*, and Eugene Lyons of *Reader's Digest* sat on the board of directors of the National Committee for a Free Europe (NCFE), which functioned as a thinly-veiled private-sector cover for channeling funds to neo-Nazi émigré groups intent on "liberating" their homeland. Other NCFE board members included CIA director Allen Dulles and former OSS chief William "Wild Bill" Donovan.

Small wonder that U.S. journalists rallied to the cause, even though several countries represented in the CIA-sponsored "captured nations" coalition were fictitious entities ("Cossackia," "Idel-Ural") that had been invented by the Nazi propaganda ministry during World War II. The U.S. media repeated the Big Lie, whitewashing the brutal, anti-Semitic nature of the CIA's East European proxies with heroic accounts of anticommunist "freedom fighters" sustained by nickel-and-dime donations from ordinary Americans. A similar ruse was later invoked by U.S. officials to explain how the Nicaraguan contras persisted when the Boland Amendment forbade military aid.

Targeting the Third World

CIA disinformation plots have been instrumental in stoking the flames of various Third World regional conflicts. John Stockwell, head of the CIA's Angola Task Force in the mid-1970s, recounted how he conjured up a gruesome tale about Cuban soldiers raping Angolan women, which the CIA planted in the African press; days later, as expected, Stockwell found his anticommunist fantasy had become a big news story in Western countries, including the United States. CIA propaganda planted in the Chilean newspaper *El Mercurio* played a crucial role in setting the stage for the U.S.-engineered coup that overthrew the democratically elected government led by Salvador Allende in 1973.

The CIA has also utilized numerous media assets in Central America, including the anti-Sandinista newspaper *La Prensa*. While Nicaraguan government censorship of *La Prensa* was decried in the U.S. media, CIA subversion of the press in neighboring states provoked little interest among mainstream reporters. During the mid-1980s, according to ex-contra leader Edgar Chamorro and Carlos Morales, former head of the Costa Rican Journalists Union, the CIA recruited dozens of prominent Honduran and Costa Rican journalists in an effort to turn the most influential media in those countries into contra propaganda outlets.

American televangelists such as Pat Robertson have used their media to lobby for aid to the Nicaraguan contras. According to federal law, a tax-exempt ministry is not supposed to engage in partisan politics or divert donations for projects unconnected with the organization's stated goals. But this didn't stop Robertson's *700 Club*—aired on the Christian Broadcasting Network, the second largest cable TV network in the U.S.—from waging a relentless crusade in support of Reagan's Central America policies. The *700 Club* held a telethon to raise money for the contras in 1985, while the Boland Amendment nixed U.S. military assistance for the CIA's mercenary army.

Another ally in the CIA's anti-Sandinista campaign was the *Washington Times*, owned and controlled by Rev. Sun Myung Moon's Unification Church. Launched in 1982, the *Times* gained a circulation of 100,000, along with the endorsement of President Reagan. Founding editor and publisher James Whelan resigned in 1984, charging that top Unification Church officials violated the paper's editorial integrity. He was replaced by former *Newsweek* correspondent Arnaud de Borchgrave, who edited the Moonie newspaper while it got embroiled in covert operations against Nicaragua.

In a National Security Council memo dated March 16, 1985, Lt. Col. Oliver North proposed setting up a tax-exempt entity called the Nicaraguan

Sandinistas, Qaddafi fund U.S. protest

By George Archibald
THE WASHINGTON TIMES

Organizers of nationwide protests and planned civil disobedience this weekend against Reagan administration foreign policies have received $3 million from Nicaragua's Marxist government, according to a source with close ties to the Managua regime.

The funds, secretly channeled by diplomatic pouch to the Nicaraguan Embassy in Washington and then to protest organizers across the country, came from grants to the Managua government from Libyan leader Muammar Qaddafi, said Carlos Rondon, an ex-Sandinista military official with ties to the regime's hierarchy.

Col. Qaddafi gave "several hundred million dollars" in military and economic aid to Nicaragua's Marxist rulers following a March visit to Tripoli by Victor Tirado Lopez, comandante of the Sandinista

revolution, Mr. Rondon said.

"Libya puts the money into a secret fund that [Nicaraguan Foreign Minister] Miguel D'Escoto manages," Mr. Rondon said in a telephone interview from Denver, where he now lives.

"Definitely untrue," said Nicaraguan Embassy spokeswoman Sara Lee. "It's just a try to discredit or diminish the value of the effort of the organizers and of the American people participating in the march and its activities," she said.

Mr. Rondon's account was corroborated by a former longtime U.S. legal attache in Central America, who called the Sandinista funding "standard operating procedure" to build public opposition to anti-Marxist policies in the United States.

Mr. Rondon broke with the regime after the Sandinista revolution that toppled former Nicaraguan strong-

see **PROTEST**, *page 14A*

Washington Times disinformation: the lead story, April 14, 1987, the day before a huge Washington, D.C., peace march

Freedom Fund to help sustain the contras. North, who coordinated his anti-Sandinista maneuvers with CIA director Casey, recommended that "several reliable" Americans lead the organization. Shortly thereafter, a tax-exempt group called the Nicaraguan Freedom Fund was established by the *Washington Times*. Its board included Jeane Kirkpatrick, Clare Boothe Luce (Time Inc.) and former Treasury Secretary William Simon. Bo Hi Pak, Moon's chief political fixer and president of News World Communications (the parent corporation of the *Washington Times* and other Moonie media assets), kicked in the first $100,000 of so-called private aid.

Congress made feeble attempts to reform the CIA in the wake of Watergate—and went through the motions once again after the Iran-contra scandal. But built-in loopholes assured that U.S. and foreign media would remain up for grabs, as far as CIA officials are concerned.

HOOVER'S HACKS

The Federal Bureau of Investigation, led by J. Edgar Hoover from 1924 to 1972, had long cultivated sympathetic contacts in the media. These included journalists such as Hearst society columnist Walter Winchell, Sam Newhouse, *Reader's Digest* editor Fulton Oursler, and Jeremiah O'Leary of the *Washington Star*.

One of the more prominent reporters who collaborated with the FBI was Jack Anderson, the widely-syndicated columnist. At first, Anderson impressed the FBI chief as "a rather nice looking fellow" and a "smooth talker"—unlike Anderson's mentor, Drew Pearson, who often antagonized Hoover. "Pearson looks like a skunk and is one," the FBI director wrote of the famous columnist in a memo dated July 1, 1969. Hoover explicitly barred his agents from speaking with Pearson "about anything." Meanwhile, the FBI continued to deal with Anderson, even though Hoover, in one of his mood swings, described Anderson and his ilk as being "lower than the regurgitated filth of vultures."

Over the years Anderson tipped off the Bureau about his and Pearson's column before it appeared in the press. Anderson also solicited Hoover's advice when writing about mutual adversaries, including Jack and Robert Kennedy. In April 1967, Anderson briefed the FBI after he had a lengthy conversation with Jim Garrison, the flamboyant New Orleans District Attorney, who was then investigating the assassination of President Kennedy. According to an FBI report, Anderson advised the Bureau that Garrison had made a convincing case that the CIA engineered JFK's death. This was quite different from Anderson's public disclosures about the JFK case, wherein he suggested that the President had been killed by a Communist plot.

A year later, Anderson proposed to the FBI that he write a column accusing Senator Robert Kennedy—not J. Edgar Hoover—of instigating the controversial wiretap on Martin Luther King. This "revelation" might have put a crimp in the electoral ambitions of Robert Kennedy, who was then seeking the Democratic nomination for President. "Kennedy should receive a death blow prior to the Oregon primary," an FBI document quotes Anderson telling the Bureau. Kennedy was murdered shortly after losing that primary.

Character assassination

Dr. Martin Luther King Jr. was the target of a sustained FBI smear campaign. The fruits of Hoover's voyeurism—photos, tapes, bedroom transcripts—were offered to dozens of reporters, editors and publishers in an effort to discredit the civil rights leader. This was irrefutable evidence that the Bureau had been tracking King day and night, but none of the journalists blew the whistle on the FBI. They were, in the words of black novelist John A. Williams, the FBI's "silent partners."

Hoover's personal vendetta against King dated back to the early 1960s, when King wrote an article in *The Nation*, which suggested, among other things, that the FBI be integrated. In 1964 the civil rights leader accused the

FBI of dragging its feet after the murders of Michael Schwerner, James Chaney and Andrew Goodman, three young civil rights workers in Mississippi. Hoover's G-men were viewed as villains by civil rights activists—in marked contrast to the 1988 film *Mississippi Burning*, which depicted the FBI's role during the movement in heroic terms. In the Hollywood version, FBI agents not only leapt into action in pursuit of the killers of Schwerner, Chaney and Goodman, but also took part as earnest supporters in civil rights marches. In real life, Hoover's men watched passively while police and Ku Klux Klansmen (oftentimes the same people in different uniforms) attacked civil rights protesters. The FBI never arrested anyone responsible for these attacks.

Among the journalists who participated in the FBI's efforts to "neutralize" King was Patrick Buchanan. While laboring on the editorial page of the *St. Louis Globe-Democrat*, Buchanan took material from the FBI and placed it in the paper. After he left the *Globe-Democrat* in 1965, that paper continued serving as a conduit for FBI plants. On April 2, 1968, two days before King was killed in Memphis, the *Globe-Democrat* ran nearly verbatim a canned editorial supplied by the FBI which accused him of being "one of the most menacing men in America." Two decades later, FAIR's Jeff Cohen confronted Buchanan on national television about his role in the FBI's smear campaign against King. Cohen compared him to "a hack writer from *Pravda* [in pre-*glasnost* days] taking information from the KGB and using it in print against a Soviet dissident." Buchanan was hardly apologetic: "All kinds of writers use information they get from government sources..."

FBI sex files on reporters

In addition to maintaining a list of friendly columnists, the FBI chief kept extensive files on writers whom he suspected of political infidelity. As explained in an FBI document: "The director expressed his concern about the prevalence of articles in publications which are severely and unfairly discrediting our way of life and praising directly or indirectly the Soviet system. The director questioned whether there might not be some subversive factors in the backgrounds of some prominent columnists, editors, commentators, authors, etc., which could be influencing such slanted views." FBI agents, accordingly, spied on many of America's most esteemed poets, playwrights, novelists and journalists.

FBI documents obtained by FAIR reveal that the Bureau's dossiers on the private lives of reporters became armaments in Richard Nixon's war against the working press. In November 1970, President Nixon's chief of staff H.R. Haldeman asked Hoover to pass along any information the Bureau had collected on homosexuals "known and suspected in the Washington press corps." Haldeman told Hoover that the President assumed this material would already be in the FBI files. "I told Mr. Haldeman I would get after that right away, and we ought to be able to send it over certainly no later than Friday," Hoover noted in a memo to his five assistants.

Haldeman wrote in his book *Ends of Power* that Hoover—Nixon's first official visitor after the 1968 election—offered the new President dirt on people whom the FBI had been watching. Nixon dispatched Haldeman to partake of this fount of data throughout his administration as part of an ongoing campaign to malign specific journalists and intimidate the press as a whole. On several occasions the FBI harassed reporters who persisted in writing stories upsetting to Hoover. A White House request for information on CBS correspondent Daniel Schorr resulted in an FBI investigation of the newsman. At the same time, Nixon's plumbers plotted to dose Jack Anderson with a hallucinogenic drug in an effort to derail the columnist's Watergate revelations.

Nixon's people knew which media pressure points to concentrate on. Following a meeting with the three network chiefs, White House aide Charles Colson stated: "They told me anytime we had a complaint about slanted coverage for me to call them directly. [CBS board chairman William] Paley said that he would like to come to Washington and spend time with me anytime I wanted... He also went out of his way to say how much he supports the President, and how popular the President is."

Nixon understood media corporations' reluctance to bite the hand that licenses them. Angered at the *Washington Post* for its role in exposing the Pentagon Papers and the Watergate scandal, the President threatened to challenge the license of a profitable television station held by the *Post*'s parent corporation. This kind of arm-twisting was part of an extensive effort by the Nixon administration to manage the press.

Thought police

The FBI's assault on free speech during the Nixon presidency included a systematic attempt to cripple the "underground press," which Hoover found loathsome because of "its depraved nature and moral looseness." Under the auspices of the FBI's Counterintelligence Program (COINTELPRO), the Bureau harassed leftist and counterculture publications that sprang up across the country during the late 1960s. Local police, right-wing vigilantes and the CIA also participated in this attack on the First Amendment. Newspaper staffs were infiltrated by spies; journalists were busted on trumped-up drug or obscenity charges; offices were broken into, ransacked and bombed; equipment was stolen and telephones tapped.

At the same time, the FBI was busy planting stories in "friendly news media" in an effort to undermine the New Left, civil rights and antiwar movements. A frequent conduit for raw and unverified FBI data was the San Diego-based Copley press, which published Bureau-inspired editorials about the Black Panthers and other groups. Some Copley employees were chagrined to learn that their executive staff was supplying the FBI with pho-

UNITED STATES DEPARTMENT OF JUSTICE

FEDERAL BUREAU   INVESTIGATION

WASHINGTON D.C. 20535

4:32 PM   November 25, 1970

MEMORANDUM FOR MR. TOLSON
                 MR. SULLIVAN
                 MR. BISHOP
                 MR. C. D. BRENNAN
                 MR. ROSEN

 Honorable H. R. Haldeman, Assistant to the President,
called. .He stated the President wanted him to ask, and he would
imagine I would have it pretty much at hand so there would be no
specific investigation, for a run down on the homosexuals known
and suspected in the Washington press corps. I said I thought
we have some of that material. Mr. Haldeman mentioned ▓▓▓▓▓
▓▓▓▓▓▓▓▓▓▓▓▓▓▓ and some of the others rumored generally
to be and also whether we had any other stuff: that he, the President,
has an interest in what, if anything else, we know.

 I told Mr. Haldeman I would get after that right away
and we ought to be able to send it over certainly not later than
Friday.

Very truly yours,

John Edgar Hoover
Director

INFORMATION CONTAINED
EREIN IS UNCLASSIFIED
TE 6/2/82 BY SP.1 CSK/RK

FBI document, November 25, 1970

tographs, reporters' notes and other information on local antiwar, black and Latino activists. Dubbed "the little FBI" inside Copley (which also worked closely with the CIA), this nest of media spies gathered articles and pictures for exclusive use by the Bureau, rather than for publication.

Photographers who once worked at Copley say they were asked to make blowups of demonstrators so that faces could be identified. Robert Learn, a former Copley photographer, remembered how he took "pictures of demonstrators, and they would never run in the papers. We shot rolls and rolls of film and would never see the photos in print." Said Learn: "Word finally filtered down that the stuff was going to government agencies. I got fed up..."

FBI snooping on law-abiding Americans continued long after J. Edgar Hoover died. During the Reagan administration, there were revelations of a major FBI spying campaign that initially targeted the anti-intervention group Committee in Solidarity with the People of El Salvador (CISPES) and soon grew to encompass a hundred other organizations, including the Southern Christian Leadership Conference (founded by Martin Luther King Jr.), National Council of Churches, United Auto Workers, and the Women's Rape Crisis Center in Norfolk, Virginia. Yet when FBI officials claimed the surveillance of CISPES was an aberration attributable to a few rogue agents, the newspapers of record accepted this explanation at face value, despite a long history of FBI corruption and political sabotage.

A *New York Times* editorial stated that the FBI's probe of CISPES "seems to have begun prudently enough [but] some agents and supervisors lost their direction." The probe "went astray," the editorial concluded, even though a *Times* news story had reported a week earlier that then-FBI-director William Webster personally overruled local field agents who sought to terminate surveillance of peace groups in their area.

DISINFORMATION, DAT INFORMATION

Editors don't make any bones about "the presidential factor." "We've got to cover what the President says and does," is the common refrain. But what happens when the President and his aides routinely lie as they try to sell their policies to the American public? Then the presidential factor is a recipe for distortion.

"Lying to the press goes back to the beginning of the republic," says David Wise, a former *New York Herald Tribune* editor who has authored a number of books on the American espionage establishment. But institutional lying took on a new dimension at the outset of the Cold War, as clandestine operations began to multiply like rabbits. The proliferation of covert actions required a plenitude of cover stories—and cover stories, lest we forget, are lies. "It used to be that policies were framed to fit events," Wise remarked in a 1987 interview about Reagan-era disinformation. "Now events are shaped and manipulated to fit policies."

Over the years, reporters have had to contend with a steady barrage of deceptions, half-truths and blatant falsehoods emanating from the White House. This deliberate perversion of the truth calls into question the fundamental character of a democratic society, which is supposed to be based on the consent of the governed. An ill-informed public can't hold officials accountable for their policies.

"Every government is run by liars, and nothing they say should be believed," said I.F. Stone. But the Reagan era was unprecedented in that it marked the first time government officials came right out and said that a president's numerous misstatements of fact and his inability to grasp detail didn't really matter. "We've been dealing with...an administration that freely states—and stated early—that literal truth was not a concern," said Bill Kovach when he was Washington news editor of the *New York Times*.

U.S. officials openly flaunted their disregard for the facts during the 1980s. "You can say anything you want in a debate and 80 million people hear it," George Bush's press secretary stated shortly after the vice presidential debate with Geraldine Ferraro in October 1984. "If reporters then document that a candidate spoke untruthfully, so what? Maybe 200 people read it."

Deception as a mode of governance

Reagan's PR managers knew how to make the Washington press corps jump through hoops. The pattern was set early in his administration: leak a scare story about foreign enemies, grab the headlines. If, much later, reporters poke holes in the cover story, so what? The truth will receive far less attention than the original lie, and by then another round of falsehoods will be dominating the headlines.

A few weeks into Reagan's presidency, Secretary of State Alexander Haig vowed to draw the line in El Salvador against Soviet expansionism. To back up its claim of Soviet meddling, the State Department released a White Paper on El Salvador which purported to document a global communist conspiracy to arm that country's leftist rebels. The news media ate it up. Typical was NBC correspondent Marvin Kalb's report on "a systematic, well-financed sophisticated effort to impose a communist system in El Salvador," involving "massive" Soviet aid "coordinated by Cuba." With the story haunting the front pages, the National Security Council approved $65 million in emergency aid for the Salvadoran government.

Months later, the White Paper was shown to be a hoax by *The Nation, Los Angeles Times* and *Wall Street Journal*. Confronted by belated media scrutiny, the State Department admitted the report was "misleading." By this time, however, the U.S. was neck-deep in the Central American quagmire—underscoring Austrian scholar Karl Kraus' dictum: "How is the world ruled and led into war? Diplomats lie to journalists and believe those lies when they see them in print."

Not long after the White Paper was debunked, Haig kicked off another disinformation scheme. In a September 1981 speech in West Berlin, he claimed to have physical evidence that the Soviets were supplying a mysterious chemical poison allegedly used against villagers in Laos, Kampuchea and Afghanistan with hideous and deadly results. The poison which supposedly fell from the sky was called Yellow Rain. "Its composition: one part bee feces, plus many parts State Department disinformation," Frank Brodhead reported in the weekly *Guardian*, "mixed with a high level of media gullibility."

Year after year, U.S. officials leveled accusations about Soviet chemical warfare atrocities, and mass media reported these charges. The Yellow Rain accusations were later refuted by scientists at Harvard University and the Army Chemical Systems Laboratory in Aberdeen, Maryland. While it lasted, however, the Yellow Rain hoax scored propaganda points for the Reagan administration.

State Department documents obtained by *Foreign Policy* disclose that U.S. strategists promoted the Yellow Rain scare even though other government analysts warned that no firm evidence existed to back up the charges. The documents show it was former *New York Times* correspondent Richard Burt, then director of the State Department's Bureau of Politico-Military Affairs, who persuaded Haig to launch the Yellow Rain campaign in the first place.

Unlike most rebuttals to official lies, the bee poop explanation got comparatively wide media play, probably because of its oddball quality. But the *Times* couldn't bring itself to admit that it had been used for politically convenient ends—perhaps because one of its ex-employees played a key role in the disinformation plot. "Nothing disproves the early charges, but contradictory evidence collected later is now only coming to light," the *Times* stated in a news article six years after the Yellow Rain story was concocted.

Even with the release of documents showing Yellow Rain to be a propaganda ploy, the *Times* and other major media suggested only that the allegations were premature and over-enthusiastic. Mainstream journalists ignored questions about whether a ruse had been consciously perpetrated by the government at a critical moment in order to justify a massive arms build-up and other hardline options. Toward this end, Reagan strategists sought any and every means of portraying the USSR as the Evil Empire. Yellow Rain and other disinformation schemes were just what the foreign policy doctor ordered.

Libya scare stories

Following the lead of U.S. officials, mass media depicted the Soviet Union as the prime mover of a worldwide terrorist network that included Libyan leader Moammar Qadaffi as a key operative. The demonizing of Qadaffi began in earnest shortly after Reagan took office. First came the lurid tales (based on "unnamed intelligence sources") of Libyan hit squads stalking President Reagan. Later came the Berlin disco bombing, which killed two people, including an American serviceman, and injured 200 in April 1986. Citing "irrefutable evidence" that Qadaffi was behind the bombing, Reagan ordered an air attack against Libya a week later. It was, as Noam Chomsky observed, the first air raid in history geared to preempt coverage on 7:00 p.m. prime-time news in the U.S.

As it turned out, the so-called "irrefutable evidence" was hardly airtight. Manfred Ganshow, chief of the Berlin Staatsschutz and head of the 100-person team which investigated the disco bombing, told *Stars and Stripes*, a publication servicing the U.S. armed forces, three weeks after the incident: "[I have] no more evidence that Libya was connected to the bombing than I had two days after the act. Which is none." This, however, did not dissuade the American media, whose rush to judgment was as dramatic as Reagan's rise in the popularity polls following the Libya raid. A *New York Times* editorial claimed that proof was "laid out clearly to the public... Even the most scrupulous citizens can only approve and applaud the American attacks on Libya."

Months later, West German authorities concluded that if any country was behind the Berlin disco bombing, it was Syria, not Libya. But that hardly seemed to matter as U.S. news media continued to blame the incident on Qadaffi. Soon another round of stories appeared, warning of new plots by Libya. Replete with 42 references to unnamed U.S. officials, a *Wall Street Journal* article by John Walcott and Gerald F. Seib disclosed that Qadaffi was planning more terrorism. This time the unnamed source turned out to be National Security Adviser John Poindexter, who was promoting what *Newsweek* later called a "disinformation program" aimed at destabilizing the Libyan government. The propaganda operation was outlined in a three-page memo, dated August 14, 1986, from Poindexter to President Reagan.

When details of the disinformation plot were leaked to the U.S. press, Secretary of State George Shultz justified the deception by quoting Winston Churchill: "In time of war, the truth is so precious it must be attended by a bodyguard of lies." The Reagan administration, Shultz said, was "pretty darn close" to being at war with Libya. Reporters and editors cried foul, expressing righteous indignation about being misled by the U.S. government—as if they had suddenly discovered something new!

Indeed, journalists should have known that the Reagan administration was lying about Libya. Five years prior to the Poindexter revelations, *Newsweek* reported on a CIA-run "disinformation program designed to embarrass Qadaffi," along with covert operations to overthrow and perhaps assassinate him.

U.S. actions—rhetorical and military—against Libya, and "counter-terrorist" rhetoric in general, were geared largely toward converting public anxiety over anti-Western political violence into support for an aggressive American foreign policy and increased intervention in the Third World. Exaggerating the threat of external demons in order to whip up nationalist hysteria at home was nothing new in American history. By focusing on Libya, the Reagan administration picked a fight it knew it could win. Seen in this context, the bombing of Libya was as much salutary medicine for Vietnam syndrome jitters as it was a plot to kill Qadaffi.

Cloaked in fiction

Even when lies by the government are exposed, U.S. reporters dutifully return to the same poisoned well, seeking information from official sources that have been publicly discredited. Former Assistant Secretary of State Elliott Abrams appeared frequently as a guest on *Nightline* and other TV news shows, despite his admission that he intentionally misled Congress regarding U.S. policy in Central America. Abrams' confession aroused little skepticism among journalists as to whether he could be trusted as a news source. Never once did Ted Koppel, who fancies himself a tough interviewer, ask Abrams: "Why, given your record of deceit, should we believe anything you say about Nicaragua?"

A cub reporter would surely grow skeptical about a courtroom defendant who continually changed alibis. Yet as soon as Reagan took office, veteran journalists pandered to his Nicaragua obsession, hardly blinking at the ever-changing explanations for why it was necessary to support the contras. First it was merely to "interdict" weapons allegedly flowing from Nicaragua to Salvadoran leftists. Next it was to force the Sandinistas to enact "democratic reforms," when all along the real motive should have been obvious—to overthrow the Nicaraguan government and destroy the popular revolution that swept the Sandinistas into power in 1979.

If journalists weren't so busy fixating on a White House chimera, they might have noticed that the weapons were actually moving in the opposite direction—from CIA-run air bases in El Salvador to the Nicaraguan contras. The Iran-contra scandal exposed Reagan's inner circle as a coterie of chronic dissemblers and schemers, revealing "a wholesale policy of secrecy shrouded in lies, of passion cloaked in fiction and deception," as Bill Moyers put it in an exceptional PBS report, "The Secret Government—The Constitution in Crisis."

Lt. Col. Oliver North, Elliott Abrams and other U.S. officials lied repeatedly as they sought to give credence to the absurd notion that Nicaragua, an impoverished country of three million, with no navy or air force to speak of, posed a serious threat to the security of the United States. The anti-

Sandinista propaganda offensive included oft-repeated allegations of Nicaraguan complicity with Khomeini's Iran—an ironic charge given that North and the CIA were secretly supplying weapons to Iran at the time. Such deliberate falsifications were part of a protracted disinformation campaign designed to manufacture a "Nicaraguan threat."

PLAY IT AGAIN, UNCLE SAM: PROPAGANDA AND PUBLIC DIPLOMACY

In March 1982, Congressman David Bonior spoke fervently about Reagan's Nicaragua policy on the House floor, warning of "a highly orchestrated propaganda effort by the administration which unfortunately the media of this country to a very large degree is buying hook, line and sinker." Referring to the legacy of U.S. support for one Nicaraguan dictator after another, Bonior complained about "a notable lack of a sense of history in this administration and in the media."

Citing several examples of "manipulated evidence" behind White House charges against Nicaragua, Bonior concluded: "Mr. Speaker, I would ask that the media of this country start focusing in on the evidence, and the manner of presentation, because I do not think the evidence bears the fruit that the administration wishes for."

Instead of heeding Congressman Bonior's plea, the U.S. media functioned virtually as a sieve for what Abraham Brumberg, formerly with the U.S. Information Agency, described as "a flood of distortions, exaggerations and plain unvarnished lies about the Sandinistas that issue forth almost daily from the administration."

Psychological warfare

Much of the propaganda against Nicaragua was coordinated by an Orwellian agency known as the Office of Public Diplomacy (OPD). Ostensibly part of the State Department, OPD actually took its marching orders from the National Security Council and indirectly from the CIA. A senior U.S. official described OPD as "a vast psychological warfare operation of the kind the military conducts to influence a population in enemy territory"—only in this case the target was the American people.

In order to elude legal prohibitions against CIA involvement in domestic operations, CIA Director William Casey transferred one of his propaganda specialists, Walter Raymond, to the National Security Council in 1982. Raymond's job was to help organize a massive public diplomacy effort that would generate grassroots support for Reagan's controversial—and hitherto unpopular—foreign policy ventures. Toward this end, OPD recruited five "psy-ops" specialists from the 4th Psychological

Sandinista leaders, including Ortega, left, in cap and glasses, celebrate in Moscow
Strident Marxism, disregard for human rights, and dependence on the Cubans.

Wrong! This photo in *Time* was actually taken in Masaya, Nicaragua

Operations Group in Fort Bragg, North Carolina. Skilled in what OPD chief Otto Reich called "persuasive communications," these psychological warfare experts prepared "studies, papers, speeches, and memoranda to support [OPD] activities."

A July 1986 memo described the crux of OPD's efforts: "In the specific case of Nica[ragua], concentrate on gluing black hats on the Sandinistas and white hats on [the contras]." The idea was to slowly turn the Nicaraguan government "into a real enemy and threat in the minds of the American people, thereby eroding their resistance to U.S. support for the contras and, perhaps, to a future U.S. military intervention in the region," a U.S. official told the *Miami Herald*.

OPD inundated the media with glossy booklets, reports and other material, while behind the scenes it planted stories, coached journalists and lobbied members of Congress. Media critic Alexander Cockburn summarized the modus operandi of Reagan's public diplomacy offensive against Nicaragua: "Erect a mountain of lies, and as members of the press examine each new falsehood, they find themselves on a foundation of older lies still taken for granted as natural features of the landscape."

Financed with taxpayers' money, OPD functioned as "an officially sanctioned leaks bureau" that sought to deceive the American people. A March 13, 1985 "Eyes Only" memo to White House Communications Director Patrick Buchanan mentioned "five illustrative examples" of OPD's ongoing "White Propaganda Operation." That week OPD helped compose a *Wall Street Journal* column about "the Nicaraguan arms build-up"; assisted in "a positive piece" on the contras by Fred Francis on *NBC Nightly News*; wrote op-ed columns for the signatures of contra leaders to appear in leading dailies; arranged a media tour for a contra leader; and prepared to leak a State Department cable to embarrass the Sandinistas. "Do not be surprised," OPD told Buchanan, "if this cable somehow hits the evening news."

One of OPD's specialties was creating a crisis to sway public opinion at a crucial moment. In November 1984, OPD officials leaked false information about an impending shipment of Soviet MIG fighters to Nicaragua. Bolstered by over 30 OPD background briefings, the MIGs story dominated the headlines for a few days until journalists began to realize that no MIGs were headed for Nicaragua. By this time, OPD had already succeeded in drawing attention away from Nicaragua's elections, which otherwise might have legitimized a government that the Reagan administration was trying to overthrow. As former contra leader Edgar Chamorro said of the phantom MIGs: "The timing was controlled. Events can be neutralized when people are confused or distracted. That's why timing is so important."

OPD operations kicked into high gear whenever a congressional vote on contra aid drew near. On December 10, 1987, the day before Congress was scheduled to decide on additional funds for the contras, OPD officials unveiled a Sandinista defector, Major Roger Miranda Bengoechea—who told a hand-picked group of four U.S. reporters that the Nicaraguan government planned to expand its military force to a half million soldiers, and that Soviet MIGs would be delivered by the early 1990s. Among those present during the Miranda briefing was AP correspondent George Gedda, who ignored State Department documents that contradicted claims of a massive Nicaraguan military build-up. Gedda and fellow practitioners of Foggy Bottom journalism broke the story without mentioning a relevant fact: The U.S. government was paying Miranda $800,000 to make his ominous disclosures. As it turned out, no major expansion of Nicaragua's regular army was being planned; the evidence actually pointed toward a troop reduction, according to *Newsday*, which picked apart Miranda's charges days after Congress passed $8.1 million in new contra aid.

A good deal of skepticism is in order whenever U.S. officials trot out defectors who spin yarns about supposed "enemy" activity.

Lies that echo

In addition to concocting scare stories and parading dubious defectors before the press, OPD planted articles in leading U.S. newspapers. An op-ed by Professor John Guilmartin ("Nicaragua Is Armed for Trouble"), appearing in the *Wall Street Journal*, pretended to offer independent confirmation of White House assertions. "The Soviet doctrinal model, which the Sandinistas are clearly following, is inherently offensive in nature," said Guilmartin, who was described as an OPD "consultant" in a secret State Department memo dated March 13, 1985. In keeping with OPD's "low profile," the memo cautioned, "officially, this office had no role in [the article's] preparation."

Guilmartin's opinion piece was rebutted a few weeks later in the *Journal*'s news pages when Clifford Kraus and Robert Greenberger obtained a once-classified 1984 intelligence report which indicated that "Soviet arms shipments to Nicaragua turned sharply upward only after the Reagan administration launched the contra war." The report asserted that Nicaragua's build-up "is primarily defense oriented, and much of the recent effort has been devoted to improving counter-insurgency capabilities." This article prompted an angry letter from OPD chief Otto Reich in which he touted Guilmartin's op-ed and attacked the *Journal*'s disclosure as "an echo of Sandinista propaganda"—a remarkable charge given that Reich himself was "echoing" propaganda his office had covertly generated.

For years, the Reagan administration alleged that Nicaragua was seeking to export its revolution by supplying arms to leftist guerrillas in El Salvador. Stories about this supposed "arms flow" continued to appear in the press even after the disclosures of David MacMichael, a former CIA analyst who resigned in protest over what he described as efforts to fake evidence of Nicaraguan military involvement in El Salvador. In June 1984, MacMichael told the *New York Times* that the CIA had "systematically" doctored evidence "to justify efforts to overthrow the Nicaraguan government." He reiterated these charges in testimony before the World Court, which ruled that the U.S. had violated international law by mining Nicaraguan harbors and directing the contra war. That same year a declassified State Department memo noted, "Intelligence officials claim that they can 'hear a toilet flush in Managua.' Yet they have not produced even a captured van or one downed plane."

In August 1987, James LeMoyne wrote in the *New York Times* of "ample evidence" that Nicaragua was supplying Salvadoran rebels. Said LeMoyne: "It is questionable how long they [the rebels] could survive without it." The media watch group FAIR publicly challenged the *Times* to share this "ample evidence" with its readers or retract LeMoyne's unsourced assertions. Fifteen months later, a humbled LeMoyne wrote that "evidence of Sandinista sup-

APPENDIX I

United States Department of State

Washington. D.C. 20520

FILE COPY

March 13, 1985

CONFIDENTIAL/EYES ONLY

```
┌─────────────────────────────────────────────┐
│ DEPARTMENT OF STATE A/CDC/MR                  │
│                                               │
│ REVIEWED BY ⎓⎓⎓⎓⎓ DATE 9-10-87                │
│                                               │
│ RDS☐or XDS☐EXT. DATE _____                   │
│ TS AUTH. ____ REASON(S) _____                │
│ ENDORSE EXISTING MARKINGS ☐                   │
│ DECLASSIFIED☑ RELEASABLE☐                     │
│ RELEASE DENIED☐                               │
│ PA or FOI EXEMPTIONS _____                   │
└─────────────────────────────────────────────┘
```

TO: Mr. Pat Buchanan
          Assistant to the President and
          Director of Communications
          The White House

FROM: S/LPD - Johnathan S. Miller

SUBJECT: "White Propaganda" Operation

    Five illustrative examples of the Reich "White
Propaganda" operation:

- Attached is a copy of an op-ed piece that ran two
  days ago in The Wall Street Journal. Professor
  Guilmartin has been a consultant to our office and
  collaborated with our staff in the writing of this
  piece. It is devastating in its analysis of the
  Nicaraguan arms build-up. Officially, this office
  had no role in its preparation.

- In case you missed last night's NBC News with Tom
  Brokaw, you might ask WHCA to call up the Fred
  Francis story on the "Contras." This piece was
  prepared by Francis after he consulted two of our
  contractors who recently had made a clandestine trip
  to the freedom fighter camp along the Nicaragua/
  Honduras border (the purpose of this trip was to
  serve as a pre-advance for many selected journalists
  to visit the area and get a true flavor of what the
  freedom fighters are doing; i.e., not baby killing).
  Although I wasn't wild about the tag line, it was a
  positive piece.

- Two op-ed pieces, one for The Washington Post and one
  for The New York Times, are being prepared for the
  signatures of opposition leaders Alphonso Rubello,

                    CONFIDENTIAL
                    Decl: OADR

Confidential OPD memo confirming its role in planting articles in the *Wall Street Journal*,
Washington Post, and *New York Times*

port for the rebels is largely circumstantial and is open to differing interpretations." Nevertheless, he tried to make his case in an article sourcing mostly unnamed "American and Salvadoran officials." The one named source was Sergio Gutierrez, who reportedly defected from the Nicaraguan military to El Salvador, where he supposedly told all before dying in a drunk driving accident when his car collided with a donkey.

Lies, when repeated often enough, begin to take on life of their own. During the 1980s, it got to the point where U.S. officials could say nearly anything about the Sandinistas, and most media would report it verbatim (assuming it was bad enough) without trying to set the record straight. Sometimes the media's sycophantic relationship with the State assumed ludicrous proportions, as when Connie Chung declared on NBC News in March 1985: "Reagan wants to remove the Sandinistas in Nicaragua, not oust them."

Coddling the contras

OPD efforts to glue white hats on the contras stuck, as many top journalists adopted White House terminology, calling the CIA's mercenary army "freedom fighters" and the "Nicaraguan Resistance." NBC News correspondent Robin Lloyd described Reagan's meeting with contra military chief Enrique Bermudez—a twenty-five year veteran of dictator Anastazio Somoza's brutal National Guard—as evidence of the President's "commitment to democracy."

AP correspondent George Gedda spoke openly of his respect for the contras. "Their leadership—I think they're a fairly decent group of people," Gedda told an audience at Georgetown University in February 1988. He didn't mention congressional reports that the CIA initially arranged for the contras to be trained in Honduras by neo-Nazi Argentine military officers, and that 16 of 17 contra commanders served in the National Guard, an organization notorious for human rights violations.

In an effort to confer legitimacy on the contras, the CIA put together a civilian directorate, which specialized in public relations. Known as the United Nicaraguan Opposition (UNO), the contra directorate was, in the words of NSC operative Robert Owen, "a creation of the USG [U.S. Government] to garner support from Congress." At all times, the CIA determined what, how, when and where the contra directors made public statements or lobbied Congress, according to ex-contra leader Edgar Chamorro. "We were told to emphasize issues that would influence specific targets: church people, Jewish groups, the private sector. Our propaganda efforts were coordinated with Washington's Office of Public Diplomacy, which disseminated false stories about how the Sandinistas were persecuting each of these groups."

Chamorro was amazed at how U.S. journalists kept accepting the State Department's version of events as fact. "I can recall times when I was speaking at contra press conferences and reporters criticized me for raising

CONTRA WEAPONS

too many questions! I'm serious. Reporters from all the big papers—the *Times*, the *Post*, the *Miami Herald*—were eager to use me as a source, but they didn't want to hear my doubts about the contras." Chamorro had a much more difficult time getting on TV news programs after he left the contras and began criticizing U.S. policy in Central America. His disclosures about CIA manipulation of the contra directorate appeared to have little impact on U.S. reporters who continued to elicit comments from the contra "civilian leadership" as if it constituted an authentic, independent political force.

A survey of the *New York Times* by University of Massachusetts professor Jack Spence showed that stories of contra infighting and corruption received far more coverage than atrocities committed against Nicaraguan civilians. Eyewitness accounts of contra war crimes were rarely reported in the U.S. media, even though such atrocities have been documented by Americas Watch, Witness for Peace and other human rights groups. "The contras systematically engage in violent abuses...so prevalent that these may be said to be their principal means of waging war," Americas Watch concluded.

Pictures of contra victims who had been tortured and mutilated weren't featured on U.S. television or in mainstream print media. When atrocities did get a mention, they were generally downplayed, as in a *Times* article headlined, "A Day's Toll Shows Contras' Ability to Strike." The military achievement referred to in the article was the murder of a government co-op director and nine civilians, including several children. A spate of unflattering portraits of the contras appeared in the wake of the Iran-contra scandal. But among major news dailies, only the *Boston Globe* denounced contra activity as "U.S.-backed terrorism" and "U.S.-subsidized butchery."

In addition to promoting disinformation, OPD sought to pressure journalists when they filed stories deemed objectionable by the Reagan administration. "I talked to reporters, editors, producers, anyone who would listen to our side," said OPD chief Otto Reich. "I had lots of meetings with editorial boards of newspapers." After National Public Radio aired a critical report about the contras, Reich paid a visit to NPR, which he called the "little Havana on the Potomac." According to NPR employees, Reich said his efforts had convinced editors at other media to change the tenor of their reporting, which resulted in journalists' being removed from the Central America beat. He also boasted that he had a team of people who monitored all NPR programs, as well as other broadcast networks. An NPR staffer described Reich's remarks as a "calculated attempt to intimidate." Reich's courtesy call succeeded in getting NPR reporters to second-guess themselves. After someone filed a story on Central America, an NPR editor asked a colleague: "What would Otto Reich think?"

Setting the media agenda

OPD spearheaded the drive to foist a particular line or frame on the media. It also pushed unwanted stories off page-one or out of the media entirely. By churning out a deluge of official information, public diplomacy operatives were able to focus media scrutiny on Nicaragua while deflecting attention from neighboring countries guilty of far worse human rights abuses. Case in point: ABC *Nightline* ran 27 programs on Central America between January 1985 and April 1988. Twenty-two of these programs dealt exclusively with problems in Nicaragua; not one focused on Honduras, El Salvador or Guatemala. This, of course, is exactly what the Reagan administration wanted, since it was not challenged to back up its contention that Nicaragua's neighbors were "fledgling democracies."

The skewed lineup of *Nightline* programs in part reflected the bias of its host, Ted Koppel, who once told *Newsweek* that he thought military aid to the contras "can serve a valuable purpose in concert with a very active diplomacy." During a brisk Q & A on *Nightline*, Nicaraguan government spokesperson Alejandro Bendana told Koppel that the American people opposed U.S. military intervention in his country. Koppel took exception: "I'm not sure that you know just what the will of the American people is. Perhaps you're better informed than I." Indeed Bendana was better informed. Numerous surveys, including ABC News polls, showed that U.S. citizens consistently opposed contra aid by a two-to-one margin.

"Like it or not," remarked reporter Ed Harriman, "most journalists have a bit of the State lodged in their brains competing with their wit and sagacity." As a result, the American press has rarely questioned the basic assumptions undergirding U.S. foreign policy. While reporters asked Reagan whether he was trying to topple the Nicaraguan government, few saw fit to ask whether the U.S. had a right to pursue such a policy. By a kind of ideological osmosis, journalists absorb the worldview promoted by Washington officials—which goes a long way toward explaining why the government can get away with so much deception.

A survey of editorial commentary in the papers of record by Noam Chomsky revealed the extent to which debate on Central America was framed in a way that kept the momentum going for the Reagan agenda. Chomsky analyzed all editorials, opinion pieces and columns on Nicaragua—a total of 85 articles—that appeared in the *New York Times* and the *Washington Post* during a three-month period before Congress approved $100 million in contra aid in June 1986. Every article was explicitly anti-Sandinista. "On that issue," said Chomsky, "no discussion was tolerable." No article mentioned that the Nicaraguan government did not systematically slaughter its population like the U.S.-backed governments of Guatemala and El Salvador, which had murdered 150,000 of their own citizens in the 1980s. The fact that the Sandinistas had carried out significant social reforms that benefited the poor majority was all but ignored.

A similar ideological conformity was evident on the TV news talkshow circuit, where corrupt contra leaders involved in drug smuggling were often equated with freedom fighters and compared to our Founding Fathers. While endorsing the Reagan administration's goal of "restoring democracy" in Nicaragua, certain media pundits and the loyal opposition in Congress at times quibbled over tactics (mining harbors, covertly funding foreign political candidates, etc.). But journalists rarely ventured beyond the narrow spectrum that prevailed on Capitol Hill. Prominent U.S. citizens who questioned the fundamental assumptions underlying U.S. foreign policy were excluded from broadcast debates and banished to the periphery of the media universe.

Public redundancy

A 1987 probe of OPD by the General Accounting Office found that the Reagan administration had engaged in "prohibited, covert propaganda activities." Rep. Jack Brooks called it an "illegal operation" designed "to manipulate public opinion and congressional action." The U.S. media quietly let the matter drop without further investigation.

OPD was disbanded at the end of 1987 as a result of the Iran-contra scandal. By this time, official lies about Nicaragua had become ingrained media truths. As a U.S. official told journalists Robert Parry and Peter Kornbluh: "They can shut down the public diplomacy office, but they can't shut down public diplomacy." Sure enough, anti-Sandinista volleys continued to rico-

chet through the mass media long after OPD was scuttled in a bureaucratic
shake-up.

And so it was that within hours after the Chinese government massacre of
student protesters at Beijing's Tiananmen Square in June 1989, an AP dispatch reported that Nicaragua and Vietnam had endorsed the crackdown. The
story was completely bogus, as any skeptical editor might have suspected.
After all, Vietnam and China had been adversaries in a brief but bloody war,
and China supplied weapons to the Nicaraguan contras at the behest of U.S.
officials. But these facts weren't mentioned in the AP wire story about
Nicaragua's alleged support for China's old guard, which was picked up and
amplified in network TV coverage, newspapers, syndicated columns and
negative editorials.

AP correspondents in Managua should have consulted *Barricada*,
Nicaragua's pro-government newspaper, which carried a prominent statement by the pro-Sandinista National Union of Students denouncing "indiscriminate repression" in China and urging that such a hideous episode never
be repeated. The Sandinista Party quickly adopted the students' statement as
its own.

Journalist Mark Cook traced the origins of the anti-Sandinista smear to the
AP's Tokyo bureau, and AP subsequently retracted the story. But corrections,
when they ran at all, received far less attention than the original lie—a com-

mon pattern in the U.S. media. Months later, the disinformation hoax was resurrected by NPR's senior news analyst Daniel Schorr, who blithely touted the discredited AP tale on the op-ed page of the *New York Times* and in his radio commentary, claiming incorrectly that Nicaraguan President Daniel Ortega had endorsed "the massacre of pro-democracy students in Beijing."

As Mark Twain once said: "A lie can go half way around the world, before the truth even gets its boots on."

6

Politicians and the Press

M ore than 20 years after Vice President Spiro Agnew's famous attack on the American press, the myth of the "liberal media" endures.

Agnew decried "the trend toward the monopolization of the great public information vehicles and the concentration of more and more power over public opinion in fewer and fewer hands." True enough, but his oratory targeted only the *Washington Post* and other major media outlets lacking enthusiasm for the Nixon administration. "Agnew was hypocritical in his attack on press monopolies," a critic later remarked. "Giant chains like Newhouse and Hearst—among the good guys in Agnew's press lord pantheon—escaped his ire."

Likewise, conservative owners of magazines with huge circulations, like *Reader's Digest* and *Parade*, received no brickbats from the White House. An outspoken Federal Communications Commissioner, Nicholas Johnson, observed at the time that Agnew was simply going public with "what corporate and government officials have been doing for years in the privacy of their luncheon clubs and paneled offices. They cajoled and threatened publishers and broadcasters in an effort to manage news and mold images."

Agnew's rhetorical barrage in November 1969 was to reverberate into the century's last decade. However deceptive, it struck a populist chord of resentment against media conglomerates. Rather than challenge the "liberal media" myth, right-leaning owners have encouraged it—and media under their control have popularized it.

The Vice President conveniently neglected to mention that a year earlier the majority of endorsing newspaper editorials backed the Nixon-Agnew ticket. And three years later, running for reelection, the same Republican duo received a whopping 93 percent of the country's newspaper endorsements. (Since 1932 every Republican presidential nominee except Barry Goldwater has received the majority of endorsements from U.S. daily newspapers. Ronald Reagan got 77 percent in 1980, and 86 percent in 1984; George Bush got 70 percent in 1988.) Before resigning in disgrace from the vice presidency, Agnew never explained why the "liberal" media so consistently favored conservative presidential candidates.

Reporters' "liberalism" has been exaggerated quite a bit, as Duke University scholar Robert Entman found when he examined the study most commonly cited by purveyors of the cliché. Entman discovered that the study relied on "a non-random sample that vastly overrepresented perhaps the most liberal segment of journalism"—employees of public TV stations in Boston,

New York and Washington. These journalists were much more heavily surveyed about their political attitudes than the personnel putting together the
far more weighty *New York Times* and national CBS television news.

The much-ballyhooed conclusion that journalists are of a predominantly
leftish bent failed to square with data compiled by researchers without a
strongly conservative agenda. A Brookings Institution study, for instance,
found that 58 percent of Washington journalists identified themselves as
either "conservative" or "middle of the road."

A 1985 *Los Angeles Times* survey, comparing 3,000 journalists to 3,000
members of the general public, found that journalists were more conservative
when asked if the government should act to reduce the gap between rich and
poor. Fifty-five percent of the general public supported such measures, compared to only 50 percent of the "news staff" and 37 percent of the editors.

But all the heated number-crunching may be much ado about little. The
private opinions of media workers are much less important than the end
products. Mark Hertsgaard has astutely pinpointed "the deeper flaw in the
liberal-press thesis"—"it completely ignored those whom journalists worked
for. Reporters could be as liberal as they wished and it would not change
what news they were allowed to report or how they could report it.
America's major news organizations were owned and controlled by some of
the largest and richest corporations in the United States. These firms were in
turn owned and managed by individuals whose politics were, in general, anything but liberal. Why would they employ journalists who consistently covered the news in ways they did not like?"

If there's a political tilt to news coverage, it derives principally from mass
media owners and managers, not beat reporters. "Admittedly," said sociologist Herbert Gans, "some journalists have strong personal beliefs and also the
position or power to express them in news stories, but they are most often
editors; and editors, like producers in television, have been shown to be more
conservative than their news staffs." To the extent that personal opinions
influence news content, Gans added, "they are most often the beliefs of the
President of the United States and other high federal, state and local officials,
since they dominate the news."

However baseless, accusations by conservatives that the media lean left
have made many journalists compensate by tilting in the other direction. In
this sense, the liberal media canard has been effective as a pre-emptive club,
brandished to encourage self-censorship on the part of reporters who "bend
over backwards not to seem at all critical of Republicans," commented Mark
Crispin Miller. "Eager to evince his 'objectivity,' the edgy liberal reporter
ends up just as useful to the right as any ultra-rightist hack."

And there are plenty of those, dominating America's highest-profile
forums for political commentary on television and newspaper editorial pages.
"In terms of the syndicated columnists, if there is an ideological bias, it's

more and more to the right," President Reagan's media point man David Gergen declared in a 1981 interview. As the decade wore on, the imbalance grew more extreme.

The syndicated likes of George Will, Patrick Buchanan, Robert Novak, William F. Buckley and John McLaughlin achieved monotonous visibility on national TV, thanks to producers casting nets wide for right-wing pundits. As a tedious ritual they were paired with bland centrists, so that supposed "debates" often amounted to center-right discussions—on PBS's *MacNeil/Lehrer NewsHour*, Gergen with the *Washington Post*'s charmingly mild Mark Shields; on ABC's *This Week With David Brinkley*, Will with the network's stylized but politically tepid Sam Donaldson; on CNN's *Crossfire*, Buchanan or Novak with somnolent ex-CIA-exec Tom Braden. (In late 1989, Braden yielded his seat "on the left" to Michael Kinsley of the *New Republic* magazine, but this didn't make the show any less unbalanced. "Buchanan is much further to the right than I am to the left," Kinsley acknowledged. As Howard Rosenberg wrote in the *Los Angeles Times*, "*Crossfire* should at least get the labeling right: Pat Buchanan from the far right and Michael Kinsley from slightly left of center.")

In early 1989, columnist Jack Newfield counted eight popular political opinion talk shows on national television. "These shows all have certifiably right-wing hosts and moderators," wrote Newfield. "This is not balance. This is ideological imbalance that approaches a conservative monopoly... Buchanan, who calls AIDS a punishment from God for sin, and campaigns against the prosecution of Nazi war criminals hiding in America, is about as far right as you can get."

A fixture on CNN, and often made welcome on the biggest TV networks, Buchanan has flaunted his admiration for prominent fascists past and present, like the Spanish dictator Francisco Franco (who came to power allied with Hitler) and Chile's bloody ruler Augusto Pinochet. "A soldier-patriot like Franco, General Pinochet saved his country from an elected Marxist who was steering Chile into Castroism," Buchanan effused in a September 1989 column, going on to defend the apartheid regime in South Africa: "The Boer Republic is the only viable economy in Africa. Why are Americans collaborating in a U.N. conspiracy with sanctions?"

Sharing much of the remaining op-ed space are others from the hard right, including former U.N. ambassador Jeane Kirkpatrick; William Safire (like Buchanan, an ex-speechwriter for the Nixon-Agnew team); erstwhile segregationist James J. Kilpatrick; Charles Krauthammer; former NBC News correspondent and Moral Majority vice president Cal Thomas; neo-conservative prophet Norman Podhoretz, and Ray Price (yet another Nixon speechwriter). Aside from a handful of left-leaning liberals, most of the other op-ed mainstays are establishment-tied middle-roaders such as Flora Lewis, David Broder, Jeff Greenfield, Georgie Anne Geyer, and Meg Greenfield.

The more honest conservatives readily admit to an asymmetry in their favor. Blunt acknowledgement has come from Adam Meyerson, editor of *Policy Review* magazine at the Heritage Foundation, the Washington think tank that drew up much of the Reaganite agenda. "Journalism today is very different from what it was 10 to 20 years ago," he said in 1988. "Today, op-ed pages are dominated by conservatives." The media market's oversupply of right-wingers was not without a drawback: "If Bill Buckley were to come out of Yale today, nobody would pay much attention to him... [His] ideas would not be exceptional at all, because there are probably hundreds of people with those ideas already there, and they have already got syndicated columns..." As for becoming an editorial writer, Meyerson could not be encouraging. "There are still a few good jobs here and there, but there's a glut of opinions, especially conservative opinions."

Factor in the proliferation of televangelists and far-right religious broadcasters, and the complaints about the "liberal media" ring even more hollow. By 1987, religious broadcasting had become a $2 billion a year industry, with more than 200 full-time Christian TV stations and 1,000 full-time Christian radio stations. This means that evangelical Christians control about 14 percent of the television stations operating in the U.S. and 10 percent of the radio stations, which bombard the American public with a conservative theo-political message. TV ministries continue to thrive, despite the widely-publicized preacher sex and money scandals of the late 1980s.

Some journalists may reject the mythology about liberal prejudice, but when addressing what *is* going on they're prone to denial. Instead of identifying the thumbs on news-media scales, the preference is to call the whole contraption neutral. "Everybody talks about media biases to the right or the left," syndicated columnist Ellen Goodman pooh-poohed in 1989. "The real media bias is against complexity, which is usually terminated with the words: 'I'm sorry, we're out of time.'" Of course, electronic news media are surface-skimming operations. Views that seriously challenge the status quo, however, have few occasions to be interrupted, since they're so rarely heard at all.

As he celebrated Thanksgiving in 1989, Spiro Agnew had reason to be pleased on the twentieth anniversary of his bombast. Agnew's polemical legacy hadn't stopped refracting the light under which journalists in Washington furrowed their brows. Tagged as "liberal" despite the evidence, mass media continued to shy away from tough, independent reporting.

OFFICIAL SCANDALS: FROM WATERGATE TO CONTRAGATE

Although big media are an integral part of the American power structure, it doesn't mean that reporters never challenge a President or other members of the governing class. A number of Presidents have gotten into nasty spats with the press, which has been credited with exposing the Watergate scandal that drove Richard Nixon from the vestibules of authority.

While the orthodox view of Watergate depicts it as the ultimate triumph of a free and independent press, there is a contrary view held by award-winning investigative journalist Seymour Hersh. "Far from rooting Nixon out in Watergate, I would say the press made Watergate inevitable," Hersh told us.

Hersh's thesis is simple. During his first term, Nixon conducted several illegal and unconstitutional policies with hardly a whimper from the mainstream media: the secret bombing of Cambodia, subversive operations that toppled Chile's democratically-elected government, CIA domestic spying against antiwar dissenters, wholesale wiretapping of American officials and other citizens. "If the press had been able to break any one of these stories in 1971," Hersh reflected, "we might have been able to save the President from himself. He might have been afraid to do some of the things he did in 1972, and this would have changed the course of history. But the press failed utterly to do anything during Nixon's first term, thereby making it easy for Nixon to walk into his own trap in Watergate."

Having gotten away with so much for so long, Nixon didn't think twice about launching a covert assault against leaders of the other established political party. When Nixon's private spies—the plumbers—were caught red-handed in the headquarters of the Democratic National Committee in June 1972, most media accepted White House claims that it was just a two-bit burglary. The pundits said there was no story there; *Washington Post* reporters Bob Woodward and Carl Bernstein were dismissed as a couple of precocious upstarts out to make trouble for the President.

Nearly all media were slow to delve into what proved to be a monumental political scandal. As Bernstein told an audience at Harvard University in 1989, "At the time of Watergate, there were some 2,000 full-time reporters in Washington, working for major news organizations. In the first six months after the break-in...14 of those reporters were assigned by their news organizations to cover the Watergate story on a full-time basis, and of these 14, half-a-dozen on what you might call an investigative basis." Bernstein added: "The press has been engaged in a kind of orgy of self-congratulations about our performance in Watergate and about our performance in covering the news since. And it seems to me no attitude could be more unjustified."

"We realize that we did a lousy job on Watergate," said United Press International's Helen Thomas of the White House press corps. "We just sat there and took what they said at face value." Television was even slower than print media. As author Donna Woolfolk Cross wrote, "TV news did not pursue the story until it was already a well-established matter of discussion in the press and among politicians. During the times when Americans might have profited most from a full exploration of the scandal—before a national election—TV news was still presenting the story as the administration billed it: a 'second-rate burglary.'"

When the Iran-contra scandal broke in November 1986, comparisons with Watergate quickly came into vogue. Once again there were tales of a crusading press corps—journalistic Davids slaying White House Goliaths. But the wrong analogy was being drawn. A more accurate appraisal of the two scandals would not have been very flattering to the U.S. media. For if members of the press corps snoozed through Nixon's first term, they also winked and nodded off during almost six years of the Reagan presidency. Small wonder there were those in the Reagan administration who felt they could get away with escapades even more outlandish than Watergate.

Nixon, of course, was eventually forced to resign from office. Reagan managed to elude such a fate, in part because his aides pursued a more sophisticated media strategy. Whereas Nixon's people were often overtly hostile to the press, waging both a public and private war against journalists, the Reagan White House eschewed brass-knuckle tactics in favor of a more amicable relationship. When the *Washington Post* persisted in publishing detrimental Watergate revelations, Nixon threatened to revoke the broadcasting license of the *Post*'s parent company. The Reagan administration tried a more enticing approach, expanding the number of lucrative broadcast affiliates that media corporations could own.

Reagan also benefited from the fact that the media's ideological pendulum had swung rightward since Nixon's final days—largely in reaction to Watergate. Media executives felt that perhaps they had gone too far when Nixon resigned. Roger Wilkins, who wrote *Washington Post* editorials about Watergate, later remarked that the press sought to prove "in the wake of Watergate that they were not irresponsible, that they did have a real sense of the national interest, that they had wandered out of this corporate club... But that essentially they were members in good standing of the club and they wanted to demonstrate that."

Nixon's fall from grace in 1974 came during a period of intense conflict within America's governing circles about the Vietnam War, economic policy and other matters. Nixon loyalists believe, probably correctly, that Woodward and Bernstein were used by unnamed U.S. intelligence sources—including their main source, nicknamed "Deep Throat"—to derail the Nixon presidency. This is not to detract from their accomplishments, but Woodward and Bernstein clearly had help from powerful, well-placed sources.

Shadowboxing in Washington

When Reagan became President in 1981, there was a high degree of consensus within America's corporate and political elites about domestic and foreign policy. Abdicating the role of a real opposition party, Democratic leaders in Congress were more eager to put on a show than put up a fight.

Sometimes the media used the passivity of the Democrats to justify their own. Either way, as Walter Karp put it, "the private story behind every major non-story during the Reagan administration was the Democrats' tacit alliance with Reagan."

It was a convenient arrangement for each of the three principals. The Reagan administration got credit for superb political smarts, and—after its nadir, the unraveling of the Iran-contra scandal—admirable resiliency. ("Howard Baker restored order to the White House," etc.) The Democrats scored points for slugging it out with the Reaganites. And the media reported the shadowboxing as a brawl instead of a contest that kept being thrown before it ever got bloody.

"For eight years the Democratic opposition had shielded from the public a feckless, lawless President with an appalling appetite for private power," Karp wrote. "That was *the* story of the Reagan years, and Washington journalists evidently knew it. Yet they never turned the collusive politics of the Democratic party into news. Slavishly in thrall to the powerful, incapable of enlightening the ruled without the consent of the rulers, the working press, the 'star' reporters, the pundits, the sages, the columnists passed on to us, instead, the Democrats' mendacious drivel about the President's 'Teflon shield.' For eight years, we saw the effects of a bipartisan political class in action, but the press did not show us that political class acting, exercising its collective power, making things happen, contriving the appearances that were reported as news."

One of the chronically contrived appearances was President Reagan's great popularity—phenomenal only in that it was a distortion. In April 1989, the *New York Times* reminded readers that Reagan was "one of the most popular Presidents in American history." Authoritative, but false—as University of Massachusetts political science professor Thomas Ferguson promptly documented for the umpteenth time. "It is tiresome," he wrote in *The Nation* magazine, "always to be pointing out that this ever-popular and seemingly indestructible refrain monumentally distorts the truth. But it does." The past half-century of polling data from Gallup Report showed Reagan's average public approval rating while in office (52 percent) to be lower than Presidents Johnson (54 percent), Kennedy (70 percent), Eisenhower (66 percent), and Roosevelt (68 percent). What's more, Reagan barely bested his three immediate predecessors—Carter (47 percent), Ford (46 percent) and Nixon (48 percent). Of the last nine Presidents, Reagan's approval ranking was a mediocre fifth.

But the Reagan popularity myth was extremely useful for all concerned. It enhanced the administration's power. It alibied the congressional Democrats' ineffectual pseudo-opposition. And it left the media—unencumbered by much authentic political conflict—free to talk about the success of the mirage on stage instead of the motives and methods of those orchestrating from the wings. "It was a win-win situation," recalled Jeff Cohen of FAIR.

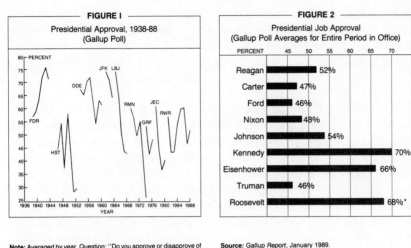

FIGURE I

Presidential Approval, 1938-88
(Gallup Poll)

FIGURE 2

Presidential Job Approval
(Gallup Poll Averages for Entire Period in Office)

	PERCENT
Reagan	52%
Carter	47%
Ford	46%
Nixon	48%
Johnson	54%
Kennedy	70%
Eisenhower	66%
Truman	46%
Roosevelt	68%*

Note: Averaged by year. Question: "Do you approve or disapprove of the way (X) is handling his job as president?"
Sources: 1938-86 follows H.W. Stanley and R.G. Niemi, *Vital Statistics On American Politics* (CQ Press); 1987 averaged from Gallup *Report*, July 1988; 1988 from Gallup *Report*, January 1989.

Source: Gallup *Report*, January 1989.
* The figures for F.D.R. begin in 1938.

"First, Reagan wins by manipulating the media and the public, then he wins by getting laudatory stories out of the media about how brilliantly he manipulates the media and the public."

In fact there was plenty of vigorous opposition to the Reagan administration, but little of it came via Capitol Hill. It was strongest at the grassroots, in a diversity of American communities, wild and wooly areas that national political reporters had little patience—or coverage—for, especially when propounded views didn't fit within the "two sides" put forward by news operations based in Washington and New York. Reagan wasn't very popular among the millions of hungry and homeless, the unemployed, racial minorities, the bankrupt farmers, the struggling single mothers or the union members forced to accept cuts in wages and benefits.

But he was popular among journalists. Sam Donaldson, nurturing his hold-on-there image as one tough inquisitor around the White House, found the commander-in-chief simply charming. "I'm gonna admit something," Donaldson said during Reagan's first term. "He's a hard President to cover for most reporters, because he is such an amiable, warm, human being." The business and financial community—especially media owners and military contractors—were even more enthused about Mr. Nice Guy in the White House, whose policies catered to the interests of corporate America.

Of course, Reaganomics had a distinct downside, as Mark Hertsgaard noted in his book *On Bended Knee*—"it deprived the many while subsidizing the few." But most of the press didn't guffaw when Reagan insisted that social spending could be slashed without hurting the poor, or that taxes could be cut and the military budget jacked up without incurring a huge deficit. When Congress approved Reagan's tax package in 1981, major news media skirted an obvious point: it constituted one of the most phenomenal give-aways to big corporations and wealthy individuals in American history.

Teflon journalism

Much of the Reagan program was directly at odds with popular sentiment. But the President's aides figured they could overcome this problem if the press adopted the Reagan agenda as its own. The goal was not simply to neu-tralize the press but to turn it into a government asset. Toward this end, a team of public relations experts utilized a deft combination of news manage-ment techniques. They played emotionally on patriotic themes ("America is Back"), repeating the same message in a variety of forms as often as possi-ble. The way issues were presented took precedence over substance, as the White House served up pre-masticated news bites and photo opportunities. Mass media bit the bait, while the President himself remained largely off-limits to reporters. Thus on television, we caught glimpses of Reagan visiting a senior citizen center or doing a cameo at the International Games for the Disabled, but journalists never got close enough to ask him why he cut pro-grams for the elderly and the handicapped.

Jeff Gralnick, executive producer of ABC *World News Tonight*, com-mented on the media's willingness to play by Reagan's rules. "It's my job to take the news as they choose to give it to us," he told Hertsgaard. "The evening news telecast is not supposed to be the watchdog on the government. It never was, never will be. We are a national front page, five days a week."

When journalists tried to do some serious reporting about Reagan, they often got flak from management. CBS News executives pressured White House correspondent Lesley Stahl to tone down what they viewed as overly negative stories, especially about the economy. As Stahl recounted, "No one said to me, 'We're being more positive, we're out to be less shrill,' if you will. When occasionally a piece would have a sharply critical close, I found it coming back changed, with editorial suggestions that took the hard edge off the piece." For the most part, critical stories that saw the light of day were scattered, one-shot affairs and, therefore, basically innocuous, as far as the White House was concerned.

On the whole, Reagan's people were quite pleased by the media coverage the President received. "I think a lot of the Teflon came because the press was holding back," said David Gergen, White House communications direc-tor during Reagan's first term. "I don't think they wanted to go after him that toughly." Reagan aide Michael Deaver felt the same way. In his memoirs, Deaver wrote that prior to the Iran-contra scandal, "Ronald Reagan enjoyed the most generous treatment by the press of any President in the postwar era. He knew it, and liked the distinction."

Soft treatment of the President was most evident at his rare news conferences, when Reagan stumbled along without the help of a teleprompter. After a while, reporters stopped trying to correct his legendary gaffes and inane statements. Journalists avoided asking difficult questions, lest they appear partisan. Following a press conference in June 1986, a White House aide remarked that the media treated Reagan "almost reverentially." Indeed, those reporters who marveled at the Teflon President were often the same ones who coated and protected him.

Mass media fawning over Reagan reached a height during Fourth of July festivities in 1986. A *Time* magazine cover story titled "Yankee Doodle Magic"—featuring a beaming Reagan haloed by fireworks—called him "one of the strongest leaders of the 20th century...who has restored the authority of the presidency." "People tend to trust him," *Time* asserted, "even if they utterly disagree with his principles." Two months later, in a cover story praising his hands-off managerial style, *Fortune* magazine hailed Reagan as a model executive—"One extraordinarily important if little-noted element of the Reagan legacy is already established: He has proved once again that the presidency is manageable." Shortly thereafter came the Iran-contra scandal, and the media bubble burst.

Not "another failed presidency"

Whether Reagan was riding high or looking shaky, mass media were eager that he not be thrown from the Oval Office saddle—and were projecting that eagerness onto the general public. "Americans do not want to see another failed presidency," columnist Haynes Johnson wrote in the *Washington Post* in January 1982. Five years later, amidst the Iran-contra revelations, many newspaper editorials emphasized the same theme with new urgency. Reporters reading their bosses' editorials could easily get the message that it was more important for the scandal to bottom out than for them to get to the bottom of it.

Although the Iran-contra affair was viewed by some as an example of muscle-flexing by the American press, it was an obscure Lebanese newspaper that first broke the story of the arms-for-hostages swap with Khomeini. Then came the announcement by Attorney General Edwin Meese about the diversion of Iranian funds to the Nicaraguan contras. Up until that time, thousands of media professionals—drawing on the resources of the nation's biggest news gathering organizations—had failed to alert the country to the far-reaching chicanery directed out of the White House basement.

To make matters worse, the press ignored the staggering implications of its own fragmentary news items. On August 8 and 9, 1985, the *New York Times* reported that the contras were "receiving direct military advice from White House officials." While mentioning that a military officer on the National Security Council who "briefs President Reagan" was running the operation, the *Times* acceded to a White House request not to publish Oliver North's name. By not following up on its own disclosures, the paper of record sent an unmistakable signal to the rest of the media that the story wasn't all that important.

On August 11, 1985, the *Chicago Tribune* referred to a "Marine Corps lieutenant colonel" instrumental in Reagan's "effort to press his [Nicaragua] policy despite opposition in Congress." Four days later, columnist Joseph Kraft named Oliver North as coordinator of White House covert involvement in Nicaragua, "a smelly operation redolent of Richard M. Nixon." Yet during two presidential news conferences the following month, not a single reporter asked Reagan about the recent indications that the White House and North were violating the law by aiding the contras. The media's reluctance to press the point may have had something to do with the fact that many journalists valued North as a confidential source on "national security" matters and they didn't want to burn that bridge. After the scandal broke, one media outlet after another—*Time, Newsweek, New York Times*, etc.—admitted their long-standing relations with North.

As for the Iranian angle of the scandal—syndicated columnists Jack Anderson and Dale Van Atta sat on a story about the secret arms-for-hostages scam after President Reagan confirmed the existence of the Iranian initiative in a February 1986 off-the-record interview. Three months later—and a half year before the scandal officially broke—Anderson and Van Atta disclosed that Israel peddled more than $250 million worth of arms and ammunition to Iran since 1981 "with the tacit approval of the CIA." But, again, there was little follow-up by other media.

As Mark Hertsgaard has written, "The essentials of the contra story and to some extent the Iran arms sales were known to individual members of the press nearly 18 months before they became headline news in November 1986. Parts of the stories were even reported in major media outlets... But the stories were not deemed worthy of vigorous pursuit, were not picked up throughout the rest of the news media, were not accorded a sufficiently high profile to attract the attention of the American public. And so they floated past largely unnoticed, fortifying Reagan administration officials in the conviction that they could conduct whatever illegal or unpopular operations they wished without fear of detection."

Ten signs of an official scandal

The Iran-contra revelations shared ten common characteristics of an official scandal:

1) The scandal comes to light much later than it could have to prevent serious harm.
2) The focus is on scapegoats and fall guys, as though remedial action amounts to handing the public a few heads on a platter.
3) Damage control keeps the media barking but at bay. The press is so busy chewing on scraps near the outer perimeter that it stays away from the chicken house.
4) Sources on the inside supply tidbits of information to steer reporters in certain directions—and away from others. With the media dashing through the woods, these sources keep pointing: "The scandal went that-a-way!"
5) After denials by government officials come well-publicized admissions of "mismanagement," "mistakes," even "improprieties." The media take, and report, these half-hearted confessions at face value.
6) The spotlight is on outraged officials—senators, congressmen, special prosecutors, federal judges—asking tough questions. (But not too tough.) As time passes, politicians and/or the judicial system take the lead in guiding media coverage.
7) Despite all the hand-wringing, the press avoids basic questions that challenge institutional power and not just a few powerful individuals.
8) Even when the proverbial "highest levels" are implicated, a journalistic fog sets in, obscuring trails that could lead to more substantial revelations, or far-reaching solutions.
9) Protracted news coverage makes a big show out of airing certain facts, over and over, but in the end the most powerful and culpable oxen remain ungored.

10) Inevitably, media pundits emphasize that despite all the past problems, the system is cleansing itself. "The system works."

And so it was during the Reagan administration. Mass media seemed oblivious to wrongdoing until the government—via the Meese announcement—certified that a scandal had occurred. And official disclosures, not aggressive independent reporting, continued to shape the evolution of the Iran-contra story.

Yes, Reagan took his lumps when he appeared before the press and tried to explain the arms-for-hostages swap. Sam Donaldson went so far as to accuse the President of "duplicity." For a while it seemed that Reagan would be subjected to the kind of probing that ought to be the norm in a democratic society. But with so much at stake, the scandal also triggered a protective impulse within the media. "Nobody wants another Nixon," declared *NBC Nightly News* commentator John Chancellor. *Chicago Tribune* editor James Squires warned his reporters not to repeat the "excesses" of Watergate. And while *Washington Post* reporters sniffed around for new leads, Katharine Graham chatted with Nancy Reagan to shore up the First Lady's spirits.

Olliemania, Olliemedia

Unable to muster the resolve for a full-fledged investigative assault, the press began to do the White House damage-control shuffle. The plan for containing the scandal was set in motion at the very moment Meese disclosed the diversion of Iranian "assets" to the contras and fingered North and Poindexter as the higher-ups responsible. Mass media picked up the cue and focused on the diversion while ignoring other crucial issues, such as U.S. government complicity in contra drug smuggling. The overriding question became, "What did the President know, and when?" It all seemed to boil down to this: If Reagan knew about the diversion, he was guilty; otherwise he was innocent. And since North and his colleagues had already shred key documents, the damage-controllers knew the paper trail would stop short of Mr. Nice Guy in the White House.

During the congressional Iran-contra hearings in the summer of 1987, PBS analyst Elizabeth Drew commented on how ironic it was that people were "searching for a smoking gun in a room filled with smoke." The televised hearings coincided with the 200th anniversary of the U.S. Constitution—yet neither Congress nor the press showed much fiber when it came to confronting those who had made a mockery of constitutional government by setting up an "off the shelf" apparatus to conduct secret missions.

A *Miami Herald* article by Alfonso Chardy disclosed that Oliver North had "helped draw up a controversial plan to suspend the Constitution in the event of a national crisis, such as...widespread internal dissent or national opposition to a U.S. military invasion abroad." Published on the eve of

North's congressional testimony, Chardy's article should have put a snag in the can-do colonel's attempt to pass himself off as a beleaguered patriot. But the papers of record and the TV networks shamelessly ignored the story. (The media silence was deafening when Congressman Jack Brooks tried to raise the issue during the hearings, only to be reprimanded by the chairman, Senator Daniel Inouye.)

Coverage of North's testimony was marked by the same superficiality that characterized White House reporting throughout the Reagan presidency. TV commentators described his chin line, his haircut, the way his voice choked up at just the right moments. Ted Koppel said North held "an entire nation enthralled." John Chancellor called it "a terrific performance" that "played in Peoria." Dan Rather praised it as "Washington theater at its best." Typically the emphasis was not on *what* North said but on *how* he said it.

TV analysts neglected to point out the most glaring contradictions. While North claimed to be an anti-terrorist, he sold missiles to the Iranian government, which backed the Islamic fanatics who pulled off the 1983 terrorist attack that killed 241 Marines in Beirut. North bragged of his role in apprehending the *Achille Lauro* hijackers, but his contra supply network utilized the services of Manzar Al-Kassar, a Syrian drug and gun runner who also supplied weapons to the group that hijacked the *Achille Lauro*. Many other such contradictions went unreported, in part because so many of the guest "experts" who provided commentary during the hearings were drawn from the ranks of hardline conservatives and intelligence operatives—people like Patrick Buchanan, John McLaughlin, former CIA agent Ray Cline and retired general John Singlaub, who was himself deeply implicated in the scandal.

In devising covert operations, spymasters create cover stories in advance to contain the damage should their schemes be exposed. North's congressional interlocutors chuckled when he revealed that his mentor, CIA director William Casey, had told him that he might not be a big enough fall guy; North's immediate superior, National Security Adviser John Poindexter, would probably also have to take the rap if it came down to that. Poindexter was a well-known dissembler on Capitol Hill, having planted disinformation in the U.S. media about Libya. Yet when it came his turn to testify about Iran-contra, he was pegged by reporters as the one person who could prove or disprove that Reagan was privy to the diversion scam. Poindexter said no. He also maintained it was his job to provide the President with "plausible deniability."

In effect, Poindexter told Congress and the media that they had been taken for a ride on a national security roller-coaster, and now the ride was over. Since there was no way to refute Poindexter's testimony, he would end up being the principal fall guy, just as CIA director Casey had planned. The Democrats in Congress, still refusing to act like an authentic opposition party, had little inclination to pursue the matter further. And the Washington press corps, peering through a cover story that had been rendered transparent, caught a vivid glimpse of its own weakness, and moved on.

A new political season was about to begin.

THE PRESIDENTIAL HORSERACE

During the 1988 presidential election campaign, certain media clichés became as stale and repetitious as the candidates' stump speeches. Journalists typically applied the "special interests" label to groups advocating for black and Hispanic Americans (46 million people), labor unionists (17 million), seniors, women, homosexuals and the poor. At the same time, mass media avoided using the pejorative "special interests" tag to describe big oil, banking, chemical, agribusiness, military and nuclear firms—and, of course, huge media corporations.

At the start of the Democratic convention in Atlanta, TV reporter Chris Wallace (then with NBC News) was mouthing media gospel with a hallowed question: "How far can Dukakis go to meet Jackson without [the Democrats'] appearing, like 1984, to be caving in to every special interest?" We caught up with Wallace at the convention a few days later and asked him why the media kept defining "special interests" as Jesse Jackson's constituencies, but not the corporate sponsors of politicians like Lloyd Bentsen or George Bush. Wallace hedged, predicting that we would also hear the phrase in network coverage of the Republican convention in New Orleans a few weeks later. Prophecy turned out not to be among Wallace's gifts.

With makeshift offices set up inside an enormous exhibit complex next to the Democrats' convention hall, some 13,500 journalists and media technicians went about their work with the news frame already well established. CBS correspondent Bruce Morton discoursed on the Democrats' need "to shed the image of the special interests." On the PBS television show *Washington Week in Review*, Howard Fineman of *Newsweek* solemnly parroted the prevalent wisdom by speaking of Dukakis' desire not to "kowtow to every special interest group whether it be labor or the teachers or black voters." (Fineman failed to explain why "black voters" comprised a "special interest group," but Southern white voters or rich voters did not.) At one point, CBS's Lesley Stahl proclaimed from the convention floor that she'd uncovered some "special interests hiding in the wings"—a reference to a couple of union officials. Influential corporate leaders in attendance were spared such negative innuendoes.

Equating deference to the party's old guard with wise pursuit of victory, media mostly applauded the choice of Senator Bentsen for the ticket. Although reporters agreed that Michael Dukakis had to be careful not to come off as "caving in" to Jackson, none referred to Dukakis' selection of

Bentsen as "caving in" to the corporate elite or conservative special interests that backed the wealthy Texan.

Mass media were distinctly unsympathetic toward Jackson's political program. Jackson called for a tax freeze on the middle class and poor, and a tax hike only for wealthy individuals and corporations. Like other reporters, NBC's Bob Kur described it simply as a platform plank "for higher taxes." When the proposal went down to defeat, journalists were virtually unanimous in characterizing it as a Dukakis victory over "special interests." It could also have been depicted as a win for big business special interests, but very few mainstream journalists played it that way—certainly not the network TV stars who are in high-income brackets themselves.

Jesse Jackson, the troublemaker

Jackson's willingness to contest platform issues during the convention appeared irksome to America's journalistic establishment, which seemed more enthused about open debate at the Soviet Communist Party's conference in Moscow the previous month. One correspondent commented that Jackson "threatened to spoil the convention" with debates over issues. Jackson delegates "are capable of causing trouble," Bill Plante reported on CBS; his network colleague Diane Sawyer added that they "have the threat of disruption over issues." To a nearly uniform extent, mass media equated Dukakis platform positions with reasoned unity, minority planks with divisiveness.

Meanwhile, the *Los Angeles Times* implied that Jackson supporters were not really part of the party at all—reporting in the lead of a July 17 page-one article that "Rev. Jesse Jackson sows frustration and anxiety throughout the Democratic Party." The sweeping statement was neither quoted nor even vaguely attributed; the *Times* simply presented it as matter-of-fact reportage in a news story.

Journalists rapidly alerted the public to Jackson's prodigious conceits. Tom Brokaw began NBC's coverage by suggesting that Jackson might be "on an ego trip." In the *Chicago Tribune*, Joan Beck opined that "his résumé is no match for his ego." They were in tune with a media crescendo that had been rising since early summer. Of all the presidential aspirants, only Jackson was subjected to attack for egotism. While their personal styles, cultural backgrounds and political agendas were different than his, it was hardly an objective truth that Michael Dukakis, George Bush and other campaigners possessed measurably smaller egos.

The media's proverbial question—"What does Jesse want?"—implied that a black candidate wanting to be President must have ulterior motives. Reporters posed the question repeatedly and answered it with ill-disguised suspicion, more bent on mystifying than explicating Jackson's worldview. For mass media institutions controlled by wealthy whites, a spokesperson for poor blacks was all the more puzzling as his appeal widened to include voters of other racial and economic backgrounds.

Unable to ignore Jackson's eloquence or huge following, press coverage was nonetheless hostile to his message. Appearing on NBC's *Meet the Press* during convention week, David Broder of the *Washington Post* declared: "There is a consensus in the Democratic Party that has moved to the center and right—and the Jackson people are way out of this consensus." And Broder spoke for many of his colleagues when he wrote of the Democratic Party: "The days of litmus-test liberalism are finished."

Such punditry ignored polling data that indicated significant public support for many positions depicted as overly "liberal" by the media. At the end of 1987, for example, a *New York Times*/CBS poll reported that 71 percent of Americans believed the federal government should see to it "that everyone who wants a job has a job"; 78 percent said "the government should guarantee medical care to everyone"; 62 percent favored "federally-sponsored day care programs"; 60 percent "reject cuts in social programs to balance the budget"; and 38 percent favored reducing military spending, while 13 percent wanted an increase. While journalists kept asking whether the Democrats were "too liberal to win," the polls suggested that on key issues Dukakis and Jackson were closer to mainstream opinion than George Bush, someone rarely stigmatized as being "too conservative" for the electorate.

Bush scandals (sort of)

The same folks who spun circles around the media during the Reagan years worked wonders for the Bush-Quayle ticket. Their strategy entailed limiting access to the candidates, staging photo opportunities, avoiding substantive policy discussions and hitting below the belt. Republican attack ads emphasized Willie Horton, a black prisoner from Massachusetts who raped a white woman while he was out on a furlough; another target was pollution in Boston Harbor. "Besides the racial overtones," noted the Toronto *Globe and Mail*, "the message was clear: Michael Dukakis was soft on crime, and George Bush, who had shown no particular interest in matters ecological, was turned into the environmentalist President."

It hardly mattered that the furlough issue was spurious, and that footage for the Boston Harbor ad was not filmed in the waterway cited in the commercial. The Bush team knew from experience that if the truth ever emerged, it would be shunted to the back pages, while they dominated the front pages and network news with another round of photo ops. ABC's Sam Donaldson was candid, if unrepentant: "When we cover the candidates, we cover the campaigns as they outline them."

When his campaign turned the corner and widened the lead against Dukakis in the early fall, the ground shook with accolades for Bush. Despite some grousing that Bush's tacticians had taken a low and tacky road, the former CIA director scored doubly. Political reporters abetted Bush's media manipulations, and praised his marvelous acumen for pulling off the manipulations so effectively. It was no coincidence that throughout the campaign important issues about Bush's record had been steadily disappearing from TV screens and newsprint.

In December 1987, the congressional Iran-contra Committee released a White House memo describing Bush's "solid" support for a "risky operation" that involved secret arms sales to Iran. During the first three months of 1988,

ɔonesbury BY GARRY TRUDEAU

as an embattled Bush struggled with fellow Republicans in the primaries, the Iran arms fiasco got major coverage—74 minutes on national CBS, ABC and NBC News broadcasts. But the issue received less than six minutes during the several months that followed. The attention span was similar at the *New York Times*, which "ran stories about Bush and Iran on 18 days in January, three days in February and March, and four in April," University of California professor Peter Dale Scott found. "In May and June, after Bush had emerged as the certain GOP candidate, there were no more such stories; the teflonizing had begun."

An aspect of the Iran-contra maneuvers ignored by mass media was George Bush's tie-in with big oil. As Professor Scott pointed out, in early 1986 Bush launched an initiative "to stabilize crude oil prices, then rapidly falling, by promoting a common price policy between the U.S. and the oil producers of the Persian Gulf, above all Iran and Saudi Arabia. Higher oil prices was an explicit goal in some of Oliver North's secret arms negotiations with the Iranians. It reflected the concerns of Bush, a former Texas oilman." Secretary of State George Shultz and Defense Secretary Caspar Weinberger were not informed about the May 1986 visit of North and Robert McFarlane to Teheran. According to the Iran-contra Select Committee, Bush not only knew of the trip, he helped plan it. Bush's oily involvement was a potential media bombshell that never went off.

Bush's office repeatedly lied about the Vice President's role in the illegal contra supply operation. At a White House meeting in June 1984, Bush, Reagan and other top U.S. officials discussed how to sidestep the will of Congress—that is to say, violate the law—by inducing foreign governments to finance the contras. Two memos written by Donald Gregg, Vice President Bush's national security adviser, stated that former CIA agent Felix Rodriguez had briefed Bush in May 1986 "on the status of the war in El Salvador and resupply of the contras." Bush later insisted he was "out of the loop," and while many journalists were skeptical, few pressed the point during the campaign.

Another scandal whitewashed by the media involved a group of former Nazi collaborators who held important positions within the Bush campaign. Two months before the November 1988 election, a small newspaper, *Washington Jewish Week*, disclosed that George Bush had appointed an ethnic coalition for his campaign that included a number of outspoken anti-Semites with Nazi and fascist affiliations. The article prompted the resignation of six leaders of Bush's ethnic outreach division. Although the resignations were widely reported, few major media investigated the actual charges or the meaning behind them.

The *New York Times*, in particular, downplayed the significance of the Nazi-GOP connection, burying the news that six Republican ethnic leaders had quit the campaign on page 24 of the D-Section under the headline, "A

Decisive Baker Puts His Mark On Bush Race." The article by Gerald M. Boyd treated the resignation of the discredited ethnic officials less as a sign of scandal than as evidence of James Baker's "authority" in running the Bush campaign. A Bush spokesperson dismissed the charges against the six ethnic leaders as "politically inspired garbage," claiming that the Republican Party looked into the allegations and "was unable to substantiate them." Most media publicized this denial unchallenged.

An exception was the *Philadelphia Inquirer*, which featured a series of investigative pieces documenting the Nazi link. A front-page lead story detailed the sordid past of men like Florian Galdau, the national chairman of Romanians for Bush, who defended convicted war criminal Valerian Trifa; Radi Slavoff, co-chairman of Bulgarians for Bush, who arranged a 1983 event in Washington that honored Austin App, author of several texts denying the existence of the Nazi Holocaust; Phillip Guarino, chairman of the Italian-American National Republican Federation, who belonged to a neofascist masonic lodge implicated in terrorist attacks in Italy and Latin America; and Bohdan Fedorak, vice chairman of Ukrainians for Bush, who was also a leader of a Nazi collaborationist organization involved in anti-Polish and anti-Jewish wartime pogroms.

A follow-up story in the *Inquirer* summarized the findings of a well-documented report published by the Cambridge-based Political Research Associates, titled "Old Nazis, the New Right and the Reagan Administration: The Role of Domestic Fascist Networks in the Republican Party and Their Effect on U.S. Cold War Politics." The report, written by Russ Bellant, showed how the Bush campaign's ethnic outreach program was rooted in a pro-Nazi émigré network dating back to the late 1940s. The GOP's ethnic leaders were among thousands of extremists from Eastern Europe who were welcomed by the U.S. government at the close of the Second World War because of their vociferous anticommunism.

Within days, the story about fascists in the GOP and the Bush campaign faded. No major broadcast media covered the story in depth. Salient facts got little publicity: Even after the Bush campaign's dismissal of individuals with anti-Semitic and fascist links, people associated with Nazi collaborationist groups continued to lead the GOP's ethnic outreach apparatus. This was the essence of an op-ed article by Bellant that the *New York Times* was ready to publish before the election. But the *Times* sat on Bellant's piece until 11 days after the election.

All in all, campaign coverage generally stuck to a simplistic script—tracking gaffes, rhetorical charges, the latest attack ads on TV, and if-the-election-were-held-today polling data ("horseracing" the presidential contest). News media showed much more interest in Bush's repeated invocation of the Pledge of Allegiance as a campaign issue than in those GOP leaders who had pledged their allegiance to swastika flags.

DAN QUAYLE, A POT DEALER AND
THE "INFORMATION POLICE"

Within days after George Bush chose Dan Quayle as his running-mate, controversies swirled around reports that Quayle's family wealth and connections enabled him to enter the National Guard to avoid military service in Vietnam, and that similar favoritism got him into law school. Most of the hullabaloo was short-lived; Republican strategists popularized the idea that journalists were unfairly picking on him.

Yet a hidden story of the 1988 campaign was the manipulation of the federal prison system for partisan political purposes, a story involving the Justice Department's collaboration with top Bush-Quayle campaign managers to suppress allegations that Dan Quayle repeatedly purchased marijuana while in law school. Mass media refused to report what was going on, imposing a virtual blackout before the election and declining to publicize dramatic new evidence that emerged afterwards.

"In a free society," *USA Today* editorialized on Election Day, November 8, 1988, "the news media are obligated to feed all the information they can to the public. People can then use that information as they wish—or they can ignore it. They don't need information police standing in the way." The editorial's clarion call for uncowed media (part of an argument favoring exit polls of voters) was terribly ironic, since it came from one of the "information police" giants standing in the way of news involving a Quayle accuser, who remained sequestered in a solitary cell even as the editorial rolled off *USA Today*'s presses.

Four days before the election that delivered George Bush to the Oval Office and put Dan Quayle a heartbeat away, the newspaper near a federal prison in Oklahoma—the *El Reno Daily Tribune*—published a startling front-page article. Written by the paper's news editor, the story disclosed that an inmate, "Brett Kimberlin of Indianapolis, Ind., claims he sold marijuana to Quayle '15 to 20' times between 1971 and 1973. Kimberlin said the sales occurred while Quayle was a law student at Indiana University." An NBC television news crew had filmed Kimberlin at the prison that morning. (The public never saw the footage.)

Journalists immediately deluged the El Reno Correctional Institution with requests to interview Kimberlin. In response, prison authorities scheduled a press conference for that evening at the penitentiary. But when reporters arrived, they were told that the press conference was cancelled. Instead of going before news reporters, Kimberlin was put in solitary confinement.

Ordinarily a local newspaper's prominent article with wide interest would have been put on news wires. But this time it didn't get beyond the *El Reno Daily Tribune*. "We checked into this story, we found no substantiation in this matter and we did not run a story," said Robert Shaw, Associated Press bureau chief in Oklahoma City, who sought to justify the news blockade when we reached him by phone. Yet Shaw was not claiming that any inaccuracies existed in the newspaper story—just that AP could not verify the truth of Kimberlin's charges and therefore refused to report on them at all.

Associated Press officials in New York were directly involved in the decision to kill the story, according to AP's national assistant managing editor, Charles Hanley, who confirmed his role in deciding to keep it off the wire. And so it was with every other major news organization in the United States. In the case of Kimberlin's allegations, and again when federal officials stopped his press conference before it started, top-level national news editors uniformly opted *not* to provide any information to the public. A media logjam continued to block Kimberlin's story.

The mass media remained silent after Kimberlin was again locked in solitary Monday morning—the day before the election—within two hours after noncommercial WBAI Radio in New York City broadcast a taped interview with Kimberlin. That morning, he was scheduled to hold a telephone news conference by way of speakerphone at the Mayflower Hotel in Washington, but his banishment back to solitary made that impossible.

Kimberlin, who'd offered to take polygraph tests, had signed two affidavits swearing that he repeatedly sold marijuana to Quayle. The inmate's assertion could have posed serious problems for the Republican ticket for several reasons. Quayle was adamant that he'd never smoked marijuana, as he reiterated on August 17 just after being named as Bush's running-mate, in answer to a question from ABC's Peter Jennings. Both Bush and Quayle had proclaimed that, as Vice President, Quayle would be in charge of the government's "war on drugs," a plan later dropped. And in his first debate with Michael Dukakis, Bush went out of his way to denounce marijuana use. "For a while, as I recall, it even seems to me that there was talk of legalizing or decriminalizing marijuana and other drugs, and I think that's all wrong," Bush declared. He added: "And we have to be tougher on those who commit crimes. We've got to get after the users more."

Mass media editors—who in the preceding months printed and broadcast totally unsubstantiated rumors that Michael Dukakis had seen a psychiatrist and that his wife Kitty had participated in the burning of an American flag—responded to our inquiries before the election by insisting that the Kimberlin allegations should remain unpublicized out of fairness to the Bush-Quayle team.

Prison politics

Six weeks after the election, more facts emerged about the inside story behind the Quayle/Kimberlin non-story. On December 19, 1988, the Washington-based weekly journal *Legal Times* front-paged an investigative report which concluded that "Kimberlin's handling by federal prison officials, and the intense interest in his activities among top GOP campaign aides, suggests that a supposedly apolitical system was being guided by political considerations." Exhaustively researched and written by staff reporter Aaron Freiwald, the *Legal Times* article stated: "The Bush-Quayle campaign certainly closely monitored the Kimberlin matter. Mark Goodin, deputy press secretary to the campaign, says he briefed campaign chairman James Baker on Kimberlin's status five times during the final days of the campaign. Goodin, who says he was in regular contact with the Justice Department about Kimberlin, also says that throughout the Nov. 4 weekend, he briefed Lee Atwater, Bush's campaign manager, and Stuart Spencer, Quayle's campaign manager."

In the midst of this intensive briefing process, Kimberlin's scheduled press conference on November 4 was abruptly cancelled by J. Michael Quinlan, director of the Federal Bureau of Prisons, an agency administered by the U.S. Department of Justice. Quinlan also gave the order that Kimberlin be isolated, away from any telephone. Those were highly unusual actions. And *Legal Times* observed that "several factors, in addition to Quinlan's personal involvement, lead to the conclusion that the decisions to silence Kimberlin were not simply the product of routine prison administration."

The Justice Department's director of public affairs, Loye Miller, conceded to *Legal Times* the purpose of the disciplinary action: "The Bureau of Prisons caught on that he was going to hold another press conference. So they put him back in." Some officials contended that inmates were simply not allowed to hold press conferences, and that by scheduling one, prison authorities in Oklahoma had violated the federal bureau's procedures. But actually, as *Legal Times* found, "inmate press conferences have been allowed in the past and are not barred by law or policy." What was more, "John Pendleton, congressional liaison for the bureau, says he cannot think of another instance in which the director of the bureau made the decision to place an inmate in administrative detention." Such matters were routinely left to the warden's office at each prison.

"Quinlan's unusual personal involvement in Kimberlin's treatment came amid a flurry of contacts throughout the pre-election weekend among the bureau, high-ranking political appointees at the Justice Department, and senior advisers at Bush-Quayle headquarters," *Legal Times* revealed. Kimberlin's sudden solitary confinement, preventing potentially dramatic press appearances, "served to contain what could nevertheless have been an explosive situation on the eve of the Nov. 8 election," said *Legal Times*. Officials at the Justice Department were acutely aware of just how concerned the campaign managers were as they closely monitored the Kimberlin matter. "Bush-Quayle spokesman Goodin says he kept in close touch with Loye Miller, director of public affairs at the Justice Department, reporting to Campaign Chairman Baker and other senior campaign officials."

While increasingly drawn into fielding pre-election media calls on the matter, Loye Miller apparently served as a savvy switchboard between Bush-Quayle strategists and the ostensibly non-political Bureau of Prisons operating under the wing of the Justice Department. After a long reportorial career that included several years of covering the Reagan White House for Newhouse News Service, Miller was not always forthright while in the employ of the Justice Department, as *Legal Times* discovered: "Miller, after first denying that he discussed the Kimberlin matter with any higher-ups at Justice, now acknowledges that he called Robin Ross, executive assistant to the attorney general. 'I think I thought if this guy was going to have a press conference, and we were going to get a story out of it, Ross ought to know,' explains Miller."

Kimberlin's legal troubles stretched back to his teens, when he was convicted as a perjurer for testimony he gave about drug dealing. At age 34, he was in his tenth year of serving a 50-year prison sentence as a result of guilty verdicts on charges of smuggling marijuana and involvement in bombings near the Indianapolis Speedway. In summer 1988, a letter to the Parole Commission from former U.S. Solicitor General Erwin Griswold noted that "Kimberlin's prison record has been good" and that "he has received a number of commendations from the prison authorities."

But after he made public his allegations about having been Dan Quayle's pot dealer, Kimberlin's problems kept mounting. In late December 1988, three days after publication of the *Legal Times* exposé, Kimberlin was back in solitary, with the explanation that he had abused telephone privileges in speaking with his attorneys. Kimberlin told us that his unwavering claim about Quayle and pot "can't help me. It can only hurt me. Like this getting thrown in solitary and getting harassed."

Whether Dan Quayle purchased marijuana is in some ways far less important than whether Bush-Quayle campaign officials—including James Baker, on his way to becoming Secretary of State—improperly used the Justice Department to put Kimberlin in solitary confinement, away from the media, for partisan political purposes.

In its detailed reporting, *Legal Times* had broken a significant story. Once *Legal Times* let the cat out of the bag, inquisitive media should have followed up with their own investigations. But that didn't happen. The information police kept standing in the way.

An editor at the Washington bureau of Associated Press received the advance text of the *Legal Times* exposé the night of December 16, more than 48 hours before publication. But the AP wire never carried a word about it. Nor did the commercial TV and radio networks, PBS, NPR, the newsweeklies, the *Washington Post* or the *Los Angeles Times*.

It was the *New York Times*, however, that may have done more than any other media to smother the *Legal Times* exposé. The nation's "newspaper of record" turned the story into old news without ever really reporting it at all.

Solitary for Quayle's Accuser

Special to The New York Times

WASHINGTON, Dec. 19 — The Justice Department said today that four days before last month's election, its senior prison official ordered solitary confinement for an inmate who tried to call news conferences to assert that he once sold marijuana to Dan Quayle.

No evidence has surfaced to document the charges by the inmate, Brett Kimberlin, who is in the Federal Correctional Facility at El Reno, Okla., serving a 51-year sentence on drug- and explosives-related charges. Vice President-elect Quayle has denied using drugs.

Loye Miller, the director of the Justice Department's public affairs office, confirmed an account of the episode today in The Legal Times, a Washington newspaper. He said Mr. Kimberlin was twice placed in administrative detention on the order of J. Michael Quinlan, head of the Federal Bureau of Prisons.

Mr. Miller said he knew of no evidence to suggest that Mr. Kimberlin

was confined to avoid any damage his statements might cause the Bush-Quayle campaign. He said the inmate had been interviewed by at least three national news organizations before he was placed in solitary confinement, adding, "It wasn't exactly as if he was kept under a rock."

Mr. Miller said Mr. Kimberlin had planned a Nov. 4 news conference at the prison after Oklahoma newspapers became aware that he had made allegations about Senator Quayle to an NBC News crew. According to The Legal Times, Mr. Quinlan said he canceled that conference because he does not permit them in Federal prisons.

Mr. Kimberlin was later placed in solitary confinement twice, once out of fear that his actions placed him in danger from other inmates and later because he violated prison regulations by trying to stage a news conference without permission, Mr. Miller said.

From the *New York Times,* December 20, 1988

The brief article, appearing on page B9, was a masterpiece of omissions and distortions. According to the *New York Times*, Kimberlin claimed "he once sold marijuana to Dan Quayle." The actual claim was "15 to 20 times." The *Times* featured Bureau of Prisons chief Quinlan's assertion that inmate news conferences were not permitted; *Legal Times* had documented that press conferences *were* permitted. The *New York Times* omitted the story's key points: the unprecedented nature of Quinlan's personal intervention resulting in the solitary confinement of a prisoner; the flurry of contacts between Bush-Quayle campaign leaders and Justice Department officials. The only individual quoted in the *Times* story was Loye Miller, the Justice Department official whose veracity about the incident had already been strongly questioned by the *Legal Times* exposé.

We later spoke with the *New York Times* reporter who wrote the article, Michael Wines. "The story had a surface appeal at the beginning because, I mean, it's almost a rule of thumb that if somebody tries to suppress a story it raises the possibility that whatever they're trying to suppress is true," he said. But the story quickly petered out, according to Wines: "I did manage to confirm the fact that they [Bush-Quayle campaign officials] were kept abreast of what this guy was doing. At which point I asked myself—'Okay, what's wrong with that?'" Wines checked with some official sources. "After making telephone calls I wound up concluding that this was basically a case of one prison inmate who was a publicity hound."

Wines said he might have pursued the story further if he had more time. "But," he hastened to add, "it was after the election and the point in any case was moot. There was a new regime coming in at the Justice Department, in more ways than one, and there was a load of other things on my plate."

BUSH-LEAGUE JOURNALISM

A lot of points were becoming moot as Ronald Reagan bid adieu to the Washington press corps. Journalists greeted his successor with homage more suitable for a coronation than an inauguration.

Depicting Bush's first full day as President, the *New York Times* strained to portray the palace at 1600 Pennsylvania Avenue as belonging to all loyal subjects. "George and Barbara Bush had a few thousand folks over this morning to show off their new house," began a front-page article about a public reception at the White House. The above-the-fold headline contained no quotation marks; it was a declaration by the *New York Times*: "The People, the Thousands, Get a Look at Their House."

In the rush to portray the new President as both ascendant to royalty and a regular guy, print journalists busily did their part. Some inaugural examples:

- "Bush Offering a Special Mix: Ivy League and Pork Rinds"—headline, *New York Times* (front page), January 20
- "George Bush embodies the patrician ideal of responsibility begotten by privilege," an "American tradition reaching back through the many Presidents more at home in mansions than log cabins, from Washington of Mount Vernon to Jefferson of Monticello to Roosevelt of Hyde Park."—R.W. Apple Jr., *New York Times* (front page), January 20
- "They have good bone structure, fine manners and a passion for understatement... Ultimately, the media microscope might uncover imperfections. But for now, the Bush family seems perfectly cast."—Eleanor Clift, *Newsweek*, January 23
- "Kind words. Gentle words. Nothing flashy or particularly memorable. Just good, plain talk from the heart... The perception has already taken hold: Bush is more sensitive and caring than Ronald Reagan..."—Michael Kramer, *Time* magazine, January 30
- "Perhaps it was only the trappings, but George Bush finally looked presidential."—Michael Kramer, *Time* magazine, January 30

America could rest assured that no imposter had reached the throne.

"In the art of creating illusion," remarked Donna Woolfolk Cross, "the media is the President's all-too-willing conspirator... Any piece of information, no matter how trivial, becomes 'news' if it is about the President—or his family." Even presidential house pets swiftly acquire mythic stature. (In 1989, the Bush family dog Millie received more publicity on TV network news than some members of the Cabinet.) It is the stylistic impressions—of being personable, in charge and, above all, "presidential"—that redound most emphatically in media evaluations.

In a media milieu touting the glories of being the best that one can be, the man who wins the presidency is the ultimate success story. Long before the victor lays his hand on the inaugural Bible, he has become a human super-achiever. Yet "this image of the mighty individual," as Mark Crispin Miller says, "is a corporate fiction, the careful work of committees and think tanks, repeatedly reprocessed by the television industry for daily distribution to a mass audience."

Taming the press corps

On the whole, the Bush team's handling of media was quite dexterous. Just after the inauguration, *New York Times* reporter Michael Oreskes noted that "since Election Day Mr. Bush has been assiduously courting the press corps he held at arm's length through the campaign." As the incoming President and the media warmed to each other, a man who had labored as press liaison for five previous administrations was blunt. "Let's face it, the Washington press in particular goes with the power," said Joseph Laitin, a public relations consultant and former reporter. "This is not a very nice commentary. But I'm afraid it's true. If a man is in a powerful position the press tends to go along to the point of being subservient."

A few weeks into 1989, columnist Russell Baker was discerning: "Last year's 'wimp' who turned into the beast of October is enjoying his third metamorphosis in less than a year and now appears in the press as a...gentle knight, precisely the kind of leader we need at this hour." That same month Barbara Walters told Bush, "So many people's view of you has changed. It's as if Clark Kent became Superman."

Although Bush's press secretary Marlin Fitzwater (a holdover from the Reagan era) contended in early spring that reporters were "competitive, cynical characters" immune from becoming presidential advocates, American journalism worked wonders for his new boss.

By using the words "competitive" and "cynical" to describe White House reporters, Fitzwater employed the same adjectives that *New York Times* reporter Bernard Weinraub had chosen for a news article published a few days into the Bush presidency. Weinraub wrote that Bush was trying "to deal with an old problem: how to deal with a highly competitive, sometimes cynical, sometimes irascible press corps that never seems satisfied." Weinraub was projecting a self-image of snarly newshounds chronically in need of housebreaking. His editors at the *New York Times* harbored similar notions, judging from the headline over Weinraub's article—"Bush Begins Perhaps His Toughest Job: Taming Press Corps."

One aspect of the media make-over was the swift emergence of Bush as a rugged sportsman. "For those Americans still clueless that a virile active President has replaced an aging enfeebled one," sociologist William Gibson commented in the spring of 1989, "the Bush administration has kindly and gently choreographed a remarkable outdoor routine for the nation's press photographers." Running, fishing, hunting and all-around sporting, Bush went from wimp to he-man in a matter of months. The media accomplished the transformation because "the drama seems irresistible; the press acquiesces to its own manipulation, and in turn shares responsibility for the reduction of democracy from discussion and action to the role of spectators watching a presidential 'Wild Kingdom.'"

The first dose of bad press for President Bush came with his attempt to install John Tower as Secretary of Defense. Journalists emphasized Tower's drinking and womanizing (activities that seemed foremost on the minds of more than a few senators who debated his nomination). Much less ink was spilled about Tower's pivotal role in the decade's huge military build-up, as a senator and then as a private consultant greasing lucrative deals for corrupt Pentagon contractors.

The Tower defeat tarnished Bush's image, but it didn't come about because of diligent digging by reporters. "No one could say the press was out to get him," wrote Mark Hertsgaard in a July 1989 *Rolling Stone* article. "There is a difference, however, between tough coverage and negative coverage, and Bush did endure a surprising amount of the latter... [Negative] stories were merely the result of the news media's responding to events and echoing the views of official Washington. Tough coverage, on the other hand, requires journalists to take the offensive, to follow up one another's stories, to highlight inconsistencies in the public record and to pursue information independent of the White House P.R. machinery. In that sense there has been little tough coverage of George Bush."

The North trial

The trial of Oliver North produced new evidence about the Iran-contra scandal. In particular, it showed that Reagan and Bush were more deeply entangled in illegal contra aid operations than had officially been acknowledged—so deeply, in fact, that Reagan's advisers worried it could get the President impeached. The most incriminating disclosure, as far as Bush was concerned, involved a trip he made to Honduras while Vice President in March 1985. Bush's meeting with Honduran President Roberto Suazo was part of a secret *quid pro quo* deal approved by Reagan whereby Honduras would get additional economic and CIA assistance if it continued to support the contras. Initialled by Reagan, the document (dated February 19, 1985) authorizing the deal was marked "cc Vice President," indicating a copy was sent to Bush.

A report by Linda Wertheimer on NPR's *All Things Considered* program typified the mass media's timid response to these revelations. Wertheimer said that new evidence from the North trial was unlikely to present much of a political problem for Bush. A once-secret memorandum "indicates that he had a more active role than was previously believed"—her passive voice implying that the wisdom of congressional and media heavies had always encompassed all reasonable beliefs—"if in fact the memo represents accurately what he did do."

President Bush "does have to explain it," Wertheimer went on. "But you also have to consider the political climate of these times. The events of Iran-contra seem a very long time ago... Peace is at hand between the President and the politicians in Washington. These are not people who are out for George Bush's blood. So I think in this political climate, he'll have some uncomfortable times trying to explain what exactly happened, but it seems to me very likely that he can explain it and put it behind him."

Every such media pronouncement helped to ensure its own accuracy. Just as they had with Reagan, the press and Congress couldn't bring themselves to say clearly and unequivocally that Bush had violated the Constitution. With few exceptions, the press didn't challenge White House assurances that Bush was innocent. Perhaps journalists feared a no-holds-barred investigation might show that Bush had committed an impeachable offense, possibly leaving Dan Quayle in charge of the country. Not a comforting thought.

The eagerness of the media to put the entire affair behind them was evident when a guilty verdict came in at the North trial. In what amounted to a slap on the wrist, U.S. District Judge Gerhard Gesell fined Oliver North and placed him on probation. The judge ruled that North could avoid serving time in prison by performing 1,200 hours of community service as an inner-city drug counsellor. North's sentence required him to address a drug problem he helped create while running the contra supply operation—an irony that few mainstream journalists pointed out. "It is clear that individuals who provided support for the contras were involved in drug trafficking, the supply network was used by drug trafficking organizations, and elements of the contras themselves knowingly received financial and material assistance from drug traffickers. In each case," a Senate Foreign Relations Subcommittee concluded, "the U.S. government had information regarding the involvement either while it was occurring, or immediately thereafter."

The lenient sentence handed down by Judge Gesell in July 1989 met with near-universal applause by U.S. mass media. Daniel Schorr, NPR's senior news analyst, apprised his listeners of the proper civic attitude. "In sparing

Oliver North from jail, Judge Gesell may also have spared the country," said Schorr, who added: "Gesell is a no-nonsense judge but not vindictive. A non-jail sentence is quite normal in the case of a first-time offender committing a white-collar crime that is not likely to repeat, and where, as Gesell said, 'jail would only harden your misconceptions.' And so now the tension abates and the pressure is off President Bush for a pardon decision that would stir further controversy, and attention turns to the pending trials and to those whom Gesell characterized as 'a few cynical superiors.'"

As with numerous other media-enthroned pundits, Schorr's tone was of beneficent forehead-crinkling concern for the well-being of the Republic. Like so many of his colleagues, Schorr went out of the way to praise the "jail would only harden your misconceptions" statement by the judge. Imagine that being said from a federal bench—much less applauded from the mass media—if a judge had told someone convicted of armed robbery or drug peddling that he or she would not be sent to prison because "jail would only harden your misconceptions."

On the day of the North sentencing, a switch from NPR to the other main "alternative" broadcast network in the country, PBS Television, brought the same watery gruel. The *MacNeil/Lehrer NewsHour* featured two commentators on the topic—former Nixon speechwriter Ray Price, and *Washington Post* columnist Haynes Johnson. Both expressed relief that North would not be going to jail. Beyond that, it was the classic mass media square-off, presenting only two sides of a many-sided story—hard-right Price versus mushy-centrist Johnson. Price contended that North had done nothing wrong; Johnson insisted that North had broken the law and was appropriately punished for his misdeeds. While Price filled the well-worn media slot customarily held open for a no-apologies conservative, Johnson tied himself in knots trying to enunciate the mainstream line of the day.

Johnson lauded the judge for "sending a signal to people in public life that if you violate the law, you usurp the Constitution, you go beyond your authority you are going to be held accountable. But in not sentencing him to jail and making him a martyr [Judge Gesell] also sent a clear signal to higher-ups that there are many more people involved. That North didn't act alone and I think in that sense it's a verdict that somehow singularly fits the case." Yet Johnson had bigger fish not to fry, going on to state that after the upcoming trial of former National Security Adviser John Poindexter, "the trail doesn't go much higher." Exoneration of George Bush was implicit.

The media's explicit judgment was that North didn't belong in jail—and that everyone worthy of mention agreed. In the *San Jose Mercury News*, a banner headline announced: "Right and Left Agree on North Sentence." The *Chicago Tribune* editorialized, "Even if his appeal fails, he'll still do no prison time. Most Americans will be grateful. No one wants him in the slammer while those above him walk free of a mess they must at the least have had some inkling of." Anyone reading the editorial who *did* want North in the slammer would doubtless be gratified to know that he or she was actually "no one." By media decree, those who felt North deserved to go to jail were beyond the realm of reasonable—or reportable—discourse.

Bush's slow start

Meanwhile, George Bush emerged nearly unscathed from the North trial. His main problem in the press was that he had "gotten off to a slow start" as President. This set the stage for Bush's historic high-jump over lowered expectations at the NATO summit in Brussels. In early June, the President returned from Europe amid great fanfare and profuse accolades—even though nothing substantive happened.

The press was in raptures. CBS News, the *Los Angeles Times*, *Chicago Tribune*, *Time* magazine and many other big media used the identical word: "triumph." Coast to coast, newspaper editorials revved the media spin at frenetic RPMs, under headlines such as "Mr. Bush Takes the Lead" (*New York Times*), "Bush Plays a Trump" (*Miami Herald*), "Bush Seized the Moment" (*San Francisco Examiner*).

The *Washington Post*'s liberal columnist Richard Cohen succumbed to the rampant use of sports metaphors for political analysis, explaining in his first paragraph that "if Bush is a natural at anything, then it has to be football. As he proved at the NATO summit, 'Crazy Legs' Bush is the greatest broken-field runner of all time." Sensing Bush's breakthrough in public relations, Cohen piled on the trite sports-reporter jargon. ("Bush did what he had to do.") Extolling the President, Cohen reduced the nuclear-periled world to a gridiron: "Triumphant, he stands where few predicted he would: in the end zone. Whether he got there by executing a plan or simply by running from his critics is, while troubling, at the moment beside the point. Either way, he's a winner. 'Crazy Legs' Bush has done it again."

Richard Cohen was wrong. The mass media, not Bush, had done it again. Transfixed with surface appearances, journalists made the trip to the NATO summit the turning point that set the press-image dominos falling. Months later, a much-touted analyst at the conservative American Enterprise Institute, William Schneider, told a reporter that the NATO summit was nothing more than a "public relations triumph...and the press fell for it."

While lacking Reagan's purported charisma, Bush was meeting much more frequently with reporters, and his blandishments were not going unrequited. "It's nice he is more accessible, but we're as managed as we were before," the senior White House correspondent, Helen Thomas of UPI, said in late summer. The Bush administration was jerking on reporters' strings like a puppeteer directs marionettes. At least Thomas was honest enough to say so publicly: "You see the manipulation and thought control."

PART III

Domestic Routines

7

Money Matters

D aily news reports indicate that American society is in trouble. Often it may seem that the news media are doing all too good a job of informing us about serious problems in our midst—from AIDS and crack-cocaine babies to rampant pollution and ozone depletion; from homelessness and poverty to street crime and violence; from rising prices and layoffs to higher interest rates and fewer government services; from Washington's corruption and budget deficits to partisan squabbles that seem more petty than principled.

While we don't lack for bad news, the reporting fits into familiar patterns. Grim effects of social ills may be evident, and movingly presented at times—but the actual causes are hazy, and so are the forces that stand in the way of major improvements. People's difficulties mostly seem to have resulted from bad luck, or character flaws, or factors beyond anyone's control. And solutions offered by the media are liable to wind up delivering much less than promised.

All in all, local and national news events frequently seem like episodes that are virtual reruns. The names may change but the stories remain more or less the same. Usually the official explanations and descriptions all but drown out the voices of those closer to the bottom of the economic heap.

Media definitions of domestic issues are especially important because they provide contexts for how we look at what we see. In the long run, we may end up discounting firsthand impressions in favor of those supplied by journalism.

What we perceive as a social crisis may not qualify as a "crisis" on TV networks or the front pages. What we know to be important obstacles to personal fulfillment may get scant—or skewed—media coverage. Overall we're unlikely to recognize many of the concerns of our daily lives in our daily newspapers. Yet marketed entertainment and news reports can be so overbearing that their outlooks supplant our own.

News media present "reality" so powerfully that we may assume they are providing more insight than our own personal and collective experiences do. Worse yet, the news media may exert tremendous influence over how we view our own day-to-day lives—to the point that our more genuine human responses are hemmed in by the parameters of media discussion.

All too often people take the media's word for how to define a situation that's close to home. Maybe that wouldn't be so bad if we could depend on the press to depict—fairly and accurately—important aspects of American society. But patterns of bias are common in coverage of domestic issues.

CLASS CONFLICT IS A NO-NO

"The lesson is this: In a nation of people with ambitions to be affluent themselves, someday, class warfare does not sell."

So wrote a reporter for the *Christian Science Monitor*, in a news article about politics and the capital gains tax. Two days earlier, a news headline in the *Washington Post* presented the identical conclusion: "Tax Fight's Class-War Rhetoric Was at Odds With American Dream." Both newspapers were summing up the considered judgment of American mass media, owned by rich people who are notably unenthusiastic about anything that smacks of class warfare against the privileged.

The wealthy are not immune from criticism in the media, of course. Everyone knows that a good deal of resentment against the rich exists in American society. Some may be selectively lampooned as overly greedy, intemperate or personally flawed. Mass media channel those ill feelings toward individuals rather than toward the system that produces multimillion-aires and corporate concentration of riches. We may be encouraged to dislike or scorn specific tycoons (though not nearly as often as hype promulgates admiration of the super rich). However, major media do little to probe how inordinate wealth and power are undermining democratic possibilities. *Newsweek* chose a vituperative (and sexist) title for its cover story on hotel billionairess Leona Helmsley—"Rhymes With Rich"—but the article condemned her personal cruelties, not her class position.

With so many advertisers preferring a well-heeled audience, composed of people less interested in lower-income communities than their own pursuits, the news media drift is toward upper-class concerns. In the general news media, it is considered gauche to expose the competing class interests; instead, the "A" sections of newspapers overlay economic topics with thick veneers of euphemism and myth. Business sections are somewhat more candid. The *Wall Street Journal* (owned by Dow Jones & Co.), informing a business world that depends on factual data, is still more straightforward. (The *Journal* also provides quality news articles about the role of big money in electoral politics—something we don't often see in daily papers or on TV news.) And perhaps most honest are conservative economic periodicals such as *Barron's* (also owned by Dow Jones), which make no bones about serving profit-hungry elites.

Rich versus poor

When the Census Bureau comes out with periodic reports on wide income gaps, the media provide fleeting reports—one-day stories that quickly sink into the ocean of news. And facts about class divisions are often buried. After the Census Bureau released 1986 income data, a *Washington Post* account included a quote from Robert Greenstein, director of the nonprofit

Center on Budget and Policy Priorities, who said the data reflected the fact that "The gap between the rich and the middle class and the rich and the poor has now reached its widest point in at least 40 years." The quotation came in the article's tenth paragraph, appearing on page A15. But the article had begun on the front page, under the upbeat headline: "Number of Poor Americans at Lowest Level Since 1980."

Most journalists are reluctant to draw attention to wide economic divisions that should be patently obvious to everybody. "Class difference in the United States has so far been the great, undiscussed elephant in the national living room," says San Francisco writer Ann Bartz. In recent years the stratification has worsened. Author Barbara Ehrenreich comments that U.S. "income distribution is now almost as perilously skewed as that of India."

Nevertheless, "class conflict" is a media no-no. To be accused of encouraging it is a damning indictment. Americans are supposed to strive to be one big happy family, even if some of the brothers and sisters are driving new Porsches and Cadillacs while others have no home. When convenient, politicians and mass media invoke family metaphors for the entire society, although it would be an odd family indeed that would allow some of its members to feast in luxury at the dinner table next to others with mere scraps on their plates.

Jesse Jackson has been one of the few people able to reach a large national audience while raising issues of basic fairness. In the United States, "most of the poor are not black and brown as projected in the media," he said in a May 1989 speech. "Of the 40 million poor, 29 million are white. The poor are mostly white, female and young. But whether white, black or brown, hunger hurts. When a baby cries out at midnight after having gone to bed supperless, it doesn't cry race, sex or religion; it cries in pain. Somebody must hear the crying babies."

On matters of poverty and wealth, America's mass media are sluggish about emphasizing realities in human terms. "The problem with economic news today is that most of it comes from economists," says author Hazel Henderson. "And economists are trained to deal with statistics, not with people." When journalists refer to the impoverished, the human dimensions are frequently submerged, as Barbara Wien of the Institute for Policy Studies noted: "The detached and abstracted manner in which television talk shows like *Wall Street Week in Review* report economic news means that we never learn about the fundamental causes and human impact of certain policy choices."

Worthy and unworthy earthquake victims

Even reporting on natural disasters often involves biases that make some victims of tragedy more important than others. The powerful earthquake that struck Northern California on October 17, 1989, brought many days of

News anchor Tom Brokaw sprays his hair into place before going on camera for earthquake coverage.

intense national publicity to the upper-crust Marina district of San Francisco. But where poor neighborhoods suffered severe damage elsewhere in the Bay area, media coverage was minimal. The anguish of black residents in West Oakland, for instance, got comparatively little press. And, a two-hour drive south, the devastation that displaced hundreds of families in Watsonville was a belated and minor story.

With several days to gather material, the three newsweeklies totally ignored the many hundreds of impoverished Latino people who'd suddenly lost their homes. In more than a dozen pages of coverage, *Time*'s only mention of Watsonville was that "the Bake-Rite Bakery caved in, fatally smashing a passerby"; the magazine's extensive photo spread included one picture from the town—a damaged church—with a caption, "Watsonville: St. Patrick's lost bricks, but not its cross." *Newsweek* skipped Watsonville entirely. So did *U.S. News & World Report*.

More than insulting, journalistic prejudices had the effect of diverting aid from communities deemed less newsworthy. Well-meaning TV viewers, and relief agencies, were inclined to earmark donations for publicized areas. "The Red Cross only will go to where the media is, the rich white areas," charged Raul Ramirez, a frustrated volunteer in Watsonville. The executive director of the city's Chamber of Commerce and Agriculture, Charlene Shaffer, was a bit more diplomatic, but sounded just as upset. "It's distressing to see hard-hit communities near the quake's epicenter...being overshadowed by the Bay area in the media's coverage," she complained. "Watsonville Community Hospital has sustained millions of dollars in damage and the economic vitality of the entire community has been jeopardized by the $325 million in damage to local businesses. Donations, which could make the difference between economic survival and devastation to a small community like ours, are pouring into San Francisco instead..."

Doing numbers on poverty

The media's numbers don't always add up. In fact, they're apt to downplay the extent of destitution. A district court concluded that the 1980 census had omitted about three-quarters of a million poor people in New York City alone. The media draw heavily on data from the Census Bureau, which undercounts the poor: English-language forms sometimes get sent to Hispanic neighborhoods; census takers may choose not to enter high-crime neighborhoods; inadequate effort goes into surveying undocumented immigrants and homeless people.

Even while understating the extent of deprivation nationwide, government statistics are staggering. In late 1989, a federal report pegged the official rate of poverty at 13.1 percent—which amounted to 31.9 million Americans. On Capitol Hill, the Joint Economic Committee said that in light of changes in economic conditions since the poverty-line was defined in the 1960s, the true number of impoverished Americans now would be 58 million people—a quarter of the entire population. And across the board, young people are hit hardest. Two-fifths of America's poor are children; half a million of those kids are homeless.

Such poverty statistics, while sometimes noted, are not pointedly matched with the other pole—inordinate wealth. The media customarily portray extremities of privation and riches as totally separate matters. And while news reports sometimes refer to a "working class," reference to a U.S. "ruling class" is a mass media taboo. The press is much better at identifying class hierarchies overseas. Although a *New York Times* news headline declared that "Japan's Ruling Elite Faces a Fed-up People," the *Times* and other American mass media avoid so bluntly identifying a "ruling elite" in the United States.

On occasion, media reports do go beyond wooden and detached accounts. A hard-hitting PBS documentary that aired in spring 1989, "Babies at Risk," showed areas of Chicago where "the rate of infant death is worse than in many Third World countries." Later in the year *Newsweek* published four pages of moving photos and text by author and activist Jonathan Kozol, who pointed out that "the gulf in income between rich and poor American families is wider than at any time since figures were recorded, starting in the 1940s." Also at a new record was "the gap between white and black mortality in children... Black children are more than twice as likely to die in infancy as whites—nine times as likely to be neurologically impaired." With federal housing funds sharply cut during the 1980s, "homeless children were seen begging in the streets of major cities for the first time since the Great Depression. A fivefold increase in homeless children was seen in Washington, D.C., in 1986 alone. By 1987 nearly half the occupants of homeless shelters in New York City were children. The average homeless child was only six years old."

Kozol called for drastic changes in priorities, noting that routine economics "condemns the children of the very poor to the implacable inheritance of a diminished destiny." But his appeals seemed doomed to be unheeded as the 1990s got underway, for reasons including the fact that his article was exceptional for a large-circulation magazine.

Mass media do not hesitate to declare crises. There are recurring hostage, energy, drug, and international crises of various stripes. But the preventable suffering of millions of children within our own borders is not a bona fide media crisis. Such a judgment was implicit when the *New York Times*, in its editorial on President Bush's first 100 days in office, stated categorically that "no national emergencies confront him at home." Powerful editors may have felt that way, but such a complacent declaration would be news to millions of Americans.

ECONOMIC FOLKLORE:
TAXES, SOCIAL SECURITY AND THE AMERICAN DREAM

Reaganomics enriched the already-rich, at the expense of most Americans. But, on the whole, that is not what mass media told us. Soon after Ronald Reagan moved into the White House, no less a mainstream authority than James Reston declared in the *New York Times* that Reagan's economic program amounted to a "serious attempt...to spread the sacrifices equally across all segments of society." Media heavies like Reston were very helpful to administration strategists eager to obscure their class warfare from the top down. As right-wing activist Paul Weyrich commented in a moment of candor: "The rural people in West Virginia don't understand Reaganomics, and frankly, if they did, they wouldn't like it."

Most people don't look kindly on regressive taxation, a setup in which the tax burden falls as income rises. Acceptance has depended on political hocus-pocus abetted by mass media unwilling to openly state the tax-code favoritism doled out to the well-to-do. Journalistic jargon on tax proposals is convoluted enough to be widely befuddling. Throughout the 1980s media often called proposals for tax breaks to the wealthy "tax reform." This inversion of usual meaning led to other absurdities. The press even went on to describe advocates of higher taxes for the rich as enemies of the "reform" enacted during the Reagan years: With a Gallup/Times-Mirror poll showing 82 percent of U.S. citizens in favor of raising taxes on incomes of over $80,000 a year, the *International Herald Tribune* cited the survey as an indication of "anti-reform rumblings."

Showing intermittent sensitivity to the poor and consistent responsiveness to rich owners, journalists often use words without clarifying their meaning. "Recession," for instance, means more people will be out of work. "Consumer confidence" sounds very upbeat—and for business people it is, since it indicates customer willingness to buy expensive things—but it also means that ordinary people are going deeper into debt.

Certain media themes never grow too stale to be repeated in a big way. For example:

This is a land of opportunity.

Media play up those who have "made it" as object lessons for people who feel the crunch of basic living costs. The implication is that difficulties making ends meet are due to individual shortcomings, rather than government priorities or economic structures.

Blame-the-unemployed messages can be direct. In September 1989, *USA Today* opened up a phone hot line for job seekers. Most of the 9,560 callers "don't know beans" about looking for work, said the newspaper, which highlighted a quote from an "outplacement expert" who scolded: "They don't know what they want or how to go about getting it."

We're all in this together.

"Our political system works best when people focus on shared values," wrote a *Newsweek* columnist, who added: "Economic opportunity and striving—the promise of the American dream—is one such basic value. It cuts across religious, ethnic and class differences." Corporate America sounds similar themes in paid ads. In its customary "advertorial" spot on the *New York Times* op-ed page, Mobil shared a stirring homily just before Labor Day 1989, headlined "Here's to us." Between its lyrical appreciation of "the panoply of race and color that makes this country such a fascinating place" and a closing quotation from Walt Whitman, the quarter-page Mobil ad got to the point: "This land, this country of ours, *works.*"

What's most important is that we be aware of the poor and empathize with their plight.

This theme is most evident around holidays like Thanksgiving and Christmas, when countless news outlets urge donations to charity campaigns.

Whether the *New York Times* is entreating readers to "Remember the neediest!" or a small-town newspaper is promoting a similar effort, such rituals often include heart-wrenching photos of the poor.

But showing dire circumstances does not necessarily help change them. "Social problems are less revealed than obscured by depiction of their effects," writes media critic Jan Grover. She adds: "The homeless become so through enormously complex mechanisms involving real-estate speculation, the flight of U.S. industry abroad, declining blue-collar wages and decreasing federal and local social-service benefits, as well as by their own more personal griefs and failures. But few photographic representations of poverty include depictions of the people and practices responsible for an economy that makes housing the enormous burden to the poor that it is. When was the last time you saw a documentary about the poor that included photographs identifying slumlords and speculators as part of the problem?" The media approach is such that "we are more likely to view the poor as a spectacle and as victims than as people caught in a crunch that implicates us all."

What happens on the stock market is big news. What happens at food stamp, unemployment and welfare offices isn't.

No news broadcast is complete without a summary of the day's events on Wall Street. Yet only two percent of the public owns half of the country's individual stock and bond holdings. Most people in the market are very small investors. And 80 percent of Americans don't play the stock markets at all. (While nearly 50 million American workers have some indirect holdings via pension funds, they have no say in how the money is invested or any direct claim in the proceeds until they retire.) The emphasis on reporting every twitch of the Dow reflects media zeal for serving people with the spending capabilities sought by advertisers.

Every daily newspaper is filled with detailed listings of stock market closings. What's more, as economist Pamela Sparr has written, "many papers, magazines, radio and TV stations have collapsed most of their [economics] coverage into business sections geared for corporate executives and private investors." And that's whose worldview gets most faithfully presented in daily newsprint. Whenever a new report on the economy is issued, the news media busily quote government officials, economists, stock analysts, employers and the like. "The financial pages of the newspapers of this country see the world through the eyes of bankers as opposed to through the eyes of bank customers," *Philadelphia Inquirer* reporter David Johnston told us.

Elitist media approaches to financial matters are typified by ABC's *Nightline* program. FAIR's study found that when shows dealt with economics, 20 percent concentrated on the stock market. Only 7.2 percent focused on labor topics. And the most frequent guests for programs on the economy were of a conservative bent: More than one out of three guests (37 percent) represented business, but only one in 20 (5.3 percent) spoke for labor. Other guests included government officials (15.4 percent), academics (13.9 percent) and journalists (12 percent). Under such circumstances, working people without social prestige are unlikely to get a word in edgewise.

The situation is no better on "public" broadcasting. PBS Television features *Adam Smith's Money World* and *Wall $treet Week*, along with the *Nightly Business Report*. And in 1989, public radio from coast to coast began airing the daily half-hour *Marketplace* program—which added General Electric as an underwriter at the start of 1990, dutifully announcing GE's "We bring good things to life" motto as part of every show. There are no comparable national programs devoted to labor or consumer interests. Even on the noncommercial networks, there's no business like dough business.

Widening gaps between the rich and poor are natural.

A Harris Poll in 1989 found 79 percent of Americans agreeing with the statement, "The rich get richer and the poor get poorer." Such trends are apt to be fairly evident based on firsthand observations. Yet the mass media rarely raise journalistic eyebrows or convey alarm at the economic disparities in the country, much less affix blame or demand substantial changes.

In spring 1989, the congressional House Ways and Means Committee came out with a report that the *New York Times* summarized this way: "From 1979 to 1987 the standard of living for the poorest fifth of the population fell by 9 percent. At the same time, the living standard of the top fifth rose by 19 percent." In a laughable front-page understatement, *Times* reporter Peter Passell went on to quickly interject that "the Reagan Administration was not entirely free of responsibility for the change." By the time the article got to its concluding paragraph, Passell and the *Times* were absolving those in power: "The actions of free markets and free people drove a giant wedge in the income distribution. Government responded by not responding, in effect leaving the rich and the poor to fend for themselves."

To close its laissez-fairy tale, the *Times* news article might have added that the rich and poor were equally free to sleep under bridges and steal bread.

When money moves in, it's a good thing.

News media look favorably on the process of gentrification that fixes up run-down neighborhoods, driving rents up—and lower-income people out. A cover story in *Time* described the gentrifiers as "democratically inspired." Said the magazine: "It is the hurly burly pleasures of democracy—pluralism incarnate—that pulled Americans back downtown." Of course, the end result of gentrification is upscale uniformity, not pluralism or democracy.

The motives of developers are anything but altruistic. "It is easier to see people moving in and out of neighborhoods than it is to see capital moving in

"Few things are more attractive to us than a rundown...abandoned neighborhood": real estate development ad in *Fortune*, July 21, 1986

and out, investment and disinvestment in a neighborhood," says Neil Smith, a Rutgers University professor of urban geography. "The mobility of capital—not people—is the key to urban change. But very few reporters make the connection between the movement of capital and the forced displacement of poor and minority households."

Large amounts of newspaper ad revenues come from landowners and developers in a metropolitan area. And realtors often sit on media company boards of directors. So it was no surprise to informed observers when the *New York Times*—years after cancelling the Sidney Schanberg column so distasteful to the city's real estate interests—was still condemning rent control. One of many *Times* editorials defending the rights of landlords in 1988 managed to blame government regulations for housing shortages and homelessness. Yet, as Smith says, "It was the outmigration of capital—by banks, landlords, homeowners and other lenders—that led to neighborhood decline in the first place."

Hang in there—the economy will improve. In the meantime, some of us will just have to grit our teeth and bear it.

"Our economic problems are stubborn, but not as stubborn as they often seem," columnist Robert J. Samuelson advised *Newsweek*'s readership. "Some have solutions, and some solve themselves. We can reduce inflation. Although the cure (a recession) is painful, it works and the pain isn't permanent." Someone like Samuelson, who began working as an economics reporter for the *Washington Post* in 1969, might find it easy to conclude that unemployment for others is a "cure" that "works." But millions of people, with their lives badly harmed by joblessness, might be surprised to hear that "the pain isn't permanent."

Evidently, the wealthier one is, the easier it is to find silver linings. In mid-1989, the editor-in-chief of the Hearst Newspapers, William Randolph Hearst Jr., wrote in his weekly column that "the prophets of doom and gloom never seem to tire of underestimating the basic economic strength of this great country of ours." The son of Citizen Hearst cited recent financial news he deemed favorable, and then added: "All this is gratifying to me because I have been consistently optimistic about our economy." If you were so rich you might be consistently optimistic about our economy too.

On the whole, big business deserves public trust.

Most Americans don't seem happy with the extent of corporate power. A 1989 Harris Poll found that 69 percent of people in the U.S. agreed that business had "too much power over too many aspects of American life."

Public opinion would be even more lopsided if mass media bothered to provide anything approaching balanced reporting of economic issues. "They just don't bother to quote, much less feature, critics of business," says Doug Henwood of the *Left Business Observer*. Instead, the array of widely-publicized opinion is so narrow that congressional leaders from the Democratic Party are the only "opponents" of big business regularly presented.

Takeover experts are admirable financial wizards.

Much coverage of corporate takeover efforts is couched in terms of chivalry and knavery, with knights of the boardroom table squaring off in legendary battle.

"Nebraska investor Warren Buffett has come calling on the takeover battle-weary Gillette Co., playing the role of squire to the twice-targeted razor company," Associated Press reported. Going on to say that "analysts hailed the move," AP quoted an investment firm broker—"It's a masterstroke." As in the case of Buffett, many financiers highly-regarded in august investment circles get high marks from the press.

As for wheeler-dealers who wind up indicted, like Drexel Burnham Lambert junk bond whiz Michael Milken, they come across as bad apples in a fairly honest barrel. (As the *Washington Post* editorialized about the stock exchanges, "keeping the game clean is desperately important.") The direct victims of the vilified inside-traders of the late 1980s were other rich people—and hell hath no media fury like an elite stung.

"The Drexelites are a vulgar and greedy lot," commented Henwood, "but their crimes are nothing compared to the crimes committed by respectable bankers when they cash an interest check from a Third World debtor. *They* have blood on their hands." And left off the lists of parties aggrieved by the indicted are "workers and communities wrecked by the leveraging madness, and the economy at large, where risk of a deflationary debt-collapse has been greatly magnified."

Social Security is an economic drain.

In 1983, the media joined politicians in labeling a bill to cut back Social Security a "rescue move." But the resulting law—freezing the cost-of-living adjustment for six months, while raising payroll taxes and setting the retirement eligibility at age 67 instead of 65—was fiscally unnecessary. Former *New York Times* reporter John L. Hess contends that foes of Social Security have scored "wide success among reporters, but virtually none among voters." As the main pension program for Americans, Social Security "is beyond doubt the most popular government program." Yet this self-financed system gets lots of media flak.

A favorite line of attack has been the notion that rich retirees are milking Social Security. Yet without it, census data show, nearly half of elderly Americans would be below the poverty line. And, not counting Social Security, households with members 65 and older had a median income of $7,005 in 1986. Fully two-thirds of the nation's elderly recipients depend on Social Security for most of their income. However, journalists can be heard complaining that within a couple of years after retirement, beneficiaries have received more than they paid into Social Security; when Capitol Hill reporter Cokie Roberts made the complaint on ABC's *This Week With David Brinkley*, none of the assembled media sages differed with her. "This ignores the employers' matching share and 50 years or so of inflation and interest on the money paid in," says Hess. "Above all, it ignores that Social Security is an insurance program."

Social Security also gets blamed for contributing to the federal deficit. A 1988 column by *Times* economics expert Leonard Silk said that one of the prime causes of the deficit was "entitlement programs such as Social Security." But Hess points out that Social Security "has never cost the

Treasury a cent. In fact, it is a source of cheap credit to the Treasury, which acts as its banker..." Media do more to cover up than cover the implications of attacks on Social Security. As Hess observes, "to reduce the budget deficit by capping Social Security pensions should be understood as an effort to transfer the tax burden, still more, from the upper to the middle and lower brackets."

"The deficit" is preventing government from solving serious problems.

Under the headline "As World Changes, U.S. Leaders Paralyzed," the *Washington Post* published two front-page articles about the intractable federal budget deficit as autumn 1989 began. The stories barely mentioned the option of raising taxes for the rich, even though annual incomes of over $200,000 were being taxed at a mere 28 percent rate. And the stories skimmed over the government department with the highest bill—the Pentagon. *Post* reporter David Hoffman explained that "Bush has resisted any further cuts in defense spending because of uncertainty over the future of the Soviet Union's internal reform efforts and its foreign policy." Hoffman didn't mention that pressure from military contractors might also be a factor. By solemnly regurgitating the official rationale as if it were his own, he certainly was not jeopardizing his good relations with White House sources.

For all the clucking and moaning about federal budget woes, it was not quite a hot topic on the Tube, as *Washington Monthly* magazine enumerated in an article about Ted Koppel and ABC's *Nightline*: "While the administration and Congress added $1.6 trillion to our children's IOUs, Koppel devoted exactly six shows out of 1,850 to the topic [of the national debt]... During the same period, the World According to *Nightline* included eight shows on strange animals and another eight on either fatness or hair loss. It offered nine on Elvis, rock 'n' roll and video."

KEEPING LABOR IN ITS PLACE

As a reporter covering labor for the *Washington Post*, Peter Perl gained admittance to a $325-a-day seminar on how to bust up unions. He was surprised to find that out of 30 participants, four were vice presidents or managers of the newspaper he worked for. The founder of the firm running the anti-union seminars told Perl that the *Post* was "a leader in this field."

What *Washington Post* bosses did to press operators, breaking their union in 1975, served as a model for media owners. Fifteen years later, unionized *Post* employees including hundreds of reporters were acutely aware that the newspaper's management continued to get its way at the bargaining table. The *Post* hierarchy showed no sign of backing away from active hostility toward unionism in its own news and advertising departments, where conditions for clerical workers remained bleak. "Most of the labor issues I wrote about of employers abusing employees can be found in [the *Post*] building in the commercial departments," said Perl. "Workers here are computer monitored, their lives are harassed by supervisors, they're unfairly discharged, and they are victims of punitive absentee policies."

And while the *Post* waxes on about the importance of free speech, independent journalist David Moberg discovered, "The fear that being pro-union hurts one's career has a chilling effect on *Post* workers. There are many cases of lower-level employees who claim they were squeezed out of jobs for joining a union demonstration, being quoted by another newspaper criticizing the *Post*, or signing a union lawsuit."

Eager to tame the power of unions they face in negotiations, most media owners are hardly enthusiastic about labor power as a general concept. In its September 1989 editorial endorsing Mayor Ed Koch for reelection, the *New York Times* specified its priorities. It was, said the great gray newspaper, a "tormenting" choice between Koch and David Dinkins, who "has the temperament to soothe the city." On the other hand, Koch had something even better—demonstrated hostility to unions: "Mr. Koch, while provocative, has proved his ability to run the city, facing up to truculent special interests." And who were *they*? "The city is still paying for unreasonably generous labor settlements that City Hall negotiated with municipal unions in the 60's," the editorial went on. Fortunately, Koch "restored stability to the city after the fiscal crisis and imposed discipline on city services and unions... His record shows he can hold the line on labor contracts..."

Most of the nation's editorial writers are of a similar bent on the need to "hold the line on labor contracts." A *Los Angeles Times* survey found that in business-labor disputes, 54 percent of newspaper editors said they generally took business' side while only seven percent sided with labor.

Labor on the decline

Concerned with labor costs, big media owners are hardly unhappy about the decline of union strength in the United States. By the end of the 1980s only 17 percent of American workers were union members—down from 40 percent in 1956. But "the decline of labor went largely unnoticed, particularly in the media," says *Washington Post* reporter Thomas Byrne Edsall. "As the power of organized labor in the United States fell, the interest of the press shifted elsewhere. In a direct reflection of the importance attached to the trade union movement, the assignment to cover labor—the labor beat—on many newspapers, which had been a high-status assignment in the heyday of labor's prestige...has been relegated to much lower status, and in many cases has been eliminated altogether."

In the society at large, Brooklyn's Auxiliary Bishop Joseph Sullivan stated in 1989, "Workers are measurably worse off than they were ten years ago."

Such a blunt declaration is far from common in mass media. "We don't get much coverage of basic conditions that working people are living with," says Laura McClure, a journalist specializing in labor issues. "Nowadays you have to have two wage earners to support a family in most cases. Cost of living allowances are usually no longer part of people's package deal from their employer, so wages are just continually dropping in value. Even though the majority of Americans are facing that situation, it's not something that you can pick up the *New York Times* and read about. In general it seems like the mainstream media try to present this as a period of prosperity."

It's no coincidence that prosperous people are usually the ones who provide "expert" commentary on TV news programs. The results can be ludicrous. "I get so annoyed," Barbara Ehrenreich remarked, "if I turn on one of the public affairs talk shows on TV and see usually four white men, well-dressed—I'm sure they earn close to six figures a year—pontificating on...the minimum wage. Now, none of them have been close to the minimum wage since they were paper boys. Why don't they have someone on who's trying to support a family on the minimum wage?"

As for joblessness, news reports routinely understate it. Not counted in the most publicized index of unemployment are "discouraged workers"—people who've given up on finding work—as well as part-time employees seeking full-time jobs. The Labor Department compiles quarterly totals that include such people. But, as we noted in Chapter Three, media concentrate on the lower "unemployment rate" announced by the Bureau of Labor Statistics.

Workplace safety

Media tend to depict trade unions as little more than power blocs and bargaining units. Yet, in the words of activist Roberta Lynch, "there is in unions of every variety a wealth of experience worthy of wider public attention. Local union members who know more than epidemiologists about cancer patterns. Union stewards who blow the whistle on secret hazardous waste disposal. Women in chemical factories who know first-hand the potential for causing birth defects of many commonly used manufacturing substances..." Workers who encounter toxic substances on the job are the first and the heaviest exposed. When journalism ignores grievances about unhealthy work environments, in effect an early-warning system for society as a whole has been short circuited. Workers' afflictions—from exposure to asbestos, radiation, fiberglass, chemical fumes and the like—spread to the broader population as carcinogenic substances pollute the air, water and soil.

In 1989, the National Safe Workplace Institute—concluding that "other industrialized nations have far superior job-safety and health records than those of the U.S."—reported an annual American death toll of 10,700 employees killed by workplace accidents, a figure that did not include traffic deaths on the job. But sudden mishaps are only part of the problem. More insidious hazards include chemicals and radioactivity. Michael Parenti points out that every year "another 100,000 die prematurely and 400,000 become seriously ill from work-related diseases. Many, if not most, of these deaths and injuries occur because greater consideration is given by management to profits and production than to occupational safety and environmental standards. Yet these crimes are rarely defined and reported as crimes by the news media."

Efforts to avoid blaming management for job hazards can lead to remarkable convolutions. In November 1989, the *New York Times* outdid itself with a front-page headline—"Boom in the Poultry Business Brings More Worker Injuries: Demand for Chicken Drives Assembly Lines"—which made it sound like consumers were responsible for the upsurge of injuries to workers in poultry processing plants. Reporter Peter Applebome began by declaring that "Americans' growing appetite for chicken has produced...a workplace that labor leaders consider among the most injurious in the nation." While the article went on to explain that conditions at the plants were contributing to the injuries, the headline and lead-off theme blamed chicken-hungry Americans. *Remember: Skimming only headlines can be hazardous to comprehension.*

When employees go on strike, the news focus is likely to be on wages, with the top of the salary range often reported as though it were the average. Less mentioned are strikers' demands about health benefits, vacation time and sick leave. (Employers have created many job slots—temporary, part-time, contract work—that avoid paying benefits altogether.) As for working conditions, media are inclined to refer to them in passing, if at all. "You don't go on strike because you're greedy. You're risking your whole job, you're doing it because there's something really wrong. But that's not the way it's portrayed in the media," said Laura McClure, who was president of a clerical workers union local before covering labor issues for the weekly *Guardian* during the last half of the 1980s.

Treating foreign labor better than our own

The U.S. media have cheered on workers organizing in Communist countries, while turning a blind eye to the suppression of labor inside our own borders. In 1981—the same year that martial law clamped down on the fledgling Solidarity union in Poland—President Reagan fired more than 11,000 striking air-traffic controllers and crushed their union. Our media condemned the repression of labor in Poland, but didn't raise strong objections when leaders of the Professional Air Traffic Controllers Organization went to jail in chains.

Near the end of the decade, when coal miners went on strike in the Soviet Union, the *New York Times* reported that their work stoppage resulted in "widespread, generally sympathetic coverage of the strike by Soviet newspapers and television." Yet at the same time, here at home, U.S. mine workers were in the fourth month of a strike that had already caused them and their families to endure more than 2,500 arrests. (Media accounts routinely referred to the arrestees as men striking the mines; in fact, many were women.) The arrests resulted from their nonviolent civil disobedience, blocking company trucks. The United Mine Workers of America and its officials had been hit with fines of $4 million. The struggle was to save unionism in the coal fields, where the Pittston Coal Group was cutting health-care and retirement benefits—and where, in contrast to the past, most coal was being mined nonunion.

The Soviet coal strike was front-page news in the United States. The American coal strike wasn't. As columnist Alexander Cockburn observed in *The Nation*, media accounts of the U.S. strike "covered the 'violence' of the miners (rock throwing, destruction of property) without examining the economic and physical violence that is waged against the miners: no coverage of the danger of going down into the pits, where many miners die; of the conditions of poverty in which many of them live." When the National Labor Relations Board, hardly pro-union, finally declared that coal company owners had failed "to bargain collectively and in good faith," it was a dud of a story as far as media managers were concerned. "The major papers," Cockburn found, "said barely a word." On the main TV networks, the nightly newscasts devoted 36 minutes to the Soviet miners in eight days—twice the coverage of the U.S. miners' strike over a four-month period.

Doing interviews in Appalachia at the time, Laura McClure talked with miners and union supporters who were "absolutely livid" at the double standard. "They'd say, 'How come the papers are full of news about these Soviet miners? We support them—but what about us? The media defends people elsewhere but thinks it's OK to trample on the rights of workers here.' That was a really infuriating thing for a lot of people."

A grievous omission was the non-coverage of a remarkable event: For the first time in half a century, according to union observers, strikers occupied a U.S. industrial plant, ejecting scabs and halting production. The nonviolent occupation lasted four days, with 99 miners holed up inside the Pittston Company's coal-processing plant near Carbo, Virginia, while about 1,000 union supporters blocked the plant gates. The occupation went virtually unreported in American mass media.

There was some good coverage of the 1989 miners' strike against Pittston. In mid-June, on NPR, *All Things Considered* delved deeply into the conflict; the result was an excellent series of reports. But such exceptions contrasted with the dreary normalcy of cliché-ridden journalism looking askance at the miners' actions. It seemed difficult for the press to fathom modern-day labor militancy in the United States.

Corporate media's passion for union-busting

During the first year of the Bush presidency, mass media hardly objected when the U.S. government allowed tycoon Frank Lorenzo to use bankruptcy laws to bust unions at Continental Airlines. Nor did media cause a fuss when Bush departed from past presidential practice and refused to set legal mechanisms in motion for a cooling-off period requested by Eastern Airlines strikers. Although Lorenzo had alienated virtually his entire work force at Eastern, he retained loyal followers among mass media owners. When Lorenzo put out full-page ads attacking the Machinists Union, he didn't have to write much ad copy; he simply reprinted chunks of editorials from leading dailies—including "Labor Threatens the President," from the *New York Times*, which warned about the "cost of appeasing" labor. In four subsequent editorials, the *Times* accused labor of "threatening" President Bush, vital transport links, airline travelers and other carriers.

In the media picture, some strikers can quickly become invisible. The Eastern strike involved machinists, pilots and flight attendants. But news reports quickly zoomed in on the high-paid professionals, especially the pilots. "It's true they had more power than any of the other workers to make the company suffer," McClure recalled, "but there are more flight attendants than there are pilots, and flight attendants' starting salaries were like $12,000 a year, and their working conditions are terrible. Sometimes the media didn't even mention the fact that the flight attendants were on strike. It makes them feel like non-entities. They're out there on strike just like everybody else, and why don't they see themselves in the news media?"

Commonly enthusiastic about "cooperative" union approaches, the news media offer plenty of thinly-veiled advice about how unions must learn to be "mature" while avoiding confrontation. Typical was a lengthy *New York Times* article that appeared on the day when the one-million-member United Auto Workers union opened its triennial convention. "To cooperate with management or to confront?" asked the lead by reporter Doron P. Levin. The *Times'* preference was clear. The 24-paragraph article included only a single paragraph quoting a union "dissident"—even though the dissidents' challenge to the mainline leadership was the primary focus of the story. Those dissidents, the article explained, "pose a significant roadblock to the expansion of joint programs, a process that many experts say has enhanced the auto industry's competitiveness."

Plant shut-downs

A few days before Christmas 1988, the largest plant closing in Wisconsin history occurred. Some 5,500 Chrysler workers in Kenosha were suddenly jobless. The next day, the *New York Times*—evidently eager to find silver linings in the Rust Belt—reported that the closure was "occasion for surprising

expressions of relief and optimism in this industrial city on Lake Michigan."
An accompanying photo of a worker had the caption "I hated my job." The
newspaper quoted Kenosha Mayor Patrick Moran asserting, "Generally, I
don't think the town's too upset."

But Roger Bybee, editor of the Wisconsin weekly newspaper *Racine
Labor*, blasted the *Times* coverage for basic omissions: "This account of the
community mood neglected to mention a September 22 meeting where
[Mayor] Moran had to leave under heavy police escort because 2,000
autoworkers furiously objected to his unwillingness to sue Chrysler for
breach of contract." Bybee added that while the *Times* portrayed the closure
as an opportunity for self-determination and economic growth, the newspaper chose not to quote a single source with "an alternative explanation—that
it signaled the community's lack of control and powerlessness in the face of
Lee Iacocca and Chrysler."

The *Times* was part of the overall media pattern. "A community-wide disaster has been treated as a minor and momentary barrier to the affluence that
lies just over the horizon," said Bybee. His assessment: "Confronted with a
blatant example of corporate malfeasance, journalists failed to convey the
real picture of impoverishment that results when a factory town loses its
largest and highest paying employer."

When more Chrysler workers lost their jobs the following year, the press
was still more attentive to their employer. "Fresh evidence that the domestic
auto industry is sliding into a recession came yesterday, when Chrysler
announced that it was laying off more than 4,000 workers in three states and
permanently closing its oldest assembly plant in the heart of Detroit," said
the lead of a November 1989 *Los Angeles Times* article. With a different
journalistic approach, the story could have begun something like this: "More
than 4,000 auto workers in three states found themselves without jobs yesterday, as new layoffs by Chrysler provided fresh evidence that more working
people will suffer from a recession as winter sets in."

News coverage provides little affirmation for working people. It's routine
for employers to receive much more respectful treatment than employees do.
Rather than focus on the well-being of workers, mass media are busy doting
on the fortunes of corporations.

LOTS OF DOLLARS, BUT NOT MUCH SENSE

Fragmentation is part and parcel of the news media game. Reports of negative trends focus much more on victims than on institutional villains.
Economic adversities faced by family farmers, industrial workers or urban
dwellers are made to sound like the results of chance events. Manipulations
by big-money interests are apt to be mentioned obliquely—with
euphemisms—if at all. And when chronic social problems get a close look,

their causes usually come across as little more controllable than bolts from the blue.

News stories about family farmers, for instance, describe their love of the soil, changes in the weather, government subsidy policies and the like. To hear mass media tell it, lots of bad luck has been plaguing America's tillers of the earth. However, in real life, small farmers have been pushed off the land just as steadily as independent news outlets have fallen prey to media conglomerates. The same corporation that owns enormous farms can also process foods, package them, and operate supermarkets where they're sold. But, after decades of expansion by agribusiness, the tightening corporate hold on the nation's food supply still gets little media attention. Misfortunes of individual farmers are likely to be presented as sad occurrences—but not as economic squeeze plays by large growers, banks and realtors who benefit from farm foreclosures.

A simplistic urban outlook was being projected onto the country's heartland when the *New York Times* reported a story from Greenfield, Iowa, under the headline "Death Is as Capricious as Life for Farm Leader." Dixon Terry, a populist rural organizer, had been struck down by a lightning bolt. Terry was a third-generation farmer who "watched his own parents lose their farm in the economic collapse of the early 1980's," the *Times* recounted. Yet the newspaper was drawn to imagery of natural rather than economic adversity. The story's third paragraph read: "In the manner of his death, some saw a metaphor for the life of the American farmer, of the capriciousness of the forces of nature that rule his days."

Crisis in education

Whether reciting ills in the countryside or cities, the mass media do little more than note the continuing indices of social disaster. At decade's end, for example, the entire federal Education Department budget for a year, $22 billion, was not close to one-tenth of Pentagon outlays—although just about every news medium or politician has mouthed platitudes about the crucial importance of education for the future of America.

Children, we hear, are our most precious resources. And most of us seem to believe it. One 1989 poll found that two-thirds of the public "favored increasing spending on public schools, and nine in ten of that group said they would accept higher taxes to pay for it. Even adults without children in school backed greater spending by nearly two-to-one." Yet when President Bush balked at spending more federal funds for education, the press dutifully touted presidential verbiage as a meaningful substitute.

Media rarely have probed the human dimensions of spending priorities perpetuated by a man who'd promised to be the Education President. "Efforts begun more than ten years ago to equalize school funding between districts have been put on the back burner," Jonathan Kozol pointed out in

1989, "and are now replaced by strident exhortations to the poor to summon 'higher motivation' and, no matter how debilitated by disease or hunger, to 'stand tall.' Celebrities are hired to sell children on the wisdom of not dropping out of school. The White House tells them they should 'just say no' to the temptations of the streets."

While millions of teens leave high schools with needs unmet and often without diplomas, the media seem drawn more to mirages than remedies. TV networks and newsweeklies glorified New Jersey principal Joe Clark when he patrolled halls with a baseball bat in one hand and bullhorn in the other, as if kicking students out of schools might amount to a solution. Rather than focus on the lack of resources provided for education, the media are inclined to blame the victims, echoing widespread frustrations of a society beset with deep problems that afflict vulnerable young people.

Fair game for big corporations, children across the country may increasingly be subjected to commercially-sponsored national video broadcasts as part of their school days. Controversial plans by Whittle Communications (a division of Time Warner), aiming to sell ads on broadcasts fed directly into classrooms as part of curricula, set off some criticism. Whether in school or not, children are buffeted by the power of money.

Volunteers of America

In the late 1980s, U.S. officials escalated hype about voluntarism. A variety of private do-gooders were to rush where the government was unwilling to tread. A year after Bush won the presidency, the *Christian Science Monitor* published a news article headlined "A Thousand Points of Light to Shine." Shucking all sobriety at the outset, the lead declared: "President Bush's goal of promoting a 'thousand points of light' is beginning to shine." The reporter gushed that the approach "will heavily involve U.S. business, since the White House will be asking every commercial establishment to join voluntarily in efforts to find solutions for such problems as illiteracy, dropouts, drug abuse, unwed teen pregnancy, youth delinquency and suicide, AIDS, homelessness, hunger, unemployment, and loneliness."

In a nation ablaze with grave crises, the White House was piously urging citizens to fill their squirt guns and go after the infernos. The news media were willing conscripts in the chief executive's propaganda army. As the *Monitor* reported, "the President's program will rely heavily on the cooperation of the media. It calls for every television and radio station, cable system, newspaper, magazine, and other media institution to promote community service 'relentlessly' as a national ethic, spotlighting successful service initiatives, profiling outstanding community leaders and institutions, and informing the public of how to get involved in community service."

The scheme was off to a good start, the newspaper went on. "Already each of the three television networks has agreed to weave the theme of community service as a way to tackle social problems into the plots of some of their top-rated shows during three weeks in December. The combined audience of these shows is 290 million people." (Apparently some super-patriotic couch potatoes could be relied upon to watch more than once.) Such an approach, while no doubt involving many sincere people, was calculated to let the country's fat-cats and their government allies off the hook.

The voluntary nature of the whole setup guaranteed that the powerless and unfortunate would remain so—at the mercy of beneficence—subject to the ebb and flow of charity resources, shifting interests and the restless media spotlight that could popularize "community service" one season and desert it the next. Even as media blathered about the "thousand points of light" in action, on the eve of Thanksgiving 1989, a nationwide network of food banks reported a substantial drop in donations to feed the hungry. Corporations, perhaps due to effects of mergers and leveraged buyouts, had cut back on contributions of food for the needy—while federal program reductions had accounted for a drop of 75 million meals for the poor.

All in all, the thousand points of light would be no match for the nation's millions of points of blight. But the twinkling rhetoric would distract from demands for substantive government action. Media owners and their corporate colleagues had good reasons to prefer volunteer scenarios, popular among the well-off since the days when tycoons like John D. Rockefeller got their pictures taken while giving shiny new dimes to little children. In the words of Stephen M. Wolf, the CEO of United Airlines, "in corporate America, economic reality often limits generosity. However, there is another option whose power to get things done is enormous—voluntarism... With each individual personally committed to doing something more than simply going about the business of the day, there is no limit to what can be accomplished."

Such words may seem benign, but they are much to do about doing next-to-nothing—fiddling with rhetoric while social problems burn. Mass media owners join in extolling altruism—in forms that will not threaten company profits. Voluntarism may suit them just fine. But as a potential solution it is, in essence, a hoax. "The much publicized volunteer literacy movement promoted for the last six years by Barbara Bush serves only 200,000 of the nation's estimated 30 million functional illiterates," says Kozol, who adds that "hope cannot be marketed as easily as blue jeans. Certain realities—race and class and caste—are there and they remain."

Savings and Loan boondoggle

Media failures had high financial costs for American society during the late 1980s. For years the warning signals were profuse that a bipartisan phalanx of officials in Washington were colluding with wealthy financiers to loot the national system of Savings and Loans. But the banking industry as a whole got little media scrutiny. In Texas, several years before the collapse of many of the state's financial institutions, a brief exception led to swift enforcement of the rule. Shortly after the *Dallas Morning News* disclosed the dire straits of a floundering bank, the newspaper's management fired the reporter who wrote the article, Earl Golz, and forced the resignation of the editor who okayed it. But blaming the journalists for the bad news did not prevent the bank from failing within two weeks. Afterwards, neither journalist was rehired.

Finally roused when the S&L ship foundered, a drowsy media establishment then featured expert commentary from many of the same quarters that had allowed the debacle to occur in the first place. "The background to the S&L scandal is rarely mentioned in media accounts, which rely on pro-deregulation mainstream economists, government officials and self-serving industry reps as sources," says Patrick Bond, economics correspondent for noncommercial Pacifica Radio News.

In early winter of 1989, a two-month study of network news detected the extent of the bias. "Of 80 on-air sources asked by the three nightly news broadcasts for their views on S&Ls between mid-December and mid-February, three-fourths were government officials and one-fourth were financial industry spokespersons or private analysts," Bond reported. "No public interest spokespersons were given an opportunity to comment on the problem."

The S&L crisis festered in an atmosphere encouraging financial speculation while calling for less federal regulation. Journalists belatedly blamed the Reagan administration—but many had been promoting a see-no-evil approach as late as Reagan's last year in office. Major newspapers were so supportive of bank deregulation proposals in 1988 that an official of the American Bankers Association claimed that out of editorials in 150 newspapers on the subject, all but ten were in favor of deregulation. "Letting [banks] diversify into additional kinds of businesses will improve stability," the *Washington Post* editorialized. "Banks need expanded powers to compete fairly in a vastly changed financial landscape," opined the *Baltimore Evening Sun*. And the *Boston Herald* was indignant: "No other country on earth strangles its banks with so many restrictions and prohibitions."

Once the Savings and Loan disaster became unmistakable, media singled out federal administrators, politicians and financial speculators as culprits. Rather than probing deeper implications of such extensive corporate clout in government agencies, the press was much more inclined to villainize specific officials, with some explicit victim-blaming tossed in for good measure. *Newsweek* economics columnist Jane Bryant Quinn wrote that the American public "is not so innocent. During the 1980s, we've happily fattened our savings accounts on the high rates of interest paid by insolvent S&Ls... Now we're being asked to give some of those unearned profits back. Rough justice, I'd say." In essence, Quinn was blaming average citizens—for keeping money in savings accounts!

Despite the magnitude of the rip-off, media avoided raising fundamental questions. "In general," Bond noted, "populist or anti-corporate perspectives were submerged beneath a chorus of 'expert' analysis which begins and ends with two crucial assumptions: 1) the taxpayers are going to foot the bill; and 2) the problem can be isolated and solved merely by throwing money around and tinkering with the regulatory apparatus."

In summer 1989, as Congress and the White House approved a "bailout" committing the government to spend at least $164 billion during the next decade to assist a thrift industry on the rocks, the press again proved much more interested in cheerleading than whistleblowing. A *New York Times* editorial praised "a promising plan to rid the industry of its rot and set surviving S&L's on a sounder path." The *Washington Post* hailed "an impressive achievement. It provides substantial assurance that this immensely expensive assault on the U.S. Treasury won't be repeated." Such plaudits kept ignoring what the mass media had been failing to highlight all year: There were alternatives to the pro-rich bias of the prevailing bailout scenario.

Instead of sticking average taxpayers with long-term costs including massive bills on interest, a quick step-up of tax rates for the wealthy and corporations could have raised $50 billion in three years, thus avoiding long-term debt. But, in the offices of journalists and politicians, a near-consensus throttled debate. ABC, CBS and NBC evening news programs, the *New York Times* and the *Washington Post* all refused to say a word about a "Report to U.S. Taxpayers on the Savings and Loan Crisis" released by Ralph Nader—who contended that the S&L bailout should be financed by economic strata benefitting from high-finance speculation, not by poor and middle-class taxpayers uninvolved in such high-roller maneuvers. The *Wall Street Journal* managed nine paragraphs on the Nader plan; *MacNeil/Lehrer NewsHour* aired a sound bite that lasted 15 seconds. A parallel attack on the S&L bailout by the "Financial Democracy Campaign"—a coalition of over 100 consumer, housing, community and women's organizations—netted little more than brief wire service stories.

With the bailout iced, National Public Radio was explaining that the legislation would "rescue hundreds of ailing thrifts." An NPR reporter extended the medical metaphor so popular in media coverage of the S&L bailout: "As the bill that legislators hope will be the cure for the Savings and Loan crisis moves to the floors of both houses of Congress, the patient remains bruised and battered. Hundreds of Savings and Loans have already died. Hundreds more are on the verge, waiting for emergency help..." In response to the mission of mercy, bargain-hungry investors licked their lips, and promptly began wolfing down S&Ls at cut-rate prices—a story that media did little to illuminate.

HUD and public housing

In 1989, after snoozing through several years of improprieties at the Department of Housing and Urban Development, mass media belatedly chronicled the costly fiasco at HUD. But coverage was inadequate when it came to connecting the scandal with the Reagan administration's hostility to public housing—and the reality that influence-peddling had stolen housing aid from poor and moderate-income Americans. Few journalists linked the HUD scandal to the profusion of homelessness at the same time corruption was milking precious federal housing funds.

By mid-1989, a theme of renewal was canned and on the media shelf: The new HUD secretary Jack Kemp, as *Newsweek* phrased the common acclaim, "has earned high marks for his candor and swift attention to the crisis." The press generally failed to spotlight Kemp's congressional past—which included recent votes against aid to the homeless and in favor of cutting budgets for several HUD housing programs. With Kemp's avid support, the Reagan presidency oversaw the slashing of $24 billion in federal housing funds.

Glowing accounts of Kemp's commitment to public housing were widespread. Media paid little heed to critics like Florence W. Roisman, a Washington attorney representing advocates of housing for the poor: "There's nothing in Kemp's record that causes me anything but deep concern. If selling off public housing is his primary legislative achievement in this field, then that's not going to help many public housing tenants. It would reduce the stock of affordable housing that is available to low-income people."

Kemp proceeded to start shutting down tainted HUD housing programs. Mainstream journalists depicted his role as salutary, and rarely probed the Bush administration's approach of providing some low-income people with HUD-financed "vouchers" to give to landlords in place of rent. "Any serious public housing program should be looking at alternatives to the market, not to new strategies for fattening the wallets of slumlords," commented *Left Business Observer* editor Doug Henwood. But with all the media outrage over HUD, little was left for victims of the government's standard not-so-benign neglect. Census Bureau figures pegged eight million renting households below the poverty level. Their average rent was 65 percent of income. Above the poverty line, the situation was also deplorable, with one-fifth of renting households giving more than half their incomes for rent.

Isn't housing a human right?

In the United States, mass media and federal government alike do not recognize housing as a human right—although the principle is articulated by the United Nations in the Universal Declaration of Human Rights. "Of the devel-

oped nations, the U.S. is by far the most egregious violator of the internationally recognized right to housing," contend Rutgers professor Neil Smith and
attorney Maureen O'Conner.

Local media tend to fret about the unsightliness of the homeless—bad for
business, unsafe or distasteful for shoppers—more than the suffering of the
homeless themselves. A front-page *New York Times* article supplied an acute
angle for looking down on the Big Apple's less fortunate, observing that
"aggressive panhandling" was "eroding the quality of life." Associated Press
put a long story on its national wire about "the predicament of fast-food
restaurants, which have become beacons for the homeless." Explained AP:
"The welcome ends if owners think the restaurant is becoming a stopgap
shelter for stinky transients." Owners do not "want their family atmosphere
disrupted by shabby creatures, sometimes lugging all their worldly possessions in shopping bags and carts."

In the summer of 1989, the *San Francisco Chronicle* reported that homelessness might be causing the fall-off of business at major hotels, and thus
was "starting to threaten the $3 billion [tourism] industry, the city's largest."
A week later, syndicated columnist Ellen Goodman described a disagreeable
visit to the city of brotherly love. At a "posh and pleasant urban space,"
Philadelphia's Rittenhouse Square, she counted "one, two, three outstretched
hands, open palms." Later, en route to a party, she found that "at every other
corner of the high-rent district there is a young man with a paper cup."

Goodman lamented that "the beggars break into the consciousness of the
middle class and confront us with poverty and drug abuse... Today, at least,
this tourist walking from one block to another, one cup to another, one city to
another wants to join in a citizens' chorus. 'Enough's enough.'" (Not enough
poverty, but enough of its visibility.) With apparent satisfaction, Goodman
noted that during her visit the *Philadelphia Inquirer* had editorialized that
"citizens should stop giving money to panhandlers and the city should adopt
a policy against sleeping on the streets."

Those are the kind of "solutions" we might expect from mass media that
accept the vast disparities of poverty and wealth in our society. Such biases
in favor of the status quo help to perpetuate widespread deprivation. And, as
the next chapter discusses, similar media biases are increasing the likelihood
that ominous environmental trends will continue to assault human health and
the planet's ecological balance.

8

Unhealthy Reporting

I n recent years, many people have become aware that intricate ecological webs, once ravaged, cannot be replaced like so many back-ordered gadgets. We cannot manufacture another Alaska coastline. Or another food chain. Or replacement genes for living beings.

Shouldn't our media serve as frontline survival mechanisms, warning us of dangers to personal and global health? As a general rule, though, American journalism has been much better at pointing to environmental victims than culprits. Even when responsibility would seem to be clear, corporate biggies usually slide right off the media hook.

Although the lethal impacts of corporate wrongdoing seem difficult for many journalists to grasp, or at least report, the actions of a lone nut are likely to be a different story. In October 1982, when several people died because somebody put poison into Tylenol capsules sold in stores, the media responded with huge coverage. Yet the same media shrugged off a much larger number of deaths (27 in the U.S. and 97 elsewhere) caused by Eli Lilly, the pharmaceutical giant, when it marketed the Oraflex "anti-arthritis pill." In 1981, the Food and Drug Administration allowed Oraflex on the market, despite an earlier FDA report indicating that Lilly was hiding data on the drug's dangerous side effects.

As Michael Parenti observed, "Clearly here was a sensational story of mass murder and skulduggery, of possible corporate malfeasance and government collusion, yet the press did not bother with it. Why the difference in handling the two stories? The Tylenol killings seemed to have been the work of deranged persons; the corporate manufacturers (and advertisers) could not be blamed. Therefore, the story was not only simple and sensational, but safe, free of any criticism of the marketing ethics of drug advertisers and of big business in general—which was not the case with Oraflex."

In reporting on matters of health and the environment, a number of media fallacies are repetitious:

- *Costly health:* A slant placing higher priority on short-term corporate profits than on long-term health consequences for humans and other life forms.
- *Staying superficial:* Instead of probing key factors responsible for widespread environmental ills, the news frame tightly constricts the picture, while protecting big business and/or government agencies by blurring their accountability for scandalous behavior.

201

- *Ecosystem-as-Monosystem:* Discussing a single part of the environment as an end in itself—without considering that all parts of an ecosystem are reliant upon each other and that damage to one part brings harm to others.
- *Not you:* A theme that presents environmental issues as concerns of a very specific area or group—even though the implications are actually broad.
- *Labeling:* A technique for discrediting the opinions of individuals opposed to government or corporate actions, by affixing a label that classifies them as outside the country's mainstream.

Loaded language can easily tilt environmental coverage. In December 1989, for example, *NBC Nightly News* ran a story on two brothers in California; one farmed with pesticides and the other used organic, chemical-free methods. Presented as a human interest story about a feud between siblings, the report noted that organic farming techniques required more work, but cost less and actually netted more per acre than fields doused with pesticides. But the closing lines imparted a curious angle to the news report, describing the brother who used pesticides as a "traditionalist," in contrast to the organic farmer. Apparently, Indians and European pioneers who farmed without chemicals are not part of the American tradition.

While the media occasionally spotlight harmful pesticides and government bureaucrats who are supposed to regulate them, the corporations that manufacture chemicals and profit from pollution don't often come under close journalistic scrutiny. Some big-name reporters have even jumped on the toxic bandwagon, lending their prestige to enhance the image of chemical polluters. Once called "the most trusted man in America," Walter Cronkite—former anchor (and later a board member) at CBS—was paid $25,000 to narrate a pro-pesticide documentary, "Big Fears, Little Risks," which aired on PBS stations in the summer of 1989. Under the sponsorship of the American Council on Science and Health, an industry-backed group, the film was indirectly funded by pesticide-makers Dow and Monsanto. Cronkite read a script dismissing consumer fears of carcinogenic pesticides as "chemophobia."

RADIATION IN THE NEIGHBORHOOD

In late 1988, the American media began to focus on major problems at nuclear warhead production plants in the United States. Suddenly the topic of radioactive dangers from making the Bomb was big news. Journalists cited numerous examples of mismanagement and deceit by private contractors and the federal government—along with dramatic signs that radioactive releases were continuing to jeopardize public health in communities across the U.S.

Some observers believed that the mass media and the nation were finally about to face up to realities of health hazards from making nuclear bombs.

A year later, little had changed. Nor was any significant change on the horizon. The official scandal had served its purpose, providing assurances of "reform" while avoiding any fundamental challenge to the basic bomb-making system. From Fernald in Ohio to Rocky Flats in Colorado, from Savannah River in South Carolina to Hanford in Washington state, the Energy Department's thermonuclear bomb factories continued to comprise local hazards and global threats. The publicity had subsided, but the dangers had not. How could that be?

Although a few radiation victims in downwind communities received some empathetic publicity, the klieg lights came to settle mostly on outraged members of Congress and a new layer of top bureaucrats vowing to clean house at the U.S. Department of Energy. Mass media isolated discrete "issues," separating the topics of nuclear bomb output and deployment policies. Safeguarding our environment at home could have dovetailed nicely with enhancing international security through halting the arms race and cutting nuclear arsenals. Instead, the key issue of the news coverage stayed narrow: How do we clean up and modernize our weapons production system?

News media highlighted efforts to update an antiquated weapons assembly line. As the officially-authorized scandal broke in October 1988, the *Washington Post* led off front-page coverage by referring to the Energy Department's "struggle to maintain production of bomb materials in its aging weapons complex." The spin was that big bucks would solve the problem. The "Week in Review" section of the *New York Times* featured a map of nuclear warhead plants with a caption of lamentation—"All the sites are old...and for many years, their managers say, the Government provided little money for maintenance, let alone improvements."

Much more journalistic empathy was devoted to nuclear managers and warhead production timelines than to the human gene pool's vulnerability to irreversible mutations. And heightened risks of cancer, leukemia and genetic damage from massive radioactive emissions, past and ongoing, were emphasized more as impediments to meeting bomb production schedules than as crucial issues in their own right. The need to continue the manufacture of nuclear bombs went unquestioned.

Deadly emissions

From the outset, most coverage stuck to faulting the federal government's nuclear overlords for a job not well done. During the same week that *Time* magazine chided them for "complacency, recklessness and secrecy," *Newsweek*'s thesaurus came up with "negligence, incompetence and deliberate deception." The *Washington Post* quickly editorialized that nuclear bomb plants "can't be allowed to remain down indefinitely." Meanwhile, U.S.

officials claimed the only alternative to continued warhead production would
be "unilateral disarmament," and journalists dutifully took up the cry. *Wall
Street Journal* reporter Paulette Thomas, appearing on PBS's program
Washington Week in Review, warned that failure to restart the military reactors would mean "unilateral disarmament." Her colleagues around the table
didn't question this assessment. Media-authorized "critics" sang the same
tune, keeping the scandal within proper bounds.

Spokespersons from anti-nuclear groups were, as usual, excluded. Thus
few Americans heard experts like Samuel H. Day Jr., former editor of the
Bulletin of the Atomic Scientists, who told us, "News reports haven't made
any connections between local environmental problems and the overall threat
posed by the weapons themselves." Day, co-director of the Nukewatch organization, added that "these facilities are inherently hazardous and inherently
prone to fall apart due to the corrosive nature of radioactive materials."

Much of the information about problems at nuclear bomb factories came
not from a vigorous press, but rather from the digging of labor unions, community activists, independent health researchers and congressional investigators. Evidence about enormous emissions of deadly radioactive isotopes from
the Savannah River Plant, for example, was available in federal document
repositories for a half-dozen years before it first appeared in mainstream
media in autumn 1988.

The spate of stories was very shocking—but only to the extent that the public had been ill-served by media in the past. The press covered itself by rewriting history. A front-page *New York Times* piece by Fox Butterfield—after
mentioning a 1970 study that found alarming plutonium levels in the Denver
area due to emissions from the nearby Rocky Flats plant—jumped over a
decade-and-a-half and declared: "Although the study attracted some attention
at the time, only in the last two or three years has public concern about Rocky
Flats become widespread in this area as a result of a number of problems."

Butterfield and the *Times* ignored a long record of public concern and scientific documentation. During the late 1970s, protest rallies near Rocky Flats
drew tens of thousands of people denouncing the plant's plutonium releases.
Nonviolent civil disobedience frequently resulted in hundreds of arrests. By
1980, Dr. Carl Johnson, then director of the Health Department of Jefferson
County (which encompasses the Rocky Flats plant), had linked the radioactive
releases to elevated cancer rates in the most heavily-contaminated neighborhoods.

The *Times* headlined Butterfield's page-one article "Dispute on Wastes
Poses Threat to Weapons Plant." Two days later, Butterfield reported more
details on this nuclear "threat"—writing that Idaho's refusal to accept more
of Rocky Flats' nuclear waste "has posed a serious threat to the continued
operations of Rocky Flats." First and foremost, the *plant* was threatened;
threats to people's health were secondary.

News magazines, complete with photos of real people living in the shadow of nuclear arms plants, did a better job of exploring the human dimensions of the scandal, but neglected to include alternative policy options. *Time*'s cover story, titled "They Lied to Us," seemed particularly schizoid—reporting that "for many, the invisible nature of radiation does stir emotions and feed paranoic imaginations," and then claiming "there is no undisputed evidence that radioactive materials released into the environment around DOE [Department of Energy] facilities have harmed anyone." The hedge word, *undisputed*, rendered the ludicrous statement technically correct. After all, when does the evidence against official power *ever* go undisputed?

Time quoted a nuclear industry apologist, Jacob Fabrikant, identified only as "an expert on the biological effects of radiation," saying that off-site contamination levels were "far too low to pose a risk to the health of individuals." Like most media, *Time* left unchallenged the notion that there is a "threshold" of radiation dosage that entails no risk—a concept with very little credence among modern health physicists.

Institutional sin and redemption

No official scandal is complete without high-profile redemption. While beginning to report on the scope of nuclear bomb-makers' sins, the media also seemed eager to bring tidings of repentance. *Time* revealed that the Department of Energy "finally seems bent on reform" and "has taken commendable steps to infuse a safety-conscious attitude at the weapons facilities." That "safe nuclear weapons production" might be an oxymoron was a concept off-limits to mass media.

Officials' public self-flagellations were taken at face value. The *Washington Post* front-paged a contrite quote from a DOE undersecretary, "We have a moral obligation to rectify past sins." The *New York Times* asserted that "the Energy Department has provided a candid account of its failings." That the DOE's effusive mea culpas might have any motive other than penance and nuclear safety was rarely suggested. Yet an underlying goal of the agency's PR strategy was to wrest major appropriations for nuclear weapons plants—reinvestments in the arms race under the guise of responding to safety concerns.

Politicians and media alike took to calling for a "cleanup" of the nation's 17 major nuclear bomb production sites in a dozen states. (Less often mentioned were 72 other badly-contaminated sites, presumably incidental since they were inactive and therefore would not be a drag on future bomb-making.) Some journalists with reputations as top-notch science writers were among the worst purveyors of illusions. Matthew L. Wald began a news article in the *New York Times* by discussing the ecosystem as though it were a mechanical device due for an overhaul. He referred to "the meager resources the federal government has devoted to repairing environmental damage at nuclear weapons plants." In the next ten paragraphs he used the words "cleanup" or "cleaning up" eight different times. It was familiar yet absurd language, denying key realities: After radioactive elements enter the food chain, they cannot be retrieved from soil, water, plants, animals or people.

The *Times* tried to be dramatic yet reassuring. A front-page headline in December 1988 declared "Wide Threat Seen in Contamination at Nuclear Units"—yet a subheadline credulously stated that "No Effect on Humans Has Yet Been Found." The *Times* was simply regurgitating the gibberish of federal bomb-makers, whose new report stated that nuclear facilities "pose serious threats to public health"—yet at the same time claimed that there was no evidence of "any harm to people from the byproducts of four decades of weapon production and research." The account was illogical—and contradicted by voluminous health studies.

The bomb complex

Two days later, a *Times* editorial, titled "The Bomb on Mr. Bush's Desk," urged the incoming President to "escape catastrophe by moving fast and setting priorities." But the "catastrophe" that the *Times* was so concerned about had nothing to do with links between radioactive emissions and cancer, leukemia and genetic damage. Nor did it have to do with the dangers of nuclear war exacerbated by perpetual bomb production. No, the "catastrophe" that the *Times* was intent on avoiding was the prospect that the government's ability to manufacture more nuclear weapons might be impeded by a shortage of tritium, a radioactive element needed for nuclear warheads. With "the operation of the bomb complex" at risk (the psychological connotation of the word "complex" was apparently inadvertent), the *Times* concluded that "Mr. Bush has only a limited time to avert its collapse."

Like the editorial, a followup top-of-page-one article by *Times* reporter Michael R. Gordon laid out in detail (as the headline put it) "How a Vital Nuclear Material Came to Be in Short Supply." It was the type of tunnel vision equally appreciated in editorial suites at the *Times* and in the Pentagon. The need for more tritium—a key nuclear weapons ingredient—was a given, its assumed shortage bemoaned. A contrary view got half a paragraph out of 43: "Not everyone is convinced that the shortage of tritium is a national emergency. Some critics of the Administration say the United States could afford dismantling some nuclear weapons to salvage the tritium it needs. But the Administration rejects this idea…" It was vintage national security reporting, with dissenting views mentioned only long enough to be dismissed as irrelevant to the subject at hand.

The nuclear priesthood

When a new cleric of the nuclear priesthood—Energy Secretary James Watkins—arrived on the scene in Washington, promising deliverance from past sins, mass media faithful were quick to laud him. Watkins' refrain of "safety first" fell on the appreciative ears of editors who were worried that negative public perceptions of the nuclear arms production line could slow it down or even stop it. A June 1989 *Washington Post* editorial hailed Secretary Watkins as one hell of a guy. "He set out a program of reforms that, judged by the history of the institution, are astounding. Safety and environmental protection will now come before weapons production." A month later, when the *MacNeil/Lehrer NewsHour* aired a 12-minute interview with Watkins, Jim Lehrer explained that the Energy Secretary had just "announced a \$20 billion five-year plan to clean up environmental and safety problems at the nation's 17 major nuclear weapons plants." Watkins put in a charming performance that advanced his goal stated early in the interview: "I think that what we're going to have now is the potential to convince the American people that we're credible."

Mass media seemed determined to make him so. The summer continued with gushes of publicity about the refreshing Admiral-turned-Energy-Secretary who was making such articulate noises about, at last, putting safety ahead of schedules for manufacturing warheads. The media applauded Watkins' rhetoric—but were considerably less attentive when, on September 7, 1989, the Energy Department issued a brief public statement that Watkins had approved plans to re-open a tritium-producing reactor before the end of 1990. In the words of a *New York Times* article, "the department refused to commit itself to completing safety testing or an environmental analysis before reopening the South Carolina plant." But the story was a blip on the screen, disappearing quickly, since it did not fit in with the by-then-established theme of Watkins the marvelous reformer, dedicated to making the nation safe for producing more nuclear weaponry.

Agencies overseeing the nuclear bomb production cycle had always claimed to be solicitous about public health. Across the country, clusters of cancer and other radiation-linked illnesses had been showing up in above-average proportions downwind and downriver of nuclear facilities. But Watkins' new promises were given enormous credence by news media apparently tiring of the topic as a major focus.

A segment on ABC *World News Tonight* concluded that a new agreement on monitoring the plutonium-triggers fabrication plant in Colorado meant that "future contamination should be diminished if not altogether cut at Rocky Flats." Meanwhile, the government was redoubling its commitment to making nuclear weapons, amid a proliferation of soothing assurances. Watkins liked to describe the "cleanup" as bolstering the mission of maintaining a "nuclear deterrent." News media, accordingly, treated nuclear bomb production as an ongoing necessity. In mid-1989, *Time* magazine set the framework for an update on nuclear arms plant hazards with this lead sentence: "For 40 years the nation's nuclear weaponry has provided enough security to allow Americans to sleep better at night."

Nevada test site cover-up

In autumn 1989, the abysmal situation at Rocky Flats resulted in a change of contractors. The new firm hired by the Energy Department, EG&G Inc., was praised as a company with a fine track record running a few other nuclear weapons operations. "An Energy official said the firm has compiled a good environmental record at those places," the *Washington Post* reported, citing no contrary view. The *Christian Science Monitor* followed suit, explaining that an Energy Department spokesperson said the agency "has never had any environmental problems at EG&G-run facilities." Whether through laziness or bias, neither newspaper gave readers so much as a hint of the horrible ecological damage actually caused by those "EG&G-run facilities." For instance, the Nevada Test Site—managed by EG&G since it opened in 1951—was severely poisoned with radioactivity and other dangerous wastes. The Energy Department itself had released a report to that effect only weeks earlier, citing the contamination of 3,000 acres.

More importantly, hundreds of nuclear bomb tests at the Nevada site had spewed deadly radiation to the winds, regularly exposing people in Utah, Nevada and Northern Arizona to carcinogenic doses of fallout. Even after the Limited Test Ban Treaty of 1963 confined test explosions underground, at least several dozen vented significant quantities of radioactivity to neighboring states. To assert that the Nevada Test Site "never had any environmental problems" required prodigious ignorance or deceit. To report such an assertion without any contrary view was, at best, incompetent journalism.

One of the most notable things about the entire media uproar on Energy Department weapons facilities was that it did not encompass the Nevada Test Site operated by the department, at a cost of about $1 billion annually. With more than ten nuclear bombs going off underground every year, and with ample evidence of radiation leaks and duplicity, the test site nevertheless escaped the glare of critical publicity—perhaps because of its great importance as the only place where the government can conduct test explosions before deploying new designs of nuclear warheads.

Although one wouldn't know it from relying on major news outlets, well-informed activists had extensive evidence that government deception about the test site was continuing. The Downwinders organization, based in Salt Lake City, got frequent coverage in Utah media for its documentation of ongoing dangers. But national media avoided test-site issues.

Accepting the views of Washington's powers-that-be about the need to produce more nuclear bombs, the mass media reduced public discourse to little more than quibbles about the most effective way to build new warheads.

PUFFING THE PEACEFUL ATOM

The same biases in press coverage of nuclear weapons plants have applied in press treatment of "the peaceful atom." Nuclear power has been vigorously promoted by many news media, which have made clear their hopes for revival of the industry in the U.S. during the last decade of this century. The *New York Times*, for instance, has been crazy about the Shoreham nuclear plant built on Long Island. In July 1986, *Village Voice* writer Jack Newfield reported that by his count the *Times* had editorialized in favor of the Shoreham plant 22 different times during the previous 40 months. He called it "the *Times*'s love affair with the nuclear power industry."

The *Times* was not interested in merely raising the dead. It wanted the country's nuclear power business to be revived well beyond the hundred-odd reactors accounting for just under 20 percent of the nation's electricity. Its editorial barrage grew more frequent and furious throughout the decade. As the Shoreham plant's chances of opening faded, the *Times* took to heaping scorn on anyone who opposed the nuke.

In May 1988, the *Times* had yet another nuclear conniption fit, denouncing politicians who'd proposed scrapping Shoreham: "That folly could threaten the nation's security, not just Long Island's, by further eroding public confidence in nuclear power." In mid-February 1989, the paper lashed one of its favorite whipping boys on the subject, New York's Governor Mario Cuomo—who "could have educated people about Shoreham, and quieted their distorted fears." A few weeks later, the *Times* was back at the nuclear pulpit, damning a familiar demon: "Governor Cuomo's festoon of fine arguments against Shoreham is spun around a falsity. The plant is not unsafe..." For good measure, the editorial blasted people for selfish unwillingness to share their island with a nuclear plant that could turn their neighborhoods into radioactive wastelands: "Long Islanders have themselves to blame, too. They made it impossible for any politician to tell them the truth. They refused to accept assurances on Shoreham..."

But along with the bombast, the *Times* offered a suggestion. Why not beat some nuclear plowshares into swords? After all, it reasoned, "Instead of acquiescing in the wasteful destruction of a $5.5 billion reactor, the Government could at least consider converting it to making tritium for nuclear weapons." If Shoreham could be retrofitted to make material for thermonuclear bombs, all would not be lost. (So much for the "peaceful atom.")

The *Times*' affection for both nuclear power and nuclear weapons was anything but coincidental. From the beginning, the military and commercial aspects of the split atom have been closely linked, depending on the same matrix of technologies and federal subsidies—along with media hype to deflect opposition. And while in theory a newspaper's editorial position is separate from what appears in the news pages, the realities are often different. In the case of the *New York Times*, the torch it was carrying for Shoreham cast a long shadow in the newsroom.

In 1982, *Times* reporter Frances Cerra wrote in a news article that LILCO, the utility company building Shoreham, faced "financial demise" because of the nuclear project. The article never appeared. A *Times* editor informed her that the article "could adversely affect LILCO's financial well-being," recalled Cerra. "He further told me that I—at the time covering Long Island for the paper—should in the future consider LILCO out of my beat. When I told him that this was unacceptable, I was punished by being removed from Long Island coverage to dangle, uncomfortably, without portfolio and anything of substance to work on." It was a time-honored form of retribution meted out by the *Times* hierarchy. Cerra responded by resigning from her job.

Seven years and several billion dollars later, the *Times* was still spinning the Shoreham news to suit its editorial stance—and the high-finance heavies on its board of directors who also sat on the boards of nuclear-invested banks and utilities. According to the Republican presiding officer of the Suffolk Legislature, Gregory Blass, an opponent of Shoreham, the *Times* coverage "has been downright negligent, disgraceful. The county's position is either misstated or not stated. The *Times* has been blatantly pro-utility, pro-bank, pro-corporate. It calls us extremist. It is the *Times* that is extremist, fanatical on nuclear power."

Three Mile Island

When the tenth anniversary of the accident at Three Mile Island rolled around in March 1989, the *New York Times* refused to publish any submitted op-ed article citing unusual clusters of leukemia, birth defects and hypothyroidism around the plant in central Pennsylvania. However, the *Times* did print an anniversary op-ed piece—headlined "Three Mile Island: The Good News"—which saw "grounds for optimism about the future of the nuclear power industry." And, it explained, "The accident was arguably a positive development. Without hurting anyone, it triggered a substantial change in nuclear utility management, emergency planning and, to a degree, regulation."

By that time, more than 2,000 residents near Three Mile Island had filed claims for cancer and other illnesses they linked to the nuclear plant. About 280 personal-injury settlements had been paid out by TMI's operating utility, including $1.1 million to the parents of a baby with Down syndrome and heart trouble, born nine months after the accident. Some media had sobered about the technology; *USA Today*, for instance, used the tenth anniversary as an occasion for an editorial urging less reliance on nuclear power. But the *Times* remained committed to a position it had staked out from the outset—that the TMI accident hadn't hurt anybody.

From the start, the *Times* had methodically pooh-poohed evidence of infant deaths and animal deformities in the Harrisburg area. One editorial, a year after the accident, scoffed at "scare stories about radiation damage," and concluded that "even in nuclear fables there are people who cry wolf." The editorial declared that fears of health damage "were effectively laid to rest by state and federal health investigators, as reported in The Times by Jane Brody." The reporting by Brody, however, was riddled with errors. A few months later the daily *Baltimore News-American* had published results of its own investigation—concluding that the government survey data cited by the *Times* were "worthless," and among other things ignored an extraordinary pattern of health damage to farm animals.

Finessing the Chernobyl disaster

In April 1986, when catastrophe struck at the Chernobyl nuclear power plant in the Soviet Union, American mass media were instantly torn between two impulses—pro-nuclear and anti-Soviet. After some wavering between the two, a *de facto* compromise was reached, blaming the Soviets for incompetence and secrecy while for the most part going along with the official U.S. line that such an event can't happen here. "This reflexive smugness in United States newsrooms could not have been sustained without the consistent application of a double standard that overlooked much of our own nuclear record, and without dissemination of much dis- and misinformation," Tom Gervasi wrote months later.

It took the Soviets two days to announce the Chernobyl accident; by then large amounts of fallout had already spread across Europe. The delay was inexcusable. The U.S. government, however, had its own record of delays and deceit, although American mass media rarely mentioned this.

From 1945 to 1962, the USA's aboveground nuclear testing had frequently taken place without warning downwind American civilians, soldiers and Pacific islanders of potential consequences. On May 11, 1969, a major fire at Rocky Flats in Colorado sent large amounts of deadly plutonium particles into surrounding communities; the government did not announce the fire for 45 days. During the Three Mile Island accident false assurances were legion; Pennsylvania's governor at the time, Richard Thornburgh (later the Bush administration's Attorney General), refused to call for evacuation of nearby pregnant women and preschoolers until two days into the accident, an unconscionable delay. And it took the U.S. government more than 36 *years* to reveal that on December 2, 1949, it *intentionally* released massive clouds of the thyroid-ravaging isotope Iodine-131 into the winds blowing from Washington state's Hanford site to populated areas. It wasn't until February 1986 that U.S. officials admitted what had happened, by declassifying a report that had been written in 1950.

The profound message of Chernobyl—the suicidal folly of nuclear fission—swiftly got lost in the American media shuffle. There were some initial descents into sensationalism; the *New York Post* filled its tabloid front page with the headline "Mass Grave for 15,000 N-Victims." In fact, the initial death total was a couple of dozen people in the Ukraine. Once that became clear, within a few days U.S. media began underplaying the disaster's long-term implications.

The American press has hardly been energetic about looking past the assurances of pro-nuclear agencies and corporations as to radiation dose impacts. Radioactivity's effects are usually delayed, with an incubation time of at least a few years for leukemia and up to several decades for solid cancers. Isotopes such as strontium, cesium and plutonium, released into air, water and soil, will remain lethal for many hundreds or thousands of years; in the shorter term they accumulate at each step of the food chain and concentrate most highly in human beings. Children are 10 to 20 times more sensitive to the carcinogenic effects of radiation than adults.

So the real story about Chernobyl's effects could only be a long-range view. Official scientific assessments—usually funded by nuclear agencies, energy corporations and the like—tended to minimize the ultimate harm, anticipating perhaps tens of thousands of cancer deaths. Other estimates, running to a half-million or more cancer and leukemia deaths, were downplayed—sometimes much more so in the American than the Soviet press.

In February 1989, the Soviet weekly *Moscow News* reported that less than three years after the Chernobyl disaster, cancer rates had doubled in the Narodichsky region 50 miles west of Chernobyl. And more than half of the children in the agricultural district developed thyroid gland illnesses. The information got brief mention in U.S. media. Coverage was hardly encouraged by American officials, committed to a policy of reassuring citizens about the atomic power and nuclear weapons plants in their midst.

Recent efforts to raise the dead

In late 1989, pro-nuclear forces stepped up efforts to resuscitate a U.S. nuclear power industry that had not seen a new domestic order for a reactor in more than a decade. As usual, high costs were being blamed on stubborn foes and burdensome regulations. But other themes were supplied by paid ads from nuclear industry front-groups such as the U.S. Council for Energy Awareness. That organization's full-page ads in newsweeklies showed a grinning Ayatollah with Uncle Sam roped around his pinky ("Imported Oil Strengthens Our Ties to the Middle East"), or a machine gun with a 55-gallon drum for a barrel labeled Foreign Oil ("America's Next Hostage Crisis"), always with the tag line: "Nuclear energy means more energy independence."

Other appeals were less crude. "Experts See Nuclear Energy as Cure for Global Warming," said a *New York Times* headline as autumn 1989 began. (All the quoted "experts" with that vision were officials of the South Korean,

British and U.S. governments—regimes devoted to nuclear power.) A wide array of coverage discussed renewed consideration of atomic options. With concern heightening about the greenhouse effect, media seemed eager that America not forget nuclear power when choosing its environmental poisons.

In the last month of the 1980s, the *New York Times* closed out the decade with a predictable editorial titled "Revive the Atom," citing the greenhouse effect as one of the "compelling reasons" to support the nuclear power industry. "The new plants now being designed put safety first," the editorial assured, while poking at "supine politicians" who had the gall to side with the majority of local residents opposed to the Shoreham facility. In sharp contrast, politicians who've knuckled under to multibillion-dollar nuclear interests are not denigrated as "supine" by the *Times*.

On NPR, an *All Things Considered* host set up a lengthy report this way: "The carbon dioxide and other gasses that result from burning fossil fuels are building up in the atmosphere, and these are likely to trap heat, like a greenhouse. The environmental movement has decided to take on 'global warming' as an issue, and this raises a dilemma for them—whether to reconsider nuclear power, which they've traditionally opposed."

What followed was a ten-minute segment by reporter Richard Harris, whose condescension was ill-disguised as he portrayed most participants at a Sierra Club international meeting as anti-nuclear dogmatists. After mentioning a bill in Congress to fund more nuclear power research, Harris introduced an Audubon Society staff physicist who, Harris said, "also recognizes that the world may ultimately have to rely more heavily on nuclear power." The scientist, described as a solar-power advocate, said: "I think we have to bite the fuel rod and leave nuclear power as an insurance policy, as an option that we should research in case solar technology does not pan out the way I and others expect it to... We're going to have to give up some of our old myths, take some risks, find some new bedfellows and get the kind of legislation that we need through. Because if we don't do it, there ain't gonna be anybody else to do it for us." Whereupon Harris closed the report with an audible shake of his head and the conclusion: "But judging by the Sierra Club gathering in Ann Arbor, few environmentalists are ready to be that pragmatic when nuclear power is the issue."

Media concern about the environment is evident. But few mainstream journalists venture to conclude that a long series of so-called "pragmatic" compromises has pushed the world to the brink of ecological destruction.

SLICK COVERAGE OF THE EXXON OIL SPILL

In the aftermath of Exxon's 11-million-gallon oil spill, U.S. news media described an Alaskan coast with countless dead animals, decimated plant life, and a massive black blanket covering nearly 1,100 miles of shoreline.

But within a few months, a different story gained currency, as reports out of Prince William Sound took on a friendly and forgiving tone. Writers and editors across the nation began to focus on the damage not done by Exxon's blunder, and heralded big oil's haphazard efforts to preserve Alaska's environment. Out of the jaws of catastrophe, Exxon snatched a media spin increasingly to its liking.

During one week in September 1989, the American people learned via cover stories in *Newsweek* and *U.S. News & World Report* that the oil spill off the Alaska coastline wasn't so bad after all. As *U.S. News* reported, "The sublime beachscapes of Prince William Sound remain startlingly beautiful" despite the "image" of ecological disaster in one of the world's most pristine areas. The very premise of that magazine's cover story—"The Disaster That Wasn't"—dismissed the seriousness of the spill, and praised Exxon's poorly organized and haphazardly executed "cleanup" effort.

Framing an image-versus-reality theme, both weeklies painted a sympathetic picture of Exxon as a well-meaning (though clumsy) corporate citizen. *Newsweek* urged that the 11 million gallons of crude oil spilled into an untouched wilderness area be put "in a more realistic perspective." The magazine boldly proclaimed that "Man has done his best...now it's nature's turn to repair the damage"—a big-type declaration certainly welcomed by Exxon. But the statement ignored many scientists and others, in Alaska and elsewhere, who questioned whether or not "man," in this case apparently a journalistic synonym for "Exxon," had actually "done his best."

While most stories detailing Exxon's pullout opened with a reference to the frigid Alaskan winter on the way, they rarely delved into whether or not the cleanup was effectively completed. The obstacles to staying in the Sound for the winter seemed to excuse Exxon's retreat. Few high-profile journalists dared to step outside the boundaries of Exxon press releases and raise serious questions about what the company called "1,087 miles of treated shoreline."

Newsweek scoffed at Exxon's use of the word "treated" as "a far cry from the brave words of...Exxon's Alaska public affairs manager, who immediately after the spill promised 'to pick up, one way or another, all the oil that's out there.'" Yet the same magazine, just one page later, featured a brightly colored "Box Score" sheet neatly listing the mileage of "contaminated" shoreline ("1,090") in comparison with the amount of "treated" shoreline ("1,087"). *Newsweek*'s chart used the word *treated* without quotation marks. Albeit with a bit of grumbling, *Newsweek* thus credited Exxon with tending to all but three miles of the shoreline affected by the spill.

Many reports from Prince William Sound routinely underplayed the significant, far-reaching effects of damaging any part of the global ecosystem. Shunning logic and available evidence while claiming that Prince William Sound was well on the biological rebound, *U.S. News & World Report* insulted their readers' common sense by suggesting that even though

the American public had been misled by "one-dimensional television images and a furious environmental community, Prince William Sound is no longer an ecological disaster zone." The reportage stayed on the same wave-length, explaining that initially "there was heavy mortality among sea birds and otters...but the long-term injury to most wildlife and marine organisms is expected to be minimal." Soothing news, if one ignores the potential consequences of wiping out half the sea otter population.

The sea otter is considered by biologists to be "a keystone species" in the Prince William Sound ecosystem. Keystone species are singled out for their vital role in sustaining the balance of the ecosystem; when such a species is absent from a given environment, the food chain breaks down and the ecosystem is destroyed. Otters eat sea urchins, which feed on kelp beds. The kelp, known as "the foundation of the coastal ecosystem," supports the entire food chain from the bottom up. *Newsweek* reported that half the otter species was destroyed, and conceded that "lose the otters . . . and there's nothing to stop the urchins from chewing the kelp down to the roots"—yet the magazine confidently proclaimed that "the food chain has survived." If the news media had made a responsible attempt to assess the potential impacts of destroying half the population of a keystone species in the delicate Prince William Sound ecosystem, Exxon might have found itself with an entirely new batch of public questions to answer.

USA Today demonstrated a similar power-friendly approach to the spill in a piece headlined "Exxon extols spill cleanup as 'fantastic'"—truly an epitome of stenography, as the company announced that the coast had been rendered "environmentally stable." *USA Today*'s laudatory sum-up of Exxon's role was characteristic of the news media's tendency to jump on the bandwagon when the government or industry has "good news" to report.

Shifting the blame

Instead of blaming those in power positions when ecological catastrophes occur, the media are apt to fault lower-level individuals. The shock of the Alaska oil spill hadn't yet abated when mass media shifted the blame from Exxon and the U.S. government to Captain Joseph Hazelwood, skipper of the *Exxon Valdez* oil tanker. Journalists showed little enthusiasm for probing the laxity of federal shipping regulations or Exxon's labor cuts which forced tanker personnel to work up to 12-hour shifts without breaks. Instead, the news media much preferred to chronicle the personal and legal problems of Captain Hazelwood. *Time* magazine ran a cover story on "Joe's bad trip," six pages that purported to expose a "wider web of responsibility" but wound up devoting almost all the space to reminiscing about Hazelwood's personal woes.

The *Newsweek* and *U.S. News & World Report* cover stories failed to mention the Federal Clean Water and Clean Harbor Act that provided for felony charges and jail terms for corporate officers of polluting companies. (This information, if reported, might raise questions about why such laws remain virtually unused.) And, like most coverage of environmental disasters, mainstream media stories about the spill did not explain that various factors—poorly enforced EPA and transit rules, federal tax deductions for corporate "cleanups," and minuscule penalties for polluters—make the legal and financial aspects of polluting actually work to the advantage of large corporations such as Exxon. In effect, it's cheaper for industries to pollute and pay token fines than to comply with minimal pollution standards.

With news media more inclined to stress the short-term economic prospects for big business than the long-term prognosis for human health and the environment, often the deepest concern seems to be extended toward embattled CEOs and public relations specialists. In a revealing reflection of mass media values, *U.S. News & World Report* summed up events along the Alaska coast by declaring that "the greatest damage done by the spill is to Big Oil's public image." Consistent with such an ideology, the U.S. press went to great lengths to make sure the American public knew how much money Exxon was spending on Prince William Sound. The media turned the workers in Alaska into "\$16.69-an-hour beach cleaners," and placed more emphasis on the costs of the "cleanup" than its effectiveness.

Among the numerous news plugs for Exxon and the oil industry were references to "a reprise of the employment bonanza during the transatlantic pipeline construction in the mid-1970's" that supposedly had positive effects on Alaska's economy. According to *U.S. News & World Report*, "Locals joke about nominating... [Captain] Hazelwood for governor because he has created more jobs than the previous four administrations." Such cues, combined with daily reminders of "cleanup" expenses, seemed calculated to evoke both pity and admiration for Exxon's effort while implying, in some perverted sense, that the short-term "economic bonanza" that Exxon brought to Alaska was worth the "unsightly rocks and beaches" marring the Alaskan coastline.

Commenting on Exxon's post-spill moves "to assuage an angry public," *U.S. News & World Report* described the company's efforts "to win the hearts and minds of environmentalists, the public and Congress," while "responding to a barrage of calls and letters from outraged animal lovers." Only two months earlier, the magazine had trumpeted the entire country's environmental devotion with a story which explained that "protecting the best of our outdoor heritage is an enduring American ethic reaching deep into the national psyche." But many media reports came to categorize vocal supporters of the "enduring American ethic" as mere "environmentalists" and "animal lovers."

At year's end, *National Geographic* provided an authoritative summary gloss for "the worst tanker spill in U.S. history and a six-month, billion-dollar cleanup effort." The cover story—"ALASKA'S BIG SPILL: Can the Wilderness Heal?"—featured 40 pages of sumptuous photos and earnestly-toned text...which never got around to faulting Exxon for much of anything. The article must have pleased execs at oil companies such as Chevron, which had a full-page ad in the same issue of *National Geographic*. "Sooner or later, through human error or simply through the perils of the sea, spilled oil will assault another shore," the magazine story stated. "And sooner or later, the damage will have to be left to nature to repair."

POLLUTING THE MEDIA ENVIRONMENT

People working hard to stop ecological damage are sometimes depicted by mass media as gratified by evidence of it. A page-one *Washington Post* headline announced, "Environmentalists Hope for Scorcher." Referring to the possibility of a long, hot summer aggravated by the greenhouse effect, the *Post* alleged that "environmentalists and their allies are praying for a sizzler. A little drought wouldn't hurt either." While fueling the stereotype of environmentalists as Machiavellian cynics, the story's underlying premise was that Congress would act quickly if only presented with clear evidence of environmental demise—another dubious representation of reality.

In cases of blatant large-scale environmental desecration, media commonly diffuse blame of the corporate sector. A *New York Times* editorial typified the approach with a remarkable assertion: "Ocean dumpers need help, not fines." Insisting that "ocean dumpers aren't villains," the *Times* identified the real problem—"Congress refuses to help" relieve the "financial burden" of treating sewage sludge.

Although adverse effects from injuries to the ecosphere are everywhere, so is media denial. Truly a master of exonerating the corporate culprit while blaming the victim, the *Times* front-paged a 1989 piece claiming that fears of environmental damage were more due to paranoia than peril. Reporter Peter Passell maintained that "Americans have never been safer." Largely ignoring relevant data, he dismissed the increase in cancer deaths over the last 20 years as "not, apparently, due to man-made hazards." Instead of scrutinizing patterns of corporate-government behavior that put private profit ahead of public health, the article shifted blame to a justifiably worried public.

Who does the EPA really protect?

An Associated Press report was sympathetic to the struggle of a small town in North Carolina against a paper products plant dumping millions of gallons of "dark, poisonous wastewater" into a river bisecting the community. But the AP article did not mention that the corporation might be resisting change simply because it's cheaper to pollute and pay measly government fines than to invest in waste treatment. So it may have seemed reasonable to readers that an Environmental Protection Agency (EPA) official had the gall to suggest "it's the classic confrontation between jobs and environmental concern." More classic was the reoccurring evidence of the EPA's unwillingness to enforce its own rules, but that angle was absent from the story.

Also absent from that story, and many like it, was an explanation of how the EPA suppressed vital information regarding the deadly poison dioxin, which was among the chemicals bleeding into the North Carolina waterway. *Greenpeace* magazine revealed that the EPA secretly worked with paper industry bigwigs to cover up the presence of dioxin in discharge from mills. As 1990 began, dioxin was still an ingredient of some paper products—including milk cartons in millions of American refrigerators.

According to former EPA press officer Jim Sibbison, the EPA regularly soft-pedals stories about pollution—and mainstream media obediently accept EPA leads, routinely concocting stories around them. "It makes no sense for the press to continue to treat the EPA as a reliable source of information," Sibbison asserts, adding that "the story now is malfeasance at the EPA itself, and the facts won't be found in a press release."

Sibbison derides the news media's "inability to see the EPA as part and parcel of the pollution story—a kind of bureaucratic smokestack, as it were." Michael Weisskopf, a reporter on the environment beat for the *Washington Post*, has conceded that journalists are often misled by the regulatory agency: "It is very easy for the EPA to snooker members of the press unless they are watching the ball all the time."

Knee-jerk acceptance of the EPA line is typical of the media's unhealthy reliance on official sources. When weather reporters on local TV news broadcasts state the air-pollution index is "low" or "moderate" today, for instance, they are really just relaying an administrative definition provided by federal and regional agencies that regularly kowtow to powerful corporate interests. Smiling weather forecasters accept government criteria on health and environment issues without question, even though independent scientists tend to be much less sanguine about pollution levels that the government says are nothing to worry about.

The high cost of public health

President Bush's proposals for controlling air pollution ("Every person has the right to breathe clean air...") caused a big news splash in early summer 1989. Although most reporters celebrated the President's air pollution scenario as a demonstration of his commitment to the environment, criticism of the plan's cost was immediate. Syndicated business writer Warren Brookes wrote that "the risk to the economy is infinitely greater than the slight health risks" which Bush's program might alleviate. Perhaps Brookes was not among the millions of people encountering difficulty breathing the air in the nation's major cities.

When the EPA mandated the use of filters for the U.S. water supply in order to destroy disease-causing microbes (which can result in Hepatitis A, among other afflictions), a *New York Times* news story dubbed the move an adoption of "costly rules." To make its point, the *Times* mentioned costliness of the measure three times in the first four paragraphs of the article. The price of the EPA mandate: $3 billion, a pittance compared to the price-tag on any number of nuclear weapons projects enthusiastically supported by the *Times*.

In November 1989, the *Times* made no secret of its go-slow attitude toward big expenditures to protect public health. A front-page article—headed "Cure for Greenhouse Effect: The Costs Will Be Staggering"—explained that a major effort to limit carbon effluent "makes little economic sense" for the United States. The cost of limiting this carbon production could be so "staggering," in fact, "one pessimistic but not implausible estimate" says the cost might "rival the current level of military spending." But not to fear, writer Peter Passell concluded, "high cost need not rule out action, of course, if the alternative is catastrophe."

Phil Shabecoff, an environmental reporter at the *New York Times* bureau in Washington, has voiced concern that media attention fails to recognize "the

Reminder: Clean air costs

All of us breathe, and air pollution is obviously a legitimate concern for government, industry, and the public alike. Auto emissions are among the many causes of air pollution. We don't quibble with the need to control these emissions, nor does any reasonable—and breathing—individual.

But reasonable people can question the methods used to attain a desirable goal. We're particularly concerned with the regulations recently adopted in a number of Northeastern states. These regulations attack the emissions problem by mandating that refiners deliver gasoline for this year's warm-weather driving season that is considerably less volatile than the gasoline motorists have been getting in past summers.

Gasoline must be volatile—capable of changing from fluid to vapor at relatively low temperatures. It's the vapor, mixed with air, that ignites within the cylinders to power your car.

Volatility is measured as Reid Vapor Pressure, or RVP. For Northeast winters, refiners usually boost the volatility so cars can start and run better in the cold. In summer, RVP normally is cut back to 11.5 in recognition of the warmer weather.

The new regulations mandate a summer RVP of 9. We know that 9 RVP gasoline will reduce pollution. But we feel compelled to inform the public that the gains in cleaner air carry a penalty. Here's what we mean:

• The rules say that 9 RVP gasoline must be in use by May 1. As a practical matter, however, such fuels will have to be at the dealers' pumps in April. Any resident of the Northeast knows that spring weather is unpredictable. On cool days, some cars may not start, and others will experience hesitation, stalling, and even backfires.

• The regulations will reduce the ability of refiners to produce gasoline this summer because making a 9 RVP product is not only more expensive, but requires more crude oil. And U.S. refiners already operate virtually at full gasoline capacity to meet peak summer demand. The Northeast has had to rely on imported fuel for part of its supply. Foreign refiners would have to produce the needed quantities of low-RVP gasoline to continue supplying the Northeast in the summer. Whether they all do or not, of course, is their decision. A tightening of supply, therefore, seems certain.

• New York State in particular has indicated it may allow exemptions for suppliers who say they're unable to obtain the 9 RVP gasoline. But a system of exemptions would trigger sharp differences in quality and cost among suppliers and dealers. Such a system would also make the exemptions themselves something of a political prize.

Fortunately, these costs of cleaner air can be minimized—and much of the environmental gain realized—if the federal Environmental Protection Agency acts promptly.

The EPA has been considering a rule calling for a phase-in of lower RVP, starting at 10.5. Another rule being considered by the EPA would enlarge the vapor-catching canisters that have been standard in automobiles for several years. An EPA order combining 10.5 gasoline and larger canisters, preempting the state regulations, would result in less pollution and less cost, while preserving car performance and avoiding the potential for supply problems. It would also keep a tight lid on the political Pandora's box of special state-granted exemptions.

As we've said, we endorse the goal of the Northeastern lawmakers. But in this instance, we feel there's a better way. We urge the EPA to move now—so all of us can breathe easier.

Mobil ad-itorial, *New York Times*, March 2, 1989

significance of the issue." Shabecoff contended that "increasingly national security is not going to be defined by the number of weapons we have, or the military budget, but by the state of our natural environment and the quality of our resources."

Free-lance writer Dick Russell interviewed many other journalists who are also eager to provide high-quality coverage of environmental news. But, as Russell noted, they work for "institutions that are increasingly dominated by corporations with a vested interest in maintaining a status quo that has perpetuated many environmental problems."

To fret or not to fret

Relying far too much on news slants provided by corporate and government PR reps, news reports on "the environment" are apt to distance people from real situations. Mass media usually don't explain how or why ecological problems are relevant to the lives of ordinary folks. Environmental issues often seem abstract because the media make them so. Sometimes a don't-worry message is overt, as when *Newsweek* suggested in the summer of 1989 that "the environment is damned near indestructible." Of course, it is just such an attitude that has accelerated the destruction of vital ecological webs that sustain life on Earth.

While some news stories say the planet will rebound no matter what, other reports foster a crisis mentality—and the net effect is confusion and widespread apathy. On the occasions that news media choose to present environmental issues as a direct concern to everyone, the crisis approach often repels the public in the same stroke. At times, mass media create a psychological barrier by overwhelming people with a laundry list of environmental tragedies, a commonly-used technique in articles reviewing the overall state of the Earth's ecological balance.

When reporters are faced with the task of summarizing an array of daunting environmental problems in a matter of a few hundred words, the product often assumes the mood of *USA Today*'s alarming headline, "Saving the environment takes on new urgency." The piece opened with a lighthearted admission, "there's nothing quite like a crisis—or a series of them—to prick public consciousness." Typical of such overviews, the *USA Today* treatment included a special section titled "A global chain of damage," which enumerated point-by-point the world's "ecological problems." An accompanying blurb listed various crises pertaining to energy, toxins, pollutants, water, and preservation of the environment. The message to readers: The whole world is going to hell and there's not much you can do.

The world's rainforests and the World Bank

Newswriters' zeal for simple leads and tidy conclusions has been evident in the U.S. media's belated coverage of massive deforestation in the

Amazon, where half the species on the globe are estimated to reside. Not big on context, mass media accounts usually omit the fact that luscious rainforests are also being grazed, burned and bulldozed (in the name of economic progress) in places ranging from Costa Rica, Haiti, Guatemala and Mexico, to Australia and even Alaska.

Those who read *National Geographic*'s lengthy feature on preserving the rainforest (in the issue with a hologram of the Earth on the front and a gold-arch McDonald's ad on the back) wouldn't have learned of the World Bank's insidious role as supplier of the money behind most of Brazil's deforestation. In the 51-page spread, five of six references to the World Bank were positive, with the magazine only able to bring itself to say in passing that "the finger of blame is often pointed at the World Bank."

U.S. news media rarely acknowledge the impact of the international monetary power structure on the environment. Nor does U.S. journalism link ecological problems to the grinding poverty and class oppression of a country like Brazil, where government policies dictate destruction of forests. Likewise, struggles for social justice and a healthy environment are kept separate. Agronomist Susanna Hecht and columnist Alexander Cockburn have pointed out that in the Amazon "tribe after tribe of Indians has been exterminated through the decades, and hundreds of rural organizers harassed and murdered across the region"—yet "such crimes have scarcely been a preoccupation of the North American media." The people and ecosystem of the Amazon are being ravaged by an exploitative social order. That the rainforest cannot be saved without overturning this social order is a reality ignored by splashy coverage in the USA.

The environment is perhaps the "biggest" story a reporter can face; that's part of the problem. "Because nobody sees the ozone layer there isn't the immediacy," said Dianne Dumanoski of the *Boston Globe*. Ecological issues that are difficult to cover—requiring more time and money to produce—can seem too amorphous and global. "Basically, it's an area that requires a great deal of work for very little visual payoff," explained Linda Ellerbee, formerly of NBC and ABC News, "exactly the kind of story TV was created to ignore."

AIDS: LOOKING THE OTHER WAY

One day in March 1986, the *New York Times* published a column by William F. Buckley Jr., under the headline "Identify All the Carriers." The article was evidently of special merit both to the editors of the *Times* and Buckley, whose syndicated column was under contract to run regularly in the competing New York *Daily News*. Despite this arrangement, the *Times* featured Buckley's article on its op-ed page. In the piece, Buckley made a proposal: "Everyone detected with AIDS should be tattooed in the upper forearm, to protect common-needle users, and on the buttocks, to prevent the victimization of other homosexuals."

Government tattooing of people for identification purposes had, of course, been done before: in Nazi Germany. Buckley's suggestion, run up the august flagpole provided by the *New York Times*, drew more outrage than salutes—enough so that Buckley, as he later recalled, "quickly withdrew the proposal for the simple reason that it proved socially intolerable." But the episode, coming several years after the AIDS epidemic became visible in the U.S., spoke loudly.

As a fatal disease that struck gay men first and most widely in the United States, AIDS arrived on the American scene associated with homosexuality. From the beginning, publicity was fraught with prejudice and evasion; the consequences were to provide a cover for the disease to spread without appropriate countermeasures. In short, mass media neglect proved deadly.

"Even a cursory look at U.S. mainstream and gay media in 1981-1982 suggests that a great deal of denial was going on about the extent and severity of the problem," health policy analyst Jan Grover wrote in the same year that Buckley made his fascistic tattooing proposal. It wasn't until May 31, 1982, that the *Los Angeles Times* reportedly became the first major newspaper to print a front-page story about AIDS. By the end of 1982 the recorded cases of AIDS in the U.S. were doubling every six months, and three-quarters of the people so far diagnosed with the disease were already dead. But, Grover recalled, "the press did little to publicize the epidemic. The mainstream press saw AIDS as a peculiarly (and perhaps justifiably) gay disease, and the gay press treated it as an internal problem that, if widely discussed, might lose gays recent hard-won political and social gains."

The straight media paid a bit more attention in 1983 when hemophiliacs began coming down with AIDS due to transfusions with contaminated blood. A growing problem with intravenous drug users became more evident in New York City and other urban areas. Meanwhile, the gay press was improving its coverage, spurred by growing anti-AIDS activism in gay communities. But to the mass media, and to most Americans, it was still a disease that happened to people one would probably never know.

It wasn't until Rock Hudson died of AIDS in October 1985 that mass media noticed the disease in a big way. Suddenly, AIDS became a cover story, a page-one topic, a scourge worthy of repeated mention on the evening news. A survey of 90 major U.S. newspapers and magazines found that in the first half of 1985, a total of 1,197 articles on AIDS appeared. During the last half of the same year, 3,810 AIDS articles appeared—more than all those printed from 1982 through 1984.

But the media fascination with AIDS dissipated after another surge following Liberace's death from the disease in February 1987. Even at its height, much of the media glare seemed preoccupied with the prospect that the fatal illness would spread among heterosexuals. Certain people in society—homosexuals, or poor junkies sharing needles—were implicitly expendable, their suffering seemingly less tragic. And precious time had already been lost.

"The media are convinced in 1987 that they're doing a great job reporting the AIDS story, and there's no denying they've grasped the horror," Paul Monette wrote in his book *Borrowed Time*. "But for four years they let the bureaucrats get away with passive genocide, dismissing a no-win problem perceived as affecting only an underclass or two. It was often remarked acidly in West Hollywood that if AIDS had struck boy scouts first rather than gay men, or St. Louis rather than Kinshasa, it would have been covered like nuclear war."

Belittling AIDS activists

Outraged by government indifference and inaction—as well as by similar journalistic attitudes—AIDS activists have marched and rallied in many communities. At times, they've militantly protested at government buildings, scientific conferences and media outlets. Some news coverage has been respectful and communicative, but more often it portrayed the demonstrators as desperate, belligerent and/or irrational. The most common response is for news media not to report on such protests at all.

When 150 people from the AIDS activist group ACT UP demonstrated outside the home and office of *New York Times* publisher Punch Sulzberger one day in summer 1989, a total of 400 police turned out. Distributing literature critiquing the *Times* treatment of AIDS issues, the activists asked such questions as: "Why, instead of actively investigating the work of federal health organizations, does the *Times* merely rewrite [their] press releases?" The demonstrators charged that "such compliance makes the *Times* a mere public relations agent for an ineffective government." Although the AP wire's daybook listed the protest, only two radio stations in the city covered the event. The *Times* didn't print a word about it. And, in the apt words of media critic Doug Ireland, "The TV blackout was total, the other dailies silent as graves."

Deficient news coverage of AIDS has paralleled other facets of media. Condom ads generally were barred from mass media until a breakthrough in 1987—several years into an AIDS epidemic that would have been slowed by wider use of condoms. The big three TV networks continued to refuse condom ads on grounds of sensitivity to some viewers' sense of morality. This excuse came from top executives in a medium constantly broadcasting blatant sexual references and innuendos in its entertainment programs as well as in commercials.

As for televised dramas, they focused largely on children and hemophiliacs. The people hardest-hit by AIDS—gays, the poor, people of color—were being rendered almost invisible on the Tube. In 1989, the executive producer of *American Playhouse* on PBS, Lindsay Law, noted that made-for-TV films "always seem to dance around the issue. You don't see the high-risk groups—it's as if AIDS is happening to everybody else."

Innocent children and guilty grownups

Much of the media fixated on the presence of AIDS in children even when it was extremely rare. Perhaps that had a positive effect of eliciting sympathy for people with AIDS. But there was an ugly undercurrent—distinguishing between "innocent" victims and others with the disease. It was an unusually direct challenge to mass media assumptions when *Newsweek* printed the comments of James Hurley in August 1987: "I caught AIDS, so to speak, out of ignorance. And I caught it at a time when no one else knew about it. It galls me when I hear one of these reporters mention that the babies who contract AIDS through their mother are the innocent victims of AIDS, as though the rest of us are somehow guilty victims... It hurts me very deeply to read that I'm not part of the general population."

The coverage of AIDS-afflicted children, Jan Grover pointed out, "masks an obvious but heavily resisted fact: everyone with AIDS is someone's child. And they will all leave grieving parents or siblings and friends behind should they die. The wall that the mainstream press uses to ward off such unpleasant recognitions is the construct of 'blame.' Young children are seen as 'innocent,' as not having willed or chosen their own infection. But did adults will their own deaths?"

According to Grover, "the biggest problem in reporting on AIDS" has been "the magnetic pull toward the atypical." Maybe this has occurred because the "typical" American with AIDS does not fit the idealized stereotypes that draw the most enthusiastic media attention. Between the lines and explicitly, in news reports and advertising, some Americans—with white skin, with money, with heterosexual public behavior—are treated as more important than others whose skin is darker, whose finances are thinner, whose sexual orientations are in a minority.

Coverage drops as death toll climbs

By mid-1989, the volume of AIDS coverage had dropped to its lowest level in three years. And little of the coverage went beyond local angles and medical research news to take a close look at federal policies. "One consequence," wrote Randy Shilts, "is that CDC [Centers for Disease Control] staffers now routinely find that many people think the AIDS epidemic has 'leveled out' or peaked. The reality, of course, is that caseloads have never been higher, with as many as 1,400 Americans a week being diagnosed with the disease. It is only the media's interest that has peaked."

Shilts, a reporter for the *San Francisco Chronicle* and author of the highly-praised book *And the Band Played On: Politics, People and the AIDS*

Epidemic, had been covering AIDS since the early 1980s. In the last year of the decade he took a critical look at the media situation: "The state of print reporting on federal AIDS policy is so dismal that several leading activists in New York—people like Mathilde Krim of the American Foundation for AIDS Research—are currently engaged in a fierce letter-writing campaign to persuade *Times* editor Max Frankel to ask his Washington bureau to write stories that acknowledge there is a federal government whose policies have something to do with the course of the epidemic." Television, Shilts went on, was so irresponsible that "no TV network has a reporter covering AIDS full-time. And the science reporters to whom the story has been entrusted have done little more than repeat what they are told by officials."

Once news editors realized that AIDS was an important story in mid-1985, Shilts recalled, they "made what proved to be a crucial error"—turning over the AIDS beat to medical and science writers. Some journalists provided insightful reports that helped to dispel myths about AIDS as a disease. But there was a downside; much of the coverage "mindlessly parroted administration press releases." As Shilts explained, "reporters have frequently demonstrated an astounding inability to investigate aggressively the problems within government agencies that are supposed to translate scientific achievements into practical advances. When it comes to this essentially political aspect of AIDS reporting, medical writers have shown themselves to be, at best, naive. More typically, they have proved so extraordinarily malleable that they end up presenting distorted and often dishonest information."

Shilts concludes that most science reporters "seem far more comfortable explaining science to their readers than challenging policy makers." And high-quality science reporting "means little if government doctors don't have the money and staff to apply it to the business of saving lives."

In June 1989, the same month that Shilts' media critique appeared in the New York magazine *7 Days*, San Francisco's Mayor Art Agnos took the occasion of a national mayor's conference to denounce the federal government for "incomprehensible" failures and foot-dragging in response to AIDS. But the national media, ignoring such complaints, kept covering the AIDS story as if by rote as the death toll climbed. In the summer of 1989, the estimated AIDS cases in the U.S. went over 100,000. Meanwhile, the number of Americans who died from AIDS exceeded the total of 58,021 U.S. soldiers who lost their lives in the Vietnam War. Worst of all, there was no end in sight for the AIDS epidemic.

Ignorance and bigotry, not just the AIDS virus, were responsible for killing so many people, Shilts noted. "Inarguably, the fact that gay men were the epidemic's first identified casualties had everything to do with how this country initially responded to the disease. Most of the institutional failures to confront the epidemic aggressively—whether in science, government or the media—can be traced to prejudice against gays."

As the AIDS tragedy widened still more, the *New York Times* made clear that mass media denial was very much alive. In a mid-1989 lead editorial—headlined "Why Make AIDS Worse Than It Is?"—the *Times* tried to reassure readers in a city where reported AIDS deaths of 10,700 people amounted to a small fraction of what seemed certain to follow. The *Times* had not criticized the Bush administration's inaction on AIDS. But the paper did see fit to editorialize that "the toll of new cases, which has been rising for years, may at last be about to level off and then decline. Gloomier numbers released this week by the General Accounting Office mask the possibility that the epidemic's worst rages may be abating."

With macabre complacency, the *Times* shrugged off new evidence that the number of Americans due to be diagnosed with AIDS by the end of 1991 was in the range of 300,000 to 485,000 people. "In certain major groups," the paper of record added, new infections "seem to be leveling off. If so, the epidemic will peak, and maybe sooner than many forecasters expect. The reason is that the disease is still very largely confined to specific risk groups. Once all susceptible members are infected, the numbers of new victims will decline." The editorial went out of its way to target anti-AIDS spending: "Advocates for people with AIDS sometimes accept good news badly; steadily rising tolls are such a powerful argument for new resources."

Insistent on asking for whom the bell tolls while drawing back from the human tragedies of AIDS, the *Times*—like so much of the mass media—continued to go along with deadly governmental neglect, as a decade of AIDS suffering ended and another began.

The *Times* editorial "comes at a time when the experts are bewailing the underfunding of treatment and care for the infected, the sick, and the dying," said *Village Voice* columnist Doug Ireland. He fittingly described the *Times'* editorial stance as "murderous optimism." When addressing issues of great importance, the most powerful media seem inclined to invert the ideal role of journalism by afflicting the afflicted and comforting the comfortable.

9

Press and Prejudice

The printed pages we read, and the broadcasts we tune in, are said to mirror society. But mass media also continue to *shape* our society—reinforcing certain attitudes and actions while discouraging others. If television, for instance, were not capable of fundamentally affecting people's behavior, then corporations would not be spending billions of dollars every month for commercials. If what appears in print had little impact on day-to-day lives, advertisers would not be so heavily invested in newspaper and magazine ads.

For many women, media messages reflect the kind of attitudes that rudely confront them on a daily basis. For people who are black, Latino, Native American or of Asian ancestry, the largely white world of U.S. mass media resonates with many of the prejudices that they repeatedly encounter in a white-dominated country. And for those whose sexual orientation draws them to people of the same gender, the main news media commonly leave them out or put them down.

Media that habitually stereotype, debase and overlook the humanity of some of us are not doing a good job of serving any of us. Rather than isolating and pigeonholing the wide diversity of people in the United States, shouldn't the mass media illuminate commonalities and differences, aiming to increase genuine understanding? Instead of recycling the dregs of past prejudicial views, media could help us all to take fresh looks at antiquated preconceptions.

All this may sound like nothing more than common sense. But despite all the progress that's been made in recent decades, common nonsense still finds its way into American mass media portrayals of issues surrounding gender and race.

WOMEN'S RIGHTS AND MEDIA WRONGS

Picture this scene at the 1987 Pan Am games: U.S. basketball player Jennifer Gillom dribbles the ball up the court as millions of people across the United States watch on TV. Then they hear CBS commentator Billy Packer say, "Doesn't Gillom remind you of a lady who someday is going to have a nice large family and is going to be a great cook? Doesn't she look like that? She's got just a real pleasant face."

Or consider what happened on NBC Television at the 1984 Democratic National Convention, as Geraldine Ferraro—the first woman nominated for national office by a major party—looked out from the podium while the convention hall erupted with cheers from the delegates. On the air, Tom Brokaw provided this narration: "Geraldine Ferraro... The first woman to be nominated for Vice President... Size six!"

When the *Washington Post*'s venerated columnist David Broder wrote that the National Organization for Women was "strident and showboating," *USA Today* founder Al Neuharth liked the comment so much that he quoted it in his own column. Only ten days earlier, another Neuharth commentary had called for the return of the "sky girls" he preferred to look at. "Many of the young, attractive, enthusiastic female flight attendants—then called stewardesses—have been replaced by aging women who are tired of their jobs or by flighty young men who have trouble balancing a cup of coffee," Neuharth complained. He yearned for the days when a flight attendant was "a nurse; unmarried; under age 25; not over 5 feet 4 inches tall; weight less than 115 pounds." This conveyed something of the mentality of the man who invented and ran *USA Today* for its first half-dozen years. His unabashed sexism so appalled many staffers at the newspaper that 175 (out of 426 in the newsroom) quickly signed a letter declaring they were "offended, outraged and embarrassed" by the founding father's column.

Male media dominance

Between the lines and between the transmitters is an invisible shrug about the status of women in America. We are told that it's improving—but usually without reference to how bad the situation remains. The mass media, ill-equipped to play a constructive role, are key contributors to the problems facing women. That's not surprising, since news media companies are bastions of male supremacy themselves.

In 1989 men held 94 percent of the top management positions in the U.S. news media. As for reporters, men had the highest profiles. A study of the front pages of ten major newspapers found that only about one-quarter—27 percent—of the bylines were women's. (*USA Today* ranked best at 41 percent; in contrast 16 percent of the *New York Times*' front-page bylines belonged to women.) On network television the picture was similar; researchers found that on the nightly news, 22.2 percent of the stories on CBS were reported by women, 14.4 percent on NBC, and 10.5 percent on ABC.

"I think women are going to continue to be a presence in broadcasting, but we've had a slowdown [at the networks] in the last eight years," Marlene Sanders said in 1989, after a long career as a reporter and producer at ABC and CBS Television. "The move for affirmative action has been played down. The pressure is off the people who hire. The women are there, but at a quarter of staff." At commercial TV stations around the country, figures for 1988 showed that 18 percent of the news directors were women.

"There are fewer women on air at the networks now than there were in 1975 when I went to work at the networks," Linda Ellerbee said in 1989. The situation farther up the hierarchy was even worse. "The reason you see us on TV is so you don't notice our absence in that room marked 'executive producer' or 'CEO' or 'network president'... You get to a certain place where you would reasonably expect that the next executive producer job will be yours, for example. Then you see younger, less qualified men promoted over you. It's much harder for the women on the management side than it is on the air." Ellerbee added that with "younger women coming into this business...I hear them saying that they'd better not make waves or they won't get anywhere because that's the way corporations work."

Media commentators are overwhelmingly male. "For all their activity now outside the home," said Fairleigh Dickinson University's dean of graduate studies, Barbara Kellerman, "women are by and large still excluded from the select group that constructs our national reality." While women are becoming more visible as news reporters, "for a female to play the role of commentator, expert, or analyst—that is, to be the resident sage—is still disturbingly rare." During presidential campaigns, for instance, "television's stock experts" are "almost invariably men." Studies of the nation's op-ed pages show a heavy preponderance of males.

Women's voices are also scarce in news coverage. Surveys of ten leading newspapers found that 11 percent of people quoted on the front page were female. (For the *New York Times* the figure was five percent.) Betty Friedan called the absence of women on front pages "a symbolic annihilation of women. I don't think it's a systematic attempt to do that by editors, but I do think it is clearly related to the style and content decisions of what makes news, and those are still being defined by men." Said Junior Bridge, a researcher for the surveys: "Is the news that appears on the front page really the news we want? We raise men in this country to believe that things in our daily lives are irrelevant, and things women do are irrelevant."

Abortion lingo and the floating fetus

One of the experiences that can only be second-hand for the men dominating the press is abortion. In 1989, the Supreme Court gave state legislatures more latitude to interfere with abortions. Like the highest court itself, those legislatures were dominated by men who could rest assured they would never get pregnant. And like the legislators, the pundits too were of a singularly uninvolved gender as they uttered assorted wisdom on the topic. "The talk shows are becoming just incredible," exclaimed Eleanor Smeal, president of the Fund for the Feminist Majority. "The major national talk shows are white male conservatives... The Washington gangs that you see on Sunday morning are all men essentially. Oh, they have a woman here and there, but it's nowhere near balanced. And on a subject like abortion, don't tell me a 55-year-old man feels like a 35-year-old woman, I mean it's just not possible."

"IN THE NEXT HALF HOUR, MY WEALTHY WHITE CONSERVATIVE MALE FRIENDS AND I WILL DISCUSS THE ANNOYINGLY PERSISTENT BLACK UNDER-CLASS, AND WHY WOMEN GET SO EMOTIONAL ABOUT ABORTION."

Labeling has been central to media coverage of abortion. In the courts and in politics, disputes center around whether abortion should be legal. Activists and others who support that option are pro-choice. But some media have insisted on calling them "pro-abortion." For instance, in an introductory segment on ABC's *Nightline*, Jeff Greenfield repeatedly used "pro-abortion." Throughout 1989, *Chicago Tribune* news articles frequently referred to "abortion supporters" and "pro-abortion" forces. And in an ironic twist the newspaper ran the headline "Abortion rights gain for fathers," over a report on backing in the Illinois legislature for a bill to "give a father the right to seek a court injunction to prevent a woman from terminating her pregnancy."

Use of the "pro-abortion" term implied that supporters of abortion rights were trying to maximize the frequency of abortions. The term also masked the realities of abortion as a last resort. "As a woman who was forced to confront this decision, I can assure you that it is a rare woman, indeed, who 'wants' to have an abortion," said Kate Michelman, executive director of the National Abortion Rights Action League. She added: "Our position, and the position of the vast majority of Americans, is pro-choice, not pro-abortion."

Sometimes bias has been stark, as when *U.S. News & World Report* made a sweeping reference to "abortion, pornography and other threats to families"—a favorite theme of many groups opposed to abortion rights.

Broadcast journalism has felt their sting, as when an ABC Radio special on the subject, hosted by Barbara Walters, aired without commercials in summer 1989. "This topic is one advertisers seem to be very cautious about," a network official explained. And before NBC broadcast a two-hour TV movie, *Roe v. Wade*, starring Holly Hunter, several advertisers pulled out as sponsors. They did so at the request of a leading gendarme of social propriety, the American Family Association based in Tupelo, Mississippi.

Abortion-rights activists have tried to buy commercial air time. But TV networks refused to run paid spots for an upcoming Washington march for legal abortion in spring 1989. The ads were blocked from the airwaves as too "controversial"—an objection that, for instance, has not impeded pro-nuclear commercials which appear regularly on television.

Eleanor Smeal charged that while "the media has been very willing to show the opposition's films, such as *Silent Scream*, it worries about showing a real abortion. The rationale is that somehow it might be viewed as not good taste... One of the things we would love them to show is what comes out of an abortion at the typical abortion. It's only two tablespoons of tissue and blood. Well, they show the grotesque pictures of the opposition, and those pictures—we don't believe are real. The pictures are always of what they *purport* to be a typical abortion, but have to be either last trimester or stillbirths, or perhaps not even an abortion, and they're grotesque. Ninety-one percent of all abortions occur in the first trimester. Less than one one-hundredth of one percent of abortions are in the last trimester. Yet to show what is the truth is somehow more controversial than the distortion."

On TV, when an anchor reports the latest abortion news, a common background graphic is a well-developed fetus. While presented as a neutral symbol of the abortion issue, the fetal logo strongly tilts the debate—perhaps as much as a drawing of a coathanger (signifying harm caused by illegal abortions) would tilt in the opposite direction. The logo is in sync with tendencies to push women almost out of the mental pictures we have of the abortion issue. "The rise of the fetus as an independent figure in our national consciousness has transformed the debate—upstaging, and sometimes eclipsing, women and their stake in the legality of abortion," Barbara Ehrenreich has observed. Media framing of the issue brought us to a point where, in her words, "the fetus is viewed almost as a freestanding individual, while women have all but disappeared."

But if concerned women were to be pushed from the abortion picture, so were women journalists—at least according to some of the most powerful newspapers in the country. The *Washington Post* reprimanded staff reporters who, on their own time, marched for abortion rights with hundreds of thousands of other Americans one Sunday in April 1989. At the *Post*—as at the *Philadelphia Inquirer* and *Chicago Tribune*—the First Amendment seemed in disrepute. The *Post* handed down a memo ordering every "newsroom professional" not to take part in any abortion-related demonstration, no matter what subject areas they reported on for the newspaper. The preference seemed to be for training journalists not to have any convictions strong enough to impel public protest on a matter of principle.

An ironic *Post*script came a few weeks after issuance of the thou-shalt-not-demonstrate memo, when the *Washington Post* published a very favorable news article headlined "Chinese Journalists Demand Freedom," about more than 1,000 reporters and editors who were publicly petitioning in China. The featured photo was of a Chinese editor speaking through a bull-horn to demonstrators against press censorship. The specter of journalists on the march was laudable in Beijing, but unprofessional in Washington.

For all the uproar about abortion, there has been little media promotion of contraception. Suggestive sexuality is unabashed in movies, TV shows, newspapers and magazines. But the rudiments of contraception—and the failures to come up with more reliable and less hazardous forms of birth con-trol—are not on the media agenda. Bloody violence and flip allusions to sex are media staples, yet somehow a straightforward and continuing flow of information about preventing unwanted pregnancies is deemed too "sensi-tive" for the mass media to implement. That the need for abortions might be appreciably lessened by such information is apparently too logical for the media powers to acknowledge.

Domestic violence and rape

In 1974, Ann Simonton was the model who appeared on the cover of the *Sports Illustrated* annual swimsuit issue. But, she now says, that type of media emphasis dehumanizes women, encouraging violence against them. In an interview, Simonton described the process this way: "The media indoctri-nates the masses to view women as consumable products. Women, now viewed as 'things,' are much easier to violate and to harm because they aren't seen as human beings." She offered the following equation: *Woman = product = consumption = what one purchases has no will of its own.*

Perhaps the situation in the USA is not much different than in France, where the government Women's Rights Minister, Michele Andre, said: "If a man beats a dog on the street, someone will complain to the animal protec-tion society. But if a man beats his wife in the street, no one moves." In the United States, a country which has no high governmental post for women's rights, the city of Chicago had three times as many shelters for animals as for battered women in 1989; the animal shelters had a total budget several times higher too.

The *Time* magazine cover story "Women Face the '90s" included poll results showing that 88 percent of American women rated rape as an issue "very important" to them. Yet nowhere else in the six-page spread did *Time* so much as mention rape—or any other form of violence against women. While the women of America are justifiably concerned, the media of America paper over the issue.

A brutal assault is apt to be written off as the product of a sick mind, unconnected to the cultural attitudes that go unchallenged and routinely fueled by the dominant media of the country. But, as former Brooklyn district attorney Elizabeth Holtzman says, "Rape is only superficially a sexual act. It is foremost an act of violence, degradation and control... Sexual violence against women exists because attitudes dehumanizing women exist." And, she adds, "Society should stop identifying sex with violence and with denigration of women, and that includes the images on television and in the other media."

According to the FBI's national statistics, a forcible rape gets reported to police once every six minutes, and one woman in ten will be raped during her lifetime—an extreme underestimate. Studies calculate that up to one-third of females in the United States will be raped during their lifetimes. Whatever the data, media usually report the figures fatalistically—as if rape were a natural occurrence.

News reporting of rape is selective. "Think of all the women," suggests poet and essayist Katha Pollitt, "who have not entered the folklore of crime because their beatings and/or rapes and/or murders lacked the appropriate ingredients for full-dress media treatment—which include, alas, being white, young, middle-class and, as the tabloids love to say, 'attractive.'" These kinds of imbalances in coverage are magnified when sensationalized stories stress rape as a black-on-white crime. In fact, most rape is *intra*racial.

Also obscured is the reality that—whatever the race of the assailant—rape is almost entirely a male-on-female crime. After the highly-publicized and extremely brutal gang rape of a woman jogging in New York's Central Park in 1989, such points were rarely discussed in mass media. That was certainly the case when six men and no women appeared on ABC's *This Week With David Brinkley* to discuss the Central Park rape—just another instance of how male voices dominate the media, defining what the "issues" are, and are not.

When a woman publicly charged that Senator Brock Adams—a longtime friend of her family—had sexually assaulted her, *U.S. News & World Report* began its account this way: "The senator is not the first politician accused of hanky-panky." A press that uses "hanky-panky" as a synonym for sexual assault is part of the nation's milieu that tacitly accepts rape.

More than half of the rapes in the United States are perpetrated by men who are not strangers to the women they attack—but you wouldn't know that from our mass media. When rape happens between people who know each other, news coverage is usually skimpy or nonexistent, says Robin Warshaw, author of the landmark book *I Never Called It Rape*. When people don't see "acquaintance rapes" or "date rapes" reported in the media, the implication is that such rapes don't happen, or that there's nothing much wrong with them when they do. And the reporting "still really focuses on what women should do, what limits they should do in order to be safe. There is very little examination of men and why they do it. The focus is on making the woman responsible for being raped."

Until the news media start reporting rape for what it is—a viciously violent crime—society will fail to treat it that way. And until the media start defining the prevalence of rape in the U.S. as a crisis, the dominant public messages about rape will imply acceptance.

OUR HOMOPHOBIC PRESS

Along with portrayals of women, media outlooks toward gay people have been slow to change. Some media continue to identify open homosexuality as a symbol of modern ills, as when a 1987 *Parade* magazine article fondly reminisced: "The '50s, viewed through the rosy prism of nostalgia, were the good old days... We had never heard of AIDS. Homosexuals stayed in the closet, not on the front pages."

While progress has been evident during the past two decades, prejudices continue to deeply influence the publicized images of lesbians and gay males in America. Clearly, journalism can provide excellent coverage about the nation's wide spectrum of gay people. Some articles and news broadcasts have shown sensitivity and insight—but such instances are much more the exception than the rule.

National Public Radio aired a superb retrospective report 20 years after gay resistance to a police raid at a bar in Greenwich Village set in motion the country's gay liberation movement. "Remembering Stonewall," a half-hour segment produced by Pacifica Radio and aired on *All Things Considered* one evening in the summer of 1989, was rich with oral history rendered vivid and alive. Those who produced "Remembering Stonewall" for a national radio audience of several million people showed that the boundaries of news media potential are far wider and more meaningful than the usual limits of American journalism.

In a city considered a mecca for homosexuals, San Francisco's morning *Chronicle* and afternoon *Examiner* have had plenty of incentive to improve news treatment of gay people. When the *Examiner* put together a 16-day "Gay in America" series—drawing on 50,000 hours of staff time—the result was 64 pages illuminating the lives and concerns of gays in the Bay area and elsewhere. The 1989 project was unprecedented for a U.S. daily paper. "I'd go to other cities and describe it to journalists and get blank looks," recalled a reporter and editor who worked on the series, Raul Ramirez. The series was notable for its broad scope and a tone affirming homosexuality as a sexual orientation as valid as any other.

The greatest success of the project, wrote a columnist for the city's alternative weekly *Bay Guardian*, "was that it dared to make visible gay men and lesbians who were real people, with all the differences and contradictions that entails." That set the *Examiner* series apart from mass media's usual cubbyhole approach, David Israels added: "For the most part, gays rarely see themselves in the newspaper or on the nightly TV news unless the story is about death (AIDS) or politics (usually the repeal of gay or AIDS rights statutes). As for the supreme arbiters of cultural acceptance—film and television—gay life is virtually nonexistent."

Attacks on lesbians and gay males

Outside of San Francisco, U.S. media coverage is frequently equivocal or worse about gays. While generally avoiding overt put-downs of people because of their gender or the color of their skin, many journalists imply that gay people may have already gained more than their fair share of human rights. "There is a myth that our community isn't oppressed any more," said *Village Voice* writer Donna Minkowitz. "On the TV news, we are a powerful minority beginning to flex its perversely huge muscles. But that image ignores much of our experience."

Underneath a thin layer of tolerance, media are routinely indifferent to day-to-day realities. Attacks unleashed on lesbians and gay men get little censure in the mainstream press. Newspapers publicized a report by the National Gay and Lesbian Task Force documenting 7,248 acts of violence that targeted homosexuals in 1988—but mass media neither dwelled on the pattern nor defined it as a serious human rights problem. The links with other types of bigotry were clear to researchers, even though the press seemed disinclined to give the connections a second glance. "There has been an increase in homophobic behavior and it is not just within the general population," warned Janet Caldwell of the Center for Democratic Renewal. "It is also an outgrowth of the activities of organized hate groups, including the Klan and the neo-Nazis."

Anti-homosexual venom doesn't seem to bother many in the media who criticize other forms of bigotry. While taking the rock group Guns n' Roses to task for racism in song lyrics, *Entertainment Tonight* appeared unconcerned by vilification of gay people. The TV show singled out a verse from a Guns n' Roses song addressing African-Americans as "niggers"—but the program ignored the same song's reference to "faggots" spreading AIDS. *Entertainment Tonight* also made no mention of the Guns n' Roses album cover's urging that people be on guard against attacks by gays.

Selling the straight life

Sometimes media aversion to gays takes the form of a not-so-soft sell for the superiority of the straight life. A *Christian Science Monitor* front-page article, headlined "Finding pathways out of homosexuality," chronicled the efforts of "ex-gays" to give others "an opportunity to change." The story, which was slanted toward a view of homosexuality as an affliction, did not mention that the newspaper itself refused to knowingly employ any homosexuals.

"The *Christian Science Monitor* is an activity of The First Church of Christ, Scientist," the paper's circulation manager explained in a letter to an angry subscriber who had learned of the policy. "Consequently, the standards of the newspaper cannot be different from those of the church. Our moral standards are based on the Bible, which for us has very clear statements on sexual conduct." After firing employee Chris Madsen because she was a lesbian, the newspaper engaged in seven years of legal battles rather than reinstate her.

While most newspapers are more accepting of employee diversity, homophobic attitudes have a way of surfacing to the printed page. The *New York Times* published a news article which cited unnamed sources and baseless innuendos suggesting that lesbian parenting could damage children: "Some clinicians speculate that in the long term, girls might have difficulty in intimate relationships with men, and boys might be uncomfortable with their roles as males. If lesbian parents are openly hostile toward men, these difficulties could be worsened." After gay activists complained, the *Times* published an editor's note admitting that the comments in question "were added to the article during editing" after reporter Gina Kolata had submitted it. "In the absence of evidence that hostility toward men is common among lesbian parents," the *Times* conceded, "the reference to such hostility was unwarranted. The article should have given lesbian parents a chance to respond."

Contributing to American homophobia are nationally televised news accounts like a 1989 story by Fox TV's *The Reporters* about a male pedophile. The show linked homosexuality with sexual abuse of boys. In response, the Gay & Lesbian Alliance Against Defamation (GLAAD) asked: "Would a segment on Ted Bundy or Charles Manson describe them as killers, rapists and heterosexuals?" As GLAAD pointed out, "Statistically the vast majority of child sexual abuse cases involve heterosexual men who abuse girls (usually family members or friends), although the media's coverage has disproportionately focused on men who abuse boys." That imbalance of coverage "serves to perpetuate the popular myth that all molesters are gay, and all gays are molesters."

On Capitol Hill, the media periodically go wild over "scandals" involving sexual conduct, gay and straight. The matter of whether sex was between consenting adults sometimes seems to count less than whether the activities were heterosexual or homosexual. Thus, in 1989, when an Ohio jury convicted U.S. Representative Donald Lukens of having sex with a 16-year-old female, the media uproar was far less sustained than the tumult that greeted Lukens' colleague Barney Frank for his relationship with a man who worked as a prostitute.

For many millions of gay Americans a recurring message is that there is something wrong with their sexual orientation. Every time a news account speaks of an "accusation" of homosexuality, or refers to someone as an "admitted" homosexual, the harmful prejudices get reinforced. When the Republican National Committee issued a news release implying that House Speaker Tom Foley was a homosexual, few of the press commentators who vocally deplored the "smear" raised the question of why homosexuality—real or invented—should amount to a smear at all.

While homosexuals often face media negativity, prejudice also manifests in omissions; gays are frequently excluded from consideration as a legitimate minority group. After a New York City redistricting hearing in 1989, for example, the *New York Times* reported calls for fair representation of the black, Hispanic, and Asian-American communities without mentioning that gay and lesbian community activists had testified with similar concerns. Protests of the exclusion seemed to have little effect on the *Times*. In a follow-up article on redistricting, written by the same reporter, the *Times* again failed to give any ink to the views of gay and lesbian groups.

While instances of sensitive reporting about lesbians and gay males have been on the rise, serious defects persist. The media's discussions of gay rights in the abstract ignore the personal dimensions of daily life impinged upon by anti-gay bigotry. If American journalism were doing a better job, it would discover reasons to pay attention to voices like that of writer Jacqi Tully: "When I don't hold hands with my lover in the grocery store, the issue isn't how much I can display affection publicly. It's freedom. My freedom. I don't have as much of it as heterosexuals do."

VIOLENCE, DRUGS AND CRIME

Our media never tire of deploring violence, drugs and crime in American society. Yet among the scourges most exacerbated by the media are...violence, drugs, and crime.

American mass media are strongly against violence, and, in doublespeak fashion, they strongly encourage it. Every decade the average TV viewer takes in more than 100,000 acts of violence. The acclimation to "solving" problems with violence starts very early.

Saturday morning cartoon shows are replete with violence, as role-model characters express anger by clobbering each other. When children watch prime-time, it's even worse. The 8:00-9:00 p.m. time period is now the most violent hour of the TV day. Overall the average child sees more than 1,000 dramatized murders on TV each year.

But does all that televised violence make children more aggressive? TV network executives say no, pointing to a study commissioned by NBC. However, says American Psychological Association official Brian Wilcox, three separate independent examinations of the study each "concluded that the network-hired researchers misinterpreted their own evidence and that NBC's own data actually showed a causal relationship between television violence and increased aggression in children." In fact, according to the Knight-Ridder news service, out of 85 major studies on the subject, the NBC study was the only one that did not find a direct connection.

"We keep pumping children with the messages that violence is the way to solve their problems—and some of it takes hold," commented Aletha C. Huston, co-director of the Center for Research on the Influence of Television on Children. As an exceptional article by Knight-Ridder reporter Carl M. Cannon concluded, "the evidence on television violence is in."

- "It comes in studies—more than 3,000 of them—almost all of which show that children who watch television violence are more prone to use physical aggression than those who don't."
- "It comes in somber warnings from child psychologists who can tell after one visit which preschool-age children watch violent television and which do not."
- "It comes in the configurations of the corpses, mutilated by disturbed teenagers to resemble victims in slasher movies that find their way onto television."

Addictive drugs

Meanwhile, a substance that contributes to many violent tragedies—alcohol—gets too little challenge from news media. "We've been engaged on a national level in a war on drugs for three years. But people aren't aware that alcohol is the biggest drug problem in the country," said Christine Lubinski, an official with the National Council on Alcoholism, which works to end alcohol's "privileged position in society."

A major obstacle continued to be the reality that mass media are on the take from breweries, wineries and distillers. Media proprietors have been pleased to pocket the enormous booze-soaked ad revenues. The same media provide little information about the dire impacts of alcohol.

While the press has gone wild reporting on tragic instances of babies born addicted to crack, it's been rare to see a major news report on a far more widespread occurrence—fetal alcohol syndrome (FAS). American news media have not hesitated to sensationalize what can happen after pregnant women use cocaine. But despite all the self-righteous hoopla about the need to stop drugs, the mass media have in effect winked at FAS, the country's most prevalent preventable birth defect. Journalistic institutions haven't done much to inform the public of the Surgeon General's conclusion that *no* amount of alcohol is safe for a woman who is pregnant or nursing a newborn.

Likewise, women can watch TV for nine months and never be told that smoking while pregnant severely jeopardizes the health of their offspring. In 1989 the Surgeon General reported that cigarettes were currently responsible for more than one out of six deaths in the United States. Such facts are treated as intermittent items in the media—but not as a "crisis."

In contrast, the American news media frequently denounce drugs like crack cocaine and heroin, commonly decrying their use as a national emergency. The "drug crisis" has become a never-ending media sensation.

When people take addictive drugs, despair is often a crucial factor. To examine that despair, however, would require deeply probing social conditions. Politicians usually aren't interested in such pursuits, and American journalism doesn't bother with them much either. A key effect of anti-drug frenzies in the media, sociologists Craig Reinarman and Harry G. Levine point out, is to "blame individual behavior and morality for endemic social and structural problems, and divert attention and resources from those larger problems."

Drug scares not only sidestep social ills; media-induced hysteria actually undercuts possibilities for really solving them. The same White House preaching anti-crack sermons "had just said NO to virtually every social program aimed at creating alternatives for inner-city young people. Unfortunately, these kids cannot 'Just say NO' to poverty and unemployment. Drug abuse...has been used as a scapegoat for crime, rebellious youth, failing productivity, broken families, urban poverty, black and Hispanic unemployment, and other social problems that have little to do with drugs and much to do with U.S. economic and social policy."

Drug hysteria

The media provided an enormous build-up for President Bush's "war on drugs" speech from the Oval Office in September 1989. By then, some news accounts mentioned that public opinion saw drugs as the nation's number-one problem. When pollsters asked Americans "What do you think is the most important problem facing this country today?" in July 1989, barely over 20 percent answered, "Drugs." Two months later, well over 60 percent gave that answer. Amazing what some media hype can do.

In Washington, an upsurge of murders tied to the drug trade generated enormous publicity in 1989. The *New York Times* reported that "the crime-and-drug crisis is the first long-running, truly local story in recent memory to draw so much national attention. News organizations are responding by pulling staff members from other assignments to roam the streets, carrying newly purchased cellular phones to keep in contact with their offices and portable police scanners to stay on top of the latest killings." During previous years, the rampant poverty in the Nation's Capital seems to have been much less important to the media managers determining the flow of news across the United States.

The problems of crack and other illicit drugs were real and horrendous enough. But while some critics said that attacking the causes of drug abuse was the only possible solution, most media echoed official evasions. Bush called for spending about two-thirds of anti-drug funds on law enforcement. The *New York Times* quickly editorialized that "there is broad agreement that as much ought to go for treatment as for law enforcement." But whether earmarking a third or a half of the money for drug treatment programs, both Bush and the *Times* were content to piddle around with non-solutions. Even William Randolph Hearst Jr., hardly a bleeding-heart liberal, noted a few days later that "95 percent of the many thousands of drug addicts who seek treatment are turned away."

It was certainly true that, as a front-page headline in the *Times* reported, "In Cities, Poor Families Are Dying of Crack." But they were also suffering and dying of many other afflictions—including preventable diseases, inadequate health care, lead poisoning, malnutrition, lousy schools, greedy landlords, a severe dearth of economic opportunities, and an overall atmosphere of institutional violence in their surroundings. Drugs were taking a heavy toll on minority communities in the U.S., but media seemed prone to mistake cause and effect.

Chicago Tribune columnist Clarence Page, interviewed for this book, cautioned that "we fool ourselves thinking that we are going to fight this 'war on drugs.' We fall prey to this war metaphor...from government sources and the media picks up on it." He added: "Our culture kind of demands that we have a war metaphor before we can deal with a social problem. We have a cultural drive to deal with this in a legalistic sense instead of a sociological sense of really caring about the people who are the victims of this problem. We're talking about illiteracy, bad schools, we're talking about alienation, we're talking about racism, we're talking about a lot of things. Social problems that are at the root of the drug problem."

Street crime and suite crime

While the roots of lawlessness get little media focus, street crime and punishment are hot topics. Severe penalties for corporate criminals, however, are non-issues—even though a single act of white-collar corruption, such as cutting corners on safety for new cars or any number of other consumer products, can cause more human suffering and death than dozens of crack dealers can. Typically, the criminal role of the banking industry has gotten little press—even though, according to the *New York Times*, "more than $100 billion a year in drug money flows through the nation's banks."

Double standards are pervasive. Although a *Newsweek* cover story observed that "the Crack Nation includes all sizes, classes and hues," white people were absent from the featured photos. Meanwhile, black people in the *Newsweek* spread "were profiled in the usual flattering positions that the media delights in showing us," wrote Earl Hutchinson, an editor based in Inglewood, California. "They were in handcuffs, stretched out on the ground, spreadeagled against a wall, in court, marching off to prisons and drug wards." *Newsweek*'s words were in sync with its pictures. According to the magazine, the crack plague "feeds on junkies and cops, hookers and babies" and must be "mercilessly destroyed." But in an accompanying story about big-money swindlers, titled "White-Collar Shame," the tone was decidedly less harsh about rich white criminals: "The harshest penalty may be the one they inflict on themselves."

News media generally recycle the judicial system's definitions of crime. "We have a system shaped by economic bias from the start," wrote Jeffrey H. Reiman, professor of criminal justice at American University. "The dangerous acts and crimes unique to the wealthy are either ignored or treated lightly, while for the so-called common crimes, the poor are far more likely than the well-off to be arrested, if arrested charged, if charged convicted, and if convicted sentenced to prison." Day to day, and year to year, news reporting looks at this status quo uncritically.

When journalists discuss thefts they are referring to individual actions—not economic manipulations by the high and mighty. As attorney Gerry Spence has written, "the cost of corporate crime in America is over ten times greater than the combined larcenies, robberies, burglaries and autothefts committed by individuals." But the magnitude of the theft bears little relation to the amount of media reporting. And when reporters refer to violent crime they mean murders, assaults and the like—not the corporate policies that result in injuries and deaths. Like other instruments of the power structure, America's mass media impart what Reiman calls "a message of enormous ideological value to those at the top in our society: the message that the greatest danger to the average citizen comes from below him or her on the economic ladder, not from above."

For every citizen who is murdered, two Americans "die as a result of unhealthy or unsafe conditions in the workplace." But the news media join in accepting the legal bias. "Although these work-related deaths could have been prevented, they are not called murders," Reiman notes, adding that "the label 'crime' is not used in America to name all or the worst of the actions that cause misery and suffering to Americans. It is primarily reserved for the dangerous actions of the poor."

The news media do little more than repeat the judgments of a system that "deals with some evil and not with others," Reiman says, "because it treats some evils as the gravest and treats some of the gravest evils as minor."

Crimes in the streets are real enough. But by downplaying the importance of crimes committed in the suites, journalists literally become little more than court reporters.

If our media were more independent and evenhanded, a TV news broadcast might include reportage like this: *Two people were killed in an armed robbery today. And in other crime news: Figures released today show that more than 20 area residents died last month because they could not get adequate medical care. At the same time, failures by local employers to provide safe working conditions resulted in the deaths of four workers.*

The color of crime

For a month, journalist Kirk A. Johnson monitored about 3,200 news stories as he studied the output of six of the largest news media in Boston—two daily papers, three TV channels and one radio station—plus four small print and radio outlets with black ownership. The contrasts were striking.

"In the major media," Johnson found in examining coverage about the city's two mainly-black sections, "most of the stories about these neighborhoods dealt with crime or violent accidents and, all in all, 85 percent reinforced negative stereotypes of blacks. Blacks were persistently shown as drug pushers and users, as thieves, as troublemakers, and as victims or perpetrators of violence."

But the black media provided a very different mix of news coverage. By contrast, "57 percent of the stories about the two neighborhoods suggested a black community thirsty for educational advancement and entrepreneurial achievement, and eager to remedy poor living conditions made worse by bureaucratic neglect. Many of these stories went unreported by the major media."

Same city. Same neighborhoods. Same profession (journalism). Very different depictions of reality.

Reporting his research in *Columbia Journalism Review*, Johnson said that taken as a whole "the evidence suggests that major-media news about Boston's predominantly black neighborhoods is biased in the direction of commonly held stereotypes about blacks and the poor. Stories featuring crime and violence dominate, almost to the exclusion of stories that would reflect the true diversity of the black community, so that a typical news consumer might easily come to associate the prevailing negative images with all inner-city blacks." Although in the major media the two neighborhoods "accounted for only seven percent of the crime news during the thirty-day period, 59 percent of all the news about these two black neighborhoods was about crime. The tacit message is that, while all criminals may not be black, most inner-city blacks are criminals."

News coverage of crime, Michael Parenti argues, "is largely determined by the class and racial background of the victim and victimizer. Affluent victims are more likely to receive press attention than poor ones, leaving the false impression that most victims of crime are from upper- and middle-class backgrounds."

Crime coverage may be slanted most of all on TV. "Television with its visual orientation loves pictures of cops and robbers, people getting arrested, blood and guts and shoot-outs and that sort of thing," says Clarence Page. "They generally go for the areas closest to them, mostly big cities and most crime in big cities is committed by blacks and Hispanics. You wind up with a lot of pictures on TV of black and Hispanic people getting busted for crimes. The problem in the public is the mentality that they confuse crime with blacks and Hispanics, so that whenever blacks or Hispanics move into their neighborhood they immediately say, 'Oh we're going to get a lot of crime'... That would be my biggest complaint. Too often crime is portrayed with a minority face on it."

During the same week in spring 1989 when a gang of black youths assaulted and raped a white woman jogging in New York's Central Park (widely publicized as the "wilding" case), 28 other women (mostly minorities) were raped in the city, including a black woman thrown from a rooftop after a brutal attack. But those tragedies were lost in the media-bias shuffle. Clarence Page later wrote of "the double standard the media and society appear to place on the value of black life. Many resent the way the mob psychology that caused commentators to brand the black boys of East Harlem 'wolves,' 'savages' and 'mutants' never applied such titles to the white boys of Howard Beach, who killed one black man and beat two others for the sin of being in their neighborhood after dark." A couple of months after the Central Park rape, "a group of middle class white kids over in New Jersey gang-raped a white girl who was a special education student," Page recalled in an interview. "None of the media referred to them as a 'wolf pack.' The media tended to portray them generally as 'misguided youths.' When it's a bunch of black kids, it's a 'wolf pack.'"

RACISM: DENIAL AND PERPETUATION

Public images of racial minorities are still largely controlled by whites in American mass media. Newsrooms regularly foster unbalanced reporting about people of color. The patterns may go unnoticed because they're so routine.

America has been called a nation of immigrants—but the news media, through language and emphasis, often give the impression that some immigrants are more welcome than others. For Hispanic people in the United States, much of the media focus is on law enforcement actions against undocumented workers, who are often listed as contributors to the nation's woes. Under the headline "US Paying Stiff Price for Porous Borders," the

Christian Science Monitor printed this subhead on its front page: "After three centuries of inattention, pressure is building to close off entry of drugs, aliens." The article's first sentence grouped together "drug traffickers, illegal aliens, smugglers, and even potential terrorists."

Likely to evoke sci-fi images at least unconsciously, the phrase "illegal aliens"—standard in the news—is dehumanizing. Linda Mitchell, spokeswoman for the Coalition for Humane Immigrant Rights of Los Angeles, calls that catch-phrase "an inflammatory way to categorize a group of people. It's a polarizing term. An alien is someone who's not human, so the message is we don't need to care about how they're being treated. The use of these words in the media ends up justifying how people are looked at: 'Illegal aliens' don't have rights because they're criminals and it's as if they're from another planet."

Customarily obscured are some key reasons why undocumented workers have come to the U.S. from south of the border. Nearly a half-million Salvadoran refugees settled in the Los Angeles area during the 1980s; news accounts rarely connected the exodus from their war-wracked homeland with massive U.S. military aid to the government of El Salvador. Nor is the press inclined to link the influx of Mexicans to their country's debt crisis and economic tailspins—even though U.S. policies have more than a little to do with those circumstances.

While posing as foes of prejudice, the mainstream media do much to sustain it. Writing in *Essence* magazine, journalist Jeri L. Love charged that the country's mass communications system "exhibits continuous indifference, ignorance and insensitivity toward the Black community." The same goes for Native Americans, and many Latino and Asian communities. Love's judgment may seem unduly harsh to those who prefer to believe that mass media side with racial understanding and social justice. But that very impression is a dangerous result of news media that have been more self-congratulatory than candid about current racial realities in the United States.

Racism at the top

Despite periodic flaps about racist statements by public figures, the mass media seem willing to accept racism in high places. The political career of Ronald Reagan is a case in point. During the battle for "open housing" in California, when blacks sought the right to live in neighborhoods of their choice, then-Governor Reagan maintained that the blacks were "just making trouble" and really had no intention of moving. When Martin Luther King Jr. was killed in 1968, Reagan implied that King had brought the assassination upon himself—that by breaking unjust laws in the interest of desegregation, King had somehow given the green light to murder. When poor blacks gathered in Oakland to receive free groceries paid as ransom in the 1974 kidnaping of Patty Hearst, Reagan quipped that he hoped for "an outbreak of botulism" among the food recipients. Media did not make an issue of these statements when Reagan ran for the presidency. Moreover, in 1982, President Reagan wrote a letter praising the publisher of overtly racist and anti-Semitic literature, Roger Pearson, but that was no big deal as far as news media were concerned.

During the 1984 and 1988 campaigns, however, the press kept after Jesse Jackson to atone for his "Hymietown" remark (which he did on numerous occasions) and to repudiate black nationalist minister Louis Farrakhan for making anti-Semitic remarks. But the media still did not hold Reagan and George Bush accountable for their tolerance of racism, even though a Reagan Cabinet member, Terrel Bell, said that racist slurs were frequently uttered by White House staffers. When Interior Secretary James Watt's racist remarks led to his resignation, the White House expressed regrets over his departure—and the media let the matter drop rather than push Reagan to denounce Watt.

Nor did the mass media confront the racist remarks that House Republican leader Robert Michel uttered nearly two months before the 1988 general election. In a TV interview taped in mid-September—but kept under wraps until six days after the election, when *USA Today: The Television Show* finally broadcast it—Michel stated that he wished he could use the word "nigger" in the song "Ol' Man River." Michel also expressed regret at the dying out of minstrel shows, and rendered an impromptu imitation of Kingfish from *Amos 'n' Andy*. Yet *USA Today*'s TV show did not consider his statements to be "news" until after the election was over. Even when the interview was aired, most national media treated it as a minor story that ended with Michel's perfunctory apology. "If a right-winger says something racially insulting, it's treated as just another day at the race track," an aide to a black member of Congress told the *Guardian*. "But if a black says something insensitive, it's considered a matter of stirring up racial animosities."

Michel went on making widely-quoted statements and writing prominent articles about congressional "ethics"—his stature and ability to do so undiminished. To many in the mass media, questions of racism do not qualify as matters of "ethics."

During George Bush's successful campaign for the White House, mass media saw to it that most voters never found out about his Caucasian-only housing covenants in Texas. On February 4, 1981, after he became Vice President, Bush bought a lot in West Oaks, Texas, as the site of a future retirement home in the all-white neighborhood. Bush signed a contract with a clause that the land could not "be sold, leased or rented to any person other than of the Caucasian race, except in the case of servant's quarters." In late 1987 *The Nation* exposed the story of Bush's racially restrictive deed—and several others he had signed since the 1950s. The magazine reported that a spokesperson for Bush said, "There's really nothing to this." Mass media agreed. It stayed a non-issue.

When a series of Supreme Court rulings in 1989 undermined civil rights, quite a few editorials decried the trend. The top court dealt major setbacks to hard-won gains—including affirmative action, equal employment opportunities, challenges to on-the-job inequities, and options to sue in response to violation of rights. Supreme Court Justice Thurgood Marshall called the rulings "a deliberate retrenchment of the civil rights agenda" that "put at risk not only the civil rights of minorities but the civil rights of all citizens." Eroding along with civil rights was the media definition of what constituted support for civil rights. Soon after several of those court decisions were handed down, ABC/NPR reporter Cokie Roberts referred matter-of-factly to "George Bush's pro-civil-rights record." Roberts did not explain how someone could be "pro-civil-rights" after serving as Vice President for eight years in an administration whose Supreme Court appointees had provided the winning margin for all those anti-civil-rights rulings.

As the 1990s began—while nearly one-quarter of U.S. citizens were black, Hispanic or Asian—only three percent of the country's national, state and local elected officials were people of color. The main news media have clear preferences for what types of candidates should break the color barriers. When Douglas Wilder became the first elected black governor since Reconstruction, his victory in Virginia caused *Time* to draw a "contrast to [Jesse] Jackson's often divisive politics of prophecy." Wilder, the magazine indicated, fit a reassuring profile for a black man: "Even during the turbulent 1960s, Wilder was far more concerned with amassing wealth (he is now a millionaire) as a trial lawyer than with civil rights protest."

Newsweek entrusted coverage of Wilder's victory to Howard Fineman, who had categorized "black voters" as a "special interest group" the previous year. Fineman praised "a new wave of black Democrats who, like Wilder, seek acceptance rather than confrontation." The journalist seemed pleased as he wrote: "The newly elected leaders...presumably will want to encourage blacks—and whites, for that matter—to dismiss race, once and for all, as a factor in public life." This was the mass media's favored proposition: A Mr. Cleanup approach that would, by fiat, expunge unsightly racial messes without difficult social change.

Minorities in newsrooms

Inside journalism, on a systematic basis, white people retain a disproportionate share of the power. That imbalance affects how the news gets reported every day. "Even when stories dealt with bald-faced injustices and black-community disenchantment," Kirk Johnson concluded in his study of Boston's mass media, "most reporters failed to acknowledge racism as an underlying mechanism. Indeed, the very word 'racism' was rarely uttered in the major media; when racism *was* mentioned, it was treated not as a continuing tradition, but as a mere historical footnote. Euphemisms such as 'the disadvantaged' and 'the underprivileged' suggested a reluctance to acknowledge the persons or institutions responsible for causing the 'disadvantage.'" Victims without victimizers—a common theme in media coverage of domestic issues.

Columnist Clarence Page, who won a Pulitzer Prize for commentary in 1989, has seen a big improvement in hiring practices since he joined the *Chicago Tribune* news staff 20 years earlier as only its second full-time minority reporter. Yet even at the end of the 1980s, the *Tribune*'s daily news operation lacked black people in supervisory positions. "I think it hurts the paper as far as having sensitivity during the day to what issues are important in the black community and also what issues are developing in the black community, and the Hispanic community too," he said.

One of the few Asian-Americans working as an editor on a sizable daily paper in the United States, William Wong, settled into writing a regular column for the *Oakland Tribune* in 1988. Says Wong: "A lot of the things I bring up are not even talked about by other columnists."

Chicago's news, Mayor Harold Washington contended, "never quite came out the way things actually happened. It came out in a skewed fashion because we didn't have Hispanics, women, blacks and other minorities to winnow out, interpret and help make the news more meaningful to the majority of people in our city." Shortly before his death, he predicted that news coverage "shall forever be biased in Chicago, until people get fed up and start demanding that something be done about it. We need to reevaluate the whole structure of the news industry—the owners, editors, anchorpersons, producers, journalists on the street."

Washington went on to say that while many policies were especially hurting black and Hispanic people, "it's difficult to get our message across when it's siphoned through newspapers and other media which in many cases are predisposed against what we're trying to say." Speaking in 1986, Washington pointed out that in many U.S. cities the "minority" is actually a majority of the population. "Yet most metropolitan newspapers do not cater to the working public within their cities; they reach out to the suburbs to embrace a more affluent readership. These papers are still based in our cities, they own city property and to a great extent they control our cities. But newspapers largely ignore the people right around them."

Many journalists have expressed similar concerns. But the profession as a whole has moved slowly in response. The 1989 figures were hardly encouraging. "Blacks, Hispanics, Asians and Native Americans now constitute 7.54 percent of all newsroom professionals, up from 7.02 percent last year," the American Society of Newspaper Editors announced. What's more, a majority of U.S. daily newspapers—54 percent—did not have a single minority person in the newsroom. And while nearly 20 percent of recently-hired newspaper journalists were from racial minorities, the hierarchy remained almost entirely white—95.5 percent.

Several months after release of the 1989 survey results, a *New York Times* article noted that recent Supreme Court decisions weakening affirmative action laws "have raised fears that expanding minority employment within news organizations may become more difficult than ever." Yet the *Times* headline gave the opposite impression: "'Sense of Muscle' for Black Journalists." The implication was that newspaper owners could hardly be expected to hire more black journalists voluntarily.

The *New York Times* managed to be somewhat sanguine, in spite of—or perhaps because of—its notably shabby record as an equal opportunity employer. A profile of the *Times*, published in the *Columbia Journalism Review* at the end of 1988, said that "despite more than 20 years of pledging to vary the color of the newsroom and despite settlement of a rancorous lawsuit eight years ago that set specific hiring and promotion goals, the paper has only six blacks who have reached positions as assistant or deputy editors or editors of special sections."

Active discrimination has been widespread—from tiny newspapers to the country's most renowned. In spring 1987, a jury found the New York *Daily News* guilty of discriminating against four black journalists on the staff. At the *Washington Post*, after 20 years of union efforts to halt discriminatory practices at the newspaper, employees filed a class-action complaint with the District of Columbia government, charging widespread bias by the *Post*'s management.

Electronic media have been a bit better. Figures for 1988 indicated that minorities comprised eight percent of the nation's news employees at commercial radio stations and 16 percent at commercial TV stations. But minorities held only five percent of supervisory positions in radio and 11 percent in TV. "The word is 'racism,'" says Linda Ellerbee. "It exists in the networks and in the media pretty much throughout."

As Barbara Reynolds of *USA Today* has observed, the fact that so many women on network television are blonde and blue-eyed is a standard that "discriminates against black and Hispanic women." After two decades as a journalist, Reynolds was among the highest-ranking black women in the newspaper business in 1989, serving on the *USA Today* editorial board, editing its Inquiry page and writing a column for the paper. "I think black women are an invisible presence," she said in an interview. "When people talk about women, they talk about white women; when they talk about blacks, they mean men." She pointed out that the American Society of Newspaper Editors was not even compiling employment data on women of color in the industry.

Reynolds—who has written that "minority women are laboring at the bottom rung of...newspaper ghettos"—said that despite her professional record, until recently she found herself often treated as a non-person at work. "Just because you're in, it doesn't mean that it reverses the disparities available.

Black women journalists have been ridiculed, humiliated, never a part of the old boy network. When you look at the top, many have decided to leave journalism because of the way they have been treated, in the Victorian way men treat women. We're always an afterthought." In newsrooms "the pressure is so great because of both of the hang-ups people have in our society with sexism and racism. It's a double-edged blade."

Blaming the victims: black families

For many children of all races, poverty is not a word but a gnawing reality. "Indeed," says Temple University professor Noel Cazenave, "there are millions of neglected and hungry children trapped in America's wretched house of mirrors, and their plight—and its real causes—have yet to become a cause célèbre to America's white corporate media." Almost half of all black children in the United States—45 percent—were living in families officially below the poverty line, a 1989 study found. Congressman George Miller, chair of the committee that issued the report, said that "for America's youngest children and their families, the 1980s have been a disaster."

Miller blamed severe cuts in government help. But all the Republicans on the committee disagreed, blaming erosion of family structures and values—an explanation buttressed by decades of mass media boosterism for the idea that black families are largely responsible for problems faced by black people in America. Morton Kondracke of the *New Republic* typified the media spin when he wrote, "it is universally accepted that black poverty is heavily the result of family breakdown." Such an assertion was akin to saying that the absence of food is heavily the result of malnutrition.

In 1986, in the midst of a decade of sharply accelerated inner-city poverty, CBS broadcast a two-hour documentary by Bill Moyers, "The Vanishing Black Family: Crisis in Black America," that was widely praised by mass media. *Newsweek* proclaimed that "Bill Moyers and CBS News look unflinchingly into the void: it's no longer only racism or an unsympathetic government that is destroying black America. The problem now lies in the black community itself, and in its failure to pass on moral values to the next generation."

The CBS documentary could be seen as an honest attempt to show the horrendous conditions of life in black ghettos. But it was expert tunnel vision, fixated on effects—unwed mothers, young black males with few job prospects, dilapidated housing—while virtually ignoring causes. As writer Barbara Omolade noted: "The concept of a pathological underclass has become the rationale for continued racism and economic injustice; in attempting to separate racial from economic inequality and [in] blaming family pathology for black people's condition, current ideology obscures the system's inability to provide jobs, decent wages, and adequate public services for the black poor."

Media stereotyping has persisted. "The incessant emphasis on the dysfunctioning of black people," says the longtime president of the National Council of Negro Women, Dorothy Height, "is simply one more attempt to show that African-Americans do not really fit into the society—that we are 'overdependent' and predominantly welfare-oriented. Quite overlooked in this equation is the fact that most black Americans are, on the contrary, overwhelmingly among the working poor."

The black family scapegoat has been invoked by politicians and news media time and again to declare limits on public responsibility for improving the oppressive circumstances that afflict millions of Americans. In the words of scientist Stephen Jay Gould: "How convenient to blame the poor and the hungry for their own condition—lest we be forced to blame our economic system or our government for an abject failure to secure a decent life for all people."

There has been some breakthrough coverage going beyond the usual blame-the-victim approach. A prime example was National Public Radio's half-hour report titled "Black Men: An Endangered Species." Produced by Verta Mae Grosvenor, written and narrated by Phyllis Crockett, the program revealed stark truths about black America:

- "There are almost as many young black men in prison as in college."
- "For the first time in American history the life expectancy for black people is declining."
- "Murder and suicide are the two leading causes of death. A young black man...stands a one in 21 chance of being murdered before he's 44; for a white man, it's one in 133."
- "The suicide rate for young black men is up and rising... White men who commit suicide tend to do it when they see themselves as 'powerless' in their 50s; for black men, 'powerless' in their 20s."
- "Even though black men make up only six percent of the U.S. population, half of all the men behind bars are black."
- "There is no federal response to what's happening to [black men] shown by the alarming rise in statistics. There are, of course, some job training programs, some education programs, but there is no focused effort on this problem."

Why are these facts so rarely articulated in major media?

The Martin Luther King Jr. we don't see on television

The mass media tell us over and over that Martin Luther King Jr. was the nation's most gifted civil rights leader. But they don't remind us that King, besides crusading for racial justice and harmony, was one of the toughest critics of America's economic system and foreign policy. To King, issues of race, poverty and peace could not be separated.

Consider the film clips of King shown on TV every January when we celebrate his birthday as a national holiday. The TV footage presents a sanitized King with only one concern—desegregation. But in other speeches, late in his life, King went further, urging that people directly confront the connections between racism, poverty and militarism. Those speeches were also filmed and recorded—but we don't see them on television or hear them on the radio or find them quoted in daily newspapers.

King explicitly linked racism and poverty at home with intervention and warfare abroad. The nation's press, which didn't like that kind of approach then any more than it does now, angrily criticized him for making such connections. For example, when King spoke out against the Vietnam War, editorials around the country faulted him for moving beyond civil rights into peace issues. In 1967, the *Detroit News* complained that "he risks his credentials as an influential civil rights leader on the questionable merits of his foreign policy statements." *Life*—then one of the nation's biggest publications—explained that King "goes beyond his personal right to dissent when he connects progress and civil rights here with a proposal that amounts to abject surrender in Vietnam…" The *Washington Post* stated that King's criticism of the war "diminished his usefulness to his cause, to his country, and to his people." *Time* accused King of "demagogic slander that sounded like a script for Radio Hanoi."

King's response: "For about 12 years now, ever since the Montgomery bus boycott, I have been struggling and fighting against segregation, and I have been working too long and too hard now against segregated public accommodations to end up segregating my moral concerns, for since justice is indivisible, injustice anywhere is an affront to justice everywhere."

What's more, King pointed out, the conduct of the American government and corporations abroad could not be separated from what was going on inside our national borders. It had become all too clear that "when a nation becomes obsessed with the guns of war, social programs must inevitably suffer. We can talk about guns and butter all we want to, but when the guns are there with all of its emphasis you don't even get good oleo. These are facts of life."

Corporate-controlled news outlets repeatedly show King's beautiful but general "I have a dream" oration, to the virtual exclusion of his later speeches—like the address in which he declared: "A true revolution of values will soon look uneasily on the glaring contrast of poverty and wealth. With righteous indignation, it will look across the seas and see individual capitalists of the West investing huge sums of money in Asia, Africa and South America, only to take the profits out with no concern for the social betterment of the countries, and say: 'This is not just.' It will look at our alliance with the landed gentry of Latin America and say: 'This is not just.' The Western arrogance of feeling that it has everything to teach others and nothing to learn from them is not just."

Martin Luther King told an audience in early 1968 that "I never intend to adjust myself to the madness of militarism." He referred to a trend that was to remain with us, aided and abetted by media giants: "A nation that continues year after year to spend more money on military defense than on programs of social uplift is approaching spiritual death."

More than two decades after King was murdered, his truth is marching on. Many festering ills in our society correlate with American foreign policy guided by "the madness of militarism." And the same powerful media institutions distorting events at home are no more trustworthy when reporting on the rest of the world.

PART IV

International Intrigues

10

U.S.-Soviet Relations

A typical nightly news broadcast on a major television network devotes about ten minutes to international stories. That's not a lot of time to cover the entire world. While reporters occasionally file insightful stories from abroad, oftentimes they are superficial, incomplete or misleading. Most viewers, however, aren't in a position to second-guess stories about events in far-off lands.

Much of the international news read on-air by TV anchors is gleaned from the wire services. There are also reports from foreign correspondents who usually have a lot of territory to cover. Even the biggest print and broadcast media can't afford to have reporters and cameras at all places where significant stories may break. Overseas news bureaus are usually located in countries deemed most important to the United States. As a general rule, if the U.S. government doesn't express interest in a foreign subject, neither will American news media, as they lurch from crisis to crisis while reinforcing Washington's vision of the world.

"It is a truism that in U.S. foreign reporting the State Department often makes the story," admitted *Washington Post* reporter Julia Preston. Even when hedged with qualifications, stories that contradict officialdom have a more difficult time getting into the news, and those that diverge sharply from the mainstream are likely to attract only fleeting attention.

Articles about other countries are often datelined "Washington," while stories emanating from abroad are apt to feature U.S. Embassy sources or unnamed officials from friendly governments. "To get the stories a lot of foreign reporters file, editors could just as well save a lot of money and send them straight to the State Department in Washington," said former *Wall Street Journal* correspondent Jonathan Kwitny. "They end up going to the U.S. Embassy for most of the information anyway."

A double standard has skewed U.S. coverage of international affairs. Consider, for instance, which stories about proceedings at the United Nations are reported by major media and which are ignored. A typical case: In November 1987, the U.N. General Assembly voted 94-2 in favor of a resolution calling for "full and immediate compliance" with the World Court ruling which found that the U.S. violated international law by mining Nicaraguan harbors; the measure also called for the termination of the contra war. This vote was not mentioned in the newspapers of record or by the three TV networks. Yet on the day before the Nicaragua vote, the *New York Times* and other media dutifully alerted the American public to the fact that the U.N.

General Assembly had approved by 123-19 a resolution calling for the with-drawal of Soviet troops from Afghanistan. Pressed for an explanation, a *Times* staffer told us, "Christ, maybe we are biased."

Whereas domestic stories in the U.S. media are replete with victims but have few culprits or solutions, international coverage abounds with cul-prits—"communists," "terrorists," "leftists"—and the solution often entails forceful intervention by the U.S. government. American meddling in the Third World is frequently depicted in benign or favorable terms, as when *New York Times* correspondent Richard Halloran described military construc-tion projects near contra base camps in a story headlined, "U.S. Army Engineers Fight Poverty in Honduras." A piece by *Times* columnist James Reston underscored the widely-held assumption of American innocence in foreign affairs: "We are constantly taken by surprise in a world we are trying to help but don't quite understand."

While the U.S. is always trying to help, bad guys like Fidel Castro are always trying to hinder the benevolent policies pursued by Washington. The Soviet Union used to be portrayed as the principal source of subversion in the mass-mediated world, but that image changed when Mikhail Gorbachev began to dismantle the so-called Evil Empire. Although the U.S. maintains hundreds of military installations all over the globe and has overthrown and propped up dozens of foreign governments, mainstream reporters rarely refer to it as the "American Empire" or scrutinize its policies from that perspec-tive. Quick to denounce "Soviet imperialism," the American press rarely dwells upon "U.S. imperialism," a phrase that almost always appears between quotation marks in print media accounts.

Few U.S. journalists did a double take when a *New York Times* article, headlined "CIA Seeks Looser Rules on Killings During Coups," discussed proposals by the Bush administration to permit a greater CIA role in violent plots against foreign leaders. (Recall how Elliott Abrams, dissembler emeri-tus, made the rounds on television after the abortive coup in Panama in October 1989, urging Congress to lift restrictions that prohibit assassina-tions.) CIA-backed coups are not only considered acceptable, they are openly applauded by many media pundits, who take for granted that the United States has a right to interfere in other countries whenever it chooses. Imagine the outraged reaction if the headline had read, "KGB Seeks Looser Rules on Killings During Coups."

BEHIND THE IRONY CURTAIN

During the first two years of the Soviet Union's existence, the *New York Times* reported that the Soviets were on the verge of collapse 91 times. "From the point of view of professional journalism," Walter Lippmann and a colleague concluded after scrutinizing every issue of the *Times* between

March 1917 and March 1920, "the reporting of the Russian revolution is nothing short of a disaster. On the essential questions the net effect was almost always misleading, and misleading news is worse than none at all." Summarizing American newspaper coverage of Russia in that era, Upton Sinclair wrote: "They published so many inventions that they couldn't keep track of them."

The quality of U.S. news reporting on the Soviet Union has improved significantly since then. And the 1980s ended with the American media sometimes providing in-depth and cogent accounts of a Soviet society in the throes of dramatic change. Yet, like a nagging flu that won't quite disappear, the Cold War virus has continued to afflict our main sources of information.

Focused on Soviet gaps between idealistic theories and actual conditions, American media are far less fascinated by such gaps in the United States. The U.S. press is pleased to conclude that over there hypocrisy reigns, while we merely have negative aberrations. An unbiased observer, from Mars perhaps, might well chuckle at the ironic blind spots that exist next to our acuity about Soviet failings—but our media would probably depict such an extraterrestrial as being soft on communism.

Americans are deluged with news coverage of the USSR, much of it pre-strained like some kind of ideological baby food. With Washington long claiming to be holier-than-Moscow 100 percent of the time, a side-effect of such divine pretensions has been the impossibility of admitting to hypocrisy. But the failings of only one superpower fascinate the American press. A righteous USA requires a far less virtuous USSR, much as a spotlight relies on darkness.

In the U.S. media, some of the most virulent stereotyping of the Soviets has been produced by people who never bothered to find out about the nation they were so eager to condemn or mock. In 1987, ABC broadcast a mini-series, *Amerika*, which dramatized the aftermath of a Soviet takeover of the United States. Despite a $35 million budget for a television production that was in the works for years, Donald Wrye—the writer, director and executive producer of *Amerika*—infused the project with willful ignorance. He had never bothered to set foot inside the Soviet Union.

Amerika fit right in with ads on the Tube—for products as diverse as Miller Lite beer, Cabbage Patch dolls, MTV and the MCI long-distance phone service—depicting Soviets as vicious, devious and idiotic oafs. The leading commercial of the genre saturated the nation's TV sets beginning a few days after the Reagan-Gorbachev summit of November 1985: In the Wendy's Restaurant spot about a Soviet fashion show, an obese model sported the same drab sack-like dress every time she walked on stage, announced by an emcee in military garb. The Soviet audience, equally fat and lifeless, applauded mechanically. "Having no choice," declared the Wendy's voice-over, "is no fun." (Cut to a colorful array of delightful toppings offered at your nearest Wendy's.) The adman behind the commercial, Joe Sedelmaier, didn't worry about reality. "I never did any research on it or anything," he told us. "I just did it."

Most American journalists actually do a lot of research when they cover the Soviet Union. Many of the several dozen based in Moscow work long hours, often providing informative news about Soviet society. But their reportage tends to slip into clichés pandering to the folks back home. When it comes to breaking free of shopworn prejudices, even America's best daily newspapers aren't good enough.

The urge to purge

During 1989 Soviet leader Mikhail Gorbachev made great progress in setting up democratic procedures while ousting old-guard officeholders, who in some cases dated back to the bloody reign of Stalin. In April, Gorbachev and his allies scored a major breakthrough—removing one-quarter of the entire voting membership of the Communist Party's most powerful body. That night, on National Public Radio, the *All Things Considered* program began with these words: "Mikhail Gorbachev purges the Central Committee." The next morning's *New York Times* front-page headline was "Kremlin Approves a Sweeping Purge..."

Beating the same drum, the *Los Angeles Times* reported that "dozens of older officials...were effectively purged in the move." Later in the week, follow-up articles in the *Los Angeles Times* and the *New York Times* again referred to Tuesday's "purge." Journalistic history was already written.

But what had happened was not a *purge* in any real sense of the word—which, especially in connection with the Soviet Union, evokes images of murderous repression. Millions of people lost their lives because of Stalin's periodic purges until his death in 1953. In contrast, the Soviets who were removed from office in 1989, as the *Times* mentioned, "were allowed to leave with effusive praise for their service and without criticism," let alone punishment. (In describing power plays and forced resignations of American politics, our media virtually never use the word "purge," due to its bloody connotations.) Despite the fresh winds blowing through the Soviet Union, the U.S. press clung to its favored rhetorical relic—even though Gorbachev's successful efforts were victories *against* old-timers who had acceded to real purges of the past.

After the spring-cleaning, the Politburo contained only one Brezhnev-era holdover—Ukrainian arch-conservative Vladimir Shcherbitsky—an impediment to Gorbachev's reform program. In June 1989, a *Wall Street Journal* commentary, written by a Radio Liberty official, charged that "Gorbachev has not shown interest in removing his Ukrainian subordinate." But a few months later, the Kremlin announced removal of a quarter of the Politburo—including Shcherbitsky and a former head of the KGB. A smashing victory for democratic forces, the story was front-page news. "Gorbachev Purges 5 From Politburo," declared the *Washington Post*'s headline. *New York Times* reporter Francis X. Clines liked the word "purge" so much that it appeared in six of his first dozen paragraphs. It was entirely possible, however, to report the story without once referring to it as a purge, as the British news agency Reuters proved in a lengthy dispatch from Moscow.

Superpower summits

Even while proclaiming that the Cold War might be over, U.S. mass media have displayed chronic ambivalence about calling a truce. Keen on ascribing laudable motives to Washington, journalists have kept ringing familiar propaganda bells. In times of superpower summitry, the media themes have become especially rigid.

Well before Gorbachev arrived in Washington to meet with Ronald Reagan in December 1987, U.S. media were allowing only three perspectives on center stage: 1) the White House view; 2) critics who believed the President was being too conciliatory toward the Soviets; and 3) the Kremlin. A dozen Americans, divided between supporters of Reagan's stance and right-wing opponents of the INF nuclear weapons treaty being signed by the superpower leaders, made the rounds of the TV networks. A press conference called by a hastily-organized "Anti-Appeasement Alliance"—which denounced Reagan as a Kremlin dupe—became a big news story. ABC's *Nightline* zoomed into the rightward fray, booking three foes of the INF treaty, including a conservative ideologue who charged that Reagan had become "a useful idiot for Kremlin propaganda."

Virtually banished from the publicized discussions were Americans who felt the Reagan administration was dragging its feet over the issue of nuclear disarmament. On the eve of the Washington summit, maverick Republican Senator Mark Hatfield delivered a blistering attack against the Reagan administration for reckless nuclear arms deployments; the national media blanked him out. Leaders of large U.S. peace groups called on the government to move toward disarmament, but received scant media attention.

When it came to longtime critics of nuclear build-ups, the U.S. press was playing a game that had been standard for the pre-*glasnost* Soviet media: Publicize government attacks on dissidents, but don't give the dissidents any ink or air time to respond. Secretary of State George Shultz did not lack for coverage when he jabbed at American peace activists, saying "I would hope that the people in the movement would admit that they were wrong. In order to have peace, you have to show some strength." But the *Washington Post*, which carried Shultz's statement, refused to give any rebuttal space to the country's largest peace group. "Shultz is given free rein to make the case against us," SANE/Freeze press secretary Brigid Shea told FAIR. "We aren't given one inch to tell our side of the story."

Media coverage left many questions unasked, such as: Why was President Reagan resisting a ban on nuclear bomb tests? Would the White House agree to a mutual halt to missile flight testing? And why was Reagan failing to pursue Soviet proposals for a ban on sea-based nuclear weapons in Scandinavian waters and a nuclear-arms-free corridor in Central Europe? Such questions were not raised because they did not conform to the mass media's news angles about a limited INF treaty that would destroy only intermediate-range missiles on European soil, less than four percent of the world's nuclear weapons.

"With rare exceptions, the media share the mind-set of the 'defense establishment' on issues of national security and nuclear policy," explained Samuel H. Day Jr., former editor of the *Bulletin of the Atomic Scientists*, who added: "In covering the INF agreement, the media ignored the real danger that the treaty will lull people into a false sense of security about the perils of still-growing nuclear arsenals."

Day maintained that official "arms control" was continuing as a way of managing the arms race, not stopping it. More nuclear arms were coming off assembly lines or in the planning stages—weapons of deadly long-range accuracy that were apt to tighten the nuclear hair-trigger. With awesome weaponry always in the pipeline, the White House was eager to keep updating America's nuclear arsenal while promoting its arms-control image too.

Gorbachev's "misconceptions about America"

American reportage seemed blasé about the deeper implications of Gorbachev's repeated moves for drastic nuclear arms cutbacks. Instead, the principal media obsession was Gorbachev's public relations acumen, as though the Kremlin had somehow cracked a prized American code. The surface adulation, projecting onto Gorbachev the mastery of smoke-and-mirrors, usually obscured the underlying value of Soviet disarmament attempts.

In addition to Gorby-as-PR-wiz, another journalistic fixation during the December 1987 Washington summit was the Soviet leader's "misconceptions about America"—particularly his notion that a "military-industrial complex" dominates the United States. *Newsweek* joined ABC's *World News Tonight* and other media in deriding Gorbachev for suggesting that President Reagan was a "pawn" of this mysterious complex. Perhaps American reporters had forgotten that it was President Eisenhower who warned, in his 1961 farewell speech, of the military-industrial complex's undue influence over U.S. policies.

Another one of Gorbachev's "misconceptions" concerned the human right of housing. When CBS anchor Dan Rather questioned a correspondent about the summit talks—"Any give on human rights?"—he was obviously not asking if Reagan had made concessions by promising structural reforms to reduce homelessness in America. CBS reporter Wyatt Andrews, who clearly understood the question as referring only to Soviet abuses, replied: "No, just boilerplate rhetoric—no give on human rights." Perhaps Rather and his colleagues had discovered a way of working in New York and Washington without stepping over the bodies of homeless people on the sidewalks. In any event, they evidently judged that shelter is no human right. (In contrast, Articles 22 to 27 of the U.N.'s "Universal Declaration of Human Rights" enumerate fundamental economic rights, including food, housing and medical care.)

One of the persistent themes—lurking as a treasured subtext—is that Soviets' shortcomings underscore our virtues; their problems prove the superiority of our system. Trapped behind an irony curtain, U.S. journalists are too often inclined to paper over abuses by their own government and inequities in their own society, while readily pointing up myriad failures of the Soviet Union.

When President Reagan traveled to Moscow in June 1988, U.S. news coverage seemed to depart from traditional Cold War reporting. But—again—the customary media biases established a three-cornered debate among Reagan boosters, U.S. hawks displeased with his mild overtures to the other superpower, and official Soviet spokespeople. In effect, our own media imposed tight constraints on substantive domestic debate—something U.S. journalists have frequently faulted Soviet media for doing inside the USSR.

"We see the limits of *glasnost*," ABC's Peter Jennings reported on *World News Tonight*. But American journalism could have used some *glasnost* of its own to widen the bounds of discussion. The *Washington Post*'s op-ed page, for example, was notable for its limited range of views on U.S.-Soviet relations in the weeks leading up to the Moscow summit.

The *Post* seemed frozen in a Cold War time-warp. A stable of regulars—including George Will, Jeane Kirkpatrick, Stephen S. Rosenfeld, Charles Krauthammer, Rowland Evans and Robert Novak—kept up a fusillade of warnings that the U.S. must not be taken in by Soviet tyranny. Former CIA agent-turned-editor Philip Geyelin stressed the perils of precipitous nuclear disarmament, cautioning against "any number of softheaded things that we and our allies could do—a dumb START treaty, a failure to follow through with necessary modernization of the 'theater' nuclear forces, or whatever." Freelance op-ed contributors included State Department alumni Al Haig and Seymour Weiss. And a *Post* column by Richard Cohen wondered how Gorbachev "feels about civil liberties when they are no longer useful to him"; the headline over Cohen's piece was "Gorbachev Is No Westerner," with "Westerner" apparently a synonym for civil libertarian.

In Moscow, U.S. journalists pounced on Kremlin surveillance of Soviet citizens while conveniently ignoring the long history of FBI and CIA harassment of dissenting Americans. "How do you feel about the fact that [Soviet officials] have kept dossiers on these dissidents with whom you met?"

NBC's Andrea Mitchell asked Reagan at his Moscow news conference. "Doesn't this contradict your new feeling of optimism about the Soviet Union?" The next day, reporter Lou Cannon pressed the issue further on the front page of the *Washington Post*: "The President ignored a question about the disclosure that the Soviets had kept dossiers on the dissidents who met with him Monday."

Of course, the FBI has routinely kept "dossiers" on many thousands of American citizens engaged in lawful political activities, including civil rights leaders, religious figures and journalists. But, in tandem with U.S. media's explicit message that Russian dissidents are admirable, a common implicit message is that American dissidents are unimportant or contemptible. The unspoken journalistic rule of thumb: Their dissidents are worth listening to; ours aren't.

Thus a blurb on the *Washington Post*'s front page—"Disgruntled U.S. peaceniks participate in Soviet leadership's counteroffensive on human rights"—summarized a lengthy news article inside about U.S. dissidents, including a group of American Indians, who visited Moscow during the June 1988 summit. Tagging the activists three times with the moldy pejorative "peaceniks," *Post* reporter Michael Dobbs strained to depict them as Kremlin stooges "paraded through the [Soviet] peace-committee offices."

The *Post* story combined '50s-style Red-baiting with what might charitably be called arrogant ethnocentrism. Perhaps racism would be a more accurate term for an article declaring that the performance of an American Indian song "turned out to be a wordless high-pitched gargle, the significance of which was lost on the assembled world press." (In fact—though *Post* readers had no way of knowing—the Indians performed a traditional native song that included words in the Lakota language.) And Dobbs' article referred to imprisoned Native American activist Leonard Peltier as a name "scarcely known in the United States." The extent to which he remained "scarcely known" said a lot about media bias; by that time Peltier's efforts toward a new trial had been publicly supported by Amnesty International, as well as more than 60 members of Congress.

Cold-warrior reporting laced with paleface chauvinism didn't seem to hurt Michael Dobbs' career. Months later, he became the *Washington Post* bureau chief in Moscow.

THE COLD WAR IS OVER...LONG LIVE THE COLD WAR

In April 1989, a *New York Times* editorial declared that "the cold war is over." But the armistice appeared shaky. Not content to describe Soviet difficulties, our news media often could not resist turning the ideological knife.

That spring a prominent news article about the opening of a soup kitchen in Leningrad appeared in the *Times* under the headline: "It Hurts to Be Old and Poor in a Classless Society." Beyond mocking the communist dream of a society without class divisions, the vintage Cold War headline implied that it does *not* hurt as much to be old and poor in an avowed class society like our own. The headline did double duty—bashing the Soviets and subtly congratulating capitalist life. A front-page *Times* headline a few days earlier did a similar number: "After Rash of Wildcat Moves, Soviets Admit Right to Strike." The word *admit* conveyed that the Soviet government had finally come around to acknowledge a right that exists beyond dispute in more enlightened societies. Yet the U.S. government has never "admitted" any absolute right to strike. In the 1980s, air traffic controllers were among quite a few Americans punished for engaging in "illegal" strikes.

Media messages are no less powerful when they are implied rather than directly stated. And with U.S. news media's acuity toward Soviet hypocrisy rarely matched by focused looks at American hypocrisy, the propagandistic impacts are cumulative and far-reaching. Since few U.S. journalists break the unwritten rule that comparisons must be favorable to the United States, it is unusual to hear about positive aspects of Soviet society. The relative lack of homelessness and unemployment went unremarked during the eighties; so did the low costs of rents, public transportation and basic foodstuffs. And despite their much lower economic standard of living, some Soviets who learn of financial uncertainties that face many elderly Americans feel fortunate that they can depend on basic social services in their future.

Ideological blinders

Many U.S. journalists continue their propaganda salvos, evidently lukewarm about ending the Cold War. The *Washington Post*'s Jim Hoagland explained that the Soviet system "has failed miserably" and "has produced nothing any modern society would think worth saving." Anyone who has made more than a superficial visit to the Soviet Union would need to have donned strict ideological blinders beforehand in order to make such a statement—expressing much more certainty than truth, while eschewing shades of gray. Within the binary black-and-white mentalities that so frequently hold sway, sweeping pseudo-journalistic comments substitute for more accurate renditions of the Soviet Union with all its complexities.

Although hardly eager to be self-critical in more than shallow terms, American mass media swoon over opportunities to point out the failings of Soviet journalism. Reporting on Soviet elections in March 1989, the *New York Times* was at pains to cite what was "conspicuously absent from national and regional newspapers" in the USSR, along with what the Communist Party newspaper *Pravda* "made no mention of" and "omitted." Yet every day the *Times*' own pages are Swiss-cheesed with absences and omissions of a political nature.

The *Times* was eager to observe that lots of Soviet candidates "seem virtually indistinguishable" (as if U.S. candidates are politically quite diverse) and that the Soviet system often "filtered out" non-traditional contestants (as if third-party and independent candidates really stand a chance in the U.S.). And *Times* columnist Flora Lewis lost no time writing that "they were carefully managed elections, not properly democratic." As in so many other instances, the American mass media supplied critiques of shortcomings of the nationwide Soviet elections in 1989—but proudly continued with myopic once-overs of situations in the USA. (After all, anything the Soviets do, we've already done better.)

In the United States the previous year, fully one-fifth of the races for seats in the House of Representatives had only one candidate. What's more, as *The Nation* pointed out, over 98 percent of House members and 85 percent of Senators won their bids for reelection, "giving Americans a collection of politicians not widely known to be unconventional contenders." Noting that "all governments warrant the skepticism of journalists," the magazine editorialized that "the U.S. media's doubt is strictly selective and rarely applied to the Democratic and Republican oligopoly that produces our homogenized politics. The nation would be far better off if its media were as critical of U.S. elections as they are of the Soviet Union's."

Ironically, the Soviet election had at least one feature sadly lacking in the U.S.—the option of voting for "none of the above" by crossing out the names of unacceptable candidates. In Leningrad and other cities, even powerful incumbents running unopposed lost their jobs when voters scratched them. Among the matters "conspicuously absent" from reporting by American media was the fact that voters in the United States do not have any such choice.

While negative toward the Soviet status quo, U.S. journalists regard the status quo at home as far more congenial. "Old guard" is a frequent derogatory name for pillars of the traditional Soviet power structure, but the term is rarely attached to the President of the United States or his political allies. Likewise, "conservatives" are bad folk in the USSR, but not in the USA; one *New York Times* headline, describing fears of regression toward past Soviet policies, read: "Gorbachev Aide Warns of Rightist Reaction Ahead." Meanwhile, "liberals" are good people in the USSR, but the "L-word" is often treated like a curse in American politics. And the term "dissident," long applied to Soviets jailed for their political activities, is not used by U.S. media to label Americans jailed for *their* political activities, such as protesters punished for trespassing on nuclear weapons sites in the United States.

Most U.S. journalists are far more eager to describe the splinters in Soviet eyes than to examine the beams in their own. *New York Times* reporter Seth Mydans decried the contents of Soviet textbooks because "they are presented in a way that will support the ideological bias that governs Soviet public life,

and they are accompanied by the catch phrases of Soviet propaganda."
Mydans was appalled at Soviet texts with assertions such as: "The U.S. economy is dominated by monopolies. In order to gain higher profits they exploit
the American workers as well as the population of the countries dependent
on the USA."

Old bias against new thinking

Slow to appreciate the depth of the Soviet "new way of thinking" propounded by Mikhail Gorbachev, the U.S. news media ultimately latched onto
the phrase with a vengeance. In Moscow, the "new way of thinking" refers to
a revised outlook on national and global security that, among other things,
recognizes that military build-ups are dangerous and unnecessary. But U.S.
officials and American media have used the phrase "new way of thinking"
not to explore its profound implications so much as to hurl it back as a taunt
at the Kremlin—to push for ever more concessions, however unreciprocated
by the White House.

"Secretary of State James A. Baker 3d said today that he viewed Soviet
cooperation in Central American peace efforts as a test of whether there is
really 'new thinking' in the Kremlin," the *New York Times* reported. In another
article, about allegations that the USSR sold bombers to Libya, a front-page
headline explained: "Deal Is Viewed as Contrary to Moscow's 'New Thinking'
on Mideast Tensions." The article quoted a source—identified only as an
administration official—saying that "It raises major questions about the
Soviets' new thinking. Indeed, the so-called new thinking in the Middle East is
turning out to look a lot like the old thinking."

It was clear from listening to Dan Rather report on the Panama invasion
that "new thinking" hadn't gotten off the dime at CBS News. Rather dismissed the Soviet Union's "predictable" condemnation of U.S. military intervention in Panama as "old-line, hardline talk from Moscow"—this at a time
when the U.S. had once again resorted to old-style gunboat diplomacy to
impose its will in Latin America.

As the 1980s drew to a close, the U.S. press seemed less open to profound
discourse than the Soviet press. Like vain dilettantes transfixed with preening
themselves in the mirror, American media remained enthralled with their own
self-image. In a rare disruption of these conceits, the *New York Times* published
an op-ed piece by David K. Shipler a few days after he returned from a visit to
the Soviet capital in November 1988. "Sad to say," Shipler wrote, "the quality
of political debate has been more intelligent and sophisticated in the world's
leading closed society than in the world's leading democracy."

Shipler, a former *Times* correspondent in Moscow who'd gone on to
become a senior associate at the Carnegie Endowment for International
Peace, added that Soviet supporters of Gorbachev's reform program "have
created an atmosphere in which every idea has weight, no utterance is empty

and each proposal and criticism reverb[er]ates with heavy implications for the country's political and economic future. There is a creative and exhilarating dialogue on the most fundamental issues concerning the individual and the state. Not so in America. We act as if we have resolved all the fundamental questions and that our role is to teach the rest of the world."

Coping with the charm offensive

It was a fairly typical Sunday morning broadcast on CBS Television in early July 1989, with the host starting off the show this way: "Welcome to *Face the Nation*. I'm Lesley Stahl. Soviet leader Mikhail Gorbachev has taken his charm offensive across Western Europe with speeches and proposals U.S. officials say are aimed at dividing the NATO alliance and throwing the American President on the defensive." (Sponsors for the program that Sunday: Raytheon Company, a military contractor; and the brokerage firm Merrill Lynch.) The same phrase—"charm offensive"—turned up months later on the front page of the *New York Times*, in a Bill Keller article that began: "MOSCOW, Sept. 13—The K.G.B. stepped up its charm offensive today…" But in fact the phrase could be traced back at least as far as the pre-

Gorbachev: snake or charmer? Two *New York Times* headlines from national (left) and New York (right) editions, December 10, 1987

vious spring, when a front-page *Times* article quoted an unnamed State Department official insisting, "If we wanted to right now, we could really pull the rug out from under Gorbachev's charm offensive."

Such phrases were lame attempts to distract from Soviet challenges to U.S. foreign policy business-as-usual. In contrast to America's mass media and reigning politicians, Gorbachev's actions indicated strong commitment to getting a disarmament process underway. This was a real worry for official Washington and the country's opinion-shapers. In a front-page article headlined "Soviets Take W. Europe by Charm," the *Los Angeles Times* fretted that "Moscow is suddenly winning the battle for world opinion in a way that few ever would have thought possible. It is a success that carries serious implications for the Western Alliance as it struggles to halt an alarming erosion of public support for the firm defense it has maintained for four decades."

U.S. officials and big media professionals seemed to figure that disparaging remarks about public relations might help provide an antidote to Gorbachev's enormous prestige. CBS News anchor Dan Rather described Gorbachev as "a great master of media and political seduction." Weeks later, *New York Times* reporter Thomas J. Friedman was writing about "'Gorby fever,' a virus that has already swept Western Europe afflicting its victims with an uncontrollable urge to reduce the military." Friedman speculated on the chances that the dire "virus" might be "beginning to spread in the United States as well."

Repeatedly, U.S. media portrayed Gorbachev's initiatives for a peaceful world as the moves of a brilliant troublemaker. *New York Times* journalist Michael R. Gordon led off a Sunday piece by reporting that "the Soviet leader managed to throw a little gasoline on the fiery arms control debate within the Western alliance about nuclear short-range missiles." What had the devious Gorbachev actually done? "In a move that once again stole the spotlight, Mr. Gorbachev disclosed that the Soviet Union would withdraw 500 missile warheads, nuclear artillery shells and nuclear bombs from Eastern Europe." Accusing the Kremlin's leader of being a spotlight-stealer wasn't up to old Cold War standards, but apparently it was the best that Gordon and the *Times* could do.

A few days later, another *Times* article noted that "the more the Kremlin leader appears to be responding to Washington's demands, the more annoyed the White House seems to become." But it was not only the White House that displayed annoyance. The U.S. press also seemed unsettled by its own failures to anticipate that profound changes would take place in the Soviet Union, with world-shaking impacts. Back in late 1985, *Washington Post* editorial page editor Meg Greenfield had blithely and arrogantly proclaimed that the West had the image game all sewed up. "I don't care how many master craftsmen image makers the Russians employ," Greenfield wrote in *Newsweek*, "the public-relations war is an ultimate loser for them."

Even when U.S. policy makers suffered a severe decline in PR fortunes,

they could rely on the Fourth Estate to pull them through. When President Bush attended the May 1989 NATO summit conference in Brussels, for the most part mass media stayed with scripted psychodrama—Could Bush prove himself a worthy competitor in the image contest? Could he assert U.S. leadership while saving NATO unity? Thousands of journalists had little or nothing to say about the profound mental distances between Bush and Gorbachev. The Soviet leader insisted that a nuclear-weapons-free Europe was desirable. And he recognized that NATO's planned "modernization" of nuclear missiles was a euphemism for escalating the arms race. But these were issues of substance, and therefore not of much interest to the U.S. press.

Most American journalists sidestepped Washington's refusal to reciprocate Soviet disarmament moves, choosing instead to frame U.S.-Soviet interactions as a continuous PR battle. Meanwhile, a grave fact got lost in all the media hocus-pocus: The U.S. government was determined to keep nuclear weapons in Europe, even if most Europeans opposed them.

THE ARMS CONTROL RUSE

America's mass media take the arms race for granted as something that must continue. As George Bush moved into the Oval Office, *Newsweek* explained to its several million readers that "not even the most visionary planner knows where the search for newfangled, gold-plated killing machines will stop." The new President "faces a debate over means and missions that could lead to far-reaching reforms of the U.S. military." But none of those "far-reaching reforms" had anything to do with ending the arms race.

Newsweek described "the Western Alliance" as a "40-year tradition of armed vigilance that has seen the emergence of a world order stabilized by the balance of nuclear terror and destabilized, from time to time, by regional conflicts like the war in Vietnam and the Soviet invasion of Afghanistan." (Of the two instances of murderous superpower imperialism, only one qualified in Newsweekspeak as an "invasion.") The magazine laid out the ruling ideology as self-evident common sense: "Like his predecessors, Bush must accept the quest for military preparedness as a permanent characteristic of the American superstate; real disarmament, it can be said, has never been a realistic option, and it is not an option now."

First-strike weapons

Our pundits griped that President Bush was lethargic in the face of bold Soviet measures. But the U.S. press also remained stuck in old ways of thinking. Typical was a July 1989 cover story in *U.S. News & World Report*—"America's Best & Worst Weapons." The magazine lamented that "too often, billions of dollars are being wasted on bad weapons," which offered an insufficiently high ratio of kill-power to cost.

When the Trident 2 nuclear missile flubbed its first sea-trial launches, media bemoaned the setback. With the issues kept technical, the desirability of the weapons system was a given. The Trident submarine system—and its $155 billion price-tag for 21 submarines and 899 nuclear missiles—got safe passage from the press, which cited bipartisan support on Capitol Hill. As usual, when the *New York Times* informed readers that the Trident 2 would be able to "carry a 475-kiloton nuclear warhead at least 4,000 miles and strike within 100 yards of its target," the newspaper didn't mention that this capability would be most useful as part of a first-strike attack on the Soviet Union. A couple of days later, a "Week in Review" piece by Richard Halloran was headlined "Even After Misfirings, Trident Is Well Liked."

Only the *Times* op-ed page offered another view—an article by Greenpeace coordinator Michael Ross, who made the point the news coverage kept avoiding: "The Trident 2's added explosive power and accuracy give the Navy the ability to destroy Soviet missiles before they have been launched. This extra capacity is useful only if the U.S. strikes first." The objection was not new. Early in the decade, for example, the United Methodist Church issued a statement through its Board of Global Ministries, warning that the Trident 2 was one of the U.S. government's key "first-strike nuclear weapons" that "escalate the danger of nuclear war through accident or misperception."

In contrast to the glum tone of reports about the Trident 2 misfiring, media were celebratory when the B-2 Stealth bomber lifted off from the Mojave Desert in a "successful" test flight on July 17, 1989. Attention riveted on whether the Northrop-built plane was worth its $70 billion price-tag. A spate of Northrop ads filled the bottom right-hand quarter of the *New York Times'* op-ed page lauding the B-2—with other Northrop ads on the same page praising its F-5 fighters.

An exceptional look at the Stealth had come from the Knight-Ridder news service back in March. Reporter Frank Greve documented how $17 billion got invested in the B-2 even though Congress "has never voted on the bomber on its merits." The exposé was an unusually piercing examination of corrupt ties between Pentagon brass, politicians and corporate officials. Yet even this fine reportage steered clear of a hard look at the Stealth's anticipated function—the fact that the plane would be most adept at slipping past Soviet air defenses undetected. Thus, like Trident, the Stealth would be well-suited as part of an American first-strike.

Days after the Stealth's maiden flight, the *Los Angeles Times* reported that the warplane was central to an aggressive new Pentagon strategy for penetrating the Soviet Union with nuclear missiles that could "decapitate" the Soviet leadership. The *Times* quoted specialists who said that the changes in the U.S. government's "Strategic Integrated Operations Plan" would increase the likelihood of triggering a nuclear war. The Bush administration was going ahead with the plan. There was scant follow-up in the press, as America's media giants, tightly interlocked with big military contractors, weren't interested in pursuing the horrific implications.

Nor have mass media dwelled upon the links between profligate military spending and severe government cutbacks in social programs to meet basic human needs. The $70 billion production project for the Stealth bomber, for instance, revved up in the same decade that saw federal housing programs cut by about 75 percent.

For the umpteenth time, the connection remained unmade when media worthies gathered around a table on the PBS television show *Washington Week in Review* days after Congress had voted to keep the Stealth project going. (The TV program—which reaches nearly seven million viewers every week plus noncommercial radio listeners nationwide—might be aptly renamed "Whitewashington Week In Review"; reporters from major newspapers and magazines take turns restating the conventional wisdoms of their colleagues.) When the Stealth came up for discussion, nary a word was said questioning the assumptions behind new multibillion-dollar military hardware. As the longtime "underwriters" of the show, Ford and Ford Aerospace (both military contractors) have had no reason to be displeased.

Judging from what they produce, the overwhelming majority of main-stream journalists who cover military policies accept Washington's prevailing attitudes. One of the most predictable reporters in the late 1980s was the *New York Times'* Michael R. Gordon, whose articles mirrored outlooks from the White House, Capitol Hill and the Pentagon with little deviation. As part of a normal day's work, when President Bush decided to go ahead with developing both MX and Midgetman land-based nuclear missiles, Gordon declared point-blank in a news report on the *Times* front page: "The decision is likely to have a generally positive effect on the strategic arms talks."

A public secret

For decades, every President has claimed that it's necessary to threaten to fire nuclear weapons in case of a non-nuclear attack on Western Europe. But, thanks to government-media coziness, this is a policy that most U.S. citizens don't even know exists.

A poll by the Public Agenda Foundation discovered that 81 percent of Americans were not aware that the United States has refused to adopt a "no first use" policy. And 78 percent did not know that the publicly-announced U.S. policy is to respond with nuclear weapons in the event of a Soviet conventional attack on Western Europe. The U.S. media have failed to illuminate these matters, which suits Washington policy makers just fine. Meanwhile, throughout the 1980s, the USSR kept issuing no-first-use pledges while urging the United States to do the same.

"The refusal of the U.S. to renounce the first use of nuclear weapons," wrote journalism analyst Jay Rosen, "is an example of what might be called a 'public secret'—a fact that is publicly known but not known by the public. Such facts mark the limits of the public as an active body in a democracy, for they make it impossible for citizens to debate and help decide the matters the 'secrets' concern. One can hardly get agitated about a policy one does not know exists. Thus, the same study that found a large majority ignorant of the first-use policy in Western Europe also found that three of four Americans oppose the use of nuclear weapons to repel a conventional attack."

To the extent that the press educates U.S. citizens about nuclear arsenals, it is primarily to promote continued acquiescence to policies of nuclear terrorism by their own government. Although present arsenals bristle with tens of thousands of nuclear warheads capable of incinerating humanity many times over, the U.S. nonetheless is pushing ahead with plans to deploy extremely accurate new missiles during the 1990s. Because accuracy encourages military minds to envision a disabling first-strike, these weapons are especially aggressive in character.

Nuclear test moratorium

Test explosions of new weapons designs are necessary before they can be deployed. For this reason, the U.S. government has steadfastly refused to go along with a nuclear test ban. This refusal has been aided and abetted by American mass media.

In the summer of 1985, the Soviet Union announced the start of a unilateral moratorium on nuclear test detonations. Mikhail Gorbachev invited the United States to follow suit. It was a Soviet step that, if reciprocated, would have meant the end of superpower nuclear testing—and a major brake on the nuclear arms race. American mass media quickly dismissed the initiative as an empty ploy.

CBS Evening News immediately depicted the Soviet move as mere "posturing." Lesley Stahl used the word "propaganda" four different times in the network's first report on Gorbachev's moratorium announcement. News articles the next morning in the *New York Times*, *Washington Post* and *Los Angeles Times* "each committed the cardinal journalistic sin of getting a basic fact flat wrong when they downgraded Gorbachev's unilateral action from a policy shift to a mere 'proposal,'" Mark Hertsgaard later observed. The *New York Times* and *Los Angeles Times* didn't even headline the moratorium—but instead featured a quickie spin-control proposal by President Reagan, inviting Soviet observers to a nuclear test in Nevada.

Then came the editorials in the national security newspapers. The *New York Times* sneered at the moratorium as "a cynical propaganda blast" that "would ring hollow even if it had not come after an energetic series of Soviet test explosions." In reality, the Soviet testing pace that year actually had been slower than in previous years, and lagged behind the 1985 rate of U.S. test explosions to date, seven compared to nine. The *Washington Post* chimed in, defending the administration's rejectionism in an editorial titled "Nuclear Tests Are Necessary."

But nuclear tests were "necessary" only to escalate the nuclear arms race. Verification of compliance with a test ban was assured, since existing technology provided adequate monitoring from afar. Nor were nuclear tests needed to confirm the reliability of existing warheads, as the Federation of American Scientists and nuclear weapons designers themselves had attested. After all was said and done, the U.S. government wanted to keep exploding nuclear bombs so that it could continue to develop and deploy ever-more-deadly weapons systems. And in that crime against humanity, the U.S. press served as a key accomplice.

While Gorbachev kept extending the moratorium, American media kept sniping. After the announcement of an extension in December 1985, Dan Rather began the CBS coverage by saying: "Well, a little pre-Christmas propaganda in the air, a new arms control offer from Soviet leader Mikhail Gorbachev." (It's doubtful that Rather has ever described statements by Reagan or Bush as "propaganda.")

More than a year into the Soviet moratorium, in yet another editorial indicative of its pathological affection for the nuclear industry, the *New York*

Times emphatically and illogically maintained that "limits on testing are highly desirable, but only after the arms race itself has been constrained." This was like saying that a house's foundation could not be laid until a roof had been properly installed. The claim was demolished by Kosta Tsipis, director of a program on international security at the Massachusetts Institute of Technology: "The arms race cannot be constrained if the nuclear weapons laboratories are allowed testing because they will promote the notion of 'third-generation' nuclear explosives. These are not more usable or useful than the present 'second-generation' variety, but given the evident ignorance about these matters even among the sophisticated press, they will be welcomed and invoked as reasons to continue development and testing of nuclear devices and thereby further animate the arms race."

But the *Times* seemed eager for such animation—and more than a little miffed that the Soviet leader kept breaking the tacit rules of the nuclear game: "What Mr. Gorbachev seeks in a test ban is a halt in the modernization of American strategic weapons, and a free ride to hamstring the President's 'Star Wars' missile defense. Nuclear tests are necessary for development of the nuclear-pumped X-ray laser, one of Star Wars' most promising components... A test ban could also freeze the quality of America's strategic deterrent and thus award the Kremlin its two mostly [sic] ardently sought objectives for nothing in return."

Freezing out the peace movement

For 19 months, the Kremlin held its nuclear-test fire while asking the White House to join in the moratorium so as to make it permanent. During that period, Southern Nevada shook with 25 nuclear explosions beneath the desert floor. News media provided little coverage of what was going on. At the same time, more than 1,400 Americans were arrested for nonviolent civil disobedience at the Nevada test grounds; the rare news accounts of these protests were spotty and fleeting. Mass media also gave minimal and sometimes disparaging coverage to other forms of dissent, such as a petition drive for a test ban treaty that gathered 1.2 million American signatures between spring and fall of 1985.

Even at the height of the grassroots citizen movement for a nuclear weapons freeze, the *New York Times* had put leaden feet down in a widely-reprinted editorial shortly before the November 1982 statewide referendums across America. In tones of wise elders lecturing errant offspring, the *Times* let it be known that because "the freeze remains a simplistic, sloganeering response to a complex issue...we urge a vote against." On Election Day, most voters ignored such conventional wisdom, approving freeze ballot measures in state after state.

But the nation's most pedigreed commentators continued to pour anti-freeze into the engines of the nuclear arms race. The *Washington Post* attacked two leading women's organizations in the disarmament movement as "Soviet stooge groups." (The charge was later retracted.) And news articles echoed editorials—Strangelovian fixations sugar-coated with verbiage about slowing the nuclear arms build-up. Someday.

Leaders of peace groups have generally been excluded from national TV debates about the arms race. The only strong opponents of U.S. nuclear weapons policies allowed on the biggest television shows are usually Soviet officials. This time-honored mass media practice—discounting many millions of Americans strongly opposed to their government's nuclear escalations—persisted throughout the 1980s.

U.S. media all but ignored disarmament activism as the decade drew to a close, while confining nuclear arms "issues" to inside-the-Beltway differences on the pace and mix of nuclear deployments. By presenting "arms control" as some kind of counterweight to the arms race, mass media have continued to further deadly confusion, since "arms control" has always aided the arms race as a reassuring euphemism for reshaping nuclear arsenals with newer weapons while discarding older ones.

On a short leash from the Oval Office, mainstream reporters do not wander off very far to sniff at nuclear weapons policies, the epitome of hallowed "national security" concerns. As a matter of routine, journalistic ears are cocked to the master's voice. And no spectrum of mass media's allowable opinion is more constricted than nuclear weapons "debates." Controversies may flare up about specific weapons systems—but not about actually putting a stop to the production of evermore deadly weaponry. Perpetual nuclear arms development remains sacrosanct to the military-industrial-media complex.

Obscuring and evading what these weapons mean, mass media whistle past a very large thermonuclear graveyard in which several billion unmarked graves have already been plotted. And news media encourage the public to do the same.

11

The Twin Scourges:
Terrorism and Narcotics

During most of the Reagan era, U.S. officials, aided by a pliant press corps, pushed the idea that the Soviet Union was Terror Central, the conspiratorial mastermind that called the shots for terrorists worldwide. The issue of terrorism was especially useful for furthering a Cold War agenda. Its efficacy as a propaganda tool has not waned with the warming of superpower relations.

Echoing the Cold War whoops of Secretary of State Alexander Haig, a 1981 *Washington Post* editorial charged that the USSR and its allies were "the principal source of terror in the world" and urged the U.S. "to improve intelligence and counterterror measures" so that Moscow would no longer have "a free ride for being the hatchery of international terrorism." That same year, however, ex-CIA-chief William Colby told Congress there was little evidence that the Soviets directed terrorist acts around the globe. Then-FBI-director William Webster declared emphatically that there was "no real evidence of Soviet-sponsored terrorism within the United States."

Nevertheless, the U.S. media continued to hype the Moscow terrorist threat. The *Post* and the *New York Times* gave prominent coverage to right-wing conspiracy theories promoted by the likes of Claire Sterling, an American journalist who had worked for a CIA-proprietary newspaper in Rome, and Paul Henze, a former CIA operative. (Henze insisted that his spy credentials not be disclosed when he appeared as a guest on the *MacNeil/Lehrer NewsHour* and other news programs, and the networks obliged him.) Sterling and Henze alleged that the Soviet KGB and its Bulgarian proxies were behind the May 1981 shooting of Pope John Paul II.

According to the so-called Bulgarian connection theory, Soviet spymasters wanted to kill the Pope because of his support for Solidarity, the opposition trade union movement in Poland. Toward this end, they supposedly recruited a Turkish neo-Nazi gunman named Mehmet Ali Agca, who fired the shots that injured the pontiff. U.S. news media, with few exceptions, failed to point out glaring inconsistencies which made the theory implausible.

In 1979, Agca publicly threatened to kill John Paul II. In July of the following year, he (and thousands of other Turks) traveled along the infamous smugglers' route through Bulgaria. There Agca was allegedly recruited by communist spies who hatched the assassination plot. One problem with this theory: Agca's Bulgarian sojourn occurred before Solidarity was even formed—which meant that the Bulgarians or the Soviets would have had to recruit Agca to kill the Pope at a time when they had no reason to attempt such an outrageous scheme. The Bulgarian connection later collapsed in a Roman court, when Agca blew what little credibility he had by proclaiming on the witness stand that he was Jesus Christ.

But the "KGB did it" theory was resurrected in November 1989 by Dan Rather in a *CBS Evening News* series called "God and Gorbachev," which coincided with the Soviet leader's historic visit to the Vatican. Rather said it was ironic that Gorbachev would be meeting the Pope when eight years earlier the Soviet Union tried to murder him. Then the camera cut to old footage of Agca shouting to reporters that the KGB was behind the papal shooting. According to Rather, unnamed "Vatican insiders" insisted the Soviets were responsible, even though this was never proven in court. CBS News could have presented footage of Agca saying he was Jesus Christ, but that would have made the CBS story look as ludicrous and dishonest as it actually was.

As Edward S. Herman and Frank Brodhead wrote in their book *The Rise and Fall of the Bulgarian Connection*: "Old, fabricated, and disproved anticommunist tales never die, they merely fade into the dimmer background of popular mythology."

WHEN AIRPLANES EXPLODE IN THE SKY

When a Soviet interceptor plane blew up a South Korean passenger jet in September 1983, U.S. media immediately condemned it as a heinous act. Editorials denouncing the KAL shootdown were filled with phrases like "wanton killing" and "reckless aerial murder." The day after the incident, a *New York Times* editorial, titled "Murder in the Air," was unequivocal: "There is no conceivable excuse for any nation shooting down a harmless airliner... No circumstance whatever justifies attacking an innocent plane."

But when Iran Air Flight 655 was blown out of the sky by a U.S. cruiser in July 1988, excuses were more than conceivable—they were profuse. Confronted with the sudden reality of a similar action by the U.S. government, the *New York Times* inverted every standard invoked with righteous indignation five years earlier.

Two days after the Iranian passenger jet went down in flames killing 290 people, the *Times* editorialized that "while horrifying, it was nonetheless an accident." The editorial concluded, "The onus for avoiding such accidents in the future rests on civilian aircraft: avoid combat zones, fly high, acknowledge warnings."

A similar double standard pervaded electronic media coverage. In the aftermath of the KAL tragedy, America's airwaves carried ritual denunciations by journalists. On CBS, for example, Dan Rather called it a "barbaric act." No such adjectives were heard from America's TV commentators when discussing the U.S. shootdown of a civilian jet.

Murder in the Air

There is no conceivable excuse for any nation shooting down a harmless airliner. After tracking the South Korean intruder for more than two hours, and then observing him at close range, Soviet air defenders had to know the identity of their target — which means someone in the Soviet chain of command is guilty of cold-blooded mass murder.

The Soviet leaders' response will affect their standing in the world for a very long time. They had better curb their customary instinct to cover up, or blame their victims, and bring the guilty to account. Any effort to justify such brutality will surely affect America's judgment of the man newly in charge of the world's other doomsday machine.

•

Why would anyone shoot an innocent jumbo jet out of the sky?

A pilot gone mad? Not when he reports the kill with such cool detachment and satisfaction, as shown by American radio intercepts.

A secret base commander afraid of aerial photographs? Not at night, surely, and not when everyone knows that satellites routinely photograph such bases, on both sides.

A higher command made paranoid about intruders that might be testing Soviet radar defenses? Soviet commanders already know that Americans read their radar over their shoulders, as Secretary Shultz freely demonstrated. They cannot in any case believe that anyone would put a planeload of innocents at risk for such a test.

There simply is no rational explanation, much less excuse. It's not as though this is the first such episode; all governments have been on notice of the danger. Bulgaria shot down an Israeli passenger plane in 1955. Israel shot down a Libyan airliner in 1973, and the Russians crippled a South Korean passenger jet in 1978. That the Soviet Union nonetheless let stand the authority to fire at commercial aircraft is unforgivable.

In the air even more than at sea, commercial pilots and passengers have a right to expect civility and humanity, especially when their craft are in trouble. That is a Soviet interest no less than an American or Korean. The tone of Moscow's statements in the next few days will show whether the Kremlin accepts its responsibility for a minimally decent international order.

To earn the right to participate in global aviation the Soviet Government needs now to demonstrate that it is determined to end such aerial murder. It needs to agree to clear, unthreatening procedures for guiding an errant plane back on course. It needs to accept arrangements for voice communication in cases of doubt or misunderstanding. Above all, it needs to change the orders to its air defenders, acknowledging that no circumstance whatever justifies attacking an innocent plane. Nothing less can even begin to atone for this wanton killing.

In Captain Rogers's Shoes

The White House's restrained expressions of regret do scant justice to the 290 victims who died at U.S. hands in the Persian Gulf Sunday. Yet while horrifying, it was nonetheless an accident. On present evidence, it's hard to see what the Navy could have done to avoid it.

Modern naval warfare and the crowded skies of the gulf have combined to make the stage conducive to tragic accidents. The first occurred in May of last year when an Iraqi plane mistakenly attacked the American frigate Stark. It's too early to assess blame for the new tragedy, the shooting down of an Iranian Airbus by the U.S. cruiser Vincennes. But if the Navy's account of events turns out even approximately correct, Captain Will Rogers of the Vincennes had little choice.

The ship was not only in a combat zone; but at that very moment was engaged in action against Iranian gunboats making high-speed runs against it. Then Captain Rogers's radar operators reported an aircraft heading toward the ship and descending, although that information has since been called into question by a report from a second Navy ship. The plane was reportedly flying five miles outside the civilian air corridor and failed to answer three warnings over the civilian distress channel.

The radar operators apparently had indications, which the Navy refuses to discuss, that the plane was a F-14 jet. That inference was tragically in error. Iran says the plane was within its corridor. Its speed, reported at 450 knots, was more typical of civilian flight than an F-14 attack. And it is not clear why sophisticated radar did not distinguish between an F-14 and a much larger Airbus.

Still, put yourself in Captain Rogers's shoes. These contrary pieces of evidence would have weighed lightly against other evidence suggesting an imminent attack. Iranian F-14's had recently been seen in the region; U.S. forces had been warned to expect attacks around July 4; Captain Rogers already had a battle on his hands. Barring surprising findings, it is hard to fault his decision to attack the suspect plane.

The episode also raises stern questions for Iran. If the Navy's version of events is largely correct, blame may lie with the Iran Air pilot for failing to acknowledge the ship's warnings and flying outside the civilian corridor. Iran, too, may bear responsibility for failing to warn civilian planes away from the combat zone of an action it had initiated.

•

Because surface warships are extremely vulnerable to missiles, American captains in the gulf are being asked to bear an appalling responsibility. If they delay too long in attacking unidentified aircraft, they risk losing their ship. Yet if they fire before an intruding aircraft can be positively identified, they risk causing a massacre.

The present rules of engagement allow a captain to fire first in defense of his ship. If that rule cannot be prudently altered, the onus for avoiding such accidents in the future rests on civilian aircraft: avoid combat zones, fly high, acknowledge warnings. Better still, no one would have to be in Captain Rogers's shoes in the first place. That prospect turns on Teheran's willingness to bring an end to its futile eight-year war with Iraq.

New York Times editorials, September 2, 1983 (top) and July 5, 1988 (bottom)

The Reagan administration exploited KAL 007 for all it was worth. As *Nightline* host Ted Koppel admitted years later, "This was at a period when the President was very much interested in portraying the Russians as being a bunch of barbarians, was very much interested in getting the Strategic Defense Initiative program going. It all fit very nicely, didn't it, to have this image of the Russians at that time knowingly shoot down a civilian airliner?"

The Soviet shootdown inspired a single-issue focus unparalleled on *Nightline* since the Iran hostage crisis had given birth to the show in 1979. *Nightline* aired eight consecutive programs on the story, with titles such as "Korean Air 'Massacre'—Reagan Reaction" and "Punishing the Soviets—What U.S. Options?" On one show, host Ted Koppel was remarkably candid: "This has been one of those occasions when there is very little difference between what is churned out by the U.S. government's propaganda organs and by the commercial broadcasting networks."

Nightline's programs on KAL 007 featured a steady parade of hawks like Richard Viguerie, William Buckley, George Will, William Safire ("a brutal act of murder"), Jesse Helms ("premeditated, deliberate murder") and John Lofton ("sever diplomatic relations with the Soviet Union"). Koppel himself stated there wasn't "any question that the Soviet Union deserves to be accused of murder, it's only a question of whether it's first degree or second degree."

On *Nightline* "007 Day Three," Koppel promoted an on-air telephone poll asking viewers whether the administration "should take strong action against the Soviets." Over 90 percent said yes. On the same show, right-wing leader Terry Dolan stated that "anyone who would suggest that the U.S. would ever consider shooting down an unarmed civilian plane is downright foolish and irresponsible."

When the U.S. shot down a civilian plane five years later, *Nightline*'s hometeam bias was evident. Instead of eight consecutive shows (followed by two more later in the month), there were only three *Nightline* programs focusing on the U.S. shootdown. No American foreign policy critics denounced the U.S. for murder; instead the discussion focused on "somber questions" about "the tragedy," occasionally implying that Iranians were to blame.

What can explain the disparity in coverage? In each case, *Nightline* meshed with the propaganda needs of the U.S. government: the Soviet action was hashed and rehashed as evidence against the Evil Empire; the U.S. action was deftly handled as a tragic mistake.

Debunking relevant comparisons

As soon as the Iranian Airbus crashed into the Persian Gulf, the Reagan administration set out to discourage what should have been obvious comparisons with the KAL incident. The *New York Times* and other media uncritically quoted the President's July 4 resurrection of his administration's time-worn deceit: "Remember the KAL, a group of Soviet fighter planes went up, identified the plane for what it was and then proceeded to shoot it down. There's no comparison."

Virtually ignored was a key finding of Seymour Hersh's 1986 book *The Target Is Destroyed*—that the Reagan administration knew within days of the KAL shootdown that the Soviets had believed it to be a military aircraft on a spy mission. Soviet commanders had no idea that they were tracking a plane with civilians on board. The *Times* acknowledged this years later in an editorial, "The Lie That Wasn't Shot Down"; yet when Reagan lied again, the *Times* again failed to shoot it down.

Instead, *Times* correspondent R.W. Apple weighed in with an analysis headlined, "Military Errors: The Snafu as History." In his lead, Apple observed that "the destruction of an Iranian airliner...came as a sharp reminder of the pervasive role of error in military history." The piece drew many parallels to the Iran jetliner's tragic end—citing examples from the American Revolution, World War II and Vietnam—while ignoring the most obvious analogy. About the KAL 007 shootdown, Apple said not a word.

In certain ways, the Iran Air tragedy was less defensible than the KAL disaster. The Iran Air jet went down in broad daylight, well within its approved commercial airline course over international waters, without ever having strayed into unauthorized air space. In contrast, the KAL jet flew way off-course deep into Soviet territory above sensitive military installations, in the dead of night.

But, as with Washington's policy makers, journalists were intent on debunking relevant comparisons rather than exploring them. The government's PR spin quickly became the mass media's—a tragic mishap had occurred in the Persian Gulf, amid puzzling behavior of the passenger jet. Blaming the victim was standard fare, as reporters focused on the plight of *USS Vincennes* commander Captain Will Rogers, whose picture appeared on tabloid covers with bold headlines—"Captain's Anguish" (*Newsday*) and "Captain's Agony" (*New York Post*).

An ABC News-*Washington Post* poll released three days after the Iran Air jet's demise found a lopsided majority of Americans believed that Captain Rogers had taken appropriate measures. Having presented events in such a way as to load sympathy and justification on the side of the attackers, the media proceeded to survey the population's response; the polling results were then cited to certify widespread public support for the Navy's action. At the same time, U.S. journalists asserted that the Iranian government was eager to exploit its new propaganda advantage.

While much of the coverage amounted to breathless summaries of U.S. government news conferences and press releases, there were some exceptions: *Newsday* editorialized that Reagan gave "the impression that his over-

New York Post (left) and *Newsday* (right)

whelming desire is to preserve Persian Gulf policy, not to discover what went wrong. And his attitude reflects a regrettable tendency to demonize the Iranians."

Day-by-day comparisons of news articles in the *New York Times* and the *Washington Post*, during the crucial first days of the crisis, reveal the *Times* coverage to be softer and more biased. On July 6, 1988, as the *Times* continued to echo government perspectives, the *Post* was beginning to raise doubts about the official fable that the U.S. Navy had reason to fear an attack on a warship by Iranian F-14 jets. The *Post* front-paged an investigative piece by George C. Wilson headlined "Pilots Question Threat Posed by F-14," with the subhead: "Warplane Designed to Attack Air Targets, Not Ships."

But media scrutiny of Pentagon accounts came days after the basic parameters of the story had been set. Even the better reportage tended to focus on technical questions while avoiding fundamental issues. Mass media coverage skirted the aggressive character of the U.S. military's presence in the Gulf, and rarely mentioned that for a year the Soviet Union had been urging the withdrawal of all foreign military vessels from the region. The Soviet proposal would have dispatched ships under the U.N. flag to the Persian Gulf to keep the shipping lanes open—the supposed purpose of the enormous (and deadly) U.S. presence there.

Sorely lacking from the outset was any semblance of soul-searching about the holier-than-thou Soviet-bashing that followed the KAL accident. The last thing that White House officials wanted was a national self-examination of this sort. U.S. media allowed their proclaimed precepts to spin 180 degrees in an instant, while discarding basic insights like the one expressed in a *New York Times* editorial six days after KAL 007 exploded: "To proclaim a 'right' to shoot down suspicious planes does not make it right to do so." Commenting on this journalistic dual standard, the Toronto *Globe and Mail* (Canada's newspaper of record) described the *Times* editorials on the KAL and Iran Air shootdowns as "jingoism" in an article headlined, "Is It Really All The News That's Fit To Print?"

Pan Am Flight 103

Media coverage of terrorism is dominated by some of the most extreme—and in light of Iran-contra revelations, most hypocritical—foreign policy rhetoric, often at the expense of examining the complexities of the issue. As soon as it was learned that a bomb destroyed Pan Am Flight 103 over Lockerbie, Scotland, in December 1988, killing all 271 people on board, reporters began asking all the usual questions: How can we punish those responsible? Will we retaliate against any government that protects terrorists who bomb civilian jets?

Reagan and Bush responded with stern language. Said Reagan: "We're going to make every effort to find out who was guilty of this savage thing and bring them to justice." Bush promised to "seek hard and punish firmly, decisively, those who did this, if you could ever find them."

What was wrong with this predictable rhetoric? As many journalists knew, the U.S. government had harbored an accused jet-bombing terrorist without doing anything to bring him to justice. This was the case with Luis Posada, a right-wing Cuban exile who worked for the CIA for many years since the ill-fated Bay of Pigs invasion. Trained by the CIA in the use of explosives, Posada was the reputed mastermind of the 1976 mid-air bombing of a Cubana Airlines passenger jet that killed all 73 people on board.

Posada and other members of the anti-Castro terror group, Command of United Revolutionary Organizations (CORU), were charged in Venezuela with the crime. Two CORU operatives who admitted planting the bomb fingered Posada as a pivotal figure behind the plot.

In 1985 Posada escaped from a high-security Venezuelan prison. Instead of hunting him down, U.S. government agents offered Posada a job at Ilopango Air Base in El Salvador. There he played a key role in overseeing efforts to resupply the Nicaraguan contras. In May 1986, a Venezuelan TV journalist interviewed Posada from "somewhere in Central America." "I feel good here," Posada exulted, "because I am involved once again in a fight against international Communism."

While based at Ilopango, Posada served as the right-hand man of longtime CIA agent Felix Rodriguez, who reported directly to Vice President Bush's office. During this period, Rodriguez met with Bush on three occasions to brief him on the illegal contra resupply operation.

What did the U.S. government do after leading U.S. dailies exposed Posada as a contra operative in El Salvador? American officials let him slip away and vanish. And the U.S. media quietly dropped the matter.

As Jeff Cohen of FAIR noted shortly after the Pan Am bombing: "Instead of clamoring for hypothetical responses to as yet unidentified terrorists behind the Pan Am explosion, journalists would do better to ask Bush some probing questions. Why has the U.S. protected Posada and his friends? If it's terrorism to blow up innocent civilians in the fight against 'Western Satanism' and 'international Zionism,' isn't it also terrorism to do the same in the struggle against 'international Communism'? And if it's justified for the U.S. to retaliate against a foreign country linked to the Pan Am terrorists, does Cuba have the right to launch an air strike against Washington because of U.S. relations with Posada and his colleagues? If U.S. officials are serious about punishing terrorists, shouldn't they start with their own?"

The bombing of Pan Am Flight 103 received a lot of media coverage, but certain aspects of the case have been downplayed, including the fact that at least six U.S. intelligence agents died during the blast. Among them were Mathew Gannon, a highranking CIA Middle East expert, and his two body-guards, Ronald Lariviere and Daniel O'Connor, all of whom were working under State Department cover. Another Pan Am victim was Charles McKee, a Defense Intelligence Agency officer specializing in Middle East counter-terrorist operations; at the time of his death, McKee was on a CIA assignment.

A special 27-page report commissioned by Pan Am in the wake of the attack confirmed that CIA officials were killed aboard Flight 103. The shocking contents of this report—prepared by a New York consulting firm called Interfor—were summarized in a November 1989 *Toronto Star* article headlined "Pan Am bomb linked to double-dealing CIA drug plot." According to the *Star*, the group of CIA agents who died on Flight 103 were en route to the U.S. to personally inform their superiors about another CIA clique (dubbed "CIA-1" in the Pan Am report) involved in an illegal arms and drugs operation to secure the release of American hostages held in Lebanon.

A pivotal figure in the hushed-up affair was Manzar Al-Kassar, the Syrian heroin dealer who supplied weapons to the Nicaraguan contras (at Oliver North's behest) and to Arab terrorists. This was the person CIA-1 was relying on to help free the hostages. Al-Kassar, the *Star* reported, also had close links with Ahmed Jibril, head of the Popular Front for the Liberation of Palestine-General Command, an anti-Arafat extremist group allegedly hired to conduct a retaliatory attack against the U.S. for shooting down Iran Air Flight 655 over the Persian Gulf.

At one point, said the *Star*, CIA-1 learned from Al-Kassar of a plot by Jibril to bomb Pan Am Flight 103, but CIA officials, fearing they might blow Al-Kassar's cover and jeopardize the hostage rescue scheme, never conveyed this information to the appropriate authorities. Congressman James Trafficant disclosed on CBS *Saturday Night With Connie Chung* that the bomb was smuggled on to the aircraft in a suitcase that was supposed to contain heroin. Ironically, CIA-1 knew about this drug smuggling network but did not interfere because it was Al-Kassar's operation.

The American spies who died on the plane flight over Scotland were on their way to the United States to discuss what they had learned about the Al-Kassar situation with other CIA officials, concludes the report—which absolves Pan Am of legal responsibility for the mishap and shifts the blame to an off-the-shelf branch of U.S. intelligence. Whether or not its findings were accurate, the Pan Am report should have stimulated some independent inquiry on the part of U.S. journalists. But the American press dropped the story like a hot potato. Major media displayed little curiosity even when Congressman Trafficant announced his intention to conduct an investigation after Pan Am had subpoenaed the CIA, FBI and the State Department.

WHO'S A TERRORIST, AND WHO'S NOT?

Over the years, U.S. media have promoted a simplistic view of the world where North Americans in white hats police the globe of black hats—usually worn by Arab terrorists. By applying the terrorism label only to anti-Western political activity and violence, mass media foster the illusion that "terrorism is alien to American patterns of conduct in the world, that it is done to us, and that what we do violently to others is legitimate counter-terrorism," said Richard Falk, a professor of international law at Princeton University.

The U.S. government's selective definition of terrorism is echoed throughout the media. In January 1989 the Pentagon released a slick, 130-page report—with photos and bar charts—called Terrorist Group Profiles. Praising it as "an effort to raise public awareness," *CBS Evening News* correspondent Terrence Smith noted that the Pentagon spent $71,000 to produce and distribute the report. "Cheap by Pentagon standards," Smith concluded, "and few are likely to question its value."

The CBS segment featured a sound bite from "terrorism expert" Ray Cline, who endorsed the Pentagon's "consciousness raising among our own people." Cline, a former CIA deputy director, is a close associate of the

World Anti-Communist League, whose Latin American affiliates include unsavory characters linked to death squads and neo-Nazi violence.

A.M. Rosenthal puffed the Pentagon report as a compilation of "all known terrorist groups" in his *New York Times* column. But a cursory glance at the report's table of contents should have been enough to discern the Pentagon's slant. The section on African terrorism lists only one organization: the anti-apartheid African National Congress. Latin American terrorists are all left-wing revolutionaries; right-wing death squads aren't mentioned. The roster from Western Europe features the defunct Direct Action from France (supposedly a leftist group), while omitting any reference to numerous neo-Nazi terror gangs that are still active on the Continent. And El Fatah, the main PLO faction, is included among Mideast terrorist organizations, despite Yasir Arafat's renunciation of terrorism.

That major U.S. news media should give their stamp of approval to such a blatantly biased Pentagon report underscores an essential point. "The American understanding of terrorism," said Professor Falk, "has been dominated by recent governmental efforts to associate terrorists with Third World revolutionaries, especially those with Arab countries... The media have generally carried on their inquiries within this framework of selective perception. As a result, our political imagination is imprisoned, with a variety of ugly and unfortunate consequences."

The Arab pariah

During a 40-month period from 1985 to 1988, ABC *Nightline* aired 52 programs about terrorism; of these, 48 focused on the Middle East. The implication of such coverage is that Arabs are by far the primary cause of international terrorism. *Nightline* and other U.S. media seem much less interested in terrorism when it happens elsewhere—even in the United States.

Consider, for example, the massive publicity that enshrined American Leon Klinghoffer as a hero after he was murdered by Arab terrorists aboard the *Achille Lauro* cruise ship in 1985. It was a brutal killing that warranted major coverage. But the press showed little interest when, three days after Klinghoffer's death, terrorists bombed the Southern California headquarters of the American-Arab Anti-Discrimination Committee, killing Alex Odeh, its regional director. Odeh, who had lit the menorah candles during Chanukah ceremonies hosted by New Jewish Agenda, was committed to dialogue and peaceful reconciliation among Arabs and Jews. His murder drew sparse national attention, perhaps because it didn't fit in with the prevailing stereotypes about terrorism.

U.S. news and entertainment media typically depict Palestinians as terrorists, not as victims of terror. "For decades, negative portraits of Arabs, unbalanced by positive images, have collectively nurtured suspicion and ignorance," said sociologist Jack Shaheen, author of *The TV Arab*.

"Palestinian caricatures are not harmless, escapist fare. History has taught us that such images inform—or disinform—the values, ideas, and actions of individuals and their governments." Shaheen noted that most U.S. political leaders refuse to condemn anti-Arab racism. (Some Reagan administration officials had denigrated Arabs as "sand-niggers.")

An unbiased press would acknowledge that terrorism comes not only from the barrels of Palestinian guns. It also comes from Israeli air strikes against Arab villages and from Israeli-backed Phalangist forces who have massacred defenseless civilians in Lebanon. Waging a campaign for a Jewish homeland after World War II, some Zionist groups (including future leaders of the Likud Party) engaged in bloody terrorist attacks. The world's first air hijacking occurred in 1954, when the Israeli military seized a Syrian passenger plane and traded the hostages for captured Israeli soldiers.

In subsequent years, Arab terrorists hijacked Israeli planes and attacked other civilian targets, provoking widespread international condemnation. But when the tables were turned, U.S. media outrage was minimal, as when the Israelis assassinated Arafat's right-hand man, Abu Jihad, in 1988. Or when Israel shot down a Libyan civilian jet lost in a sandstorm over the Sinai in 1973, killing 110 people. "No useful purpose is served by an acrimonious debate over assignment of blame," the *New York Times* editorialized about the downing of the Libyan plane. In the world according to mass media, Israel responds to terrorism, but never initiates it.

The CIA's secret deal with the PLO

In December 1988, when the U.S. government finally recognized Arafat's recognition of Israel and his call for negotiations to establish a Palestinian state, numerous commentators expressed doubt as to whether the PLO chief's peace overtures were genuine. "Has Arafat really renounced terrorism?" was the common refrain. No national news media outlet pointed out an important fact that had been reported years earlier in a *Wall Street Journal* story by David Ignatius.

During the mid-1970s, according to the *Journal*, Arafat entered into a secret agreement with the CIA, whereby the PLO vowed to protect U.S. Embassy employees from attacks by Arab extremists. Arafat's security chief, Ali Hassan Salameh, began warning the CIA of plots by rival Palestinian groups. Salameh (later murdered by Israeli intelligence) also shared information with Western European governments concerning links between European terrorists and Arab hardliners.

In other words, Arafat and the PLO were helping the U.S. defend itself against Arab terrorists. This arrangement continued until Israel invaded Lebanon in 1982 and destroyed the PLO infrastructure in Beirut. With the PLO no longer a major military factor, U.S. Embassy personnel in Beirut were henceforth highly vulnerable to terrorist attacks. By dislodging Arafat's moderate forces, the Israeli invasion precipitated a bloody tit-for-tat war between CIA "counterterrorist" commandos and Arab extremists whose attacks included the 1983 car-bombing which killed 271 Marines. Those who died aboard Pan Am Flight 103 may also have been victims of this clandestine war.

As told by mass media, only America's enemies practice terrorism. When the battleship *New Jersey* lobbed mortars into Lebanese villages in 1984, causing numerous civilian casualties and arousing intense anti-American feelings, few journalists suggested that this was also a form of terrorism. The idea that terrorist attacks against Americans might be a response to actions by the U.S. government seemingly never crosses the minds of most reporters. Instead, news stories depict terrorism as random madness, with neither roots nor origin. In so doing, mass media promote the officially sanctioned view that the U.S. is unfairly targeted by bloodthirsty fanatics who deserve swift retribution.

Terrorism and counter-terrorism are often two ways of describing the same activity. As Richard Falk wrote in *Revolutionaries and Functionaries: The Dual Face of Terror*, "The terrorist is as much the well-groomed bureaucrat reading the *Wall Street Journal* as the Arab in desert dress looking through the gunsights of a Kalashnikov rifle." Indeed, the activities of both are symbiotically linked, with U.S. officials invoking the specter of revolutionary violence in Third World countries as a pretext to preserve "national security" through state terrorism.

Selective definitions of terrorism

Because the U.S. government dominates the media agenda, Third World revolutionary violence continues to exert a distracting hold on the American imagination, while U.S.-backed state terrorism in countries like Guatemala, El Salvador, the Philippines and Indonesia is downplayed. Consider the headline of a December 1988 *New York Times* article by Lindsey Gruson: "Salvador Rebels Step Up Terrorism." The lead reported on the leftists' "use of terrorism"—a reference to the killing of eight mayors in the previous eight months. One learned only in the last paragraph (of a 22-paragraph story) that Americas Watch, an independent human rights organization, found the U.S.-backed government was responsible for two out of every three civilian deaths in El Salvador during this period.

When tracking abuses of civilians by rebel groups in Central America, independent human rights organizations long identified the Nicaraguan contras as the worst offenders. A once-secret 1982 Pentagon report explicitly described the contras as a "terrorist" group. A CIA-authored assassination manual actually instructed the contras to target elected mayors in Nicaragua. Despite this evidence, the *New York Times* never referred matter-of-factly in a news story to "contra terrorism" or ran a headline like "Nicaraguan Rebels Step Up Terrorism"—a blatant double standard in light of *Times* reporting on El

Salvador. Instead, an October 1989 *Times* editorial used the word "pinpricks" to describe contra terrorist attacks, which had killed over 140 Nicaraguan civilians since a cease fire supposedly went into effect 18 months earlier.

As government-allied death squad murders escalated in El Salvador, the *Times* whitewashed U.S. responsibility for the violence. "*Despite U.S. training programs*," read a *Times* editorial, "the Salvadoran military played into leftist hands with indiscriminate attacks on peasants [emphasis added]." As Allan Nairn documented in *The Progressive*, it was U.S. intelligence that organized and tutored the Salvadoran security forces involved in death squad activity that killed tens of thousands since the 1960s.

Jude Wanniski, former associate editor of the *Wall Street Journal* and author of the annual *Media Guide*, is an ardent defender of Salvadoran death squad leader Roberto D'Aubuisson, widely believed to be the mastermind of the assassination of Archbishop Oscar Romero in 1980. Wanniski dismissed the notion that D'Aubuisson has anything to do with the death squads, calling it "one of the most successful hoaxes of the decade." Those like former U.S. ambassador Robert White and ex-Salvadoran President José Napoleón Duarte, who have linked D'Aubuisson to the death squads, were guilty, in Wanniski's words, of "a McCarthyist tactic, pure and simple." Wanniski didn't mention D'Aubuisson's admiring comment about Adolf Hitler told to a German reporter and another European journalist: "You Germans were very intelligent. You realized that the Jews were responsible for the spread of communism, and you began to kill them."

The kind of terrorism the U.S. media pay most attention to is committed by small groups on planes, ships, or at airports—what Edward S. Herman has described as "retail terror"—compared to "wholesale terror" that occurs with U.S. financial assistance and military support in countries like Guatemala, El Salvador, and the Philippines (where human rights abuses have persisted under Corazon Aquino's government at a level rivaling, if not exceeding, the Marcos era). Although their numbers are much smaller, the victims of Third World revolutionary violence often receive far more news coverage than victims of U.S.-backed state terror.

A notable exception occurred when Salvadoran soldiers murdered six Jesuit priests and two associates in November 1989. Although depicted as an aberration, this incident was actually part of a long-standing pattern of religious persecution by U.S.-backed regimes, which have kidnaped, tortured and murdered scores of progressive church activists in Latin America during the past decade.

THE CONTRA COCAINE NON-STORY

In July 1989, four high-ranking Cuban military officers were executed by firing squad after a show trial—in which they had no right of appeal—convicted them of drug trafficking. It was a sensational story that grabbed big headlines in the United States.

A week after the Cuban officers died, another sensational drug-related story emerged. An in-depth investigation by a Costa Rican Congressional Commission on Narcotics found that the contra resupply network run by Lt. Col. Oliver North was deeply connected to narcotics smugglers. North, Poindexter, Richard Secord, former CIA station chief Joseph Fernandez, and former U.S. ambassador Lewis Tambs were subsequently barred from entry into Costa Rica by an executive order from Costa Rican President Oscar Arias.

Unlike the Cuban drug connection, North's involvement with narcotraffickers in Costa Rica received hardly any attention in the United States. It should have. On July 22, 1989, an Associated Press wire story carried news of the Costa Rican government's findings into nearly every American newsroom, but the North drug link was downplayed or ignored entirely by mass media. The *Washington Post* and the *Miami Herald* relegated it to a few muddled sentences on the back pages, while the *New York Times* and the three commercial TV networks didn't say a word about the story. One noteworthy exception was the *San Juan Star*, which ran a lengthy version of the AP dispatch.

The story certainly wasn't downplayed for lack of interest. After all, 1989 news polls showed a majority of U.S. citizens viewed drugs as the most important problem facing the country. The ·American people probably would have been interested to know that U.S. government officials were providing cover for a major drug-running operation in Central America. This media-obscured fact helps to explain the four-fold increase in cocaine entering the U.S. during the Reagan administration, while Veep Bush was titular head of the "war on drugs."

How the story slipped out

The U.S. press, acting more as a gatekeeper than an aggressive proponent of truth, skipped lightly over the highly embarrassing and potentially explosive contra drug connection for a long time. The first comprehensive exposé of contra drug trafficking appeared in late 1985, when the Associated Press ran a story by Robert Parry, a career AP reporter, and Brian Barger, who had covered Central America for ABC News and the *Washington Post*. (Earlier that year, Barger won the Polk Award for breaking the story on the CIA assassination manual distributed to contra troops in 1984.) As it turned out, the contra drug story got onto the wire by accident after their boss tried to kill the story.

"It was probably the most heavily edited story in the history of the bureau," recalled one AP staffer in Washington. "They start out questioning sources. They weaken and weaken, then they say 'Why is the AP doing this story?' Which, by then, is a good question since all the good stuff is on the cutting-room floor, so to speak." Parry told Joel Millman of the *Columbia Journalism Review* that he had "bitter" arguments with AP editors about the story. Each rewrite was sent up to AP headquarters in New York for approval. Only much later did the two reporters find out that Oliver North was speaking with their boss, Charles J. Lewis, on a regular basis.

Just when it looked like the story was going nowhere, an editor working overnight at the AP's Spanish-language wire called up the text on the computer and, without checking to see if it had been okayed for publication, translated the latest draft and sent it out over the wire. The next morning Spanish-language papers in New York, Miami, and throughout Latin America picked up the story, which quoted a U.S. law enforcement official saying that drug smuggling had become an established practice among "virtually all" contra groups in Costa Rica. Three days later, on December 20, 1985, the AP ran a heavily-edited English-language version, which omitted the quote from the U.S. official linking "virtually all" contra factions to the narcotics trade. This version bore the earmarks of damage control, as it focused only on the soon-to-be-expendable contra group led by Eden Pastora—a spin undoubtedly preferred by Lt. Col. North, who had grown increasingly frustrated with Pastora's refusal to unite with contra forces in Honduras.

Even though the piece had been watered down considerably by management, the Parry-Barger revelations were still sensational. But, while the story ran in the *Los Angeles Times*, *Newsday* and the *Philadelphia Inquirer*, it didn't get much more exposure. The *New York Times*, which published other AP riffs on the contras, let it slide; the *Washington Post* held it for a week, then buried it in the middle of the paper. Aside from a passing mention by Tom Brokaw on *NBC Nightly News*, none of the networks touched the story.

In March 1986 *San Francisco Examiner* reporter Seth Rosenfeld documented links between cocaine traffickers and top officials of the main contra group in Honduras. But it was just another drop in the big media bucket. A year would pass before CBS *West 57th* broadcast the first incisive TV news report on the contra drug connection. *West 57th* interviewed convicted American drug pilots who told of flying weapons to contra base camps in Honduras and backloading cocaine and marijuana to the United States. PBS *Frontline* also presented an in-depth report on the role of U.S. intelligence in the narcotics trade. But these disclosures came and went without causing much of a stir—in large part because U.S. officials, for obvious reasons, were not inclined to push the story.

Instead, the Reagan administration sought to divert attention from the contra connection by claiming that the Nicaraguan government was involved in drug trafficking. Whereas U.S. media were squeamish about publicizing contra smuggling, they eagerly embraced allegations of a Sandinista cocaine link, despite a lack of evidence to back up the charges.

The Sandinista cocaine hoax

It was the Rev. Moon-owned *Washington Times*—which worked in tandem with the National Security Council in covert operations against Nicaragua—that first alleged in July 1984 that Sandinista officials were involved in the coke trade. The *New York Times*, the *Washington Post*, the major wire services and TV networks immediately gave the charges prominent coverage, invariably citing anonymous "senior administration officials." These officials, *Newsweek* later revealed, were propaganda specialists from the Office of Public Diplomacy.

Over the years, U.S. media frequently repeated the same charges, sometimes with a new twist, as when a Nicaraguan defector told *CBS Morning News* that Interior Minister Tomas Borge used narcotics profits to buy cars and women. During a nationally-televised speech in March 1986, shortly before Congress was to vote on contra aid, President Reagan underscored his anti-Sandinista pitch by displaying a blurry black-and-white photo that purported to show a Nicaraguan official named Federico Vaughn loading duffel bags of cocaine onto a C-123 cargo plane. "I know every American parent concerned about the drug problem will be outraged to learn that top Nicaraguan government officials are deeply involved in drug trafficking," Reagan declared.

The story began to unravel shortly thereafter when Joanne Omang of the *Washington Post* and Joel Brinkley of the *New York Times* quoted U.S. Drug Enforcement Administration officials who said they had no information implicating the Nicaraguan government in the drug business. Undaunted by these denials, *U.S. News & World Report* portrayed the Sandinistas as "narco-terrorists" in a lurid 1987 cover story that reeked of disinformation.

Wall Street Journal reporter Jonathan Kwitny looked into the matter and found that the U.S. intelligence agent who took the blurry photo shown during Reagan's speech had been working closely with North's secret arms network and contra drug-running operations. Moreover, the C-123 cargo plane which transported the cocaine subsequently crashed in Nicaragua during a weapons drop for the contras, leading to the capture of Eugene Hasenfus—a grunt in North's supply network—in October 1986.

Evidence presented during 1988 hearings of the House Judiciary subcommittee on crime, chaired by William Hughes, strongly suggested that the entire Sandinista coke connection was a U.S. intelligence fabrication. Particularly suspicious was the role of Federico Vaughn, the supposed Sandinista official involved in the coke trade, who appeared to have been a U.S. spy all along. Congressional investigators called Vaughn's Managua telephone number (found in Oliver North's notebooks) and spoke to a "domestic employee" who said the house had been "continuously rented" by U.S. Embassy personnel and Western diplomats since 1981.

Aside from a segment on *CBS Evening News*, no word of the Hughes hearings appeared on network television or in the papers of record. Instead, the stenography department at the *New York Times* ran a short item a few days later quoting President Reagan's weekly radio broadcast about how Nicaraguan officials were involved in drug trafficking.

Hearings on Capitol Hill

Congressional probes of contra drug dealing have consistently been distorted by the U.S. press. The headline of a July 1987 *Washington Post* article was unequivocal: "Hill Panel Finds No Evidence Linking Contras to Drug Smuggling." It was also false, according to Charles Rangel, chairman of the House Select Committee on Narcotics Abuse and Control. In a letter-to-the-editor which the *Post* refused to publish, Rangel wrote: "Your headline says we drew one conclusion, while in fact we reached quite a different one... We did not conclude that there was no evidence of contra involvement in drug smuggling." Based on the information presented, Rangel added, Committee members determined there was "a strong need for further congressional investigation" into contra drug allegations. Rangel's letter was subsequently published in the *Congressional Record*.

The Iran-contra Committee assiduously avoided the drug issue during public hearings in the summer of 1987, even though it had access to Oliver North's handwritten notes which stated: "$14 million to finance [contra arms] came from drugs." Out of 2,848 pages in North's notebooks on the contra resupply operation, 543 pages contained references to drug trafficking. Even when this information was made public, most media continued to "just say no" to investigating contra dope peddlers.

A pattern of selective reporting helped to defuse many a bombshell during hearings of the Senate Subcommittee on Terrorism, Narcotics and International Operations, chaired by John Kerry. Ramon Milian Rodriguez, a key money-launderer for the Medellin cocaine cartel, testified in February 1988 that he worked with the CIA, but this wasn't mentioned by the *New York Times*, the *Washington Post* or the major networks in their coverage of the hearings, which were broadcast live on CNN and C-Span.

New York Times correspondent Elaine Sciolino minimized some of the more delicate aspects of Rodriguez's testimony in an article headlined "Accountant Says Noriega Laundered Billions." Omitting any reference to the CIA, Sciolino focused primarily on Rodriguez's description of Panamanian General Manuel Noriega's extensive dealings with the Medellin cartel. She also neglected to mention Rodriguez's testimony about his secret meetings with representatives of U.S. banks in Panama, including Citicorp and the Bank of America, which eagerly and knowingly welcomed the drug cartel's patronage.

During his testimony, Rodriguez stated on a number of occasions that drug money was donated to the contras. This bit of information was tucked away on page six of the *Times*; the same edition featured a front page above-the-fold article ("Military Officers in Honduras Are Linked to the Drug Trade") by James LeMoyne, who quoted unnamed "American officials" claiming that the Medellin cartel "has close ties with...some Sandinista officials in Nicaragua." No evidence to support this allegation was provided by LeMoyne. While journalists wedded to official sources kept pointing the finger at the Nicaraguan government, the Senate hearings on narco-terrorism showed that the contras were the meal ticket for drug traffickers, who operated with virtual impunity as long as they helped the CIA's so-called freedom fighters.

NARCO-TERRORISM, NARCO-CYNICISM

The U.S. news media showed little interest in scrutinizing Panamanian General Manuel Noriega until May 1986, when a *New York Times* series by Seymour Hersh disclosed Noriega's links to the CIA, the narcotics trade and other corrupt activities. At first, *Times* higher-ups were hesitant to publish the story. Why? Because no other paper had it!—not even "Brand X," as *Times* editors half-jokingly referred to the *Washington Post*. (Some people at the paper of record were apparently more comfortable with pack journalism than aggressive investigative reporting.) Hersh's story eventually ran—and turned out to be one of the biggest scoops of the year. It proved highly embarrassing to the Reagan administration and the CIA, which had kept Noriega on its payroll throughout his tenure as a dope pusher.

A year after Hersh's exposé, Noriega was again in the news. This time U.S. media featured the allegations of Panamanian Colonel Roberto Diaz Herrera, who had recently been fired as Noriega's chief of staff. In an AP dispatch published in the *New York Times*, Diaz Herrera accused Noriega of conspiring with the CIA to assassinate Panama's leader Omar Torrijos by planting a bomb aboard his aircraft which crashed in 1981. But two days later, there was no reference to the CIA when Diaz Herrera's charges were recounted by Stephen Kinzer in the *New York Times* and by Julia Preston in the *Washington Post*. Henceforth, the press put forward a sanitized version of the Torrijos murder plot as alleged by Diaz Herrera; the CIA connection vanished down a memory hole.

U.S. intelligence was aware of Noriega's drug dealing since the mid-1970s. Nevertheless, he was subsequently enlisted in the contra cause by Lt. Col. Oliver North. But TV commentators and newspaper columnists were far more harsh in their condemnation of the Panamanian dictator than of his U.S. collaborators—the CIA, Pentagon, State Department, Vice President Bush, and the American banks that fattened themselves with drug money during Noriega's reign.

CIA drug connection

Some pundits expressed concern that the U.S. government may have placed too much emphasis on fighting communism when more attention should have focused on an even greater threat to our national security: international narcotics trafficking. This was the upshot of a spate of *New York Times* editorials in 1988, with headlines such as "A Hemisphere at Risk From Drugs," "For Drugs: A Monroe Doctrine," "The Drug Flames Rise Higher" and "Ten Months Left to Fight Drugs." That year the *Times* ran a total of 45 editorials and 34 op-eds on the drug problem. Conspicuously absent from all of these articles was any mention of the CIA's perennial role in aiding and abetting drug traffickers.

The *Times* and other major media have been reluctant to delve too deeply into this subject, despite well-documented evidence that Air America (an airline owned and run by the CIA) transported opiates from the Golden Triangle in Southeast Asia during the Vietnam War. *Times* columnist C.L. Sulzberger reacted in disbelief when poet Allen Ginsberg challenged him to write about the CIA-heroin link in the early 1970s. But Sulzberger later wrote a letter to Ginsberg, dated April 11, 1978: "I fear I owe you an apology. I have been reading a succession of pieces about CIA involvement in the dope trade in Southeast Asia and I remember when you first suggested I look into this I thought you were full of beans. Indeed you were right."

It's no coincidence that the Golden Crescent in Southwest Asia became a major source of heroin in the 1980s while the CIA supported the mujahadeen guerrillas fighting to topple the Soviet-backed government in Afghanistan. The role of CIA-backed Afghan rebels in the dope business has occasionally been referred to in *Times* news stories—but never in editorials about the drug plague. "The cheapest and most efficient method of stopping foreign drugs flowing into the country is at the source, not at our borders," wrote *Times* columnist A.M. Rosenthal without a hint of irony. Neither Rosenthal nor any other *Times* editor has mustered the courage to state an obvious truth: The war on drugs will be futile as long as U.S. intelligence supports groups that peddle narcotics.

Corporate pushers

Few subjects evoke more hypocritical media tirades than drugs. Although countless editorials and news reports wail about international drug trafficking, massive U.S. exports of cigarettes get restrained coverage—even while tobacco companies wage enormous campaigns to sell their lethal product abroad. A former chairperson of the U.S. Federal Trade Commission has lamented that in the Third World, "toward which the cigarette companies have directed the full force of their advertising prowess, and where cigarette ads dominate the media, the amount of cigarette smoking is rapidly increasing."

To the *New York Times*, this was unfortunate, but nothing to fret about. While noting that "many people in these countries will now die because they smoke American cigarettes," a *Times* editorial shrugged off the issue: "As long as cigarettes are legal in America, it will remain legal to export them." The newspaper said it was "hard to object" to spreading U.S. cigarette sales to still more countries. The *Times'* solution: "Wherever the U.S. Trade Representative opens a market, let the Surgeon General follow, issuing his annual report on smoking, and nagging and scolding foreign governments as well as his own."

Just below that editorial was another one. But suddenly the *Times* had lost its tone of tolerance for pushers of addictive substances: "America pays a terrible price for cocaine addiction…" In other words, promoting cigarettes that kill millions in countries around the world is somehow okay, but cocaine causes the U.S. to pay a "terrible price." The *Times* editorial writer didn't mention that for every cocaine-related fatality, hundreds of people die from tobacco and alcohol-related causes.

Aside from tobacco and alcohol, many legal pharmaceuticals cause physical and psychological damage due to over-prescription by doctors and overuse by patients. "Newspapers are full of stories about huge profits made in the illegal drug trade, and about aggressive acts that drug dealers commit to protect their turf," wrote a Sacramento-based columnist, Dan Walters. "But there's big money to be made in the legal drug trade as well. Drug companies are no less anxious to protect and enhance those profits, even if it means bulldozing public officials into doing their bidding. Their methods may be a little more genteel, but their motivations are precisely the same."

While Dan Rather and other famous reporters may spend 48 hours on crack street, they haven't been very inquisitive about spending 48 hours on Wall Street to see who is profiting from government-approved addictive chemicals.

Hidden agenda of the War on Drugs

While corporate pushers were given license to kill, reporters and pundits echoed sounds of "Charge!" in the anti-drug battle. Military metaphors were bipartisan and virtually across the mass media spectrum. Consigned to the margins were those who feared that the call to arms might be an excuse to justify armed intervention abroad, particularly in Latin America, as well as closer to home. "In the Bush era," warned *Village Voice* journalist James Ridgeway, "dope is replacing communism as both the rationale for American hegemony abroad and for a crackdown against minorities and dissidents here at home. Where 'national security' and 'terrorism' once were enough to get an FBI investigation going against U.S. citizens, now it's all in the name of epidemiology."

Colombia is one of the Latin American countries in which U.S. intervention has deepened as a result of the "war on drugs." Nearly every time someone is murdered in Colombia, U.S. journalists automatically blame the drug cartels. But as Amnesty International has documented, narco-traffickers have forged deadly links with sectors of the Colombian military; together they've been waging a dirty war against left-leaning politicians, social justice activists and other law-abiding civilians. Human rights violations by the Colombian military are rarely mentioned in the drug-crazed U.S. media.

When a Colombian death squad led by a military commander committed a massacre in November 1988, the *Los Angeles Times* described it this way: "Colombian guerrillas, firing on anything that moved, killed 42 civilians and wounded 57 in an attack on the northern mining town of Segovia, military authorities said. It was an indiscriminate attack on the population, whatever its age or sex... They were just intent on sowing blood, terror."

Compare this description to Amnesty International's account of the same event, which was not sourced to "military authorities," and contained no reference to guerrillas: "Fifteen heavily armed men...opened fire on people in the streets. Grenades were thrown into bars and the church and one group of assailants went from house to house searching for political opposition and union leaders. A bus was intercepted close to the military battalion 'Bombona,' based just outside the town and several passengers were killed. The regular garrisons of police and military stood by while the gunmen moved freely through the town for over an hour... Not only [did] the armed forces fail to intervene, but army and police personnel, including the battalion commander, directly participated in the preparation of the massacre. Forty-three people, including three children, were killed."

According to major media, the U.S. government has been sending military assistance to Colombia and neighboring countries to help them fight against the narco-traffickers. Reporters haven't written much about the Colombian death squads composed of military personnel allied with the drug cartels—death squads that utilize U.S.-supplied weapons to murder nonviolent political opponents. This is part of the untold story behind the so-called war on drugs in Latin America.

12

Human Rights and Foreign Policy

I n February 1988 the *New York Times* ran a story by correspondent James LeMoyne who told a gruesome tale of Salvadoran guerrillas executing two peasants in a remote village because they wanted to vote in upcoming elections. Although the article gave the impression that LeMoyne had interviewed villagers with firsthand information about the alleged guerrilla atrocity, he actually had lifted the story from a right-wing newspaper in San Salvador, which—unlike LeMoyne—attributed the report to the Salvadoran military command. A number of independent sources, including free-lance journalist Chris Norton and media critic Marc Cooper, subsequently disclosed that the story had been fabricated by psychological warfare specialists in the Salvadoran military. Six months after the original article, the *Times* acknowledged LeMoyne's mistake in a lengthy editor's note.

LeMoyne's error underscores how easily reporters can be led astray when they rely too heavily on official sources. Even when they get the facts straight, U.S. journalists commonly layer their stories with dubious statements from unnamed U.S. diplomats spouting familiar rhetoric about our commitment to freedom and democracy throughout the world. The end result is contradictory and misleading news coverage, as when *Times* correspondent Lindsey Gruson described a massive crackdown on international relief groups, religious workers, labor unionists and other civilians by U.S.-backed Salvadoran security forces in a December 1989 article—while also citing unnamed "diplomats" who spoke of "Washington's attempts to foster democracy" in that country.

The structure of a news article can convey a distinct ideological bias. In reporting on El Salvador, for example, Gruson has often quoted U.S. officials at the beginning of a story, enabling them to set the agenda and frame the discussion. In the middle come statements by Salvadoran government officials, who usually affirm what their sponsors in Washington say. And toward the end of the story are brief comments by the FMLN guerrillas. *Take careful note when official sources are emphasized in story leads, while critical or opposition sources are confined to the caboose.*

In reporting on Third World regional conflicts, U.S. journalists often depict their government as a mediator or peace advocate in someone else's war, even when the U.S. has been instrumental in fomenting and perpetuating the strife. In a news article headlined "Lonely Peacemaker," the *Times* portrayed Secretary of State George Shultz and the U.S. government as crusaders for peace—from Central America to the Middle East to Southern Africa. Although the U.S. and South Africa had been arming guerrilla forces in Angola for over a decade, American news media cast the Reagan administration as a champion of peace, not as a major party to the bloody conflict.

When it comes to peace talks, the onus is usually on enemies of the U.S. government to prove their sincerity. When Central American leaders signed a peace accord in August 1987, U.S. journalists kept asking: "Can the Sandinistas be trusted to negotiate?" Yet the record shows that Washington, not Nicaragua, had failed to negotiate in good faith. Typical of the media's misplaced skepticism was Ted Koppel's comment to a Nicaraguan official that his government should offer "some serious proposals," not "more rhetoric." Koppel did not ask U.S. officials about a once-secret November 1984 memo from John Poindexter to National Security Adviser Robert MacFarlane on peace talks with Nicaragua: "Continue active negotiations but agree on no treaty and agree to work out some way to support the contras either directly or indirectly. Withhold true objectives from staffs."

TIANANMEN SQUARE AND OTHER MASSACRES

A wave of exhilaration surged through the crowd when the first contingent of Chinese workers joined student hunger strikers in Tiananmen Square. Three thousand students started their protest in May 1989, two days before Mikhail Gorbachev arrived for historic talks with China's rulers. *New York Times* correspondent Nicholas Kristof said it was "largely coincidental" that people seized the streets during Gorbachev's visit. CNN anchor Bernard Shaw also felt the timing was an "accident."

But it was hardly an accident that many of the protesters were inspired by Gorbachev's reforms in the Soviet Union. Pictures of the Russian leader circulated among the assembled masses. By the time he left Beijing, demonstrations had spread to 20 Chinese cities. They kept coming in droves, young and old, farmers, teachers, more workers, journalists, even the police, singing "We Shall Overcome" and "The Internationale," the socialist anthem. Millions of people were celebrating, marching for human rights, empowered by their wildest hopes and dreams as they faced down a reluctant army.

Tears of communitarian joy turned to terror and grief with the crackdown in June. Scenes of tanks crushing makeshift barricades and mangled bodies lying in pools of blood were shown on television across the globe, as foreign journalists continued to send footage out of the country via satellite until the plug was pulled by Chinese censors. Working 'round-the-clock with hardly any sleep, American journalists provided a riveting chronicle of events as they unfolded. But the U.S. media, which excelled at blow-by-blow descriptions, failed to give a cogent analysis of why China was suddenly on the brink.

Instead we heard platitudes about Deng Xiaoping's wonderful economic reforms, which supposedly liberated China from the dungeons of Maoism and ushered in a new era of free enterprise and capitalist incentives. But students got upset because political reform was lagging—or so the pundits told us. "The Chinese people are furious with a system of government that promised utopia and has delivered hell," explained Claudia Rosett, editor of the *Asian Wall Street Journal*'s editorial page. "Their only relief has come by way of Mr. Deng's economic liberalization of the past 11 years."

Far from relief, Deng's economic liberalization delivered record-high 30 percent inflation, unemployment, hunger and rampant corruption among privileged elites. A stable society in the countryside, where 80 percent of the population resided, was turned upside down, resulting in the mass migration of peasants to beleaguered urban centers. The social dislocation caused by Deng's reforms was even cited in the official Beijing *People's Daily*, the nation's leading newspaper, as a key reason why workers flocked to the side of student protesters. Among popular protest slogans were: "Eradicate privilege" and "Down with official racketeering." The huge demonstrations in China were in many ways a repudiation of the government's vaunted "free-market" policies, but the U.S. media, with few exceptions, failed to point this out.

American journalists did not examine what role foreign (including U.S.) capital may have played in exacerbating conditions that led to the uprising in China. *New York Times* correspondent Fox Butterfield expressed concern on *Nightline* that the formation of independent trade unions in China (along the lines of Poland's Solidarity) might be a major obstacle to economic modernization. Apparently labor unions are fine if they challenge a Soviet-dominated government, but not if they bother U.S. corporations doing business in China.

Encumbered by their own ethnocentric and ideological biases about communism and capitalism, most U.S. journalists were unable—or unwilling—to understand the Chinese protesters on their own terms. The assumption was that pro-democracy demonstrators aspired to be like Americans. Reporters rarely explored what democracy might mean in a Chinese context, and few put the movement in a historical perspective.

China news blackout

The massacre at Tiananmen Square was the climax of a momentous human rights drama that had been building for years in China. But the U.S. media had rarely mentioned human rights violations in China since the Democracy Wall Movement was crushed in 1979 and its leaders were thrown in jail. "Look at Wei Jingshen," Deng said of a prominent Democracy Wall dissident. "We put him behind bars and the democracy movement died. We haven't released him, but that did not raise much of an international uproar."

Wei Jingshen remained in prison throughout the 1980s, his exact whereabouts unknown.

Shortly after the suppression of the Democracy Wall Movement, Deng introduced economic and legal reforms. "A wave of euphoria swept through U.S. government and media circles," recalled Roberta Cohen, who served as Deputy Assistant Secretary of State for Human Rights under Carter. "The enthusiasm for free market initiatives and other reforms became the new rationale for turning a blind eye to the continuing repression in China." Between two and five million people languished in Chinese labor camps and prisons, and an untold number of dissidents were executed. Fox Butterfield of the *Times* reported on the existence of Chinese gulags when he was based in China in the early 1980s, but there wasn't much follow-up in the American press.

U.S. media remained tight-lipped when—despite serious human rights abuses by the Chinese government—President Reagan approved sales of police equipment to China's internal security force, expanded military ties and encouraged loans and investment. The brutalization of Tibet and the relentless suppression of dissent in China were off the press agenda until late in Reagan's second term. Meanwhile, according to Amnesty International, hundreds of Chinese political prisoners were being tortured, while others faced illegal arrest, unwarranted search and seizures, and other forms of harassment.

Journalists were outraged when Deng & Company imposed severe press restrictions during the June 1989 crackdown, but U.S. reporters appear to have practiced a form of self-censorship with respect to Chinese human rights violations for nearly a decade. "American administrations yawned at reports of repression of basic freedoms in China... So, much too often, did American journalism," A.M. Rosenthal wrote in the *New York Times* shortly after the massacre at Tiananmen Square. Rosenthal's complaint rings hollow, for it was during his tenure as *Times* executive editor that reporting on Chinese abuses virtually ceased. No news stories on China and human rights are listed in the *New York Times* index from 1984 through 1986. Ditto for *Time* magazine, which selected Deng Xiaoping as "Man of the Year" in 1985. *Newsweek* managed only one story on the subject for those three years.

The media silence was all the more deafening in light of what transpired in China during this period. Vice President Bush visited the People's Republic in 1985, but this evoked none of the concern for political prisoners that journalists displayed when U.S. officials met with Soviet leaders. And another round of student protests was put down in December 1986 by Deng Xiaoping, who stated at the time: "When necessary one must deal severely with those who defy orders. We can afford to shed some blood." This is the man Bush hailed as a "forward-looking" leader.

When Bush visited Beijing again in February 1989, Chinese authorities prevented Fang Lizhi, a prominent human rights advocate, from attending a banquet at the U.S. Embassy, even though he had received a highly publicized invitation. President Bush subsequently failed to raise the human rights issue with Chinese officials. The best he could muster was a statement of regret channeled through his press spokesperson, Marlin Fitzwater. In a case of too little too late, editorials in major dailies chided Bush for not taking a tougher stand in Beijing.

Fang Lizhi, who took up residence in the American Embassy, went a step further, accusing the U.S. government of practicing a double standard with respect to human rights. Why, he wondered, were U.S. officials reluctant to criticize human rights abuses in China, when the Soviet Union was never treated with such deference? Lizhi might have added other questions: Was it because China had sided with the U.S. in various regional conflicts, supplying arms to the Afghan mujahadeen, the bloodthirsty Khmer Rouge in Cambodia, UNITA rebels in Angola, and the Nicaraguan contras? Did human rights take a back seat while U.S. intelligence operated electronic listening posts along the Sino-Soviet border?

During the Cultural Revolution in the late 1960s, Fang Lizhi was confined to a cow shed for more than a year because, as a dissident intellectual, he supposedly belonged to the "stinking ninth category" of society. Fang Lizhi may have been reminded of that barnyard odor when Richard Nixon, Henry Kissinger and Bush administration officials shamelessly came to the defense of the Chinese regime in the wake of the Tiananmen bloodbath. "The caricature of Deng...as a tyrant is unfair," Kissinger wrote in the *Los Angeles Times* a few months after the massacre. During a subsequent trip to Beijing, he told Deng, "You will never be without great influence." "Are you opposed to it?" Deng asked. "I am for it," said Kissinger, whose consulting firm represented numerous U.S.-based corporations with major investments in China. Nixon praised President Bush's "measured response" to the crackdown—a reference to Bush's selective enforcement of economic sanctions and the continuing cooperation between U.S. intelligence and the Chinese government.

How did the U.S. media respond when the Bush administration's collusion with the butchers of Tiananmen Square became too obvious to ignore? There was some criticism in the American press, since in this case many Democrats and even some conservative Republicans voiced their displeasure with Bush's China policy. (Before the massacre, the Democrats didn't criticize American support for China's repressive ruling elite; hence it wasn't an issue in the U.S. press.) Foreign policy pundits chided the President for "caving in" to the Chinese leadership, but no major media took Bush to task for "caving in" to the U.S. corporate elite—represented by Kissinger & Associates—which had big bucks invested in China. Kissinger's pals were in it for the money, yet journalists rarely examined the role of U.S. corporate interests in shaping American foreign policy.

New York Times correspondent Thomas Friedman asserted that, amidst all the critical publicity, pragmatic U.S. diplomatic experts quietly endorsed Bush's China overtures. Tacit acceptance was reflected in the headline of a front-page December 1989 *Times* news article which framed Bush's China policy as a test of his assertiveness: "Bush's Gamble With Beijing," with the subhead "His Dispatch of Aides Is Attempt at Boldness." The "he's trying not to be a wimp" spin derived from unnamed U.S. officials who were quoted throughout Andrew Rosenthal's article. Of course, there were other ways of describing U.S. support for China's brutal ruling clique. A less accommodating headline might have read: "Bush's Collusion With Beijing—His Dispatch of Aides Is Setback for Freedom and Democracy."

Double standard on human rights

The media's soft treatment of China prior to the Tiananmen massacre raises broad questions about reporting on human rights. Are U.S. "strategic interests" paramount in determining whether abuses are scrutinized? What other factors influence coverage of human rights issues? Why does the U.S. press remain a quiet spectator in some countries, while violations in other parts of the world receive prominent attention? *New York Times* correspondent James LeMoyne, who covered Central America during the mid-1980s, provided a clue when he told a Hunter College audience in New York City in November 1988 that human rights reporting was "policy-driven."

Thus, when Jimmy Carter became President and started to talk about making human rights the centerpiece of his foreign policy, the issue received a dramatic boost in media attention—even though a coherent human rights policy never emerged during his administration. The *Los Angeles Times* index shows a sharp increase in the number of articles listed under "human rights," with 16 references in 1976 compared to 230 in 1977, Carter's first year in office. Data from *CBS Evening News* show a similar trend: six segments indexed under "human rights" in 1976 compared to 93 segments in 1977. This was significantly higher than the average number listed during the Reagan administration, which declared at the outset that "counter-terrorism" would replace human rights as the guiding theme of U.S. foreign policy.

Right from the start, Reagan flaunted his disregard for human rights by nominating Ernest W. Lefever to be his first Assistant Secretary of State for Human Rights. A congressional inquiry disclosed that Lefever ran an institute that received money from the South African government to circulate views favorable to the apartheid state. So Elliott Abrams got the job instead, and human rights became a potent weapon in a full-fledged ideological war. The Reagan administration loudly decried abuses in the USSR and other "enemy" states, while pursuing a quiet policy of "constructive engagement" with South Africa, China, Guatemala, Indonesia, Turkey and other "friendly" regimes whose brutalities were often overlooked.

This dual standard was reflected in media coverage of human rights. When the Nicaraguan government temporarily closed the U.S.-financed opposition paper, *La Prensa*, it was widely reported in the U.S. media as an example of Sandinista totalitarianism. By contrast, major media were virtually silent when U.S.-backed Salvadoran security forces murdered the editor of *La Cronica del Pueblo* and destroyed the offices of *El Independiente* in El Salvador. Similarly, the bombing of the independent Guatemalan journal *La Epoca* in June 1988 received next to no coverage in the United States. Looking at U.S. coverage, London *Times* correspondent David Gollob wrote that Guatemala's closing of a TV station "did not create an international scandal, while Nicaraguan moves to silence opposition media are headline news."

Edward S. Herman and Noam Chomsky compared repression in Communist Poland and anticommunist Guatemala, and found a significant disparity in press attention. Example: For months the U.S. media doggedly followed the case of Jerzy Popieluszko, the activist priest killed in 1984 by Poland's security forces. Yet in the early 1980s, more than a dozen priests were assassinated by government-sponsored death squads in Guatemala, and this was virtually ignored by major U.S. media. Americas Watch called Guatemala "a nation of prisoners," but it never got admitted into the pantheon of "captive nations" by the papers of record, which reserved such appellations for Poland, Czechoslovakia and other Communist countries.

Writing about Poland in May 1988, A.M. Rosenthal offered this description of a "captive nation" in his *New York Times* column: "Its economic and political systems, both distasteful to its people, were imposed by another state. Its economic fortunes are shaped by the regular pressure or occasional benevolence of that state. Its leadership cannot survive without the approval of the greater power. Year to year and decade to decade, the threat of intervention—economic or military—varies in immediacy but never vanishes. If the danger of intervention disappeared entirely, the people would dismantle the imposed government and the structure on which it perches, fast." Rosenthal's description of a captive nation could also have applied to Guatemala and El Salvador—albeit with an important distinction: The violence visited upon Central Americans by their anticommunist governments has been far more severe than in Communist Eastern Europe.

While human rights abuses in Eastern Europe were regularly traced back to Soviet domination, U.S. media rarely explained Guatemalan state terror as a product of continuous U.S. intervention since 1954, when a CIA-sponsored coup overthrew a democratically-elected government. One exception was a two-part series on PBS's *Kwitny Report*, which examined the U.S. role in Guatemalan human rights abuses. Jonathan Kwitny provided historical context as he interviewed human rights activists and exiled Guatemalan opposition leaders, as well as U.S. officials, in a hard-hitting exposé that linked

U.S. business interests to death squad activity in that country. Fred Sherwood, former president of the U.S. Chamber of Commerce in Guatemala, was heard telling journalist Allan Nairn: "Why should we do anything about the death squads? They're killing commies. I'd give them more power! I'd give them cartridges if I could..." A few months after airing this segment, *Kwitny Report* was dropped by PBS for lack of funds.

Guatemala has one of the worst human rights records in the Western Hemisphere, yet it receives far less media attention than Nicaragua or, for that matter, El Salvador, where the U.S. government has invested heavily in a war against leftist rebels. This underscores another key point about the way in which human rights reporting is policy-driven. As Michael Posner, executive director of the New York-based Lawyers Committee for Human Rights, explained: "Countries that loom large in East/West regional conflicts get a lot more press than countries that aren't perceived in the same geopolitical terms." El Salvador and Nicaragua loomed in the 1980s, while Guatemala—where an estimated 50,000 people were murdered by security forces early in the decade—faded into hellish obscurity.

Friendly dictators

If the gravity of human rights violations were the sole factor in determining the amount of coverage a country received, reporting on human rights would be substantially different. Consider, for example, the case of Indonesia, a nation where political and civil rights have been systematically suppressed during President Suharto's 24-year dictatorial rule. Although Indonesia is the world's fifth most populated country, it gets scant attention in the U.S. media—partly because of tight restrictions on journalists, but also because Indonesia, a U.S. ally, is not a focal point of East/West conflict. Despite a continuing record of torture, disappearances, summary executions and thousands of political incarcerations, Suharto was described as a "moderate leader" by the *Christian Science Monitor*. The Indonesian dictator got a free ride in the press when he visited Washington in June 1989 to discuss economic matters.

Press coverage was minimal even when the Indonesian army massacred an estimated half-million people in 1965. And the silence continued when Indonesia, armed by the U.S., invaded neighboring East Timor and slaughtered a third of the population in the mid-1970s. While these atrocities by a "friendly" anticommunist government were being ignored, the American press was filled with stories about the killing fields in Cambodia, where the Khmer Rouge, led by the maniacal Pol Pot, butchered more than a million people. The Communist Khmer Rouge were eventually ousted by Vietnamese troops, whereupon the Reagan administration quietly shifted its support to Pol Pot's army—a cynical and outrageous foreign policy maneuver that provoked little comment in the U.S. media at the time.

In January 1990, after Vietnam had withdrawn its forces, the *New York Times* rewrote history in a chronology headlined "Two Decades of Suffering in Cambodia." But the chronology skipped five grief-stricken years—from March 1970 to April 1975. This was a period of massive American bombing of the Cambodian countryside that left the country in ruins, with hundreds of thousands dead and millions displaced. A Finnish government commission of inquiry on Cambodia referred to the entire 1970s as the "decade of genocide," but the *Times* omitted any reference to the genocidal violence perpetrated by the United States.

Of the 35 signatory nations of the 1975 Helsinki accords, Turkey is one of the most egregious human rights violators, yet it's a low priority for American media. When the Turkish government, a staunch U.S. ally and NATO member, figures in human rights stories, they are usually about the brutal mistreatment of the Kurdish ethnic minority. But very little is said about the Turkish government's ongoing oppression of its own people.

"The coverage of Turkey is terrible," Helsinki Watch director Jeri Laber told us. "It's amazing how little gets into the press." Laber has spoken with U.S. journalists who filed human rights stories from Turkey (the fourth largest recipient of U.S. aid), only to have them killed by editors more interested in travel articles about Turkey. Ironically, freedom of movement is a right many Turks cannot exercise. Since the military coup in 1980, as many as 300,000 Turkish citizens have been denied passports, and, according to Amnesty International, 250,000 political prisoners were detained and nearly all were tortured; 200 Turks died while in custody because of torture.

One would think that U.S. news organizations might show more interest when their own employees are brutalized by Turkish authorities. But the U.S. media didn't publicize the case of Ismet Imset, a UPI reporter who was beaten and imprisoned on trumped-up charges in 1984. (Imset was fired by UPI after he criticized how it responded to the incident.) Nor have U.S. media shown much concern for the 2,000 reporters and editors tried in Turkish courts since a civilian government was installed in 1983, or the 41 journalists in jail as of 1989.

Labor unions have also been a prime target of Turkish government repression. Martial law in Turkey put an end to collective bargaining in the early 1980s, and the trade union movement was decimated by mass arrests, torture and executions. This occurred at a time when the fledgling Solidarity movement in Poland was a major story in the American media. Driven more by U.S. policy interests than by a concern for human rights, mass media averted their eyes from the nightmare in anticommunist Turkey, and thereby helped to perpetuate it.

Perhaps the human rights situations would have improved in countries like Turkey, Guatemala and Indonesia if they had received the kind of U.S. media attention that was given to Poland or the Soviet Union. While good investigative journalism occasionally brings human rights abuses to light, media coverage of U.S.-allied countries tends to be episodic and crisis-oriented. Near-insurrection seems to be a prerequisite for serious reporting on friendly dictatorships.

Such was the case in the mid-1980s, when the Reagan administration, in last-minute policy shifts, took credit for engineering the departure of Philippine President Ferdinand Marcos, who had been toasted in 1981 by Vice President Bush for his "adherence to democratic principle." So too with the departure of Haitian dictator Jean Claude Duvalier. A July 1985 *Washington Post* headline read: "U.S. Praises Duvalier for Democratic Commitment." Yet seven months later, after Duvalier fled the country, the *Post* reported that the Reagan administration claimed it "laid the ground-work" for his departure. This contradiction went unnoted in coverage of the grim situation in Haiti, as U.S. support for successive military juntas contin-ued in the post-Duvalier era, despite massive human rights abuses.

State Department fudge

A *New York Times* editorial in December 1988 spoke of President Reagan's human rights "conversion" in the waning days of his administra-tion. The editorial praised the State Department for issuing "candid annual reports on human rights." Said the *Times*: "There is now an American con-sensus that a plausible human rights policy has to strive for a single standard of judgment."

Unfortunately, U.S. media—the *Times* included—have not applied a single standard of newsworthiness to human rights violations around the world. Instead, coverage has often mirrored the geopolitical priorities of the State Department, which is obliged to provide yearly reports on the status of human rights in countries throughout the world. (If abuses are found to be increasing, Congress may be required to cut off foreign aid to the offending government.) But Mark McLeggan, a State Department official, has admitted that the annual "Country Reports" are edited to take into account political and diplomatic considerations. Hence, they are not quite as "candid" as the *Times* editorial claimed. If these assessments were truly candid, it would not be necessary for Human Rights Watch and the Lawyers Committee for Human Rights to publish a detailed critique of the numerous omissions, errors and distortions contained in the State Department's Country Reports.

While the *New York Times* gave its stamp of approval to the State Department's Country Reports on Human Rights Practices, a *Chicago Tribune* news story by Ray Moseley offered a different appraisal. Citing numerous examples from the 1988 State Department survey by Human Rights Watch and the Lawyers Committee for Human Rights, he stated: "It may help explain why the State Department is widely known, even to its own diplomats, as the Fudge Factory."

Reagan's so-called human rights "conversion" was mostly a matter of expediency, as U.S. strategists scrambled to keep up with momentous changes around the globe, particularly in the Soviet Union. Concurrent with the release of hundreds of political prisoners and the emergence of thousands of grassroots organizations, Soviet television began showing photos of skeletons dug up from mass graves in an effort to exorcise long-suppressed demons from the Stalin era. This national soul-searching had significant implications for human rights throughout Eastern Europe and beyond. But as new reforms were being implemented in the Soviet Union, old myths were kept alive by the U.S. media.

When President Bush flew to Paris to meet with Western leaders in July 1989, ABC News correspondent Brit Hume summed up the official consensus by declaring, "These are good times in the Free World"—in contrast to life behind the "Iron Curtain." And when the Berlin Wall was rendered obsolete a few months later, CNN anchor Bernard Shaw repeatedly spoke of East Germans visiting "the Free World." The use of such loaded jargon was a reminder that the U.S. media's human rights spotlight is still aimed at selective targets abroad. (The "Free World" presumably includes such anticommunist allies as Turkey, South Africa and Guatemala.) Likewise, U.S. abuses such as homelessness, poverty, the oppression of Native Americans and FBI harassment of domestic dissidents are not framed in terms of human rights by the mainstream American press. For this would be tantamount to acknowledging that human rights problems exist in the United States, and such an admission would belie a cherished myth about life in "the Free World."

DEMOCRACY AND ELECTIONS, CENTRAL AMERICAN STYLE

In August 1987, *New York Times* editorial writer Karl Meyer reminisced about Major Smedley Butler, describing him as the U.S. Marine hero who tried to bring "true democracy" to Nicaragua 75 years earlier. Repeated U.S. interventions in Nicaragua had been motivated by our desire to spread democracy, said Meyer. As proof he cited a communiqué from Washington that Major Butler carried with him to Nicaragua: "America's purpose is to foster true constitutional government and free elections."

Butler, however, saw his role somewhat differently than the historical revisionists at the *Times*. He admitted rigging Nicaragua's 1912 election on behalf of the Taft administration, which entailed rounding up 400 Nicaraguans who could be counted on to vote for the U.S.-controlled dictator, Adolfo Diaz. Only those 400 were told of the election, and as soon as they cast their ballots the polls were closed. "Today," Butler wrote home to his wife, "Nicaragua has enjoyed a fine 'free election,' with only one candidate being allowed to run... To the entire satisfaction of our State Department, Marines patrolled all the towns to prevent disorders."

After Butler retired, according to editorial writer Meyer, he "lamented the futility of his own interventionist missions." Not exactly. Butler attacked the motivation behind U.S. meddling. The *New York Times* didn't see fit to print Butler's speech before the American Legion on August 21, 1931, in which he stated: "I spent 33 years being a high-class muscle man for Big Business, for Wall Street and the bankers. In short, I was a racketeer for capitalism.

"I helped purify Nicaragua for the international banking house of Brown Brothers in 1909-1912. I helped make Mexico and especially Tampico safe for American oil interests in 1916. I brought light to the Dominican Republic for American sugar interests in 1916. I helped make Haiti and Cuba a decent place for the National City Bank boys to collect revenue in. I helped in the rape of half a dozen Central American republics for the benefit of Wall Street.

"I had a swell racket. I was rewarded with honors, medals, promotions... I might have given Al Capone a few hints. The best he could do was to operate in three cities. The Marines operated on three continents."

Nixing Nicaragua

Throughout this century, successive U.S. administrations have talked about bringing democracy and economic advancement to Latin American. But during the reign of the Somoza family in Nicaragua, a handful of wealthy landowners, bolstered by U.S. corporate interests, dominated the economy, while the nation as a whole remained underdeveloped and most people lived in abject poverty. Such conditions still persist throughout the region—although this isn't stressed in rose-colored media accounts of Central America's "burgeoning democracies." How democratic can a country be—few journalists ask—if its population is largely illiterate and hungry? Having suffered under the U.S.-backed Somoza dictatorship, Nicaraguans were not overly impressed by Washington's sudden concern for democracy when the Sandinistas took power in 1979.

Although rigged elections during the Somoza era raised hardly an eyebrow in the U.S. media, Nicaragua's November 1984 election was uniformly denounced by U.S. officials and the mainstream press. "It was not a very good election... It was just a piece of theatre for the Sandinistas," State Department public relations spokesperson John Hughes (now a columnist for the *Christian Science Monitor*) told *Time* magazine, which denigrated the vote: "The Sandinistas win, as expected... The outcome was never in doubt."

Indeed, the Sandinista victory was not surprising, given the social advancements in Nicaragua since the 1979 revolution. After five years of Sandinista rule, infant mortality dropped to the lowest level in Central America. Over 85 percent of the population had learned to read and write at least on a third-grade level as a result of a crash literacy program acclaimed by UNESCO. The number of schools had doubled since the overthrow of Anastazio Somoza. ("I don't want educated people," he once declared, "I want oxen.") The Sandinistas also initiated sweeping agrarian reform, emphasizing basic grains and crops for local needs rather than export—a development strategy that brought Nicaragua close to food self-sufficiency.

In addition, the Nicaraguan government banned DDT and other harmful sprays, while neighboring states still serve as dumping grounds for U.S.-made chemical toxins. Strides in Nicaraguan health care won praise from the United Nations and other international groups. The World Health Organization lauded Nicaragua's success in nearly eliminating polio, measles and diphtheria, and reducing infant mortality. But many of these achievements were subsequently eroded—along with the Sandinistas' popularity—as the Nicaraguan government diverted its resources in an effort to defend itself from attacks by U.S.-financed mercenary forces. "Unfortunately," said former contra leader Edgar Chamorro, "the contras burn down schools, homes and health centers as fast as the Sandinistas can build them."

While the U.S. media followed Washington's lead in dismissing the 1984 Nicaraguan elections as meaningless, the vast majority of independent observers considered it to be a free and fair vote. The British *Guardian* summed up the results in a news story headlined "A Revolution That Proved Itself at the Polls." A report by an Irish parliamentary delegation stated: "The electoral process was carried out with total integrity. The seven parties participating in the elections represented a broad spectrum of political ideologies." The general counsel of New York's Human Rights Commission described the election as "free, fair and hotly contested."

Thirty-three percent of the Nicaraguan voters cast ballots for one of six opposition parties—three to the right of the Sandinistas, three to the left—which had campaigned with the aid of government funds and free TV and radio time. Two conservative parties captured a combined 23 percent of the vote. They held rallies across the country and vehemently criticized the Sandinistas. Most foreign and independent observers noted this pluralism in debunking the Reagan administration charge—prominent in the U.S. press—that it was a "Soviet-style sham" election.

Shortly after the vote, the *Washington Post* published portions of a "secret-sensitive" National Security Council briefing paper which outlined a "wide-ranging plan to convince Americans [that the] Nicaraguan elections were a 'sham.'" The crux of the U.S. strategy was to focus media attention away from those conservative parties actively campaigning and toward Arturo Cruz, who was anointed leader of "the democratic opposition" by the White House and the U.S. press. Cruz had hardly lived in Nicaragua since 1970 and had dubious popular support, but the U.S. media made his candidacy the litmus test of whether the election was free and fair.

"An election without [Cruz's] participation will be judged a charade," declared a *Washington Post* editorial a few weeks prior to the vote. Sure enough, Cruz dropped out of the race after Washington convinced him not to participate (a decision Cruz later regretted). A recipient of CIA funds, Cruz joined the contras after boycotting the vote. U.S. officials admitted to the *New York Times* that the White House "never contemplated letting Cruz stay in the race" because "legitimate" elections would have undermined the contra war. Leaders of all three right-of-center parties which competed for votes complained to election observers of having been pressured or bribed by the U.S. Embassy to quit the race.

Although the U.S. boycott strategy had been exposed, it still worked to perfection on leading editorial pages. The *New York Times* proclaimed, "Only the naive believe the election was democratic or legitimizing proof of the Sandinistas' popularity."

El Salvador's "fledgling democracy"

While the U.S. media fixated on the CIA-financed candidate who was pressured to withdraw from Nicaragua's election, virtually no explanation was offered as to why the leftist opposition chose not to participate in 1984 Salvadoran elections. The reason was simple: Right-wing death squads had murdered tens of thousands of Salvadorans—unionists, students, church activists—and anyone campaigning for progressive change or for human rights would have risked his or her life. But ongoing state terror, which precluded an open campaign essential for a free and fair vote, didn't figure in the U.S. media as a factor that had any bearing on the Salvadoran election—an event designed to put a happy-face on a government drenched in blood from massacring its own people. Few U.S. journalists featured the protests of Maria Julia Hernandez, a leading Salvadoran human rights monitor: "These elections have been imposed by the U.S. State Department to legitimize the government so it can get more U.S. military aid. All this will mean is more deaths, more violations of human rights."

Edward S. Herman's analysis of *New York Times* coverage showed that reporting on El Salvador's 1984 elections relied almost exclusively on noncritical U.S. and Salvadoran government officials, while 80 percent of the *Times* sources about the Nicaraguan election were critical U.S. officials and Nicaragua's boycotting opposition. Herman found that issues of press freedom and limits on opposition candidates were discussed in most articles about Nicaragua's elections, but these topics were ignored in articles about elections in El Salvador, where local journalists were murdered and newspapers bombed out of existence. Moreover, U.S. media often cited threats by Salvadoran rebels to disrupt the elections in that country, but rarely mentioned that the contras had urged Nicaraguans not to vote and killed several election workers.

U.S. officials trumpeted the elections in El Salvador, won by Christian Democrat José Napoleón Duarte, as a triumph for democracy. And mainstream media reported it that way, undaunted by the fact that elections don't guarantee civilian control over the military. Journalists avoided basic issues, such as what democracy could mean in a country where death squads routinely carved up people (including priests and human rights monitors) and no officers were punished for human rights offenses. As Ken Roth of Human Rights Watch noted, "Elections are certainly a crucial step toward democracy, but you can't talk about authentic democracy unless there is also the rule of law. This apparently hasn't sunk in with much of the press."

The rule of law didn't apply in El Salvador during Duarte's term in office (1984-89). Although death squad killings persisted, Duarte was exonerated by U.S. media, which depicted the Salvadoran President as pursuing a moderate course between violent extremists on the left and right. This widely-accepted notion ignored well-documented evidence that the vast majority of killings were committed by death squads connected to the Salvadoran government.

"It is sometimes very hard to tell the difference between the death squads and the government security forces in El Salvador," explained Holly Burkhalter of Americas Watch, "because frequently the security forces will abduct people in unmarked vans, wearing plainclothes." Under the circumstances, Burkhalter said journalists would be more accurate referring to Salvadoran death squads as "government-controlled."

Amnesty International characterized the Salvadoran death squads as "official personnel acting in civilian clothes under the direction of superior officers." A 1989 Amnesty report, El Salvador "Death Squads"—A Government Strategy, identified a "persistent pattern of gross human rights violations by the Salvadoran armed forces" including "arbitrary arrest, torture, disappearance and extrajudicial execution."

Although human rights groups have continually linked death squad activities to the Salvadoran government, most U.S. media have reported on death squads as if they were a mysterious, independent force. This convenient fiction allows the U.S. government to continue providing massive military aid to the Salvadoran government as it commits horrendous cruelties—all in the name of promoting "democracy." In May 1989 Meg Greenfield rhapsodized over "the worldwide democratic surge" in Newsweek, going so far as to describe El Salvador as a "democracy, or at least a pretty good approximation of it."

The idea that El Salvador's civilian leaders were do-gooders caught between two violent extremes stretched the limits of credulity when Alfredo Cristiani of the far right ARENA party was elected to succeed Duarte as the President of El Salvador. The March 1989 elections were also marred by government violence. Reporting on the vote, the New York Times indicated at

Quayle Stresses Human Rights at Meeting in San Salvador

Vice President Dan Quayle with Defense Minister Gen. Humberto Laris, left, and Col. Emilio Ponce, Army Chief of Staff, in San Salvador, where he also met with Roberto d'Aubuisson, the rightist leader. Mr. Quayle is holding a Soviet-made flame thrower reportedly confiscated from guerrillas. Page 3.

Quayle Meets With Salvadoran Leaders

Vice President Dan Quayle with Defense Minister Gen. Humberto Laris, left, and Col. Emilio Ponce, Army Chief of Staff, in San Salvador, where he also met with Roberto d'Aubuisson, the rightist leader. Mr. Quayle is holding a Soviet-made grenade launcher reportedly taken from guerrillas. Page A3.

In its late edition the *New York Times* noticed the irony in "stressing human rights" with artillery. The *Times* failed to notice that Quayle was pointing the weapon the wrong way.

the end of a lengthy news article that three journalists (one foreign, two Salvadoran) had been killed by military personnel during the elections. But the trigger-happy military men were transformed into leftist rebels in a *Times* editorial, which described the killings as follows: "Cristiani has been at pains to present ARENA as a mainstream conservative alliance. He says the true extremists in El Salvador are Marxist guerrillas who terrorize the countryside and did their best to disrupt an election in which 33 were killed, including three journalists."

And that was it. Not a word about what had been reported in the news pages regarding the murder of the journalists. The editorial made it sound like the guerrillas were responsible. When we asked about the misleading statement, *Times* editorial writer Karl Meyer acknowledged that the sentence was "clumsily written." He promised a correction would be printed the next time the newspaper ran an editorial on the subject, but no such correction was forthcoming.

With Cristiani at the helm, at least in a titular sense, the U.S. media took pains to distinguish him from his party's sickening reputation as a death squad haven. One of the distinctions, according to *Times* reporter Lindsey Gruson, is that Cristiani-types in the ARENA party are "conservative, American-trained technocrats"—implying that U.S. training made a crucial difference. But Roberto D'Aubuisson, founder of ARENA and key force behind the Salvadoran death squads, was also trained by the U.S.

The *Times'* State Department correspondent Robert Pear also drew spurious distinctions when he wrote that ARENA's "leaders now include far-rightists like Mr. D'Aubuisson and moderates like Mr. Cristiani." Pear didn't mention that the two men were close friends and poker partners. Nor did he explain why a so-called moderate would represent a party that was launched in 1980 as a paramilitary organization modeled after the Nazis and whose "honorary president for life," Roberto D'Aubuisson, is an admirer of Adolf Hitler.

Death squad murders began to increase soon after Cristiani was sworn in as President. Yet even when uniformed Salvadorans tortured and assassinated six priests and two others at the Jesuit University in November 1989, many U.S. journalists kept framing the issue as though moderate Cristiani was trapped in a crossfire between violent extremes that threatened a fragile democracy.

Meanwhile, as Nicaragua's 1990 elections approached, the American press once again put itself at the U.S. government's disposal, resurrecting myths about U.S. foreign policy. "Before the Feb. 25 election," a *Christian Science Monitor* news story reported, "the [Bush] administration wants to do as much as it can to strengthen the democratic process inside Nicaragua." Toward this end, according to the *Miami Herald*, the State Department began "funding classroom courses for the Nicaraguan contras about a subject the rebels hope will come in handy someday—democracy."

In article after article about the upcoming 1990 elections, U.S. journalists asserted that if the Sandinistas played by the rules, it would be the first free and fair election in Nicaraguan history. Reporters ignored what Virgilio Godoy, a vehement foe of the Sandinistas who was the U.S.-supported vice presidential candidate in the 1990 election, told the *Christian Science Monitor* about the last election five years earlier: "If the U.S. administration said that the Guatemalan and Salvadoran elections were valid ones, how can they condemn elections in Nicaragua, when they have been no worse and probably a lot better? The elections here have been much more peaceful. There were no deaths as in the other two countries, where the opposition were often in fear for their lives."

The main tactical issue mulled over in the U.S. press with respect to Nicaragua's 1990 elections was how to channel millions of dollars to the political opposition—covertly via the CIA or openly through the National Endowment for Democracy. That such meddling—whether overt or covert—might compromise the integrity of the Nicaraguan electoral process was never mentioned by most mainstream journalists, who seemingly took for granted that it's perfectly fine if the U.S. government interferes in the affairs of other countries. Funding foreign political candidates is a common CIA practice, constituting one of the largest categories of covert projects undertaken by the Agency. Recent beneficiaries of the CIA's largess have included Duarte's Christian Democrats in El Salvador, opponents of Costa Rican President and Nobel Peace Laureate Oscar Arias, and candidates running against General Manuel Noriega's cronies in the May 1989 Panamanian presidential election.

Finding "just cause" in Panama

Shortly before the vote in Panama, President Bush declared that Noriega was preparing to rig the results. *New York Times* correspondent Bernard Weinraub reported the President's comments in an article headlined, "Bush Warns Panama on Election Fraud." In the same article, Weinraub mentioned that "the Central Intelligence Agency was funnelling millions of dollars" to support Panamanian opposition candidates. A week later, after Noriega had nullified the election results when they didn't go his way, the *Times* front-paged an article by R.W. Apple Jr. with the headline "Bush's Trap on Panama: Can He Avoid Label of Gringo Meddler?"—as if CIA financing of the opposition was not already a form of meddling.

Well-publicized election-day violence marked the voting in Panama. A report by *Nightline*'s Judd Rose featured vivid footage of a journalist gasping for air after being injured by Noriega's goons. In his voice-over, Rose referred sarcastically to "democracy, Panamanian style." By contrast, when the Salvadoran military killed three journalists during that country's elections two months earlier, there were no sarcastic references to "democracy, Salvadoran style."

A *New York Times* editorial, "Stern but Steady on Panama," attacked "General Noriega's insult to democracy." Noting that fraudulent balloting had once been standard practice in Central America, the editorial continued: "Starting with the leftist threat in Nicaragua a decade ago, however, Washington began to show real concern for democratic elections. North Americans can now credibly cry foul over General Noriega's theft and seek justice for his people."

Noriega's behavior certainly was an insult to democracy; so was the *New York Times'* hypocritical editorial. For the *Times* showed no "real concern for democratic elections" in Panama just five years earlier, when Noriega's hand-picked candidate, Nicolas Ardito Barletta, became President through a rigged vote in which 14 Panamanians were killed and scores wounded. How did the Reagan administration respond to these events? Secretary of State George Shultz attended Ardito Barletta's inauguration and praised the country's "democratization." In 1987, after Noriega had fallen out of favor with the U.S. government, Julia Preston tidied up the official record in the *Washington Post*: "The lack of fair elections [in Panama] has troubled Washington."

During the Panamanian elections in 1989, U.S. journalists frequently described Noriega as a "dictator" and a "thug." But no such epithets were heard in 1984, when he stole the presidential election and brutalized his political opponents. It seems that U.S. reporters will talk bluntly about a dictatorial thug when the U.S. government is trying to sack him, but not when Uncle Sam is propping him up.

The U.S. invasion of Panama in December 1989 unleashed a torrent of Orwellian linguistics in the press. The bias was unmistakable. On *NBC Nightly News* one correspondent referred to U.S. soldiers—who had descended upon Panama with guns and bullets—as engaged in "peacekeeping chores." On the same broadcast, another correspondent referred to Latin American diplomats who denounced the invasion as a "lynch mob." And while many TV journalists mocked the phrase "Dignity Battalions," as Noriega called his fiercest supporters, few saw any historical irony in the codename for the invasion—"Operation Just Cause."

By and large, journalists took their cues from official sources while covering the invasion. After a briefing by high-level Pentagon brass, a wide-eyed Dan Rather effused that viewers couldn't have asked for a better report on an ongoing military operation. The footage of the attack provided by the U.S. Defense Department ran on all the major networks, while ad-libbing reporters—barred from scenes of battle by military decree—reverted to familiar scripts.

Swept up in a decade-ending spasm of jingoism, network anchors began making "we we" on camera: "We haven't got him yet," NBC's Tom Brokaw said of Noriega before he turned up in the Vatican Embassy. There were a few embarrassing moments for the Bush administration, as live split-screen coverage by ABC, CBS and CNN showed Bush smiling and joking at a presidential press conference juxtaposed with images of American coffins being unloaded at Dover Air Force Base—a faux pas that prompted a quick apology from Peter Jennings. But this incident also underscored one of the glaring weaknesses of news accounts: The fixation on casualty figures only extended to U.S. troops and Panamanian combatants, while hundreds of civilian casualties were ignored. With nine U.S. soldiers confirmed dead, John Chancellor couldn't suppress his satisfaction on NBC: "We lose numbers like that in large training exercises."

CBS law correspondent Rita Braver quickly pronounced the invasion legal "according to all the experts I talked to." Apparently Braver's legal experts were unfamiliar with the charter of the Organization of American States (OAS). At least NBC's John Dancy mentioned Article 20 of the OAS charter, which states unequivocally that Latin American countries "may not be the object, even temporarily, of military occupation or of other measures of force taken by another state directly or indirectly on any grounds whatever."

But most journalists were not inclined to quibble over minor points like international law. As *Village Voice* media critic Doug Ireland noted in a column on coverage of the invasion: "When the flag is unfurled, all reason is in the trumpet." Thus we heard Diane Sawyer on ABC *Primetime Live* mouthing official rhetoric about "Panama's lurching struggle toward democracy." And *New York Times* reporter R.W. Apple described the Panama assault as Bush's "presidential initiation rite"—as if violent intervention in Third World countries were a necessary and expected expression of manhood for an American commander-in-chief.

Restoring democracy, nabbing a drug runner and protecting American lives were invoked repeatedly as just cause for U.S. military attack. Yet few reporters saw fit to pursue disclosures by Jonathan Marshall, editorial page editor of the *Oakland Tribune*, who documented extensive involvement in drug money laundering by associates of Noriega's successors, Panamanian President Guillermo Endara and Vice President Guillermo Ford. (For example: Carlos Eleta, the Panamanian CIA agent who disbursed millions of U.S. dollars to Endara's political party, was arrested in April 1989 in Macon, Georgia, for conspiring to bring more than half a ton of cocaine each month into the United States. Endara was Eleta's lawyer for 25 years.) Once again it appeared that the U.S. government and the press were willing to tolerate drug profiteering so long as the guilty parties remained steadfastly pro-United States.

As for protecting Americans (a rationale applauded by the *New York Times*), Bush didn't send 25,000 troops to Guatemala when Diana Ortiz, an American nun, was abducted and sexually abused by U.S.-backed Guatemalan security officers a few weeks before the Panama attack. Likewise, administration officials showed little concern about protecting American lives when U.S.

clergy were killed in Nicaragua a few weeks after the invasion. Colleagues of the murdered clergy blamed the contras, but most U.S. journalists were too busy exulting in the Panama "success" to press the point.

Mexico's President: wimp or death squad symp?

The Mexican presidential elections in December 1988 were also marked by extensive fraud. Carlos Salinas de Gortari of the ruling PRI party took office after claiming to have won slightly more than 50 percent of the vote, amid charges of massive irregularities at the ballot box in regions where opposition candidates of the left and right were popular. U.S. media acknowledged that fraud had occurred, but this hardly put a damper on their enthusiasm for the new Mexican leader.

Salinas had been President barely a month, but already the U.S. government and press were praising him. A *Miami Herald* article, headlined "Salinas signals that he's not a wimp," cited the arrest of Mexico's "oil workers' boss" and other "shows of force" by the new government as evidence that Salinas is a tough, assertive leader.

"Salinas signals he's soft on human rights abusers" would have been a more appropriate headline; the other "shows of force" referred to by the *Herald* (part of Knight-Ridder, the second largest U.S. newspaper chain) included a massacre by police following a prison uprising that left 25 dead, with several inmates allegedly killed "after they surrendered," and Salinas' appointment of hardliner Miguel Nazar Haro as police intelligence chief of Mexico City. "Nazar," wrote Knight-Ridder correspondent Katherine Ellison, "is reportedly also the ex-chief of the White Brigade, a secretive paramilitary team believed to be responsible for the torture and disappearance of hundreds of suspected leftists in the 1970s."

Ellison noted that Nazar had been indicted in 1982 by a U.S. grand jury in San Diego, which linked him to a luxury car-theft ring. Jailed briefly in the U.S., Nazar fled after posting $200,000 bail. On the day after disclosing details of Nazar's checkered past in its news pages, the *Herald* ran an editorial that hailed President Salinas for putting his "foes on notice that he means to make good on his campaign promises to curb corruption."

The *New York Times* followed suit with an editorial ("Mexico's President Gets Tough") stating, "Salinas' crackdowns [on Mexico's labor unions] deserve support." Acknowledging that Salinas' legitimacy had been "tainted by the fraud used...to inflate his vote tally" (a subtle way of soft-pedaling allegations that he stole the election), the *Times* editors warned that "unless Mr. Salinas faces down the obstacles to reform early in his six-year term, his chance to achieve change from within could collapse." Ironically, the "obstacles" mentioned include "vote-riggers" and corrupt public officials.

A month after Salinas took office, a front-page story in the *Times* by Larry Rohter discussed government-sponsored political executions in Mexico. "In the first public acknowledgment of death squad activity in Mexico," the article began, "a former Mexican Army soldier is maintaining that he was part of a secret military unit that executed at least 60 political prisoners here in the late 1970s and early 1980s." Two top Salinas appointees were linked to the death squads: Miguel Nazar, the police intelligence chief under indictment in the U.S. for car theft; and Deputy Interior Minister Fernando Gutierrez Barrios, who commanded the forces that massacred several hundred demonstrators in Mexico City days before the 1968 Olympics. Nazar resigned shortly after Rohter's article appeared in the *Times*, but Gutierrez kept his post in the Mexican government.

While this may have been the first time the paper of record referred to death squad executions in Mexico, it was certainly not the "first public acknowledgment" of such activity, as Rohter asserted. *Inside the League,* a book by Scott Anderson and Jon Lee Anderson, discussed the Tecos, a bizarre neo-Nazi cult based in Guadalajara that coordinated its death squad operations with other paramilitary groups in Latin America. The Tecos comprised the Mexican chapter of the World Anti-Communist League, an organization which later played a key role in providing aid to the Nicaraguan contras.

Nor did death squad activity in Mexico cease in the early 1980s, as the *Times* suggests. Within weeks after Salinas took office in December 1988, there were 40 political assassinations in Mexico, according to the Mexico City daily *La Jornada.* Most of the victims were rural supporters of leftist Cuauhtemoc Cardenas, Salinas' principal political rival. However, these killings were virtually ignored by major U.S. media which, like the U.S. government, preferred to laud Salinas as a great reformer.

Despite widespread charges that Salinas' ruling PRI party had committed fraud in July 1989 regional elections, the *Times* again hailed Mexico's chief in an editorial titled, "Winning by Losing in Mexico." The "losing" was a reference to PRI's acknowledgement that it had been beaten by a right-wing candidate in Baja California. This showed that Salinas was dedicated to "preparing his party and his country for a future of democratic pluralism," according to the *Times*.

But Salinas' party refused to concede defeat in Michoacan, a Cardenista stronghold plagued by widespread voting irregularities, prompting *Proceso*, a Mexican magazine, to declare, "Selective democracy: Baja California yes, Michoacan no." By contrast, the *Times* editorial concluded: "Even the boldest reforms are devalued when regimes rig the rules against real opposition. Mr. Salinas knows that. His vision and courage deserve U.S. support." Once again, the *Times* editors were echoing Washington officials.

"Controlled democracy" and the debt crisis

For decades, the U.S. government has sanctioned fraudulent elections in Latin America and other areas of the Third World. U.S. administrations have also instigated coups that toppled democratically-elected leaders when the results were not to their liking: Iran, 1953; Guatemala, 1954; Brazil, 1964; Chile, 1973. Yet few mainstream journalists ever question whether promoting democracy and human rights is the actual objective of U.S. foreign policy.

"There is kind of an unconscious constraint among journalists that's related to the official American definition of the situation," said Cynthia Brown of Americas Watch. "Some influential reporters and editors have not made the distinction between elections and democracy. Instead they adopted the Reagan administration's jargon, which has become the general parlance. It's dangerous because the subtext is that we don't have to worry about Latin America anymore. They are electing civilian governments and therefore everything must be fine."

Many astute Latin American observers take Washington's professed concern for democracy with a large grain of salt. Father Luis Perez Aguirre, a leading Uruguayan human rights activist, drew attention to a significant factor jeopardizing the process of democratization in Latin America—the debt crisis. Said Perez Aguirre: "The debt is more than just an economic problem; it is also a political problem. The creditors are aware of this, and they try to maintain our countries in submission by keeping the dependency system."

The results are grim: Half a million children died in 1988, according to UNICEF, as families in the developing world slid into severe poverty, while their governments imposed strict austerity measures at the behest of the International Monetary Fund and the World Bank. This was the standard prescription for servicing the foreign debt—much of which had accrued in Latin America while U.S.-backed dictators looted their own treasuries, siphoning loans into various secret bank accounts. Yet the loans kept coming.

In our conversation with Father Perez Aguirre, he talked about the transition from Latin American military dictatorships of the 1970s to electoral democracies of the 1980s, emphasizing a truth rarely spoken in the U.S. media: "The national security regimes are becoming obsolete, but the policies of the International Monetary Fund and the World Bank haven't changed. Transnational and U.S.-based corporations are seeking to maintain the same unjust policies without propping up overtly repressive regimes. Accordingly, the U.S. government is promoting a new doctrine, not very well known yet, called *democracia tutelaria*, or 'controlled democracy.' This doctrine tries to avoid the brutal image of military rule, but the oppression of our people continues."

THIRD WORLD TROUBLE SPOTS

In June 1987, millions of South Koreans protested nonviolently against military rule in that country, forcing the government to announce that it would hold elections by the end of the year. Several U.S. senators and congressmen who traveled to Seoul to observe the elections reported evidence of counterfeit ballots, vote-buying, political harassment and the beating of election monitors. Amidst charges of fraud, former general Roh Tae Woo, the military's hand-picked candidate, claimed victory.

After the elections, U.S. media quickly closed ranks behind Roh, glossing over irregularities at the polls that had been reported by members of Congress. A *Wall Street Journal* headline read, "Koreans Elect Roh as President in Easy Victory; Little Is Found to Confirm Charges of Wide Fraud Made by the Opposition." The next day, a *Washington Post* editorial stated, "The air is thick with complaints of fraud, but the proof offered so far is thin."

U.S. media largely ignored the fact that South Korean police had shut down an independent vote-counting center staffed by the National Coalition for Democracy, which kept a computer tally for comparison with the official government figures. When police intervened and closed the Coalition's offices, only 60 percent of the vote had been counted. Nor did major American media report that police had raided the Christian Broadcast Company on election eve, closing down the only independent national television network in Korea. As a result, Korean citizens and American journalists relied solely on state-controlled media for the election results.

The official count gave Roh 36.6 percent of the vote, while the opposition candidates, Kim Young Sam and Kim Dae Jung, divided 55 percent of the tally between them. Even though a majority of Koreans had voted for major change from past abusive rule, *Time* magazine called the results a "Vote for Stability."

Roh Tae Woo was sworn in as South Korean President in February 1988. His decision to fill most of his cabinet with recently-retired generals and other holdovers from the U.S.-backed military regime provoked widespread dismay among Koreans. So did Roh's decision not to follow through on a much-repeated campaign promise to free all political prisoners, many of whom had been tortured. "We cannot but be overwhelmed by disappointment," the nation's largest newspaper, *Dong-A-Ilbo*, editorialized.

This disappointment was not shared by major U.S. media, which hailed Roh's inauguration as a great step forward for democracy. A *Chicago Tribune* editorial praised the "peaceful transfer of power from a military autocrat to a democratically-elected civilian. Roh Tae Woo, elected President in a free and fair election in December, has shown the vision needed to consolidate public support and avert military interference."

The *Tribune* editorial was wrong on all counts. The election of Roh was marked by fraud, and the notion that he would hold the military at bay didn't square with the cabinet appointments he had already made. Moreover, the editorial's claim of a "peaceful transfer of power" was contradicted by a *Chicago Tribune* news story from the same day: "Students who oppose Roh in Seoul and several other cities clashed with riot police in scenes reminiscent of protests last summer that eventually led to the election."

A *New York Times* editorial, "Not So Regressive in Korea," praised President Roh Tae Woo in March 1989 after he postponed a plebiscite he had promised voters during his election campaign. "Friends of South Korean democracy shouldn't be alarmed," assured the *Times*. "In his first year in office, President Roh has already laid to rest doubts about his democratic convictions... He has let workers struggle for long-denied union rights and kept the powerful security forces leashed."

A few days later, the *Times* ran a brief Reuters dispatch which stated: "More than 10,000 riot police, firing tear gas and in full battle gear, stormed [South Korea's] biggest shipyard early today and arrested workers... Strikers fought back with stones, gasoline bombs and clubs. About 700 people were arrested and 20 wounded..." So much for keeping the security forces "leashed" and letting workers "struggle for long-denied union rights."

Israelis and Palestinians

Another example of discontinuity between editorials and news stories can be found in the *Washington Post*'s coverage of human rights violations in the Israeli-occupied West Bank and Gaza Strip. Correspondent Glenn Frankel has often brought abuses to the fore, quoting human rights groups, Palestinian detainees, Israeli officials and U.S. State Department sources in his articles. Meanwhile, the *Post*'s editorial page offered palliatives with this ideological two-step: "What counts most, however, is the nature of the system... That Israel is at heart a democratic country remains its core strength."

John Healey, executive director of Amnesty International USA, responded to these remarks with a letter to the *Post*. "Visualize the arm of a teenager held out by soldiers and broken at midshaft," said Healey, "a rock-thrower lying dead with a bullet in his back or an infant in her cradle asphyxiated by tear gas. Next, record the name and age of each person who has been abused—and chronicle dozens of deaths as a result of plastic bullets and many thousands of wounded people. Finally, count the thousands imprisoned without trial and the scores tortured. Now, turn to an editorial by the *Post* and read, 'What counts most, however, is the nature of the system.'"

The outbreak of the *intifada* (the Palestinian uprising) in December 1987 came as a surprise to U.S. media, which had long ignored serious human rights abuses in the Occupied Territories. For 20 years Israeli forces had been detaining people without charge, closing universities, censoring Palestinian publications, torturing political prisoners, blowing up Arab homes, and operating military courts which made a mockery of justice. Yet prior to the *intifada*, the *New York Times* called the military occupation "benign" and praised Israel (the largest recipient of U.S. government aid) as "a society in which moral sensitivity is a principle of political life."

The killings, beatings and daily humiliation of a people under occupation were not deemed worthy of coverage in the U.S. press until the *intifada* erupted with full fury. It was only then that American journalists began to pay unflattering attention to the poverty and degradation suffered by many Palestinians, whose "towns are short of hospitals, sewers, paved roads and schoolrooms," as *Newsweek* put it. ABC News correspondent Dean Reynolds portrayed the Palestinians as victims of an unjust occupation, drawing parallels between the West Bank and the black South African township of Soweto. Most Palestinians, said Reynolds, "live in refugee camps, stateless and homeless. They work low-paying jobs that Israelis refuse. Most are under 20, and have spent their whole lives under Israeli rule. They watch helplessly as Israeli settlements in the territories expand... The tragedy of the Palestinians is they seldom get attention to their problems unless they're killing someone, or someone is killing them."

The sense of frustration and desperation among Palestinians was compounded by the fact that repeated peace overtures by the PLO—viewed as "the sole and legitimate representative of the Palestinian people" by 93.5 percent of Arabs in the Occupied Territories, according to a 1986 *Newsday* poll—were rejected by Israel. For years PLO chief Yasir Arafat had been advocating a negotiated settlement with Israel, based on the principle of "exchanging land for peace," but this was consistently ignored by major U.S. media.

The PLO reiterated its position on several occasions, sometimes ambiguously and sometimes quite clearly, but the U.S. media turned a deaf ear to Arafat's conciliatory words. In the spring of 1984, for example, Arafat issued a series of statements in Europe supporting "direct negotiations between the Israelis and ourselves," which would lead to "mutual recognition between two states." This was reported by the *London Observer*, *Le Nouvel Observateur* in Paris, and the *Jerusalem Post*, but not by the *New York Times* or the three major U.S. networks.

In December 1987, shortly after the *intifada* erupted, the Hebrew press in Israel gave prominent coverage to Arafat's assertion that he was "ready for direct negotiations with Israel." But this offer was ignored by the *New York Times*, which also slighted Arafat's statement on January 14, 1988, that the PLO would "recognize Israel's right to exist if it and the United States accept PLO participation in an international Middle East peace conference." Instead the *Times* editorialized, "Until the PLO summons the courage and wisdom to accept peace with Israel in return for some kind of Palestinian homeland, it would be folly for Israel to bargain."

In May 1988, Bassam Abu Sharif, one of Arafat's closest advisers, submitted an article outlining the PLO's moderate stance to the *Washington Post*, which reportedly solicited the piece for its op-ed page. But Abu Sharif's carefully crafted position paper didn't sit well with the *Post*'s editors, who refused to print it. His article—explicitly calling for a two-state solution, with a Palestinian state coexisting in peace alongside Israel—was subsequently included in a PLO press kit given to journalists covering the Palestinian summit conference in Algiers in June. A brief account of Abu Sharif's article ran in the *Wall Street Journal*, and a *Boston Globe* editorial quoted snippets from his statement, characterizing it as one of "exemplary moderation."

Nothing about Abu Sharif's peace overture appeared in either of America's newspapers of record until two weeks after it was first mentioned in the *Wall Street Journal*. The *Washington Post* ran an AP story from Cyprus which focused on the fact that anti-Arafat Palestinian fringe groups had rejected Abu Sharif's moderate position. This was how *Post* readers first learned about his declaration. The next day a critical column by *Post* editor Stephen Rosenfeld focused on those fringe groups rather than Abu Sharif's position.

The *New York Times* did somewhat better, running a news report on rejectionist criticism of Abu Sharif near the front of the newspaper, along with a summary of the main points of his article on its editorial page. The *Times* also printed a laudatory column by Anthony Lewis, who described Abu Sharif's article as "one of the most important documents in the tormented history of conflict between Israelis and Palestinians." Yet it was never mentioned during network news coverage of the Algiers summit conference.

In November 1988, the PLO issued a declaration of Palestinian independence that once again affirmed Israel's right to exist in peace as part of a two-state Mideast solution. The PLO also rejected "terrorism in all its forms." The Palestinian communiqué was greeted by media across the country and abroad with cautious optimism. WNBC-TV in New York summed it up: "PLO recognizes Israel, but many obstacles remain." A *Christian Science Monitor* editorial was headlined, "A welcome move by the PLO."

But the *New York Times* kept insisting that the PLO had not actually recognized Israel. The rest of the world had been suckered by the PLO, but the *Times* knew better. According to a *Times* editorial, "The PLO: Less Than Meets the Eye," Arafat merely sought to appear conciliatory, when he actually wasn't. The PLO announcement "will do little to strengthen the hand of Israelis who search for a basis of negotiations," said the editors. "The fine print [of the PLO declaration] plays directly into the hands of the Likud bloc and its leader, Yitzhak Shamir, who totally opposes any settlement based on trading land for peace." Actually, it was the fine print of the *New York Times* that played right into the hands of Israeli rejectionists.

As the days passed and the PLO continued to receive accolades from Western Europe and elsewhere, *Times* correspondents joined their editors in verbal contortions to minimize the PLO declaration. Robert Pear employed no less than four minimizing clauses in one sentence when he reported that the PLO "*appeared* to *some* to have *implicitly* taken *a step toward* accepting Israel's right to exist [emphasis added]."

The *Times* steadfastly refused to accept the PLO declaration until weeks later, when the green light came from the State Department. It was then that the paper of record finally acknowledged that the PLO had made the proper minuscule word changes that it had requested. At which point the *Times* editors asserted that the PLO underwent a "seismic shift of attitude...towards a serious negotiating position." Joel Brinkley, the *Times* correspondent in Jerusalem, described it as a major breakthrough: "Yasir Arafat, the PLO leader, is saying openly for the first time that he wants to solve the Palestinian problem through negotiation." In fact, Arafat had been saying so openly for years. It was the State Department that shifted its position, not the PLO. Brinkley and his editors were guilty of seriously distorting the historical record.

Although the Israeli government continued to reject negotiations with the PLO, the *Times* placed much of the responsibility for the logjam on the Palestinians. When Israeli hardliner Ariel Sharon called for assassinating Arafat as a precondition for "peace," his threat was buried inconspicuously in the middle of a *Times* article headlined, "Israel Asserts Threats by PLO Imperil Bid to Revive Peace Plan." Israeli Prime Minister Shamir warned that Palestinians resisting occupation would be "crushed like grasshoppers," with their heads "smashed against the boulders and walls." Yet in his August 1988 *New York Times* magazine profile of Shamir, Joel Brinkley stated: "Shamir is a tactician. He's not a man of volatile emotions, subject to such dangerous feelings as hate."

By this time, coverage of violence in the Occupied Territories had become repetitive, almost numbing, with a few more Palestinian youths dying each week, their bodies embalmed in cold statistics and "buried in shallow, two-paragraph graves," as media critic Dennis Perrin put it. After yet another fatal clash between Israeli troops and Palestinians in the West Bank, Israeli minister Yitzhak Peretz was quoted as saying in a cabinet meeting that Israel could not allow "every dirty Arab" to infringe on Israeli access to religious sites in the Old City of Jerusalem. *Washington Post* reporter Edward Cody described Peretz's racial slur as "a measure of the bitterness" Israeli officials feel toward Palestinians. If someone had used the phrase "dirty Jew," it would rightly have been characterized as a blatant expression of anti-Semitism. But when an Israeli official says "dirty Arab," the *Washington Post* discerns only bitterness, not racism.

Seeing red in Southern Africa

For all its deficiencies, U.S. press coverage of repression in the Occupied Territories has increased substantially since the *intifada*. This is more than can be said about reporting on human rights abuses in most of sub-Saharan

Africa. When 400,000 Somalians fled their war-torn East African country in the summer of 1988, it barely entered public consciousness in the United States. Initially backed by Moscow in its conflict with Ethiopia, Somalia later turned to the U.S. government, which became its principal military supplier. With American backing, Somalia has committed mind-boggling atrocities against unarmed civilians. Similarly, a 1988 massacre in Burundi came and went with hardly any follow-up in the U.S. press.

Such incidents in "obscure" places receive little coverage, partly because they have only minor impact on U.S. economic interests or East/West relations. Racial bias is also a factor. As one network news reporter commented, "TV news executives figure that the American population cares less about what happens to people the darker their skin is." According to former CBS correspondent Randy Daniels, "The preponderance of news from Africa is clearly from a white point of view and deals primarily with whites."

Africa is consistently the most under-reported area in the world, as far as U.S. media are concerned. Journalists quip that you have to add a few zeros to the number of casualties in Africa before it is deemed newsworthy. The exception is South Africa, where coverage of violence by the apartheid government has catalyzed worldwide protests, including calls for economic sanctions and divestment. Media attention helped turn the struggle inside South Africa into an international cause. Pretoria responded by imposing harsh press restrictions in 1985 that succeeded in limiting coverage of the unrest.

"There is no formal censorship system," *New York Times* then-foreign-editor Joseph Lelyveld said of the South African press regulations. "I don't think we have ever submitted a line of copy. It's a system of self-censorship... Some use the government's pressure of close scrutiny as an excuse for not doing a hell of a lot."

It is often said that if U.S. journalists defied the press rules, they would be expelled from the country. But former ABC News reporter Ken Walker feels that the U.S. media have been complicit in Pretoria's media manipulation. He contends the same fear of getting tossed out was not present in Eastern European countries where government restrictions were routinely challenged, and where expulsion was often a badge of honor. Walker points to a lack of black network correspondents assigned to South Africa as a sign of widespread reluctance to challenge the status quo.

A South African journalist told *Africa Report* magazine that a reporter's political outlook is as crucial as his or her racial sensitivity. "South Africa is viewed as one of us, as a Western democracy, and the correspondents operate as if it was one," he asserted. "Western reporters cover South Africa from the point of view of the people who run it, not from the point of view of those who suffer it." Indeed, while the U.S. media described the protesters in Eastern Europe and China as "pro-democracy" demonstrators, black South

Africans demanding a system based on one-person one-vote were rarely, if ever, referred to as "pro-democracy" activists.

A Cold War frame has skewed U.S. reporting on the war in Angola, a target of South African aggression since the mid-1970s. Mainstream media have obscured the origins of the Angolan conflict, depicting South Africa and the U.S. as responding to Soviet-Cuban "expansionism" in Southern Africa. Typical was a *Los Angeles Times* news article, which claimed that "within weeks of Angolan independence, Cuban troops arrived to support the new government, and South Africa, worried about the Soviet-backed Cuban troops' threat to Namibia, sent its own troops into Angola to help the National Union for the Total Independence of Angola [UNITA]."

Not so, according to John Stockwell, head of the CIA's Angolan task force during the mid-1970s. Stockwell maintains that Cuban forces entered the fray *after* some 5,000 South African troops invaded Angola and drove 500 kilometers toward the Angolan capital of Luanda in a week. This is what prompted the Angolan government to request the assistance of Cuban soldiers, who helped stave off the South African attack and defeat the CIA-supported rebels.

UNITA was resurrected as a guerrilla force during the Reagan administration, which armed the South African-backed rebel army at a time when military assistance was prohibited by Congress. Scattered reports in the U.S. media provided evidence of a Southern African connection to the clandestine operations run by CIA director William Casey and Lt. Col. Oliver North. This was one of the hidden stories of the Iran-contra affair, but the U.S. press again neglected to pursue mounting evidence of illegal covert actions.

From the outset, UNITA leader Jonas Savimbi was treated with kid gloves by the American media, which rushed to sanctify him as a legitimate anti-colonial leader. Yet in the early 1970s, Savimbi had collaborated with neofascist mercenaries employed by the Portuguese secret service, in assassination attempts against rival Angolan guerrilla leaders who were fighting the Portuguese colonial regime. This was not reported by the mainstream press.

During 15 years of civil war in Angola, U.S. journalists paid little attention to human rights abuses by UNITA forces. In 1986, for example, the Africa Faith and Justice Network reported that UNITA had kidnaped 60 priests as part of an ongoing U.S.-backed terror campaign, but this was ignored by most media. UNITA's indiscriminate use of land mines maimed thousands of civilians, prompting a *Wall Street Journal* reporter to describe central Angola as the "amputee capital of the world." But the *Journal* and other U.S. media didn't mention that UNITA targeted medical clinics, attacking an artificial limb center in Huambo four times during the war.

UNITA atrocities, including the use of starvation as a weapon, had long been cited by church groups and human rights monitors. But it wasn't until

March 1989, when peace talks between the warring parties were underway, that major media began to acknowledge the sinister side of Savimbi and UNITA. A front page *New York Times* article by Craig Whitney and Jill Jolliffe featured a UNITA defector who asserted that Savimbi had ordered the torture and killing of dissenters. In another case of reporting too little too late, the *Times* referred to eyewitness accounts from an Amnesty International study which said that Savimbi—hailed as a "freedom fighter" by the Reagan administration—burned some of his opponents at the stake after accusing them of being "witches."

The other side of the Afghanistan story

The soft-pedaling of UNITA abuses exemplified a longstanding pattern of U.S. media coverage, which has often downplayed atrocities by U.S.-backed forces in various regional conflicts around the world. This was certainly the case when anticommunist mujahadeen rebels battled Soviet troops in Afghanistan. Those who followed American reporting on the war learned a lot about Soviet and Afghan government atrocities, but there wasn't much news of widespread abuses committed by the guerrillas, who received over $2 billion in weapons from the CIA to conduct their decade-long *jihad*, or holy war.

Over one million people have died in the war in Afghanistan, mostly due to aerial bombardments by the Soviet and Afghan government forces. The U.S. media, however, didn't report on rebel human rights abuses that began before Soviet tanks rolled into Afghanistan in 1979. For example, the Afghan government's literacy campaign for women sparked demonstrations by Islamic fundamentalists, culminating in a revolt in the western city of Herat in which several Afghan officials and Soviet advisers were slaughtered. Civilian massacres by the mujahadeen continued throughout the war, as when Afghan rebels captured a government-controlled village in Kunar province in January 1989, murdered many inhabitants, raped 40 women and engaged in extensive looting. These war crimes were largely ignored by major U.S. media.

While American journalists wrote about Afghan government "press gangs" forcibly recruiting among reluctant civilians, little was said about forced conscription commonly practiced by the rebels. A double standard was also at work in coverage of indiscriminate bombings by both sides in the conflict. When bombs exploded in Pakistani havens of the mujahadeen, the *Washington Post* and other media described them as "terrorist" attacks—a characterization absent when Afghan civilians were killed by rebels who indiscriminately shelled the capital city of Kabul.

Similarly, the U.S. press often charged that communist forces were torturing political prisoners, but the torture of POWs (some of whom were skinned alive) by the mujahadeen was seemingly not fit to print. As author Steven Galster noted, "In 1986 and 1987, the BBC [British Broadcasting Corporation] aired a film in which a member of the National Islamic Front of Afghanistan, a rebel faction consistently described as a 'moderate' party by the U.S. media, disclosed that he sentenced six to seven thousand prisoners of war to death." Again, not a word of this ran in the newspapers of record.

Why did Afghan guerrilla atrocities largely escape scrutiny by American reporters? In part because Soviet and Afghan government abuses were so horrendous, but also because of what Galster described as "an excessive reliance on 'Western diplomatic' and rebel sources." Even after the Soviets withdrew their forces, *New York Times* correspondent Paul Lewis cited unnamed "diplomats" who argued that President Najibullah of Afghanistan, with backing from Moscow, was intent on "retaining power by force instead of seeking a compromise with the opposition." In fact, the Soviet Union had already committed itself to a negotiated settlement, but the U.S. government balked at such a prospect, prompting BBC Radio World Service to ask, "Is the United States willing to give peace a chance in Afghanistan?"

A minor media scandal erupted in September 1989 when the *New York Post* disclosed that *CBS Evening News* had aired fake combat footage and false news reports about the war in Afghanistan a few years earlier. According to the *Post*, a free-lance cameraman staged scenes of guerrilla sabotage and made a Pakistani jet on a training run appear to be a Soviet plane bombing Afghan villages. CBS News also aired a segment in 1987 showing a bomb made to look like a toy, which the network said was planted by Soviet soldiers to injure Afghan children. The *Post* cited a BBC reporter who claimed that the bomb-toy had been created for the CBS cameraman.

In the wake of these disclosures, news professionals scolded CBS for sloppy journalism. But as Fairness & Accuracy in Reporting pointed out, "It was sloppiness in the service of a cause—the so-called Afghan freedom fighters." The problem did not simply stem from a network's hunger for "good pictures," nor could it be remedied by using less footage from free-lancers. "The problem was deeper," said FAIR. "CBS coverage of Afghanistan often resembled partisan war propaganda more than reporting."

CBS anchor Dan Rather, acting more like a cheerleader for the rebels than a journalist, had abandoned any pretense of objectivity while covering the Afghan conflict. Imbued with a deep-rooted anticommunist bias, CBS News functioned as a public relations arm for the mujahadeen cause. In this sense, CBS was not much different than other major media, which neglected to explore important questions, such as: How many U.S.-backed mujahadeen leaders were followers of the Ayatollah Khomeini? Which U.S.-armed guerrilla factions were committed to creating a society modeled after the Islamic Republic of Iran? How did the rebels view the role of women in Afghan society? To what extent has heroin trafficking by rebel groups contributed to the drug problem in the United States? Were American intelligence officers complicit in drug smuggling by the mujahadeen?

The main beneficiaries of the CIA's multibillion-dollar covert aid program—the Afghan fundamentalist rebel parties and their Pakistani military sponsors—had never distinguished themselves as democrats in any sense of the word. Yet, with few exceptions, U.S. journalists also turned a blind eye to extensive human rights violations perpetrated by Pakistan's military regime. Led by General Mohammed Zia ul-Haq until his death in August 1988, Pakistan became the third largest recipient of U.S. foreign aid during the Reagan administration. Asked by *Time* magazine about the prospects for a more democratic regime in Kabul, General Zia asserted that he would never accept an Afghan government that came to power "riding on Soviet tanks." *Time* failed to mention that Zia had also come to power via a military coup and then repeatedly reneged on pledges to hold democratic elections.

In 1989 Mikhail Gorbachev and other Soviet leaders admitted that the invasion of Afghanistan was illegal and immoral. Media in the United States reacted as if to say, "See, we told you so." But there are few mass media pundits with sufficient honesty and courage to denounce the U.S. government's death squad diplomacy in Central America as illegal and immoral. Likewise, few U.S. commentators have condemned the forced transfer of $275 billion from the poorest to the richest countries in the world since the debt crisis broke in the early 1980s. Primed to see evil in Red tyranny, U.S. media are much less critical when injustice reigns under Red, White and Blue domination.

CONCLUSION

Toward an Uncensored Future

On a warm spring day in 1988, we visited George Seldes, then 97 years old, at his home in Hartland-4-Corners, Vermont. The man I.F. Stone called "the dean and 'granddaddy' of us investigative reporters" stood slightly hunched on the porch of his modest brick house where he lived by himself. We were greeted with handshakes and a ready smile, as he ushered us inside. For the next six hours, he regaled us with vivid recollections of a remarkable journalistic career that spanned eight decades.

As a reporter for the *Chicago Tribune*, in 1921 Seldes went to Russia where he interviewed Bolshevik leaders Lenin and Trotsky. He covered the Soviet Union for two years until his stories about the suppression of non-Bolshevik revolutionaries got him ousted. A tireless freethinker, he spent two years in Italy before being thrown out because of his unflattering portraits of Fascist dictator Mussolini. He served as the *Tribune*'s bureau chief in Berlin. And during the Spanish war in the 1930s—which he insists was not a civil war since Hitler and Mussolini aided General Franco with so many troops, tanks and planes—Seldes and his wife Helen wired dispatches to an East Coast newspaper chain. But the chain stopped running the Seldes' pieces after U.S. Catholic prelates who favored Franco called for a boycott by readers and advertisers.

That decade saw the rise of ad agencies which undermined ambitious plans for a magazine slated to be the first illustrated, mass-circulation American weekly "one step left of center." Seldes had been hired as one of the editors, but the magazine's support for progressive causes, such as the Spanish Republic's struggle against Nazism and fascism, displeased Madison Avenue, and a lack of advertising revenue killed the project.

Shortly thereafter, Seldes published *Lords of the Press*, a book filled with startling revelations about the corruption and political bias of American journalism. Not surprisingly, the book was shunned by mainstream newspapers and magazines. Undaunted, Seldes kept taking on the privileged and the powerful, including big-money interests like the tobacco industry. Beginning in the late 1930s, he vehemently denounced the American press for covering up the dangers of smoking while raking in millions from cigarette ads.

In 1940, Seldes started a weekly newsletter, *In fact*, the world's first regular publication devoted entirely to press criticism. During its ten-year life, circulation rose to over 175,000—with kudos from Eleanor Roosevelt, among others—before *In fact* was Red-baited to death by McCarthyites "who rode top saddle in the nation's press in those days," Seldes recalled. A few decades later, he was writing of that "imaginary institution called 'freedom of the press,' a phrase that means, or should mean, not only the right of the owners to publish without government control or Moron Majority censorship, but the right of the buyer of a paper to read hitherto suppressed news."

In his hundredth year, Seldes remained an American individualist in the best sense, combining an unpretentious, fiercely independent, intellectual ethic with an unwavering commitment to social justice. For us he was a living inspiration, someone who had supreme confidence in the power of ideas and the capacity of people to see through the hypocrisy of politicians and media pundits. Seldes never stopped believing that the essence of a democratic society is an enlightened, well-informed citizenry. And he continued to do his part by closely monitoring the press, even though he was well past the age when most would have retired. Toward the end of our conversation, he pointed to a stack of news clips and said, "There are too many to file. I can hardly keep up with them."

For Seldes, being skeptical of news media was nothing less than a civic duty. But the very nature of mass media in our society discourages such a critical disposition. Newscasts share a half-hour continuum with high-budget commercials that intersperse the con and the come-on, mixing messages whose net effect is to inculcate confusion and passivity. Taking in the world of the foreign crisis and the yellowed kitchen floor, heart-rending disasters and new cars, severe domestic ills and great light beer, TV viewers are conditioned to be passive about nearly everything that can't be purchased. While commercials emphatically encourage shopping sprees, television imparts little enthusiasm for grassroots activism, least of all for Americans who might endeavor to significantly alter a society with unforgivable extremes of wealth and poverty, a poisoned ecology and other festering injustices.

For hucksters marketing products as antidotes to the daily dose of "bad news," personal insecurity is a desirable trait, to be egged on and exploited ad infinitum, so that social life becomes a guided tour from on high, arranged by mega-media complexes that prey upon Americans who are glued to the Tube an average of 31 hours each week. ("Who is watching the direction of society, if we are all at home watching re-runs?" asked Ralph Nader.) Ubiquitous media beseech that we do little except keep watching, reading, listening...and buying. Excitement is reserved for, or at least associated with, spending money. One dollar, one vote: in mass media's gilded cage of "demogracy," some people are more affluent, and therefore more equal, than others.

Linguicide

The intersection of Madison Avenue, Wall Street and Pennsylvania Avenue is a heavily-trafficked zone, where lies and facts cohabitate as convenience and opportunism dictate. With reporters serving mainly as messengers for corporate PR reps and government officials who try to fog up reality, it's no wonder "the news" leaves so many people feeling confused.

The world according to mass media is not supposed to make sense; it is supposed to make money. When we watch news on television, Mark Crispin Miller has written, "we come to feel, not only that the world is blowing up, but that it does so for no reason, that its ongoing history is nothing more than a series of eruptions, each without cause or context. The news creates this vision of mere anarchy through its erasure of the past, and its simultaneous tendency to atomize the present into so many unrelated happenings, each recounted through a sequence of dramatic, unintelligible pictures. In short, the TV news adapts the world to its own commercial needs, translating history into several mad occurrences, just the sort of 'story' that might pique the viewer's morbid curiosity... And so we have the correspondent, solemnly nattering among the ruins, offering crude 'analysis' and 'background,' as if to compensate us for the deep bewilderment that his medium created in the first place."

The resulting renditions of the world—from special reports about earth-shaking events to local TV news happy-talk—are disorienting, which suits backers of the status quo just fine. Confusion "keeps us powerless and controllable," psychotherapist Anne Wilson Schaef notes. "No one is more controllable than a confused person; no society is more controllable than a confused society. Politicians know this better than anyone, and that is why they use innuendos, veiled references, and out-and-out lies instead of speaking clearly and truthfully."

While sometimes echoing public skepticism or even disdain toward politicians, news media grant them continuous access—endlessly featuring, quoting, summarizing and propagating their opinions. As with histrionic wrestlers on TV, journalists and political players make various noises, encouraging viewers to mistake the embraces for mortal combat. But when the President wants reporters to jump for a story, they are much less interested in asking "Why?" than "How high?"

The symbiotic relationship between officialdom and the press has debased public discourse. We could call this process "linguicide"—the ongoing destruction of language as an instrument of meaning. Linguicide occurs when journalists say "tax reform" but actually mean huge giveaways to the wealthy. It occurs when an economic system dominated by gigantic monopolies is erroneously described as "free enterprise." Or when building new weapons of mass destruction is called "modernization" of a "deterrent." Or when a Central American government murders 50,000 of its own people, including priests and human rights monitors, but is routinely sanctified as a "democracy"—that, too, is an example of linguicide.

Ultimately, the denuding of issues is what linguicide is about: "news" as a hazy defoliant, stripping away substance. "Covering" current events, the media blanket is more opaque than translucent—smothering issues rather than ventilating them. Like the prisoners in Plato's cave who can see only flickering shadows on the wall, our picture of the world is filtered through the mass media and we are apt to mistake this distortion for reality.

Media governance

The examples and patterns of news bias documented in this book are not aberrations; they are fundamental to the political and economic system that sustains—and is sustained by—the mass media of the United States. A central function of the American press is to keep legitimizing the country's most powerful institutions, as exemplified by that post-Bush-inaugural headline on the front page of the *New York Times*—"The People, the Thousands, Get a Look at Their House." In this respect, certain "noncommercial" news programs provided by PBS and NPR can be particularly insidious, posing as alternatives without really fulfilling that function.

In projecting elite opinion, the U.S. press plays a crucial role in molding popular opinion; it serves as a channel that converts the former, however imprecisely, into the latter. And while mass media can't always dictate our political and social attitudes, they never stop telling us what our views supposedly are—or should be. *USA Today* has popularized the royal "We" in news headlines—"We like..." "We support..." "We're happy about..." etc.—keeping the public informed about the outlooks that constitute being in step.

American media are perhaps best understood as institutions of governance that have broken new ground in addressing what Aldous Huxley described as "the problem of making people love their servitude." That so many of us take for granted the freedom and independence of the U.S. press is an index of the extent to which we've become accustomed to a subtle kind of oppression.

If we're looking only for hard-as-nails prohibitions usually associated with despotism, we may not recognize the spikes being driven by familiar forces. Edward S. Herman and Noam Chomsky have pinpointed the dilemma in their book *Manufacturing Consent*: "In countries where the levers of power are in the hands of a state bureaucracy, the monopolistic control over the media, often supplemented by official censorship, makes it clear that the media serve the ends of a dominant elite. It is much more difficult to see a propaganda system at work where the media are private and formal censorship is absent. This is especially true where the media actively compete, periodically attack and expose corporate and governmental malfeasance, and aggressively portray themselves as spokesmen for free speech and the general community interest."

Are there contradictory aspects of mass media? Of course. The sheer volume of information conveyed by the press on a daily basis guarantees that fragments of the truth will keep surfacing; otherwise the facade of credibility would collapse. Vigorous journalism or vibrant artistry can pierce the veils of commercialism, but these are notable exceptions in a society inundated by mass-mediated themes. Something essential to journalism at its best—the courageous investigative passion that drove people like George Seldes, Lincoln Steffens, Ida Tarbell and I.F. Stone—is a conspicuous rarity.

The present-day horizons of American journalism are as truncated as its short paragraphs and brief sound bites. News reports offer glimpses of a wide world—but shredded, as if confetti for a tacit celebration of an "open" society that remains woefully insular and ill-informed. The most powerful restraints on reporters, internalized and implemented as self-censorship, are rooted in media ownership patterns. Stories that challenge official viewpoints or powerful vested interests are given short shrift by the mainstream press and thus have little impact, while policy-driven themes are hammered home over and over again until they become synonymous with public opinion. Amidst the incessant clatter of corporate and government PR machinery, dissenting voices are barely audible.

In *1984*, George Orwell described a society in which "it was seldom possible to follow a heretical thought further than the perception that it *was* heretical." Consider America's largest news magazines, with all their color-splashed glitz. The ultimate heresies—ideas which, if acted upon, could truly undermine the power of corporate empires such as Time Warner—are ignored, disparaged, misconstrued. Like other forms of mass media, the big newsweeklies are filled with propaganda salvos, expertly aimed and continuously fired; tracing the trajectories across slick pages, it is, indeed, "seldom possible to follow a heretical thought." When mega-media speak, most thinking is done—and the rest is relegated to the margins.

Oligarchy made easy

"The news media in America do not tell the American people that a political whip hangs over their head. That is because a political whip hangs over their head."

So wrote Walter Karp shortly before his death in 1989. He named mass media's most forbidden topic: "In the American republic the fact of oligarchy is the most dreaded knowledge of all, and our news keeps that knowledge from us. By their subjugation of the press, the political powers in America have conferred on themselves the greatest of political blessings—Gyges' ring of invisibility. And they have left the American people more deeply baffled by their own country's politics than any people on earth. Our public realm lies steeped in twilight, and we call that twilight news."

What Karp called the "invisibility" of American political power is a ghostly shield guarding against exposure and deflecting critical attacks. Major media steadfastly refuse to acknowledge what underlies so many reported events—"the fact of oligarchy." When brought to light, specific abuses come across as episodic—perhaps attributable to corrupt individuals in high places, but not the result of overall corporate domination.

Eager to please their bosses in an era of staff cutbacks and bottom-line budget slashing, journalists are integral to the closed loops of social denial. Thus we hear precious little about the fact that one percent of the population in the U.S. owns nearly one-half of the country's wealth, and one percent of all industrial corporations in America account for nearly 90 percent of total sales. It is seemingly taboo for journalists to examine the implications of such figures.

"Financial accumulation is admired," political scientist Paul Goldstene points out. "That it influences politics is dimly understood and vaguely resented: that economic concentration is, in fact, political power is understood by modern liberals hardly at all." But it is surely understood by today's media owners and their wealthy corporate brethren. Beholden most of all to big business, mass media mystify who controls what, how and why, taking people on detours every day—away from clarity about power in our society.

As Ben Bagdikian observed, "Monopolistic power dominates many other industries, and most of them enjoy special treatment by the government. But media giants have two enormous advantages: They control the public image of national leaders who, as a result, fear and favor the media magnates' political agendas; and they control the information and entertainment that help establish the social, political and cultural attitudes of increasingly larger populations." This built-in institutional bias "does more than merely protect the corporate system. It robs the public of a chance to understand the real world."

Rather than probing the extent to which U.S. corporations influence foreign policy, American media typically cover political developments abroad (revolutionary movements, military coups, etc.) as if they were divorced from economics. On the home front, there is hardly any in-depth reporting about what has caused the widening gap between rich and poor, of which millions of homeless Americans are only the most glaring symptom. And when the roots of social ills are obscured, people have a tendency to blame the victim or look for scapegoats; inevitably this fuels xenophobia and racial hatred.

"There is a fundamental contradiction between a corporately owned press and a press fulfilling its duties as a critical social institution," said Alexander Cockburn. But reporters are loath to explore this contradiction, preferring safer controversies that usually amount to pseudo-tempests in media teapots. Take, for example, the brouhaha over TV news "simulations." Widespread condemnation of this practice has been ironic, given that so much of the news blurs fact and fiction on a routine basis. When programs like CBS *Saturday Night With Connie Chung* air contrived footage of supposedly real events, they are re-enacting what happens regularly—albeit more subtly—on network news broadcasts.

The cross-hatch of video simulations and disinformation has spawned a new form of fakery—"disinfotainment." The term was coined by political satirist Paul Krassner in reference to the network trend toward docu-dramas (about Oliver North, Richard Nixon, etc.) and away from serious documentaries. "Disinfotainment" is a concept that may be applicable to ABC *World News Tonight*'s presentation of "hidden camera" surveillance pictures of an actor posing as Felix Bloch, a U.S. diplomat, handing a briefcase to another actor portraying a Soviet KGB agent. The voice-over by ABC national security correspondent John McWethy cited unnamed U.S. officials who claimed that Bloch had been photographed in a European capital delivering a briefcase to a Soviet spy. In real life, Bloch had not been charged with any crime.

Print media were especially self-righteous in their criticisms of ABC News. The *New York Times* declared that "the fakery insulted viewers, ethics and journalism." *USA Today* thundered against TV news simulations in an editorial with a stirring punch line: "Most newspapers, including *USA Today*, don't like distorting the facts. They have strict rules against tampering with the truth." Is such a statement deluded vanity or outright mendacity? Honest belief or conscious deception? In the semi-Orwellian world of present-day mass media, these possibilities are not mutually exclusive.

Democratizing the media

During a *Nightline* show in late 1989, Ted Koppel engaged in a bit of candor: "Is the news media reporting the news or simply playing the role of cheerleader? They call it pack journalism, instant consensus, the pied piper syndrome. Who sets the agenda for the American news media? Is it really a matter of independent news judgment or skillful manipulation by the White House?" Then came a frank admission: "We are a discouragingly timid lot. By we, I mean most television anchors and reporters and most of our colleagues of the establishment press... We tremble between daydreams of scooping all of our competitors and the nightmare of standing alone with our scoop for too long... People whose job it is to manipulate the media know this about us. They know that...many of us are truly only comfortable when we travel in a herd."

The herd of mainstream reporters is adept at steering clear of certain issues—most notably, the impact of concentrated corporate ownership on mass communications. Omitted, played down, painted in comforting hues, spun into benign shapes, above all, are basic facts about oligarchy and media power. On this subject, the traditional five "W"s of intrepid journalism—*Who? What? When? Where? Why?*—do not apply.

Mass media self-criticism may at times make salient points, but attacks on prerogatives of corporate ownership are almost never among them. Many pundits have played, in effect, "let's pretend"—that high-tech developments are not unfolding at the service of consolidated, centralized power. The best-selling predictions by futurist Alvin Toffler in the early 1980s discerned "a truly new era—the age of the de-massified media...instead of masses of people all receiving the same messages, smaller de-massified groups receive and send large amounts of their own imagery to one another." For good measure, Toffler contended that as a result "opinions on everything from pop music to politics are becoming less uniform."

But newer technologies like cable TV, which Toffler and others envisioned as forces for decentralizing mass media, are dominated by the same corporate clique. Although American citizens appear to be surrounded by an abundance of news sources, the range of cultural and political opinion deemed legitimate by information conglomerates is pathetically narrow. While paying lip-service to free speech and democratic values, modern-day press lords are, in Bagdikian's words, "just as ready as any dictatorship to suppress or de-emphasize news or entertainment that might seriously question their power."

It is no small irony that sizable outlets for dissident voices and alternative ideas are dwindling in the United States at a time when people in the Soviet Union and Eastern Europe are infused with vibrant debate about restructuring their societies. In covering these momentous changes abroad, American media have been quick to highlight the failures of centralized economic and political power in Communist countries. But silence reigns when it comes to discussing negative aspects of concentrated corporate power in the United States.

We face a formidable task of reinvigorating the First Amendment and promoting *glasnost* in this country when the mass media are controlled by a handful of corporate titans concerned most of all with boosting their profits. It is a sad but telling commentary that Philip Morris, a mammoth cigarette company, could pay the U.S. government $600,000 (quite a bargain) to feature the Bill of Rights in a slick ad campaign designed to polish the firm's nicotine-stained image. "The freedom to say and think what we believe... That's our birthright," the commercial declared, thereby reducing the principle of free speech to an advertising gimmick.

Such a travesty underscores the need to reclaim the airwaves as a public trust. Lest we forget, commercial broadcasters do not own the airwaves; they rent them. According to the Federal Communications Act, a broadcasting license can be revoked if a network fails to serve the "public interest." But this stipulation is never enforced because powerful groups prefer that it not be enforced. The same is true for antitrust regulations which, if applied, could require a company like General Electric to divest itself of NBC, or a monopolistic newspaper chain like Gannett to part with many of its holdings.

There was a time during the radio days of the 1930s when the corporate media monopoly was seriously challenged by a citizens movement led by parent-teacher groups, college presidents, librarians, union leaders and ministers. Decrying the commercialization of the airwaves, the public interest coalition rallied around a Senate bill known as the Wagner-Hatfield Amendment, which would have nullified all existing station licenses and allotted 25 percent of broadcast channels to "educational, religious, agricultural, labor, cooperative, and similar non-profit-making associations." Corporate broadcasters responded with a massive lobbying effort and the bill was defeated on the Senate floor.

Among those who supported this grassroots movement for more democratic media was the American philosopher John Dewey. In considering ways to challenge mass media bias, it is helpful to recall Dewey's essay "Our Un-Free Press," written in the mid-1930s. "The only really fundamental approach," Dewey argued, "is to enquire concerning the necessary effect of the present economic system upon the whole system of publicity... The question, under this mode of approach, is not how many specific abuses there are and how they may be remedied, but how far genuine intellectual freedom and social responsibility are possible on any large scheme under the existing economic regime."

Over 50 years later, American mass media are more powerful than ever before. While inextricably linked to big-money interests, today's information conglomerates are not completely immune to pressures from an aroused public. Attempts at reform should be pursued, but there are inherent limits as to how much press performance can improve when a small number of media corporations wield such enormous influence. This stifling power imbalance won't change until a broad-based democracy movement emerges in the United States on a scale comparable to recent popular upheavals in China and Eastern Europe. If that happens, it will be quite a story indeed.

A Call to Media Activism

Interview with Jeff Cohen

While the task of confronting the media establishment is a daunting one, we wrote this book in hopes that it would spur people to take action in behalf of more responsive and democratic media. Many individuals and organizations are already engaged in media activism. One of these is the media watch group FAIR (Fairness & Accuracy in Reporting). We asked Jeff Cohen, FAIR's founder and executive director, to discuss what active citizens can do to promote media pluralism.*

Q. In the face of concentrated media power, what can an individual do to make changes or improvements in the media?

A. The first thing to do is to snap out of the mode of passive media consumer. When you watch TV or read a newspaper, be alert and skeptical. In other words, don't take the media lying down. Be conscious of who the sponsors and advertisers are. Remember when you're watching NBC, you're watching the network owned by GE. Remember that the other broadcast networks and mass publications are owned by big business. And remember who doesn't own or sponsor the news. When you see a report about a labor/management dispute, for example, be conscious that no unions own any daily papers or TV stations.

If you're informed about the impact of media ownership, pass on your knowledge to friends, family, co-workers—because it's not the kind of information they'll readily pick up from *Newsweek* or *Nightline*.

Besides watching and reading the news in an alert fashion, take action. Become an active citizen who speaks up. Write letters and make calls to the media, both local and national. If, for example, you see a news story on an NBC station involving General Electric, contact the station or the network to ask why the viewers were not informed that GE owns NBC. The question can be phrased simply: "Our society demands that politicians and government officials disclose their financial involvements; why shouldn't the media disclose theirs?"

---

*The authors have been associated with FAIR in various capacities. Martin Lee is the publisher of FAIR's journal, *Extra!* Norman Solomon has been FAIR's Washington coordinator, and is a member of its advisory board.

If you support equality for women and you regularly watch a TV news panel show which rarely includes women as panelists, contact the program's producers to ask why they're having so much trouble finding women experts. Ask the editors of opinion pages why there are so few women writing political columns. Opponents of racism should be asking similar questions of media forums which typically exclude racial minorities. Individuals concerned about the environment, consumer rights or other causes should be complaining directly to media outlets which exclude their advocates. The media always tell us what a great pluralistic society we have. We won't see this wonderful diversity reflected in the news media until they begin to hear from an aroused public. Until then, the viewpoints of conservative elites will continue to dominate the news.

Q. Can anyone challenge the media, or does one need special expertise?

A. Anyone who's read this book has the expertise to challenge media practices. If you regularly read a certain newspaper or watch a certain news program, you have a right and a duty to talk back to the journalists who put out that paper or program. Media managers are counting on people to be intimidated by their assertion of authority. It's clear that those who own the media would rather have us be a nation of mindless consumers than a nation of active citizens. But if you're the kind of person who believes you can fight City Hall—and victories by community activists across the country have proven it—then you should also be talking back to the media. Media outlets, like City Hall, are political institutions. You don't have to be a communications professor to talk back to the media any more than you need be a political scientist to take on City Hall.

Q. What's the evidence the media will listen to an aroused public?

A. There's evidence the media listen quite closely. Many of those who work in the media see themselves as "majoritarians"—offering the stories and opinion that most viewers or readers want. Media owners and journalists are aware that media outlets are businesses selling access to their viewers or readers. More than news and entertainment, what they're selling is advertising time or space to corporations seeking customers. It is very important for them to attract and keep viewers and readers so that advertisers will buy ads.

But the media have not heard enough from thoughtful individuals demanding tough journalism and wide-ranging discussions of the issues. Instead, they've heard thunderous clamor from well-organized right-wing and religious fringe groups. With a few thousand letter-writers, these groups have sought to convince the media that the public is dominated by conservatives who want censorship and conformity.

Q. How much success have these right-wing groups had in moving the media?

A. These groups made a big impact up through their heyday in the early 1980s, getting independent journalists muzzled and getting adventurous TV programs killed. But their power is waning. While they still can get the attention of conservative media owners, their intimidation tactics have begun to backfire with members of the working press. Journalists have learned that these groups, with their orchestrated campaigns using pre-printed post cards, usually represent a narrow fringe. A PBS programmer told me she came to realize that the right-wingers calling to harangue her about this or that documentary had rarely seen the program they were complaining about.

Q. How can people who want to lodge complaints with the media distinguish themselves from the organized right-wing fringe?

A. That's easy. First, contact the media only about stories or programs or issues you're actually familiar with. Second, don't join the right wing in calling for censorship of viewpoints you disagree with. At FAIR, we advocate for the inclusion of new, balancing viewpoints, not the exclusion of old, conservative ones. In other words, don't ask TV networks to cancel their many shows offering the business agenda; instead, ask for new programs offering the balancing agendas of other constituencies—civil rights, ecology, labor, consumers, etc. Don't ask that TV networks or op-ed pages censor the voices of hard-line conservatives like William Buckley, Patrick Buchanan, Robert Novak and all the rest. Instead ask them to open their pages and airwaves to the balancing voices of outspoken, unapologetic progressives. Fighting to get new voices into the media, fighting for free speech and an invigorated First Amendment, is exhilarating; working to silence someone is censorial and depressing.

Finally, avoid the right wing's intimidation tactics. An ABC News staffer told me of an incident in which a right-wing "watchdog" made a haranguing phone call to a network producer's hospital room hours after he emerged from intensive care. Don't harass people. Try to gain the respect of media professionals, to win them over through persuasion and documentation. Remember there are still some reporters who are respectful of the old journalistic ethic: "Dig out and present the facts no matter whom it offends." These people in the working press, not the media owners, are the public's natural allies. They need to hear from us, and know that we're out here. Hopefully, it will embolden them to fight more resolutely for controversial stories or viewpoints.

Q. What's the evidence that there's a split between the working press and the higher-ups?

A. One of the best pieces of evidence is the 1985 survey commissioned by the Associated Press Managing Editors which found two distinct types of journalists in the mainstream media. Those at the higher levels of their newspapers, labeled the "older natives," tended to hold conservative views—believing that there was too much investigative journalism, too much negative news. On the other hand, rank-and-file members of the working press, labeled the "younger transients," believed the press was not aggressive enough, particularly when it came to covering wealthy, conservative elites. So it's obvious that those of us who want a more aggressive press should be cultivating and supporting this type of rank-and-file journalist.

Owners and managers ultimately call the shots at any corporate institution. But the day-to-day work at media outlets is carried out by journalistic hired-hands. The news staffs have influence. They make certain decisions. Media businesses, even more than other businesses, are not monolithic institutions. There are good, ethical people working at every media outlet...even the ones taken over by conglomerates. In fact, I've yet to come across an NBC News staffer who's expressed happiness that his or her boss is GE.

Q. What specific requests or demands can an individual make in the interests of media pluralism?

A.   That answer is as varied and diverse as the American public. It depends on what issues concern the individual. Women and minorities should be demanding greater representation at every level of the media—from hosts and panelists on news talkshows, to expert sources quoted in news stories, to reporters and columnists. If white men had a lock on wisdom, our country wouldn't have the problems it does. There is no more democratic demand than the one calling for new and diverse voices to be heard in the media. This demand has been winning out throughout Eastern Europe. We should bring it home.

If you are a member of a labor union, you might ask your local daily why the paper has a business section but no labor section. One could argue that labor, not business, represents the bulk of active participants in our economy. If there is regular space for the latest news from the world of business and finance, why is no space set aside for the world of labor, and issues like child care, parental leave, job stress, health insurance, the decline in real wages of the average worker, factory closings, job sharing between spouses, and other developments affecting millions of Americans? Why are there dozens of syndicated columnists who regularly promote the positions of groups like the Chamber of Commerce and National Association of Manufacturers, but not one columnist who can be clearly identified with the positions of the labor movement? Why are there numerous national TV talkshows on business, and not one on labor? (In England, one of the major TV networks offers a regular labor show.) The demand should be for some semblance of balance.

These same questions about the predominance of pro-business columnists, business sections in newspapers and business programs on TV, can be raised by those concerned about the environment or consumer rights. Media managers are very big on studying demographics; yet they have largely ignored

polls showing protection of the environment to be among the biggest concerns Americans have. It's not a fringe issue. Why isn't there a single weekly
show on national TV devoted to the environmental agenda?

Syndicated columnists are famous for grinding axes: Patrick Buchanan
crusaded for individuals accused of Nazi war crimes; George Will was a
trumpeter for nuclear power; Abe Rosenthal took on the cause of the Afghan
mujahadeen, while Charles Krauthammer carried a torch for the Nicaraguan
contras. Why is there no recognizable columnist, published in hundreds of
papers like Buchanan and Will, who is known as the consumer rights advocate or the environmental crusader?

It's questions of balance like these that we should be asking.

*Q. Besides issues of balancing viewpoints, what are the kinds of questions
people ought to be raising about the way news is reported?*

A. I know of dozens of changes made because FAIR members or
unaffiliated individuals communicated one-on-one with journalists by letter
or phone. Again it depends on what issues concern you. Feminists have been
challenging TV news programs for adopting a graphic image straight from
the "right-to-life" movement. It's that graphic which appears behind the TV
anchors as they announce that day's news from the abortion battle: a (seemingly 11-month-old) fetus floating in space, unconnected to a woman's body.
Feminists say abortion is a woman's issue and a woman's choice, but there's
no woman to be found in the picture. The image also distorts reality since
over 90 percent of abortions occur within the first three months of pregnancy.

During the 1988 campaign, journalists regularly hung the "special interests" label on the Democratic Party's mass constituencies—blacks, women,
labor unionists, environmental activists—without ever hanging the negative
label on the corporate interests in either party. It was often done without mal-
ice or premeditation. After the bias was pointed out to them, several journalists at the *New York Times* and the *Christian Science Monitor* reappraised
their use of the label.

In covering political campaigns, journalists always report how much
money each candidate has raised (as if money-raising were a measure of
merit), but rarely do they tell us where the money has come from. Which
special interests are behind which candidate is important information to a
voter. And it's available to reporters on forms filed with election offices.
Activists have had success demanding that the media report not just the "how
much" of campaign finances but the "from whom."

Active media watchers have also complained about the "no culprits, no
solutions" style of journalism found in many reports on the environment or
poverty. In this type of journalism, reporters thoroughly lay out a problem,
then throw up their hands in desperation at the possibility of a
solution—carefully avoiding the issues of who caused the mess and what

solutions are being proposed by independent, public interest experts. An environmental problem is often detailed; the polluters who caused it aren't named. The increasing homeless population is dramatically shown; how Reagan/Bush housing policies contributed to the problem is avoided. Upon seeing this type of report, activists should contact the media outlet demanding a follow-up story that names names and offers solutions. A letter-to-the-editor which commends the reporter for thoroughly describing the problem, and then goes on to offer a strong view on who is to blame or what is to be done, may get published.

This type of "good but go further" letter raises another important point: Don't just complain to journalists! Commend them when they deserve it. Let them know when you've been informed or enlightened by their work. Media professionals appreciate compliments from the public. And it may make them more receptive the next time you have a beef.

Q. Which raises the question of the tone of one's communications with the media.

A. Whenever possible, try to offer constructive criticism. If you contact a media outlet to complain about the narrow range of sources or viewpoints which it presents, give the names of individuals or groups whose views you want to see reflected in that media.

If you're involved in the peace movement and you see a foreign policy story in a local newspaper or on a TV station based exclusively on official U.S. sources, contact the reporters—even if it means calling Washington—and ask if they are aware that a leading academic or peace spokesperson is located in their hometown ready to offer a differing view. Suggest that the next time they do a story heavily based on official sources, they seek out this policy critic for a balancing perspective.

When you criticize reporters or news editors, do so on the basis that they've fallen short of their professed standards of neutrality, balance and independence from the state—not that they have lousy politics. You're not trying to convince them to adopt your advocacy position but to consult and quote experts with these perspectives as sources in their reporting.

Q. What can people do to get media outlets to reveal their potential conflicts-of-interest?

A. Progress will be slow on this front until the media hear from more of the public. In April 1987, after GE acquired NBC, the network aired a pro-nuclear power documentary about France's nuclear industry. In FAIR's view, Tom Brokaw should have made a disclosure when he introduced the program, such as: "NBC's corporate parent, GE, has substantial investments in nuclear power, but the work on this documentary was done by NBC News alone." After the documentary aired, I called NBC and asked a veteran news producer to comment on whether such a brief disclaimer would have been appropriate. He gave it some thought and replied: "Good idea. Absolutely." When it dawned on him that he could get into trouble if such a quote appeared in print, he called me back, begged me not to use it, and pleaded that I get a comment instead from a corporate spokesperson. When I did, I got a platitude about the disclaimer being unnecessary since "the news division operates independently of our parent."

NBC and other media simply haven't heard enough complaints about the "C" word: Conflict-of-interest. Henry Kissinger, for example, is a walking, talking conflict-of-interest. He appeared repeatedly on TV to apologize for the Chinese government in the months following the Tiananmen Square crackdown on pro-democracy protesters without mention of his various economic ventures with China. Like so many other veterans of the "defense establishment," Kissinger has numerous entanglements with foreign governments and multinational corporations. But in their regular appearances on TV to pontificate about foreign policy, these men are introduced only as former secretaries of state or defense...as if they hold no current jobs or board memberships that the viewer need be informed of.

Q. Do letters-to-the-editor really matter?

A. Informed, non-hysterical letters can matter, and they need not be published to have impact. Sometimes your letter will be passed on to the relevant journalists at a media outlet even if it's not published. If you take the time to write a letter, send copies of it to two or three places within that media outlet—perhaps to the reporter, his or her immediate editor, as well as the letters-to-the-editor department.

If media outlets get letters from a dozen people raising the same issue, they may tend to publish one or two of them. If, instead, they receive only one or two total, they may just toss them in the trash, figuring, "No big issue here." So even if your letter doesn't get into print, it may help another one with a similar point-of-view get published. Surveys of newspaper readers show that the letters page is among the most closely-read parts of the paper.

Q. What other kinds of "free media" can people make use of?

A. Besides letters-to-the-editor, don't forget call-ins to radio and TV talkshows. An articulate advocate calling in for two minutes on a radio talk show will be listened to more closely than the station manager reading another boring editorial. When you're turning the radio dial and you stumble across someone talking passionately about an issue, you tend to stop and listen.

Unfortunately, public interest folks often believe that call-ins and other "free media" are beneath them. Meanwhile, it seems to be a requirement of membership in certain right-wing groups to write letters-to-the-editor or make call-ins to talkshows every day about the commie conspiracy.

It's true that right-wingers dominate as hosts of radio talkshows, but they need controversy and they'll often let you finish your sentences when you call in. I know from my guest appearances on even the craziest right-wing talkshows that there are open-minded people in the audience. Some listen because they "love to hate" the host.

And don't forget to call-in to the better quality talk shows—for example, on C-SPAN cable TV or Larry King's national shows on radio and CNN.

Q. Speaking of cable TV, what about free media there?

A. Even though the cable industry has been taken over by the same companies that own the broadcast industry, in many locales there is still "public access," where community groups can put on their own TV programs. Union activists have programs in various cities. So do peace and environmental groups. Cable companies in some places are trying to extinguish public access channels, so activists are fighting to save them. In most places it's virtually free. Often there are long waiting lists, but once you get your turn, you're given a program, cameras, and you can put almost anything on the air. Thanks to "Paper Tiger/Deep Dish TV" in New York and other non-profit producers [see Appendix C], there's alternative programming you can get, add a local focus to, and plug into your time slot.

Q. Most of what you've been talking about is individual action. What action can groups take?

A. Organizations are in a more powerful position to dialogue with media. Various groups—feminist, peace, civil rights—have set up projects to monitor media coverage of issues concerning them. Some groups focus their scrutiny on the biggest media outlet in town. Other groups have divided up the media so that each news outlet is scrutinized by at least some of their members.

In the early 1980s, the Machinists Union involved its membership in an eye-opening project monitoring the way workers and unions were represented on national TV. They found that production workers were usually denigrated, that prostitutes were 16 times more likely to appear on TV than mine workers, and that fashion models were ten times more prevalent than farm workers.

After a period of monitoring, your group should approach the media to discuss ways coverage could be improved or made more balanced. If you can link up with other groups that have similar criticisms of the media outlet you're targeting, consider approaching that outlet as a coalition. You'll have more clout.

Even without having done organized monitoring, if you do represent a group with dozens or hundreds of members, make sure you point this out in your communications with media—whether for publication or not.

Q. How do media activists get the information they need to stay on top of the issues?

A. A key part of media activism is informing oneself, and helping others to inform themselves. Active citizens must look beyond corporate-generated news and seek out alternative sources of information. Many cities and towns have alternative weekly or monthly newspapers owned locally and independently, not by big, distant corporations. Alternative weeklies include the *L.A. Weekly*, *San Francisco Bay Guardian*, Detroit's *Metro Times* and Phoenix's *New Times*. The Association of Alternative Newsweeklies [see Appendix C] will tell you of such a publication near you.

Pacifica Radio, with listener-sponsored stations in Berkeley, Los Angeles, New York, Washington, D.C., and Houston, calls itself America's Free Speech network. Since the 1950s, Pacifica has been an adjunct to every movement for change—civil rights, peace, labor, civil liberties, feminism, gay rights, ecology. During the Reagan era when the FCC opened the way to unprecedented media mergers in the name of small government, it continued to investigate and harass Pacifica stations over the content of their programming. The FCC has been a Big Brother growling at Pacifica, and a little kitten purring at the media conglomerates.

Dozens of community and public radio stations air some Pacifica programs. But most NPR-affiliated stations don't air any. If you're a loyal listener to a public radio station, make sure it avails itself of Pacifica programming. Many community and public stations are underfunded or otherwise in need of innovative programs. Pacifica maintains a huge radio archive and program service in North Hollywood, California. Other alternative radio programs are the Philadelphia-based *Consider the Alternatives* which emphasizes peace and justice issues; the D.C.-based *New Voices Radio* which focuses on public interest activism; the investigative program *Undercurrents* out of New York which specializes in issues such as CIA and FBI abuse, covert action and the Third World; and *American Dialogues*, hosted by actor/director Robert Foxworth [see Appendix C].

Q. Are you including NPR as an alternative news source?

A. Not so much lately. Despite in-depth reports that won't be found on mainstream radio, NPR news shows like *All Things Considered* and *Morning Edition* have softened over the years, losing their independent tone. Increasingly, NPR relies on the same established sources as the corporate networks, and looks to the same tired pundits. In places where NPR has been the only alternative, it amassed an extremely loyal listenership. But many listeners have grown disaffected as it's moved to the mainstream. The good news is that many news staffers came to NPR because they saw themselves as independent journalists and they may be very open to constructive criticism from the public. NPR is dependent on the support of its loyal listeners. Instead of complaining to FAIR, I wish NPR listener/supporters would spend more time communicating their complaints directly to NPR's staff.

Q. What do you tell people in cities or towns that have neither an alternative weekly nor access to Pacifica radio programs?

A. If there are no local alternative outlets, active citizens can at least work to insure that national alternative media are available locally. Work closely with your public or university library system; librarians are generally open to appeals to diversity and balance. Make sure that alongside conservative, corporate magazines like *Time* and *Newsweek*, there are progressive, non-corporate (or anti-corporate) publications. *The Nation*, a New York-based weekly which has been publishing for 125 years, and *The Progressive*, a Madison, Wisconsin-based monthly which has been publishing for over 80 years, are both indexed in the *Reader's Guide to Periodical Literature*. If these magazines are not in your local library, you should ask why.

Reader's Digest is in virtually every library; you should encourage libraries to also subscribe to the fast-growing (200,000 circulation) *Utne Reader*, which is the digest of the alternative press. Another publication that should be in your library is *Mother Jones*, a magazine that has exposed countless scandals, including the unsafe design of the Ford Pinto, and the corporate practice of "dumping" unsafe products on developing countries after they've been banned in the U.S.

Many libraries receive the right-wing *National Review*; there is no reason they shouldn't also get national left-wing newspapers like *In These Times* or the *Guardian*. If your library carries religious publications, see if they will carry progressive journals such as the weekly *National Catholic Reporter*, the Protestant monthly *Sojourners*, or the Jewish bimonthly *Tikkun*.

If you're interested in labor issues, make sure that your local library has some labor-oriented publications to complement all the business publications. Civil rights advocates and feminists should request publications that cover their issues. We are all "consumers"; make sure your library carries not only *Consumer Reports*, which helps us decide what to buy, but publications like the monthly *Public Citizen*, launched by Ralph Nader, which informs consumers about how to act politically to expand their rights.

Remember: You're not demanding that the library convert to militant advocacy of any cause; you're simply asking for balance and diversity. These same appeals should be made to your local bookstores or magazine stands. There are magazine distributors in various locales who specialize in disseminating alternative publications to newsstands and stores.

If you're the kind of person who makes call-ins to talkshows, get in the habit of naming the alternative media that helped you learn things that weren't in the mainstream news. Alternative publications can use the free publicity since they don't have the ad budgets of *Time* or *Newsweek*.

Q. Explain what FAIR is.

A. FAIR is the media watch group that challenges the narrowing range of news and views presented by the corporate-owned media. We educate the public about who owns the media. We've worked hard to let the average American know that GE owns NBC. But we don't just educate; we also agitate. FAIR and its members fight so that public interest voices—peace spokespersons, consumer advocates, environmentalists, social justice activists—get access to the media.

FAIR is an anti-censorship organization, meaning we confront the main culprits of censorship in U.S. society: the corporations that own the media. Unlike some other countries, censorship in the U.S. is caused less by government or religion than by business interests. Not surprisingly this kind of censorship is not recognized as such by the media. When Warner executives ordered the destruction of thousands of copies of a book criticizing U.S. foreign policy, there was no outcry in the U.S. media. This was just a business prerogative exercised by corporate managers. If Soviet state publishers or the ayatollahs of Iran had destroyed books, U.S. media would have taken umbrage. FAIR exists so that when journalists or authors or viewpoints are suppressed, the American public hears about it.

Q. Can you give an example?

A. FAIR waged a campaign on behalf of a hard-hitting documentary about the religious right, *Thy Kingdom Come, Thy Will Be Done*, after PBS executives had shelved it for mysterious reasons during the height of the Jim and Tammy Bakker scandal. We screened the film in front of overflow audiences. We sent letters and petitions to PBS. Our campaign provoked articles in publications like *TV Guide* and the *Los Angeles Times*. After a few months, PBS executives took the documentary off the shelf. The film's producer is convinced that if it weren't for FAIR, his film would not have aired on PBS.

Q. How does FAIR distinguish itself from all the right-wing media watchdogs that came before it?

A. Watch "dog" is the proper term since the purpose of these right-wing groups is to "hound" independent journalists and to "bark" up the wrong tree. Groups like AIM (Accuracy In Media) are funded by oil and chemical companies, for example, to harass journalists who dare to produce stories critical of those industries. AIM went positively mad in support of the pesticide industry after *60 Minutes* aired reports on the dangers of Alar, the chemical additive used on apples. The best thing one can say about AIM is that they call attention to the fact that some journalists, too few for our liking,

persist in the face of great obstacles to get stories out which offend government or corporate power. Journalists are correct to see it as a badge of honor
if AIM or similar groups attack them.

FAIR, on the other hand, sees itself as an ally of the working press and of
independent journalism. When reporters get muzzled, when their stories get
censored or watered down, we do our best to turn a spotlight on the abuse
and support the reporter. There's a New York-based group, the Committee to
Protect Journalists—whose board includes media heavyweights like Walter
Cronkite and Dan Rather—which scours the globe documenting instances
when reporters are censored, jailed or murdered. Reporters are rarely jailed
or murdered in the United States. But FAIR was once approached by people
active in the Newspaper Guild, a union that represents reporters, for advice
in setting up a "committee to protect journalists" here at home from political
censorship or harassment by their bosses. Such a group is needed.

Q. What triggered the birth of FAIR?

A.   FAIR was formed in mid-1986 as the media were continuing to drift
rightward, ownership was becoming more and more concentrated, right-wing
watchdogs were increasingly vociferous and the exclusion of progressive
viewpoints was reaching absurd proportions.

Media treatment—or mistreatment—of the nuclear freeze movement was
key in bringing FAIR into existence. It was an appalling example of media
exclusion. The movement for a bilateral nuclear weapons freeze was
arguably the biggest grassroots movement of the 1980s with many thousands
of volunteers working in hundreds of groups across the country, spearheaded
by national organizations with recognizable national leaders. But in those
rare instances when the freeze was debated on national television, the people
chosen to debate on behalf of the freeze were defense establishment "moderates" like former Secretary of Defense Robert McNamara and former CIA
chief William Colby. These guys were deemed the "responsible" freeze
spokespersons by the media, and the actual freeze leaders who'd built this
huge movement—many of whom were women—were rarely heard from on
national TV. They were locked out of the national debate, unable to speak for
themselves. That kind of exclusion hurt the freeze movement, and played a
big role in the birth of FAIR.

Q. Has FAIR found allies on the exclusion issue?

A.   Yes, TV critics for major dailies have increasingly joined us in criticizing TV news shows for offering as experts "all the usual suspects" from conservative elites. TV critics complain that the Tube's narrow spectrum of
experts is not only bad for democratic discourse, it's horribly boring television. FAIR calls it the Kissinger-Haig syndrome—the belief in TV news that
you've fully covered a foreign policy issue if you've had Kissinger dis-

cussing with Haig whether they agree with Brzezinski. When military or
weapons issues are discussed, we want to see debates between officials from
the Defense Department and spokespersons for peace groups like
SANE/Freeze or Greenpeace. On nuclear power issues, representatives from
GE and Westinghouse should square off against representatives from Ralph
Nader's Critical Mass Project. These kinds of discussions would more fully
ventilate an issue, and would be exciting, democratic television.

*Q. What if the establishment representatives won't agree to face their tough-
est critics on TV?*

A.   Leave an empty chair with GE's name on it. Let the critics of GE or of
nuclear power have a full show to themselves two or three times, and I pre-
dict the establishment voices will come running back to debate on future
shows. The better TV public affairs shows—such as PBS's *Kwitny Report*
and the New York PBS show *The Eleventh Hour*—have not allowed establishment guests to exercise veto power over who their debating opponents
will be. At these programs, journalists decide who the best advocates are for
each side. This is not the case at programs like *Nightline* where powerful
guests have refused to go on the air with certain critics and the producers
have reacted by either dropping the critic or scurrying around to find an
"acceptable"—often meaning wimpy—opponent. In these cases, journalists
have surrendered their responsibility over the program to the powers that be.
Elliott Abrams, the Reagan aide who admitted lying to Congress about
Central America, is one official the media bowed down to when he refused to
face certain opponents in debate.

*Q. Given that conservative corporations like GE and AT&T sponsor these
programs, and given the other pressures being exerted to exclude anti-estab-
lishment guests, how can you be confident that things will change?*

A.   Because I believe the frustration level is at a breaking point. Something
has to give. Nothing's more frustrating than being locked out. Look at recent
history: being locked out of society's mainstream is what produced the powerful civil rights and feminist movements. FAIR is part of a new movement
protesting another lock-out: the virtual exclusion of public interest leaders
from mainstream TV. This new movement for an open, pluralistic media is
just beginning to take off.

Consider the huge reaction to FAIR's study, "Are You on the *Nightline*
Guest List?"—which showed that the country's most influential news show
generally favored white, male conservatives while generally excluding
women, people of color, progressives and public interest leaders. Individuals
and groups across the country are distributing the report. It's been requested
by libraries, universities, foreign news outlets. On the day it was released,

U.S. dailies gave it major, sympathetic coverage...some to the point of ridiculing *Nightline*. The mainstream daily in Bethlehem, Pennsylvania, ran a wire story about FAIR's study with a photo of Ted Koppel seated next to Kermit the Frog [*Nightline* once used the Muppets to explain economics], and the photo's caption read, "Ted Koppel during a rare appearance with a minority group member." While that caption was a bit of a low blow, it highlights the fact that when persuasion and documentation are insufficient to end media censorship, ridicule and public embarrassment may become effective tools.

Originally, FAIR was just a research and educational project. We've become a membership organization due to popular demand. So things are growing.

Q. For a group set up to criticize the media, doesn't FAIR have a lot of friends in the media?

A. That was a conscious strategy of ours, in keeping with our view that the media are not monolithic, and that many in the working press are FAIR's potential allies. Our common foe is media conglomeration and callous media owners.

FAIR's goal from the beginning has been to critique the media in the pages and airwaves of the biggest media we could fight our way into. Since a number of media professionals believe FAIR offers constructive, well-documented criticism, they've seen to it that our views have been heard. We've appeared on leading TV news and talk shows; our columns are sometimes published in major dailies.

Progressive media criticism had for too long been marginalized in undercirculated books or magazines. FAIR has put this critique directly under the noses of the mainstream journalists. Our publication, *Extra!*, is widely read at some national media; I've been told that friends at certain outlets leave copies of *Extra!* in the lavatories near the newsrooms. FAIR staffers got to know some media employees by meeting them at picket lines when they went on strike against the TV networks in the wake of the corporate takeovers.

One strategy for getting our message out is to critique Media A in Media B, and then turn around and expose Media B in Media A. FAIR's criticism of television, for example, has been well covered in newspapers. When we wanted to publicize our critique of the conservative "aditorials" which Mobil Oil pays for in various publications, we wrote a critical opinion column and sent it to the secondary papers in cities where the primary daily accepted the Mobil ads. The *New York Times* runs the ads; *New York Newsday* ran our critique of the ads. The *Los Angeles Times* runs the ads; the *Los Angeles Herald* ran our column. [Unfortunately, the *Herald* no longer provides an alternative to the *Los Angeles Times* since it folded in 1989.]

Q. What if well-documented criticism, even ridicule, doesn't work in bringing change?

A. Treat the media like you would any other political institution—whether it be City Hall or a company polluting your neighborhood. If dialogue doesn't work, there are many lawful, nonviolent ways of escalating one's tactics. Public demonstrations often focus attention on a problem. In Los Angeles, FAIR set up a picket line outside KABC to protest its lineup which featured the views of a right-wing commentator unbalanced by a partisan of the left. Picketers carried signs: "You can't fly a plane with just a right wing." KABC savaged the protest, but the newspapers gave it major coverage, and we were invited to debate the issue on the talkshows.

There have been spirited demonstrations outside the *New York Times* in protest of that paper's party-line coverage of Central America. A favorite slogan has been: "Two-four-six-eight...Separate the press and state." Picket lines have been most successful in the late afternoon when news staffers are leaving work. At a demonstration protesting *Times* coverage of El Salvador, dozens of protesters chanted "Remember Ray Bonner!" upon seeing Abe Rosenthal scurrying from the *Times* front door toward his waiting limousine. Rosenthal was the executive editor who removed Bonner from Salvador after his reporting on death squads had offended the White House.

Q. What about the tactic of boycotting sponsors to put pressure on a particular TV program?

A. We've avoided it because it's a tactic that smacks of censorship and has long been associated with right-wing and religious fanatics. Right-wing groups, because of their ideological closeness to certain corporate sponsors, have an easier time getting their attention. FAIR operates differently: we take our complaints directly to the media, directly to the journalists. We haven't brought sponsors into our disputes with the media, nor have we brought in the state. Our commitment to civil liberties makes us wary of tactics aimed at punishing a TV program for airing a point of view we find offensive. Instead of working to suppress a program, our demand is for a new program offering a balancing view. Not less speech, but more.

Q. Explain FAIR's position on PBS.

A. PBS is one of FAIR's main targets. It calls itself "public broadcasting" but tends to take the public for granted while catering to big business. PBS is the TV network most vulnerable to public pressure because about one-third of its funding comes from individual members...the same amount it receives from corporations. As PBS executives know very well, most of these individual donations are not coming from right-wingers. They come from progressives, non-conformists and others who want a real alternative to the corporate-owned networks. If PBS does not move quickly to broaden its weekly public affairs lineup, there will be a massive walkaway by the public.

Hundreds of individuals across the country have notified PBS stations that they will not renew their PBS memberships until it takes steps to end the conservative, pro-corporate slant of its public affairs talkshows.

Each and every week, PBS stations air three programs hosted by editors connected to the same right-wing magazine, the *National Review*. I'm speaking of William Buckley's *Firing Line* and John McLaughlin's *One on One* and the *McLaughlin Group*. A fourth weekly show, *American Interests*, is hailed by PBS as the only show devoted exclusively to foreign affairs; it's hosted by foreign policy hawk Morton Kondracke. In the interests of balance, FAIR is demanding that PBS launch at least one weekly show hosted by a progressive. Pressure from PBS members has moved the programming executives on this issue—at first, they claimed that the talkshow lineup didn't create a balance problem, later saying that the network would be very open to a progressive-oriented show if funding could be found. A big "if" given the conservative, corporate interests that fund so much PBS programming. FAIR has urged PBS executives to go out and help find the funding for such a show.

PBS also airs three regular programs offering the business agenda: *Wall $treet Week* hosted by conservative Louis Rukeyser, *Adam Smith's Money World*, and the *Nightly Business Report*. Yet PBS does not air one weekly show presenting the agendas of public interest constituencies—consumer rights, environment, labor—which often conflict with big business. FAIR is asking PBS to air a weekly "public interest show."

Q. What are the chances that PBS will broaden its lineup?

A. Chances are better. Executives at PBS and local public stations have been hearing these complaints from their members for so long they know the complaints will not soon be going away. If changes aren't made, their members will go away.

PBS did add two bold programs to its weekly lineup: *South Africa Now* and the *Kwitny Report*, probably TV's toughest investigative news program. Both shows regularly brought stories to TV that aired nowhere else. Both shows have been plagued by funding problems which have put their futures in jeopardy. In city after city, grassroots advocacy from PBS members and media activists helped convince local PBS stations to carry these programs.

Q. What about the political talkshow lineup on Ted Turner's CNN?

A. It offers the same center-to-right spectrum as PBS. Ted Turner is a maverick media owner in that he sometimes speaks out on environmental and world peace issues, but there's nothing original about CNN's talkshow lineup. Opponents of the environmental and peace movements are everywhere on CNN, proponents nowhere. Right-winger Patrick Buchanan co-hosts *Crossfire* every night, and hosts *Capital Gang* every week. Right-winger Robert Novak and sidekick Rowland Evans host a weekly CNN show, while Novak is a panelist and producer on *Capital Gang*.

Who represents the "left" on *Capital Gang*? People like Al Hunt, Washington bureau chief of the *Wall Street Journal*. Who represents the "left" on *Crossfire*? For years, it was the unrepentant CIA official Tom Braden; now it's Michael Kinsley from the centrist *New Republic* magazine, who admits that he's not a reliable advocate for the left.

FAIR's beef with CNN is not that there are too many rightists, but that there are no genuine left advocates—besides the fact that all these hosts and panelists are white men. CNN apparently allowed Patrick Buchanan to veto potential *Crossfire* co-hosts who would have more forcefully represented the opposite pole. And with the likes of Bob Novak producing the *Capital Gang*, it's no wonder that a *Wall Street Journal* bureau chief represents the "left wing."

One of FAIR's goals is to end TV's censorship of the left end of the political spectrum, and to break the taboo against genuine left partisans hosting national TV programs. CNN's Ted Turner, and network executives at PBS and elsewhere will be hearing these complaints until the censorship ends.

Q. What are FAIR's short-term targets and long-term campaigns?

A.   In the short term, we will maintain our focus on programs like the *MacNeil/Lehrer NewsHour* and *Nightline* until they end their virtual exclusion of public interest leaders, progressives, women and people of color as guests. And until these groups are allowed to host and produce their own programs and talkshows, we will continue to pressure PBS, CNN and the other networks.

In terms of news reporting, FAIR's immediate goal is to mobilize citizens to demand that reporters cease their over-reliance on official sources. Major public interest groups—whether environmental, consumer rights, public safety, women's rights or whatever—work closely with technical experts, economists, scientists. These are sources of information the American people must be allowed to hear. Can journalists trust public interest experts to dispense accurate information? History shows—from Vietnam to Watergate to Irangate—that it would be difficult to find sources any more deceptive and duplicitous than the official sources journalists have relied on for so long. FAIR is asking for some *glasnost* in U.S. journalism. If there's "new thinking" going on in our country, we tell journalists, it's quite possible they won't find it in Washington or on Wall Street.

As a nationwide movement of media activists reaches a certain critical mass, FAIR will consider long-term campaigns aimed at a democratic restructuring of the media. One campaign might call for a total restructuring—and refinancing—of public broadcasting in an effort to establish several well-funded public TV and radio networks, serving all sectors of our pluralistic society, and run by journalists and programmers insulated from undue government and corporate pressure. Western Europe offers models for such a system. Plentiful funding for truly public broadcasting could come from a variety of sources: a tax on imports and factory sales of radios, TVs and VCRs; a tax on TV and radio commercials; a fee charged to private broadcast owners when they acquire or renew their licenses from the federal government.

Governing bodies for public broadcasting would be chosen not just from corporate elites, but from a wide spectrum of Americans. Programming would have one mandate: pluralism. Shows would be aimed not just at corporate investors and managers, but at consumers and employees. Political shows would be hosted not just by conservatives and centrists, but by progressives as well. Programs would be presented by and about blacks, Latinos, Asians, Native Americans, Arab and Jewish Americans, gays and lesbians, and others. And pluralism would infuse cultural programming: Where commercial broadcasters have, for example, offered a spectrum weighted to pop, rock and country music, public stations would also feature blues, jazz and classical music. This kind of public broadcasting system would set high programming standards that could enhance the overall quality of U.S. media.

Another long-range FAIR campaign would seek to get GE to divest itself of NBC. A divestment campaign would have great value in educating Americans about how ever-concentrating media ownership threatens to undermine the founding principles of our Constitution and First Amendment.

Q. How optimistic are you?

A. In an era when largely nonviolent movements have brought down corrupt governments throughout Eastern Europe and elsewhere, there are real grounds for optimism. Ironically, the same U.S. media pundits who are breathless supporters of democracy movements in Eastern Europe would be petrified at the prospect of a pro-democracy movement challenging elite structures here in the United States. Let's not forget that in country after country—whether Czechoslovakia, Romania or the Philippines—movements to throw aside corrupt elites have targeted much of their efforts against media outlets associated with the old rulers, sometimes engaging in physical confrontations in order to seize TV or radio stations. My point is that if a pro-democracy movement emerges in the United States against entrenched concentrations of power, the battle over the media will be center stage.

If you come across glaring examples of media bias, pass them along to FAIR. Include newspaper or magazine clips or citations of broadcast news reports with your letter. Of course, don't hesitate to contact directly the media outlet in question.

FAIR
130 W. 25th Street
New York, NY 10001
212-633-6700

Appendices

Appendix A: Recommended Reading

Aronson, James. *The Press and the Cold War*. Boston: Beacon Press, 1970. Shows key role of media in promoting Cold War stereotypes, myths and hatreds.

Bagdikian, Ben. *The Media Monopoly*. Boston: Beacon Press, 1990 (third edition). The classic study of concentrated corporate ownership and its impact on mass media.

Barnouw, Erik. *The Sponsor: Notes on a Modern Potentate*. New York: Oxford University Press, 1978. Examines the influence of advertising on broadcast media.

Bennett, W. Lance. *News: The Politics of Illusion*. New York: Longman, 1988. Explores why, in a society with so much information, people are so confused about politics, and how media practices—not public apathy—are key to this dilemma.

Cockburn, Alexander. *Corruptions of Empire*. London: Verso, 1988. A collection of essays by a gifted polemicist and media critic.

Cross, Donna Woolfolk. *Mediaspeak: How Television Makes Up Your Mind*. New York: Mentor, 1983. A telling look at TV's wide range of manipulative techniques.

Diamond, Sara. *Spiritual Warfare: The Politics of the Christian Right*. Boston: South End Press, 1989. Analyzes televangelists and right-wing religious broadcast media.

Entman, Robert M. *Democracy Without Citizens: Media and the Decay of American Politics*. New York: Oxford University Press, 1989. A deft academic examination of how institutional patterns deprive us of a "free press."

Gans, Herbert. *Deciding What's News*. New York: Vintage, 1980. A sociologist takes apart the functional criteria for what qualifies as "news."

Gitlin, Todd. *The Whole World Is Watching: Mass Media in the Making and Unmaking of the New Left*. Berkeley: University of California Press, 1980. A study of how mass media catalyzed and eventually undermined the New Left movement of the 1960s.

Hallin, Daniel C. *Uncensored War*. New York: Oxford University Press, 1986. The definitive history of the media's role in the escalation and demise of the U.S. war in Vietnam.

Herman, Edward S. and Brodhead, Frank. *The Rise and Fall of the Bulgarian Connection*. New York: Sheridan Square Publications, 1986. A case study of "free world" disinformation and the shooting of Pope John Paul II.

359

Herman, Edward S. and Chomsky, Noam. *Manufacturing Consent: The Political Economy of the Mass Media.* New York: Pantheon, 1988. A probing exposé of biased reporting on human rights and foreign policy issues.

Hertsgaard, Mark. *On Bended Knee: The Press and the Reagan Presidency.* New York: Farrar Straus Giroux, 1988. The definitive work on U.S. media performance during the Reagan era.

Mander, Jerry. *Four Arguments for the Elimination of Television.* New York: William Morrow, 1974. Examines the destructive impact of television on American society.

McClain, Leanita. *A Foot in Each World: Essays and Articles.* Evanston, IL: Northwestern University Press, 1986. A wrenching book about modern racism, written by a young black editor at the *Chicago Tribune* before her suicide.

Miller, Mark Crispin. *Boxed In: The Culture of TV.* Evanston, IL: Northwestern University Press, 1988. A witty and astute critique of the television medium in America.

Parenti, Michael. *Inventing Reality: The Politics of the Mass Media.* New York: St. Martin's, 1986. A concise and insightful analysis of U.S. news media bias.

Peck, Abe. *Uncovering the Sixties: The Life and Times of the Underground Press.* New York: Pantheon, 1985. A history of the role of the underground press in the 1960s, and its continuing legacy.

Rapping, Elayne. *The Looking Glass World of Nonfiction TV.* Boston: South End Press, 1987. How mass culture—news, sports, commercials, game shows—promotes the ideological bias of media owners.

Schiller, Herbert I. *Culture, Inc.: The Corporate Takeover of Public Expression.* New York: Oxford University Press, 1989. Analyzes the corporate structure of mass communications and how it constrains expression in a wide range of news and entertainment media. See also Schiller's *The Mind Managers*, Beacon Press, 1973.

Seldes, George. *Witness to a Century.* New York: Ballantine, 1987. The dean of American media criticism reflects on eight decades of journalism.

Shaheen, Jack. *The TV Arab.* Bowling Green, OH: Bowling Green State University Popular Press, 1984. A probing study of racial stereotyping in news and entertainment.

Stone, I.F., *The Haunted Fifties, In a Time of Torment,* and *Polemics and Prophesies.* Boston: Little, Brown, 1989. Three-volume series of edited writings from an eminent media critic.

Washburn, Patrick S. *A Question of Sedition: The Federal Government's Investigation of the Black Press During World War II.* New York: Oxford University Press, 1987. Documents official steps against the black press, including FBI efforts to stigmatize black reporters who protested discrimination.

Appendix B: The Media Business

The world's ten biggest media companies:

1. Time Warner
2. Bertelsmann, A.G. (West Germany)
3. CapCities/ABC
4. Thomson (Canada)
5. News Corporation Ltd. (Murdoch)
6. Hachette (France)
7. Gannett Company
8. Knight-Ridder Inc.
9. Pearson PLC (Great Britain)
10. Maxwell Communication Corp. (Great Britain)

[Source: *MacLean's* 7-17-89]

The 23 dominant corporations that control most of the U.S. media (newspapers, magazines, books, television, and motion pictures, in alphabetical order):

1. Bertelsmann, A.G. (books)
2. Capital Cities/ABC (newspapers, broadcasting)
3. Cox Communications (newspapers)
4. CBS (broadcasting)
5. Buena Vista Films (Disney; motion pictures)
6. Dow Jones (newspapers)
7. Gannett (newspapers)
8. General Electric (television)
9. Paramount Communications (books, motion pictures)
10. Harcourt Brace Jovanovich (books)
11. Hearst (newspapers, magazines)
12. Ingersoll (newspapers)
13. International Thomson (newspapers)
14. Knight-Ridder (newspapers)
15. Media News Group (newspapers)
16. Newhouse (newspapers, books)
17. News Corporation Ltd. (newspapers, magazines, motion pictures)
18. New York Times (newspapers)

19. Reader's Digest Association (books, magazines)
20. Scripps-Howard (newspapers)
21. Time Warner (magazines, books, motion pictures)
22. Times Mirror (newspapers)
23. Tribune Company (magazines)

[Source: *The Media Monopoly*, Ben Bagdikian]

The companies that dominate the daily newspaper industry:

1. Gannett Company—*USA Today* and 87 other dailies.
2. Knight-Ridder, Inc.—*Philadelphia Inquirer, Miami Herald* and 27 others.
3. Newhouse Newspapers—*Staten Island Advance, Portland Oregonian*, and 24 others.
4. Tribune Company—*Chicago Tribune*, New York *Daily News* and 7 others.
5. Times Mirror—*Los Angeles Times* and 7 others.
6. Dow Jones & Co.—*Wall Street Journal* and 22 Ottaway newspapers.
7. International Thomson—120 dailies (mainly in Canada).
8. New York Times Company—*New York Times* and 26 others.
9. Scripps-Howard Newspapers—Denver *Rocky Mountain News* and 22 others.
10. Hearst—*San Francisco Examiner* and 13 others.
11. Cox—*Atlanta Journal and Constitution* and 19 others.
12. News Corp. Ltd—*Boston Herald* and 2 others.
13. Media News Group—*Dallas Times Herald* and 17 others.
14. Ingersoll Newspapers—*New Haven Register* and 36 others.

The three dominant corporations in the magazine business:

1. Time Warner—*Time, People, Sports Illustrated, Fortune*, etc.
2. News Corp.—*TV Guide, Seventeen, New York, Premiere*, etc.
3. Hearst—*Good Housekeeping, Cosmopolitan, Esquire*, etc.

The six companies that dominate book publishing:

1. Paramount Communications—Simon & Schuster, Pocket Books, etc.
2. Harcourt Brace Jovanovich

3. Time Warner—Little, Brown, Warner Books, Book-of-the-Month Club
4. Bertelsmann, A.G.—Doubleday, Bantam, Dell, etc.
5. Reader's Digest Association
6. Newhouse—Random House, Ballantine, etc.

The four firms that dominate the motion picture industry:

1. Buena Vista—Disney
2. Paramount Communications—Paramount Pictures
3. Murdoch—20th Century Fox
4. Time Warner—Warner Brothers

[Source: *The Media Monopoly*, Ben Bagdikian]

The 15 top network television advertisers—January through June 1989:

1. General Motors
2. Philip Morris Companies, Inc.
3. Procter & Gamble Co.
4. Kellogg Co.
5. McDonald's Corp.
6. Ford Motor Co.
7. Unilever N.V.
8. Johnson & Johnson
9. Pepsico, Inc.
10. Kohlberg Kravis Roberts & Co.
11. Anheuser-Busch Companies, Inc.
12. American Home Products Corp.
13. Chrysler Corp.
14. Sears Roebuck & Co.
15. Coca-Cola Co.

[Source: Television Bureau of Advertising]

Appendix C: Alternative Media

National alternative print media:

Black Scholar
485 65th Street
Oakland, CA 94609
415-547-6633

Guardian
33 W. 17th Street
New York, NY 10011
212-691-0404

In These Times
2040 N. Milwaukee
Chicago, IL 60647
312-772-0100

Mother Jones
Foundation for National Progress
1663 Mission Street
San Francisco, CA 94103
415-558-8881

The Nation
72 Fifth Avenue
New York, NY 10011
212-242-8400

National Catholic Reporter
115 E. Armour Boulevard
Kansas City, MO 64111
816-531-0538

New Directions for Women
108 West Palisade Avenue
Englewood, NJ 07631
201-568-0226

The Progressive
409 E. Main Street
Madison, WI 53703
608-257-4626

Public Citizen
2000 P. Street, NW, #700
Washington, DC 20036
202-293-9142

Sojourners
Box 29272
1321 Otis Street, NE
Washington, DC 20017
202-636-3637

Tikkun
5100 Leona Street
Oakland, CA 94619
415-482-0805

Utne Reader
The Fawkes Building
1624 Harmon Place
Minneapolis, MN 55403
612-338-5040

Village Voice
842 Broadway
New York, NY 10003
212-475-3300

Zeta
Institute for Social and Cultural
Communications
116 St. Botolph Street
Boston, MA 02115
617-266-0629

To find out about local newsweeklies in your area, contact:

Association of Alternative
Newsweeklies
c/o Jane Sullivan
Bay Guardian
520 Hampshire Street
San Francisco, CA 94110
415-255-3100

Alternative news services:

Alternet
2025 Eye Street, NW, #1104
Washington, DC 20006
202-887-0022

College Press Service
2505 W. Second Avenue, Suite 7
Denver, CO 80219
303-936-9930

Insight Features
Networking for Democracy
3411 W. Diversey, Suite 5
Chicago, IL 60647
312-384-8827

InterPress
400 Madison Avenue
New York, NY 10017
212-832-2839

National Student News Service
Box 3161
Boston, MA 02101
800-833-NEWS

Pacific News Service
450 Mission Street, Room 506
San Francisco, CA 94105
415-243-4364

For recommended journals that cover specific subject areas—environment, economics, etc.—consult Utne Reader or contact FAIR.

Alternative broadcast media:

Radio:

American Dialogues
Robert Foxworth
8033 Sunset Boulevard, #967
Los Angeles, CA 90046
213-550-3949

Common Ground
Stanley Foundation
216 Sycamore Street, Suite 500
Muscatine, Iowa 52761
319-264-1500

Consider the Alternatives
5808 Greene Street
Philadelphia, PA 19144
215-848-4100

National Federation
of Community Broadcasters
1314 14th Street, NW
Washington, D.C. 20005
202-393-2355

New Voices
Public Interest Video Network
1642 R Street, NW
Washington, DC 20009
202-797-8997

Pacifica (Program Service)
3729 Cahuenga Boulevard West
North Hollywood, CA 91604
818-985-2711

Radio for Peace International
Box 10689
Eugene, OR 97440
503-741-1794

Second Opinion
Erwin Knoll (host)
c/o The Progressive
409 E. Main Street
Madison, WI 53703
608-257-4626

Undercurrents (carries FAIR's weekly
   radio show)
   130 W. 25 Street
   New York, NY 10001
   212-691-7370

WINGS
   Women's International News
   Gathering Service
   P.O. Box 5307
   Kansas City, MO 64131
   816-361-7161

Television and Video:

Alternative Views
   Box 7279
   Austin, TX 78713
   512-477-5148

Empowerment Project
   1653 18th Street, Suite 3
   Santa Monica, CA 90404
   213-828-8807

GlobalVision
   361 West Broadway
   New York, NY 10013
   212-941-0255

Media Network
   121 Fulton Street
   New York, NY 10038
   212-619-3455

Paper Tiger/Deep Dish
   339 Lafayette Street
   New York, NY 10012
   212-420-9045

Video Databank
   37 S. Wabash
   Chicago, IL 60603
   312-899-5172

The Video Project: Films and Videos for
   a Safe and Sustainable World
   5332 College Avenue, Suite 101
   Oakland, CA 94618
   415-655-9050

Appendix D: Media Analysis Groups & Publications

Adbusters: A Magazine of Media and
Environmental Strategies
The Media Foundation
1243 W. Seventh Avenue
Vancouver, British Columbia
V6H 1B7 Canada
604-736-9401

Columbia Journalism Review
700 Journalism Building
Columbia University
New York, NY 10027
212-854-1811

Communications Consortium
1333 H Street, NW, 11th Floor
Washington, DC 20005
202-682-1270

Deadline
Center for War, Peace and the News
Media
New York University
10 Washington Place, 4th Floor
New York, NY 10003
212-998-7960

Essential Information
P.O. Box 19405
Washington, DC 20036
202-387-8034

Extra!
FAIR (Fairness & Accuracy in
Reporting)
130 W. 25 Street
New York, NY 10001
212-633-6700

GLAAD
Gay and Lesbian Alliance Against
Defamation
80 Varick Street
New York, NY 10013
212-966-1700

Independent
625 Broadway, 9th Floor
New York, NY 10012
212-473-3400

Lies of Our Times
Institute for Media Analysis
145 W. 4th Street
New York, NY 10012
212-254-1061

Media & Values
Media Action Research Center
Center for Media & Values
1962 South Shenandoah
Los Angeles, CA 90034
213-559-2944

Mediafile
Media Alliance
Fort Mason Center, Building D290
San Francisco, CA 94123
415-441-2557

Media Watch
1803 Mission St., #7
Santa Cruz, CA 95060
408-423-6355

Project Censored
Communications Studies Program
1801 E. Cotati Avenue
Sonoma State University
Rohnert Park, CA 94928
707-664-2149

Propaganda Review
Media Alliance
Fort Mason Center, Room D290
San Francisco, CA 94123
415-441-2557

Quill
53 W. Jackson Boulevard, Suite 731
Chicago, IL 60604
312-922-7424

St. Louis Journalism Review
  8380 Olive Boulevard
  St. Louis, MO 63132
  314-991-1699

Tyndall Report
  135 Rivington Street
  New York, NY 10022
  212-674-8913

The Democratic Communiqué
  Union of Democratic
  Communications
  P.O. Box 1220
  Berkeley, CA 94701
  415-596-3589

Washington Journalism Review
  2233 Wisconsin Avenue, NW
  Washington, DC 20007
  202-333-6800

Women's Institute for Freedom of the
  Press
  3306 Ross Place, NW
  Washington, DC 20008
  202-966-7783

Appendix E: Journalism Organizations

American Society of Newspaper Editors
P.O. Box 17004
Washington, D.C. 20041
703-648-1144

Article 19
90 Borough High Street
London SE1 1LL, United Kingdom
01-403-4822

Black Press Institute
7917 South Exchange Avenue, Suite 205
Chicago, IL 60617
312-375-8200

Center for Investigative Reporting
530 Howard Street, 2nd Floor
San Francisco, CA 94105
415-543-1200

Committee to Protect Journalists
16 E. 42 Street, 3rd floor
New York, NY 10017
212-983-5355

Fund for Investigative Journalism
1755 Massachusetts Avenue, NW
Room 519
Washington, D.C. 20036
202-462-1844

Journalists Without Borders
Antonio Maria Claret 133,
First Floor, Door Three
08025 Barcelona, Spain
34-265-5167

National Alliance of Third World Journalists
P.O. Box 43208
Washington, DC 20010
202-462-8197

National Association of Black Journalists
11600 Sunrise Valley Drive
Reston, VA 22091
703-648-1270

National Association of Hispanic Journalists
National Press Bldg.
Suite 1193
Washington, DC 20045
202-785-6228

National Writers Union
13 Astor Place, Seventh Floor
New York, NY 10003
212-254-0279

Newspaper Guild
8611 Second Avenue
Silver Spring, MD 20910
301-585-2990

Society of Professional Journalists
53 W. Jackson Boulevard,
Suite 731
Chicago, IL 60604
312-922-7424

Appendix F: National News Media

Here are some important media addresses and phone numbers that you may want to write, call or telegram your own complaints about imbalanced coverage. You might also want to supplement this list with addresses of your local media.

ABC World News Tonight
7 West 66th Street
New York, NY 10023
212-887-4040

Associated Press
50 Rockefeller Plaza
New York, NY 10020
National Desk (212-621-1600)
Foreign Desk (212-621-1663)
Washington Bureau (202-828-6400)

CBS Evening News
524 W. 57th Street
New York, NY 10019
212-975-3693

CBS This Morning
524 W. 57th Street
New York, NY 10019
212-975-2824

Christian Science Monitor
CSM Publishing Society
One Norway Street
Boston, MA 02115
800-225-7090

CNN
One CNN Center
Box 105366
Atlanta, GA 30348
404-827-1500

CNN
Washington Bureau
111 Massachusetts Avenue, NW
Washington, DC 20001
202-898-7900

Crossfire
CNN
111 Massachusetts Avenue, NW
Washington, DC 20001
202-898-7951

Face the Nation
CBS News
2020 M Street, NW
Washington, DC 20036
202-457-4321

Good Morning America
ABC News
1965 Broadway
New York, NY 10023
212-496-4800

Larry King Live TV
CNN
111 Massachusetts Avenue, NW
Washington, DC 20001
202-898-7900

Larry King Show—Radio
Mutual Broadcasting
1755 So. Jefferson Davis Highway
Arlington, VA 22202
703-685-2175

Los Angeles Times
Times-Mirror Square
Los Angeles, CA 90053
800-528-4637

MacNeil/Lehrer NewsHour
P.O. Box 2626
Washington, DC 20013
703-998-2870

MacNeil/Lehrer NewsHour
  WNET-TV
  356 W. 58th Street
  New York, NY 10019
  212-560-3113

Meet the Press
  NBC News
  4001 Nebraska Avenue, NW
  Washington, DC 20016
  202-885-4200

Morning Edition/All Things Considered
  National Public Radio
  2025 M Street, NW
  Washington, DC 20036
  202-822-2000

NBC Nightly News
  30 Rockefeller Plaza
  New York, NY 10112
  212-664-4971

New York Times
  229 W. 43rd Street
  New York, NY 10036
  212-556-1234
  212-556-7415

New York Times
  Washington Bureau
  1627 Eye Street, NW, 7th Floor
  Washington, DC 20006
  202-862-0300

Newsweek
  444 Madison Avenue
  New York, NY 10022
  212-350-4000

Nightline
  ABC News
  47 W. 66th Street
  New York, NY 10023
  212-887-4995

Nightline
  Ted Koppel
  ABC News
  1717 DeSales Street, NW

Washington, DC 20036
202-887-7364

This Week With David Brinkley
  ABC News
  1717 DeSales Street, NW
  Washington, DC 20036
  202-887-7777

Time magazine
  Time Warner, Inc.
  Time & Life Building
  Rockefeller Center
  New York, NY 10020
  212-522-1212

Today Show
  NBC News
  30 Rockefeller Plaza
  New York, NY 10112
  212-664-4249

United Press International
  1400 Eye Street, NW
  Washington, DC 20006
  202-898-8000

U.S. News & World Report
  2400 N Street, NW
  Washington, DC 20037
  202-955-2000

USA Today
  1000 Wilson Boulevard
  Arlington, VA 22229
  703-276-3400

Wall Street Journal
  200 Liberty Street
  New York, NY 10281
  212-416-2000

Washington Post
  1150 15th Street, NW
  Washington, DC 20071
  202-334-6000

Washington Week in Review
  WETA-TV
  P.O. Box 2626
  Washington, DC 20013
  703-998-2626

Notes

Chapter One: Mixed Messages

3   Critic on "constant violence…": Ben Bagdikian, "The Lords of the Global Village," *The Nation*, 6-12-89

3   TV on for average of nearly seven hours: 1989 Nielsen Report

3   Thirty-one hours a week viewer average cited in *Boston Globe*, reprinted in *San Francisco Chronicle*, 5-19-89

3   Acts of violence figure, *Time* magazine, 6-12-89, p. 55

3   Number of commercials viewed: Bagdikian, *The Nation*, 6-12-89

3   Whatever the impact of TV, newspapers still occupy a central place in most American homes. Almost two-thirds of the country's adults read a newspaper each day, according to *Editor & Publisher* International YearBook (cited in *U.S. News & World Report*, 8-28-89).

3   Survey on identifying judges, *Washington Post*, 6-23-89

3   Ellerbee, "That is the biggest fallacy…", quoted in *Mother Jones*, June 1989

4   *Los Angeles Times*, 6-4-89; Meisler's article ran in the Sunday "Opinion" section.

4   Meisler, *Los Angeles Times*, 6-4-89

4   Howard Rosenberg, *Los Angeles Times*, 5-20-89

5   Smoking's annual death toll, "Reducing the Health Consequences of Smoking: 25 Years of Progress," A Report by the Surgeon General, 1989

5   Tobacco company retaliation against *Mother Jones* cited in *The Media Monopoly*, Ben H. Bagdikian, p. 171

5   Tobacco company retaliation against Saatchi cited by Ben Bagdikian in *The Nation*, 6-12-89

6   Koop's allegation received brief mention in the *New York Times* (1-12-89). The big three newsweeklies (1-23-89) gave short shrift to his criticism. *Newsweek* said only that Koop had noted "that dependence on tobacco-advertising dollars effectively bars many magazines from publicizing the hazards of smoking." *Time* and *U.S. News & World Report* skipped that aspect of Koop's presentation entirely.

6   In 1988 *TV Guide*'s tobacco ad income totalled $30,715,885, accounting for 9.16 percent of all the magazine's ad revenues. (*TV Guide* manager of advertising services John Rettew, authors' interview, 8-24-89)

6   Andrew Mills, authors' interview, 8-8-89

6   *Playboy*, September 1989; Barry W. Lynn, "Censoring Tobacco Ads"

6   Authors' interview, Mark Klein, *Playboy* Magazine Research Department, New York, 8-17-89.

6   Women have been special targets of cigarette advertising. Women's magazines such as *Redbook*, *Self*, *Cosmopolitan*, *Ladies Home Journal* and *Mademoiselle* have kept printing cigarette ads—while staying away from articles about smoking dangers. The editor of *Cosmopolitan*, Helen Gurley Brown, has made clear that her candor far outstrips her decency: "Having come from the advertising world myself, I think 'Who needs somebody you're paying millions of dollars a year to come back and bite you on the ankle?'" (*Washington Post*, 12-11-85)

6   A minority of major magazines *do* refuse to accept cigarette ads, including *Good Housekeeping*, *Saturday Evening Post*, *Reader's Digest* and *Prevention*.

6   Authors' interviews with Brian Brown, *Time* magazine publicity manager, 8-15-89; Gary

Gerard, *Newsweek* spokesman, 8-31-89; Beth Kseniak, *U.S. News & World Report* publicity manager, 8-30-89.

7   Brown, authors' interview, 8-31-89

7   "Deeply influences the subjects...", Bagdikian, *The Media Monopoly*, p. xi; henceforth all citations of Bagdikian will be from *The Media Monopoly* unless otherwise indicated.

7   Allen Neuharth quoted in *The Making of McPaper*, Peter Prichard, pp. 298-300

8   St. Pauli Girl ad campaign, *New York Times*, 4-10-89

8   Beer target profile, *New York Times*, 4-10-89

9   Ellerbee on cover of *Mother Jones*, May 1989

9   Savan, *Village Voice*, 6-13-89

10   "I did it for the money...", Ellerbee quoted in *Village Voice*, 6-13-89

10   Early 1970s salary range cited in *New York Times*, 2-20-89

10   Mudd quoted in *Extra!* (newsletter published by Fairness & Accuracy in Reporting, based in New York City), June 1987

14   AP article on survey, in *San Francisco Chronicle*, 6-6-89

14   Gelb memo quoted in *Columbia Journalism Review*, November/December 1988, "The 'Max' factor at The New York Times," Bruce Porter

Chapter Two: Consider the Sources

15   Los Angeles Times, 8-25-89

16   Bagdikian, pp. 179-180

16   Chung quoted in *San Jose Mercury News* by that paper's television columnist Ron Miller, 6-7-89

16   Evening news programs on ABC, CBS and NBC were drawing in a total of 32.3 percent of the USA's 90.4 million households in 1989. (*TV Guide*, 7-8-89)

17   Donaldson quoted in *Orange County (CA) Register*, 4-12-87

17   Rather quoted in *Los Angeles Times*, 8-25-89

17   Shaw, *Los Angeles Times*, 8-25-89

17   Robert M. Entman, *Democracy Without Citizens: Media and the Decay of American Politics*, p. 19

17   *Harper's* magazine, July 1989, "All the Congressmen's Men: How Capitol Hill controls the press," Walter Karp

17   Sampling of 2,850 articles cited in Michael Parenti, *Inventing Reality*, p. 51

17   Study of *All Things Considered* by WAMM Media Committee, Minneapolis, Minnesota; issued 1-12-89

18   Wicker quoted in Karp, *Harper's* magazine, July 1989

18   Alter, *Newsweek* , 5-23-88

18   Karp, *Harper's* magazine, July 1989

19   For details about Nazi spies on the CIA payroll, see *Blowback*, Christopher Simpson

19   Entman, p. 20

19   David Johnston, *Columbia Journalism Review*, November/December 1987, "The Anonymous-Source Syndrome."

19   McCartney quoted in ibid.

20   Jeff Cohen, authors' interview, 9-14-89

20   Bradlee quoted in Mark Hertsgaard, *On Bended Knee*, p. 101

20   Armstrong interview in *Extra!*, July 1987

21   Harwood's role at *Trenton Times* described in Howard Bray, *The Pillars of the Post: The Making of a News Empire in Washington*, p. 201

21   Harwood column in *Washington Post*, 7-16-89

21   Nader quoted in *The Progressive*, February 1989, "The Union-Busting Post," John Hanrahan

22   Hamill, *Village Voice*, 10-1-85

22   *Brookline Citizen* interview with Schanberg; quoted in *Village Voice*, 10-1-85

22   Gruson reply quoted in *Columbia Journalism Review*, November/December 1988, "The

'Max' factor at The New York Times," Bruce Porter

23 AP total audience cited in *Los Angeles Times*, 4-3-88. Edward S. Herman and Noam Chomsky note that "the four major Western wire services—Associated Press, United Press International, Reuters, and Agence-France-Presse—account for some 80 percent of the international news circulating in the world today." (Herman and Chomsky, *Manufacturing Consent: The Political Economy of the Mass Media*, p. 335)

23 *Los Angeles Times*, 4-3-88

23 *Los Angeles Times*, 4-4-88

23 *Columbia Journalism Review*, November/December 1987, "AP: The Price of Purity," Jim Sibbison

23 AP and NBC deferral to censorship request discussed in *Los Angeles Times*, 4-4-88, and in Hertsgaard, *On Bended Knee*, p. 225

24 *Washington Post* role in Pelton story cited in Hertsgaard, *On Bended Knee*, p. 226

24 Scoop killed by top AP editors, *Los Angeles Times*, 4-4-88

24 Meetings between AP's bureau chief Lewis and Oliver North described in *Los Angeles Times*, 4-4-88

24 Blocking of Parry-Barger also described in *Columbia Journalism Review*, November/December 1987, "AP: The Price of Purity," Jim Sibbison

24 Walter Mears memo quoted in *Los Angeles Times*, 4-4-88

24 *Boston Globe*, 10-26-88

25 Gregory Gordon quoted in *New York Times*, 5-31-89

25 *Newsweek*, 6-15-87

26 Koppel quoted in *Newsweek*, 6-15-87

26 *Columbia Journalism Review*, March/April 1989, "Ted Koppel's Neutrality Act," Michael Massing

26 Koppel, on Kissinger, quoted in *Columbia Journalism Review*, March/April 1989, "Ted Koppel's Neutrality Act," Michael Massing

26 *Nightline*, "American Options in the Hostage Crisis" (8-3-89)

26 Kissinger and Kalb, on Koppel, quoted in *Newsweek*, 6-15-87

26 Koppel on his qualifications, quoted in *Life* magazine, October 1988

26 "Are You On the Nightline Guest List?: An Analysis of 40 months of Nightline Programming," By William Hoynes and David Croteau, February 1989, prepared for Fairness & Accuracy in Reporting. The study researched all transcripts of *Nightline* broadcasts from January 1, 1985 to April 30, 1988.

29 Jennings quoted in *Boston Globe* magazine, 11-6-88

29 Kaplan quoted in *New York Times*, 2-6-89

29 Koppel, on FAIR study, quoted in *Los Angeles Times*, 2-6-89; and in *Washington Times*, 2-6-89

29 Jeff Cohen, op-ed, *Los Angeles Herald Examiner*, 2-17-89

30 Stone column, *Philadelphia Daily News*, 2-7-89

30 Clarence Page column, *Chicago Tribune*, 2-12-89

30 Rosenberg column, *Los Angeles Times*, 11-28-86

31 Maynes quoted in *Newsday*, 3-19-89

31 Wilkins quoted in *Newsday*, 3-19-89

Chapter Three: Media Con Games

32 Gore Vidal, The Nation, August 7 & 14, 1989

32 *New York Times* 5-6-89 and *USA Today* 5-8-89 cited in *New Republic*, 5-15-89

32 *Newsday* 4-13-89 and *New York Times* 4-13-89

32 *New York Times* 12-10-87 and *Boston Globe* 12-10-87, cited in *New Republic*, January 4 and 11, 1989

33 *New York Times* and *Washington Post* on Southern Africa (9-30-88) cited in *New Republic*, 10-31-88

33 *St. Louis Post-Dispatch* (4-30-89) cited in *New Republic*, 5-29-89

33 *New York Times* on Uganda (6-15-89) cited in *New Republic*, July 17 & 24, 1989
33 AP report on Hammarskjold in *New York Times*, 9-17-61
33 AP report on South Africa in *San Juan Star* and *New York Times*, 8-20-89
33 AP report on Afghanistan, *New York Times* and *San Juan Star*, 8-20-89
34 Erdrich and Dorris, *New York Times* Sunday magazine, 9-4-88; see also Winona LaDuke, "White Earth Land Struggle: Omissions and Stereotypes," *Extra!*, Summer 1989
34 Erdrich and Dorris, letter to the editor, *Minneapolis Star Tribune*, 9-10-88
34 AP report on North and cocaine, *San Juan Star* (7-22-89) and *Washington Post* (7-23-89)
35 *New York Times* articles on Reagan, 6-1-88 and 6-2-88
35 Preston, *Washington Post*, 2-4-88
35 *Miami Herald* on Filipino mail order brides, 7-21-89
36 McCarthy headlines cited in Edwin R. Bayley, *Joe McCarthy and the Press*, p. 64
36 *Washington Post* editorial, 9-23-88; *Washington Post* news article, 7-11-88
36 *New York Times* editorial on South Africa, 5-28-88
37 *San Francisco Examiner*, 10-7-89
37 Jo Thomas, *Columbia Journalism Review*, May/June 1988
37 *New York Times*,"After 20 Years, Ulster's Hopes Fade," 8-14-89
37 Schmemann, *New York Times*, 5-14-89; Rosenthal, *New York Times*, 5-16-89
37 Gordon, *New York Times*, 5-14-89
38 *Washington Post*, nuclear allergy in Australia, 2-8-85; see *Extra!*, June 1987
38 "A touch of Hollanditis," *Washington Post*, 7-19-84
38 *New York Times* editorial on South Pacific, 5-20-87
38 Haberman, *New York Times*, 12-17-88
38 *San Francisco Chronicle*, 6-19-89
38 *New York Times* editorial, "Hiding Behind Hormones in Milk," 5-5-89
39 *Washington Post* on "humanitarian aid," 2-21-88
39 *Miami Herald* article on abortion rights, 2-22-89
39 *International Herald Tribune*, 4-10 and 4-11-89
39 "Pro and anti-abortion activists," WNBC-TV, 2-8-89
39 Serge Schmemann on Berlin elections, *New York Times*, 1-30-89
40 Jonathan Fuerbringer, *New York Times*, 12-13-87
40 *New York Times* correction, 12-20-87
40 "Democratic countries in Central America," *New York Times*, 6-29-88
40 Tom Mintier, CNN, 4-4-89
40 AP story on Korea in *New York Times*, 6-9-88
40 Lobe letter to *New York Times*, 2-12-89
41 Mary Laughlin, CNN, 12-21-89
41 Brokaw, *NBC Nightly News*, 3-26-87
41 Sam Donaldson quoted in *Extra!*, June 1987
42 Rather, *CBS Evening News*, 4-20-87
42 LeMoyne on Nicaraguan link to Medallin cartel, *New York Times*, 2-12-88
43 Joel Brinkley, *New York Times*, 3-19-86
43 Paul Lewis, *New York Times*, 3-7-89
43 Roth letter to *New York Times*, 3-26-89
43 Koppel, *Nightline*, 1-8-85
44 Gruson on contras, *New York Times*, 11-5-87
44 *CBS Evening News* on Noriega, 3-29-88
46 D.D. Guttenplan, "Round Up the Usual Suspects," *Newsday*, 3-19-89
46 Kissinger's business connections in China, John Fialka, *Wall Street Journal*, 9-15-89
46 Kissinger's defense of the Chinese regime, *Los Angeles Times*, 8-1-89
46 Richard Cohen, *Washington Post*, 8-29-89
47 Boyer, *Who Killed CBS?*, p. 143
47 CNN on Palestine Aid Society, 7-21-88
49 Mood music, NPR, see Parenti, p. 225
49 *New York Times* on Chile coup, 8-12-84; cited in Parenti, p. 222
49 *Washington Post* on Turkey, 4-23-83; cited in Parenti, pp. 222-223
49 *Christian Science Monitor*, 7-9-80; cited in Parenti, p. 222

50   "Scanting of content," Parenti, p. 223
50   Wald on Exxon spill, *New York Times*, 4-22-89
50   Brody, *Miami Herald*, 4-2-89
50   *Nightline* on King's birthday, *Extra!* November/December 1988
51   Ben Gay ads during "Roots," *Variety*, 1-26-77; quoted in Erik Barnouw, *The Sponsor*, p.114
51   GM story and ad in *Wall Street Journal*, 9-28-87
51   "Good Health" supplement, *New York Times* Sunday magazine, 9-27-87; see Joe McDonald in *Extra!*, March/April 1988
51   *National Geographic*, December 1988; see also Nicolas Hentoff, *The Nation*, 12-26-88
51   GE sponsored show on Vietnam vets, NBC, 5-29-88
52   Serrin in *The Nation*, 1-23-89
54   State Department claims of 2,500 to 3,500 Cuban military personnel and 6,000 Cuban civilians in Nicaragua, *Los Angeles Times*, 12-6-85
54   Trainor, *New York Times*, 7-26-87
54   Schiller, *The Mind Managers*, pp. 110, 121-122
54   Roper poll, Erik Barnouw, *The Sponsor*, p. 94
55   National Public Radio on Gallup affiliate in Costa Rica, 3-24-86
55   Irving Brown obit in *New York Times*, 2-11-89
56   *Miami Herald* on Huey Newton, 8-23-89
56   Lucille Ball's death, *The Nation*, 5-22-89
56   Harriman, *Hack*, p. 185

Chapter Four: The Media Cartel

59   Coverage of 1988 Winter and Summer Olympics, Extra!, March/April 1988 and November/December 1988
59   *NBC Nightly News* ran 38 stories (totalling 91 minutes) on the Summer Olympic games, while ABC *World News Tonight* aired 13 stories (41 minutes) and *CBS Evening News* presented only 8 stories (26 minutes).
59   Newspaper space reserved for ads, Bagdikian, p. 153
60   Volume of TV commercials, FCC press release, 6-28-84
60   Keld quoted in Parenti, p. 49
60   Audubon Society program aired without commercials, *Wall Street Journal*, 9-25-89
60   Domino's Pizza withdraws ads, *Wall Street Journal*, 4-11-89
61   Writers Guild poll on entertainment programs, *Mediaspeak*, Donna Woolfolk Cross, p. 94
61   Examples of entertainment script tampering, Cross, p. 88, and Bagdikian, p. 158
61   Proctor & Gamble memo, quoted in Erik Barnouw, *The Sponsor*, p. 112
61   Prudential Insurance, quoted in Bagdikian, p. 158
61   Herskovitz quoted in Stephen Farber, *New York Times* Sunday magazine, 5-7-89
61   Herskovitz: "I would rather have…", quoted in *USA Today*, 7-24-89
62   ABC booklet: "Some people are more valuable…", Barnouw, p. 114
62   DuPont to FCC, Bagdikian, p. 160
62   MacGuyver episode aired on 11-21-88; see *Extra!*, November/December 1988
62   "We will not allow…", *New York Times* Sunday magazine, Stephen Farber, 5-7-9; see also *Extra!* November/December 1988
62   Tommy Smothers quoted in *Chicago Tribune*, 5-25-89
63   "Advertisers have a perfect right…", Thomas R. King, *Wall Street Journal*, 6-21-89
63   Ad executive in *USA Today*, 7-28-89
63   NBC News employee, quoted in *Extra!*, August/September 1987
63   *Rolling Stone* manager quoted in Bagdikian, p. 110
63   Henwood, *Left Business Observer*, 1-17-89; *Extra!*, March/April 1988
63   *Business Week* ad in *New York Times*, 6-2-89
64   *Newsweek* ad in *New York Times*, 5-30-89
64   *Newsweek* ad in *Los Angeles Times*, 5-30-89

64   *New York Times* and the auto industry, Parenti, p. 48
64   "On the back of advertisements," Parenti, p. 62
64   *Vanity Fair* stories on advertisers, Doug Ireland in *Village Voice*, 5-30-89
65   Alter, "Art of the Deals," *Newsweek*, 1-9-89
65   "The wall of separation...", Bagdikian, p. 231
65   Davis, Pacific News Service, 6-9-89
65   Gitlin, quoted in ibid.
66   Culip study, quoted in Jeff and Marie Blyskal, *PR: How the Public Relations Industry Writes the News*, p. 50
66   Bagdikian, p. 165
66   Topping quoted in Blyskal, p. 46
66   Staebler quoted in Blyskal, p. 47
66   *Columbia Journalism Review*, Joanne Angela Ambrosio, March/April 1980
66   PR Newswire figures, Blyskal, pp. 88-89
66   Aerosol spray manufacturers, Blyskal, p. 172
67   Dow Chemical in *Newsweek*, 7-11-83, and *Fortune*, May 1983; quoted in Blyskal, p. 226
67   Agent Orange suit, Blyskal, p. 164-167
67   CBS *60 Minutes*, 5-3-87; see also *Extra!*, August/September 1987
67   *New York Times* and *Newsday* on Union Carbide, 8-11-86
68   Mobil advocacy ads, Jeff Cohen, *Los Angeles Herald Examiner*, 9-3-86
68   *USA Today*, 5-30-89
68   "It looks like the Rolling Stones...", *Miami Herald*, 7-22-89
69   Bagdikian, *The Nation*, 6-12-89
70   *New York Times*, 3-7-89
71   Munro quoted in *Boston Globe*, 3-5-89
71   Record sales, Steven Wishnia, *The Nation*, 10-24-87
71   CBS and K-Mart, Doug Henwood, *Left Business Observer* 8-15-89; *Extra!* October/November 1989
71   Carman, *San Francisco Chronicle*, 6-20-89
71   Gannett assets, Bagdikian, *The Nation*, 6-12-89
72   Neuharth quoted in Bagdikian, p. xxi
72   Surveys of newspaper quality, Bagdikian, p. 83
72   McClatchy quoted in *New York Times*, 1-31-88
72   Donaldson on *David Letterman*, 7-19-89
72   Cronkite quoted in *Los Angeles Times*, 7-21-89
73   *Broadcasting* magazine, 7-24-89
73   Porter quoted by Lou Chapman in *New York Observer*, 6-19-89
73   Stone, *The Truman Era*, p. 217
73   Numbers of newspapers in foreign capitals, Bagdikian, pp. 118-119
74   Haberman, *New York Times*, 4-24-89
74   Bagdikian, pp. 6, 223, 237
74   "Private Ministry of Information," Bagdikian, p. xx
74   Cross, p. 3
75   "What the public learns...", Bagdikian, pp. x
75   The effort to eliminate the Fairness Doctrine received near unanimous support in editorial columns of America's major newspapers in 1987. With few exceptions, these newspapers neglected to mention that their corporate parents also own broadcasting properties and, therefore, would be directly affected by the FCC action. For example, *New York Times* columnist A.M. Rosenthal attacked the Fairness Doctrine without informing his readers of the Times Company's five TV stations. The *Chicago Tribune* editors didn't point out that Tribune Broadcasting owns six TV and four radio stations. Ditto for the *Miami Herald* (parent Knight-Ridder owns ten stations), *San Francisco Examiner* (Hearst owns 13) and the *Atlanta Constitution* (Cox Enterprises, 20). In each case the newspapers did not give any hint of a conflict of interest, even though one clearly existed.
75   Book censorship by Time and Warner, *Extra!*, March/April 1989
75   *The Press*, A. J. Liebling, p. 32
75   Eisenhower quoted in *INFACT Brings GE to Light*

76   GE corruption, *INFACT*
77   Langley quoted in John S. Saloma, *Ominous Politics*, p. 64
77   GE layoffs, *INFACT*
77   NBC *Today* show censorship, *New York Times*, 12-3-89; *Chicago Tribune*, 12-2-89
78   *Christian Science Monitor* cited in *Extra!*, June 1987
78   Westinghouse award to NBC, *Extra!*, January/February 1988
80   GE's Midwest nuclear reactors, Lee Daniels in the *New York Times*, 6-9-89; AP, 6-3-87; see also *Business Week*, 6-15-87; *Extra!*, July 1987
80   *New York Times*, 11-30-88, "GE Charged in $22 Million Pentagon Fraud," Andrew Rosenthal
80   GE and Star Wars, *New York Times*, 5-13-88
81   Disgruntled NBC employee quoted in *Extra!*, August/September 1987
82   Wilson quoted in *INFACT*
83   GE communications manager quoted in Bagdikian, p. 160
83   Media outreach by the Center for Strategic and International Studies, *Washington Post Weekly Edition*, 5-26-86
84   University of Windsor survey of news sources, *Washington Times*, 12-15-87
84   South Korean intelligence and the Heritage Foundation, *The Nation*, 1-23-89
85   Pace on public TV and riot control, Barnouw, p. 64
85   Moyers, quoted in David M. Stone, *Nixon and the Politics of Public Television*, p. 152
85   Oil company underwriting of PBS in Saloma, p. 107
86   Friendly quoted in Saloma, p. 107
86   Made in USA, *Extra!*, November/December 1988
86   "Free to Choose," Saloma, pp. 34, 74
86   Aufderheide, *The Progressive*, January 1988
87   *The Economist* cited in Edward S. Herman and Noam Chomsky, *Manufacturing Consent*, p. 17
87   MacNeil quoted in Cross, p. 79
88   Lehrer quoted in *The Progressive*, July 1987
89   PBS election specials, *Extra!*, March/April 1988
89   Cohen at PBS, *Extra!*, June 1987
89   Chase quoted in *The Progressive*, March 1988
90   Kwitny quoted in Howard Rosenberg, *Los Angeles Times*, 6-9-89
91   "Hollywood's Favorite Heavy," see *Extra!*, June 1987
91   Oil companies and uranium, Barnouw, p. 164
91   Schmertz quoted in Blyskal, p. 150
92   Bagdikian, p. 48
92   Ruder and Finn survey, Bagdikian, p. 57
92   "No sacred cow...", Bagdikian, p. 47
92   "...hostile to independent journalists...", Bagdikian, p. 65
92   Parenti, p. 43
92   Johnson quoted in Dennis Bernstein, *Extra!*, September/October 1988
93   Bagdikian, pp. 84-85
93   Chandler quoted in Parenti, p. 44
93   Seldes, *Witness to a Century*, pp. 307, 327
93   Hearst cartoons, Piers Brendon, *The Life and Death of the Press Barons*, p. 145
94   Steele quoted in Edwin R. Bayley, *Joe McCarthy and the Press*, p. 67
94   Pulitzer quoted in Bayley, p. 140
94   Luciano on Annenberg, quoted in *Extra!*, September/October 1988
95   *Boston Globe*, 6-13-88
96   Little Steven (Van Zandt) quoted in *Extra!*, September/October 1988
96   Murdoch interview, *Cosmopolitan*, July 1986
96   Bagdikian, p. 217
96   Catledge quoted in Parenti, p. 43
96   American Society of Newspaper Editors survey cited in Bagdikian, p. 30
97   Mark Dowie, *Mother Jones*, November/December 1985, "How ABC Spikes the News"
97   Goldin quoted in *Mother Jones*, June 1989

98   Vieira quoted in *Mother Jones*, June 1989
98   *New York Times* magazine cover story on Newhouse, 9-10-89
98   Newhouse tax evasion trial, *The Nation*, 3-13-89
98   Welles quoted in Parenti, p. 39
98   Nader quoted in Andy Boehm, *L.A. Weekly*, February 20-26, 1987
98   Johnson quoted in *Extra!*, September/October 1988
99   Jensen quoted in *Extra!*, September/October 1988
99   Frank quoted in *Extra!*, September/October 1988
99   "People are even more careful...", *Extra!*, September/October 1988
100 "I don't want the same thing...", Joel Millman, *The Progressive*, October 1984
100 *In These Times*, March 1-14, 1989
100 Dedman quoted in *In These Times*, March 1-14, 1989
100 Barnouw, p. 151
101 Cirano, quoted in Cross, p. 115

Chapter Five: Fourth Estate or Fourth Branch of Government?

102 "It was difficult to tell...", *New York Times*, 6-5-89
102 Forbes' birthday party, *New York Times*, 8-28-89
103 Radio & Television Correspondents banquet, *Washington Post*, 4-10-87
103 David Broder's 1988 award at the National Press Club, Alexander Cockburn, *In These Times*, March 1-14, 1989
104 Johnson quoted by Karp, *Harper's* magazine, July 1989
104 Marro, *Columbia Journalism Review*, March/April 1985
104 Wicker and Moyers quoted in Blyskal, p. 61
104 Air Force press releases, Herman and Chomsky, *Manufacturing Consent*, p. 22
104 13,000 PR people work for federal government, Stephen Hess, *The Government/Press Connection*, cited in Blyskal, p. 189
104 Abelson quoted in Karp, *Harper's* magazine, July 1989
104 Deaver quoted in Blyskal, p. 198
105 Pentagon PR arsenal, Blyskal, p. 9
105 DOD nixing peace organizations on NPR, Herman and Chomsky, p. 22
105 Knightley, *The First Casualty—From Crimea to Vietnam: The War Correspondent as Hero, Propagandist, and Myth Maker*, quoted in Blyskal, pp. 39-40
105 Dorman, *Bulletin of Atomic Scientists*, August 1985
106 *New York Times* editorial, 8-30-87
106 Friendly: "shield the audience..." quoted in Herman and Chomsky, p. 200
106 Friendly: "I must confess..." quoted in Cross, p. 79
106 De Borchgrave, *Newsweek*, 10-10-66
106 *Huntley-Brinkley Report* quoted in Herman and Chomsky, p. 200
106 Hersh's attempts to publicize the My Lai massacre, Adam Hochschild, *Mother Jones*, September/October 1981
107 *Washington Post* editorials, quoted in Bray, *The Pillars of the Post*, p. 40
107 Bray, pp. 55-6
107 *Boston Globe* survey of editorials on Vietnam, 2-18-68
108 Chomsky, *Propaganda Review*, Winter 1987-88
108 Snepp quoted in Peter Biskind, *Seven Days*, January 1978
108 Koppel, authors' interview, 1-10-90
109 Koppel profile on Laotian pilot, ABC TV News, 3-6-71
109 Peter Dale Scott, *The War Conspiracy: The Secret Road to the Second Indochina War*, p. 5. See also Scott's account of the war in Laos, pp. 27-47 and pp. 173-187
109 Koppel's omissions in reporting from Pakse were in sync with Nixon administration goals. As Peter Dale Scott wrote at the time, "The main problem Washington sees in Southeast Asian policy is that the war has become too public; the idea now is to hang on by reemphasizing the covert while publicly 'Vietnamizing' the war to dull popular

concern. Nixon is again stepping up our undercover involvements in Southeast Asia, with special focus in Laos and Cambodia, battlefields rarely penetrated by nosy TV camera teams." (*The War Conspiracy*, p. 23) The war in Laos took an estimated 350,000 Laotian lives, more than a tenth of the country's entire population.

109   Walter Smith, authors' interview, 11-15-89

109   Karp, *Harper's* magazine, July 1989

109   Walters' collaboration with the Reagan White House, *New York Times*, 3-17-89; *Wall Street Journal*, 3-16-89

110   Article by Trainor in *New York Times*, 7-17-87

110   "Ex-General to Join the Times," *New York Times*, 9-16-86

111   Gelb with the State Department, Alexander Cockburn, *The Nation*, 11-10-84; Walter Pincus, *Washington Post*, 10-23-84

111   *Bulletin of Atomic Scientists*, William Dorman, August 1985

111   The United States Information Agency spends close to a billion dollars annually "to tell the world about America."

112   Boyer, *Who Killed CBS?*, p. 143

112   Donaldson quoted in *San Francisco Chronicle*, 6-16-89

112   Graduates from NPR and PBS, supposedly an alternative to mainstream media, have served faithfully in various administrations, both Republican and Democratic. Douglas Bennett, president of NPR, was director of the State Department's Agency for International Development under Carter. The chairman of the Corporation for Public Broadcasting in the mid-1970s, W. Allen Wallis, became Undersecretary of State for Economic Affairs during the Reagan years. Sometimes reporters switch parties as easily as they slip through the revolving door: Susan Morrison, an off-air Capitol Hill reporter for the *MacNeil/Lehrer NewsHour*, became deputy communications director of the Bush for President campaign in 1980 after leaving her position as communications director for the Democratic National Committee.

113   Greenfield quoted in James Fallows, *New York Review of Books*, 6-12-86

113   The revolving door also turns easily for public regulators of private media corporations. Newton Minnow, FCC Commissioner during the 1960s, is on the board of directors of CBS. One study indicated that 65 FCC commissioners and high-level staffers who left the FCC between 1945 and 1970 had emerged from the private-communications sector before their FCC service, and 34 went into private-firm service after leaving the FCC.

114   CIA cooked data, according to former CIA analyst David MacMichael, authors' interview, Summer 1988

114   CBS chief Paley and CIA, Bernstein, *Rolling Stone*, 10-20-77

114   GE and CIA, *INFACT*

114   Bernstein, *Rolling Stone*, 10-20-77

115   Cline quoted in Charles B. Seib, *Washington Post*, 1-3-78

115   Colby quoted in *Rolling Stone*, 10-20-77

116   Keely's scoop from CIA, Joe Trento and Dave Roman, *Penthouse*, August 1977

116   Luce, Muir and CIA, *Rolling Stone*, 10-20-77

116   Braden, *Saturday Evening Post*, 5-20-67

116   Geyelin, the CIA and the *Washington Post*, Bray, pp. 144-145

116   Geyelin quoted in Marro, *Columbia Journalism Review*, March/April 1985

116   Katharine Graham quoted in Bray, p. 150

116   C.L. Sulzberger's column in *New York Times*, 9-13-67

117   *New York Times* series on the CIA and the media, December 25-27, 1977

117   Examples of English-language newspapers operated by the CIA included the *Rome Daily American*, *Bangkok Post*, and *Manila Times*. The most widely circulated CIA news service in the 1970s was Forum World Features. Based in London and owned by right-wing financier Richard Mellon Scaife, it syndicated to 300 media outlets around the world. In addition to serving as a conduit for CIA money, the Scaife Mellon Foundation has been a major supporter of Old and New Right projects, including conservative think tanks with high media profiles like Heritage Foundation, American Enterprise Institute and the Center for Strategic and International Studies.

117   "Broad and comprehensive...": "Report of Special Meeting held in [deleted] on 1 June

1951, Matters relating to CIA Project 'BLUEBIRD.'"

117 Anti-Soviet disinformation by the CIA, Biskind, *Seven Days*, January 1978; *New York Times*, 12-25-77

117 *The Penkovsky Papers*, Bray, p. 141

117 *The Penkovsky Papers* was one of at least 1,200 books subsidized in whole or part by the CIA, including 250 English-language titles. The CIA assisted in the preparation of a book on the KGB by *Reader's Digest* editor John Barron. Sometimes books supported by the Agency have been reviewed by CIA operatives in major media such as the *New York Times*. (Biskind, "How the CIA Manages the Media," *Seven Days*, January 1978)

117 Dulles at Princeton, Martin A. Lee and Bruce Shlain, *Acid Dreams: The CIA, LSD and the Sixties Rebellion*, p. 27

118 "No indication of Red use...", 3 December 1953 (title deleted)

118 "Apparently their major emphasis...", 14 January 1953 (title deleted)

118 CIA document regarding U.N. Ambassador Lodge, 5-11-53

118 U.S. Army study of brainwashing, Alan W. Scheflin and Edward M. Opton Jr., *The Mind Manipulators*, p. 89

118 CIA memo on subliminals, "Report Concerning Certain Techniques in Hypnosis, 17 January 1958"

119 Nixon on CIA subliminals, William R. Corson, *Armies of Ignorance*, p. 37

119 "Document on Terror," Christopher Simpson, *Blowback*, pp. 134-135; see also Martin A. Lee, *Propaganda Review*, Spring 1989

120 Stockwell, authors' interview, December 1988

120 *El Mercurio* and the CIA, Fred Landis, *Covert Action Information Bulletin*, March 1982; see also Martha Honey, "Contra coverage—paid for by the CIA," *Columbia Journalism Review*, March/April 1987; "CIA Back In," *Common Cause* magazine, September/October 1986

120 CIA and the Central American press, *Columbia Journalism Review*, March/April 1987; for information on the CIA and religious broadcasters in the Third World, see Sara Diamond, *Spiritual Warfare*, pp. 6-9

120 Pat Robertson and the contras, Diamond, pp. 16-19, 39-40

121 *Washington Times* and the NSC, Fred Clarkson, *Extra!* August/Septempber 1987

121 Unlike his predecessor Bill Casey, CIA director William Webster hasn't made public threats against journalists. Maybe that's because most reporters aren't inclined to rock the boat these days. William A. Baker, who left the Agency for a high post at the FBI, spoke of cordial relations between Webster's CIA and leading U.S. media. He told a Harvard University audience in 1989 that the *Wall Street Journal* had killed a story about counterterrorist operations in the Middle East at the CIA's request. And a *New York Times* correspondent agreed to delay a story about an alleged American double agent. Another example cited by Baker: The *Washington Post* altered a story about CIA property holdings in Virginia when asked to do so. (*Boston Globe*, 8-22-89, "Restraining the media at the CIA.")

122 Hoover on Anderson and Pearson, J. Edgar Hoover's Personal Files, 7-1-69

122 "Lower than the regurgitated filth of vultures," J. Edgar Hoover, quoted in Athan Theoharris, *The Boss*, p. 282n

122 Anderson on Jim Garrison, FBI document, 4-4-67

122 Anderson on Robert Kennedy, FBI document, 5-21-68; see also *Extra!*, November/December 1988

122 Williams quoted in Jeff Cohen, "The White House War Against Martin Luther King," *The Rebel*, 11-22-83

123 Cohen and Buchanan on *The Morton Downey Show*, 6-14-88

123 FBI document, "The director expressed his concern...", quoted in Herbert Mitgang, *Dangerous Dossiers*, p. 8

123 FBI sex files, *Extra!*, December 1987

124 Colson quoted in David L. Paletz and Robert M. Entman, *Media Power Politics*, p. 62

124 Attacks on the underground press, Lee and Shlain, *Acid Dreams*, p. 225

126 Copley and the FBI, Trento and Roman, *Penthouse*, August 1977

126 Compare the *New York Times* editorial (2-6-88) on the surveillance of CISPES to its new

story a week earlier (1-30-88). See also Ross Gelbspan's excellent articles on this subject in the *Boston Globe* (2-29-88, 3-15-88, 7-26-88).

126 Wise quoted in *Newsweek*, 10-13-87

127 Stone quoted in Marro, *Columbia Journalism Review*, March/April 1985

127 Kovach quoted in Marro, *Columbia Journalism Review*, March/April 1985

127 "You can say anything...", quoted in Marro, ibid.

127 Kalb quoted in Parenti, p. 202; see also Jeff Cohen and Martin A. Lee, *Newsday*, 1-21-87

127 James Petras, *The Nation*, 3-28-81; John Dinges, *Los Angeles Times*, 3-17-81; Jonathan Kwitny, *Wall Street Journal*, 6-8-81

127 Kraus quoted in *Extra!*, October/November 1987

128 Brodhead, *Guardian*, 9-16-87

128 Julian Robinson, Gene Guillemin and Matthew Meselson, "Yellow Rain: The Story Collapses," *Foreign Policy*, Fall 1987

128 *New York Times* on yellow rain, 8-31-87

129 Libya scare stories, Andrew Breslau, *Africa Report*, March/April 1987

129 Ganshow quoted in *Africa Report* March/April 1987

129 *New York Times* editorial on Libya, quoted in *Africa Report*, March/April 1987

129 The *Times* Sunday magazine subsequently published an article by Seymour Hersh on the U.S. plot to assassinate Qadaffi. As Hersh explained in an interview with FAIR: "There was manipulation of intelligence at the highest level. There were distortions and lies by the U.S. government about the true intent of the bombing raid. The Reagan administration claimed they were targeting tents and a house, and they had reason to believe that Qadaffi might be in those places. But they said they weren't trying to kill him. That's their position, and it's accepted by everybody. I'm not the social conscience of America, but I'm troubled by the fact that the Secretary of Defense can get up and make a statement like that and not have the reporters say, 'Come on.'" (*Extra!*, June 1987)

129 Syria behing the disco bombing, Cohen and Lee, *Newsday*, 1-21-87

129 Walcott and Seib, *Wall Street Journal*, 8-25-86

129 *Newsweek* on Libya disinformation, 10-13-86

129 After U.S. jets shot down two Libyan MIGs over the Gulf of Sidra in December 1988, a spate of news reports mentioned the U.S. attack on Tripoli following the 1986 La Belle disco bombing. *Time* (1-16-89) stated matter-of-factly that a "Libyan-backed terrorist bombed a disco in West Berlin," thereby provoking the U.S. "retaliatory" bombing. This was the official line put out by the White House, though the "irrefutable" evidence supporting the claim never materialized. A December 1988 AP dispatch disclosed that West Berlin authorities had officially ended their investigation of the La Belle disco bombing. But the five-paragraph version of the AP dispatch that ran in the *New York Times* (12-22-88) neglected to mention that West German officials found no proof of a Libyan connection.

129 Shultz quoting Churchill in *Newsweek*, 10-13-86

129 Early reports about CIA disinformation regarding Libya, *Newsweek*, 8-3-81

130 Bill Moyers, *The Secret Government—The Constitution in Crisis* (transcript)

131 Bonior quoted in *Extra!*, October/November 1987

131 Brumberg quoted in *Extra!*, October/November 1987

131 "A vast psychological warfare operation...", *Miami Herald*, 7-19-87

131 Raymond and the Office of Public Diplomacy, Peter Kornbluh, *Extra!*, Summer 1989

132 White hats and black hats, Kornbluh, *Extra!*, Summer 1989

132 "Into a real enemy and threat...", *Miami Herald*, 11-20-85

132 Cockburn, *Wall Street Journal*, 2-28-85

133 "Eyes only" memo to Buchanan, *Extra!*, October/Novembver 1987

133 Chamorro quoted in *Extra!*, October/November 1987

133 *Newsday* on Miranda, December 16 and 17, 1987

134 Guilmartin op-ed, *Wall Street Journal*, 3-11-85

134 Clifford Kraus and Robert Greenberger, *Wall Street Journal*, 4-3-85

134 Reich's letter in *Wall Street Journal*, 4-19-85

134 MacMichael quoted in *New York Times*, 6-14-84

134 State Department memo quoted in *Extra!*, October/November 1987

134   "Ample evidence," LeMoyne, *New York Times*, 8-13-87
136   "Evidence of Sandinista support...", LeMoyne, *New York Times*, 11-24-88
136   Connie Chung, NBC News, quoted in Holly Sklar, *Washington's War on Nicaragua*, p. 260
136   Lloyd, *NBC Nightly News*, 8-22-87
136   Owen quoted in *Extra!*, October/November 1987
136   Chamorro quoted in *Extra!*, October/November 1987
137   Spence survey, *Extra!*, October/November 1987
137   Americas Watch quoted in *Extra!*, October/November 1987
137   "A Day's Toll Shows Contras' Ability to Strike," *New York Times*, 11-13-86
138   *Boston Globe* on contra terrorism, 6-4-87
138   Reich, quoted in *Extra!*, June 1987
138   Reich visits NPR, *Extra!*, June 1987
138   *Nightline* programs on Central America, *Extra!*, January/February 1989
138   A similar slant was evident in *New York Times* coverage during the 90-day period following the signing of the Central American peace plan on August 7, 1987. FAIR research associate Chris Burke tallied the column inches of 215 articles in the *Times* and found a clear pattern. The *Times* devoted 3.6 times more column inches to Nicaragua than to three of its neighbors combined. The ratio of Nicaragua coverage to that of El Salvador was 5 to 1; Honduras 22 to 1; and Guatemala 26 to 1. This was a period of assassination and human rights reversals in El Salvador, rejection of the peace accord in Honduras and intensified warfare in Guatemala. Consider the coverage of a single week: The brief detetentions of oppositionists in Nicaragua were reported far more prominently in the *Times* (1-16 through 1-20-88) than the murder of human rights monitors in Honduras.
138   Koppel quoted in *Newsweek*, 6-15-87
138   Harriman, *Hack*, p. 186
139   Oliphant quoted in Hertsgaard, p. 258
139   Chomsky op-ed survey, *Propaganda Review*, Winter 1987-88
139   Reich memo, quoted in Kornbluh, *Extra!*, Summer 1989
139   GAO report on OPD, *Washington Post*, 10-5-87
139   Brooks quoted in *Washington Post*, 10-11-87
139   "They can shut down...", Kornbluh and Robert Parry, "Iran Contra's Untold Story," *Foreign Policy*, Fall 1988
140   AP report on Nicaraguan support for China crackdown, *Boston Globe*, 6-6-89; *Wall Street Journal*, 6-12-89
141   Schorr, *New York Times* op-ed, "Daniel Ortega: Our Man in Managua?", 11-5-89
141   Mark Twain quoted in Cook, *Extra!*, Summer 1989

Chapter Six: Politicians and the Press

142   Agnew speech to the Montgomery Chamber of Commerce in Alabama, November 20, 1969; text in *Frankly Speaking*, Spiro T. Agnew, p. 79
142   "Agnew was hypocritical...", Howard Bray, *The Pillars of the Post*, p. 94
142   Nicholas Johnson quoted in Bray, p. 93
142   Majority of 1968 endorsing editorials for Nixon-Agnew ticket cited in Bray, p. 93
142   History of newspaper endorsements for president in *Editor & Publisher*, 11-4-72; 11-3-84 10-29-88; 11-5-88
142   Entman critiqued the research of academics Stanley Rothman, S. Robert Lichter and Linda Lichter. (L. Lichter, S. R. Lichter and Rothman, "The Once and Future Journalists,' *Washington Journalism Review*, December 1982; see also, S. R. Lichter and Rothman, "Media and Business Elites," *Public Opinion*, October/November 1981) "There is no consensus formula for obtaining a sample that properly represents the national media," Entman concluded, "but this one is clearly skewed." (*Democracy Without Citizens*, Entman, p.32) Sociologist Herbert J. Gans, a senior fellow at the Gannett Center for Media Studies, wrote that Rothman and the Lichters "hide a political argument behind a

seemingly objective study, highlighting the data which support that argument," while "their approach often diverges sharply from scientific methodology." (Herbert J. Gans, "Are U.S. Journalists Dangerously Liberal?", *Columbia Journalism Review*, November/December 1985)

143 For an analysis of differences between the attitudes of younger journalists and older colleagues who are more likely to be editors, see *Editor & Publisher*, 11-16-85, "Debunking the liberal media bias belief," John Consoli.

143 Brookings Institution study (issued in 1981) cited in Bagdikian, p. 56.

143 *Los Angeles Times* survey: Gans, *Columbia Journalism Review*, November/December 1985

143 Hertsgaard, pp. 85-86

143 Gans, *Columbia Journalism Review*, November/December 1985

143 Mark Crispin Miller, op-ed, *New York Times*, 11-16-88

144 Gergen in *Public Opinion* magazine, December 1981 - January 1982; quoted in Hertsgaard, p. 97

144 Kinsley quoted in Rosenberg, *Los Angeles Times*; reprinted in *San Francisco Chronicle*, 9-4-89

144 Rosenberg column, *Los Angeles Times*; reprinted in *San Francisco Chronicle*, 9-4-89

144 Newfield column, New York *Daily News*, 2-27-89

144 "A soldier-patriot like Franco...", Buchanan column, *New York Post*, 9-17-89

145 Meyerson interview in *Newslink*, Collegiate Network, November 1988

145 Christian broadcasting statistics: Sara Diamond, *Spiritual Warfare: The Politics of the Christian Right*, pp. 1-2

145 Ellen Goodman, syndicated column; in *San Francisco Chronicle*, 4-14-89

146 Hersh, authors' interview, April 1987

146 Bernstein, speech at Institute of Politics, Harvard University, 3-20-89

146 "We realize that we did...", Helen Thomas quoted in Walter Spear, *The Presidents and the Press*, p. 195

146 Donna Woolfolk Cross, *MediaSpeak*, p. 80

147 Wilkins quoted in Bray, p. 154

147 Deep Throat's leaks to Woodward and Bernstein bore the earmarks of what historian William R. Corson, a former intelligence official, called "a highly skillful, organized counter-espionage operation whereby another intelligence service—the *Washington Post*—was manipulated in a classic manner." Corson wrote: "As the White House role in the Watergate cover-up was revealed in a series of stories in the *Washington Post* by Woodward and Bernstein, the suspicion that their 'Deep Throat' source was somehow connected with the intelligence community someplace in the White House or the NSC [National Security Council] became quite real... [F]rom a close reading of the *Post* series and *All the President's Men* it is possible to distill the essence of Deep Throat's information and the manner by which Woodward and the *Washington Post* were run... [I]t is significant to note the counterespionage techniques the secret source employed. Besides the examples of tradecraft employed in the meetings and information drops, these were used to manipulate Woodward et al. by giving them instructions where to look rather than providing the information directly... Deep Throat's ability to alter national policy and bring about a change in events is a clear and important statement of the power of intelligence information." (William R. Corson, *Armies of Ignorance*, p. 433)

148 Karp, *Harper's* magazine, July 1989

148 *New York Times*, 4-20-89

148 Thomas Ferguson, *The Nation*, 5-22-89

148 Gallup Report, January 1989; cited by Ferguson, *The Nation*, 5-22-89

148 Jeff Cohen interviewed in *In These Times*, March 15-21, 1989

149 Donaldson quoted in Mark Crispin Miller, *Boxed In*, p. 84

149 "It deprived the many...", Hertsgaard, *On Bended Knee*, p. 131

150 Gralnick quoted in Hertsgaard, *On Bended Knee*, pp. 62-63

150 Stahl quoted in Hertsgaard, pp. 162, 166

150 Gergen quoted in Hertsgaard, p. 203

150 Deaver quoted in Hertsgaard, p. 4

151   *Time*, 7-7-86
151   *Fortune*, 9-15-86; the cover story was titled "What Managers Can Learn From Manager Reagan"
152   Haynes Johnson, *Washington Post*, 1-24-82; cited in Elliot King and Michael Schudson, "The Myth of the Great Communicator," *Columbia Journalism Review*, November/December 1987
152   Anderson and Van Atta column, 4-28-86
.153   Hertsgaard, *On Bended Knee*, p. 302
154   Drew quoted in Hertsgaard, p. 332
154   *Miami Herald*, 7-5-87
154   According to the North-assisted plan to suspend the Constitution, control of the U.S. was to have been turned over to the national crisis-management unit, the Federal Emergency Management Agency, directed by Louis Guiffrida. He was the same administrator who had written a memo recommending the internment of all "American Negroes" in "assembly-centers or relocation camps," in the event of major civil disorder. (Noam Chomsky, *The Culture of Terrorism*, p. 42)
155   Manzar Al-Kassar's links with North and Arab terrorists, *Newsday*, 4-17-87
155   During Olliemania week, *Nightline* had Richard Secord, another Iran-contra conspirator, on solo. Host Ted Koppel's close friend, Noel Koch, had founded the Richard Secord Defense Committee.
156   Morton, CBS, 7-16-88
156   *Washington Week in Review*, PBS, 7-15-88
157   Plante and Sawyer, CBS, 7-16-88
158   Beck column, *Chicago Tribune*, 7-18-88
158   Broder, NBC, *Meet the Press*, 7-17-88
158   Broder column, *Washington Post*, 7-14-88
158   Poll results, *New York Times*, 12-1-87. On some key issues such as military spending, Dukakis was arguably to the right of public opinion. In early 1989 the Gallup Organization found that "the American public favors sharp reductions in military spending to reduce the budget deficit," and opposes cuts in education, Social Security, Medicare and health programs. (*Los Angeles Times*, 3-9-89; *New York Times*, 3-12-89)
159   Toronto *Globe and Mail*, 4-29-89
159   Donaldson, *This Week With David Brinkley*, 11-6-88
159   Bush's "solid" support for arms shipments to Iran, *New York Times*, 12-18-87
160   Minutes of national TV news devoted to arms-for-hostages scandal, contained in study by the Conference on Issues and Media (*Marin Independent Journal*, 9-6-88)
160   Peter Dale Scott, "George Bush: The Teflon Candidate," *Extra!*, September/October 1988
160   Peter Dale Scott provided details of Bush's oil-price-fixing agenda in *Extra!*, September/October 1988
160   *New York Times*, 9-13-88
161   "Politically inspired garbage," Bush spokesperson quoted in *Philadelphia Inquirer*, 9-13-88
161   Front-page story, *Philadelphia Inquirer*, 9-10-88
161   Follow-up story, *Philadelphia Inquirer*, 9-18-88; see also Russ Bellant, "Old Nazis, the New Right and the Reagan Administration," Political Research Associates (Cambridge, MA: 1988)
162   *El Reno* (Okla.) *Daily Tribune*, 11-4-88
162   "We were just told that it was due to unforeseen circumstances, that it had to be cancelled," prison staff duty officer Ed Rubes explained to us at the time. (Authors' interview, 11-7-89) Kimberlin's sister Cynthia maintained that "the press conference was cancelled and Brett was put into solitary confinement to prevent him from communicating with the media." (Authors' interview, 11-7-89)
162   Robert Shaw, authors' interview
163   Hanley, authors' interview, 11-6-88
163   "I had not put [the Kimberlin story] on the air because I couldn't corroborate his story with sources that I felt were sufficiently credible," National Public Radio reporter Nina Totenberg told us. But if the news conference had occurred "it probably would have" enhanced the possibilities of NPR's broadcasting the story, she said, "if it had been carried

elsewhere" in the media. "If the story wasn't going to hold and it was going to be splashed all over the front pages, we weren't—you know, we had an interview with the guy and we had to be prepared to go with it." In Totenberg's opinion, the cancellation of the press conference "certainly" lowered the chances that Kimberlin's claims would get coverage. In the end NPR opted not to air a word about any aspect of the Kimberlin matter. In retrospect, Totenberg told us a year later, "I think we did the right thing." (Authors' interview, 10-11-89)

163 Kimberlin's second stint in segregation lasted seven days. All in all, beginning four days before the presidential election, Kimberlin was kept in solitary incommunicado from November 4 to November 14 except for a 36-hour break from a Saturday night (November 5) to Monday morning.

163 Bush-Dukakis Debate Transcript, *Washington Post*, 9-26-88

163 *Legal Times*, 12-19-88, "Isolation for Inmate With Quayle Claims," Aaron Freiwald. Unless otherwise noted, quotations from *Legal Times* are from the 12-19-88 article. For follow-up stories also by Aaron Freiwald, see: *The Recorder* (San Francisco), 12-27-88, "Back to Solitary." Also, *Legal Times*, 1-30-89, "Prisons Director Defends Quayle Accuser's Isolation." Nine months after his exposé appeared in *Legal Times*, Freiwald told us that none of the people involved had contacted the newspaper to dispute the accuracy of the article. (Authors' interview, 9-21-89)

164 "The purpose of the detention, [Bureau of Prisons director] Quinlan says, was to protect the prisoner, not to stifle or punish him because of his highly charged, unproven allegations about Quayle," *Legal Times* reported. But the article went on to point out that "the basis for the detention order is shaky." The man in charge of public relations for the Justice Department, Loye Miller, "says his belief that Kimberlin needed protection came from a conversation he had with NPR reporter Nina Totenberg. Miller says Totenberg, who had interviewed Kimberlin by phone, related that Kimberlin was concerned for his safety. But Totenberg denies she ever made such a claim. And Kimberlin, in a phone interview from prison, says that when prison authorities came to put him in solitary confinement, he denied being in any danger. 'I told them I'm the one who has to worry about my protection,' says Kimberlin. 'I told them to leave me out, that I'd sign a waiver.'" When we interviewed Totenberg she reiterated that prison officials had claimed to be "relying on my say-so—something that I didn't say." She added that when she talked with Kimberlin just before his solitary isolation, "he was definitely worried, but he was not worried from the prison population, he was worried about the authorities after they cancelled his press conference, he was worried what *they* would do to him." (Authors' interview, 10-11-89)

164 Loye Miller does not dispute that he gave inaccurate information to *Legal Times* reporter Aaron Freiwald. Miller's explanation: "In his initial questioning, Freiwald pressed to know who above me at Justice had been informed about the Kimberlin affair as it unfolded through the weekend. I told him that I hadn't told anyone. Later he informed me that [the attorney general's executive assistant Robin] Ross contradicted that, by telling Aaron that I had informed him about Kimberlin Friday afternoon [November 4]. I conceded that Ross was indeed correct, that I had forgotten that I had talked to Ross, and that I stood corrected." (Miller memo to authors, 10-11-89)

164 A revealing sidelight is Loye Miller's revolving-door trek from the Washington press corps to government agencies to an armaments manufacturer. During the 1960s and 1970s, Miller was a political reporter for *Time* magazine, Knight-Ridder Newspapers, *Chicago Sun-Times* and Gannett News Service. Then he covered the White House for Newhouse News Service for a half-dozen years until 1985—when he joined the Reagan administration. In spring 1989 he moved on from his post as spokesman for the U.S. attorney general—to work as a public relations executive for the Northrop Corporation, one of the nation's leading military contractors. The special utility of a journalist like Loye Miller, as a PR operative for federal or corporate employers, was well articulated by *New York Times* reporter Michael Wines at one point in our interview. After we cited the *Legal Times* article's evidence that Miller had dissembled when he initially denied having discussed the Kimberlin matter with the attorney general's office prior to the election, Wines responded: "Most people who know Loye Miller—who was a reporter and a

respected reporter for about 20 years in this town, for a variety of publications including *Time* magazine and Newhouse Newspapers and some others—do not think of him as a guy who's a dissembler." (Authors' interview, 8-29-89)

165   Griswold's letter was dated 6-2-88; quoted in *Legal Times*, 12-19-88

165   Brett Kimberlin, authors' interview, 11-6-88

165   *Newsday* (12-21-88) published a staff-written four-paragraph item under the headline "Prison Move Confirmed." The article did not scratch the surface of the *Legal Times* revelations.

166   "Solitary for Quayle's Accuser," main edition, *New York Times*, 12-20-88

166   Meanwhile, the *New York Times* wire service version contained a brief addition that still evaded the crux of the *Legal Times* exposé: "A Bush-Quayle campaign official, Mark Goodin, was quoted in the *Legal Times* as saying he had been in touch with the Justice Department about Kimberlin's contentions." The wire story appeared in the *San Francisco Chronicle* and other newspapers, 12-20-88.

166   Michael Wines, authors' interview, 8-29-89.

167   "The People, the Thousands, Get a Look at Their House," *New York Times*, 1-22-89.

168   Cross, *Mediaspeak*, pp. 191-192

168   Mark Crispin Miller, *Boxed In*, p. 88

168   "Since Election Day…", *New York Times*, 1-22-89

168   Laitin quoted in *New York Times*, 1-22-89

168   Baker column, *New York Times*, 1-25-89

168   Walters quoted in *New York Times*, 1-22-89

168   Fitzwater quoted in *New York Times*, 4-2-89

168   "Bush Begins Perhaps His Toughest Job: Taming Press Corps," *New York Times*, 1-26-89

169   Gibson, *Extra!*, March/April 1989

169   *Rolling Stone*, July 13/27, 1989

169   "U.S. Came Through On Honduras Deal, Documents Show," *San Francisco Chronicle*, 5-2-89

170   Wertheimer, National Public Radio, *All Things Considered*, 4-15-89

170   U. S. Senate Subcommittee on Terrorism, Narcotics and International Operations, "Drugs, Law Enforcement and Foreign Policy," December 1988

170   Schorr, National Public Radio, *All Things Considered*, 7-5-89

171   *MacNeil/Lehrer NewsHour*, 7-5-89

171   *San Jose Mercury News*, 7-6-89

171   *Chicago Tribune* editorial, 7-6-89

172   Editorials: *New York Times*, 5-31-89; *Miami Herald*, 5-31-89; *San Francisco Examiner*, 6-4-89

172   Richard Cohen column in *Miami Herald*, 6-3-89

172   Schneider quoted in *Los Angeles Times*, 8-25-89

172   Thomas quoted in *USA Today*, 8-18-89

Chapter Seven: Money Matters

176   *Christian Science Monitor*, 10-6-89. The article, "Bush Successes Baffle Opposition," was by reporter Marshall Ingwerson.

176   The *Washington Post* article (10-4-89) declared that some Democratic leaders in Congress had made a mistake by using "class-warfare rhetoric" in fighting the Bush administration's proposal to reduce the capital gains tax.

176   "Rhymes With Rich," *Newsweek* , 8-21-89

177   "Number of Poor Americans At Lowest Level Since 1980," *Washington Post*, 7-31-87

177   Ann Bartz, *San Francisco Chronicle*, Book Review Section, 8-13-89

177   Barbara Ehrenreich, *Fear of Falling: The Inner Life of the Middle Class*, p. 8

177   Excerpts from Jesse Jackson's speech, at a banquet sponsored by the American Jewish Committee in Beverly Hills, appeared as an op-ed piece in the *Los Angeles Times*, 5-20-89

177   Hazel Henderson, *Media & Values* magazine, Media Action Research Center, Los

Angeles, Summer 1989

177   Barbara Wien, *Media & Values*, Summer 1989

178   *Time, Newsweek , U.S. News & World Report*, 10-30-89

178   Ramirez quoted in weekly *Santa Cruz Sun*, 10-27-89

179   Shaffer, letter, *Newsweek* , 11-20-89

179   Official poverty rate: *Washington Post*, 10-19-89. The headline was "Poverty Level
       Stabilizes at 31 Million," rounding the 31.9 million figure downward along the way. The
       article, reporting on statistics compiled for 1988, said that "a family of four was
       considered poor if cash income was below $12,092."

179   Joint Economic Committee estimate of poverty, *Washington Post*, 10-30-89

179   Children's poverty statistics: Children's Defense Fund, Coalition for the Homeless

179   "Japan's Ruling Elite Faces a Fed-up People," *New York Times*, 7-23-89

179   "Babies at Risk," *Frontline*, PBS, 5-30-89

179   Jonathan Kozol, *Newsweek* , Winter/Spring 1990 (special issue)

180   "President Bush's Hundred Days," editorial, *New York Times*, 4-23-89

180   James Reston, *New York Times*, 2-22-81; quoted in Herman, *Zeta*, June 1988

180   Weyrich quoted in Edward S. Herman, *Zeta*, June 1988

181   *International Herald Tribune*, 4-13-89

181   *USA Today*, 9-20-89

181   Robert J. Samuelson, *Newsweek* column, reprinted on *Washington Post* op-ed page, 7-19-
       89

181   Mobil op-ed ad, *New York Times*, 8-31-89

182   Jan Grover, *Artweek*, 1-24-87

182   Pamela Sparr, *Media & Values*, Summer 1989

182   David Johnston, authors' interview, 8-23-89

182   "Are You On the *Nightline* Guest List?: An Analysis of 40 months of *Nightline*
       Programming," By William Hoynes and David Croteau, February 1989, prepared for
       Fairness & Accuracy In Reporting.

183   Harris Poll, *San Francisco Chronicle*, 10-30-89

183   Article by Peter Passell, *New York Times*, 7-16-89

183   Gentrification, *Time* magazine, 11-23-87

184   Neil Smith, "How the Press Gentrifies," *Extra!*, January/February 1988

184   Pro-landlord editorial, *New York Times*, 1-16-88

185   Neil Smith, "How the Press Gentrifies," *Extra!*, January/February 1988

185   Samuelson's *Newsweek* column was reprinted on the *Washington Post* op-ed page, 7-19-89.

185   William Randolph Hearst Jr. column, *San Francisco Examiner*, 5-28-89

185   The Harris Poll on business power was conducted for *Business Week*; reported in *San
       Francisco Chronicle*, 5-19-89

185   Doug Henwood, authors' interview, 11-19-89

185   Associated Press, in *San Francisco Chronicle*, 7-22-89

186   "Keeping the game clean...", *Washington Post* editorial, 8-5-89

186   Doug Henwood, *Left Business Observer*, 1-17-89

186   John Hess, *Extra!*, January/February 1988

186   Median incomes figures: Joan B. Bernstein and Merton C. Bernstein, letter, *New York
       Times*, 6-2-89

186   Cokie Roberts, *This Week With David Brinkley*, ABC, 1-17-88

186   John Hess, *Extra!*, January/February 1988

186   John Hess, *The Nation*, 1-16-88

187   Article by David Hoffman, *Washington Post*, 9-24-89

187   "The Case Against Ted Koppel," *Washington Monthly*, May 1989

187   Peter Perl was quoted in an article on *Washington Post* labor practices, written by *In
       These Times* senior editor David Moberg for *Union* magazine and adapted in *Extra!*,
       May/June 1989.

188   Moberg, *Extra!*, May/June 1989

188   For management's view, see "ombudsman" Richard Harwood's column in the *Washington
       Post* (9-17-89); for an employee response, see letter by lead plaintiff Tom Sherwood in the
       Post (9-24-89).

188 Editorial endorsing Koch, *New York Times*, 9-3-89
188 *Los Angeles Times* survey cited in *A Workers Guide to the Media*, published by the United Auto Workers
188 Thomas Byrne Edsall, *The New Politics of Inequality*, p. 150
188 Auxiliary Bishop Joseph Sullivan quoted by Scripps-Howard News Service, *San Francisco Examiner*, 9-3-89
189 McClure, authors' interview, 11-13-89
189 Barbara Ehrenreich, "Diane Rehm Show," WAMU-FM Radio, Washington, D.C., 11-7-89
189 Roberta Lynch, *In These Times*, July 15/28, 1981
189 National Safe Workplace Institute report cited in four-paragraph item by UPI, *Chicago Tribune*, 9-3-89
190 Parenti, *Inventing Reality*, p. 12
190 *New York Times*, 11-6-89
190 McClure, authors' interview, 11-13-89
190 "Widespread, generally sympathetic...", *New York Times*, 7-14-89
191 Alexander Cockburn, *The Nation*, 8-21-89
191 TV coverage of Soviet and U.S. miners: *Extra!*, October/November 1989
191 McClure, authors' interview, 11-13-89
191 One of the outstanding NPR reports on the Pittston strike was aired 6-17-89 on *All Things Considered*.
191 For a detailed account of the occupation of the Pittston plant near Carbo, Virginia, see *Guardian*, 10-11-89.
192 "Labor Threatens the President" editorial, *New York Times*, 2-24-89. For details on media treatment of the Eastern strike, see *Extra!*, May/June 1989.
192 McClure, authors' interview, 11-13-89
192 Doron P. Levin article on U.A.W., *New York Times*, 6-18-89
192 Kenosha coverage in *New York Times*, 2-22-88
193 Bybee writing in *Extra!*, March/April 1989
193 *Los Angeles Times*, reprinted in *San Francisco Chronicle*, 11-4-89
194 "Death Is as Capricious as Life for Farm Leader," *New York Times*, 6-2-89
194 Poll on school spending, conducted by Media General and Associated Press; AP, *San Jose Mercury News*, 6-20-89
194 Jonathan Kozol, *Newsweek*, Winter/Spring 1990 (special issue)
195 *Christian Science Monitor*, 11-7-89. The article, datelined Boston, was by reporter David R. Francis.
196 Food banks reported that their supplies were down 16 percent nationwide during the Thanksgiving season of 1989. (NPR, *All Things Considered*, 11-22-89)
196 Stephen Wolf, *Vis a Vis* magazine, September 1989
196 Jonathan Kozol, *Newsweek*, Winter/Spring 1990 (special issue)
197 *Dallas Morning News* firing and forced resignation described by Bagdikian, p. 37; see also *The Progressive*, August 89
197 Patrick Bond, *Extra!*, March/April 1989
197 American Bankers Association claim on editorial ratio, *Extra!*, July/August 1988
197 Banking deregulation editorials: *Washington Post*, 4-1-88; *Baltimore Evening Sun*, 5-10-88; *Boston Herald*, 5-16-88
197 Quinn, *Newsweek*, 2-27-89
198 Bond, *Extra!*, March/April 1989
198 "A promising plan...", editorial, *New York Times*, 8-9-89
198 "An impressive achievement...", editorial, *Washington Post*, 8-6-89
198 *Wall Street Journal*, 2-16-89; *MacNeil/Lehrer NewsHour*, 2-15-89
198 *All Things Considered*, NPR, 8-2-89
199 Kemp "has earned high marks," *Newsweek*, 8-21-89
199 Roisman quoted in *St. Louis Post-Dispatch* article reprinted in *San Juan Star*, 12-22-88
199 Henwood, *Left Business Observer*, 7-27-89
199 Renter statistics: *Left Business Observer*, 7-27-89. The Census Bureau figures are from 1985, the latest data available.
200 Smith and O'Conner, *Extra!*, Summer 1989

200 "Aggressive panhandling...", *New York Times*, 7-29-88
200 Associated Press, *Santa Cruz Sentinel*, 2-17-89
200 *San Francisco Chronicle*, 7-24-89
200 Ellen Goodman, *San Francisco Chronicle*, 8-4-89

Chapter Eight: Unhealthy Reporting

201 Parenti, *Inventing Reality*, p. 55
202 *NBC Nightly News*, 12-7-89
202 For a critique of "Big Fears, Little Risks" see *Columbia Journalism Review*, September/October 1989
203 "Struggle to maintain...", *Washington Post*, 10-12-88
203 Week In Review section, *New York Times*, 10-23-88
203 *Time* and *Newsweek* , 10-31-88
203 "Can't be allowed to...", editorial, *Washington Post*, 10-14-88
204 *Washington Week in Review*, PBS, 10-21-88
204 Samuel H. Day Jr., authors' interview, 11-16-88. Nukewatch is based in Madison, Wisconsin.
204 "Dispute on Wastes Poses Threat to Weapons Plant," Fox Butterfield, *New York Times*, 10-21-88
205 "They Lied to Us," *Time*, 10-31-88
205 "We have a moral obligation...", *Washington Post*, 10-12-88
205 "The Energy Department has provided...", *New York Times*, 10-16-88
205 "The meager resources...", Matthew L. Wald, *New York Times*, 12-3-88
206 "Wide Threat Seen in Contamination at Nuclear Units," *New York Times* 12-7-88.
206 The claim that "no effect on humans has yet been found," headlined as fact by the *Times* (12-7-88), would have been false a decade earlier, let alone in 1988. (For details, see the 1982 book *Killing Our Own: The Disaster of America's Experience With Atomic Radiation*, by Harvey Wasserman and Norman Solomon.)
206 "The Bomb on Mr. Bush's Desk," editorial, *New York Times*, 12-9-88
206 "How a Vital Nuclear Material Came to Be in Short Supply," *New York Times*, 12-31-88
207 "He set out a program...", editorial, *Washington Post*, 6-30-89
207 Watkins on *MacNeil/Lehrer NewsHour*, PBS, 8-2-89
207 "The department refused to commit...", *New York Times*, 9-8-89
207 ABC *World News Tonight*, 6-16-89
207 *Time*, 7-3-89
208 "An Energy official said...", *Washington Post*, 9-23-89
208 *Christian Science Monitor*, 10-2-89
208 Energy Department report on Nevada Test Site described in *Los Angeles Times*, 8-5-89
209 Newfield, *Village Voice*, 7-22-86
209 "That folly could...", editorial, *New York Times*, 5-13-88
209 "Could have educated people...", editorial, *New York Times*, 2-17-89
209 "Governor Cuomo's festoon...", editorial, *New York Times*, 3-11-89
210 Frances Cerra, letter to *Quill* magazine, March 1984; cited by Karl Grossman, *Extra!*, May/June 1989
210 Blass quoted by Grossman, *Extra!*, May/June 1989
210 As in news articles about beleaguered nuclear arms plants, reporters have taken to using the word "troubled" to describe nuclear power projects under fire. In the *New York Times* business section (7-31-89), a piece under the headline "Delay and Shoreham" started referring to "those fighting to keep the troubled reactor alive." In San Francisco the daily *Examiner* (3-28-89) used the same adjective while also personalizing the nuclear plant as though it could experience emotions, as one headline read: "Troubled Rancho Seco fears it may be shut down."
210 "Three Mile Island: The Good News," Thomas H. Pigford, op-ed page, *New York Times*, 3-28-89

211   "Scare stories about radiation...", editorial, *New York Times*, 4-18-80

211   Jane Brody, "3 Mile Island: No Health Impact Found," *New York Times*, 4-15-80

211   "Three Mile Island's Second Accident: How Government Failed," *Baltimore News-American*, 7-20-80. The exposé produced by a journalistic team, was primarily written by Laura T. Hammel. The *News-American* is no longer in business.

211   The shoddiness of Jane Brody's "investigation" into the TMI aftermath was later documented in *Killing Our Own*, Wasserman and Solomon, pp. 250-253.

211   For in-depth investigative journalism about the health fallout from Three Mile Island eight years after the accident, see Harvey Wasserman's article "Three Mile Island Did It," *Harrowsmith* magazine, May/June 1987.

211   Tom Gervasi, *Deadline* magazine, Center for War, Peace, and the News Media, New York University, July/August 1986

212   *New York Post*, 5-2-86

212   *Moscow News* article was summarized by Associated Press; *Seattle Times*, 2-16-89

212   For a sample of U.S. Council for Energy Awareness ads, see *Time*, 11-20-89, p. 85

212   "Experts See Nuclear Energy as Cure for Global Warming," *New York Times*, 9-25-89

213   "Revive the Atom," editorial, *New York Times*, 12-8-89

213   Richard Harris, *All Things Considered*, NPR, 8-23-89

214   *Newsweek* , 9-18-89; *U.S. News & World Report*, 9-18-89

214   *U.S. News & World Report*, 9-18-89

214   "The Disaster That Wasn't," *U.S. News & World Report*, 9-18-89

214   "Alaska After Exxon," *Newsweek* , 9-18-89

214   *Newsweek* , 9-18-89

214   *U.S. News & World Report*, 9-18-89

215   *Newsweek* , 9-18-89

216   *USA Today*, 9-16-89

216   "Joe's bad trip," *Time*, 7-24-89

216   *Newsweek* and *U.S. News & World Report*, both 9-18-89

217   "The greatest damage...Locals joke about nominating...Unsightly rocks and beaches...To assuage an angry public...", *U.S. News & World Report*, 9-18-89

217   *U.S. News & World Report*, 7-3-89. The story was titled "The Battle for the Wilderness."

217   "Alaska's Big Spill: Can the Wilderness Heal?", *National Geographic*, January 1990

217   "Environmentalists Hope for Scorcher," *Washington Post*, 6-21-89

218   "Ocean Dumpers Need Help, Not Fines," editorial, *New York Times*, 7-22-89

218   "Americans have never been safer...", *New York Times*, 5-8-88

218   "Filthy river creates two-state dilemma—Jobs vs. Health," Associated Press, *San Francisco Chronicle*, 6-19-89

218   *Greenpeace*, May/June 1988

218   Jim Sibbison, *Columbia Journalism Review*, November/December 1988

219   Weisskopf quoted in Sibbison, *Columbia Journalism Review*, November/December 1988

219   Warren Brookes, *San Francisco Chronicle*, 8-1-89

219   "Costly rules," *New York Times*, reprinted in *San Jose Mercury News*, 6-23-89

219   "Cure for Greenhouse Effect: The Costs Will Be Staggering," *New York Times*, 11-19-89

219   Shabecoff quoted in *Extra!*, May/June 1988

221   Russell, *Extra!*, May/June 1988

221   "The environment is damned near indestructible," *Newsweek* , 7-24-89

221   "Saving the environment...", *USA Today*, 6-1-89

222   "Brazil's Imperiled Rain Forest," *National Geographic*, December 1988

222   Susanna Hecht and Alexander Cockburn, *Extra!*, Summer 1989. See also their book *The Fate of the Forest: Developers, Destroyers, Defenders of the Amazon*

222   Dumanoski and Ellerbee quoted in *Extra!*, May/June 1988

222   William Buckley, op-ed page, *New York Times*, 3-18-86

223   "Quickly withdrew the proposal...", Buckley, op-ed column, *Washington Post*, 4-23-89

223   *Los Angeles Times* 5-31-82 front-page story on AIDS cited in article by James Warren, *Chicago Tribune*, 5-21-89

223   Grover, *High Performance* magazine, 1986, Issue 36

223   Survey of AIDS articles: Centers for Disease Control, cited in chart accompanying article

by Randy Shilts in *7 Days* magazine, 6-7-89

224 Paul Monette, *Borrowed Time: An AIDS Memoir*, p. 110

224 Doug Ireland, *Village Voice*, 8-8-89

225 Lindsay Law, quoted in *New York Times*, reprinted in *Datebook* magazine of the *San Francisco Chronicle*, 7-23-89

225 James Hurley, "I'm Dying—AIDS Is Your Problem Now," *Newsweek* , 8-10-87

225 "Masks an obvious…", Grover, *Extra!*, March/April 1989

225 *Newsweek* (3-14-88) proclaimed the advent of an AIDS assault on heterosexuals with a cover-story excerpt of a book by researchers Masters, Johnson and Kolodny. Their study, small and poorly designed, warned that "the AIDS virus is now running rampant in the heterosexual community." The Surgeon General was expressing a scientific near-consensus when he condemned the report as "irresponsible." Equally irresponsible was a featured *Cosmopolitan* magazine article (January 1988) that staked out the other extreme position, dangerously reassuring women not to be concerned about being infected with AIDS from unprotected vaginal intercourse.

225 Randy Shilts, "Invisible Ink: The AIDS Story the Media Keep Missing," *7 Days*, 6-7-89

226 Mayor Agnos quoted by UPI, *San Francisco Chronicle*, 6-21-89

226 "Inarguably, the fact…", Randy Shilts, *San Francisco Chronicle*, 7-10-89

227 "Why Make AIDS Worse That It Is?", *New York Times*, 6-29-89. The editorial appeared five days after the U.S. General Accounting Office released a study that had taken two years to prepare. The study "predicts that 300,000 to 485,000 Americans will have been diagnosed with AIDS by the end of 1991, a range far higher than the federal government's estimate of 195,000 to 320,000." (*Washington Post*, 6-25-89)

227 Doug Ireland, *Village Voice*, 7-11-89

Chapter Nine: Press and Prejudice

228 Billy Packer quoted in *Ms.* magazine, "You Call This Adorable?", October 1988

229 Brokaw, quoted in Miller, *Boxed In*, p. 107

229 Neuharth column quoting David Broder, *USA Today*, 8-11-89

229 Neuharth column on "sky girls," *USA Today*, 7-28-89

229 "Offended, outraged and embarrassed," letter appearing in *USA Today*, 8-1-89

229 Figures on women within the journalism profession from studies by the University of Missouri and the Washington-based Communications Consortium

229 Marlene Sanders quoted in *Chicago Tribune*, 4-9-89

229 The percentage of female TV news directors was cited by Vernon A. Stone in *Communicator*, August 1989. At radio stations the figure was 26 percent.

229 Linda Ellerbee interviewed in *USA Today*, 4-10-89

230 Barbara Kellerman, op-ed page, *Christian Science Monitor*, 7-20-88

230 The *New York Times* op-ed page writers are mostly male—by a lopsided margin. Out of 309 opinion pieces by outside contributors in the *Times* during the first six months of 1989 (excluding Sundays), only 13 percent were by females. (*Mother Jones*, January 1990)

230 Figures on women's treatment in news coverage: Study released by Communications Consortium, April 1989

230 Betty Friedan quoted in *New York Times*, 4-11-89

230 Junior Bridge quoted in *San Francisco Bay Guardian*, 5-31-89

230 Smeal on FAIR/*Undercurrents* program, WBAI-FM Radio in New York City, 5-26-89

231 Jeff Greenfield, *Nightline* , ABC, 7-3-89

231 For examples of use of "abortion supporters" and "pro-abortion" labels, see news articles in *Chicago Tribune*, 4-23-89, 7-6-89, 7-18-89.

231 "Abortion rights gain for father," *Chicago Tribune*, 5-12-89

231 Kate Michelman, letter, *New York Times*, 5-4-89

231 *U.S. News & World Report*, 2-6-89

232 "This topic is one…", network official quoted in *Chicago Tribune*, 6-20-89

232 "Roe v. Wade" on NBC TV, cited in *New York Times*, 5-15-89

232 Smeal on FAIR/*Undercurrents* program, WBAI, 5-26-89

232 Barbara Ehrenreich, op-ed page, *New York Times*, 4-28-89

232 Newspaper bars on reporters in abortion protests: *New York Times*, 4-16-89

233 "Chinese Journalists Demand Freedom," *Washington Post*, 5-10-89

233 Simonton, authors' interview, 12-19-89

233 Michele Andre quoted in Reuters, *San Francisco Chronicle*, 11-27-89

233 Chicago shelters figure cited by Clarence Page, *Chicago Tribune*, 12-14-88

233 "Women Face the '90s," *Time*, 12-4-89

234 Elizabeth Holtzman, op-ed page, *New York Times*, 5-5-89

234 Katha Pollitt, *New York Times* magazine, 6-18-89

234 *This Week With David Brinkley* show cited in *New Directions for Women*, July/August 1989

234 "The senator is not...", *U.S. News & World Report*, 10-10-88

234 A National Crime Survey found that 41.7 percent of rapes are by a man who the woman knows well; another 3.8 percent by casual acquaintances; 6.5 percent by the current husband and 4.8 percent by an ex-husband. (Figures cited by Joan Beck, *Chicago Tribune*, 2-9-89)

234 Robin Warshaw, interviewed by our research associate Paula Kamen, 11-14-89

235 "Would You Trade Today for Life in the '50s?", *Parade*, 12-6-87

235 "Remembering Stonewall," *All Things Considered*, NPR, 7-1-89

235 Raul Ramirez quoted in *San Francisco Bay Guardian*, 6-7-89

236 David Israels, *San Francisco Bay Guardian*, 7-26-89

236 Donna Minkowitz, *Village Voice*, 6-27-89

236 Janet Caldwell quoted in *New York Times*, 6-8-89

236 *Entertainment Tonight*, 9-27-89

237 "Finding pathways out of homosexuality," *Christian Science Monitor*, 3-3-88

237 *Christian Science Monitor* policy against gay employees: *Gay Community News*, October 4/10, 1987; letter from the *Monitor*'s circulation manager, David E. Els, to Steven Rhodes, 1-22-88; authors' interview, *Christian Science Monitor* spokesman Thomas Johnsen, 1-5-90

237 "Lesbian Partners Find the Means to be Parents," *New York Times*, 1-30-89; editor's note, 2-3-89

237 Several corporations pulled about $1.5 million worth of commercials from ABC television's *thirtysomething* in November 1989. The network lost the ad revenue for an episode that showed two men in bed together after making love. "Advertisers generally either pre-screen shows or they or their agencies are informed of the subject matter by the networks so they can decide whether shows meet their criteria," the *New York Times* (11-14-89) reported.

237 "Omar The Evil," *The Reporters*, Fox TV, 3-11-89

237 GLADD letter to Gerald Stone, executive producer, *The Reporters*, 3-13-89

237 GLADD letter to Victor Neufield, executive producer, 20/20, ABC News, 3-23-89

238 Redistricting article, *New York Times*, 5-30-89

238 Follow-up redistricting article, *New York Times*, 8-6-89

238 Jacqi Tully, *San Francisco Examiner*, 6-4-89

238 Prime-time violence and dramatized murder figure: Carl M. Cannon, Knight-Ridder Newspapers, *Washington Post*, 9-19-89

239 Wilcox quoted in Cannon, *Washington Post*, 9-19-89

239 Huston quoted in Cannon, *Washington Post*, 9-19-89

239 Lubinski and National Council on Alcoholism quoted in *USA Today*, 5-31-89

239 In an exceptional article, *New Age Journal* devoted several pages to fetal alcohol syndrome. "Because most of the alcohol a mother drinks passes through the placenta, by the time a woman feels the effects of her drinking, the baby may well have passed out," the magazine explained. The key point: "The Surgeon General of the United States counsels that there is no safe amount of liquor for a pregnant woman or a nursing mother. Abstinence is the only safeguard." (*New Age Journal*, November/December 1989)

240 Craig Reinarman and Harry G. Levine, "The Crack Attack" chapter, Joel Best (editor), *Images of Issues: Typifying Contemporary Social Problems*, p. 130

240 A nationwide study, released in December 1989, directly contradicted the racial assumptions that have long guided news coverage of drugs. Drawing on interviews with more than 350,000 students in 38 states, the National Parents' Resource Institute for Drug Education came to startling conclusions. "Despite countless stories about how crack cocaine has ravaged black urban America," said one newspaper report, the new study "shows that white teenage students are more likely to use drugs and alcohol than their black counterparts." (*San Francisco Chronicle*, 12-19-89)

240 Poll data on drugs, gathered by CBS News and the *New York Times*, was reported in the *Times*, 9-12-89. As sociologists Craig Reinarman and Harry G. Levine have written: "In opinion polls in 1986 and 1988 more people picked 'drugs' as the 'most important problem facing the country.' However, these opinion poll results *followed* rather than led media coverage and political rhetoric. In 1987, between elections, when the drug scare was not fueled by election rhetoric and so much media coverage, only 3-5 percent of those surveyed picked drugs as our most important problem." (*Images of Issues*, p. 129)

240 "The crime-and-drug crisis...", *New York Times* News Service, *San Francisco Chronicle*, 4-14-89

241 "There is broad agreement...", editorial, *New York Times*, 9-7-89

241 Hearst, *San Francisco Examiner*, 9-10-89

241 "In Cities, Poor Families Are Dying of Crack," *New York Times*, 8-11-89

241 Clarence Page, interviewed by our research associate Paula Kamen, 9-27-89

241 "More than $100 billion...", *New York Times*, 8-27-89

242 Cover story on crack, *Newsweek* , 11-28-88

242 Hutchinson, *Extra!*, May/June 1989

242 Jeffrey H. Reiman, *The Rich Get Richer and the Poor Get Prison: Ideology, Class, and Criminal Justice* (Second Edition), p. xi

242 Gerry Spence, quoted in *The Nation* (11-20-89), from his book *With Justice For None: Destroying an American Myth*. Spence was drawing on an estimate by the Bureau of National Affairs.

242 Reiman, p. xii

242 Murder and workplace death rates, Reiman, p. 34

242 "Although these work-related deaths...", Reiman, p. 35

243 Kirk A. Johnson, *Columbia Journalism Review*, May/June 1987. The two mostly-black neighborhoods in the study were Roxbury and Mattapan. The major media monitored were the *Boston Globe*, the *Boston Herald*, WGBH-TV, WBZ-TV, WCVB-TV and WBCN-FM Radio. The black-owned media monitored were the *Bay State Banner*, *Roxbury Community News*, *Boston Greater News* and WILD-AM Radio.

243 Parenti, *Inventing Reality*, p. 12

244 Clarence Page, interviewed by Paula Kamen, 9-27-89

244 Clarence Page column, *Chicago Tribune*, 5-14-89

244 Clarence Page, interviewed by Paula Kamen, 9-27-89

244 "U.S. Paying Stiff Price for Porous Borders," *Christian Science Monitor*, 10-10-89

245 Linda Mitchell, authors' interview, 11-26-89

245 *Essence*, July 1988

245 Reagan racist comments cited in *Extra!*, March/April 1988

246 Roger Pearson letter cited in *Village Voice*, 5-7-85. During the 1970s Pearson was president of the U.S. section of the World Anti-Communist League, an international umbrella organization composed of neo-Nazis, anti-Semites and death squad leaders.

246 Racist slurs in White House, *Extra!*, March/April 1988

246 Watt racist comments cited in *Extra!*, March/April 1988

246 *Guardian*, 12-14-88

246 Robert Michel had no trouble touting himself as an expert on bringing ethics to Congress in the months that followed exposure of his racist comments. The *New York Times* published two of his op-ed articles on the subject during the first half of 1989—"This House Needs Cleaning" (1-5-89) and "Full Repairs for the Broken House" (6-18-89). It was no surprise that neither article mentioned racism as being among the "ethical" problems in Congress.

246 *The Nation*, 11-28-87

247 Marshall quoted in *New York Times*, 9-9-89
247 Cokie Roberts, *All Things Considered*, National Public Radio, 6-25-89
247 Racial composition of elected officials: *San Francisco Examiner*, 8-13-89
247 *Time*, 11-20-89
247 Howard Fineman, *Washington Week in Review*, PBS, 7-15-88
247 *Newsweek* , 11-20-89
247 Kirk A. Johnson, *Columbia Journalism Review*, May/June 1987
248 Clarence Page, interviewed by Paula Kamen, 9-27-89
248 Wong quoted in *City On A Hill*, University of California at Santa Cruz, 4-6-89
248 Harold Washington, from a speech to the National Association of Black Journalists in Miami, August 1986; excerpted in *Extra!*, December 1987
248 American Society of Newspaper Editors, press release, 4-11-89. The 1989 breakdown of newspaper journalists was: 2,310 blacks (4.1 percent); 1,160 Hispanics (2.1 percent); 620 Asian-Americans (1.1 percent); and 146 Native Americans (.25 percent).
249 "'Sense of Muscle' for Black Journalists," *New York Times*, 8-21-89
249 *Columbia Journalism Review*, November/December 1988, "The 'Max' Factor at The New York Times," Bruce Porter
249 For summary of New York *Daily News* discrimination case, see *Christian Science Monitor*, 4-20-87
249 Electronic media figures: Vernon A. Stone, *Communicator*, August 1989
249 Linda Ellerbee and Barbara Reynolds, *USA Today*, 4-10-89
249 Reynolds, interviewed by our research associate Paula Kamen, 11-28-89
250 Noel Cazenave, writer of the afterword to *Race and Media: The Enduring Life of the Moynihan Report* by Carl Ginsburg, p. 76
250 George Miller and Republican reply quoted in *Washington Post*, 10-2-89
250 Kondracke, *New Republic*, 2-6-89; quoted in Carl Ginsburg, *Race and Media*, p. 2
250 Moyers documentary first aired on CBS, 1-25-86
250 "Bill Moyers and CBS News...", *Newsweek* , 1-27-86
250 Barbara Omolade, *Village Voice*, 7-15-86
251 Dorothy Height, *The Nation*, July 24/31, 1989
251 Stephen Jay Gould, *Ever Since Darwin*, p. 239; quoted in Ginsburg, p. 73
251 "Black Men: An Endangered Species," part of the *Horizons* series, National Public Radio, broadcast in October 1989; aired on KQED-FM Radio, San Francisco, 10-29-89
252 Martin Luther King Jr. speeches and anti-King editorials quoted by Ada Sanchez and Norman Solomon, op-ed, *San Jose Mercury News*, 4-3-83
252 For details on TV's selective depictions of Martin Luther King Jr., see Jeff Cohen's article in *Extra!*, March/April 1988

Chapter Ten: U.S.-Soviet Relations

257 Julia Preston quoted in Parenti, p. 174
257 Jonathan Kwitny quoted in Hertsgaard, p. 193
257 U.N. vote on Afghanistan, *New York Times*, 11-11-87
258 "Christ, maybe we are biased," *Extra!*, December 1987
258 "U.S. Army Engineers Fight Poverty in Honduras," *New York Times*, 4-17-88
258 James Reston, *New York Times*, 6-23-85; quoted in Hertsgaard, p. 300
258 "CIA Seeks Looser Rules...", *New York Times*, 10-17-89
258 Walter Lippmann and Charles Merz, *New Republic*, 8-11-20
259 Upton Sinclair, *The Brass Check*, Cornwall edition, p. 387
260 Joe Sedelmaier, authors' interview, December 1985
260 *New York Times*, 4-26-89
260 *Los Angeles Times*, 4-26-89
260 *Los Angeles Times*, 4-27-89, *New York Times*, 4-28-89
260 *Wall Street Journal*, 6-6-89; the article, "Red Storm Rising in the Ukraine," was by Roman Solchanyk.

261 *Washington Post*, 9-21-89

261 *New York Times*, 9-21-89

261 Reuters, 9-21-89. Ironically, the 31-paragraph Reuters dispatch appeared in the right-wing *Washington Times*.

261 *Nightline*, 12-4-87

261 Shultz quoted in *Washington Post*, 12-15-87

261 Shea quoted in *Extra!*, December 1987

262 Samuel H. Day Jr., *Extra!*, December 1987

262 *Newsweek* , 12-14-87; ABC *World News Tonight*, 12-6-87

262 Rather and Andrews, CBS, 12-8-87

263 Jennings, ABC *World News Tonight*, 5-31-88

263 Geyelin op-ed, *Washington Post*, 6-1-88

263 Richard Cohen op-ed, *Washington Post*, 5-26-88

264 Andrea Mitchell, Moscow news conference, 6-1-88

264 Lou Cannon, *Washington Post*, 6-2-88

264 Michael Dobbs article, *Washington Post*, 5-31-88

264 *New York Times* editorial, "The Cold War Is Over," 4-2-89

265 "It Hurts to Be Old and Poor in a Classless Society," *New York Times*, 5-20-89

265 "After Rash of Wildcat Moves, Soviets Admit Right to Strike," *New York Times*, 5-4-89

265 Hoagland op-ed, *Washington Post*, 10-20-88

265 "Vote Chagrins a Taciturn Soviet Press," *New York Times*, 3-29-89

266 *New York Times* quotes, "seem virtually indistinguishable" and "filtered out," cited in *The Nation* magazine, 4-17-89

266 Flora Lewis op-ed, *New York Times*, 4-5-89

266 *The Nation* magazine, 4-17-89

266 "Gorbachev Aide Warns of Rightist Reaction Ahead," *New York Times*, 6-18-89

266 Article on Soviet textbooks by Seth Mydans, *New York Times*, 8-29-85

267 Baker view on "new thinking," *New York Times*, 4-13-89

267 Bombers to Libya article, *New York Times*, 4-5-89

267 Shipler op-ed, *New York Times*, 11-14-88. Shipler's commentary, headlined "The Russians Shame Us," drew the line at frank discussion of social stratification inside the United States—complaining of "Michael Dukakis' divisive plays to class antagonisms" and thus frowning on even the Democratic presidential nominee's mild criticisms of economic inequities in the U.S.

268 Lesley Stahl, *Face the Nation*, CBS, 7-9-89

269 Article quoting unnamed State Department official, *New York Times*, 4-12-89

269 "Soviets Take W. Europe by Charm," *Los Angeles Times*, 6-9-89

269 Rather quoted in *New York Times*, 4-5-89

269 Friedman article on "Gorby fever," *New York Times*, 4-25-89

269 "The Soviet leader managed to throw a little gasoline...", *New York Times*, 5-14-89

269 "The more the Kremlin leader appears...", *New York Times*, 5-18-89

269 Meg Greenfield, *Newsweek* , 11-4-85

270 *Newsweek* , 1-23-89

271 "America's Best & Worst Weapons," *U.S. News & World Report*, 7-10-89

271 "Carry a 475-kiloton nuclear warhead...", *New York Times*, 8-18-89

271 Halloran article on Trident, *New York Times*, 8-20-89

271 Michael Ross op-ed, *New York Times*, 8-25-89

272 Examples of Northrop ads for B-2 Stealth: *New York Times* op-ed pages of 7-9-89 and 7-14-89

272 The Knight-Ridder exposé by Frank Greve appeared in the *San Jose Mercury News* (3-12-89) and other newspapers.

272 Exposé of aggressive new Pentagon nuclear strategy, *Los Angeles Times*, 7-23-89

272 *Washington Week in Review*, PBS, 7-28-89

273 Gordon front-page article, *New York Times*, 4-21-89

273 Public Agenda Foundation poll cited in article by Jay Rosen, *Deadline*, November/December 1988

273 Jay Rosen, *Deadline*, November/December 1988

274 In 1963 the superpowers joined in a Limited Test Ban Treaty that barred nuclear test explosions in the atmosphere, under water or in outer space. That left underground nuclear tests.

274 Hertsgaard, *On Bended Knee*, p. 290

274 Nuclear test editorial, *New York Times*, 7-31-85

274 Nuclear test editorial, *Washington Post*, 9-2-85

274 "Well, a little pre-Christmas propaganda...", Dan Rather quoted in Hertsgaard, p. 292

275 "Limits on testing...", editorial, *New York Times*, 9-25-86

275 Kosta Tsipis, *Deadline*, November/December 1986

275 "What Mr. Gorbachev seeks...," editorial, *New York Times*, 9-25-86

275 Among the aspects of nuclear testing virtually ignored by U.S. media is its role in undermining efforts to dissuade other countries from acquiring nuclear weapons. "Unless you have a comprehensive test ban, you're never going to stop proliferation," a former assistant director of the U.S. Arms Control and Disarmament Agency, Herbert Scoville, told us in a 1980 interview. More than 100 nations are signatories of a nonproliferation treaty pledging "to pursue negotiations in good faith on effective measures relating to cessation of the nuclear arms race." With the U.S. committed to continuing nuclear tests, its message to the Third World amounts to: Do as we say, not as we do.

275 Editorial against the freeze appeared in the Sunday *New York Times*, 10-25-82; reprinted in *Los Angeles Herald Examiner*, 10-26-82

276 "Soviet stooge groups" editorial, *Washington Post*, 10-6-82

Chapter Eleven: The Twin Scourges

277 *Washington Post* editorial, 1-27-81; quoted in Parenti, pp. 148-9

278 Dan Rather, "God and Gorbachev," *CBS Evening News*, 11-29-89

278 Edward S. Herman and Frank Brodhead, *The Rise and Fall of the Bulgarian Connection*, p. xv

278 Editorial on KAL shootdown, *New York Times*, 9-2-83

278 Editorial on Iran Air shootdown, *New York Times*, 7-5-88

278 Rather quoted in *Extra!*, July/August 1988

280 "This was a period...", *Nightline*, 8-25-86

280 *Nightline* coverage of KAL shootdown, 8-31 to 9-9-83

280 *Nightline* programs on Iran Air shootdown, 7-4, 7-6, 7-11-88

281 Reagan, *New York Times*, 7-7-88

281 "The Lie that Wasn't Shot Down," editorial, *New York Times*, 1-18-88

281 R.W. Apple, *New York Times*, 7-5-88

281 Tabloid covers *Newsday* and *New York Post*, 7-5-88

281 *Newsday* editorial, 7-7-88

283 Toronto *Globe and Mail*, 10-8-88

283 Reagan and Bush on Pan Am Flight 103, quoted in *Extra!*, March/April 1989

283 Posada and Cubana airliner, *New York Times*, 12-10-86

283 Posada at Ilopango, *Miami Herald*, 10-21-86

284 Posada interviewed by Venezuelan TV, *Extra!*, March/April 1989

284 Cohen, *Extra!*, March/April 1989; *Extra!* article adapted in part from Cohen's *Los Angeles Times* op-ed, 1-9-89

284 Rodriguez briefing Bush on contra resupply, *CBS Evening News*, 1-25-88

284 Gannon, Lariviere and O'Connor, *Washington Post*, 12-26-88

284 McKee, *Philadelphia Inquirer*, 1-6-89

284 "Pan Am bomb linked to double-dealing CIA drug plot," John Picton, *Toronto Star*, 11-2-89

285 Falk, *Revolutionaries and Functionaries*, p. xiii

285 Smith, *CBS Evening News*, 1-10-89

285 Cline and the World Anti-Communist League, Anderson and Anderson, *Inside the League.*

286 A.M. Rosenthal on Pentagon terrorism report, *New York Times*, 2-10-89

286 "The American understanding of terrorism...", Falk, p. 11
286 *Nightline* on terrorism, *Extra!*, January/February 1988
286 Murder of Alex Odeh, Norman Solomon, op-ed, *Cleveland Plain Dealer*, 10-18-85
286 Media images of Arabs, Shaheen, *Extra!*, January/February 1988
287 Israeli hijacking of plane, Noam Chomsky, *The Fateful Triangle*, p. 77
287 Israeli shootdown of Libyan jet, Chomsky, *Thoreau Quarterly*, vol. 16
287 Ignatius, *Wall Street Journal*, 2-10-83
288 "The terrorist is as much...", Falk, p. 28
288 Gruson, *New York Times*, 12-26-88
288 1982 Pentagon report, cited in Chomsky, *Culture of Terrorism*, p. 81
289 Contra attacks as "pinpricks," *New York Times* editorial, 10-31-89
289 "Despite U.S. training programs," *New York Times* editorial, 1-23-89
289 Nairn, *The Progressive*, May 1984
289 Wanniski on D'Aubuisson, *Extra!*, September/October 1988
289 D'Aubuisson on Hitler, *El Dia*, Mexico, 2-11-82
289 Wholesale versus retail terrorism, see Edward S. Herman, *The Real Terror Network*
289 Persecution of Latin American religious activists, see Penny Lernoux, *Cry of the People*
290 Costa Rican Congressional Commission on North-contra-drug link, *Washington Post*, 7-23-89; *Miami Herald*, 7-22-89; *San Juan Star*, 7-22-89
291 Millman, *Columbia Journalism Review*, September/October 1986
291 North and Lewis, Jefferson Morley, *Rolling Stone*, 9-10-87
291 Rosenfeld, *San Francisco Examiner*, 3-16-86
291 *West 57th*, CBS, 4-6-87
291 PBS *Frontline*, "Guns, Drugs and the CIA," 5-17-88
292 *Washington Times*, 7-17-84
292 OPD disinformation about Nicaragua and drugs, *Newsweek*, 10-12-87
292 *CBS Morning News*, 3-12-86
292 Reagan's televised speech, 3-16-86
292 Omang, *Washington Post*, 3-18-86; Brinkley, *New York Times*, 3-19-86
292 *U.S. News & World Report* cover story, 5-4-87
292 Kwitny, *Wall Street Journal*, 4-22-87
293 *CBS Evening News*, 7-28-88
293 Reagan's weekly radio broadcast, *New York Times*, 7-31-88
293 *Washington Post*, 7-22-87
293 Rangel letter, *Congressional Record*, 8-6-87
293 North notebook entry, 7-12-85
293 "Drugs, Law Enforcement and Foreign Policy," Senate Foreign Relations Subcommittee Report, December 1988, p. 145
293 CNN and C-Span, 2-11-88
293 Sciolino, "Accountant Says Noriega Laundered Billions," *New York Times*, 2-12-88
294 LeMoyne, "Military Officers in Honduras are Linked to the Drug Trade," *New York Times*, 2-12-88
294 Coverage of Ramon Milian Rodriguez's testimony, *Extra!*, March/April 1988
294 Hersh, *New York Times*, 5-12 and 5-13-86
294 Colonel Roberto Diaz Herrera allegations, AP dispatch in *New York Times*, 6-10-87
294 Kinzer, *New York Times*, 6-12-87; Preston, *Washington Post*, 6-12-87
295 *New York Times* editorials: "A Hemisphere at Risk From Drugs," 2-20-88; "For Drugs: A Monroe Doctrine," 3-1-88; "The Drug Flames Rise Higher," 3-3-88; "Ten Months Left to Fight Drugs," 3-6-88
295 C.L. Sulzberger letter to Ginsberg, *Extra!*, March/April 1988
295 Rosenthal, *New York Times*, 3-15-87
295 Federal Trade Commission chair: Michael Pertschuck, *The Nation*, 3-7-87
296 Editorials on cigarette exports and cocaine, *New York Times*, 8-7-89
296 Cocaine, tobacco and alcohol-related fatalities, Craig Reinarman and Harry G. Levine, "The Crack Attack" chapter, Joel Best (editor), *Images of Issues: Typifying Contemporary Social Problems*, p. 120
296 Dan Walters, *San Francisco Examiner*, 6-30-89

296 Ridgeway, *Village Voice*, 9-12-89
297 *Los Angeles Times*, 9-9-88, and Amnesty International quoted in Robin Kirk, *Extra!*,
     Summer 1989

Chapter Twelve: Human Rights and Foreign Policy

298 LeMoyne and Salvadoran military disinformation, *Extra!*, July/August 1988
298 *New York Times* editor's note regarding LeMoyne article, 9-15-88
298 Gruson on Salvadoran repression, *New York Times*, 12-8-89
298 Gruson articles on El Salvador, *New York Times*, November 13-16, 1989; see also Reese
     Erlich, *San Francisco Bay Guardian*, 11-29-89
298 "Lonely Peacemaker," *New York Times*, 2-21-88
299 Memo from Poindexter to McFarlane, 11-23-84, quoted in *Extra!*, October/November
     1987
300 Rosett, *Wall Street Journal*, 5-22-89
300 Economic dislocation in China, *Extra!*, Summer 1989; see also Henwood, *Left Business
     Observer*, 6-13-89
300 ABC *Nightline*, 5-25-89; cited in *Left Business Observer*, 6-13-89
300 Deng on Wei Jingshen, *The Progressive*, March 1987
301 Authors' interview with Roberta Cohen, quoted in *Extra!*, Summer 1989; see also Roberta
     Cohen, "People's Republic of China: The Human Rights Exception," University of
     Maryland Law School, 1988
301 Between two and five million in Chinese labor camps and prisons, State Department's
     1987 Country Reports on Human Rights Practices
301 "Repression of basic freedoms in China," A.M. Rosenthal, *New York Times*, 6-13-89
301 "When necessary...", Deng Xiaoping, *The Progressive*, March 1987
302 Editorials criticizing Bush visit to China: *Miami Herald*, 2-28-89; *New York Times*, 3-1-89
302 Chinese arms to contras, David Corn and Jefferson Morley, *The Nation*, 5-1-89
302 Kissinger, *Los Angeles Times*, 8-1-89
302 Kissinger to Deng: "You will never be without great influence..." quoted in AP/*Miami
     Herald*, 11-11-89
303 "Bush's Gamble with Beijing," *New York Times*, 12-13-89
303 LeMoyne: "policy-driven," *Extra!*, Summer 1989
303 *Los Angles Times* survey and *CBS Evening News* survey, Anne E. Geyer and Robert Y.
     Shapiro, "The Polls—A Report on Human Rights?", *Public Opinion Quarterly*, 1988
304 David Gollob, London *Times*, 7-14-88
304 Coverage of Poland versus Guatemala, Edward S. Herman and Noam Chomsky,
     Manufacturing Consent, pp. 75-85
304 A.M. Rosenthal, *New York Times* column on captive nations, 5-10-88
305 The *Kwitny Report*, WNYC-TV, 2-15 and 2-22-89
305 Authors' interview with Michael Posner, June 1989; *Extra!*, Summer 1989
305 Suharto a "moderate leader," *Christian Science Monitor*, 2-6-87
305 "Two Decades of Suffering in Cambodia," *New York Times*, 1-8-90
306 Jeri Laber on Turkey coverage, authors' interview, quoted in *Extra!*, Summer 1989
306 Ismet Imset, "Civilized Censorship Under the Sword of Damocles," Committee to Protect
     Journalists, 1985
307 July 1985 *Washington Post* headline, "U.S. Praises Duvalier for Democratic
     Commitment," cited in *Extra!*, Summer 1989
307 Reagan administration "laid the groundwork" for Duvalier's departure, *Washington Post*,
     2-8-86
307 *New York Times* editorial on Reagan's human rights "conversion," 12-10-88
307 Mark McLeggan, State Department official, cited in Arthur Helton Jr., *Extra!*, Summer
     1989
307 Ray Moseley, *Chicago Tribune*, 7-2-89
308 Brit Hume, "Free World," ABC *World News Tonight*, 7-13-89

308 Karl Meyer on Smedley Butler, *New York Times*, 8-24-87
309 Smedley Butler, quoted in *Extra!*, October/November 1987
309 Hughes quoted in *Time*, 11-19-84
309 Social advances in Nicaragua, *Extra!*, October/November 1987
310 Somoza: "I don't want educated people…", *Extra!*, October/November 1987
310 Authors' interview with Edgar Chamorro, *Extra!*, October/November 1987
310 British *Guardian* headline, quoted in Mark Cook, *Extra!*, October/November 1989
310 NSC briefing paper, *Washington Post*, 11-6-84
311 "An election without [Cruz's] participation…", *Washington Post*, 9-17-84
311 Cruz a recipient of CIA funds, *Wall Street Journal*, 4-23-85
311 White House "never contemplated letting Cruz stay in the race," *New York Times*, 10-21-84
311 "Only the naive believe…", *New York Times*, 11-7-84
311 Maria Hernandez, quoted in *Extra!*, Summer 1989
311 Edward S. Herman, *Covert Action Information Bulletin*, Spring 1984
312 Authors' interview with Ken Roth, quoted in *Extra!*, Summer 1989
312 Burkhalter quoted in Dennis Bernstein, *Extra!*, Summer 1989
312 Amnesty report on El Salvador, quoted in Bernstein, *Extra!*, Summer 1989
312 Meg Greenfield in *Newsweek*, 5-29-89
314 *New York Times* editorial on Salvadoran election, 3-21-89
314 ARENA's "leaders now include far-rightists like Mr. D'Aubuisson…", Pear, *New York Times*, 6-14-89
314 *Christian Science Monitor* on Nicaraguan elections, 10-3-89
314 "Classes teach rebels about democracy," *Miami Herald*, 8-18-89
315 Virgilio Godoy, on 1984 Nicaraguan election, *Christian Science Monitor*, 11-5-84
315 CIA funding political candidates common practice, Sean Gervasi, *Covert Action Information Bulletin*, Summer 1989
315 Weinraub, "Bush Warns Panama on Election Fraud," *New York Times*, 5-3-89
315 R.W. Apple Jr., "Bush's Trap on Panama: Can He Avoid Label of Gringo Meddler?", *New York Times*, 5-1-89
315 Judd Rose, "democracy, Panamanian style," *Nightline*, 5-8-89
316 *New York Times* editorial, "Stern but Steady on Panama," 5-10-89
316 Preston on Panama in *Washington Post*, 6-12-87
316 Dan Rather on Pentagon press briefing, *San Francisco Chronicle*, 12-21-89
316 "We haven't got him yet," Tom Brokaw, NBC News, 12-20-89
317 Peter Jennings' apology for split screen coverage of Panama, *San Francisco Chronicle*, 1-6-90
317 John Chancellor, NBC News, 12-20-89
317 Braver on CBS and Dancy on NBC cited in Doug Ireland, *Village Voice*, 1-2-90
317 Sawyer, ABC *Primetime Live*, 12-28-89
317 "An initiation rite," R.W. Apple, *New York Times*, 12-21-89
317 Jonathan Marshall, "Panama's Drug, Inc.," *Oakland Tribune*, 1-5-90
317 Diana Ortiz abducted in Guatemala, Noam Chomsky, WBAI *Undercurrents*, 12-22-89
318 "Salinas signals that he's not a wimp," Ellison, *Miami Herald*. 1-13-89
318 "Foes on notice", *Miami Herald* editorial on Salinas, 1-14-89
318 "Mexico's President Gets Tough," *New York Times* editorial, 1-20-89
319 Rohter on Mexican death squads, *New York Times*, 2-19-89
319 40 political assassinations in Mexico, *La Jornada*, 1-26-89
319 "Winning by Losing in Mexico," *New York Times* editorial, 7-7-89
320 Cynthia Brown quoted in *Extra!*, Summer 1989
320 Luis Perez Aguirre interviewed by Martin A. Lee and Pia Gallegos, *Extra!*, Summer 1989
321 "Koreans Elect Roh as President in Easy Victory…", *Wall Street Journal*, 12-18-87
321 National Coalition for Democracy vote center closed, in David Easter, *Extra!*, March/April 1988
321 "Vote for Stability," *Time*, 12-28-87
321 "We cannot but be overwhelmed by disappointment," *Dong-A-Ilbo*, quoted in *Oregonian*, 2-23-88
321 *Chicago Tribune* editorial on Roh Tae Woo, 2-25-88

322 *New York Times* editorial, "Not So Regressive in Korea," 3-25-89
322 Korean labor dispute, Reuters in *New York Times*, 3-31-89
322 *Washington Post* editorial on Israel, 2-8-89
322 John Healey, letter to the *Washington Post*, 2-17-89
322 Israeli repression before the intifada, see Cockburn, *The Nation*, 1-16-88
322 Israel "a society in which moral sensitivity...", *New York Times*, quoted in Noam
      Chomsky, *Zeta*, March 1989
323 Palestinian "towns are short of hospitals, sewers, paved roads and schoolrooms,"
      Newsweek, 1-4-88
323 Dean Reynolds, *Nightline*, 12-23-87
323 London *Observer*, 4-29-84; *Le Nouvel Observateur*, 5-4-84; *Jerusalem Post*, 5-16-84
323 PLO on Israel's right to exist, Toronto *Globe and Mail*, 1-15-88, quoted in Chomsky,
      Zeta, May 1988; see also *Los Angeles Herald*, "Arafat Offers Deal with Israel for Role in
      Peace Talks," 1-15-88
323 "Until the PLO summons...", *New York Times* editorial, 3-2-88
324 Abu Sharif's article mentioned in *Wall Street Journal*, 6-8-88; *Boston Globe* editorial, 6-
      11-88
324 Stephen Rosenfeld column on Sharif, *Washington Post*, 6-23-88
324 *New York Times* news story and Anthony Lewis' column on Sharif statement, 6-23-88; see
      also Rashid Khalidi, "The PLO and the Uprising," *Middle East Report*,
      September/October 1988
324 WNBC-TV New York on Arafat declaration, quoted in *Extra!*, November/December 1988
324 *Christian Science Monitor* editorial on Arafat declaration, 11-16-88
324 "The PLO: Less Than Meets the Eye," *New York Times* editorial, 11-16-88
325 Robert Pear, *New York Times*, 11-23-88
325 "Seismic shift of attitude...", *New York Times* editorial, 12-21-88
325 Joel Brinkley, Arafat "saying so openly for the first time...", *New York Times*, 1-29-89
325 "Israel Asserts Threats by PLO Imperil Bid to Revive Peace Plan," *New York Times*, 7-18-
      89; quoted in Doug Ireland, *Village Voice*, 8-1-89
325 "Crushed like grasshoppers," quoted in Chomsky, *Zeta*, May 1988
325 Brinkley on Shamir, *New York Times* magazine, 8-21-88
325 Cody, *Washington Post*, in *International Herald Tribune*, 4-12-89
326 Human rights in Somalia, *Extra!*, Summer 1989
326 "TV news executives figure...", quoted in Cross, p. 68; see also John Weisman, "Blind
      Spot in the Middle East," *TV Guide*, 10-24-81
326 Randy Daniels, quoted in Cross, p. 68
326 Lelyveld and Walker quoted in Danny Schechter, *Africa Report*, March/April 1988
326 "South Africa is viewed as one of us...", quoted in *Africa Report*, March/April 1988
327 *Los Angeles Times* on Angolan independence, 12-14-88
327 John Stockwell, authors' interview, December 1988
327 Southern Africa connection to Iran-contra affair, *Extra!*, August/September 1987
327 Savimbi collaborated with neofascist mercenaries, Martin A. Lee and Kevin Coogan,
      Village Voice, 12-24-85; *The Nation*, 12-7-85
327 Africa Faith and Justice Network, *National Catholic Reporter*, 5-23-86
327 Angola "amputee capital of the world," *Wall Street Journal*, 2-10-87
327 UNITA attacking medical clinics, Rakiya Omaar, *Africa Report*, May/June 1989
328 Craig Whitney and Jill Jolliffe, *New York Times*, 3-11-89
328 Afghan and Soviet atrocities, Asia Watch report, 2-27-89, cited in Steven Galster, *Extra!*,
      Summer 1989
328 Bombs in Pakistan called "terrorist" attacks, *Washington Post*, 4-17-88
328 Galster citing BBC, *Extra!*, Summer 1989
329 "Is the United States willing to give peace a chance in Afghanistan?", BBC, 6-22-89
329 Paul Lewis, *New York Times*, 10-6-89
329 CBS fake footage in Afghanistan, *Extra!*, October/November 1989
329 "It was sloppiness...", FAIR press release, 9-28-89
330 General Mohammed Zia ul-Haq, quoted in *Time*, 4-13-83
330 $275 billion debt transfer, Doug Henwood, *Extra!*, Summer 1989

Conclusion: Toward an Uncensored Future

331 Mainstream media shun Seldes books, "The Press Lords Retaliate," *New Republic*, 2-15-39
331 McCarthyites "who rode top saddle...", Seldes, *Witness to a Century*, p. xx
332 Nader, *Public Citizen*, September/October 1987
333 Miller, *Boxed In*, p. 158
333 Schaef, *When Society Becomes an Addict*, p. 65
334 *New York Times* inaugural headline, 1-22-89
334 Herman and Chomsky, *Manufacturing Consent*, p. 1
335 Orwell, *1984*, Signet edition, 1961, p. 252
335 Karp, *Harper's* magazine, July 1989
336 One percent of the population owns over one-half the country's wealth, Bernard Sanders, op-ed, *Miami Herald*, 11-18-89
336 Paul N. Goldstene, *The Collapse of Liberal Empire: Science and Revolution in the Twentieth Century*, p. 23
336 Bagdikian, *The Nation*, 6-12-89
336 Bagdikian, p. xvi
336 Alexander Cockburn, *In These Times*, February 17-23, 1988
337 Footage of Bloch simulated on ABC *World News Tonight*, 7-21-89
337 *New York Times* editorial on ABC News simulations, 7-28-89
337 *USA Today* editorial on TV news simulations, 8-4-89
337 Ted Koppel, *Nightline*, 9-27-89
337 Alvin Toffler, *The Third Wave*, p. 165
338 "Just as ready as any dictatorship...", Bagdikian, *The Nation*, 6-12-89
339 Dewey quoted in Cockburn, *In These Times*, February 17-23, 1988

ACKNOWLEDGMENTS

While working on this book, we have received help from hundreds of people. Above all, we wish to thank our friend and colleague Jeff Cohen, who has astutely challenged media bias for many years. His enormous support has been invaluable.

Daniel Levy, our editor at Lyle Stuart, suggested the idea for this book. His unwavering enthusiasm has literally made *Unreliable Sources* possible. And few authors have the benefit of working with an independent publisher like Steven Schragis, who never questioned our editorial judgment.

Special thanks to FAIR and its New York staff. Hollie Ainbinder, Gloria Channon, Sanford Hohauser, Steve Rendall and William Shepard were always responsive and helpful.

We are deeply grateful to Pia Gallegos for her feedback and support throughout the many stages of this project. Offering ideas and encouragement in response to early chapters of the manuscript were Louise Rubacky and Ada Sanchez.

Especially tenacious in sticking with vital research tasks were Frances Massimino and Steve Rhodes. Neil Michel's labors on environmental issues are reflected in Chapter Eight. We also appreciate the input we received from Kim Deterline, Robert Gardner, Nancy Graham, Doug Henwood and Colleen McGuire.

Among a team of dedicated interns and volunteers, we wish to thank: Michael Benhoff, Cory Clar, Jessica Emilie Denevan, Scott Failor, Farnaz Fatemi, Barbara Jean Flowers, Sondra Friedman, Rob Grocholski, Catherine Guttman, Courtney Hunter, Paula Kamen, Sarah Lenoue, Faye Levine, Tony Michels, Amy Sarch, Scott Sherman, Roger Smith, Rick Vetrone, Allen White and David Wilkirson.

For no-strings funding that made a sizable dent in our research expenses, we thank the Fund for Investigative Journalism, as well as Carol Bernstein Ferry and W.H. Ferry. And we also thank Geri Thoma of the Elaine Markson Literary Agency.

In the category of counter-assistance, two natural disasters in autumn 1989—Hurricane Hugo and the earthquake in Northern California—each interrupted our work for several long and difficult days. We learned, also, from them.

PERMISSIONS

Index

Central Intelligence Agency. *See* CIA
Central Park jogger, 234, 244
Cerra, Frances, 210
Chamorro, Edgar, 120, 133, 136–37, 310
Chancellor, John, 111, 154, 155, 317
Chandler, Otis, 93
Chaney, James, 123
Chardy, Alfonso, 24, 154–55
Chase, Barry, 89
Chase Manhattan, 83
Chernobyl, 25, 211–12
Chevron, 217
Chicago Tribune, 30, 152, 154, 158, 171, 172, 231, 232, 241, 248, 307, 321, 331
Chile, 40, 47, 49, 91, 120, 144, 146, 320
China, 12, 16, 233, 299–303, 326; Kissinger connection, 46; Tiananmen Square, 45, 46, 140, 299–301
Chomsky, Noam, 31, 75, 108, 129, 139, 304, 334
Christian Broadcast Co. (South Korea), 321
Christian Broadcasting Network, 120
Christian Science Monitor, 49, 78, 111, 116, 176, 195, 208, 236–37, 245, 305, 309, 312, 315, 324, 344
Chrysler, 192–93
Chung, Connie, 16, 136, 285, 336
Churchill, Winston, 129
CIA, 18, 19, 31, 41, 42, 44, 55–56, 76, 83, 88, 99, 102, 108–9, 111, 120–21, 129, 131, 134, 144, 146, 152, 155, 159, 160, 170, 263, 277, 283–85, 290, 293, 294, 311, 315, 317, 348, 356; Afghanistan, 328, 330; Angola, 120, 327; behavior modification, 118–19; Bush administration, 258; Central America, 120, 136, 288, 304–5; drug trafficking and, 294–95; former Nazis, 119–20; and the media, 114–21, 124, 126; Operation MK-ULTRA, 118; and Pan Am Flight, 103, 284; PLO pact with, 287–88
Cigarettes, 4–7, 75, 240, 295–96, 331, 338
Cirano, Robert, 101
CISPES, 126
Citibank/Citicorp, 83, 293
Clark, Joe, 195
Class conflict, 176–80
Clean Harbor Act, 216
Clean Water Act, 216
Cleveland Plain Dealer, 80
Clifford, Clark, 76
Clift, Eleanor, 167
Cline, Ray, 115, 155, 285
Clines, Francis X., 261
Cluett Peabody, 84
CNBC, 82, 89
CNN, 15, 31, 40, 41, 45, 47, 56, 68, 83, 144, 293, 299, 308, 317, 347, 355–56
Coalition for Humane Immigrant Rights, 245
Coal strikes, USSR vs. US, 190–91
Cockburn, Alexander, 132–33, 191, 222, 336
Cohen, Jeff, 20, 29–30, 89, 121, 148, 284; interview with, 340–58
Cohen, Richard, 46, 172, 263
Cohen, Roberta, 301

COINTELPRO, 56, 124, 126
Colby, William, 115, 277, 351
Cold War, 105, 106, 264–70
Colombia, 293, 294, 297
Columbia Broadcasting System. *See* CBS
Columbia Journalism Review, 19, 23, 26, 37, 66, 243, 249, 291
Con Edison, 82
Conflicts-of-interest, 345–46
Congressional Record, 293
Conservative Political Action Conference, 87
Consider the Alternatives, 348
Consumer Reports, 349
Continental Airlines, 192
Contraception, 233
Cook, Mark, 140
Cooper, Marc, 298
Coors, Joseph, 84
Copley chain, 115, 124, 126
Corporation for Public Broadcasting, 84–87
Corporations, 59–60, 84–87, 185–86, 241–44
Corriere della Sera, 74
Cosby, Bill, 9
Cosmopolitan, 96
Costa Rica, 34, 55, 120, 222, 290, 291, 315
Council on Foreign Relations, 82
Counter-Revolutionary Violence, 75
Coups, U.S.-supported, 320
Cox Enterprises, 93, 100
Cristiani, Alfredo, 312, 314
Critical Mass Project, 352
Crockett, Phyllis, 251
La Crónica del Pueblo, 304
Cronkite, Walter, 10, 72, 73, 102, 107, 108, 202, 351
Cross, Donna Woolfolk, 74, 146, 168
Cross, William R., 82
Crossfire, 31, 56, 83, 112, 116, 144, 356
Croteau, David, 27
Cruz, Arturo, 310–11
C-SPAN, 293, 347
Cuba, 33, 40, 54, 115, 283, 289–94, 327
Culip, Scott M., 66
Cuomo, Mario, 209

Daily Compass, 73
Daily News (New York), 222, 249
Dallas Morning News, 197
Damage control, 18–19
Dancy, John, 317
Daniels, Randy, 326
D'Aubuisson, Roberto, 289, 314
Day, Samuel H. Jr., 204, 262
Deaver, Michael, 105, 150
DeBeers, 50
De Borchgrave, Arnaud, 106, 120
Debt crisis, third world, 319–20
Deficit, federal budget, 187
Delaney, Steve, 78
Delaware Supreme Court, 68, 70
Del Pino Diaz, Rafael, 54
Democracia tutelaria, 320
Democrats and Reagan, 147–49, 155

ABOUT THE AUTHORS

MARTIN A. LEE is the author of *Acid Dreams: The CIA, LSD and the Sixties Rebellion*. An investigative journalist and media critic, his articles have been published in *Rolling Stone, Newsday, Village Voice, San Francisco Chronicle, The Nation, Cleveland Plain Dealer, Le Monde Diplomatique*, and *Sydney Morning Herald*. A frequent radio commentator, Lee has also been interviewed on the CBS, NBC, ABC, CNN and C-Span television networks. He is currently the publisher of *Extra!*, the journal of FAIR (Fairness & Accuracy in Reporting).

NORMAN SOLOMON is co-author of *Killing Our Own: The Disaster of America's Experience with Atomic Radiation*. His news analyses and commentary articles have been published in the *Los Angeles Times, Boston Globe, Chicago Tribune, Baltimore Sun, International Herald Tribune* and many other newspapers, as well as in such magazines as *The Nation, The Progressive*, and *New Statesman*. Solomon has been a guest on numerous TV and radio programs, including *Good Morning America, Crossfire* and *All Things Considered*.